Writing Workshop Teacher's Guide

GRADE 4

Program Author

Joyce Armstrong Carroll

Welcome to
HMH Into Reading™
Writing Workshop

The *HMH Into Reading*™ Writing Workshop from Houghton Mifflin Harcourt represents a new generation of writing instruction. Developed through years of classroom experience and research, this method puts the writing workshop theory into practice. Teachers will find explicit modeling and instruction in process, technique, and the integration of grammar. Students have the chance to hone their craft through daily writing practice and regular conferences with teachers and peers. The Writing Workshop encourages students to grow into their own voices and share their ideas with the world.

PROGRAM OVERVIEW

HMH Into Reading™ Writing Workshop

PROGRAM AUTHOR

My Very Dear Teachers,

How I would have reveled in *HMH Into Reading™* 60 years ago when I walked into that third-grade classroom in Emma Arleth Elementary for my first year in teaching! Then we had Dick and Jane readers, but nothing for or about writing. Oh, we had isolated grammar exercises that put the yawn in teaching and made kids actually hate writing anything. But now we have a handle on writing as a process, and we know how to integrate grammar within that process. So hug this book and use it. Nowhere will you find so consistent a writing scaffold, so integrated a curriculum, such a research-based and pedagogically proven approach to teaching ELAR. You are lucky indeed!

With my deepest respect for you all,

—*Joyce Armstrong Carroll, a.k.a. Dr. JAC*

Joyce Armstrong Carroll, Ed.D., H.L.D.

In her 60-year career, Joyce Armstrong Carroll has taught every grade level from primary through graduate school. In the past 40 years, working in tandem with her husband Edward Wilson, she has trained thousands of teachers, who, in turn, have taught hundreds of thousands of students. A nationally-known consultant, she has served as president of TCTE and on NCTE's Commission on Composition and its Standing Committee Against Censorship. Recipient of the Edmund J. Farrell Lifetime Achievement Award in Education and the Honorary Doctorate of Humane Letters for her work in Education, Dr. Carroll has written numerous articles and over twenty books—most on teaching writing. She and her husband have authored a national writing and grammar series as well as *AbydosPRO: An Integrated Writing and Grammar Curriculum*. She co-directs Abydos Literacy Learning.

Teaching Writing Workshop

The *Into Reading* Writing Workshop focuses on the writing process and the use of mentor texts, emphasizing student ownership of their own writing.

WRITING PROCESS

- Teacher's Guide provides explicit modeling and instruction for each stage of the writing process.
- Routines build strong habits.
- Recursive development of ideas and language encourages the development of voice.

STUDENT OWNERSHIP

- Students write daily, exercising their choice of topics.
- Students set and own their writing goals.
- Students confer regularly with teachers and peers.

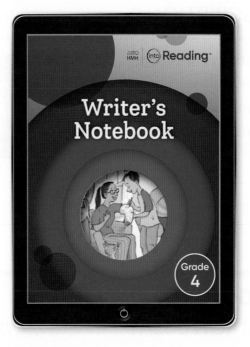

MENTOR TEXTS

- Twelve focal texts—authentic trade literature—serve as mentor texts, modeling the development of themes, topics, and writing techniques.
- The focal texts double as a student choice trade library.
- Aspirational writing models provide strong examples of responses to module prompts.

WRITING WORKSHOP • MODULES

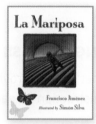

HMH *Into Reading*™ Writing Workshop

Lesson at a Glance

The Writing Workshop Teacher's Guide holds the blueprint for each day's lesson.

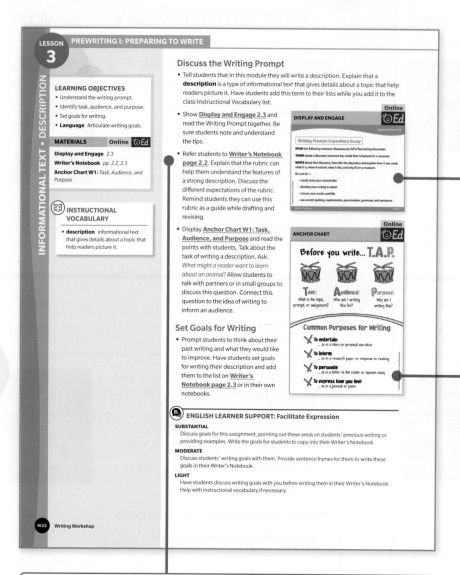

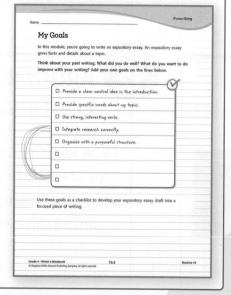

Writer's Notebook
Direct support for student writing—no abstract practice or busy work

Display & Engage Projectable content for whole-class instruction

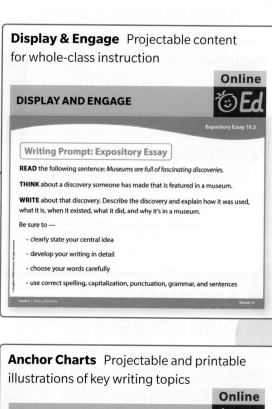

Anchor Charts Projectable and printable illustrations of key writing topics

Scaffolded Writing Instruction for English Learners

As English learners participate in the Writing Workshop, scaffolded instruction helps the teacher meet them at their own language proficiency levels and leverage what they already know.

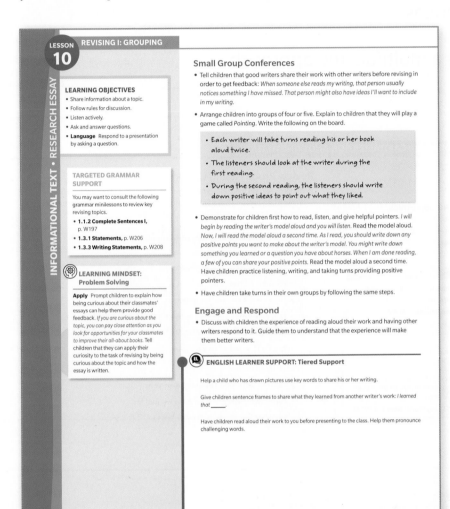

Support English learners using a variety of research-based strategies to

- focus on academic language and vocabulary

- link background knowledge and culture to learning

- increase comprehensible input

- support language output with sentence frames

- promote classroom interaction

 ENGLISH LEARNER SUPPORT: Tiered Support

SUBSTANTIAL
Help a child who has drawn pictures use key words to share his or her writing.

MODERATE
Give children sentence frames to share what they learned from another writer's work: *I learned that _____.*

LIGHT
Have children read aloud their work to you before presenting to the class. Help them pronounce challenging words.

Grammar in the Context of Writing

Grammar is most effectively taught in the context of writing instruction. The revising and editing stages of the writing process present the best opportunities for students to master the grammar skills needed to write strong, clear sentences.

Into Reading Writing Workshop provides a multifaceted approach to grammar:

INTEGRATED Writing Workshop lessons teach grammar in the context of revising and editing. Grammar minilessons supplement the revising and editing lessons as students' needs dictate.

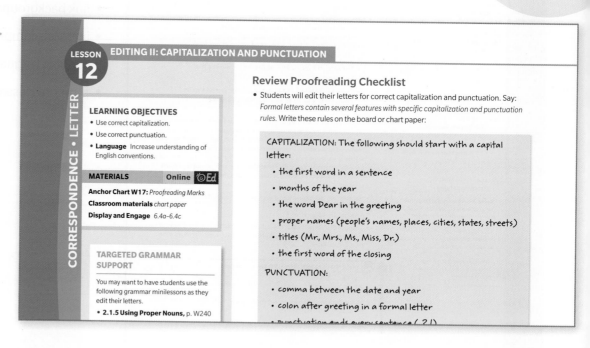

DIFFERENTIATED Grammar minilessons provide customized support for students who need help with other grammar and language skills.

SYSTEMATIC Teachers who want a comprehensive, systematic grammar curriculum can teach the minilessons according to the scope and sequence.

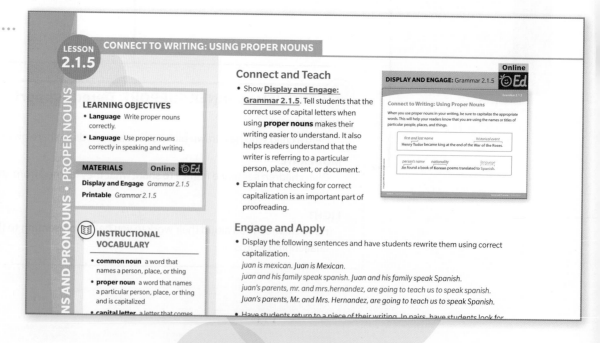

GRAMMAR MINILESSONS • TOPICS AND SKILLS

Writing Conferences and Assessment

Integrated into daily instruction, various types of assessment enable teachers to target individual needs, helping writers grow into their own voices.

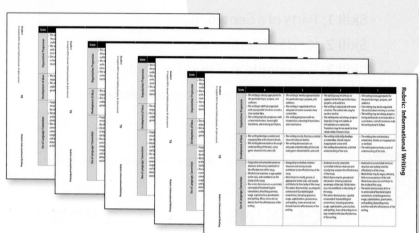

RUBRICS

Multi-trait rubrics provided at point of use offer focused guidance to score and guide student writing. One rubric for every mode is provided.

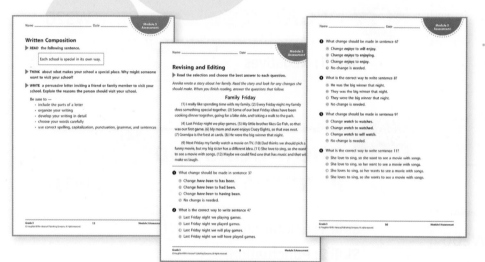

WEEKLY AND MODULE ASSESSMENTS

- Weekly Assessments include editing tasks that assess application of key grammar skills.

- Module Assessments include editing tasks and writing prompts that assess each Module's key grammar and writing skills.

WRITING CONFERENCES

As students work on their writing, teachers circulate the room and offer targeted assistance on the day's lesson, another writing topic, or an area of grammar that needs work. These regular, informal conferences provide students with actionable feedback to help them on their path to becoming great writers.

WRITING WORKSHOP • MODULES

WRITING WORKSHOP • MODULES

Mar 10, 2023

MODULE 9
INFORMATIONAL TEXT
RESEARCH REPORT

Focal Text: *The Case of the Vanishing Honeybees: A Scientific Mystery,* by Sandra Markle

Focus Statement:
Understanding our world helps us protect it.

MODULE 10
INFORMATIONAL TEXT
EXPOSITORY ESSAY

Focal Text: *The Museum Book: A Guide to Strange and Wonderful Collections,* by Jan Mark; Illustrated by Richard Holland

Focus Statement:
Discoveries, big or small, personal or from others, are exciting.

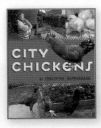

The Writing Conference

There can be no substitute for the writing conference. For teachers, it is an unbeatable opportunity to stay in touch with student work in progress. For students, it's a precious chance to have a conversation with their teacher about their writing and feel noticed as a writer.

Knowing that they have an actual audience gives students a reason to write; knowing how that audience is responding to their work gives them a reason to improve.

What happens during a writing conference?

A good writing conference is a conversation between teacher and student. This conversation has several parts:

1. **Listen** The first step is always to ask the student about his or her writing and pay close attention to the answer.

2. **Affirm** Based on what you hear, offer praise for some element of the student's writing to reinforce his or her strengths. This is essential.

3. **Teach** Focus on a general principle rather than providing a specific correction. Draw upon the focal text, writing model, or other familiar texts to provide clear examples of the principle.

4. **Apply** Finally, suggest that the student try it out for him- or herself.

How often should I confer with my students?

During independent writing time, circulate the room and confer with a few students every day, as time allows. A focused four- or five-minute conference gives you enough time to listen, deliver personalized instruction, and show students that you are paying attention.

What can I possibly cover in four or five minutes?

You don't have to do it all—focus on one or two writing elements based on the day's lesson and what the student shows you in his or her work. Provide a teaching strategy and a way to try it out. Don't edit for grammar or mechanics; use this valuable time to explore ideas, text structure, and language techniques.

Can I hold conferences with small groups?

Students with similar needs can benefit from informal small-group conferences. Feel free to call an impromptu small-group discussion during independent writing time, based on what you have seen during your individual conferences.

What about peer conferences?

During revising and editing lessons, this Teacher's Guide provides explicit direction for peer conferences. Students do best when prompted to focus on a limited set of writing traits or features in a given conference.

When is the best time to correct students' grammar?

Teaching grammar in the context of revising and editing shows students how writing good sentences will improve the clarity and impact of their writing. Rather than correcting errors, look for opportunities to emphasize principles taught in the day's grammar lesson. You can also bring in a minilesson for individual students or small groups based on demonstrated need.

What do I do with students who are sensitive to feedback?

Research shows that all students learn best from affirmative, targeted instruction about their writing. Writing is an emotionally charged activity; students who feel safe and confident will write more freely and with greater meaning.

Personal Narrative

FOCUS STATEMENT All of our experiences help us grow and learn.

FOCAL TEXT

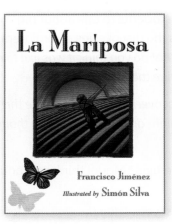

La Mariposa

Author: Francisco Jiménez

Illustrator: Simón Silva

Summary: A migrant worker boy finds his place in school as he watches a cocoon grow and become a butterfly.

WRITING PROMPT

READ this sentence: *All of our experiences help us grow and learn.*

THINK about a time you learned a lesson from something that happened to you.

WRITE a personal narrative about that time. Use descriptive language.

LESSONS

1. **Introducing the Focal Text**
2. **Priming the Text and The Read**
3. **Vocabulary**
4. **The Writing Process**
5. **Prewriting I: Choosing a Topic**
6. **Prewriting II: Narrative Structure**
7. **Drafting I: Beginning the Draft**
8. **Drafting II: Elements of a Narrative**
9. **Drafting III: Concluding the Draft**
10. **Revising I: Integrating Grammar and Punctuation**
11. **Revising II: Conferencing**
12. **Revising III: Sentence Sense and Direct Address**
13. **Editing I: Peer Proofreading**
14. **Publishing**
15. **Sharing**

**LEARNING MINDSET:
Growth Mindset**

Display **Anchor Chart 31: My Learning Mindset** throughout the year. Refer to it to introduce Growth Mindset.

LEARNING OBJECTIVES

- Apply knowledge of affixes to understand new words.
- Make connections to the topic and theme.
- **Language** Describe feelings using precise vocabulary.
- **Language** Discuss personal connections to literature.

MATERIALS   Online

Display and Engage *1.1*

Priming the Students

Explore the Topic

- Tell students that they will learn about discoveries that people make in their own lives.

- Write the word *discover* on the board. Draw a box around the prefix *dis-*. Explain that the Latin prefix *dis-* means *the reverse*. *Cover* means *hide*, so to *discover* means *to uncover or become aware of something.*

- Lead a class discussion about discoveries. Ask students to talk about big discoveries that they may know about, such as the discoveries of explorers or scientists. Ask follow-up questions, such as: *What do you think it was like to make such a big discovery? How did the discovery change the world?*

- Explain that not all discoveries are big: *Little discoveries may not change the world, but they may still be important or exciting. You might discover a book you thought you had lost or find a frog in your backyard.*

- Ask: *What does it feel like to find or discover something?* Model thinking about a discovery.

  THINK ALOUD *I remember the first cold day last year. I dug through my closet to find my warm coat. It was pushed way in the back. I put it on as I walked out the door. The wind was cold, so I tucked my hands into the pockets. When I reached in, I felt something in my left pocket. I pulled it out. It was a dollar I'd forgotten about. I was so excited!*

- Point out that sometimes a discovery is seeing something ordinary from a new perspective. A discovery can also be a greater understanding of something or someone, even ourselves.

- Ask: *Have you ever discovered something? What did you discover? How did you feel about it?* Prompt students to describe their feelings as precisely as possible with either/or questions: *Were you worried or excited? Were you proud or relieved?*

Discuss the Focus Statement

- Tell students that good writers jot down their ideas, thoughts, and interesting words in a notebook to help them later. Have students prepare a notebook that they will use throughout the year. Have them add any ideas as they write.

- Show **Display and Engage 1.1**. Read the Focus Statement with students. Have them talk with a partner about what the Focus Statement means to them.

EL **ENGLISH LEARNER SUPPORT: Support Discussion**

ALL LEVELS If students have difficulty describing feelings, list adjectives on the board such as *excited, nervous, proud, worried,* and *shy*. Point to the words and say them aloud as students repeat after you. Then use gestures and facial expressions to represent the different feelings, such as hiding your face to demonstrate *shy*.

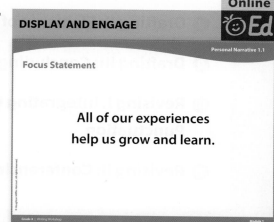

DISPLAY AND ENGAGE   Online

Personal Narrative 1.1

Focus Statement

All of our experiences help us grow and learn.

Priming the Text

Prepare to Read

- Display the cover of *La Mariposa*. Point to and read the names of the author and the illustrator. Explain that *la mariposa* means "the butterfly" in Spanish. Explain that *La Mariposa* is a book about discoveries.

- Introduce the genre to students. Say: La Mariposa *is realistic fiction. This means that the story is made up, but it describes things that could happen in real life. The characters and settings are realistic—they're like people and places you might find in the real world.*

La Mariposa

Build Instructional Vocabulary

- Turn to the glossary in the back of the book. Write the word **glossary** on the board. Ask: *How did the glossary help you as you read* La Mariposa? *What is a glossary?* Work together to agree upon a definition, and write it on the board.

- Tell students that throughout the year they will encounter words like *glossary* that are important to remember as they write. Have them create an Instructional Vocabulary Glossary section of their notebooks, making *glossary* the first entry.

- Guide students to add the words **realistic fiction, symbolism**, and **personal narrative** to their Instructional Vocabulary Glossary. You may also want to create a class Instructional Vocabulary list on chart paper to display for students. Save this list for use in future modules.

The Read

Read the Focal text

- As you read *La Mariposa*, stop to show the pictures and give students time to analyze them. When you come to a Spanish word or phrase, take a moment to model using the glossary at the end of the book to translate. Also stop from time to time to ask comprehension questions.

- After reading, lead a discussion about the importance of the image of the butterfly in the story. Write *symbolism* on the board. Explain that **symbolism** is a literary device. Say: *A symbol expresses an idea. For example, the heart is a symbol for love.*

  » Display the cover of the book again and point to the butterfly. Ask: *What does the butterfly symbolize in* La Mariposa? Guide students to connect the butterfly with the illustration of the boy flying over the field.

- Direct students' attention to the author's name on the cover. Explain that Francisco Jiménez, like many authors, based many of his stories on his own life but changed some things to make the story fictional. Ask: *Have you ever used something from your own life in a story you've written? Did you keep it the same or did you change some things?*

- Ask: *What are some elements of a story? (characters, plot, setting, dialogue)* Guide students to understand that a **personal narrative** has the same elements as other stories, except that the events described really happened to the author. Add *personal narrative* to the class Instructional Vocabulary list.

LEARNING OBJECTIVES

- Discuss genre features of personal narrative.
- Use reference materials to determine word meaning.
- Interpret the meaning of symbols in a text.
- **Language** Participate in discussions about the text.

MATERIALS   Online

Focal Text *La Mariposa*

INSTRUCTIONAL VOCABULARY

- **glossary** list of important words to know and their definitions
- **realistic fiction** story that includes people and places that could exist in the real world
- **symbolism** the use of an image to represent a larger idea
- **personal narrative** story of an important event or time in the author's life

LEARNING MINDSET: Growth

Introduce Explain that any new skill or talent takes time to learn. *Learning something new takes time, and the more complicated something is, the longer it takes to learn. You'll read about Francisco in* La Mariposa *and how he grew throughout the school year. He practiced drawing day after day. Eventually, he drew so well that he won an award!* Tell students that most things are hard to do at first, but with practice and hard work, they become easier to do well.

LEARNING OBJECTIVES

- Read and understand domain-specific vocabulary.
- **Language** Explain reasoning for category choices.

MATERIALS   Online

Writer's Notebook *p.1.1*

Focal Text *La Mariposa*

TEACHER TIP

Before students sort the words in the Word Bank, reassure them that there may be many different categories for each word. Let students know that they are not looking for a "right answer" but instead should be looking for connections between words.

Review the Focal Text

- Have students turn to the Word Bank on **Writer's Notebook page 1.1** or create a Word Bank in their own notebooks. Then revisit *La Mariposa,* stopping after each page to allow students the opportunity to add words from the page to their Word Banks. Write sample words on the board as well, such as:

overalls	recesses	prize
whizzing	swollen	swarm
suspenders	catch	clenched
cocoon	disrespectful	motioned
flannel	sketched	fluttering

- Tell students they will categorize the words they found. Model categorizing words from the Word Bank:

  THINK ALOUD *I see the word* overalls. *I know that overalls are things you can wear. I look through the words in the Word Bank. Are there any other words for things you can wear? Yes! I see the word* suspenders. *I can put* overalls *and* suspenders *in the same group. They are both things that you can wear. That is their connection.*

- Divide the class into small groups and issue this challenge: *Divide these words into groups so that all the words in the group share something in common.* As students complete the challenge, circulate the room and offer assistance, as needed.

Engage and Respond

- Have students explain the categories they chose and what those words have in common. Encourage students to rearrange the words into new groups.

 ENGLISH LEARNER SUPPORT: Tiered Support

SUBSTANTIAL

Provide images for as many Word Bank words as possible. Allow students to sort the words with images into categories to complete the task.

MODERATE

Have students sort the Word Bank words into predetermined categories, such as *things you wear* or *things you do.*

LIGHT

Encourage students to sort the Word Bank words by part of speech, guiding them to distinguish between nouns, verbs, and adjectives.

LEARNING OBJECTIVES

- Understand the steps in the writing process.
- Set goals for writing.
- **Language** Discuss writing tasks with academic language.

MATERIALS Online

Display and Engage *1.2*

Writer's Notebook *pp. 1.2, 1.3*

LEARNING MINDSET: Growth

Apply Tell students that working through the writing process will help them grow as writers. Following the steps from prewriting to sharing will allow them to think through their ideas, experiment with those ideas, and work hard at presenting them in the strongest way possible. Encourage students to focus on each step of the writing process as they come to it and not to rush through the process.

○ *Professional Learning*

BEST PRACTICES

Students learn more when they are directly involved and clearly understand their own goals and objectives. Explain to students that they will be returning to the goals they set as they work.

See the **GPS guide** to learn more.

Explain the Writing Process

- Introduce students to the writing process as you write the following steps on the board. Alternatively, you may write on chart paper to display in the classroom.

> 1. Prewriting: choose a topic and organize your ideas
> 2. Drafting: write your ideas down
> 3. Revising: make improvements to the ideas, organization, and style of your writing
> 4. Editing: correct errors in grammar, spelling, and punctuation
> 5. Publishing/Sharing: share your completed work with others

- Share that writers may need to return to earlier steps throughout the process as they work to develop their ideas: *Francisco Jiménez may have written and revised many drafts of* La Mariposa *before he published the story. He also likely had an editor that helped him edit his revised drafts a few times.*

Discuss the Writing Prompt

- Remind students they will write a personal narrative, or a true story, about a time in their lives.

- Show **Display and Engage 1.2** and read the Writing Prompt together. Note the tips.

- Distribute **Writer's Notebook page 1.2**. Explain that the rubric can help them understand the features of a strong personal narrative. Discuss the different expectations of the rubric. Remind students they can use this rubric as a resource while drafting and revising.

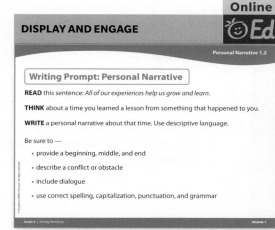

DISPLAY AND ENGAGE Online Ed

Personal Narrative 1.2

Writing Prompt: Personal Narrative

READ this sentence: *All of our experiences help us grow and learn.*

THINK about a time you learned a lesson from something that happened to you.

WRITE a personal narrative about that time. Use descriptive language.

Be sure to —
- provide a beginning, middle, and end
- describe a conflict or obstacle
- include dialogue
- use correct spelling, capitalization, punctuation, and grammar

Set Goals for Writing

Point out that good writers think about what they want to improve with each new piece they write. Have students think about what goals they would like to set for their personal narratives. Have them set their goals by adding to the list on **Writer's Notebook page 1.3** or in their own notebooks.

 ENGLISH LEARNER SUPPORT

SUBSTANTIAL
Allow students to use their home language in writing goals.

MODERATE
Discuss students' writing goals. Provide sentence frames to write their goals as needed.

LIGHT
Pair English learners and have them brainstorm goals together.

NARRATIVE WRITING • PERSONAL NARRATIVE

LEARNING OBJECTIVES
- Generate topic ideas.
- **Language** Discuss moments of discovery.

MATERIALS Online

Focal Text *La Mariposa*
Writer's Notebook p. 1.4

TEACHER TIP

Encourage students to list as many ideas as they can. Remind them that the ideas don't have to be well-developed at this stage.

Discuss Examples

- Explain that in this lesson students will begin prewriting their personal narratives, which is like a slice of their lives. They will do this by choosing a topic to write about.

- Reread page 37 of *La Mariposa*. Point out the moment of discovery as Francisco sees the butterfly take flight for the first time.

- Invite the students to close their eyes and think about how exciting it is to discover something. *Imagine finding something new and unexpected. Maybe it's a baby bird in a nest outside your window or a new friend that just moved in on your block. Maybe you just found out something about yourself, such as a hidden talent for free-throws or a new type of music that you like.* Have students share what these experiences have in common and what makes them possible personal narrative topics.

Generate Ideas

- Explain that the first step in choosing a topic is to come up with a variety of ideas to choose from. One way to do this is to make an abecedarian list. In this list, each letter of the alphabet stands for something discovered or found. Model generating a few ideas:

  THINK ALOUD *First I write an A. Then I think about something that I once found that begins with the letter A. I write* ant hill. *Next, I think about something that begins with the letter B. I once found an old baseball card in my grandpa's house. I add that to the list.*

  > A: ant hill
  >
  > B: baseball card
  >
  > C: coin

- Have students complete the Abecedarian List on **Writer's Notebook page 1.4** or create one in their own notebooks. Tell students that they can skip letters if they get stuck. When students have completed their lists, invite volunteers to read their entries to the class.

- Finally, have students circle three things worth writing about. Provide enough time for students to carefully consider the items on their lists. Ask: *Which topics on your abecedarian list did you circle? Why did you circle those choices?*

Choose a Topic

- Invite students to think about the three things they circled. Have them consider the following questions about each:

  » What do I remember about the discovery?

  » How excited was I about the discovery, or what about made it interesting?

  » What effect did the discovery have on me?

- Encourage students to choose the topic for which they have the best answers to those three questions.

LEARNING OBJECTIVES

- Identify narrative structure.
- Create a story map.
- **Language** Recount a memory.

MATERIALS
Online Ed

Anchor Chart W3: *Narrative Elements*
Display and Engage *1.3*
Writer's Notebook p. 1.5

 INSTRUCTIONAL VOCABULARY

- **introduction** the beginning of a piece of writing
- **characters** the people in a narrative
- **conflict** the problem or struggle characters face in a story
- **setting** where and when a story takes place
- **events** what happens in a story
- **conclusion** the ending of a piece of writing

Organize Ideas

- Tell students that they will begin organizing their ideas for their personal narrative. Have partners Turn and Talk as they share which topic they chose for their response to the prompt. Encourage them to provide a summary of the memory that they will write about.

- Display **Anchor Chart W3: Narrative Elements** and read the points with students. *A narrative has an introduction, a setting, events, and a conclusion. An **introduction** is how the narrative begins. It introduces the reader to the **characters** and the main **conflict**, or problem, of the story. The setting is also introduced. The **setting** is where and when the story takes place. The **events** include everything that happens in the story. The **conclusion** is how the narrative ends. The conclusion is when the main conflict is resolved. Sometimes a lesson is learned.*

- Add these terms to the class Instructional Vocabulary list, and have students add them to their own glossaries.

- Connect the points with what students recall from *La Mariposa*. Have them find an example of each narrative element in the story.

- Tell students that they can plan their own narrative by identifying the different parts of the story they want to tell. Use **Display and Engage 1.3** to walk students through organizing their thoughts.

  THINK ALOUD *I plan to write about discovering an old baseball card at my grandpa's house. The characters in my personal narrative are my grandpa and I, so I write that on the story map. For the conflict, I am going to write about how Grandpa and I often don't have anything to talk about. The setting is Grandpa's house. In the Events box, I will list the events that I plan to include in my narrative. Finally, I will tell what the discovery meant to me in the conclusion.*

- Distribute **Writer's Notebook page 1.5** and allow students time to complete the Story Map as they plan their narratives.

- Invite volunteers to share their Story Maps with the class.

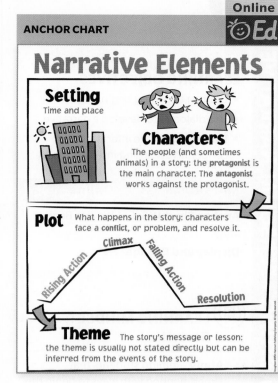

Online Ed

ANCHOR CHART

Narrative Elements

Setting Time and place

Characters The people (and sometimes animals) in a story: the **protagonist** is the main character. The **antagonist** works against the protagonist.

Plot What happens in the story: characters face a **conflict**, or problem, and resolve it.
Rising Action — Climax — Falling Action — Resolution

Theme The story's message or lesson: the theme is usually not stated directly but can be inferred from the events of the story.

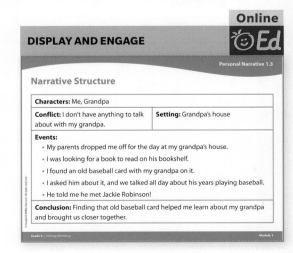

Online Ed

DISPLAY AND ENGAGE

Personal Narrative 1.3

Narrative Structure

Characters: Me, Grandpa	
Conflict: I don't have anything to talk about with my grandpa.	**Setting:** Grandpa's house

Events:
- My parents dropped me off for the day at my grandpa's house.
- I was looking for a book to read on his bookshelf.
- I found an old baseball card with my grandpa on it.
- I asked him about it, and we talked all day about his years playing baseball.
- He told me he met Jackie Robinson!

Conclusion: Finding that old baseball card helped me learn about my grandpa and brought us closer together.

Grade K | Writing Workshop Module 1

LEARNING OBJECTIVES

- Craft an engaging beginning.
- Use dialogue to develop a narrative.
- **Language** Share information in cooperative learning interactions.

MATERIALS   Online Ed

Anchor Chart W6: *5+1 Ways to Begin a Story*

Display and Engage *1.4*

LEARNING MINDSET: Growth

Apply Remind students that experimenting with ways to begin the narrative can help them grow as writers. Even if they think they know how they want to start the story, trying a few different ways can strengthen their skills and generate ideas for future writing projects.

● *Professional Learning*

RESEARCH FOUNDATIONS

Why does mindset matter? Students with a learning mindset are curious, challenge-seeking students who recognize that taking on challenges and learning from mistakes creates opportunities to develop their intelligence, practice skills, and increase their potential to be successful.

See the **GPS guide** to learn more.

Prepare to Draft

- Tell students they will learn different ways to start a narrative. Say: *Often starting a narrative is one of the hardest parts. Don't worry if you can't decide how to start right away. You can always try a few different approaches to see how they work.*

- Display **Anchor Chart W6: 5+1 Ways to Begin a Story**. Read through the different ways: *Action, Reaction, Dialogue, Setting, Glimpse of Character,* and *Combination*. Ask: *In which of these ways did* La Mariposa *begin?*

- Show **Display and Engage 1.4** and read through the model beginnings. Ask: *Which beginning do you like best? Why?*

- Guide students to realize that sometimes they can combine different beginnings to start a narrative. *I could begin with the* Action *scene, and then add the* Setting *followed by the* Dialogue.

Begin to Draft

- Have students choose three of the six ways to begin a story and use them to write three different beginnings to their own narratives.

- As students finish writing, divide them into small groups to share their three beginnings. Have group members offer feedback on which beginning is the most engaging. After sharing, you may wish to encourage students to try combining their three beginnings.

- Have students choose their favorite narrative beginning and continue drafting their narrative using the story map they completed in prewriting.

ANCHOR CHART — Online Ed

5 + 1 Ways to Begin a Story

Action — an exciting event
My bike sped toward the lake!

Reaction — a response to an event
The crowd cheered.

Dialogue — what characters say
"when are we launching?" "Our spaceship will launch soon."

Setting — the time and place of a story
The ocean sparkled under the summer sun.

Glimpse of Character — a character's traits
Grandpa loved every animal he met.

Combination — two or more ways (such as action and reaction)
The ball sailed toward the goal, and we all held our breath.

DISPLAY AND ENGAGE — Online Ed

Personal Narrative 1.4

Model Beginnings

Setting: It was my first day of first grade. I was eager to go to school, but I never thought the first day would be so exciting. I vividly remember my first day of school because I made a discovery.

Dialogue: "My name is Ms. Agnes, and I am going to be your teacher. Look here, I am giving you big sheets of paper and fat pencils. I want you to write me something. Fill the paper with writing."

Action: Mom and I walked up the big stone steps. I craned my neck to see the huge school building. I jumped and twirled around in my excitement to start my first day of first grade.

Try writing several different beginnings to your personal narrative. Share your options with a partner or small group and see which one they find most engaging and interesting.

Grade 4 | Writing Workshop   Module 1

LESSON 8

DRAFTING II: ELEMENTS OF A NARRATIVE

LEARNING OBJECTIVES
- Structure a draft purposefully.
- **Language** Use domain-specific vocabulary.

MATERIALS Online

Display and Engage *1.5a–1.5c*

Writer's Notebook *p. 1.6*

INSTRUCTIONAL VOCABULARY

- **chronological order** the order in which events happen or steps in a process should be done

Introduce the Skill

- Remind students that one way to recognize a personal narrative is by its text structure. *When you write a narrative, you should follow the narrative text structure to help develop your ideas.* Review the following parts of a narrative structure. Have students identify each part.

beginning/ introduction setting	middle plot	end/conclusion conflict

- Show **Display and Engage 1.5a–1.5c** and read the model with students. Have students follow along with **Writer's Notebook page 1.6**. Then ask the following questions and prompt students to mark their pages in crayon or colored pencil:

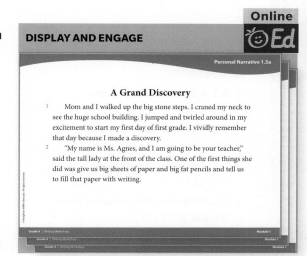

  » *What happens in the beginning? Middle? End? Circle each event in green.*

  » *Who are the characters? Underline them in blue.*

  » *What is the setting? Draw a red box around it.*

  » *What is the conflict, or problem?*

  » *How is the conflict resolved?*

- Explain that when a story is told in the order in which the events happen, it is in **chronological order**, or time order. Ask: *What is the benefit of telling a story in chronological order? (Events are in a logical order as they happen.)*

- Point out the parallel structure and repetition in the sentence *I made straight lines, I made crooked lines, I made short lines, and I made long lines.* Have students identify which words are repeated and which words are varied. Explain that writers use parallel structure and repetition to create a rhythm in their writing and sometimes to move the story along more quickly.

Apply the Skill

- Tell students to think about their own narratives. Have them draft a middle and end that follows from the beginning they have already written. Have them consider the conflict in the narrative and how it will be resolved.

NARRATIVE WRITING • PERSONAL NARRATIVE

LEARNING OBJECTIVES

- Develop a satisfying conclusion.
- **Language** Use descriptive words and phrases.

TARGETED GRAMMAR SUPPORT

You may want to consult the following grammar minilessons to review key editing topics.

- **6.1.4 Review Quotations,** p. W334
- **1.3.1 Sentence Fragments,** p. W226
- **1.3.2 Run-On Sentences,** p. W227
- **3.3.4 Review Progressive Verb Tenses,** p. W279

LEARNING MINDSET: Growth

Extend Explain to students that after every writing assignment, their writing will get a little bit stronger, and writing will become just a little bit easier for them. Remind them that they can go back and revise their prewriting ideas or take their drafts in a new direction at any time. Encourage them to stretch themselves as writers by trying something new.

Draft Conclusions

- Remind students that the narrative needs a conclusion, or ending, that follows from the events that came before it. The conclusion should show that the conflict is resolved and wrap up the story. Explain that there are different ways to do this. Write the following approaches on the board:

> Reflect on the events.
>
> Describe how you changed.
>
> Identify a future discovery you hope to make.
>
> Include dialogue that makes the resolution clear.

- Have students choose one approach to writing a conclusion for the narrative and jot down their ideas before adding the conclusion to the draft.

Circulate the Room

- Remind students that they can use different resources, including their prewriting notes, dictionaries, and thesauruses, to assist them with their writing.

- Have students continue drafting their narratives.

- Offer assistance to students, as necessary, allowing them to talk through an event or a description in order to articulate it before attempting to write it.

- As you circulate, group students who need support on similar grammar topics. Use the grammar minilessons or the students' own writing to provide targeted review and support.

 ENGLISH LEARNER SUPPORT: Scaffold Writing

ALL LEVELS Have English learners work together as they complete their conclusions. Encourage students to discuss their ideas and ask for feedback as they write.

REVISING I: GRAMMAR AND PUNCTUATION

LEARNING OBJECTIVES

- Revise writing to properly punctuate dialogue.
- Use direct and indirect dialogue in writing.
- **Language** Write direct and indirect dialogue with proper punctuation.

MATERIALS   Online ⊙Ed

Display and Engage *1.6, 1.5a–1.5c*

TARGETED GRAMMAR SUPPORT

You may want to consult the following grammar minilessons to review key editing topics.

- **6.1.1 Quotation Marks with Direct Speech,** p. W331
- **6.3.1 Commas with Direct Speech and Names,** p. W341

INSTRUCTIONAL VOCABULARY

- **direct dialogue:** the exact words that a character says
- **dialogue tag:** the words near dialogue that tell who is speaking
- **indirect dialogue:** a rewording or summary of what a character says

Introduce the Revision Skill

- Tell students that using dialogue is a great way to make characters come alive and get readers interested in a story. However, emphasize that they shouldn't overdo their narratives with dialogue. Point out that good narratives strike a balance between description, action, and dialogue.

- Show **Display and Engage 1.6** and discuss the rules for **direct dialogue**. Add the term to the class Instructional Vocabulary list. Have students add it and the other new terms in this lesson to their own glossaries.

- Explain that a **dialogue tag** introduces the dialogue by telling readers who is speaking. It can also tell readers how the person is speaking. Write several examples on the board. Then, ask students to give suggestions for other tag lines, and write them on the board as well:

> Dialogue tags:
>
> I said,
>
> Jerry whispered,
>
> shouted Penny.
>
> Serena replied with a smirk.

- Revisit the model on **Display and Engage 1.5a–1.5c** and ask: *Where does the author use direct dialogue?* When students choose a section of dialogue, have them point out the grammar rules that the author followed. (*indent, tag line, comma, quotation marks, punctuation inside the quotation marks*)

- Point students to the **indirect dialogue** in the model and show that there is no indentation or quotation mark. Ask: *Why does this dialogue follow different rules?* (*It is indirect dialogue that tells about what someone says but doesn't use someone's exact words.*)

Revise Dialogue

- Have students revise their writing to properly indent and punctuate dialogue.

- Circulate the room and assist students with revising. If students need help with a grammar topic, direct teach.

- As you circulate, group students who need support on similar grammar topics. Use the grammar minilessons or the students' own writing to provide targeted review and support.

NARRATIVE WRITING • PERSONAL NARRATIVE

LEARNING OBJECTIVES

- Conference with peers about written work.
- Revise drafts based on feedback from peers.
- **Language** Share information in cooperative learning interactions.

MATERIALS   Online

Display and Engage *1.7*
Writer's Notebook *pp. 1.7, 1.8*

TEACHER TIP

As the groups work on the Say Back exercise, circulate the room and monitor groups to ensure they are sticking to positive feedback.

LEARNING MINDSET: Growth

Apply Instruct students that when they give feedback, their job is to help their classmates grow as writers. *It is a big responsibility to give a writer feedback. When you speak, give the writer encouragement for all the work he or she has done so far. Then give suggestions to help the writer make the work even better.*

Introduce the Revision Skill

- Tell students they will listen to each other's personal narratives and provide feedback. Explain that writers will use the feedback to revise their work.

- Show **Display and Engage 1.7** and walk through the steps of the *Say Back* exercise.

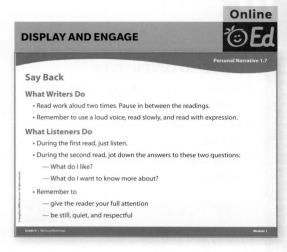

DISPLAY AND ENGAGE   Online

Personal Narrative 1.7

Say Back

What Writers Do
- Read work aloud two times. Pause in between the readings.
- Remember to use a loud voice, read slowly, and read with expression.

What Listeners Do
- During the first read, just listen.
- During the second read, jot down the answers to these two questions:
   — What do I like?
   — What do I want to know more about?
- Remember to
   — give the reader your full attention
   — be still, quiet, and respectful

Grade 6 | Writing Workshop   Module 1

- Explain that listeners should make specific comments. One way to do this is to write down just a few of the writer's exact words.

   THINK ALOUD *If I am listening to a writer read a personal narrative and he or she says,* The sunrise looked like a party to celebrate morning, *I could jot down* I like the description of the sunrise. *However, it is much better if I jot down the reader's exact words. When I give the writer my feedback, I read back the exact words. I say,* I like when you called the sunrise "a party to celebrate morning."

- Divide the class into groups of four or five students and assign each group member a number. Writer 1 will go first, then Writer 2, and so on.

- As the groups work on the *Say Back* exercise, circulate the room and monitor groups to ensure they are sticking to positive feedback.

- Have students turn to **Writer's Notebook pages 1.7 and 1.8** or have students take notes in their notebooks.

- After the *Say Back* activity, tell students to consider adding what listeners say they would like to hear more about. Remind writers that they do not have to act on every comment they receive.

- Give writers some time to study the feedback and circle comments they want to work into their revision.

Revise Based on Conference

- Have students revise their personal narratives based on conference feedback.

- Offer to be available to help students who get stuck or are unsure what to do with the feedback.

- In this workshop environment, some students may be revising, some still working in groups, and some conferencing with the teacher.

EL **ENGLISH LEARNER SUPPORT: Facilitate Discussion**

ALL LEVELS Work with students during the *Say Back* exercise. After a writer reads, help the other students provide feedback by answering yes/no questions, such as: *Would you like to hear more about how the horse looked? Does the story have a clear beginning, middle, and ending?*

LEARNING OBJECTIVES

- Edit drafts using complete sentences.
- Use a variety of sentence types in writing.
- Use commas when writing direct addresses.
- **Language** Use a variety of sentence types in writing.

MATERIALS   Online

Display and Engage *1.8*

 INSTRUCTIONAL VOCABULARY

- **direct address** when a person or thing is directly named in a sentence

TARGETED GRAMMAR SUPPORT

You may want to consult the following grammar minilessons to review key editing topics.

- **1.2.1 Declarative and Interrogative Sentences,** p. W221
- **1.2.2 Imperative and Exclamatory Sentences,** p. W222
- **1.2.3 Identify Kinds of Sentences,** p. W223

Introduce Revision Skill

- Explain that students will be looking carefully at each sentence in their writing to make sure every sentence makes sense.

- Show **Display and Engage 1.8** and go over the sentence types.

- To practice recognizing sentence types, have volunteers generate simple sentences to say aloud. Then, have students categorize each sentence according to the types shown in **Display and Engage 1.8**.

- Tell students they will also examine their writing for **direct address**. Write the following example sentences on the board:

> "Christine, can you please bring me some water?"
>
> "I really want to help you, Miguel, but I am not sure what you need."
>
> "I had a really great time, Mom."

- Read the three sentences and emphasize the person being addressed. Ask: What do these three sentences have in common? (*All address a person by name or title.*)

- Tell students that this is called *direct address*. Have students add the term to their Instructional Vocabulary glossaries.

- Ask: What do you notice about the punctuation that sets the name apart from the rest of the sentence? (*commas*) Help students understand that commas surround the name when it is in the middle of a sentence. However, at the beginning or the end of a sentence, the name is set apart by only one comma.

Revise for Sentence Sense and Direct Address

- Have students revise their writing for sentence sense and direct address.

- Circulate the room and assist students with revising. If students need help with a grammar topic, direct teach.

- As you circulate, group students who need support on similar grammar topics. Use the grammar minilessons or the students' own writing to provide targeted review and support.

DISPLAY AND ENGAGE — Online • Ed

Personal Narrative 1.8

Sentence Sense

Sentence Type	What does the sentence do?	Example
Declarative	makes a statement (declares)	I have a red bicycle.
Interrogative	asks a question (interrogates)	Do you have a bicycle, too?
Imperative	gives a command (orders)	Take your bicycle and go home.
Exclamatory	shows strong emotion (exclaims)	Someone took my bicycle!

Revise your narrative to improve sentence structure by making sure each sentence makes sense.

Grade 4 | Writing Workshop   Module 1

LEARNING OBJECTIVES

- **Language** Edit drafts for correct spelling, punctuation, and grammar.
- **Language** Share information in cooperative learning interactions.
- **Language** Edit writing for standard grammar and usage.

MATERIALS — Online

Writer's Notebook *p. 1.9*

Display and Engage *1.9*

TARGETED GRAMMAR SUPPORT

You may want to consult the following grammar minilessons to review key editing topics.

- **1.3.1 Sentence Fragments,** p. W226
- **2.1.3 Capitalizing Languages, People's Names, and Nationalities,** p. W238
- **6.3.1 Commas with Direct Speech and Names,** p. W341

TEACHER TIP

Not only does clocking teach students worthwhile habits of proofreading and editing, but it also sharpens their awareness of details and places responsibility upon them for an acceptable final copy.

Clocking Activity

- Tell students they will be doing a peer revising activity called *Clocking*.

- Have students sit in concentric circles. Distribute **Writer's Notebook page 1.9** and tell students to write their names at the top of the editing page. The page will travel with their personal narratives.

- As students receive a peer's personal narrative, they become the editor of that paper. Editors write their names to the left of the item they are checking.

- Show **Display and Engage 1.9** and call out which item is to be checked by the editor. *Is there a name on the paper? Are there opening and closing quotation marks around direct dialogue?*

  THINK ALOUD *If I find an error in the paper I am editing, I write it down on the lines following the item I am checking. I include details to help the writer find the error. For example, I might write:* Sentence 2 in paragraph 2 is a run-on.

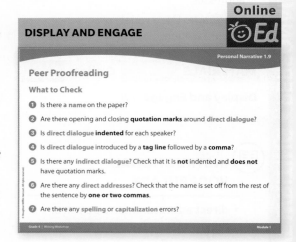

- After a couple of items, have students stand up and move—like a clock—so that each paper is read by several editors.

- No marks are made on the personal narrative drafts themselves. All notes are made on the Writer's Notebook page.

- When the editing process is completed, have students take the editing page and make any necessary corrections to their narratives.

Edit Writing

- Have students do a final pass through their personal narratives, integrating any appropriate notes from the clocking activity into their own writing.

LEARNING OBJECTIVES

- Publish personal narratives.
- **Language** Identify and use homophones and multiple-meaning words.

MATERIALS
Online

Display and Engage 1.10

 INSTRUCTIONAL VOCABULARY

- **quire** four sheets of paper that are folded to form eight leaves.

TEACHER TIP

Have students use colorful pencils, crayons, or markers to make attractive covers for their quires. The covers should include the title of the narrative and the writer's name. If time allows, give students the option of illustrating their personal narratives.

Prepare the Final Copy

- Say the word **quire** and ask: *Who can spell the word* quire? Students will likely spell *choir*.

- Write the two words on the board and tell students they are homophones, which are two words that sound the same but have different spellings and meanings. Ask: *Does anyone know the definitions of* choir *and* quire? Students may know how to define *choir* but not *quire*. Write the definitions on the board.

- Underline *leaves* in the definition of *quire*. *Does anyone know what* leaves *means here?* (*pages in a book*) Tell students that the word *leaves* is a multiple-meaning word because it has more than one completely different meaning. Add these definitions to the board.

> choir: a group of singers
>
> quire: four sheets of paper that are folded to form eight leaves
>
> leaves: foliage on a tree
>
> leaves: pages in a book

- Tell students they will make quires. Show **Display and Engage 1.10** and review the directions with students.

- Distribute paper to students. Model each step as students go through the process.

- Once quires are made, tell students to copy their personal narratives inside, using their best handwriting.

Publish Writing

- Display the quires in the classroom.

- Label the display *WRITING IS DISCOVERY!*

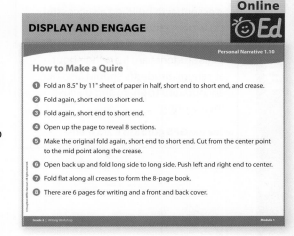

DISPLAY AND ENGAGE

Online

Personal Narrative 1.10

How to Make a Quire

1. Fold an 8.5" by 11" sheet of paper in half, short end to short end, and crease.
2. Fold again, short end to short end.
3. Fold again, short end to short end.
4. Open up the page to reveal 8 sections.
5. Make the original fold again, short end to short end. Cut from the center point to the mid point along the crease.
6. Open back up and fold long side to long side. Push left and right end to center.
7. Fold flat along all creases to form the 8-page book.
8. There are 6 pages for writing and a front and back cover.

Grade 6 | Writing Workshop Module 1

LEARNING OBJECTIVES

- Share personal narratives.
- Speak loudly and clearly at an understandable pace.
- Listen actively.
- **Language** Practice and present a narrative.

MATERIALS Online

Display and Engage *1.11*

Writer's Notebook *p. 1.10*

● Professional Learning

BEST PRACTICES

Parents, caretakers, and friends are critical to the learning process. Communication with those at home is essential to building a successful classroom environment. Caretakers should be aware of the topics and skills students are learning about at school. Students should also be encouraged to share and discuss their writing.

See the **GPS guide** to learn more.

TEACHER TIP

If time is limited, divide students into small groups to share their personal narratives.

Share Writing

- Tell students they will share their personal narratives with the class.

- Show **Display and Engage 1.11** and review the tips for readers and listeners.

- Revisit the model or use another text of your choice to demonstrate the tips for readers. As you read the model, purposely make presentation mistakes, such as:

  » Read slowly and clearly but keep your eyes only on the paper. Ask: *Which tips am I following? Which did I forget about?*

  » Read dialogue with inappropriate expression. Ask: *Did I read the dialogue correctly?* Have students help you figure out how the character would say the dialogue.

Online

DISPLAY AND ENGAGE

Personal Narrative 1.11

Sharing: Tips for Readers and Listeners

Readers
- Read slowly and clearly and make eye contact with listeners.
- Use expression for dialogue. Think: *How would my character say this?*
- If you included illustrations, remember to show them at the end of each page.
- After you are finished, ask if anyone has questions.

Listeners
- Take everything off your desk and keep your eyes on the reader.
- If you are called on, tell the reader **what you liked** about his or her story or presentation.
- Be polite. Remember, not everyone will get a chance to make comments.

Grade 4 | Writing Workshop   Module 1

Engage and Respond

- Conclude with a debriefing. Distribute **Writer's Notebook page 1.10** or write the following questions on the board and have students answer them in their own notebooks.

> 1. What did you like best about writing your personal narrative? Why?
>
> 2. What did you like least? Why?
>
> 3. What did you learn about writing? How did you learn it?
>
> 4. What did you learn about grammar? How did you learn it?
>
> 5. What did you learn about punctuation? How did you learn it?
>
> 6. Did you learn any new vocabulary words? What are they and how did you learn them?

(EL) ENGLISH LEARNER SUPPORT: Support Presenting

SUBSTANTIAL

Work individually with students to practice presenting. Assist students with pronunciation by modeling and having students repeat difficult words.

MODERATE

Work individually with students to practice presenting. Assist students with pronunciation and fluidity by modeling and having students repeat difficult words and sentences, copying your tone.

LIGHT

Have students practice presenting with a partner. Be available to help with pronunciation, as well as with fluid and expressive reading.

Description

FOCUS STATEMENT Amazing creatures live in this world.

FOCAL TEXT

Apex Predators

Author and Illustrator: Steve Jenkins

Summary: This informational text gives detailed information about many different predators, including extinct species.

WRITING PROMPT

READ this sentence: *Amazing creatures live in this world.*

THINK about an animal that you think is amazing.

WRITE a description about that animal. Use facts and details to show why that animal is amazing.

LESSONS

1. **Introducing the Focal Text**

2. **Vocabulary**

3. **Prewriting I: Preparing to Write**

4. **Prewriting II: Choosing a Topic**

5. **Prewriting III: Identifying Details**

6. **Drafting I: Beginning the Draft**

7. **Drafting II: Integrating Descriptive Language**

8. **Drafting III: Completing the Draft**

9. **Revising I: Integrating Grammar and Punctuation**

10. **Revising II: Conferencing**

11. **Revising III: Adding Descriptive Details**

12. **Editing I: Mechanics and Spelling**

13. **Editing II: Peer Proofreading**

14. **Publishing**

15. **Sharing**

LEARNING MINDSET:
Noticing

Display **Anchor Chart 31: My Learning Mindset** throughout the year. Refer to it to introduce Noticing and to reinforce the skills you introduced in previous modules.

INFORMATIONAL TEXT · DESCRIPTION

LEARNING OBJECTIVES

- Make connections to the topic and theme.
- Identify central ideas.
- Recognize a pattern of organization in a text.
- **Language** Describe personal connections to an informational text.
- **Language** Explain author's use of text structure.

MATERIALS   Online

Classroom materials *photos or videos of animals*

Display and Engage *2.1*

Focal Text *Apex Predators*

Priming the Students

Explore the Topic

- Tell students that they will explore the many ways that animals survive in the world and how amazing animals can be.

- Find and show photographs or video clips online of several interesting animals (e.g., seahorse, tiger, penguin, octopus). Ask students to describe what is amazing or interesting about the animals. Write descriptive language that students use and display it on the board or chart paper.

- Show a picture of a familiar, large predator such as a *Tyrannosaurus rex*, a lion roaring, or a grizzly bear with claws displayed. Ask: *What animal is this?* Invite students to talk about what they know about the animal and how it lives.

- Have students create a list of words that they would use to describe the animal. Write the words on the board. Ask: *Are there any other animals that could be described this way?*

Discuss the Focus Statement

- Show **Display and Engage 2.1**. Read the Focus Statement with students. Have them write a few sentences in their notebooks describing an example of an amazing animal that they know about. Encourage them to write about an animal not already covered in the class discussion.

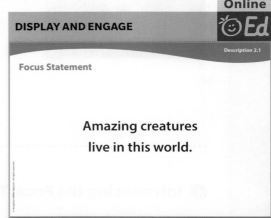

DISPLAY AND ENGAGE   Online

Description 2.1

Focus Statement

Amazing creatures live in this world.

EL **ENGLISH LEARNER SUPPORT: Build Vocabulary**

ALL LEVELS Supply a word list of descriptive terms for students to choose from, ranging from simple, lower-level words (e.g., *strong, fast*) to higher-level words (e.g., *powerful, vicious, meat-eating*).

Priming the Text

Prepare to Read

- Explain that students are going to become researchers and investigate an animal like the ones they have just described.

Apex Predators

- Show the cover of *Apex Predators*. Explain that *Apex Predators* is about particular animals called predators. Explain: *Each animal in the book is special in its own way. The things that make it special help it to get food and survive in its particular time and place.*

- Read the definition of *predator* in the first sentence of the book.

- Thumb through the book, showing pictures of the different predators. Point out the banner heads at the tops of the pages that organize the animals according to the time they lived. Explain that these headings create a text structure that helps readers understand the information more easily. Create a class Instructional Vocabulary list for this module. Write and define **text structure** as *the way information in a text is organized to help readers understand it.* Have students create an Instructional Vocabulary list in the back of their notebooks and add the term to it.

- On a world map or globe, point out locations of apex predators mentioned in the text.

  » South America: terror bird, electric eels, marsupial saber-tooth, giant *Teratorn*, *Titanoboa*

  » Asia: Siberian tiger, giant freshwater ray

  » Pacific Islands: Komodo dragon

  » Africa: African wild dogs, fossa

  » North America: giant short-faced bear, *Daedon*

- Draw students' attention to the diagram of each predator's size compared with a human.

- Display the bibliography and list of websites at the end of the book. Tell students that these books and websites provide more information about the predators discussed in the book. Explain that research about the predators could start at those websites.

Engage and Respond

- Have students Turn and Talk to a partner. Have them discuss which predator they are most interested in reading about and why.

 ENGLISH LEARNER SUPPORT: Facilitate Understanding and Discussion

SUBSTANTIAL
Simplify language by rephrasing it. For example, rephrase *modern-day predator* as *predator that is alive today*.

MODERATE
Provide sentence frames for students in Turn and Talk: *I'm most interested in _____ because _____.*

LIGHT
Partner students with similar language proficiency for the Turn and Talk.

 INSTRUCTIONAL VOCABULARY

- **text structure** the way information in a text is organized to help readers understand it

 LEARNING MINDSET: Noticing

Introduce Throughout the module, students will be asked to look closely at something or to read details carefully. Say: *Authors draw readers' attention to important details in different ways, such as through headings, images, captions, and text structures.* Explain that some things are harder to notice but are important too. *The more carefully you read, the more likely you are to notice important ideas and connections.* Give feedback as students offer descriptions by highlighting responses where students noticed something specific or interesting.

 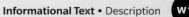

● *Professional Learning*

RESEARCH FOUNDATIONS

A student's mindset is how he or she feels about learning. A learning mindset is a set of beliefs—including growth mindset, belonging, and purpose and relevance—that drive students to seek challenges, feel school is a safe space to make mistakes, and believe that there is value in working hard.

See the **GPS guide** to learn more.

The Read

Read the Focal Text

- Read *Apex Predators* with expression, showing how language and sentence structure create a tone that draws in readers. As you read, stop at these points to highlight the organization of the text:

  » Read these pages: "Top predators of today . . ." and "and yesterday." Point to the opposing banner heads at the top of the pages that show two different categories of predators. Explain that the word *extinct* means that there are no more of that creature alive today. Ask: *What kinds of apex predators do these headings show you the book will be about?*

  » Have students study the illustrations on these pages. Ask: *Why do you think the animals in these two illustrations are facing each other?*

  » Read these pages: "Island monster" and "Jaws." Have students look at the two section heads and note that the author uses the section heads to introduce each new animal.

  » Read these pages: "Sea monster." Have students look carefully at the illustration of the *Tylosaurus*. Have them describe additional details about the *Tylosaurus* that they notice in the illustration that are not included in the text. Then ask: *What animal that is alive today does the* Tylosaurus *remind you of? What about them is similar?*

  » After reading the book, ask: *How is the information in the book organized? (It is divided into modern-day predators and predators that became extinct millions of years ago.)*

- Model visualizing one of the extinct animals after reading about it.

  THINK ALOUD *I read that the giant short-faced bear was faster than any other animal its size and could chase deer. The picture shows me that it looks like a large grizzly bear. Grizzly bears are big and can run twice as fast as people, but they can't run long enough to chase a deer! The comparison diagram shows me that the giant short-faced bear was more than twice the size of an average person. Its paw is bigger than a person's head. I think this is a terrifying predator!*

- Discuss how facts and illustrations can be used together to write a description that allows readers to learn about an animal and to visualize what the animal is like in real life.

Engage and Respond

- Display the last page of the text and ask a volunteer to read aloud the section on humans. Have small groups discuss their answers to these questions: *How are humans described? How does this information about humans fit into the organization of the book?*

LEARNING OBJECTIVES

- Read and understand domain-specific vocabulary.
- Identify proper nouns, common nouns, and adjectives.
- **Language** Identify and label parts of speech.
- **Language** Use new vocabulary to describe.

MATERIALS

Online Ed

Writer's Notebook *p. 2.1*

Focal Text *Apex Predators*

Display and Engage *2.2*

Review the Focal Text

- Guide students to start a Word Bank on **Writer's Notebook page 2.1** or in their own notebooks. Page through *Apex Predators*, pausing after each page to allow students the opportunity to add words from the page to their Word Banks. Examples of the words students may choose are:

WORD BANK

apex	Asia	fierce	scavenger
venomous	habitat	South America	extinction
canine	Spinosaurus	agile	fearsome

- Tell students to make three columns in their notebooks or a separate sheet of paper, labeling the first column *Proper Nouns*, the second column *Common Nouns*, and the third column *Adjectives*.

- Have students sort their Word Bank words into the three categories.

- When finished, invite each student to choose a word and present it to the class by using it in a different context than it is used in the book. Show **Display and Engage 2.2** and read the directions for the activity with students.

- Model presenting one of the Word Bank words: *The word I choose is fearsome. Fearsome is an adjective. It means frightening. The Dimetrodon is described as a fearsome predator in the book. This means that the Dimetrodon was intimidating and scary. A tornado is a fearsome sight and means that you must take cover.*

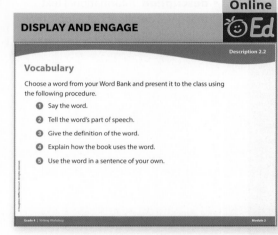

Online Ed

DISPLAY AND ENGAGE

Description 2.2

Vocabulary

Choose a word from your Word Bank and present it to the class using the following procedure.

1. Say the word.
2. Tell the word's part of speech.
3. Give the definition of the word.
4. Explain how the book uses the word.
5. Use the word in a sentence of your own.

Grade 4 | Writing Workshop — Module 2

Engage and Respond

- Have students vote for the top three terms they think are most interesting and descriptive.

EL **ENGLISH LEARNER SUPPORT: Facilitate Response**

SUBSTANTIAL

Allow students to point to where the word they chose is used in the book.

MODERATE

Place students into small groups where each group member takes one step of the presentation.

LIGHT

Have students write their sentences down. Have partners exchange sentences and offer feedback before presenting.

INFORMATIONAL TEXT • DESCRIPTION

LEARNING OBJECTIVES

- Understand the writing prompt.
- Identify task, audience, and purpose.
- Set goals for writing.
- **Language** Articulate writing goals.

MATERIALS　　Online Ed

Display and Engage *2.3*

Writer's Notebook *pp. 2.2, 2.3*

Anchor Chart W1: *Task, Audience, and Purpose*

 INSTRUCTIONAL VOCABULARY

- **description** informational text that gives details about a topic that help readers picture it.

Discuss the Writing Prompt

- Tell students that in this module they will write a description. Explain that a **description** is a type of informational text that gives details about a topic that help readers picture it. Have students add this term to their lists while you add it to the class Instructional Vocabulary list.

- Show **Display and Engage 2.3** and read the Writing Prompt together. Be sure students note and understand the tips.

- Refer students to **Writer's Notebook page 2.2**. Explain that the rubric can help them understand the features of a strong description. Discuss the different expectations of the rubric. Remind students they can use this rubric as a guide while drafting and revising.

- Display **Anchor Chart W1: Task, Audience, and Purpose** and read the points with students. Talk about the task of writing a description. Ask: *What might a reader want to learn about an animal?* Allow students to talk with partners or in small groups to discuss this question. Connect this question to the idea of writing to inform an audience.

Set Goals for Writing

- Prompt students to think about their past writing and what they would like to improve. Have students set goals for writing their description and add them to the list on **Writer's Notebook page 2.3** or in their own notebooks.

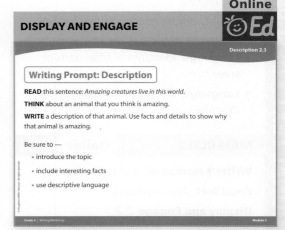

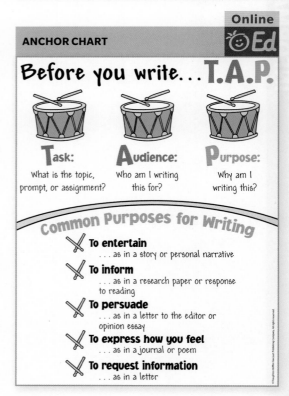

 ENGLISH LEARNER SUPPORT: Facilitate Expression

SUBSTANTIAL

Discuss goals for this assignment, pointing out these areas on students' previous writing or providing examples. Write the goals for students to copy into their Writer's Notebook.

MODERATE

Discuss students' writing goals with them. Provide sentence frames for them to write these goals in their Writer's Notebook.

LIGHT

Have students discuss writing goals with you before writing them in their Writer's Notebook. Help with instructional vocabulary if necessary.

INFORMATIONAL TEXT • DESCRIPTION

LEARNING OBJECTIVES

- Choose a topic.
- Use prewriting strategies.
- **Language** Discuss details about a potential topic.

MATERIALS   Online Ed

Writer's Notebook *p. 2.4*
Display and Engage *2.4*

 INSTRUCTIONAL VOCABULARY

- **freewriting** a strategy for getting ideas onto paper without worrying about structure or grammar.

 LEARNING MINDSET: Noticing

Apply Tell students that researching a topic in order to write about it can present new opportunities for discovery. Say: *You can find interesting facts and exciting ideas if you take the time to slow down, notice things, and enjoy the process.* Encourage students to explore a few different animals and pay close attention to what they find, making note of their observations and sharing them with a partner or small group.

Choose a Topic

- Point out to students that they have discussed animals that they think are amazing as well as the kinds of things a reader might want to read about an animal.

- Remind students that a topic is the subject of a piece of writing. Refer students to the list on **Writer's Notebook page 2.4**. Tell them to put a check next to any animal they may want to explore in their description. Encourage them to write the name of another animal they may want to write about.

- Model choosing a topic.

  THINK ALOUD *I checked both African wild dogs and Utahraptors. I think it's amazing how both these animals work in groups. I want to know more about how those groups work. I know that Utahraptors are extinct, so I may not be able to find much information about them. I will choose African wild dogs since more information is available.*

- Allow students to talk with a partner about what they find interesting or amazing about the animals they checked before deciding on a topic. Have them circle their final choice.

Explore the Topic with Freewriting

- Conduct a freewriting exercise to help students generate ideas.

  » Explain that **freewriting** is a strategy for getting ideas onto paper without worrying about structure or grammar. *Freewriting is a prewriting strategy that allows you to record any and all ideas about your topic before you begin drafting.* Have students add the term to their lists as you add it to the class Instructional Vocabulary list.

  » Show **Display and Engage 2.4** and have students choose a question as the starting point for their freewriting.

  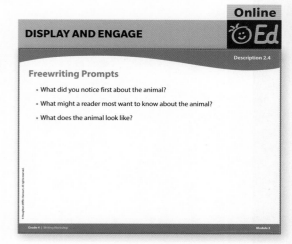

  » Remind students that the point of freewriting is to write whatever ideas come to mind without stopping to fix, edit, or organize. Say: *Try to keep your pen or pencil moving the entire time.*

  » Set a time or watch the clock for four minutes as students freewrite in their notebooks.

Gather Information

- Explain to students that by learning as much as they can about the animal they chose, they will be able to write stronger, more interesting descriptions.

- For students who chose an animal from *Apex Predators*, have them begin gathering information by rereading the section on their chosen animal, taking notes on what the text says and what they notice in the illustration.

- Depending upon resources, take students to the library or computer lab or provide texts such as encyclopedias and nonfiction books. Encourage students to take plenty of notes in their own words about the information.

- Point out that students may also want to add some of the ideas from their freewriting exercise to support their research.

Identify Audience and Purpose

- Remind students to once again consider who they are writing for and what they want their readers to know. Have students complete **Writer's Notebook page 2.5** to help them identify their audience and purpose.

- Explain that a writer's purpose guides the **main idea** of the writing, or the main point that the writer wants the reader to know. The **details** that support the main idea include specific facts. Say: *For a description, these details should include facts that help your reader picture the animal. Specific, interesting details also help engage the reader. Don't you prefer to read interesting facts?* You may want to add *main idea* and *detail* to the class Instructional Vocabulary list and have students add these terms to their own lists.

Choose Details

- With audience and purpose in mind, guide students to read through their notes and freewriting exercise to identify the most relevant and interesting details that they discovered, such as what the animal looks like, where it lives (and when it lived, if extinct), and what makes it amazing.

- Allow students time to complete the web on **Writer's Notebook page 2.6** with the interesting details they want to include in their descriptions. Encourage them to add circles for details if they wish.

- Invite volunteers to share their webs.

 ENGLISH LEARNER SUPPORT: Facilitate Research

ALL LEVELS Some online encyclopedias offer versions in languages other than English. You may also wish to show students how to use online translation dictionaries, especially those that include audio pronunciations. Help specifically with rephrasing information so that unintentional plagiarism is avoided.

LEARNING OBJECTIVES

- Develop an engaging idea.
- Craft facts and details into a description.
- **Language** Compare descriptions.

MATERIALS

Online

Display and Engage *2.5a–c*
Writer's Notebook *pp. 2.2, 2.7*

LEARNING MINDSET:
Noticing

Apply Tell students to pay attention to what they need to do in order to notice the differences between the two samples of descriptive writing. Then ask: *How does noticing what's good about the model description help you write your own description? How does noticing what is lacking in the second example help you write your own description?*

● *Getting Started*

CLASSROOM MANAGEMENT

Behavioral issues during collaborative conversations may stem from students' excitement to share and participate. Be proactive by reviewing discussion rules prior to starting the conversations. Quietly redirect students who get off track, and remind them of positive behavior.

See the **GPS guide** to learn more.

Prepare to Draft

- Tell students that they will now take the details they have gathered and begin to write their descriptions of amazing animals in their own words.

- Show **Display and Engage 2.5a–c** and read the model aloud as students follow along on **Writer's Notebook page 2.7**. Ask: *Does the model sound like it was copied from an encyclopedia? Does it sound like just a list of facts? Why or why not?*

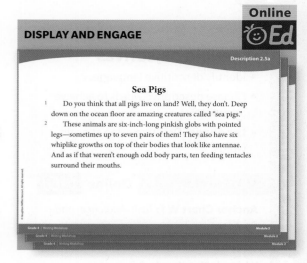

Online
DISPLAY AND ENGAGE

Description 2.5a

Sea Pigs

1   Do you think that all pigs live on land? Well, they don't. Deep down on the ocean floor are amazing creatures called "sea pigs."
2   These animals are six-inch-long pinkish globs with pointed legs—sometimes up to seven pairs of them! They also have six whiplike growths on top of their bodies that look like antennae. And as if that weren't enough odd body parts, ten feeding tentacles surround their mouths.

- Write the following sample text on the board and invite students to compare it with the model:

> Sea pigs live in the ocean. They are round. They are six inches long. They have pointed legs. They eat what they can find in mud.

- Ask: *How are these two descriptions different?* Guide a whole-group discussion about which sample is more interesting and why. Suggest students use the rubric for descriptive writing on **Writer's Notebook page 2.2** to discuss which description is better.

- Explain: *Writing is as much about <u>how</u> you say something as <u>what</u> you say.* Point out how the tone of the model is informal and engaging. The author is clearly interested in the topic. Guide students to identify parts of the model that have a clear voice and personality, such as the opening and closing paragraphs. Ask: *How would you explain your animal to a friend? What would you tell him or her first? What words would you use?* Tell students to capture that voice and excitement in their writing.

Begin to Draft

- Review the ways that students have learned to make a description interesting and have students write them in their notebook:

  1. Choose an amazing animal.

  2. Include the most interesting details.

  3. Craft those details into engaging text.

- Help students realize that facts alone do not make a good description. Say: *It's the way the facts are written that makes us want to read on.*

- Suggest that students write a sentence or two introducing their animal to help guide them as they write the description. They can return to these sentences and craft an engaging introduction when they revise.

LEARNING OBJECTIVES

- Identify descriptive language.
- Choose descriptive words to achieve a purpose.
- **Language** Describe using specific words.

MATERIALS   Online Ed

Anchor Chart W1: *Task, Audience, and Purpose*

Display and Engage *2.5a–c*

Writer's Notebook *2.7*

● *Professional Learning*

BEST PRACTICES

Review recently acquired vocabulary as needed to reinforce instruction and to assist students with their writing.

See the **GPS guide** to learn more.

Introduce Descriptive Language

- Review the elements of a good description. Post **Anchor Chart W1: Task, Audience, and Purpose** and discuss how descriptive language helps writers achieve their purpose and engage their audience. Say: *That's why it's important to use descriptive language when you write.*

- Show **Display and Engage 2.5a–c** and have students refer to the model on **Writer's Notebook page 2.7**. Say: *Let's see how descriptive language is used in the model.* Have students draw a red box around the topic of the description ("sea pigs") and underline in blue all the descriptive language. As a group, talk about what descriptive language students found and what the descriptive language adds to the writing.

- Guide students to recognize how facts and specific details work together with a writer's word choice to develop a strong description.

Apply the Skill

- Allow students time to think about their descriptions. Encourage them to make a written plan to use strong action verbs as well as specific details from the facts they found to describe their amazing animal. Then have them continue to draft their descriptions.

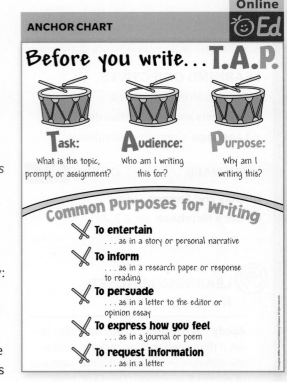

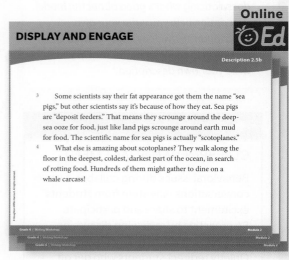

(EL) ENGLISH LEARNER SUPPORT: Expand Vocabulary

SUBSTANTIAL

Ask simple specific questions for which students produce descriptive language they can use in their writing when answering, such as *What color is it? How many legs does it have? Is it huge or tiny?*

MODERATE

Supply word banks of descriptive terms relevant to chosen topics.

LIGHT

Suggest students list words belonging to parts of speech—verbs, adjectives, adverbs—that they can use to describe their animal. Assist as necessary.

LEARNING OBJECTIVES

- Refine an introduction.
- Write a conclusion.
- **Language** Discuss and evaluate structure of writing.
- **Language** Compose an introduction and conclusion.

MATERIALS

Online

Display and Engage *2.5a, 2.5c*

 INSTRUCTIONAL VOCABULARY

- **conclusion** a statement or paragraph at the end of a piece of writing that sums up the main idea and leaves the reader with a final thought

TEACHER TIP

Explain that *conclusion* has a very general meaning: *end*. Remind students that when they read, they end up with a conclusion when they put together something in the text with what they already know in order to think of something that isn't stated. When they write, they end their writing with a conclusion when they wrap up their main idea.

Organizing with Structure: Introductions

- Say: *When you have completed the description of your animal, you should go back and write your introduction and conclusion.*

- Explain that an introduction should grab the reader's attention. Show the model on **Display and Engage 2.5a** and have a volunteer read the introduction. Ask how the model begins (*with a question*). Point out how this engages readers and makes them want to read on.

- Tell students they can craft an introduction by expanding the sentences they jotted down when they began their draft.

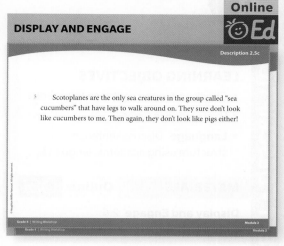

Organizing with Structure: Conclusions

- Next, explain that the best **conclusions** restate the author's main point and leave the reader with something to think about.

- Show the model on **Display and Engage 2.5c** and have a volunteer read the conclusion. Ask: *What makes this an effective conclusion?* Discuss how the conclusion appeals to the audience and how it meets the purpose of describing and giving information about an amazing animal.

- Write the following on the board.

> Like most birds, the tiny hummingbird can fly forward. But it can also fly like no other bird can. A hummingbird can rocket straight up. It can drop straight down. It can even hang in the air. In this way, it's like a helicopter.

- Model how to write a concluding sentence for the description.
  THINK ALOUD *I want a conclusion that wraps up the idea of how the hummingbird can fly. I want the reader to remember that it's like a helicopter. That will be my conclusion, but I'll put it in the form of a question: Is it any wonder the hummingbird is called the helicopter of the bird world?*

- Add *conclusion* to the class Instructional Vocabulary list, and suggest that students add it to their individual Instructional Vocabulary lists.

- Have students return to their descriptions and craft introductions and conclusions.

 ENGLISH LEARNER SUPPORT: Support Language Structures

SUBSTANTIAL
Review students' descriptions and provide appropriate concluding frames for them to use.

MODERATE
Discuss with students ways in which they might conclude their descriptions.

LIGHT
Have partners discuss ways in which they might conclude their descriptions. Monitor and offer feedback.

INFORMATIONAL TEXT • DESCRIPTION

LEARNING OBJECTIVES

- Check and repair sentence fragments.
- Vary sentence types.
- **Language** Discuss sentence structure using academic language.

MATERIALS   Online

Display and Engage *2.6*

Writer's Notebook *p. 2.7*

 LEARNING MINDSET:
Noticing

Expand Point out to students that noticing is not limited to seeing. Say: *There's plenty to notice with our ears, too. Read your sentences "aloud" inside your head. Do they sound incomplete? Do they sound varied and interesting?* Tell students that all their senses can help them notice.

TARGETED GRAMMAR SUPPORT

You may want to consult the following grammar minilessons to help students as they revise.

- **1.2.3 Identify Kinds of Sentences,** p. W223
- **1.3.1 Sentence Fragments,** p. W226

Revising to Strengthen Sentences

- Tell students that today they will begin revising their drafts by focusing on crafting the best sentences possible. Say: *Your ideas won't make sense to your readers unless your sentences work together correctly and well.*

- Use rewritten excerpts from the model to prove your point. Project **Display and Engage 2.6** and read the examples. Point out that readers can't be exactly sure what the writer means because the sentences are incomplete, or fragments. Necessary parts are missing. Have students compare the fragments with the model on **Writer's Notebook page 2.7**. Elicit and discuss the solutions to the problem: *The first fragment needs the verb* is *and the article* a. *The last fragment could use the subject* it. *The middle fragment can be attached to the first.*

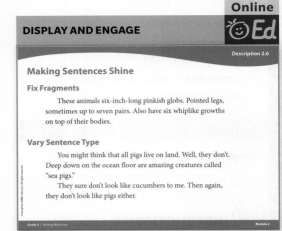

DISPLAY AND ENGAGE   Online

Description 2.6

Making Sentences Shine

Fix Fragments
    These animals six-inch-long pinkish globs. Pointed legs, sometimes up to seven pairs. Also have six whiplike growths on top of their bodies.

Vary Sentence Type
    You might think that all pigs live on land. Well, they don't. Deep down on the ocean floor are amazing creatures called "sea pigs."
    They sure don't look like cucumbers to me. Then again, they don't look like pigs either.

Grade 4 | Writing Workshop   Module 2

- Write this text, and guide students in finding and fixing the fragments. (first, third, and fifth sentences) Use the proofreading marks to make changes:

> Armadillo "little armored one" in Spanish. The animal is called that for a reason. Has bony plates on its back, head, legs, and tail. Armadillos have long sticky tongues. For catching and eating bugs in the ground. Ants and termites are their favorites.

- Remind students that they cannot achieve their purpose if readers are confused or don't understand the writing.

- Next, discuss sentence fluency and achieving it by varying sentence type. Read the examples on **Display and Engage 2.6** and have students compare them with the opening and ending paragraphs of the model. *What differences do you see?* Point out the change in sentence types from declarative to interrogative and exclamatory and the end punctuation that is involved. Discuss how the question and exclamation make the writing more engaging. Model making such a change:

THINK ALOUD *How could I revise the sentences in the armadillo text to make the writing more engaging? The second sentence just states that there's a reason. I could change it to a question to ask:* Why is the animal called that? *That makes the reader want to read on to find the answer.*

- Have a volunteer change the final sentence to an exclamation.

- Tell students to return to their drafts and look for fragments to correct and places where they can vary sentence types. Encourage students to use the proofreading marks as they work.

- As students work, be available for consultation. As you circulate, group students who need support on similar grammar topics. Use the grammar minilessons or the students' own writing to provide targeted review and support.

LEARNING OBJECTIVES
- Discuss drafts with peers.
- **Language** Discuss writing using academic language.

MATERIALS Online

Writer's Notebook *p. 2.8*

TEACHER TIP

Writers can take notes on what their listeners say directly on their drafts.

Analytic Talk

- Tell students that it is time to read their classmates' writing and provide feedback.

- Use Analytic Talk for this conferencing. Analytic talk enables students to share their writing in order to elicit specific responses in areas of concern. This strategy works best when the writing has been through several drafts and is ready for final polishing.

- Divide the class into groups of four or five students.

- Explain that each student in a small group will read his or her letter aloud, pause, and then read it again. Upon the second reading, listeners make notes and then share them.

- Read **Writer's Notebook page 2.8** with students before they begin their conferences to be sure they understand the role of listener.

- Walk among the groups to offer support as needed.

- After each reading, have group members discuss the draft. Post the following questions to guide the discussion.

> - What descriptive language helped you picture the animal?
> - Did the writer achieve the purpose of describing an amazing animal?
> - How interesting was the description to readers?

- Tell students that they will use the feedback from the conferencing groups to revise their writing during the next lesson.

EL **ENGLISH LEARNER SUPPORT: Support Oral Presentation**

ALL LEVELS Provide an opportunity for students to practice reading their descriptions to you or to another student before they read aloud in their small groups.

LEARNING OBJECTIVES

- Incorporate feedback from peer reviews.
- Expand descriptive details.
- **Language** Describe with precise language.

MATERIALS   Online Ed

Display and Engage 2.7
Focal Text *Apex Predators*
Writer's Notebook p. 2.9

TARGETED GRAMMAR SUPPORT

You may want to consult the following grammar minilessons to review key editing topics.

- **4.1.1 Adjectives,** p. W296
- **4.2.1 Adverbs,** p. W301

TEACHER TIP

You may want to demonstrate the use of a thesaurus to help students choose precise words. Students may also want to do more research for details to add.

Adding Descriptive Details

- In this lesson, students will revise their writing by adding descriptive details.
- Remind students that their purpose in writing is to describe an amazing animal so well that their readers can picture it and will be impressed by it. Say: *Descriptive details perform this job. Descriptive details include precise terms, vivid verbs, and sensory words that appeal to a reader's five senses.* Write the following on the board:

> precise terms
>
> vivid verbs
>
> sensory details (sight, hearing, taste, smell, touch)

- Show students the impact of descriptive language:

  » Project **Display and Engage 2.7** and have a volunteer read the description of an electric eel.

  » Read aloud this description from *Apex Predators*: *The electric eel lurks in the rivers and streams of tropical South America. It zaps fish, amphibians, and other small animals with a powerful electric charge, then gulps them down while they are stunned and helpless.*

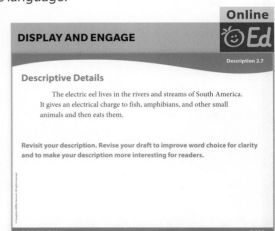

  » Ask: *Which of the two descriptions would you rather read? Why?* Explore how students are better able to picture the eel and its behavior with the description in *Apex Predators*. List on the board the vivid verbs it has. (*lurks, zaps, gulps*)

- Have small groups find examples in *Apex Predators* of precise terms and sensory details. Then, come back together to share and write their examples on the board.

Revising for Descriptive Details

- Have students revise their descriptions by adding more descriptive details. Read **Writer's Notebook page 2.9** with students. Remind them to use this checklist as they revise their descriptions. Suggest they also use their conferencing feedback to help pinpoint areas where descriptive details would improve their writing.

EL **ENGLISH LEARNER SUPPORT: Expand Language**

SUBSTANTIAL
Help students target two sentences that could be improved by adding descriptive details. Work together to add them by asking specific questions. Invite students to try to add other details on their own.

MODERATE
Supply word banks for students relevant to their chosen topics from which they can choose precise terms.

LIGHT
If students cannot determine where they might add descriptive details, tell them to add information that answers *What does it look like? How does it act?* Support use of a thesaurus.

LEARNING OBJECTIVES

- Proofread writing for subject-verb agreement.
- Proofread writing for capitalization.
- Proofread writing for punctuation.
- Proofread writing for spelling.
- **Language** Edit for English grammar, mechanics, and spelling.

MATERIALS   Online

Anchor Chart W13: *Editing Checklist*
Anchor Chart W17: *Proofreading Marks*

 LEARNING MINDSET:
Noticing

Apply Tell students to notice the kinds of mistakes they tend to make when they write and to add elements to their own editing checklist.

TARGETED GRAMMAR SUPPORT

You may want to consult the following grammar minilessons to review key editing topics.

- **1.1.3 Subject-Verb Agreement,** p. W218
- **6.2.4 Review Punctuation,** p. W339
- **7.3.5 Connect to Writing: Using Correct Spelling,** p. W365

Editing for Grammar, Mechanics, and Spelling

- Remind students that readers can get confused if their writing includes mistakes. Say: *The writer's message won't come through if readers stumble over sentences with misused or misspelled words and incorrect punctuation. That's why we edit our writing. There are two tools you can use to edit your writing.*

- Display **Anchor Chart W13: Editing Checklist**. Explain how using a checklist helps writers make sure they have reviewed their writing for all the possible mistakes they might have made. Say: *When you edit, you will be correcting capitalization, punctuation, spelling, and usage, such as making sure verbs agree with subjects.*

- Tell students to edit their descriptions for subject-verb agreement, capitalization, punctuation, and spelling. Point out that they can use the editing checklist on the Anchor Chart or create their own editing checklist in their notebooks if they'd like.

- Display and review **Anchor Chart W17: Proofreader's Marks**.

- As you circulate, group students who need support on similar grammar topics. Use the grammar minilessons or the students' own writing to provide targeted review and support.

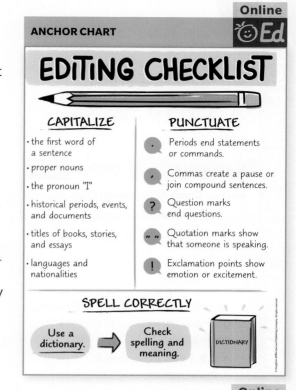

ANCHOR CHART   Online

EDITING CHECKLIST

CAPITALIZE
- the first word of a sentence
- proper nouns
- the pronoun "I"
- historical periods, events, and documents
- titles of books, stories, and essays
- languages and nationalities

PUNCTUATE
- Periods end statements or commands.
- Commas create a pause or join compound sentences.
- Question marks end questions.
- Quotation marks show that someone is speaking.
- Exclamation points show emotion or excitement.

SPELL CORRECTLY
Use a dictionary. → Check spelling and meaning. DICTIONARY

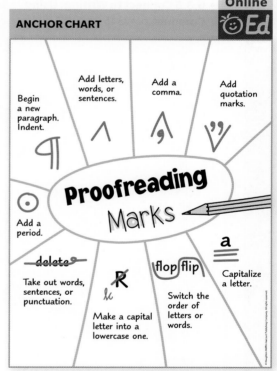

ANCHOR CHART   Online

Proofreading Marks

- Begin a new paragraph. Indent.
- Add letters, words, or sentences.
- Add a comma.
- Add quotation marks.
- Add a period.
- delete — Take out words, sentences, or punctuation.
- Make a capital letter into a lowercase one.
- flop/flip — Switch the order of letters or words.
- Capitalize a letter.

 ENGLISH LEARNER SUPPORT: Support Editing

ALL LEVELS Review students' writing with them. As you encounter a grammatical error, discuss its correction. Have students add this particular item to a personal editing checklist.

LEARNING OBJECTIVES

- Proofread peers' letters.
- **Language** Edit writing with peer support.

MATERIALS   Online

Anchor Chart W13: *Editing Checklist*

TARGETED GRAMMAR SUPPORT

You may want to consult the following grammar minilessons to review key editing topics.

- **6.2.1 End of Sentence Punctuation,** p. W336
- **6.3.5 Connect to Writing: Using Commas,** p. W345

Clocking Activity

- Tell students they will help each other proofread their writing by using an activity called clocking.

- Display **Anchor Chart W13: Editing Checklist** and quickly review the items. Keep the checklist visible during the clocking exercise.

- Explain the rules for clocking.

  » Each writer prepares a cover page with his or her name at the top. The page is divided into several sections labeled 1–5. Each number corresponds to an editing task.

  » Students form concentric circles. Students in the inner circle trade papers with their peer in the outer circle. As students receive a peer's paper, they become its editor.

  » Editors do not mark the actual paper. Instead, each editor writes his or her name in a section on the cover page and makes comments on each editing task.

  » Call out which item is to be checked by the editor: (1) subject-verb agreement; (2) capitalization; (3) punctuation within sentences; (4) punctuation at the end of sentences; (5) spelling.

  » After you call out the full set of editing tasks, have students collect their letters and move to another editor. Keep repeating until each section of the cover page is used.

Edit Writing

- When the editing process is completed, the cover page and paper are returned to the writer. The writer then uses the cover page to make further changes.

- As you circulate, group students who need support on similar grammar topics. Use the grammar minilessons or the students' own writing to provide targeted review and support.

EL   ENGLISH LEARNER SUPPORT: Support Editing

SUBSTANTIAL
Share sample sentences that contain a highlighted grammar point that students need to practice. Have students copy the sentences to provide practice with the grammar point and then write a sentence of their own.

MODERATE
Provide sentences with blanks where grammar choices that students need to practice need to be made. Have students work together to complete the sentences.

LIGHT
Help students identify a grammar point that they need to practice. Have them write a few sentences with it and exchange papers with a peer to edit.

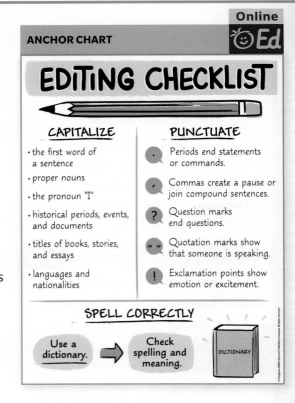

ANCHOR CHART   Online **Ed**

EDITING CHECKLIST

CAPITALIZE
- the first word of a sentence
- proper nouns
- the pronoun "I"
- historical periods, events, and documents
- titles of books, stories, and essays
- languages and nationalities

PUNCTUATE
- Periods end statements or commands.
- Commas create a pause or join compound sentences.
- Question marks end questions.
- Quotation marks show that someone is speaking.
- Exclamation points show emotion or excitement.

SPELL CORRECTLY
Use a dictionary. ➡ Check spelling and meaning.   DICTIONARY

LEARNING OBJECTIVES
- Use technology to assist with writing.
- Publish writing.
- Reflect on writing.
- **Language** Articulate response to one's writing.

MATERIALS   Online

Writer's Notebook p. 2.10

Prepare the Final Copy

- Tell students they are now ready to prepare their final draft to share with others.

- Explain that they can choose between two ways of publishing: writing or typing on a computer.

- If students write on paper, post and discuss the following points. Emphasize that they follow these guidelines to make their writing attractive to their readers. Say: *Readers can't or won't want to read writing that is messy or all over the page.*

> Write neatly.
>
> Leave margins at the top, bottom, left, and right.
>
> Write your title across the top.
>
> Write the word "by" and your name below the title.

- If students type their writing on a computer, post and discuss the following points.

> Choose a font that is attractive and easy to read.
>
> Leave margins at the top, bottom, left, and right.
>
> Type your title across the top and center it.
>
> Type the word "by" and your name below the title and center this byline.

Illustrating

- Give students the option of drawing pictures or downloading photographs to illustrate their descriptions. If students choose to use photographs, assist as necessary.

Reflect on Writing

- Say: *Now it is time to think about your writing—what you did to produce it and what you learned while producing it.*

- Allow time for students to think and answer the questions on **Writer's Notebook page 2.10**.

EL   ENGLISH LEARNER SUPPORT: Facilitate Expression

SUBSTANTIAL
Supply simple sentence frames for students to reflect and respond: *I think _____ is amazing. I learned _____. I like _____.*

MODERATE
Supply more complex sentence frames for students to reflect and respond: *The most amazing thing about my animal was _____. One thing I learned about writing a description is _____. I most like _____ about my description.*

LIGHT
Supply sentence frames for students that encourage additional thought and expression: *I think _____ was amazing about my animal because _____. One thing I learned about writing a description is _____. I like _____ best about my description because _____.*

LEARNING OBJECTIVES

- Share descriptions.
- Hold a collaborative discussion.
- **Language** Discuss using academic language.

MATERIALS	Online

Display and Engage *2.8*

Writer's Notebook *pp. 2.3, 2.11*

TEACHER TIP

After the Author's Chair activity, display students' descriptions along with their drawings or illustrations or compile them to make an anthology called *Amazing Animals.*

Professional Learning

BEST PRACTICES

At regular intervals, request family conferences to share students' independent writing progress and assignments. Positive reinforcement of progress outside of the classroom supports the development of a student's identity as a writer.

See the **GPS guide** to learn more.

Share Writing with an Author's Chair

- Tell students that they will now get the chance to share their descriptions of amazing animals. Explain that students will be presenting their writing from an Author's Chair. This activity, sometimes called a "share chair," gives students the opportunity not only to read their writing aloud, but also to elicit responses to their writing from an audience.

- Before the activity, write and discuss these reminders of good listening and feedback skills:

  > Give the author your full attention.
  >
  > Listen quietly and respectfully.
  >
  > Be positive in your feedback.
  >
  > Be specific in your feedback.

- Conduct the Author's Chair activity:

  » Obtain a special chair that is used exclusively by an author sharing his or her writing. A high director's chair, if attainable, would make the activity particularly appealing to fourth-graders. You might also decorate a chair, have student authors autograph it, or paint it in the school's colors. Place the chair where students may gather on a rug or carpet squares.

  » Invite a student to share his or her description. Have the student sit in the Author's Chair and read his or her description aloud. The student author may also invite a friend to help display any accompanying drawings or photographs.

  » After reading, have the student author ask, *"What did you like about my writing?"* and call on one to three students.

  » Have the student author ask, *"What do you want to know more about?"* and call on one to three students.

  » Allow the student to choose the next author to share.

- Use **Display and Engage 2.8** to prompt students on the questions to ask about their writing.

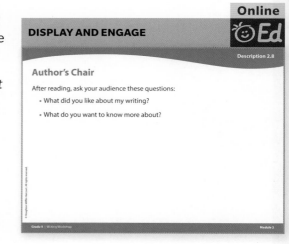

Engage and Respond

- Have students revisit the list of goals they set on **Writer's Notebook page 2.3**. Then have them turn to **Writer's Notebook page 2.11** to make notes about whether they feel they met their goals and what goals they might set for the next writing assignment.

EL **ENGLISH LEARNER SUPPORT: Support Presentations**

ALL LEVELS Before students sit in the Author's Chair, allow them to practice reading their descriptions aloud to themselves or to a partner.

3/4/2023

Opinion Essay

FOCUS STATEMENT Friends and family can work together to overcome challenges.

FOCAL TEXT

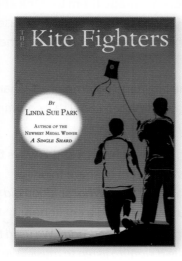

The Kite Fighters

Author: Linda Sue Park

Summary: Two Korean boys overcome challenges through friendship.

WRITING PROMPT

READ this sentence: *Friends and family can work together to overcome challenges.*

THINK about a time when you and a friend overcame a challenge together.

WRITE an opinion essay about why it's important to rely on friends when faced with a challenge.

<hr>

· · · · · · · · · LESSONS · · · · · · · · ·

1. **Introducing the Focal Text**

2. **Vocabulary**

3. **Prewriting I: Preparing to Write**

4. **Prewriting II: Choosing Support**

5. **Drafting I: Beginning the Draft**

6. **Drafting II: Integrating Persuasive Language**

7. **Drafting III: Completing the Draft**

8. **Revising I: Punctuation for Effect**

9. **Revising II: Conferencing**

10. **Revising III: Adding Strong Support**

11. **Revising IV: Using Transitions**

12. **Editing I: Mechanics and Spelling**

13. **Editing II: Peer Proofreading**

14. **Publishing**

15. **Sharing**

LEARNING MINDSET: Seeking Challenges

Display **Anchor Chart 31: My Learning Mindset** throughout the year. Refer to it to introduce Seeking Challenges and to reinforce the skills you introduced in previous modules.

LEARNING OBJECTIVES

- Establish a purpose for reading.
- Make and describe personal connections to sources.
- Explain the author's use of text structure in a literary text.
- Refer to text details to explain what it says explicitly and to make inferences.
- **Language** Describe connections to sources by using the vocabulary word *challenges*.
- **Language** Discuss the author's use of text structure by employing cooperative learning and note-taking.

MATERIALS — Online Ed

Classroom materials *chart paper*
Display and Engage *3.1*
Focal Text *The Kite Fighters*

Priming the Students

Explore the Topic

- Tell students that in this module they will explore the different ways friends and family can work together to overcome challenges.

- Point out that everyone faces challenges in life. Mention, for example, that some people may struggle to learn a new skill, while others have conflicts with people.

- To help students make connections to this topic, encourage them to think about challenges they have faced in their own lives. Have volunteers describe these challenges. Ask follow-up questions: *How did this make you feel? How did others react to it?*

- Add the examples of students' challenges to the left-hand column of a T-Chart titled *Our Challenges*, either on the board or on chart paper. Label this column *Challenge*.

- Label the right-hand column *How I Overcame It*. In this column, list the ways that students overcame their challenges by asking volunteers to share their experiences. Prompt students with the following question: *What solution did you find to your challenge?* Model how to think about overcoming a challenge:

  THINK ALOUD *When I was young, my sister and I shared a bedroom. We used to argue because I'd want to read in the room and she'd want to listen to music. We finally came up with a solution. I would have the room to myself at certain times of the day, and so would she. That way, we didn't bother each other.*

Discuss the Focus Statement

- Show **Display and Engage 3.1**. Read the Focus Statement with students. Have students write a short response to the statement, explaining their thoughts about it. Then have small groups share and compare their responses with each other.

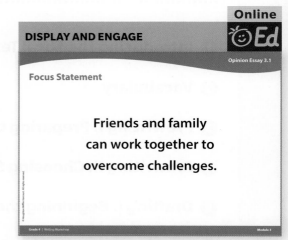

Online Ed

DISPLAY AND ENGAGE

Opinion Essay 3.1

Focus Statement

Friends and family can work together to overcome challenges.

Grade 4 | Writing Workshop   Module 3

(EL) ENGLISH LEARNER SUPPORT: Facilitate Discussion

SUBSTANTIAL
Clarify for students that the word *challenges* in this context means difficulties or struggles. Allow students to draw an example of a challenge they have faced and then describe it to a partner.

MODERATE
Provide sentence frames: *One challenge I faced was when _____. I overcame it by _____.*

LIGHT
Have students work with partners to discuss challenges they have faced before sharing them with the class.

Priming the Text

Prepare to Read

- Show the cover of *The Kite Fighters*. Point out the different parts of the kite. Have volunteers who have flown kites tell how they did it.

- Have students think about what it might mean to fight with kites.

- Point out that this is a fictional text featuring characters, settings, and a plot consisting of events. Flip through the book with students.

- Point out the chapters and the setting that the author introduces before the story begins. Prompt students to explain this text structure. Ask: *Why do you think the author tells us the book's setting before we start reading? (It helps us understand right away where the story takes place. It also tells us the events happened a long time ago.)*

- Continue paging through the book with students. Allow them to make additional observations about the text's structure and to familiarize themselves with the material. Note students' observations either on chart paper or the board.

- Point out the illustrations at the beginning of each chapter. Ask: *What do these show? (different types of kites) What details do you see in them? (Some have faces. Others are objects, like boxes, hats, or scrolls.)*

- Have students look at the author's note. Ask: *Why might an author include a note at the end of a book? (Responses may vary.)*

Engage and Respond

- Have students Turn and Talk to a partner. Ask them to predict what they think is going to happen in *The Kite Fighters*.

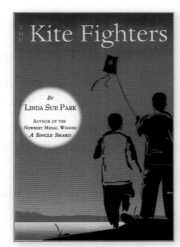

The Kite Fighters

 LEARNING MINDSET: Seeking Challenges

Introduce Explain to students that each challenge teaches us something. *When we learn something new—such as a skill, hobby, or sport—we often struggle at the beginning. Once we gain some practice, though, we gradually get better. You'll learn in The Kite Fighters how two brothers face multiple challenges. They manage to triumph over them by working through their difficulties and discovering new approaches to solving problems.* Tell students that when they face a challenge while writing, they should remember how the brothers confronted their challenges and learned new skills in the process.

The Read

Read the Focal Text

- As you read *The Kite Fighters,* stop at these points to help explain the author's use of text structure and features.

  » Read pages 3 and 4. Point out that the story begins by introducing two brothers. The older brother, Kee-sup, has received a kite as a present.

  » Ask: *How does Young-sup feel about his older brother getting this present?* (*He's jealous.*) *What has Young-sup wanted to do since Kee-sup got the kite?* (*go along with him to fly it*)

  » Read page 5. Ask: *What challenge does Kee-sup face?* (*He can't get the kite to stay in the air.*) *What happens when Young-sup takes a turn?* (*At first, he can't get the kite to stay in the air. But then he figures out how to fly it.*)

  » Read through to page 8. Ask: *What does the dialogue help you to understand about the brothers as they try to fly the kite together?* (*Responses may vary.*)

  » Reiterate that, in this first chapter, the author has introduced the main characters and their challenge. She has also used dialogue to help readers understand how the characters relate to each other.

- Continue reading *The Kite Fighters* with students and discussing the author's use of text structure and other narrative elements.

Engage and Respond

- Have students write three or four sentences that answer this question: *Did you find the plot's events believable? Why or why not?* Have volunteers share their ideas with the class.

(EL) ENGLISH LEARNER SUPPORT: Elicit Participation

SUBSTANTIAL

Rephrase questions to allow for yes/no answers: *Is Young-sup jealous of his older brother? Is Kee-sup able to keep the kite in the air?*

MODERATE

Provide sentence frames to support students' responses. For example, *I thought the plot was believable because _____.*

LIGHT

Allow student pairs time to practice their responses aloud with each other before sharing with the group.

ARGUMENT • OPINION ESSAY

LEARNING OBJECTIVES

- Use print or digital resources to determine a word's meaning.
- **Language** Use context to determine a word's meaning.
- **Language** Acquire and use academic and domain-specific words and phrases.

MATERIALS   Online

Focal Text *The Kite Fighters*

Writer's Notebook p. 3.1

Review the Focal Text

- Review with students the first chapter of *The Kite Fighters*. Explain that the text features many interesting vocabulary words relating both to kite-flying and the challenges the brothers face. See examples in the first column below.

- Page through *The Kite Fighters* and have students identify additional words they find interesting, noting their locations in the book. See examples of possible words and their locations in the second and third columns below. Pause to discuss why the words are interesting. Then have students add them to the Word Bank on **Writer's Notebook page 3.1**.

eagerness (p. 5)	impatience (p. 11)	progressed (p. 17)
reel (p. 5)	plummeted (p. 12)	accomplishment
launched (p. 5)	frustration (p. 16)	(p. 32)
experimented	joints (p. 17)	endeavor (p. 41)
(p. 6)		opponent (p. 50)

- Have students choose a selection of words from the list and use a dictionary or other resource to look up their meanings.

- Next, have students select a word from the list they have not yet defined. In the story, reread the sentence in which the word appears, along with any surrounding sentences necessary for context.

- Have students use this context to determine the word's meaning. Model using this example: *On page 5 it says, "Young-sup felt a river of eagerness surge through him as he took it." I'd read earlier that Young-sup* really *wanted to fly his brother's kite. So I think* eagerness *means an excitement to do something.* Allow students to share their thoughts about the meaning of the word they selected.

- Ask students to review their lists and identify other words with definitions that reflect emotions. Have volunteers share these with the class.

- Point out that these words might be useful as they write their opinion essays or a future piece of writing, so they should keep the Word Bank as a reference source.

Engage and Respond

- Have student pairs choose a word from the Word Bank that they think is particularly interesting. Have them use it in a sentence, and then explain to their partner why they find the word interesting.

 ENGLISH LEARNER SUPPORT: Build Vocabulary

SUBSTANTIAL
Discuss with students the meanings of unfamiliar words. Then allow students to draw pictures reflecting their meanings.

MODERATE
Have students work in pairs to review the context in which unfamiliar words appear. Provide sentence frames for students' definitions: *The word _____ means _____. I think this because _____.*

LIGHT
Use a Closed Sorts routine to help pairs categorize words in their lists. Select from students' lists any words that relate to emotions or actions. Then have pairs sort them into one of these two categories.

ARGUMENT • OPINION ESSAY

LEARNING OBJECTIVES

- Learn new vocabulary associated with argumentative texts.
- Discuss the features of argumentative texts.
- Plan the first draft of Parts.
- Use the guidance of peers and adults to assist in the planning process.
- **Language** Plan writing.

MATERIALS   Online Ed

Display and Engage 3.2
Anchor Chart W8: *Parts of an Argument*
Writer's Notebook pp. 3.2, 3.3, 3.4

📖 INSTRUCTIONAL VOCABULARY

- **opinion** ideas or beliefs that cannot be proven
- **argument** a reason or set of reasons that supports an idea
- **reasons** a statement or fact that explains an idea
- **facts** information that can be proven to be true
- **supporting evidence** detail in a text that helps to explain the central idea

Discuss the Writing Prompt

- Show **Display and Engage 3.2** and read the Writing Prompt together. Note the tips.

- Explain that an **opinion** essay is a type of **argument** writing that expresses the writer's personal views on a topic. Display **Anchor Chart W8: Parts of an Argument** and read the points with students. Explain that in an opinion essay, a writer uses **reasons**, **facts**, and examples as **supporting evidence** for his or her points. The writer hopes to persuade the reader to agree with him or her.

- Add these words to the Instructional Vocabulary List and have students add them to their glossaries.

- Distribute **Writer's Notebook page 3.2** and read the rubric with students. Point out that the rubric is like a roadmap that tells them what they should do as they write their essays.

Set Goals for Writing

- Have students consider the goals they would like to set for their opinion essays. Then have them add these goals to the list on **Writer's Notebook page 3.3** or write them in their own notebooks.

Begin Prewriting

- Have students begin to plan their first draft by first deciding what they will write about. Use this model:

  THINK ALOUD *Before I start to write, I'm going to think about a challenge I overcame with a friend or family member. I remember a time when a friend and I really wanted to attend a music camp together but we needed to raise money to pay for it. So we decided to have a yard sale together. The sale was a huge success, and we were able to attend the camp.*

- As a group, brainstorm challenges to write about. Review the rules of brainstorming.

- Have students consider additional ideas on their own. Students should then review all of their options and narrow them down to one chosen topic. Once they have made their selections, have students add the topic to **Writer's Notebook page 3.4**. Students should then write any ideas that immediately come to mind about their topics to use as a starting point for planning their writing.

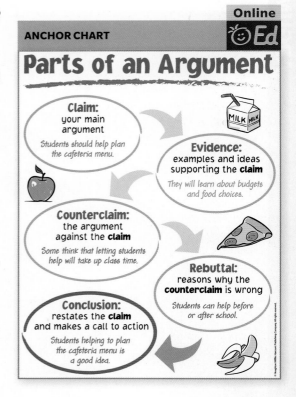

LEARNING OBJECTIVES

- Plan the first draft of an opinion essay.
- Select an audience and purpose for the essay.
- Use a graphic organizer to assist in the planning process.
- **Language** Share information using the vocabulary words *audience* and *purpose*.

MATERIALS Online

Writer's Notebook pp. 3.5, 3.6

 LEARNING MINDSET:
Seeking Challenges

Model Model for students how they might seek challenges for themselves through writing. Provide them with this sentence starter: *One thing I want to learn more about is* _____. Give an example of a writing challenge. Then tell students to complete the sentence with a writing challenge they would like to overcome. Remind students that trying difficult things is part of the process of learning, and that everyone has to face this challenge to improve their knowledge.

Discuss Audience and Purpose

- Now that students have determined which topic they will write about in their first draft, and written some initial notes, discuss the importance of considering their intended audience and purpose.

- Tell students that different forms of writing serve different purposes. For example, the purpose of a story is to entertain, while the purpose of a newspaper article is to inform.

- Explain that forms of writing can also have different intended audiences. The author of a science article, for example, might write for an audience of scientists, whereas the author of a novel might write for the general public.

- Explain that audience and purpose affect not only the content of writing but its style as well. Have students consider how they might alter their writing depending on their audience and purpose. Ask: *How would you write a story meant to entertain your friends? Would your writing be serious or playful? (Responses will vary.)*

- Have student pairs discuss the audience and purpose for their opinion essays. Use a model:

   THINK ALOUD *To determine my audience, I'm going to think about the person who will be reading my writing. Will it be friends, family, my classmates, or someone else? Next, I'm going to think about why I might write an opinion statement. Am I trying to entertain people or persuade them to agree with me? Do I have another purpose?*

- Distribute **Writer's Notebook page 3.5**. Have students complete the form. Then have them share their information with the class. Monitor students' understanding that opinion essays are meant to persuade.

Choose Appropriate Support

- Remind students that an opinion essay's supporting evidence consists of the reasons, facts, and examples the writer uses to argue a point. Without providing enough support, a writer will be less likely to convince readers to agree.

- Explain that the type of support a writer should provide depends on the text's audience and purpose. Use a model:

   THINK ALOUD *Because I'm writing an opinion essay, I know the purpose of my essay is to persuade my audience to agree with my opinion. This means I'll need to include reasons, facts, or examples that support my opinion and help convince my audience to agree with me.*

- Distribute **Writer's Notebook page 3.6**. Point out that a graphic organizer such as this one can help them organizer their reasons before they begin writing. Have students complete the graphic organizer.

- Circulate the room as students continue to plan their opinion essays and offer guidance and ideas, as needed.

- Let students know they will be developing support for their essays later in the writing process.

ARGUMENT · OPINION ESSAY

LEARNING OBJECTIVES

- Develop a first draft by using a purposeful organizational structure
- Develop a first draft with an engaging central idea and topic sentence.
- Write an introduction to an opinion essay.
- **Language** Explain an opinion by using sentence stems.

MATERIALS Online Ed

Writer's Notebook *pp. 3.2, 3.6, 3.7–3.8*
Display and Engage *3.3a–3.3c*
Classroom materials *crayons or colored pencils*

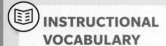 **INSTRUCTIONAL VOCABULARY**

- **transition words** words and phrases that link ideas together

Prepare to Draft

- Revisit the rubric for the opinion essay on **Writer's Notebook page 3.2**. Let students know these are the elements their opinion essays should feature. Review any terms students may be unfamiliar with as you review each point with the class.

- Show the model on **Display and Engage 3.3a–3.3c** and distribute **Writer's Notebook pages 3.7 and 3.8**. Read through the model essay with students. Have them identify the introduction, body, and conclusion.

- Have them draw a red box around the opinion in the introduction. Point out how it draws readers in by first asking a question. Ask: *Which statement in the introductory paragraph expresses an opinion telling why it's important to rely on friends when facing a challenge?* (*"This is because friends make challenges rewarding and fun."*)

- Next, review the model's body. Have students locate the reasons, facts, or examples that support the opinion and draw green circles around them. Have them then identify how the conclusion relates to the rest of the essay.

- Throughout the essay, have students identify **transition words** and phrases such as *because, for example, another,* and *as a result* that link ideas. Discuss the ideas they join. Point out that good writers use these transition words to help readers understand how reasons are connected and support the idea.

Begin to Draft

- Have students review the topic they chose and ideas related to it. Then have students decide what the experience taught them about the importance of relying on friends or family members when faced with a challenge. Ask: *How did friends or family members help? How might the challenge have been more difficult without their assistance?* (*Responses will vary.*)

- In their notes, have students write an opinion that explicitly states what they learned from the experience. You may also want to provide students with a graphic organizer to help them organize their ideas, such as the Idea-Support Map on **Writer's Notebook page 3.6**.

- Have students begin to draft introductions for their opinion essays, incorporating their opinion statement. Have them craft an effective opening using descriptions, a question, a surprising statement, or another method to draw the reader in.

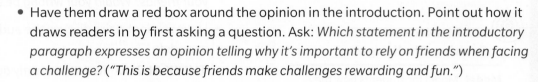

Online Ed

DISPLAY AND ENGAGE

Opinion Essay 3.3a

Friends Make Challenges Fun

1   Do you like challenges? Many people avoid them. Sometimes, they're even afraid of them because challenges can be difficult. But I've discovered that challenges are easier to overcome when you have a friend to face them with you. This is because friends make challenges rewarding and fun.

 ENGLISH LEARNER SUPPORT: Scaffold Writing

SUBSTANTIAL
Clarify for students that relying on someone means depending on them. Provide students with some examples of reasons why relying on friends or family is important, such as *they can comfort you* or *they can help you fix a problem.*

MODERATE
Provide a sentence frame: *It's important to rely on friends and family members because _____.*

LIGHT
Have students write their own opinion statements, then meet with a partner to discuss them.

DRAFTING II: INTEGRATING PERSUASIVE LANGUAGE

LEARNING OBJECTIVES

- Use persuasive language to convey an engaging idea supported by reasons.
- Compose an argumentative text featuring a purposeful organizational structure.
- **Language** Express ideas by using persuasive language.

MATERIALS　　　Online Ed

Writer's Notebook *p. 3.1*

INSTRUCTIONAL VOCABULARY

- **persuade** to try to convince someone of an idea or to try to get the person to do something

---

TEACHER TIP

Explain to students that a writer's statements in an opinion essay should be confident but never insulting to the audience.

Introduce the Skill

- Explain to students that in an opinion essay, writers **persuade** their audience by convincing them of an idea or to do something. Persuasive language helps contribute to the structure of an opinion essay by allowing the writer to effectively convey his or her opinion and then support it.

- Add *persuade* to the class Instructional Vocabulary list, and encourage students to add it to the Word Bank on **Writer's Notebook page 3.1**. Students can also add the word and their own definition to their glossaries.

- Provide an example of how you have used persuasive language to convince readers about something. Use this model:

  THINK ALOUD *I used to volunteer at an animal shelter, and one of my jobs was to write descriptions of the animals available for adoption. In my writing, I would choose words that I knew would appeal to people looking to adopt. Rather than describing the animals as just* nice *or* fun, *I'd say things like* adorable, playful, *or* energetic. *I'd also make strong statements that showed excitement, like,* You must come see them for yourself! *to convince people to visit the shelter.*

- Explain that words such as *adorable* appeal to reader's emotions, while commands featuring strong verbs, such as *you must* or *you should*, help influence readers by directly telling them what you would like them to do.

- Tell students that the type of persuasive language they use in their writing will depend on their topic and audience. When students express their opinions in an essay, they should first consider what their audience already knows about the topic and how they might feel about it.

- Point out that the example above features positive words to attract an audience that is most likely already interested in adopting pets. As a group, work together to brainstorm positive words that would convince readers to adopt a pet.

Review Use of Persuasive Language

- Ask students to review their introductions for examples of persuasive language.

- Have volunteers read aloud any examples. Then discuss the examples as a class, identifying how they help make the writing more persuasive.

Continue to Draft

- Have students continue incorporating persuasive language to develop their ideas and support the essay's structure.

- Circulate the room, offering assistance to students as needed.

ARGUMENT • OPINION ESSAY

LEARNING OBJECTIVES

- Develop a draft with a purposeful structure that includes an introduction, body, and conclusion.
- Group related ideas into paragraphs.
- Develop an opinion essay by providing reasons for the opinion.
- **Language** Express opinions and reasons using a variety of sentence types.

MATERIALS
Online Ed

Display and Engage *3.3c*

Writer's Notebook *pp. 3.6, 3.8*

 LEARNING MINDSET:
Seeking Challenges

Apply Instruct students to continue seeking challenges as they draft their essays. For example, encourage students to use more difficult sentence structures or new vocabulary words that add interest to their writing. Let students know that taking risks like these ultimately helps them to grow as writers. They can correct mistakes later in the writing process, if necessary.

Review Essay Structure

- Remind students that an essay's structure consists of an introduction, a body, and a conclusion.

- Review that the body of an opinion essay consists of one or more paragraphs that contain reasons, facts, and examples the writer uses to support his or her opinion.
  THINK ALOUD *The conclusion then summarizes the information discussed in the essay. Good writers also end their essays by leaving readers with a strong statement that reinforces the main idea.*

- Have students review the model's conclusion by using **Display and Engage 3.3c** and **Writer's Notebook page 3.8**. Point out how, in the conclusion, the writer summarizes the information discussed in the body of her essay. This summary helps to support and reinforce her opinion that *friends make challenges rewarding and fun*. The writer then wraps up the conclusion with a statement that leaves readers with a strong final impression: *With their laughter and conversation, friends definitely make challenges less challenging.*

Circulate the Room

- Have students continue working on their drafts. Remind them that they can use the model, the Idea-Support Map on **Writer's Notebook page 3.6**, and any other notes they have taken to assist them as they continue writing.

- Students should be sure to provide support for the opinion statement by including reasons, facts, or examples in the body of the essay, and they should craft an effective conclusion that summarizes the information.

Share Drafts

- Once their drafts are completed, have volunteers share them with the class.

- Have the class provide feedback on whether the students' conclusions effectively summarize the information in their essays. Ask: *Does the conclusion reflect the opinion the writer shares in the essay? Does it make an impression on you?*

 ENGLISH LEARNER SUPPORT: Scaffold Writing

SUBSTANTIAL
Clarify that a *reason* is why a person feels a certain way or does something. To help students establish reasons for their opinions, provide pairs with a sentence stem and have them work together to complete it: *I feel this way because _____.*

MODERATE
Use a Think-Pair-Share routine to help students establish reasons for their opinions. Pose the following question and have students think about it independently before discussing it with a partner: *What are the reasons you feel this way?* Afterwards, have students share their answers. Then have them incorporate the reasons into their essays.

LIGHT
Pair students and have them provide periodic feedback to each other as they draft their essays.

LEARNING OBJECTIVES

- Use the revising process to edit drafts.
- Revise drafts by using punctuation for effect.
- **Language** Revise writing by using a variety of sentence types.

MATERIALS   Online

Display and Engage *3.3a, 3.4*
Writer's Notebook *p. 3.7*

INSTRUCTIONAL VOCABULARY

- **rhetorical question** a question that a writer or speaker uses for effect

TARGETED GRAMMAR SUPPORT

You may want to consult the following grammar minilessons to review key revising topics.

- **1.2.1 Declarative and Interrogative Sentences,** p. W221
- **1.2.2 Imperative and Exclamatory Sentences,** p. W222
- **1.2.3 Four Kinds of Sentences,** p. W223
- **6.2.1 End of Sentence Punctuation,** p. W336
- **6.2.3 Punctuation for Effect,** p. W338

Introduce the Revision Skill

- Remind students that persuasive language helps writers convince readers to believe or do something. Then explain that punctuation and sentence types can serve a similar purpose for writers.

- Review the four types of sentences—declarative, exclamatory, interrogative, and imperative—and their accompanying punctuation.

- Show **Display and Engage 3.4**. Have students review the two sets of sentences shown. Then, review their purposes and punctuation.

- Read aloud each set of sentences. Then ask: *How do the two sentences sound different?* (*Responses will vary.*)

- Mention that including a variety of sentence types in an opinion essay makes it more effective and forceful. Point out how much livelier the exclamatory and interrogative sentences are than the declarative sentences you just read.

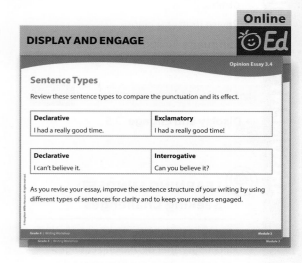

- Explain to students that a **rhetorical question** is one type of interrogative sentence. Unlike other interrogative sentences, however, a rhetorical question is used strictly for effect, with no answer expected. It is asked to capture the audience's attention and get them thinking about the topic.

- Show the model introduction on **Display and Engage 3.3a** and have students review it on **Writer's Notebook page 3.7**.

  THINK ALOUD *The first sentence of the model's introduction,* Do you like challenges? *is an example of a rhetorical question. The writer doesn't expect readers to answer the question. Instead, she's using the question to get her audience interested in the topic and to make them think.*

Revise for Sentence Types and Punctuation

- Encourage students to revisit their writing to revise for sentence types and punctuation.

- Circulate the room and assist students with revising. If students need help with a specific grammar topic, do a direct teach.

- As you circulate, group students who need support on similar grammar topics. Use the grammar minilessons or the students' own writing to provide targeted review and support.

LEARNING OBJECTIVES

- Use the support of peers and adults to strengthen writing during revision.
- Show value for the contributions of others.
- Revise drafts for clarity.
- **Language** Respond to the drafts of others by using note-taking.

MATERIALS   Online

- **Display and Engage** *3.5*

LEARNING MINDSET: Seeking Challenges

Apply Say: *Revising can be a challenge. After all, making changes isn't always easy. But if you try to do your best with your writing by gradually improving it, your hard work will result in a much more polished draft.*

Small Group Conferences

- Show **Display and Engage 3.5**. Point out the checklist and read it with students. Tell them they will use this checklist to guide their small group conferences.

- Tell students it is time to read each other's essays and provide feedback.

  » Divide the class into small groups of four or five for the *Say Back* strategy.

  » Writers read. Pause. Read again.

  » Listeners listen. During the second reading, they jot down two things:

    1. What they liked

    2. What they want to know more about

  » Listeners *say* these *back* to the writer.

- Debrief with the class. Discuss students' responses to the following questions.

  - What have you learned about writing an opinion essay?
  - How do opinion essays help you express your thoughts?
  - What did you learn from reading or listening to other students' opinion essays?

Online Ed

DISPLAY AND ENGAGE

Opinion Essay 3.5

Conferencing

As you listen to your group's essays, think about these questions.

1. Did the introduction draw you in?
2. Did the writer include an opinion statement in the introduction?
3. Did the writer provide support for his or her opinion?
4. Did the writer include a variety of sentence types?
5. Did the conclusion summarize the writer's opinion?

Grade 4 | Writing Workshop   Module 3

Continue to Revise

- Have students continue to revise, using the feedback they gained in the small group conferences.

 ENGLISH LEARNER SUPPORT: Facilitate Discussion

SUBSTANTIAL
During the *Say Back* strategy, have students answer questions with yes/no responses, such as *"Did you like . . . ?"* and *"Do you want to know more about . . . ?"*

MODERATE
Provide sentence frames for students to use during the *Say Back* strategy: *I liked _____. I want to know more about _____.*

LIGHT
Have students take notes during the *Say Back* strategy's first reading to help them determine what they liked and didn't like during the second reading.

ARGUMENT • OPINION ESSAY

LEARNING OBJECTIVES
- Revise drafts to strengthen support and provide clarity.
- Provide reasons supported by facts and details.
- Link opinions and reasons using words and phrases.
- **Language** Revise writing by using increasingly complex grammatical structures.

MATERIALS Online
- **Display and Engage** *3.3b*
- **Writer's Notebook** *p. 3.9*

TARGETED GRAMMAR SUPPORT

You may want to consult the following grammar minilessons to review key editing topics.
- **4.6.1 Prepositions,** p. W321
- **4.6.2 Prepositional Phrases,** p. W322
- **1.4.1 Compound Sentences,** p. W231

Introduce the Revision Skill

- Remind students that strong support—in the form of reasons, facts, and examples—helps a writer convince readers to do or believe something.

- Use an everyday situation to model how to decide whether a reason is convincing.
  THINK ALOUD *A friend was trying to convince me to attend a summer festival with her. The reason she gave for wanting to go was that we didn't have any other plans that day, so why not go? I didn't think this was a convincing reason because she didn't try to make the festival sound appealing to me. If she had talked about festival events she knew I'd be interested in, for example, I would've found the idea more convincing.*

- Revisit the body of the model essay on **Display and Engage 3.3b**.

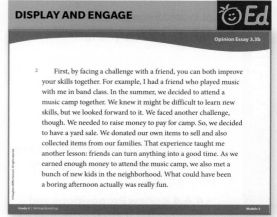

- In the first sentence, have students identify the reason the writer gives for her opinion that *friends make challenges rewarding and fun.* (*a chance to improve skills together*) Discuss how the reason supports the opinion. Then identify the details and examples the writer uses to explain the reason.

- Have students identify the second reason the writer gives later in the essay. (*Friends can turn anything into a good time.*)

- Discuss how this reason supports the opinion. Then identify the details and examples the writer uses to explain this reason.

- Distribute **Writer's Notebook page 3.9** and have read the page with students. Have them use the prompts to evaluate the strength of their reasons.

- Point out that as they revise their essays, students may discover they need to add additional reasons, facts, or examples to strengthen their support. Remind them that they should be sure to link their reasons with their opinion.

Revise for Support

- Have students revise and strengthen their support.

- As you circulate, group students who need support on similar grammar topics. Use the grammar minilessons or the students' own writing to provide targeted review and support.

 ENGLISH LEARNER SUPPORT: Support Comprehension

SUBSTANTIAL
After the class identifies the writer's reasons in the model, slowly read the reasons aloud and have students join in. Explain why these are considered reasons.

MODERATE
Have pairs work together to identify the details and examples in support of each reason before discussing them as a class.

LIGHT
Give students additional time to respond during the discussion.

ARGUMENT • OPINION ESSAY

LEARNING OBJECTIVES

- Revise drafts to provide clarity.
- Use transitions to link opinions, reasons, and other details.
- **Language** Revise writing by using transitions such as *for example* and *because*.

MATERIALS

Online

Display and Engage *3.3b*

Writer's Notebook *p. 3.10*

TARGETED GRAMMAR SUPPORT

You may want to consult the following grammar minilessons to review key editing topics.

- **4.6.4 Review Prepositions and Prepositional Phrases,** p. W324
- **4.6.5 Using Prepositions and Prepositional Phrases,** p. W325
- **1.4.2 Complex Sentences,** p. W232

Introduce the Revision Skill

- Explain to students that, in an opinion essay, good writers establish a connection between the opinion and the reasons that support it. Good writers also elaborate on these reasons by using facts, examples, and details.

- Tell students that *transitions*—words or phrases that link ideas together—help to establish these connections between the opinion and the writer's reasons, facts, examples, and details.

- Say: *Transitions work like links in a chain; they join one idea to another idea. They also help establish the exact relationship between the ideas. In this way, transitions make ideas stronger than they would be on their own.*

- Mention that writers can use transitions for many purposes, such as to compare and contrast, to establish causes and effects, and to indicate sequence. Provide students with some examples of transitions.

also	for example
another	however
because	so
first	then
as a result	in addition
but	next

- Show the body of the model essay on **Display and Engage 3.3b**.

- Explain that the writer uses the transition word *first* to introduce a reason for her opinion that *friends make challenges rewarding and fun*. She then elaborates on the reason using the transition phrase *for example*.

- Mention that the transition word *another* is used to discuss the second reason for her opinion, *friends can turn anything into a good time*.

Online Ed

DISPLAY AND ENGAGE

Opinion Essay 3.3b

2   First, by facing a challenge with a friend, you can both improve your skills together. For example, I had a friend who played music with me in band class. In the summer, we decided to attend a music camp together. We knew it might be difficult to learn new skills, but we looked forward to it. We faced another challenge, though. We needed to raise money to pay for camp. So, we decided to have a yard sale. We donated our own items to sell and also collected items from our families. That experience taught me another lesson: friends can turn anything into a good time. As we earned enough money to attend the music camp, we also met a bunch of new kids in the neighborhood. What could have been a boring afternoon actually was really fun.

Grade 4 | Writing Workshop   Module 3

- Have students identify other transition words and phrases they see in the model and explain how they link ideas together.

Revise for Organization

- Distribute **Writer's Notebook page 3.10**. Read the revision checklist aloud with students. Tell them to use this checklist as they revisit their drafts.

- Have students revise for transitions and clarity.

- Circulate the room and assist students with revising. If students need help with a specific grammar topic, do a direct teach.

ARGUMENT • OPINION ESSAY

LEARNING OBJECTIVES

- Edit drafts to maintain complete sentences and subject-verb agreement.
- Edit drafts to ensure correct capitalization, punctuation, and spelling.
- **Language** Revise writing by employing proofreading marks.

MATERIALS   Online

Anchor Chart W13: *Editing Checklist*

TARGETED GRAMMAR SUPPORT

You may want to consult the following grammar minilessons to review key editing topics.

- **1.3.3 Writing Complete Sentences,** p. W228
- **6.2.1 End of Sentence Punctuation,** p. W336
- **1.4.3 Commas in Compound Sentences,** p. W233
- **6.4.1 Capitalization and Writing Titles,** p. W346

Review Proofreading Checklist

- Display **Anchor Chart W13: Editing Checklist**.
- Review the items on the Editing Checklist. Review how to use proofreading marks.
- As needed, revisit grammar topics to which students may need additional review or practice.

Proofread Writing

- Have students independently edit their writing for spelling, mechanics, punctuation, and grammar.
- Circulate the room and provide assistance, as needed.
- As you circulate, group students who need support on similar grammar topics. Use the grammar minilessons or the students' own writing to provide targeted review and support.

ANCHOR CHART   Online

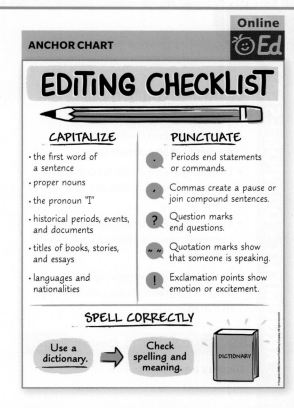

EL ENGLISH LEARNER SUPPORT: Support Comprehension

SUBSTANTIAL

Use visual supports to assist students' understanding of grammar topics, such as by showing an illustration of people performing activities to help explain the concept of subject-verb agreement.

MODERATE

Distribute a list of commonly misspelled words for students to use as a reference when checking their spelling.

LIGHT

Have students take notes during the discussion on grammar topics.

LEARNING OBJECTIVES

- Work respectfully with others.
- **Language** Edit drafts to check for elements of an opinion essay
- **Language** Edit drafts for correct capitalization, punctuation, and spelling.
- **Language** Edit drafts to maintain complete sentences and subject-verb agreement.
- **Language** Revise writing by correcting grammar and usage errors in a draft.

MATERIALS   Online

Display and Engage 3.6

TARGETED GRAMMAR SUPPORT

You may want to consult the following grammar minilessons to review key editing topics.

- **1.3.3 Writing Complete Sentences,** p. W228
- **6.1.1 Quotation Marks with Direct Speech,** p. W331
- **6.3.1 Commas with Direct Speech and Names,** p. W341
- **6.4.1 Capitalization and Writing Titles,** p. W346

Clocking Activity

- Review the rules for clocking.

  » Students form concentric circles or sit opposite each other in rows. As students receive a peer's paper, they become that paper's editor.

  » Call out what item is to be checked by the editor: spelling, capital letters, use of quotation marks, and so forth, using **Display and Engage 3.6**.

  » You may also want the students to move after a couple of items so that each student's paper is read by several editors.

  » No marks are made on the actual paper. All papers should have an editing page with the writer's name at the top.

  » Each editor places his or her name next to the number in turn and writes the concept to be checked.

  » When the editing process is completed, the students take their editing page and make any corrections. If there is a problem, they may discuss it with their editor or the teacher.

- Show **Display and Engage 3.6** and discuss the items to be checked during the clocking activity.

- Confirm that students understand each item in the checklist before beginning the clocking activity. If students need to review specific grammar topics, use the minilessons at left or others in the Grammar section.

Edit Writing

- Have students do a final pass through their opinion essays, integrating the notes from the clocking activity into their own writing.

ⓔⓛ ENGLISH LEARNER SUPPORT: Scaffold Writing

SUBSTANTIAL
Clarify the meanings of any terms in the editing checklist that students might not understand. Have pairs work together to integrate the changes into their essays.

MODERATE
Have pairs work together to integrate the changes into their essays.

LIGHT
Have pairs exchange their essays with each other for a final review after they have independently integrated their changes.

DISPLAY AND ENGAGE | Online ⓔ**Ed**

Opinion Essay 3.6

Editing Checklist

As you edit your opinion essay, use this checklist.

☐ Check that there is a name on the paper.

☐ Check that the essay includes an opinion statement in the introduction.

☐ Check that the body of the essay includes support for the opinion.

☐ Check that the conclusion relates to the opinion.

☐ Check that each sentence begins with a capital letter.

☐ Check that words are spelled correctly.

☐ Check that each sentence ends with proper punctuation.

LEARNING OBJECTIVES

- Publish written works as part of the writing process.
- Use technology, such as the Internet, to produce and publish writing.
- **Language** Share publishing plans by using academic language.

Prepare the Final Copy

- Tell students to consider different ways to publish their essays. Provide a few examples:

> a. They could produce neat, handwritten copies of their essays.
>
> b. They could use a word-processing program to type their essays.
>
> c. They could use the Internet to post their essays to a school or class website.
>
> d. They could compile their essays and present them in a book, along with photos of the friends or family members they discuss in the essays.

Publish Writing

- Have student pairs work together to plan their final copies. Circulate the room and give tips to students.
- Have students use the remainder of the time to work on the final copy and publishing format.

LEARNING OBJECTIVES

- Speak clearly and audibly at an understandable pace.
- Listen actively and ask specific and relevant questions.
- Answer questions to clarify information.
- Work respectfully with others.
- **Language** Share writing by using a variety of sentence structures.
- **Language** Ask questions by using interrogative sentences.

MATERIALS   Online

Writer's Notebook *pp. 3.3, 3.11*

Share Writing

- Have students share their opinion essays by reading them aloud.
- Ask students to speak clearly and audibly and to maintain an appropriate pace. Also have them maintain eye contact with the audience.
- Have audience members listen actively to the presenter and ask specific and relevant questions about the presentation. Then have the presenter clarify information by answering the questions.

Engage and Respond

- Conclude with an informal debriefing about whether students felt they successfully persuaded the audience to agree with their opinion.
- Have students turn to **Writer's Notebook page 3.3** and revisit the goals they set before they began writing. Have them Turn and Talk with a partner about how they feel they met their goals and take notes about what goals they might set for the next writing assignment. Then have students write a brief self-evaluation on **Writer's Notebook page 3.11**.

 ENGLISH LEARNER SUPPORT: Scaffold Writing

SUBSTANTIAL
To help guide students' responses to their goal evaluation, ask yes/no questions, such as *Do you think you met your goal to . . .* and *Do you think you need to work on . . .*

MODERATE
Provide sentence frames for students' responses: *I met my goal to _____. I need to improve _____.*

LIGHT
Have partners discuss what they did well and what they need to improve upon before independently completing their goal evaluations.

Story

FOCUS STATEMENT It takes courage to make a difference.

FOCAL TEXT

Love Will See You Through: Martin Luther King, Jr.'s Six Guiding Beliefs (as told by his niece)

Author: Angela Farris Watkins

Illustrator: Sally Wern Comport

Summary: Martin Luther King, Jr.'s niece uses examples of his life to show a life well-lived.

WRITING PROMPT

READ the following sentence: *It takes courage to make a difference.*

THINK about someone you know who has made a difference.

WRITE a story about how that person made a difference.

LESSONS

1. **Introducing the Focal Text**

2. **Vocabulary**

3. **Prewriting I: Preparing to Write**

4. **Prewriting II: Features of a Narrative**

5. **Prewriting III: Plotting Events**

6. **Drafting I: Beginning the Draft**

7. **Drafting II: Integrating Narrative Elements**

8. **Drafting III: Completing the Draft**

9. **Revising I: Integrating Grammar and Punctuation**

10. **Revising II: Conferencing**

11. **Revising III: Adding Transitions**

12. **Editing I: Mechanics and Spelling**

13. **Editing II: Peer Proofreading**

14. **Publishing**

15. **Sharing**

**LEARNING MINDSET:
Resilience**

Display **Anchor Chart 31: My Learning Mindset** throughout the year. Refer to it to introduce Resilience and to reinforce the skills you introduced in previous modules.

LEARNING OBJECTIVES

- Establish a purpose for reading.
- Make and describe personal connections to sources.
- Explain the author's use of text structure in an informational text.
- Use text details to predict information.
- Identify the main idea of an informational text.
- **Language** Discuss a thematic idea using sentence frames.
- **Language** Describe the features of an informational text by using visual and contextual support.

MATERIALS   Online

Display and Engage *4.1*

Focal Text *Love Will See You Through: Martin Luther King Jr.'s Six Guiding Beliefs*

Priming the Students

Discuss the Focus Statement

- Tell students that in this module, they will examine how stories can teach us about making a difference.

- Show **Display and Engage 4.1**. Read the focus statement with students. Model thinking about what makes someone courageous:

  THINK ALOUD *I think people who stand up for something they believe in or defend someone who needs their support have a lot of courage. I once had a friend in school who always defended people who were being bullied. I thought she was very courageous for doing that.*

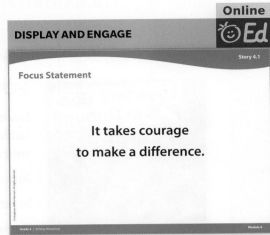

- Have students consider examples of courage that characters have displayed in stories. Allow students to use books in the classroom library to refresh their memories. Ask: *What are some acts of courage you have read about in books?* Write students' suggestions on the board or on chart paper.

- Ask students guiding questions to help them make connections between the stories' characters and real people. Ask: *What did the characters do that showed courage? Can you name a public figure or someone in your personal life who has done something similar? What did the person do?* Add their contributions to the board or chart paper.

- As a class, decide on a definition for *courage*.

- Return to the focus statement. Point out the phrase "make a difference." Model identifying how someone uses courage to make a difference:

  THINK ALOUD *The friend I was just telling you about made a difference by providing support to the person she was defending and by modeling kind behavior for other people to follow.*

Engage and Respond

- Ask partners to choose one of the examples of courage from the board or chart paper. Have them discuss how the characters or people made a difference.

 ENGLISH LEARNER SUPPORT: Facilitate Discussion

SUBSTANTIAL
Clarify the meaning of "make a difference" in the focus statement by rephrasing it as "make positive changes" or "help improve people's lives."

MODERATE
Provide a sentence frame to help students participate in the Engage and Respond activity: _____ *made a difference by* _____.

LIGHT
Provide sentence frames to help students participate in the Engage and Respond activity: *I chose* _____, *whose act of courage was* _____. *This person/character made a difference by* _____.

Priming the Text

Prepare to Read

- Discuss Martin Luther King Jr. with students by having them share what they know about him.

- If possible, show students a video clip of one of King's speeches, along with other items, such as photographs or books about King that you might have available in the classroom.

Love Will See You Through: Martin Luther King Jr.'s Six Guiding Beliefs

- Show the cover of *Love Will See You Through: Martin Luther King Jr.'s Six Guiding Beliefs* with students. Mention that King's niece, Angela Farris Watkins, is the author. Read aloud the introduction she included at the beginning of the book on page 3.

- Ask: *In what ways does Watkins say her uncle made a difference in people's lives?* (*by working to end segregation and discrimination; by making America better*)

- Flip through the book with students. Give them time to look over the pictures. Ask: *What do you see in the pictures?* (*Martin Luther King Jr., people holding hands and kneeling, police, a jail cell*)

- Point out the six numbered statements on pages 4, 10, 14, 18, 22-23, and 26. Then have students review the book's subtitle. Ask: *What do you think these numbered statements in the book are?* (*They're King's six guiding beliefs.*) *Why do you think the author included these in the book?* (*She wanted people to understand the principles her uncle stood for.*)

Engage and Respond

- Have students Turn and Talk to a partner. Ask them to predict what the book will be about, based on their preview.

ENGLISH LEARNER SUPPORT: Support Discussion

SUBSTANTIAL

During the discussion, rephrase questions to allow for yes/no answers, such as asking: *Do you see Martin Luther King Jr. in the pictures?*

MODERATE

Provide a sentence frame to help students express their prediction: *I think the book will be about* _____ .

LIGHT

Give students extra time to consider their discussion answers before speaking.

LEARNING MINDSET: Resilience

Introduce Explain to students that, just as our bodies get stronger when we exercise, our brains get tougher when we take on challenges. Say: *Our brain is made of tiny neurons. As we work, the neurons connect. We can make the neurons grow by taking on challenges. We can actually change our brains!* You'll learn in Love Will See You Through *how Martin Luther King, Jr. took on challenges throughout his life. Despite facing many difficulties, King always kept trying to make things better.* Tell students that when they encounter difficulties while writing, they should remember that learning always takes effort. They have to keep trying, just like King did.

INSTRUCTIONAL VOCABULARY

- **transition words** words that identify the relationship between ideas

The Read

Read the Focal Text

- As you read *Love Will See You Through: Martin Luther King Jr.'s Six Guiding Beliefs,* stop at these points to discuss text features and structure.

  » Read to page 9. Call students' attention to the **transition words**, or words that identify the relationship between ideas. Point out how *first* and *then* help explain the order of events. Ask: *What does King do when he gets home?* (*He checks on his family and then tells people to put down their weapons.*) *What point does King want to make by doing this?* (*He wants people to maintain a spirit of love.*)

  » Read page 13. Emphasize the italicized words in the first two paragraphs. Ask: *Why do you think King thought it was important to tell people* how *to love their enemies and the reasons* why *they should?* (*People don't normally love their enemies, so they probably wouldn't know how or why they should.*)

  » Read pages 19–21. Ask: *What happened to King after he voted?* (*Someone attacked him.*) *How did President Johnson respond?* (*He offered King his help and eventually signed the Voting Rights Act.*) *How does this action relate to King's fourth guiding principle on page 18?* (*After seeing King get hurt for voting, the president wanted to help him.*)

- Continue reading the book with students. Have students identify the book's main idea and examples of organizational patterns in the book.

- Write a definition for *transition words* on the class Instructional Vocabulary list. Have students write the definition in their glossaries.

- Write the following reminders about the content and structure of the book on chart paper. Post the list in the classroom for reference:

  - The important thing about M.L.K. Jr.'s six guiding beliefs is LOVE WILL SEE YOU THROUGH.

  - It is true his first guiding belief is HAVE COURAGE.

  - And his second guiding belief is LOVE YOUR ENEMIES.

  - Another of his powerful beliefs is FIGHT THE PROBLEM, NOT THE PERSON WHO CAUSED IT.

  - It is certainly true that WHEN INNOCENT PEOPLE ARE HURT, OTHERS ARE INSPIRED TO HELP.

  - Although M.L.K. lived all his beliefs, he suffered the most from his fifth belief: RESIST VIOLENCE OF ANY KIND.

  - He preached and proved his sixth belief: THE UNIVERSE HONORS LOVE.

Engage and Respond

- Have students write two or three sentences that answer this question: *What personality traits do you think King needed to have to live by these guiding principles?* Have students share their responses with a partner.

LEARNING OBJECTIVES

- Use print or digital resources to determine a word's meaning.
- **Language** Use context to determine a word's meaning.
- **Language** Acquire and use academic words and phrases.

MATERIALS Online

Focal Text *Love Will See You Through: Martin Luther King Jr.'s Six Guiding Beliefs*
Writer's Notebook *p. 4.1*

📖 INSTRUCTIONAL VOCABULARY

- **antonym** a word that is opposite in meaning to another word

TEACHER TIP

Before students begin identifying antonyms for the Word Bank, provide them with some simple examples such as *good/bad, right/wrong,* and *up/down* to help them understand the concept.

Review the Focal Text

- Review with students the first few pages of *Love Will See You Through: Martin Luther King Jr.'s Six Guiding Beliefs*. Point out that the text includes many words that help describe King's courage and how he made a difference.

- Continue paging through *Love Will See You Through: Martin Luther King Jr.'s Six Guiding Beliefs* and have students identify additional words they find interesting, such as those below. Pause to discuss why the words are interesting. Then have students add them to the Word Bank on **Writer's Notebook page 4.1**.

adversity (p. 5)	protesting (p. 14)	honors (p. 27)
boycott (p. 5)	inspires (p. 19)	prevail (p. 27)
segregation (p. 5)	discrimination (p. 19)	legacy (p. 27)
resisted (p. 9)	outlawed (p. 21)	tribute (p. 27)

- As a class use the context in which the words appear to determine their meanings.

- After defining the words, have the class use a thesaurus or other resource to locate each word's **antonym**—a word that is opposite in meaning. Explain to students that knowing a word's antonym or antonyms can help them understand the meaning of the word itself.

- Write a definition for *antonym* on the class Instructional Vocabulary list. Have students write the definition in their glossaries.

- Have students identify how some of the Word Bank words might be used in a story.

Engage and Respond

- Have partners choose two or three words from the list that they find interesting. Then have them write a few sentences using these words.

 ENGLISH LEARNER SUPPORT: Scaffold Writing

ALL LEVELS After partners choose the words they will use to write their sentences, provide them with sentence frames to use with the words.

LEARNING OBJECTIVES

- Engage in writing as a process.
- Use guidance from adults during the planning stage.
- **Language** Explain goals for writing.

MATERIALS Online Ed

Anchor Chart W1: *Task, Audience, and Purpose*

Display and Engage *4.2*

Writer's Notebook *pp. 4.2, 4.3*

Discuss the Writing Prompt

- Display **Anchor Chart W1: Task, Audience, and Purpose** and read the points with students. Explain that students should always consider their task, audience, and purpose as they plan their writing.

- Ask: *What do you think Angela Farris Watkins's purpose was for writing* Love Will See You Through: Martin Luther King Jr.'s Six Guiding Beliefs? (*Responses may vary.*)

- Show **Display and Engage 4.2**. Read the writing prompt together and note the tips.

- Distribute **Writer's Notebook page 4.2**. Discuss the different expectations of the rubric. Remind students that they can use this rubric as a resource while drafting and revising.

Set Goals for Writing

- Point out that good writers think about improvements they would like to make to their writing before they begin a new piece. Have students consider the goals they would like to set for their stories. Then have them add these goals to the list on **Writer's Notebook page 4.3** or write them in their own notebooks.

ANCHOR CHART — Online Ed

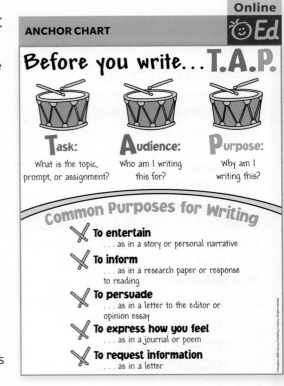

DISPLAY AND ENGAGE — Online Ed

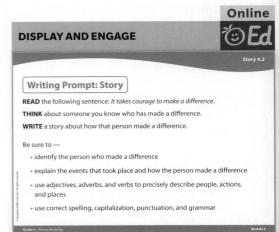

 ENGLISH LEARNER SUPPORT: Scaffold Writing

SUBSTANTIAL

Ask yes/no questions to help guide students to possible goals they would like to set.

MODERATE

Provide sentence frames to help students consider what their goals will be: *I want to make sure I _____.*

LIGHT

Have students work in pairs to complete their list of goals.

LEARNING OBJECTIVES

- Plan the first draft of a story.
- Narrow the topic of the story.
- Select an audience and purpose for the story.
- Use the guidance of peers and adults to assist in the planning process.
- **Language** Describe writing plans by using the vocabulary words *audience* and *purpose*.

MATERIALS   Online 🍎 Ed

Anchor Chart W3: *Narrative Elements*
Display and Engage *4.3a–d*
Writer's Notebook *pp. 4.4, 4.5, 4.6*

 LEARNING MINDSET:
Resilience

Normalize Explain to students that it's normal to feel a little overwhelmed when starting a new piece of writing. Say: *As you begin planning your story, you may struggle to think of ideas or grapple with how to organize them. It's normal to feel a little lost at the beginning of a project. But remember—the important thing isn't to get it right the first time. It's to put in the effort and keep trying.* Remind students that Martin Luther King Jr. had many setbacks in his struggle for justice. But he never let those experiences deter him.

Review Elements of a Narrative

- Display **Anchor Chart W3: Narrative Elements** and read the points with students. Talk about different narratives students have read. Have them note features they liked about those texts, focusing on the setting and plot. Write their ideas on the board.

- Show **Display and Engage 4.3a–d** and distribute **Writer's Notebook pages 4.4** and **4.5**. Read the model text with students.

- At the beginning of the model, have students draw a red box around the setting.

- Then go to the body of the model. Have students circle the transition words in yellow and underline the main events in green.

Begin Prewriting

- Distribute **Writer's Notebook page 4.6**. Have students start planning their story by identifying the person they are writing about and their audience and purpose for writing. Explain that students will complete the information about the story's conflict and resolution later in the writing process.

- Circulate the room as students plan their stories and offer guidance and ideas as needed.

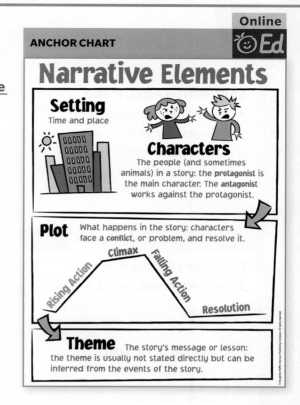

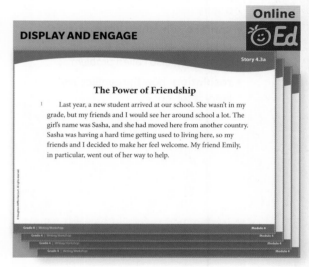

 ENGLISH LEARNER SUPPORT: Scaffold Writing

SUBSTANTIAL
Have pairs discuss and complete their writing plans together.

MODERATE
Provide sentence frames to help students with their planning: *I will write about _____.*

LIGHT
Pair students to discuss their ideas before having them independently complete their writing plans.

LEARNING OBJECTIVES
- Engage in writing as a process.
- Summarize the events in a story.
- Plan the first draft of a story.
- **Language** Plan a first draft by using the vocabulary words *event, conflict,* and *resolution.*

MATERIALS Online

Display and Engage *4.3a–d*
Writer's Notebook *pp. 4.4, 4.5, 4.6, 4.7*

INSTRUCTIONAL VOCABULARY

- **event** something that happens in a story
- **conflict** something in a story that creates a challenge for the characters; also called *problem*
- **resolution** how the conflict in a story is solved

Review Event, Conflict, and Resolution

- Review the meaning of **event** with students by explaining that it is something that happens in a story. Tell students that a story typically consists of multiple events.

- Explain that every story has a **conflict**, or something that creates a challenge for the characters or people in the story. An author will typically introduce the conflict at the beginning of a story.

- Explain to students that a story's **resolution** tells how this conflict is solved. The events that take place throughout the course of a story gradually lead to its resolution.

- Write a definition for *event, conflict*, and *resolution* in the class Instructional Vocabulary list. Have students write the definitions in their glossaries.

- Have students return to **Writer's Notebook page 4.6** to identify their story's conflict and resolution.

Examine the Model

- Revisit the model on **Display and Engage 4.3a–d** and **Writer's Notebook pages 4.4** and **4.5**.

- Create a flow chart on the board. As a class, plot the model's events in the flow chart.

- To help students determine the order of events in their own stories, you may want to provide a graphic organizer, such as the flow chart on **Writer's Notebook page 4.7**. Remind students that their events should flow from the story's conflict and lead to its resolution.

 ENGLISH LEARNER SUPPORT: Scaffold Writing

SUBSTANTIAL
To help students determine their story's conflict, explain that it is the main problem discussed in the story. Provide the following sentence frame for students to complete: *The problem in my story is _____.*

MODERATE
To help students arrange their story's sequence of events, provide sentence frames such as the following: *The first thing that happens is _____. The second thing that happens is _____.*

LIGHT
Have partners discuss their writing plans with each other before they independently complete them.

LEARNING OBJECTIVES

- Develop a first draft by using a purposeful organizational structure
- Develop a first draft with an engaging central idea.
- Develop real events in a narrative.
- Write routinely over extended time frames.
- **Language** Describe the setting of a story by telling where and when it takes place.

MATERIALS Online

Display and Engage *4.3a*
Writer's Notebook *pp. 4.6, 4.7*

 INSTRUCTIONAL VOCABULARY

- **setting** where and when a story takes place

Prepare to Draft

- Remind students that they should demonstrate how the person they are writing about shows courage and makes a difference.

- Show **Display and Engage 4.3a** and point out the story's beginning.

- Write the following items on the board to demonstrate how the model's author first developed prewriting ideas before writing her story:

  - Sasha comes to school as a new student.
  - We try to think of ways to include her.
  - Emily overcomes her shyness by inviting Sasha into our group.

- Point out how the author could have used some of these ideas to craft a first sentence in the model. Discuss how the author chose to begin the story by introducing the **setting**, or where and when the story takes place:

  THINK ALOUD *The author could have started her story with a question, such as* How do you make someone feel welcome? *Or she could've started with a strong statement, such as* Being new to a place can be scary. *Because the author wanted to establish the setting right away, though, she began with a statement that made the information clear:* Last year, a new student arrived at our school. *This tells when and where the story takes place and also helps draw readers in by making them wonder who this new student is.*

- Have students identify the time and location in which the model takes place. Remind students to organize their story by establishing the setting in the beginning. This helps readers understand when and where it happens.

- Write a definition for *setting* on the class Instructional Vocabulary list. Have students write the definition in their glossaries.

Begin to Draft

- Have students return to **Writer's Notebook page 4.6** and **Writer's Notebook page 4.7**. Tell students to begin to draft their stories, using the notes and graphic organizers from their notebooks.

- Circulate the room and offer assistance as needed.

 ENGLISH LEARNER SUPPORT: Scaffold Writing

SUBSTANTIAL
To help students establish their settings, ask questions requiring short responses: *When does your story take place? Where does it take place?*

MODERATE
Help students construct their stories' first sentences to ensure they include details about setting.

LIGHT
Have partners work together to establish the settings in their stories.

NARRATIVE · STORY

LEARNING OBJECTIVES

- Identify the types of conflict in literary texts.
- Engage in writing as a process.
- Compose the first draft of a story by clearly organizing the events to convey a central idea.
- **Language** Discuss stories by using the vocabulary word *conflict*.

MATERIALS   Online

Anchor Chart W5: *Types of Conflict*

Display and Engage *4.3a*

LEARNING MINDSET:
Resilience

Apply As students continue drafting, remind them that effort is a reward in and of itself. Say: *If you're finding that something isn't working out the way you want as you draft your story, just keep trying until you find something you're happier with. It's okay to change your plans if you think of new ideas along the way. The important thing is to put the effort into doing the best you can.* As you circulate the room, provide specific feedback to students and acknowledge their progress as they draft. Highlight new skills students are developing as a result of their effort.

Introduce Types of Conflict

- Display **Anchor Chart W5: Types of Conflict** and read the points with students. Discuss each type of conflict, clarifying their meanings as necessary. Ask them to review the types of conflicts listed in the chart and determine which types were featured in other stories they have read.

- Revisit the model on **Display and Engage 4.3a**. Ask: *What conflict does the narrator discuss at the beginning of the story?* (*A new girl at school named Sasha was having problems fitting in. The narrator and her friends tried to figure out how to help her.*) Ask: *Which type of conflict does this describe?* (*character vs. self*)

- Have students review their plans for their stories and what they have written so far. Have them determine their story's conflict and categorize its type. Ask volunteers to share their thoughts with the class.

Continue to Draft

- As students continue to organize and develop their drafts, remind them to make their conflicts clear to readers.

- Circulate the room and offer assistance as needed.

🔵 ENGLISH LEARNER SUPPORT: Support Comprehension

SUBSTANTIAL

Use actions and gestures to help students understand the different types of conflict. Assist them in determining the type of conflict their stories feature.

MODERATE

Provide students with sentence frames to help them describe the conflict in their stories: *My story's conflict is _____. This is a _____ type of conflict.*

LIGHT

Give students additional time to consider the type of conflict their stories feature before asking them to share their thoughts with the class.

LEARNING OBJECTIVES

- Develop a draft with a purposeful structure.
- Write related paragraphs on a topic.
- Provide a conclusion that follows from narrated events.
- **Language** Describe a text's organization by using the vocabulary word *conclusion*.

MATERIALS   Online ⦿ Ed

Focal Text *Love Will See You Through: Martin Luther King Jr.'s Six Guiding Beliefs*

Display and Engage *4.3a, 4.3d, 4.4*

Review Conclusions

- Revisit pages 4–9 of *Love Will See You Through: Martin Luther King Jr.'s Six Guiding Beliefs*. Review the material the author discusses in this section. Have students pay specific attention to the section's conclusion on page 9.

- Ask: *Do you think that was a satisfying conclusion to the story about the bus boycott? Tell why or why not.*

- Show **Display and Engage 4.4**. Remind students that a story's conclusion should resolve its conflict. In other words, the conclusion should summarize the solution to the problem presented in the story.

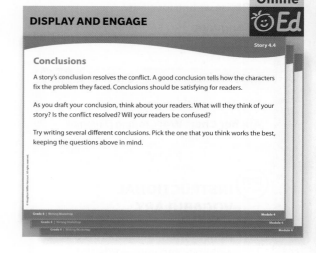

DISPLAY AND ENGAGE   Online ⦿ Ed

Story 4.4

Conclusions

A story's **conclusion** resolves the conflict. A good conclusion tells how the characters fix the problem they faced. Conclusions should be satisfying for readers.

As you draft your conclusion, think about your readers. What will they think of your story? Is the conflict resolved? Will your readers be confused?

Try writing several different conclusions. Pick the one that you think works the best, keeping the questions above in mind.

- Show **Display and Engage 4.3a**. Remind students of the story's conflict: Sasha, a new girl, was having problems fitting in. Show **Display and Engage 4.3d**. Ask: *How does the story's conclusion resolve this conflict?* (*It tells how Sasha became friends with the narrator and her friends as a result of their efforts. Sasha is a lot happier now, and the narrator and the rest of the group have made a new friend.*)

Continue to Draft

- Have students continue writing their first drafts. Remind students they can continue using their prewriting materials to assist them with their writing.

- Circulate the room, offering assistance to students as needed.

 ENGLISH LEARNER SUPPORT: Facilitate Discussion

SUBSTANTIAL
To help students participate in the discussion about the focal text's conclusion, ask questions that allow for yes/no responses, such as: *Does the conclusion tell how the problem of bus segregation was solved?*

MODERATE
Ask students guiding questions to help them determine the effectiveness of the focal text's conclusion: *What problem does this section discuss? How is the problem solved?*

LIGHT
Provide a sentence frame for students to use in response to the focal text: *I think this conclusion (is/is not) satisfying because _____.*

LEARNING OBJECTIVES

- Engage in writing as a process.
- Develop and strengthen writing by revising.
- Revise writing for clarity.
- **Language** Revise drafts by correctly using punctuation.

MATERIALS   Online

Display and Engage *4.5*

Anchor Chart W4: *Crafting Dialogue*

 **INSTRUCTIONAL VOCABULARY**

- **punctuation** the marks used in writing to separate words and sentences (for example, periods, commas, question marks, and exclamation points)

TARGETED GRAMMAR SUPPORT

You may want to consult the following grammar minilessons to review key revising topics.

- **6.1.1 Quotations Marks with Direct Speech,** p. W331
- **6.2.1 End of Sentence Punctuation,** p. W336
- **6.3.1 Commas with Direct Speech and Names,** p. W341

Discuss Punctuation

- Write on the board why **punctuation**, or marks used in writing to separate words and sentences, is important to readers and writers. Have students copy these sentences into their notebooks.

> Punctuation is important. It is a tool of writing. It helps readers understand the writer's meaning. It helps writers show what they mean.

- Write a definition for *punctuation* on the class Instructional Vocabulary list. Have students write the definition in their glossaries.

- Show **Display and Engage 4.5**. Review and discuss the different types of punctuation and their functions.

- Display **Anchor Chart W4: Crafting Dialogue** and read the examples. Discuss the use of commas, end punctuation, and quotation marks, and their placements. Point out the use of tags in the last three examples.

- Divide students into groups and write these sample sentences on the board:

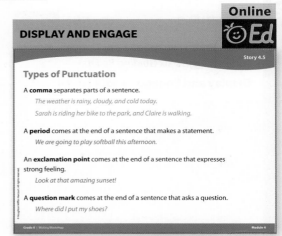

> Slow down children may be at play
>
> Did you do your homework asked my father
>
> Don't scratch Sally cried Tom
>
> No swimming is allowed

- Have the groups punctuate these sentences. Then have the groups share them with the class.

Revise Punctuation

- Have students revisit their own writing to correct punctuation.

- As you circulate the room, group students who need support on similar grammar topics. Use the grammar minilessons or the students' own writing to provide targeted review and support.

Small Group Conferences

- Have students turn to **Writer's Notebook page 4.8** Point out the conferencing checklist and read it with students. Tell them they will use this checklist to guide their small group conferences.

- Tell students that it is time to read their classmates' writing and provide feedback.

  » Divide the class into small groups of four or five.

  » Writers read. Pause. Read again.

  » Listeners listen. Upon the second reading, they jot down images they like.

  » After the reading, listeners repeat back these images.

  » Writers highlight these images on their papers.

  » After the reading, the group comments, suggests, advises, and discusses by using **Display and Engage 4.6**.

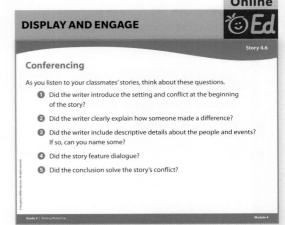

- Debrief with the class. Discuss students' responses to the following questions.

  - What have you learned about writing a story?
  - What did you enjoy the most about it?
  - What other topics would you like to write a story about?

Continue to Revise

- Have students continue to revise, using the feedback they gained in the small group conferences.

 ENGLISH LEARNER SUPPORT: Support Discussion

SUBSTANTIAL
Clarify for students that a story's images consist of descriptions the writer provides. As they listen to their classmates' stories, students should pay attention to specific words and phrases that stand out to them.

MODERATE
Provide a sentence frame for students to use during the discussion: *The images I liked were _____.*

LIGHT
Give students additional time to identify the images they liked in their classmates' writing.

LEARNING OBJECTIVES

* Revise drafts to provide clarity.
* Use the support of peers and adults to revise writing.
* **Language** Revise writing by using transition words to manage the sequence of events.

MATERIALS   Online Ed

Display and Engage 4.3a–d, 4.7
Writer's Notebook pp. 4.4, 4.5, 4.7

TARGETED GRAMMAR SUPPORT

You may want to consult the following grammar minilessons to review key editing topics.

* **1.4.5 Using Compound and Complex Sentences,** p. 235
* **4.6.2 Prepositional Phrases,** p. 322

Introduce Adding Transitions

* Revisit the model on **Display and Engage 4.3a–d** and **Writer's Notebook pages 4.4 and 4.5**.

* Have students review the transition words they had previously circled on their Writer's Notebook pages. Discuss with students how the words make it easier for readers to follow the order of events.

  THINK ALOUD *By quickly scanning the transition words in the model, we can easily understand the order of events in the story. The words also help join the sentences together by creating transitions between them. Imagine how much more difficult it would be to follow the story without these words.*

* Explain to students that good writers use transition words like these to convey how one event leads to another event in a particular sequence.

* Show **Display and Engage 4.7**. Point out to students that these are some examples of transition words and phrases they can use in their stories.

* Have students copy these transitions into their notebooks for reference as they revise their stories and work on future assignments.

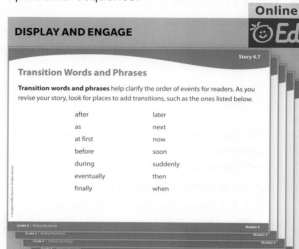

* Next, have students revisit their flow charts on **Writer's Notebook page 4.7**. Mention to students that these charts may help them determine places in their stories where they might add transitions. Point out to students that the areas between boxes, for example, may be appropriate locations for adding them.

Revise for Transition Words

* Have students revise by adding transition words.

* Circulate the room and assist students with revising. If students need help with a specific grammar topic, do a direct teach.

 ENGLISH LEARNER SUPPORT: Scaffold Revision

SUBSTANTIAL
Guide students to find a place in their stories where they could add a transition word. Help them choose an appropriate transition from the list.

MODERATE
Have partners work together to identify places in their stories where transition words might be helpful. Then assist them in determining which words might be the best choices.

LIGHT
Have students independently identify places in their stories where they might add transition words. Then have partners work together to choose appropriate words from the list.

LEARNING OBJECTIVES

- Edit drafts to maintain complete sentences and subject-verb agreement.
- Edit drafts to ensure correct capitalization, punctuation, and spelling.
- **Language** Edit writing by correcting grammar, punctuation, and spelling errors in a draft.

MATERIALS   Online Ed

Anchor Chart W13: *Editing Checklist*

TARGETED GRAMMAR SUPPORT

You may want to consult the following grammar minilessons to review key editing topics.

- **1.1.5 Using Sentences with Subject-Verb Agreement,** p. W220
- **1.3.5 Using Complete Sentences,** p. W230
- **6.4.5 Using Proper Mechanics,** p. W350
- **7.3.5 Using Correct Spelling,** p. W365

Review Editing Checklist

- Display **Anchor Chart W13: Editing Checklist**.

- Review the items on the Editing Checklist. Review how to use proofreading marks.

- As needed, revisit grammar topics to which students may need additional review or practice.

- Remind students they can also use other resources, such as dictionaries or grammar books, to check their spelling and mechanics.

Edit Writing

- Have students independently edit their writing for punctuation, including commas and quotation marks, spelling, capitalization, and subject-verb agreement.

- Circulate the room and provide assistance, as needed.

- As you circulate, group students who need support on similar grammar topics. Use the grammar minilessons or the students' own writing to provide targeted review and support.

 ENGLISH LEARNER SUPPORT: Support Editing

SUBSTANTIAL
Allow partners to work together to edit their writing.

MODERATE
Create a word wall of commonly misspelled words for students to use as a reference when independently checking their spelling.

LIGHT
Help identify errors in students' writing. Then have students independently decide how to correct the errors.

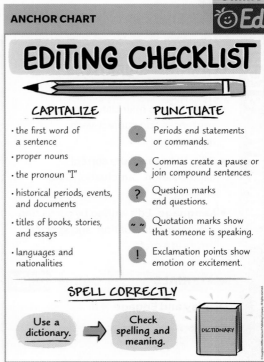

ANCHOR CHART   Online Ed

EDITING CHECKLIST

CAPITALIZE
- the first word of a sentence
- proper nouns
- the pronoun "I"
- historical periods, events, and documents
- titles of books, stories, and essays
- languages and nationalities

PUNCTUATE
- Periods end statements or commands.
- Commas create a pause or join compound sentences.
- Question marks end questions.
- Quotation marks show that someone is speaking.
- Exclamation points show emotion or excitement.

SPELL CORRECTLY
Use a dictionary. → Check spelling and meaning.

LEARNING OBJECTIVES

- Work respectfully with others.
- Edit drafts to maintain complete sentences and subject-verb agreement.
- Edit drafts to ensure correct capitalization, punctuation, and spelling.
- **Language** Edit writing by correcting grammar, punctuation, and spelling errors in a draft.

MATERIALS Online Ed

Display and Engage 4.8

TARGETED GRAMMAR SUPPORT

You may want to consult the following grammar minilessons to review key editing topics.

- **2.1.5 Using Proper Nouns,** p. W240
- **3.2.3 Consistent Use of Tenses,** p. W273
- **4.6.5 Using Prepositions and Prepositional Phrases,** p. W325

Use the Clocking Activity

- Review the rules for clocking.

  » Students form concentric circles or sit opposite each other in rows. As students receive a peer's paper, they become that paper's editor.

  » Call out what item is to be checked by the editor: spelling, subject-verb agreement, use of quotation marks, and so forth.

  » You may also want the students to move after a couple of items so that each student's paper is read by several editors.

  » No marks are made on the actual paper. All papers should have an editing page with the writer's name at the top.

  » Each editor places his or her name next to the number in turn and writes the concept to be checked.

  » When the editing process is completed, the students take their editing page and make any corrections. If there is a problem, they may discuss it with their editor or the teacher.

- Show **Display and Engage 4.8** and discuss the suggestions for editing a story.

Online
Ed

DISPLAY AND ENGAGE

Story 4.8

Editing

As you edit your story, use this checklist.

☐ Check that each sentence has proper subject-verb agreement.

☐ Check that quotation marks and commas are used correctly in dialogue.

☐ Check that verb tenses are consistent.

☐ Check that proper nouns are capitalized correctly.

☐ Check that each prepositional phrase is correctly placed in the sentence.

Grade 4 | Writing Workshop   Module 4

Edit Writing

- Have students do a final pass through their stories, integrating the notes from the clocking activity into their own writing.

- Circulate the room and provide assistance, as needed.

- As you circulate, group students who need support on similar grammar topics. Use the grammar minilessons or the students' own writing to provide targeted review and support.

(EL) ENGLISH LEARNER SUPPORT: Support Editing

ALL LEVELS Circulate as students participate in the clocking activity. Assist students by clarifying any grammatical terms they may not understand and helping students identify errors in classmates' papers.

LEARNING OBJECTIVES

- Publish written works as part of the writing process.
- Evaluate written work and re-consider writing goals
- Work respectfully with others.
- **Language** Describe responses to writing by using academic vocabulary.

MATERIALS   Online Ed

Focal Text *Love Will See You Through: Martin Luther King Jr.'s Six Guiding Beliefs*

Writer's Notebook *pp. 4.3, 4.9*

 LEARNING MINDSET:
Resilience

Reflect Encourage students to reflect on how resilience helped them during the writing process. Say: *Did you find that facing challenges and working through them helped you progress with your writing? You can learn a lot when you make the effort to confront and overcome problems.*

Prepare the Final Copy

- Page through *Love Will See You Through: Martin Luther King Jr.'s Six Guiding Beliefs* with students, pointing out how the author uses illustrations to depict the story's events.

- Tell students to review their own stories to develop some ideas about how to publish them. Provide a few examples:

> a. They could produce neat, handwritten copies of their stories.
>
> b. They could use a word-processing program to type their stories.
>
> c. They could include hand-drawn illustrations to accompany the text.
>
> d. They could turn their stories into a book by folding sheets of paper in half, numbering each page, and handwriting their stories on them. They could then provide either illustrations or photographs to accompany the text.

Publish Writing

- Discuss with students the different publishing options they have available.

- Have partners work together to plan their final copies. Circulate the room and give tips to students.

- Have students work on the final copy and decide how they will publish it.

- Then have students turn to **Writer's Notebook page 4.3** and revisit the goals they set before they began writing. Have them Turn and Talk with a partner about how they feel they met their goals and take notes about what goals they might set for the next writing assignment.

- Have students write a brief self-evaluation on **Writer's Notebook page 4.9**.

 ENGLISH LEARNER SUPPORT: Support Self-Evaluation

SUBSTANTIAL
Ask students yes/no questions to help guide them in their self-evaluations, such as: *Do you think you did well describing the person? Do you think you need more help with spelling?*

MODERATE
Provide students with sentence frames to help them complete their self-evaluations, such the following: *I did well _____. I need to improve _____.*

LIGHT
Have partners work on their self-evaluations together.

LEARNING OBJECTIVES

- Tell a story using descriptive details.
- Speak clearly and audibly at an understandable pace.
- Maintain eye contact with the audience.
- Work respectfully with others.
- Listen actively
- Ask and answer questions.
- **Language** Share stories by reading aloud.

Share Writing

- Divide the class into groups of three or four. Have students read their stories aloud to the group. Then have groups discuss any publishing ideas they derived from the focal text, such as using illustrations to enhance their story.

- Ask students to speak clearly and audibly and to maintain an appropriate pace as they read their stories. Also have them maintain eye contact with their group.

- Instruct group members to listen actively to the reader. After each reader shares his or her story, have group members identify how the person in the story demonstrated courage and made a difference.

Engage and Respond

- Conclude with an informal debriefing about how students felt about writing and presenting their story.

 ENGLISH LEARNER SUPPORT: Elicit Participation

SUBSTANTIAL
Choral read students' stories with them as they share them with the group.

MODERATE
Allow partners to practice reading their stories to each other before reading them to the group.

LIGHT
Have students practice reading their stories silently to themselves before they read them to the group.

INFORMATIONAL TEXT

Expository Essay

FOCUS STATEMENT People are extraordinary.

FOCAL TEXT

Mr. Ferris and His Wheel

Author: Kathryn Gibbs Davis

Illustrator: Gilbert Ford

Summary: A biography that tells about the events leading to the construction of the Ferris Wheel.

WRITING PROMPT

READ the following sentence: *People are extraordinary.*

THINK about an artist you know about.

WRITE an expository essay about that artist. Use facts and details to show how that artist is talented.

LESSONS

1. **Introducing the Focal Text**

2. **Vocabulary**

3. **Prewriting I: Preparing to Write**

4. **Prewriting II: Crafting a Central Idea**

5. **Prewriting III: Organizing Ideas**

6. **Drafting I: Beginning the Draft**

7. **Drafting II: Integrating Expository Features**

8. **Drafting III: Completing the Draft**

9. **Revising I: Connecting Ideas**

10. **Revising II: Conferencing**

11. **Revising III: Combining Sentences**

12. **Editing I: Mechanics and Spelling**

13. **Editing II: Peer Proofreading**

14. **Publishing**

15. **Sharing**

LEARNING MINDSET: Belonging

Display **Anchor Chart 31: My Learning Mindset** throughout the year. Refer to it to introduce Belonging and to reinforce the skills you introduced in previous modules.

LEARNING OBJECTIVES

- Brainstorm words and phrases on a topic.
- Use background knowledge to prepare to read.
- Read informational text with purpose and understanding.
- **Language** Discuss features of text with academic language.
- **Language** Speak using content-area vocabulary.

MATERIALS   Online Ed

Focal Text *Mr. Ferris and His Wheel*
Display and Engage *5.1*
Writer's Notebook *p. 5.1*

Priming the Students

Explore the Topic

- Tell students that in this module they will investigate people who created amazing objects and structures.

- Show **Display and Engage 5.1**. Read aloud the focus statement.

- Have students brainstorm examples of interesting works of art or inventions that extraordinary people have created. Ask follow-up questions, such as: *What makes these items so remarkable? What qualities do their creators have?*

- List appropriate words and ideas on the board or on chart paper. Encourage students to add some of these ideas to their Word Banks on **Writer's Notebook page 5.1** or in their own notebooks.

- Point out that designing and creating impressive and interesting buildings and structures, such as the Sydney Opera House in Australia and Mount Rushmore in South Dakota, takes an extraordinary amount of thought, creativity, and hard work. Show pictures of these landmarks from online resources, books, or magazines.

- Write the word *architect* on the board or chart paper. Explain that an architect is someone who plans, designs, and reviews the construction of buildings. Extraordinary architects created and designed these buildings.

- Then show pictures of structures such as bridges and machines such as locomotives or spacecraft. Ask: *If an architect designs buildings, then who designs structures and machines like these?* Write the word *engineer*. Explain that an engineer designs and builds bridges, roads, or large machines.

- Show students a mechanical classroom object, such as a pencil sharpener. Discuss the complexity of the object.

  THINK ALOUD *I did some research and found out that the mechanical pencil sharpener is made up of two simple machines: a wheel and axle and a wedge. The handle is a crank that turns an axle attached to a wheel inside the case of the pencil sharpener. The pencil sharpener may be small, but its designers were extraordinary!*

Discuss the Focus Statement

- Have partners discuss the focus statement on **Display and Engage 5.1**. Ask them to name an artist, architect, or engineer they admire and to list two reasons why.

 ENGLISH LEARNER SUPPORT: Facilitate Discussion

SUBSTANTIAL
Ask yes/no questions to help students discuss the concept. For example: *Does an architect design buildings?* (yes) *Did an engineer design the Golden Gate Bridge?* (yes)

MODERATE
Have students use sentence frames to discuss the images of impressive buildings and structures. For example: *The person who created _____ is extraordinary because _____.*

LIGHT
Have each student choose a building or structure and explain to a partner why it is impressive.

Priming the Text

Prepare to Read

Mr. Ferris and His Wheel

- Show the cover of the Focal Text *Mr. Ferris and His Wheel*. Tell students that they are going to read an informational text about the first Ferris wheel. Have volunteers describe a Ferris wheel. Encourage them to use the image on the cover in their description.

- Explain that the text takes place during the 1893 World's Fair in Chicago, Illinois. Tell students that world's fairs were huge international showcases of scientific, cultural, and manufacturing goods and ideas. Use online resources to show pictures and videos from past World's Fairs.

- Do a book walk with students. On page 3, note the caption. Define **caption** and have students add it to their Instructional Vocabulary glossaries. Ask: *Why do you think the captions are set in a different font? (to set them apart from the main text; to show that they give more information about events in the main text)*

- Point out the illustration of the first skyscraper on page 7 and read the caption. Explain that before the mid-to-late 1800s, there weren't many very tall buildings or structures because architects and engineers didn't have the technology or materials to build them yet.

- Have students look at pages 8–9. Explain that this image shows George in his office working on a blueprint of his design with his engineering partner. Point out George's drawing board and the other tools in his office, including the pencil sharpener. Then point out his drawings. Remind students that architects and engineers do many calculations and create many drafts before their designs are final.

- Continue paging through the book, pointing out the illustrations of the workers constructing the Ferris wheel. Invite students to comment on how difficult the work looks, as well as the progress the workers make.

- Focus on the observers' expressions in the illustration on page 25. Ask: *What expressions do you see on the people's faces? How do you think they feel? (surprised, excited) Why do you think they feel that way? (They have never seen anything like the Ferris wheel before.)*

- Look at page 38 and point out how the author explains where the quotations in the text come from. Then point out the Selected Bibliography and discuss why the author might have included it. *(so that readers can learn more about the topic)*

Engage and Respond

- Have students write a few sentences about why they think George Ferris might have been extraordinary, based on their preview of the text. Have them share their work with a partner.

ENGLISH LEARNER SUPPORT: Facilitate Language Connections

ALL LEVELS Point out the following Spanish cognates to Spanish-speaking students.

- architect: *arquitecto*
- engineer: *ingeniero*
- fair: *feria*

INSTRUCTIONAL VOCABULARY

- **caption** words or sentences about an illustration or a photograph

LEARNING MINDSET: Belonging

Introduce Explain to students that belonging means being part of a group, such as a family or a class. *Every student in this class is a valuable member of our learning community. You each have something important to offer to the rest of the group.* Tell students that their contributions to discussions and other learning activities throughout this unit will benefit everyone in the class. Connect to the focus statement that people are extraordinary.

The Read

Read the Focal Text

- As you read *Mr. Ferris and His Wheel,* stop at these points to discuss content and how the author uses cause and effect throughout the text. Create a cause-and-effect diagram to show the interconnected events. Add to the diagram as you read the text.

  » Read the quotation on the opening page that comes before the copyright page: "Make no little plans; they have no magic to stir men's minds." Invite students to share their thoughts about the quotation.

  » Read **page 6**. Ask: *Why did most of the plans look like a larger Eiffel Tower? (It was so successful that American engineers wanted to make something similar.)*

  » Read **page 8**. Ask: *What might happen if George and his partner made a mistake in their measurements? (Their invention might crash or fall down.)*

  » Read **page 12**. Ask: *Why did the judges agree to let George build his structure? (They didn't have any better applications; they couldn't decide among applications.)*

  » Read **pages 14–15**. Ask: *What happened to the construction work because the ground was so cold? (The shovels broke; the men had to use pumps to keep out the water and use steam to thaw the sand and stones.)*

  » Read **page 18**. Discuss what "losing hope" means. Then read William Gronau's quote on **page 19**. Ask: *Why was George's partner losing hope? (There was a lot to do; there were so many parts to put together, and there wasn't much time left.)*

  » Read **page 26**. Discuss why the people who rode on the Ferris wheel wanted to go around again, and how their reaction affected the wheel's popularity at the Chicago World's Fair.

- Continue reading *Mr. Ferris and His Wheel* with students as time permits. Discuss how the author shows the ways that George Ferris was extraordinary.

- Have students write interesting words and phrases related to the extraordinary actions of Mr. Ferris, his partner, and the construction workers in their Word Banks.

> **TEACHER TIP**
>
> As you look at the illustration on **page 17**, point out that the man is shown much smaller because the Ferris wheel was so much larger than a person. Browse through the book with students to find other examples of this perspective.

Engage and Respond

- Have students write three or four sentences about how they might have felt if they had been able to ride on the first Ferris wheel at the Chicago World's Fair. Have students share their thoughts with a partner.

(EL) ENGLISH LEARNER SUPPORT: Elicit Participation

SUBSTANTIAL

Ask questions to allow for yes/no answers, such as: *Did the American engineers want to make towers like the Eiffel Tower? (yes) Was building the Ferris wheel easy? (no)*

MODERATE

Provide sentence frames to help students discuss examples of cause-and-effect. For example: *Because the Eiffel Tower was successful, the Americans _____. / The effect of making a mistake in the math calculations might be _____. / The weather was very cold, so _____.*

LIGHT

Review words that signal cause and effect, such as *because, therefore, so,* and *as a result.* Encourage students to use these words in their responses to the discussion questions.

LEARNING OBJECTIVES

- Read and understand domain-specific vocabulary.
- Use context to determine meaning.
- Use print or digital resources to determine a word's meaning.
- **Language** Identify and use synonyms.
- **Language** Use strategies to learn new language.

MATERIALS

Online

Focal Text *Mr. Ferris and His Wheel*

Writer's Notebook *p. 5.1*

Display and Engage *5.2*

INSTRUCTIONAL VOCABULARY

- **synonym** a word that means the same or almost the same as another word
- **shades of meaning** small differences between words that mean almost the same thing

Review the Focal Text

- Page through *Mr. Ferris and His Wheel* and have students identify additional words and phrases that they find interesting. Have students add them to their Word Banks on **Writer's Notebook page 5.1**.

- Show **Display and Engage 5.2**. Read the definition of a **synonym** with students. Point out that good writers will think about synonyms for words they use in their drafts to make their writing more precise or interesting.

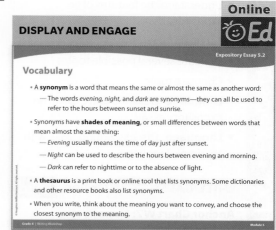

DISPLAY AND ENGAGE

Online

Expository Essay 5.2

Vocabulary

- A **synonym** is a word that means the same or almost the same as another word:
  — The words *evening, night,* and *dark* are synonyms—they can all be used to refer to the hours between sunset and sunrise.
- Synonyms have **shades of meaning**, or small differences between words that mean almost the same thing:
  — *Evening* usually means the time of day just after sunset.
  — *Night* can be used to describe the hours between evening and morning.
  — *Dark* can refer to nighttime or to the absence of light.
- A **thesaurus** is a print book or online tool that lists synonyms. Some dictionaries and other resource books also list synonyms.
- When you write, think about the meaning you want to convey, and choose the closest synonym to the meaning.

- Next, read the definition of **shades of meaning** from **Display and Engage 5.2**. Use a Think Aloud to analyze a sample of shades of meaning.

  THINK ALOUD *I could say that Mr. Ferris's wheel was big. But the word* big *doesn't give a clear mental image of the structure. I would use* immense *to describe it. To me,* immense *means "tall and wide," and that describes the Ferris wheel. When you think about the shades of meaning of synonyms to use in your writing, you give sharper, more detailed information to the reader.*

- Guide students to explore synonyms for the word *pretty*. Suggest that they use a print or an online thesaurus, dictionary, or other resource to assist in their work. Make a list of the words and discuss their shades of meaning.

breathtaking, p. 2	judges, p. 6	boldly, p. 13
impress, p. 4	ambitious, p. 7	hope, p. 18
famous, p. 4	dazzle, p. 8	precision, p. 20
contest, p. 4	mistake, p. 8	enormous, p. 22

Engage and Respond

- Have student pairs choose one of the descriptive words they wrote in their Word Banks on **Writer's Notebook page 5.1**. Tell them to list as many synonyms as they can. Remind students to use print and online resources as they create their lists. Then have them group their words by shades of meaning. Have volunteers share their lists and explain their rationales for grouping.

 ENGLISH LEARNER SUPPORT: Build Vocabulary

SUBSTANTIAL
Help students find synonyms by giving them two words and having them choose the synonym. For example, say: *The word is pretty. Which word is a synonym for pretty: beautiful or plain?*

MODERATE
Provide sentence frames for students to use as they choose synonyms. *The word _____ is a synonym for _____ because _____.*

LIGHT
Provide sentence frames for partners to use to discuss shades of meaning. *The word _____ is better to use in this sentence because it means _____.*

LEARNING OBJECTIVES

- Understand the features of an expository essay.
- Set goals for writing.
- Evaluate several possible topics.
- Choose a topic.
- **Language** Describe and explain an expository essay.
- **Language** Discuss writing tasks with academic language.

MATERIALS   Online Ed

Anchor Chart W7: *Elements of Informational Text*

Display and Engage *5.3*

Writer's Notebook *pp. 5.2, 5.3, 5.4*

TEACHER TIP

Show students images of some extraordinary artists and other people, as well as images of their achievements. Invite students to point to their choice and say a few words about the person.

Review the Writing Process

- Tell students that in this module, they will write an expository essay, which is a type of informational text.

- Display **Anchor Chart W7: Elements of Informational Text** and read the points with students. Talk about different informational texts students have read.

- Show **Display and Engage 5.3** and read the prompt together. Explain the bullet points in more detail as needed.

- Explain that students will write an expository essay to give accurate, factual information about the achievements of someone who has designed or created something extraordinary.

Set Goals for Writing

- Distribute **Writer's Notebook page 5.2**. Remind students they can use this rubric as a resource while drafting and revising.

- Discuss goals that students might want to set for their expository essays. Then have them write their goals on **Writer's Notebook page 5.3** or in their own notebooks.

Brainstorm and Choose a Topic

- Tell students that the first step in writing an expository essay is choosing a topic. Explain that before they choose, they should brainstorm ideas about possible topics. They can narrow their choices by weighing the *pros*, or positive points, and *cons*, or negative points, about each topic.

- Draw a three-column chart on chart paper or the board with the headings *Topic, Pros, Cons*. Then model how to use the chart to help narrow the focus:

  THINK ALOUD *Filling in the chart will help me think about the people on my list and decide which one to write about. I'll start with George Ferris. Pros:* He had a brilliant idea. He worked hard to convince others to let him build the Ferris wheel. He was successful. *Next, I'll think about the cons:* We just read about him. I may want to find someone else who is not as well known to my class.

- Tell students to use **Writer's Notebook page 5.4** to help them choose a topic. Explain that they will choose three possible topics and use the three-column chart to write the pros and cons about them. After they review their charts, they can choose a topic.

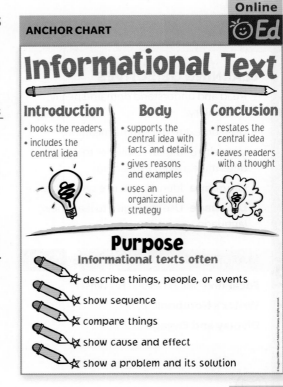

Online Ed

ANCHOR CHART

Informational Text

Introduction
- hooks the readers
- includes the central idea

Body
- supports the central idea with facts and details
- gives reasons and examples
- uses an organizational strategy

Conclusion
- restates the central idea
- leaves readers with a thought

Purpose
Informational texts often

- describe things, people, or events
- show sequence
- compare things
- show cause and effect
- show a problem and its solution

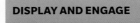

DISPLAY AND ENGAGE   Online Ed

Expository Essay 5.3

Writing Prompt: Expository Essay

READ the following sentence: *People are extraordinary.*

THINK about an artist or another extraordinary person you know about.

WRITE an expository essay about that person. Use facts and details to show how that person is talented.

Be sure to:

- conduct thorough research on your topic
- describe what the person created or accomplished
- explain why the person is extraordinary in your own words
- use correct spelling, capitalization, punctuation, grammar, and sentences

Grade 4 | Writing Workshop   Module 5

LEARNING OBJECTIVES

- Understand features of an expository essay.
- Create a research plan.
- Identify a central idea about a topic.
- **Language** Describe and explain an expository essay topic.
- **Language** Discuss writing tasks with academic language.

MATERIALS   Online

Anchor Chart W2 *Research Sources*

Display and Engage *5.4*

Writer's Notebook *p. 5.5*

 INSTRUCTIONAL VOCABULARY

- **central idea** the main idea of a text or what the text is mostly about
- **detail** a fact or idea that supports or tells more about a central or main idea
- **research** to study and find out about a subject
- **research plan** a plan for how you will learn about topic in depth

 LEARNING MINDSET: Belonging

Model Recognize that sometimes students don't feel like they belong. Say: *In our classroom, we know that everyone is different, and we look for ways to help each other feel a sense of belonging.*

Choose a Central Idea

- Explain that students' next step is to choose a **central idea** for their essay. Tell students that the central idea is the main idea, or what the essay is mostly about.

- Point out that after they choose the central idea, they will need to find **details**, or facts, that support the central idea. To find the most important details, they will create a research plan.

Create a Research Plan

- Show students **Anchor Chart W2: Research Sources**. Discuss the kinds of research sources they might want to use for their expository essay.

- Show **Display and Engage 5.4**. Model using the steps of the research plan by using the topic of the model essay:

  THINK ALOUD *My topic is the American painter Mary Cassatt. The question I want to answer is: How did she pursue her dream of becoming an artist? When I used her name in an Internet search, I found several websites about her. Then I looked at a print encyclopedia, but it only had a few details about her life. But I did find many details about her in a book about artists. I decided to use a website and the book as my main sources. I'll read them carefully and take notes. Then, I'll draft my expository essay.*

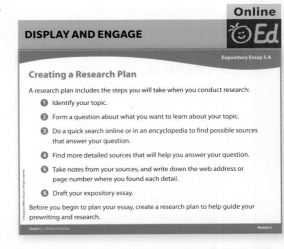

DISPLAY AND ENGAGE   Online

Expository Essay 5.4

Creating a Research Plan

A research plan includes the steps you will take when you conduct research:

1. Identify your topic.
2. Form a question about what you want to learn about your topic.
3. Do a quick search online or in an encyclopedia to find possible sources that answer your question.
4. Find more detailed sources that will help you answer your question.
5. Take notes from your sources, and write down the web address or page number where you found each detail.
6. Draft your expository essay.

Before you begin to plan your essay, create a research plan to help guide your prewriting and research.

- Have students turn to **Writer's Notebook page 5.5** to create a research plan.

- Allow time for students to conduct their research, and provide more resources as needed.

 ENGLISH LEARNER SUPPORT: Research Support

SUBSTANTIAL

Write the following questions on chart paper or the board and have students repeat them after you: *What did the person I'm writing about design or create? How did the person make the design or creation? Why is the person extraordinary?* Work with students to form their own research questions.

MODERATE

Suggest that students use the question words *what, how,* or *why* to form their research questions. Provide sentence frames: *What did the person I'm writing about _____ ? How did the person _____ ? Why is the person _____ ?*

LIGHT

Have students form their research questions independently, and then read them aloud in small groups. Tell group members to listen for a question word and to suggest questions if necessary.

INFORMATIONAL TEXT • EXPOSITORY ESSAY

LEARNING OBJECTIVES

- Identify the central idea and key details in a text.
- Identify the transition words in a text.
- Identify the conclusion in a text.
- **Language** Discuss parts of an informational text.
- **Language** Discuss writing tasks with academic language.

MATERIALS — Online

Display and Engage *5.5a–5.5c*
Writer's Notebook *pp. 5.6, 5.7*

INSTRUCTIONAL VOCABULARY

- **transition words** words in a sentence or paragraph that make the order of events more clear
- **conclusion** a statement you make or an idea you have about a text based on thinking about the information in the text

LEARNING MINDSET:
Belonging

Normalize Challenge students to think of real-life people or characters in books who felt they did not belong. *Did the person you are researching feel left out sometimes? What advice would you give him or her about belonging?*

Discuss the Model

- Show **Display and Engage 5.5a–5.5c** and distribute **Writer's Notebook page 5.6** . Read the model essay with the students.

- Review the definitions of *central idea* and *key details* from the previous lesson. Then review the definitions of **transition words** and **conclusion**. Add the words to the class Instructional Vocabulary list, and have students add the terms and their own definitions to their glossaries.

- Work through the model with students.

  THINK ALOUD *I'm going to examine this model to help me figure out how to do a good job writing my essay. The central idea is that Mary Cassatt was extraordinary because she pursued her dream to become an artist. What are the key details that support this? Let's see. She went to school even though her father didn't want her to. She paid for her own supplies. She studied alone when she could not go to art school. Also, she painted in her own style, which people really liked. Some of the transition words are* when, finally, soon, *and* after a while. *The conclusion is the last paragraph.*

- Also point out that the conclusion repeats the central idea and some of the key details, and it doesn't add any new information.

Begin Prewriting

- Explain that the research students have completed will give them an idea of what to include in their expository essay.

- Distribute **Writer's Notebook page 5.7**.

- Tell students to use their research to complete the flow chart. Explain that they can use the flow chart as they begin drafting their expository essay.

- Circulate the room as students work, and help them identify the key elements in their research and complete the flow chart.

EL ENGLISH LEARNER SUPPORT: Build Vocabulary

ALL LEVELS Work with students to make a list of words that indicate things people do that are extraordinary. The list could include words such as *try, strive, aim, work, pursue, help,* and *study.* Then provide a sentence frame for students to use as they describe the person they are writing about: _____ *is extraordinary because he/she* _____.

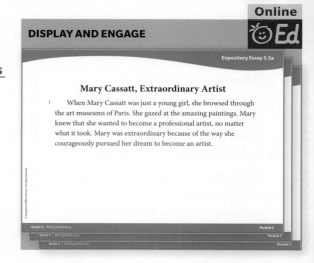

Online Ed

DISPLAY AND ENGAGE

Expository Essay 5.5a

Mary Cassatt, Extraordinary Artist

1   When Mary Cassatt was just a young girl, she browsed through the art museums of Paris. She gazed at the amazing paintings. Mary knew that she wanted to become a professional artist, no matter what it took. Mary was extraordinary because of the way she courageously pursued her dream to become an artist.

LEARNING OBJECTIVES

- Draft multi-paragraph expository essays.
- Use literary devices in an expository essay.
- **Language** Identify key features of text.

MATERIALS Online

Display and Engage 5.6

Focal Text *Mr. Ferris and His Wheel*

INSTRUCTIONAL VOCABULARY

- **hook** a literary device, usually at the beginning of a story, which keeps readers engaged

Prepare to Draft

- Remind students that the focus statement is "People are extraordinary." The prompt asks them to write an expository essay about an extraordinary person, using facts and details to show how that person is talented.

- As students prepare to draft, explain that their expository essay should start with a **hook** that will make readers want to keep reading. Add the word *hook* to the class Instructional Vocabulary list, and have students add it to their glossaries. Remind students that the hook will also refer to the prompt: "People are extraordinary."

- Show **Display and Engage 5.6**. Read the text with students. Talk about the five ways authors hook readers. Invite students to tell why each type of hook might capture their attention. Have students write the five types of hooks in their notebooks.

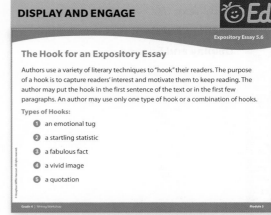

- Point out that a text may have more than one hook. This decision is up to the author.

- Read the first two paragraphs of the Focal Text *Mr. Ferris and His Wheel* on pages 2 and 4. Model how to identify the hook and to analyze why the hook is effective.

   THINK ALOUD *The paragraph on page 2 tells us about an exciting event: the last World's Fair and the soaring Eiffel Tower that was its star attraction. The paragraph on page 4 uses questions to make me wonder about the next World's Fair. I want to turn the page and find out the answers!*

- Refer to **Display and Engage 5.6** again. Ask: *Which type or types of hooks does the author use in the first paragraphs of* Mr. Ferris and His Wheel? *Use details from the paragraphs in your responses.* (*Sample answers: an emotional tug about the last fair and the upcoming one; a startling statistic that the Eiffel Tower was the tallest building in the world; a fabulous fact that the Eiffel Tower was 81 stories tall; a vivid image of seeing all of Paris from the top of the tower*)

Begin to Draft

- Have students begin to draft their expository essays using the notes and graphic organizers from their prewriting. Remind students to include at least one hook and clearly tell their readers what the topic is. Circulate the room as students work and provide support as needed.

 ENGLISH LEARNER SUPPORT: Spanish Cognates

ALL LEVELS Help Spanish-speaking students understand hooks by discussing cognates of words that appear on **Display and Engage 5.6**.

- emotion: *emoción*
- statistic: *estadística*
- fabulous: *fabuloso*
- vivid: *vívido*

INFORMATIONAL TEXT • EXPOSITORY ESSAY

LEARNING OBJECTIVES

- Identify the central idea in a text.
- **Language** Learn and use terms related to expository features.
- **Language** Discuss expository features.

MATERIALS Online

Focal Text: *Mr. Ferris and His Wheel*

Anchor Chart W9: *The Central Idea*

Display and Engage *5.7*

Introduce the Skill

- Tell students that good writers make a **promise** to readers. Ask: *What does a promise have to do with writing?* Explain that a promise is a vow or a pledge to do something. Add the word *promise* to the class Instructional Vocabulary list, and have students add it to their glossaries.

- Reread aloud the opening pages in *Mr. Ferris and His Wheel*. Use a Think Aloud to connect the idea of a promise to the central idea of the text.

   THINK ALOUD *In* Mr. Ferris and His Wheel, *the author, Kathryn Gibbs Davis, promised that she would tell about "America's turn to impress the world" at the Chicago World's Fair. She did that when she told the story of George Ferris building his wheel.*

- Display **Anchor Chart W9: The Central Idea** and read it with students. Encourage them to ask questions about anything they don't understand, and then to summarize the information in their own words.

- Show **Display and Engage 5.7**. Have students identify the promise. (*The author promises to explain what Mary did to pursue her dream of becoming an artist.*)

- Then read the weaker version at the bottom of the page. Ask: *Does the writer make a promise?* (*no*) *How do you know?* (*The writer doesn't describe any actions that Mary took.*)

- Have volunteers tell what their promise to the reader is.

Continue to Draft

- Remind students to include a clear promise in the draft. Circulate the room as students work, offering assistance as needed.

- Warn students not to *plagiarize* material—in other words, to copy someone else's writing and pass it off as their own. Say: *Another promise you make to the reader is to present your own words, not someone else's.* Tell students that it is fine to *paraphrase*, which means restating others' ideas in students' own words.

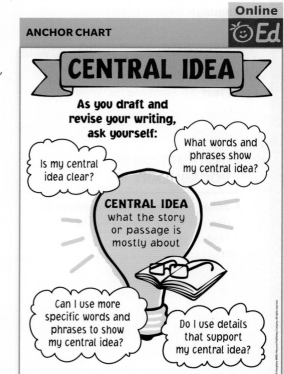

ANCHOR CHART Online

CENTRAL IDEA

As you draft and revise your writing, ask yourself:

Is my central idea clear?

What words and phrases show my central idea?

CENTRAL IDEA what the story or passage is mostly about

Can I use more specific words and phrases to show my central idea?

Do I use details that support my central idea?

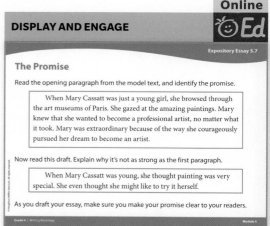

DISPLAY AND ENGAGE Online

Expository Essay 5.7

The Promise

Read the opening paragraph from the model text, and identify the promise.

> When Mary Cassatt was just a young girl, she browsed through the art museums of Paris. She gazed at the amazing paintings. Mary knew that she wanted to become a professional artist, no matter what it took. Mary was extraordinary because of the way she courageously pursued her dream to become an artist.

Now read this draft. Explain why it's not as strong as the first paragraph.

> When Mary Cassatt was young, she thought painting was very special. She even thought she might like to try it herself.

As you draft your essay, make sure you make your promise clear to your readers.

Grade 4 | Writing Workshop   Module 5

ENGLISH LEARNER SUPPORT: Scaffold Writing

ALL LEVELS Pair students and provide a sentence frame: *My promise is _____.* If the promise is not clear, have pairs revise it together.

LEARNING OBJECTIVES
- Identify the conclusion in an informational text.
- Draft a conclusion.
- **Language** Use teacher and peer support to draft a conclusion.

MATERIALS   Online

Display and Engage 5.5c
Focal Text *Mr. Ferris and His Wheel*

TARGETED GRAMMAR SUPPORT

You may want to consult the following grammar minilessons to review key editing topics.
- **1.3.1 Sentence Fragments,** p. W226
- **2.6.1 Pronoun Contractions,** p. W261
- **3.4.2** *Would, Should,* **and** *Must,* p. W282

Introduce the Skill

- Review the word **conclusion** with students. Explain that every expository essay has to have a conclusion. The conclusion restates the central idea and sums up the key details. Its main purpose is to let the reader know that the expository essay is finished.

- Show **Display and Engage 5.5c** and reread the conclusion.

- Provide a Think Aloud to explain why this is a satisfying conclusion.

  THINK ALOUD *The conclusion restates the central idea: that Mary Cassatt was extraordinary. It restates the main details about what she accomplished. It does not introduce any new information. Also, the conclusion shows that the author kept his or her promise from the beginning of the essay. I feel like I have read a complete essay, that I understand what the writer wanted to do, and that I am ready to stop reading.*

- Read aloud page 37 of *Mr. Ferris and His Wheel*. Ask: *Is this a satisfying conclusion? Why or why not?* (Sample answer: *Yes. It restates the central idea and a few of the key details from the text. It shows that the author kept her promise.*) Discuss how the conclusion helps the reader remember why Mr. Ferris was extraordinary.

Complete the Drafts

- Tell students it is time to complete their drafts. Remind them to include transition words and interesting synonyms.

- Point out that they can still refer to their notes and sources to check on information.

- Circulate the room and offer assistance as necessary. As you circulate, group students who need support on similar grammar topics. Use the grammar minilessons or the students' own writing to provide targeted review.

 ENGLISH LEARNER SUPPORT: Elicit Participation

SUBSTANTIAL
Have students point to the conclusion in their expository essays. Ask yes-or-no questions to help them evaluate it, such as: *Is this a good conclusion? Does it tell the central idea? Does it include key details?*

MODERATE
Have students use sentence frames to talk about their conclusions with partners, such as: *This is a good conclusion because _____. My conclusion still needs _____. I will revise my conclusion so that it _____.*

LIGHT
Have students explain to partners how they crafted their conclusions. Have partners either confirm that the conclusion is effective or offer suggestions for revision.

REVISING I: CONNECTING IDEAS

LEARNING OBJECTIVES

- Identify chronological order.
- Revise drafts.
- **Language** Identify and use transition words.

MATERIALS
Online Ed

Display and Engage 5.5a–5.5c, 5.8a–5.8b, 5.9

 INSTRUCTIONAL VOCABULARY

- **chronological order** the order in which events happened or steps in a process should be done
- **coherent** logical, sensible

Introduce the Skill

- Define **chronological order**. Add the word to the class Instructional Vocabulary list, and have students add it to their glossaries.

- Explain that an effective way to help readers follow the order of events in their writing is to tell them in chronological order and to use transition words.

- Show **Display and Engage 5.8a**. Tell students the events are from the model. Point out that the events are out of chronological order. Now show **Display and Engage 5.8b** and point out that events in the flow chart are in chronological order.

- Use a Think Aloud to describe the effects of reading events that are out of order.

  THINK ALOUD *When I read the events, I get confused because they are jumbled. I can't tell when Mary Cassatt did things that helped her become a great artist. When I read the flow chart, the events are easy to follow.*

- Define **coherent**. Add the word to the class Instructional Vocabulary list, and have students add it to their glossaries. Explain that when their writing is coherent, it follows a logical, sensible order and flows easily from one sentence to the next.

- Show **Display and Engage 5.9**. Explain that transition words show the reader how ideas are connected. In other words, they help make the writing coherent.

- Read the words with students. Use some of the words in sentences. Have students copy the transition words into their Writer's Notebooks or their own notebooks.

- Show **Display and Engage 5.5a–5.5c**. Have students identify the transition words that the model uses. Invite them to suggest more or different transition words that might also work.

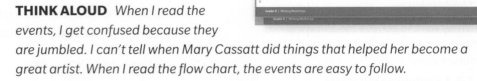

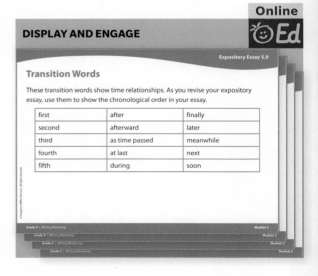

Revise for Transition Words

- Have students revise their own writing to add or change transition words. Circulate the room and offer individual assistance as necessary.

 ENGLISH LEARNER SUPPORT: Scaffold Revising

ALL LEVELS Say a series of sentences, omitting a transition word. Give students a choice of two words to complete the sentence. For example: *First, Mary visited museums. Second, she went to art school. _____, she moved back to Paris. (Sample answers: third, next, then)*

INFORMATIONAL TEXT • EXPOSITORY ESSAY

LEARNING OBJECTIVES
- Revise an expository essay.
- **Language** Discuss writing in small group conferences.

MATERIALS   Online

Writer's Notebook *p. 5.8*
Anchor Chart W12 *Revising Checklist*

 INSTRUCTIONAL VOCABULARY

- **summarize** to restate the most important information, or main ideas, in a text in your own words

TEACHER TIP

If you wish, project the essays on a monitor so students can follow along more easily.

 LEARNING MINDSET:
Belonging

Review Say: *We all get stuck on our work sometimes. If we think that everyone else gets it but we don't, we may feel as if we don't belong. Remember that our classroom is a safe place where everyone belongs. If you get stuck in your writing, ask for help.*

Small Group Conference

- Show **Anchor Chart W12: Revising Checklist**. Tell students they will have time during this lesson to revise their expository essays according to the checklist.

- Explain that before they begin revising, they are going to complete a summarizing activity that will give them feedback about their essays. They will use the feedback and the Revising Checklist to revise their drafts.

  THINK ALOUD *When you summarize a piece of writing, you restate the main idea or ideas in your own words. This summarizing activity will let you know what stands out in the essay. Your input is important because it will help the writer craft a more effective expository essay.*

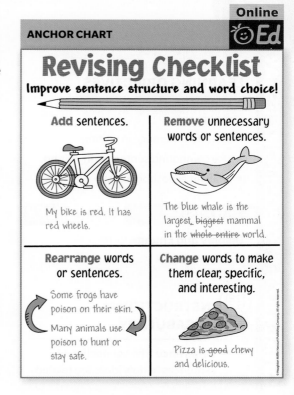

- Tell students that they will work in groups. Each writer in the group will read his or her entire essay, pause, and then read it again.

- Explain that students will use **Writer's Notebook page 5.8** to help them summarize after the second reading. Review the steps with students: focus on the central idea, write the central idea in a single sentence, choose one word to express the central idea, and think of a synonym to express that idea.

- Divide students into groups of five. Have them begin their group work. Spend a few minutes with each group to make sure they are able to follow the steps.

- When students have finished, have them share their summaries with the class.

Continue to Revise

- Encourage students to consider the feedback they received. In this workshop environment, some students may be revising, some still working in groups, and some conferencing with the teacher.

EL **ENGLISH LEARNER SUPPORT: Support Revision**

SUBSTANTIAL
Remind students that the main idea sentence should include the name of the person who is the topic of the essay plus a verb that tells what he or she did.

MODERATE
Provide sentence frames: *I think _____ is the best synonym to use because _____. I don't think _____ is a good synonym to use because _____.*

LIGHT
Brainstorm a list of nouns that students might want to use to express the main ides, such as *hope, creativity,* or *determination.* Encourage students to draw from the list as they work.

REVISING III: COMBINING SENTENCES

LEARNING OBJECTIVES

- **Language** Discuss writing in a group.
- Identify coherence in writing.
- Use compound sentences in writing.
- Draft an expository essay.

MATERIALS   Online

Display and Engage *5.10*

 INSTRUCTIONAL VOCABULARY

- **coherence** the connection of sentences to how ideas are related

TARGETED GRAMMAR SUPPORT

You may want to consult the following grammar minilessons to review key editing topics.

- **1.4.3 Commas in Compound Sentences,** p. W233
- **3.2.4 Review Verb Tenses,** p. W274
- **6.4.3 Commas before Coordinating Conjunctions,** p. W348

Introduce the Revision Skill

- Tell students that it is time to talk about **coherence,** or what we call the "glue of writing." Just as glue sticks two surfaces together, so sentences must stick together, each one to the previous one. Sentences have to be connected to make the whole piece. Also, each sentence has to show a progression of thought.

- Tell students to think of constructing a paragraph like stringing beads. The string starts with one bead and beads continue to be added to create a string of beads. Sentences work the same way. Each sentence adds some new information or insight to the one before. The paragraph develops, or gets longer, with each additional sentence.

- Explain that one way to increase connections is to combine short, related sentences into one longer sentence.

- Show **Display and Engage 5.10**. Read the definition of a compound sentence. Read the sample compound sentences. Point out how the conjunction joins the two simple sentences and that the two parts of the compound sentence have related thoughts.

- Explain how you might create a compound sentence related to the model.

  THINK ALOUD *Listen to these two simple sentences:* Mary Cassatt painted women and children. Many people liked her new approach. *They sound choppy. Since the ideas are related, I can create a compound sentence:* Mary Cassatt painted women and children, and many people liked her new approach. *I like the way the new compound sentence flows.*

- Invite students to say compound sentences using *and, but,* and *or*. Write the sentences and circle the conjunctions.

Continue to Revise

- Circulate the room and help students revise. Group students who need support on similar grammar topics. Use the grammar minilessons or the students' own writing to provide targeted review and support.

 ENGLISH LEARNER SUPPORT: Scaffold Revisions

SUBSTANTIAL

Give students two simple, related sentences and have them practice using the conjunction *and* to join them. Repeat several times until students are comfortable forming the compound sentences. Continue with *but* and *or*. Then have students choose two simple sentences in their essay to combine.

MODERATE

Have partners work together to find sentences they can combine. Encourage them to use at least two of the conjunctions.

LIGHT

Have partners read their compound sentences to each other and explain why they chose the conjunction they used for each one.

LESSON 12

12/16/2022

LEARNING OBJECTIVES

- Edit drafts using complete sentences, correct subject-verb agreement, capitalization, punctuation, and spelling.
- Use both a print and an online dictionary to check spelling.
- **Language** Proofread writing for spelling.
- **Language** Edit writing for capitalization, punctuation, and mechanics.

MATERIALS   Online

Anchor Chart W13 *Editing Checklist*

TARGETED GRAMMAR SUPPORT

You may want to consult the following grammar minilessons to review key editing topics.

- **2.1.2 Capitalizing Titles,** p. W237
- **2.2.3 Apostrophe Use in Possessive Nouns,** p. W243
- **2.5.3 Reflexive Pronouns,** p. W258

Review Proofreading Checklist

- Display **Anchor Chart W13: Editing Checklist**.

- Review the items on the Editing Checklist. Review how to use proofreading marks.

- Remind students that using correct spelling and mechanics helps their readers better understand what they are writing about.

- Point out that they should use reference sources, such as print dictionaries and online resources, to help them check their spelling.

- Model how to use print and online dictionaries to check spelling.

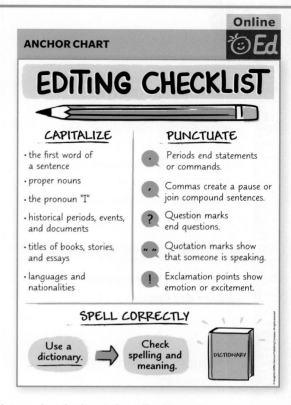

THINK ALOUD *I want to use the word* determined *when I describe Mary Cassatt. I'm not sure how to spell it, so I look in the print dictionary. I know the first three letters are d, e, and t, and I use the sounds of the rest of the letters to guess how the word might be spelled. Then I go to the page in the dictionary that has words starting with det-. I scan the pages until I find the word* determined. *I write the correct spelling in my notebook. Now let's use the online dictionary. In the search bar, I type the word* determined *the way I think it's spelled. A message pops up letting me know that the word is misspelled. Under the message is a list of possible words. I see that* determined *is at the top of the list, so I click the word and go to the page that has the spelling and definition.*

- Invite students to reread their drafts and circle any words they want to check in the dictionary. Provide time for students to use either print or online dictionaries.

Proofread Writing

- Have students independently edit their writing for spelling, mechanics, punctuation, and grammar. Circulate the room and assist students as needed.

- Group students who need support on similar grammar topics. Use the grammar minilessons or the students' own writing to provide targeted review and support.

EL   **ENGLISH LEARNER SUPPORT: Support Editing**

SUBSTANTIAL
Guide students as they use the dictionary. Provide beginning dictionaries if possible. Have students keep a list of the words they edit.

MODERATE
Review alphabetical order to the third letter with students before they begin their dictionary work. Have them work with partners to look up the spellings. Then have students spell the words aloud to each other.

LIGHT
Have students discuss the changes they made to words after they checked the dictionary. Provide sentence frames, such as: *I used the letter _____, but the correct spelling uses the letter _____.*

LEARNING OBJECTIVES

- Proofread classmates' writing for capitalization, punctuation, and correct spelling.
- **Language** Proofread writing for grammar, usage, and mechanics.
- **Language** Edit writing with peer support.

MATERIALS   Online Ed

Anchor Chart W17 *Proofreading Marks*

Display and Engage *5.11*

TARGETED GRAMMAR SUPPORT

You may want to consult the following grammar minilessons to review key editing topics.

- **1.1.3 Subject-Verb Agreement,** p. W218
- **1.4.1 Compound Sentences,** p. W231
- **2.1.3 Capitalizing Languages, People's Names, and Nationalities,** p. W238

Use the Clocking Activity

- Review the rules for clocking with students.

  » Students form concentric circles or sit opposite each other in rows. As students receive a peer's paper, they become that paper's editor.

  » Call out the item to be checked by the editor.

  » Remind student editors that they do not make marks on the actual paper. Instead, the student editors put their comments on an editing page.

  » Each editor places his or her name next to the number and writes the item to be checked.

  » When the editing process is completed, the students take the editing page and make any corrections.

  » If there is a problem, students discuss it with their teacher or the editor.

Review Proofreading Checklist

- Present **Anchor Chart W17: Proofreading Marks** and review with students how to mark up a text as they proofread.

- Show **Display and Engage 5.11**. Review the proofreading checklist with students.

- Remind students of the importance of using correct subject-verb agreement and correctly punctuating compound sentences.

> **Online**
> **Ed**
>
> **DISPLAY AND ENGAGE**
>
> Expository Essay 5.11
>
> ### Proofreading Checklist
>
> As you proofread your expository essay, use this checklist:
>
> ☐ There is a name on the paper.
> ☐ Each sentence has subject-verb agreement.
> ☐ Each sentence begins with a capital letter.
> ☐ Each sentence ends with the correct type of punctuation.
> ☐ The first letter of each proper noun is capitalized.
> ☐ All words are spelled correctly.
> ☐ Compound sentences have a comma and a conjunction.
>
> Grade 4 | Writing Workshop   Module 5

Edit Writing

- Have students do a final pass through their expository essays, integrating the notes from the clocking and proofreading activities into their own writing.

- Remind students to choose synonyms that have the shades of meaning they want to convey.

- Remind students to check that the chronological order is correct and that they have used transition words correctly.

EL ENGLISH LEARNER SUPPORT: Scaffold Proofreading

SUBSTANTIAL

Work with students as they edit. Use prompts to help them identify the items on the checklist. For example: *Point to a compound sentence. Point to the comma and the conjunction.*

MODERATE

Have students work in small groups to edit each other's expository essays. Have them use sentence frames as they discuss their editing: *This sentence (does/does not) have subject-verb agreement. In this compound sentence, the _____ is correct, but you need to add a _____.*

LIGHT

As students proofread, ask them to share one proofreading tip with the others in their group. After each student has shared, have them discuss how using all of the tips helps their proofreading.

LEARNING OBJECTIVES

- Publish writing.
- **Language** Discuss glossary words.

MATERIALS   Online

Focal Text *Mr. Ferris and His Wheel*
Writer's Notebook p. 5.9
Classroom materials *paper, stapler*

INSTRUCTIONAL VOCABULARY

- **glossary** an alphabetical list of words and their meanings in the back of a book

TEACHER TIP

Page through a glossary and a thesaurus to show students the difference.

TARGETED GRAMMAR SUPPORT

You may want to consult the following grammar minilessons to review key editing topics.

- **2.1.2 Capitalizing Titles,** p. W237
- **2.4.1 Possessive Pronouns,** p. W251
- **3.5.1 Irregular Verbs,** p. W286

Prepare the Final Copy

- Tell students they will make their own books by folding paper and stapling the folded pages together. They can make the quire, or folded paper book, any size they want.

- Distribute materials and have students make their books. Remind them to follow the format of *Mr. Ferris and His Wheel* and include a front and back cover and a copyright page. They should also leave a blank page at the end for a glossary. Invite them to include one quotation at the front of the book and one at the end.

- Then have students copy their expository essays in their best handwriting.

Add a Glossary

- Remind students that a **glossary** is an alphabetical list of words and their meanings that is often found in the back of a nonfiction book. Show examples of glossaries in books from the classroom library. Add the word to the class Instructional Vocabulary list, and have students add it to their glossaries.

- Explain that while *Mr. Ferris and His Wheel* doesn't have a glossary, many of its words could be included in a glossary. Browse through the first few pages of *Mr. Ferris and His Wheel*. Model choosing a few words to add to a glossary.

   THINK ALOUD *I want to add words that are important to understanding the story but may be difficult for or unfamiliar to some readers. Words related to science and engineering will be good choices. On page 5, I choose* technologies *because readers might not know what it means. On page 7, I choose* mechanical engineer. *On page 10, I choose* construction chief. *After I finish my list, I'll add the definitions.*

- Work through the rest of the book with students. Guide them as they make a list of words they think would be appropriate for a glossary of the book. Then have them work in pairs to write the definitions.

Reflect on the Process

- Have students turn to **Writer's Notebook page 5.9**. Read the reflection questions with students, and give more explanations as necessary. Have students complete the questions independently.

Publish Writing

- Allow time for students to add glossaries to their own expository essays. Suggest that they include between three and six entries.

- Remind them to add quotations like the ones in *Mr. Ferris and His Wheel*.

- If there is time, have students illustrate their writing or design a cover for their expository essay.

LEARNING OBJECTIVES

- Share writing.
- Hold a collaborative discussion.
- **Language** Ask and answer questions using academic language.

MATERIALS   Online

Writer's Notebook p. 5.10

Share Writing

- Before students begin sharing their expository essays, discuss the best ways to listen to an essay that is full of details and facts, and possibly some dates and technical language.

- Explain to students that they may want to try to mentally associate names with two or three key words that describe the person's actions or accomplishments. They may also want to take brief notes as they listen or just after the speaker finishes.
  THINK ALOUD *I want to remember what I learned about Mary Cassatt. Which words should I associate with her? She created paintings, so it makes sense to associate the word* artist *with her. Also, she became an artist even though many obstacles stood in her way. What word should I use to describe that? Determined works well. I'm going to write both of those words next to her name.*

- Suggest that when they hear dates in the expository essay, students should mentally associate the date with a few key words about the important events that took place on each date. They may also want to mentally arrange the dates in sequential order—that way they can make connections about the events. Students may want to jot down key dates or make timelines.

- Have students share their expository essays.

- Allow time after each expository essay for students to ask questions. Remind students to ask questions that refer to facts and details from the essay, and to ask their questions in a pleasant and respectful manner. Point out that their goal is to better understand the life and works of the extraordinary person they just heard about. Encourage the presenter to answer with details from their essay or from their research into the person.

Engage and Respond

- Conclude with an informal debriefing about how students felt about doing research; including facts, details, and dates; creating an exciting hook for their essay; compiling a glossary; and presenting their essay to the class.

- Display the following sentence starters. Invite students to respond and to explain their responses. Then discuss their ideas and responses as a group.

  > 1. Expository essays are _____.
  >
  > 2. When writing this essay, I learned _____.
  >
  > 3. My favorite word during this module was _____ because _____.

- Finally, have students turn to **Writer's Notebook page 5.10** or the list of goals they set at the beginning of this writing workshop. Have them revisit the goals and then TURN AND TALK with a partner about their results. Encourage them to take notes about goals they might set for their next writing assignment.

EL **ENGLISH LEARNER SUPPORT: Practice Fluent Reading**

ALL LEVELS Before they share their expository essays with the class, allow students time to practice reading their essays with a student who is a more proficient English speaker. Have the proficient speaker read the essay aloud, one sentence at a time. Have the less proficient student echo read each sentence. Then have both students choral read.

Letter

FOCUS STATEMENT Earth's natural wonders can teach us a great deal.

FOCAL TEXT

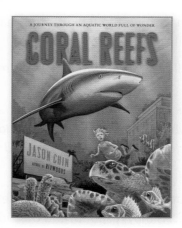

Coral Reefs

Author and Illustrator: Jason Chin

Summary: A girl visits a library to learn facts and detailed information about coral reefs.

WRITING PROMPT

READ this sentence: *Earth's natural wonders can teach us a great deal.*

THINK about a natural wonder you are interested in.

WRITE a letter to an expert in that field of study asking for more information. Use formal language and show that you already have some knowledge on your topic.

•••••• LESSONS ••••••

1. **Introducing the Focal Text**

2. **Vocabulary**

3. **Prewriting I: Types of Correspondence**

4. **Prewriting II: Choosing a Topic**

5. **Drafting I: Beginning the Draft**

6. **Drafting II: Elements of the Genre**

7. **Drafting III: Completing the Draft**

8. **Revising I: Conferencing**

9. **Revising II: Strengthening Ideas**

10. **Revising III: Strengthening Word Choice**

11. **Editing I: Grammar**

12. **Editing II: Capitalization and Punctuation**

13. **Editing III: Peer Proofreading**

14. **Publishing**

15. **Sharing**

**LEARNING MINDSET:
Wonder**

Display **Anchor Chart 31: My Learning Mindset** throughout the year. Refer to it to introduce Wonder and to reinforce the skills you introduced in previous modules.

CORRESPONDENCE · LETTER

LEARNING OBJECTIVES

- Describe personal connections to text.
- Establish purpose for reading.
- Recognize central idea in informational text.
- Explain use of text structure.
- Recognize organizational patterns in informational text.
- **Language** Use accessible language to learn new words.
- **Language** Speak using content-area vocabulary.

MATERIALS   Online Ed

Writer's Notebook p. 6.1
Display and Engage 6.1
Focal Text *Coral Reefs*

 INSTRUCTIONAL VOCABULARY

- **glossary** an alphabetical list of words and their meanings
- **graphic feature** a visual that gives information or supports text
- **index** a list of major topics and their page numbers
- **text organization** the way a text is arranged to help readers understand the information
- **inference** a smart guess that readers make, based on clues in text and what they already know

Priming the Students

Explore the Topic

- Tell students they will learn about one of Earth's natural wonders: coral reefs.

- Write the word *wonder* on the board. As a group, brainstorm words that relate to *wonder*, such as synonyms or examples. Ask: *What places or things fill you with wonder? (Possible answers: a place I went on vacation, a monument I read about in social studies class)*

- If students need more guidance, prompt them to think about places they have traveled to or things they have read about. Write ideas on chart paper.

- Point out that many natural features of Earth fill people with wonder. Use a model to describe a natural feature.
  THINK ALOUD *I remember when I visited Glacier National Park in Montana. Mountains were all around me, and I made snowballs in the middle of July. The lakes were incredibly blue, and there were many waterfalls. I saw colorful flowers and birds, mountain goats, and even a grizzly bear!*

- Show students pictures or videos of natural features, such as volcanoes, oceans, or jungles. Have students describe what they see. As they respond, add their ideas to the list.

- As you look at the pictures, ask: *If you were a scientist, what questions would you try to answer about this natural wonder?* Encourage students to add these ideas to the Word Bank on **Writer's Notebook page 6.1** or in their own notebooks as a resource for writing. Remind students that writing things down expands memory.

Discuss the Focus Statement

- Show **Display and Engage 6.1**. Read the Focus Statement with students. Connect the idea of natural wonders to their own knowledge and experiences. Ask students to name some other natural wonders. Encourage students to explain why each of their choices is a natural wonder.

DISPLAY AND ENGAGE   Online  Ed

Letter 6.1

Focus Statement

Earth's natural wonders can teach us a great deal.

- Then have students work in small groups to share their thoughts about the Focus Statement. Encourage them to add their ideas to their notebooks.

 ENGLISH LEARNER SUPPORT: Facilitate Discussion

ALL LEVELS If students have difficulty describing features of a national wonder, model expected output for students before you ask them to speak. Encourage them to select a feature from the photographs or websites to describe. You may want to learn key vocabulary words from students' home languages, such as *montaña* and *glaciar* (Spanish for *mountain* and *glacier*).

Priming the Text

Prepare to Read

- Show the cover of *Coral Reefs*. Point out the illustrations on the cover. Ask: *Where do you think most of this text will take place?* (*underwater*) Point out the buildings and the student swimming. Explain that although this text provides facts and details about real-life sea creatures, the book is illustrated as if these creatures could come right into our daily lives.

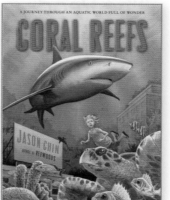

Coral Reefs

- Explain that this informational text will give detailed information about coral reefs and all the animals that live there. Point out all the animals and labels on the inside front cover and read about them with students.

- Turn to the title page. Ask: *Where is the girl?* (*a library*) *Why might she be there?* (*Possible answers: to learn more about a subject that interests her; to ask a librarian for help with research; just to find something fun to read*)

- Page through the book with students. Have students describe what they see in the illustrations.

- Ask: *Why do you think this book shows the girl right next to the ocean features?* (*Possible answer: to show how fascinated she is by what she is reading*)

- Turn to the heading *The Threat to Coral Reefs*. Point out that this section is printed inside a book. Discuss why the author may have put this text on an illustrated book. (*Possible answers: to show that there is more to the story; to encourage students to read more about protecting coral reefs*)

- Turn to the book list. Read the titles of the other books in the list. Ask: *Why do you think the author included this information?* (*to show where he found the information he used to write the book; to help readers who want to learn more about this topic*)

Engage and Respond

- Have students Turn and Talk to a partner. Invite them to describe what they want to learn by reading *Coral Reefs*. (*Possible answers: where coral reefs exist in the world, what threatens them, why they are wonders, why they are so colorful*)

    THINK ALOUD *I find that I get more out of a book when I think about why I want to read it. I'm definitely interested in these colorful illustrations, but I also want to find out what kinds of sea creatures there are and what I can do to protect them.*

ENGLISH LEARNER SUPPORT: Facilitate Discussion

SUBSTANTIAL
Students may have trouble understanding that although the book gives factual information about coral reefs, the illustrations are fantastical. If your students are Spanish speakers, you may wish to introduce the cognates *realidad* and *fantasîa* (Spanish for *reality* and *fantasy*).

MODERATE
Help students structure their verbal responses by providing sentence frames: *The girl is in the _____. The pictures are surprising because _____.*

LIGHT
If possible, provide a bilingual dictionary and a visual dictionary so students can identify sea creatures in their home languages and discuss them in English.

The Read

Read the Focal Text

- As you read *Coral Reefs*, stop at these points to discuss content and domain-specific terms.

  » Read pages 2–3. Point out that the author has defined what coral is right at the beginning of the text. Ask: *Why did the author define coral so quickly?* (*Some readers might not know any details about coral. Coral is going to be important for the reader to know about later in the text.*) Ask a follow-up question: *How do you know coral is going to be important to know about?* (*The title of the book is* Coral Reefs.)

  » Read pages 4–6. After each page, stop and ask students what interesting words, sentences, or ideas they heard. Encourage them to add words and ideas to their Word Banks.

  » Ask: *What have you learned from coral just from looking at the illustrations?* (*Possible answers: Coral comes in many colors and shapes. Coral is strange-looking but beautiful.*)

  » Ask: *Why do more and more ocean features keep appearing in the library?* (*Possible answers: to show how much more interesting and alive coral reefs are becoming for the girl; to show that reading an interesting book can make you feel as if you are in another world*)

  » In their Instructional Vocabulary glossaries, have students define **inference**: *a smart guess that readers make, based on clues in the text and what they already know.* Point out that when they answered the question about the ocean figures appearing in the library, they made an inference about why the illustrator chose to show the ocean features that way.

- Continue reading with students. Periodically, stop to have students describe the illustrations. Prompt them to use more and different descriptive words.

Engage and Respond

- Tell students to write two or three sentences about what they found the most intriguing in *Coral Reefs* and what they would like to know more about. Have students share their ideas with a partner.

TEACHER TIP

Before you read each page, show students the page to help them visualize what the text is about.

(EL) ENGLISH LEARNER SUPPORT: Support Comprehension

SUBSTANTIAL

As you read *Coral Reefs*, discuss the unique features of the undersea creatures, using simplified language. If possible, provide visual dictionaries to help students learn words related to the ocean or to undersea wildlife.

MODERATE

Use simplified language to discuss the different features of coral. Write relevant words and phrases on the board, and have students repeat them with you. If necessary, provide sentence frames to guide students through the Engage and Respond activity: *I was surprised that coral is _____. I want to learn about _____*

LIGHT

As you read *Coral Reefs*, encourage students to write down unfamiliar words. After reading, have them work with a partner to define each word using a dictionary or the glossary.

LEARNING OBJECTIVES

- Read and understand domain-specific vocabulary.
- Use context to determine meaning.
- Use word-reference materials.
- Use word parts to clarify meaning.
- **Language** Use strategies to learn new language.
- **Language** Identify and use word parts.

MATERIALS　　　Online

Focal Text *Coral Reefs*

Writer's Notebook *p. 6.1*

Review the Focal Text

- Review with students the pages in *Coral Reefs* that you read aloud. Point out that the text is rich with vocabulary related to the natural wonders of life on a reef. Use the following model.

    THINK ALOUD *This book has lots of words that I don't use in everyday conversation. When I read text that has lots of unfamiliar words in it, I write down interesting words and phrases. I also try to figure out how different words are connected because that helps me understand them better and remember them later.*

- Have students return to their Word Bank on **Writer's Notebook page 6.1** or in their own notebooks. As you review the pages, have students identify additional words and phrases they find interesting, and add them to their Word Banks. Examples:

intricate	web	protection
builders	chain	shelter
prey	predator	survive
complex	evading	common

- Remind students that keeping track of interesting words can help them as they write.

- Point out that one way to help remember words and their definitions is to think about how they are related. Use the following model.

    THINK ALOUD *The words* prey *and* predator *are related. A predator chases prey to eat. To help evade a predator, prey often look for shelter to stay safe.*

- Draw a web on the board. Demonstrate connecting words together in the web, using the words in the Think Aloud.

- If students need more reinforcement before working together in pairs, ask the class to figure out a connection between the words *shelter* and *survive*.

Engage and Respond

- Have student pairs work together to link ideas from their own Word Banks in a web and then in a few short sentences.

 ENGLISH LEARNER SUPPORT: Build Vocabulary

SUBSTANTIAL

Pair students who have similar English language abilities. Invite them to include simple pictures as well as words in their webs. Students may also include words from their home languages to help remind them what the English terms mean.

MODERATE

Provide sentence frames: *The words _____ and _____ are similar. They both _____.* Review pairs' webs and sentences, and confirm that each student in the pair can make logical connections between terms. If your students are Spanish speakers, point out that the word *predator* has a cognate in Spanish (*depredador*), as does *prey* (*presa*). Also, the word *coral* has the same spelling in Spanish and English.

LIGHT

Invite pairs to discuss what they do to remember unfamiliar words and concepts, both in their home languages and in English. Do webs help, or do they prefer rhymes or other methods?

LEARNING OBJECTIVES

- Understand features of correspondence.
- Understand parts of a formal letter.
- **Language** Distinguish between formal and informal English.

MATERIALS   Online

Display and Engage 6.2

Anchor Chart W11: *Parts of a Formal Letter*

Writer's Notebook p. 6.2

 INSTRUCTIONAL VOCABULARY

- **formal language** a style for speaking or writing, following the rules of English
- **informal language** a style for speaking or writing that you use with people you know, such as friends and family

Review the Writing Process

- Review the steps of the Writing Process. Remind students that good writers carefully complete each step before moving to the next step.

- Show **Display and Engage 6.2**. Read the different types of correspondence, discussing samples of each that they might have sent.

- Ask: *How would the language you use to write to a family member differ from the way you write to a scientist you don't know?* (*Answers may vary, but discuss any responses that are questionable.*)

- After students respond, review the definitions of **formal** and **informal language** in the Instructional Vocabulary Glossary. Model language they might use in a letter.

- Ask students for examples of formal and informal questions.

- Tell students that they will write a **formal letter** to an expert, asking for information about a natural wonder.

- Display **Anchor Chart W11: Parts of a Formal Letter** and read it with students.

- Help students understand they write their own information for the sender and that the recipient is the person who receives the letter—the person they are writing to. Discuss the use of titles, such as *Mr.*, *Ms.*, or *Dr.* Point out the colon after the greeting. Briefly discuss the contents of the body.

Set Goals for Writing

Point out that effective writers set goals before writing. Have students think about their goals for their formal letters, and add those goals to the list on the **Writer's Notebook page 6.2** or in their own notebooks.

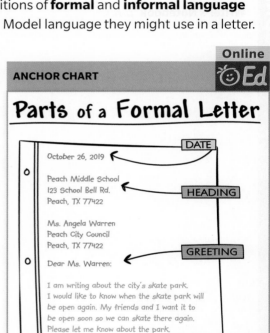

ANCHOR CHART   Online

Parts of a Formal Letter

- October 26, 2019 — DATE
- Peach Middle School / 123 School Bell Rd. / Peach, TX 77422 — HEADING
- Ms. Angela Warren / Peach City Council / Peach, TX 77422
- Dear Ms. Warren: — GREETING
- I am writing about the city's skate park. I would like to know when the skate park will be open again. My friends and I want it to be open soon so we can skate there again. Please let me know about the park. Thank you.
- Respectfully,
- Marco Rivera — SIGNATURE — CLOSING
- BODY: 1. Purpose 2. Specific Request 3. Summary

 ENGLISH LEARNER SUPPORT:

SUBSTANTIAL
Review students' last piece of writing with them. Talk about goals they can work toward. Write the goals for students, and have them copy the goals into their Writer's Notebooks.

MODERATE
Discuss students' writing goals. If needed, provide sentence frames for writing goals, such as: *I will write a letter that is _____ and _____.*

LIGHT
Have student pairs discuss their goals before writing them down. Encourage students to consult a dual-language dictionary if they need help with goal-related words.

LEARNING OBJECTIVES

- Use multiple prewriting strategies to plan writing.
- Conduct research for writing.
- **Language** Use academic language to discuss writing tasks.

MATERIALS   Online

Display and Engage *6.3*

Writer's Notebook *pp. 6.1, 6.3, 6.4*

TEACHER TIP

Students may narrow the topics in their Word Bank by crossing out words and topics in which they are less interested.

Discuss the Writing Prompt

- Show **Display and Engage 6.3** and read the Writing Prompt together.

- Distribute **Writer's Notebook page 6.3** and review the rubric with students. Point out they can use this rubric as a resource as they write.

- Review the Word Bank on **Writer's Notebook page 6.1** or in students' notebooks. Tell students they can choose from three topics they listed in the Word Bank to write their letters. Have them narrow their list to the three topics that most interest them.

- Encourage students to discuss their choices with a partner and then choose one topic for their letters. Then have students write in their notebooks, describing what they already know about the topic.

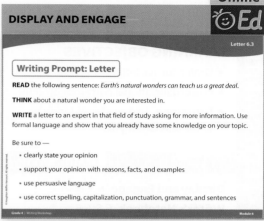

DISPLAY AND ENGAGE   Online ⓔ Ed   Letter 6.3

Writing Prompt: Letter

READ the following sentence: *Earth's natural wonders can teach us a great deal.*

THINK about a natural wonder you are interested in.

WRITE a letter to an expert in that field of study asking for more information. Use formal language and show that you already have some knowledge on your topic.

Be sure to —
- clearly state your opinion
- support your opinion with reasons, facts, and examples
- use persuasive language
- use correct spelling, capitalization, punctuation, grammar, and sentences

Conduct Research

- Remind students that their letters must show that they already know something about the topic. Model how you begin research by doing an Internet search. Show how to identify and enter keywords into a search and how to select a trustworthy website that has the information you want or need.

   THINK ALOUD *I did a search for* grizzly bear tracking *and found a website for the Interagency Grizzly Bear Study Team. The site had detailed information, and I jotted down facts, details, and examples. I also found contact information for the study team, so now I know where to send my letter. Here is a sample of what I wrote down:*

   - The study group began putting radio collars on bears in Yellowstone in 1975.
   - By collaring female bears, scientists learn how many cubs they have, how many cubs survive, and where mothers and cubs hibernate.
   - Humans cause more than 80% of all bear deaths.

- Depending upon resources, take students to the library or computer lab, or work out a schedule for students to use the classroom library and technology.

- Demonstrate how to do an Internet search for students' topics by name or keyword and how to look up their topic in books using the index and table of contents. Your library may subscribe to databases that are designed for young students.

Begin Prewriting

- Have students begin researching. Remind them to take notes on **Writer's Notebook page 6.4** or on index cards.

- Point out that the audience is the scientist to whom they send the letter, and the purpose is to get more information about the chosen topic.

LEARNING OBJECTIVES

- Draft a formal letter.
- Use organizational patterns correctly.
- **Language** Use academic language to discuss writing tasks.

MATERIALS   Online

Display and Engage *6.3, 6.4a–c*

Writer's Notebook *6.5, 6.6*

TEACHER TIP

Students may have difficulty finding names and addresses for experts. Guide them to find the names and addresses using safe websites.

Prepare to Draft

- As students move from their notes to their drafts, focus their attention by reviewing the prompt on **Display and Engage 6.3**. Underline the four key parts of the prompt or write them on the board.

  » Write a letter to an expert in the field.

  » Ask for more information.

  » Use formal language.

  » Show that you already have some knowledge on your topic.

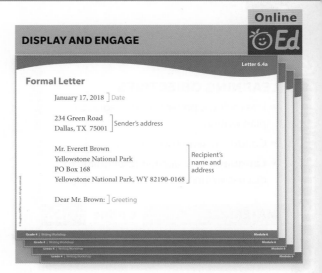

- Show **Display and Engage 6.4a** and distribute **Writer's Notebook page 6.5**. As you work through the model, have students find the matching parts in their formal letter outline.

- Explain that this shows the correct way to begin a formal letter.

  » Point out that the heading has three parts: the name and address of the sender (the student), the name and address of the recipient (the expert), and the date.

  » As you discuss the recipient, explain the use of the title (*Mr., Ms., Dr.,* and so on) and point out that the title is part of the greeting.

  » Ask students how this differs from the greeting in an informal letter to a friend or family member.

  » Point out the colon (not a comma) that follows the greeting in a formal letter.

- Show **Display and Engage 6.4b**. Explain that this shows the first two sections of the body of the letter. Point out that each paragraph is indented to show that it is the beginning of a new thought. Ask students to find examples of three parts of the prompt.

  THINK ALOUD *The writer describes the topic and asks for information in the introductory paragraph. He sounds very polite and uses the word* please. *In the next paragraph, the writer shows that he already knows something about the topic.*

- Show **Display and Engage 6.4c**. Point out that students should always thank the person because they are asking someone to take extra time to provide information. Discuss different closings they might use. Tell students to be sure to both sign the letter and print their name so that it is easy to read.

Begin to Draft

- Have students begin to draft their formal letter, using their notes and their formal letter outline.

- You may want to provide a graphic organizer to help students organize their ideas, such as the idea-support map on **Writer's Notebook page 6.6**. Remind students that many writers find using graphic organizers to be a helpful prewriting strategy. Review how to complete the idea-support map using the model letter.

CORRESPONDENCE • LETTER

LEARNING OBJECTIVES

- Draft a formal letter.
- Write using organizational patterns.
- Use formal language.
- **Language** Distinguish between formal and informal English.

MATERIALS Online

Display and Engage 6.5

 INSTRUCTIONAL VOCABULARY

- **genre** a type or category of writing, such as fiction, informational text, or opinion writing

---

Focus on Formal Language

- Explain that letter writing is a **genre**—a type or category of writing, such as fiction, informational text, or opinion writing. Have students add the word to their Instructional Vocabulary glossaries.

- Talk about how the features of a letter differ from a poem or an essay. Ask: *What are some features of a letter?* (Possible answer: heading, greeting, body, closing)

- Point out that both friendly letters and formal ones share some features. For example, friendly and formal letters usually include the date and a greeting. But the greetings have a different level of formality.

  THINK ALOUD *When I write a friendly letter, I might use a greeting like* Hi, Annie. *But if I wrote to our mayor, I would say* Dear Ms. Lee. Hi *is informal language that you use when talking to friends. A business, or formal, letter uses formal language.*

- In a friendly letter, the writer usually signs his or her first name, not the full name.

- Show **Display and Engage 6.5**. Point out the different types of formal language, such as verbs, transition words, and emphasis words. Work through each of the examples, and help students understand the difference between formal and informal language. Remind students to avoid slang. You may wish to have students add these examples to their notes.

DISPLAY AND ENGAGE Online

Letter 6.5

Informal and Formal Language

	Informal	Formal
Verbs	look at find out	examine discover, learn
Transition words	In a nutshell, Also,	To summarize, In addition,
Emphasis words	lots of really, very	much, many certainly
Contractions	I'm, isn't, haven't	I am, is not, have not
Greetings/closings	Hi Bob! Love,	Dear Sir or Madam, Sincerely, Respectfully,

Grade 4 | Writing Workshop   Module 6

Engage and Respond

- Have each student write a brief letter to a friend, using informal language. Then have students exchange papers and rewrite the letter using formal language. Circulate to check comprehension and provide help when needed.

Continue to Draft

- Tell students to continue to draft their formal letters, using their notes and their formal letter outline. Circulate the room, offering assistance as needed. Encourage students to refer to the formal letter outline to make sure they include all the parts.

EL **ENGLISH LEARNER SUPPORT: Support Comprehension**

SUBSTANTIAL
Review the writing prompt to be sure students understand the task. Provide model sentences or paragraphs for students before they are expected to write their own. You may wish to learn key words in students' home languages, such as *carta formal* (Spanish for *formal letter*).

MODERATE
Provide formal and informal letter frames for student use. Have students of similar ability work together as they draft their letters.

LIGHT
Have students describe their topics and explain what they plan to include in their letters. Help with any subject-specific words that may be difficult for them.

LEARNING OBJECTIVES

- Draft a formal letter.
- Write using organizational patterns.
- Use formal language.
- **Language** Write using new vocabulary.

MATERIALS   Online Ed

Writer's Notebook pp. 6.2, 6.3

 LEARNING MINDSET: Wonder

Apply Remind students that wondering about Earth's natural features led them to do research on a topic and write a letter asking for more information. *As you draft your letter, you might also wonder how you might make it better. You might wonder how to make your request more specific and clear. Try writing each sentence in several ways to see which one sounds best.* Tell students that wondering about their own actions is another way to grow and learn. Encourage students to consider other parts of their draft that they might wonder about.

Complete the Draft

- Have students finish drafting a formal letter. Encourage students to leave space between lines as they write their drafts to allow room for editing.

- Point out that students can continue to use different resources to help them with their writing. These resources include their prewriting notes, the formal letter outline, their Word Banks, dictionaries, and the Internet.

- Suggest that students keep the recipient of their letters in mind as they write. For example, *What might you say if you were talking to the person? How would you say the same thing using formal language?*

- Remind students to make sure the closing paragraph provides a strong concluding statement and thanks the expert for his or her help and information.

- Continue to circulate to offer help where needed.

- Some students may have problems locating the name and address of their expert. Work with them individually to help them complete this information. If a web search is not enough, you may need to consult a reference librarian. If an expert has written a book, it may be possible to contact the expert through his or her publisher.

Review the Draft

- When students feel they are finished, encourage them to compare their letters with the formal letter outline. Tell students to check off each part when they have completed it.

- Encourage students to revisit the goals they set on **Writer's Notebook page 6.2** and reflect on whether they have met their goals. If not, encourage them to continue improving their draft.

- Revisit the rubric on **Writer's Notebook page 6.3**. Tell students to review their letters to make sure they have responded to every item in the prompt.

- Have students reread their letters as if they are the expert to whom the letter is written. *How do you think the letter will make the expert feel? Does everything make sense? Will the expert understand what you want?*

 ENGLISH LEARNER SUPPORT: Scaffold Writing

SUBSTANTIAL

Have students describe what they want to say in the letter in simple language. Help them form complete sentences. Write these down, and then have students copy them into their Writer's Notebooks. Students can use these ideas as they draft their letters.

MODERATE

Have each student read his or her letter aloud, sentence by sentence. Point out any problems, such as incorrect word order or tense. Discuss how to correct the problems. If necessary, provide students with sentence frames: *I would like to know more about _____. Have you studied _____?*

LIGHT

Help students with any new basic or subject-specific words that they find difficult. Ask students what part of the letter they feel needs the most work, and help them with specific issues.

LEARNING OBJECTIVES
- Work collaboratively to improve writing.
- **Language** Express opinions.

MATERIALS Online

Writer's Notebook *p. 6.7*

TEACHER TIP

Differentiate between helpful (or constructive) and unhelpful criticism. Model commenting on a sentence in the focus text in a constructive and non-constructive way. *An example of constructive criticism is, "I think this sentence is confusing because. . . ." An example of unhelpful criticism is, "Why would anyone write that?" Which one would you rather hear about your work?*

Small-Group Conferences

- Distribute **Writer's Notebook page 6.7**. Read the questions and checklist and discuss how students can use the form to rate a formal letter.

  THINK ALOUD *When I write a formal letter, I like to have someone else read it before I send it. A second set of eyes can often find problems I don't see. Is what I wrote clear or confusing? Did I use formal language? Did I provide enough information? Having another person read your work is a great resource!*

- Tell students that they will be reading their classmates' letters and providing feedback.

- Divide students into groups of four. Within each group, have students form two sets of partners.

- Have partners exchange the drafts of their letters. Tell students to read the letters silently and add notes to the conferencing form on page 6.7. When both partners have finished, encourage students to spend a few minutes discussing the letters. Partners should give their finished forms to each other.

- Then, have partners switch so that each student is working with a new partner. Repeat the previous step with the new partner's paper.

- Debrief with the class. Focus on how students can use the peer review to improve their writing. Discuss students' responses to the following questions.

> - In what ways is having a partner read your paper helpful?
> - What did you learn about your partners as you read their letters?
> - How will this process help you revise your writing?

Begin to Revise

- Have students begin to revise their writing using the feedback they gained in small-group conferences.

EL **ENGLISH LEARNER SUPPORT: Facilitate Discussion**

SUBSTANTIAL
Allow students to give feedback to partners in their home language first.

MODERATE
You may want to learn key phrases in students' home languages. For instance, the Spanish phrase for *constructive criticism* is *crítica constructiva*.

LIGHT
Invite students to discuss levels of formality in their home languages. Would they use formal or informal language in a letter to an expert? What about when reviewing a classmate's work?

CORRESPONDENCE · LETTER

LEARNING OBJECTIVES
- Use strategies to revise a draft.
- **Language** Self-correct writing.

MATERIALS	Online

Display and Engage 6.6
Writer's Notebook p. 6.8

 LEARNING MINDSET:
Wonder

Apply Point out that the questions writers ask themselves during the revision process are a great example of curiosity or wonder. Good writers reflect on their writing and ask themselves how to make it stronger and more interesting. Invite students to describe what their writing might sound like if they accepted the first words they put on paper. (*Possible answers: confusing, uninteresting*)

Introduce the Revision Skill

- Remind students that *revision* is the part of the writing process in which the writer reflects on a writing assignment and decides how to make it stronger.

- Point out that, in revision, students should focus on the content rather than spelling, punctuation, and grammar. Model how to think about revising.

  THINK ALOUD *When I start to revise, I begin by asking myself questions about what I have written. I want to make sure that the reader will understand my ideas and will enjoy reading what I wrote. Therefore, I ask: Is my topic narrow and manageable? Does the order of ideas make sense? Do the details support the ideas? Does my writing have an interesting beginning and ending?*

- Show **Display and Engage 6.6**. Explain that this chart shows four methods students can use to strengthen their writing—adding, deleting, combining, and rearranging.

- Read the questions in the first column of the first row. In some cases, a writer may decide that he or she has enough detail and doesn't need to add anything. However, if there is a problem, the writer can revise by adding details, connecting words, or both. Read the *before* and *after* sentences in the example box, and discuss the changes the writer made. Talk about why the revised sentence is stronger than the original sentence.

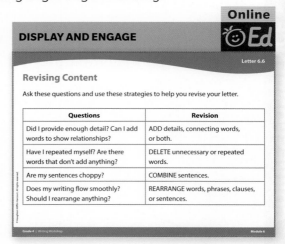

- Work through the rest of the table in the same way. Discuss how each of the revisions makes the writing stronger and easier to understand.

- Distribute **Writer's Notebook page 6.8** and read the tips with students. Tell them they can use this page to help them improve the coherence and clarity of their letters.

Revise for Content

- Have students revise their letters to improve sentence structure by adding, deleting, combining, and rearranging ideas.

- Circulate the room, monitoring student progress and offering suggestions where needed.

 ENGLISH LEARNER SUPPORT: Scaffold Writing

SUBSTANTIAL

Working with students individually or in small groups, read students' writing aloud, sentence by sentence. Discuss whether each sentence shows the intended meaning. Ask students if they can think of a clearer or more interesting way to say the same thing. Work together to revise ideas and strengthen writing.

MODERATE

Have students form pairs. Have one student read each sentence in the other's letter aloud, pausing after each sentence to discuss whether the sentence serves its intended purpose. If not, the pair should work together to revise the sentence before continuing.

LIGHT

Have student pairs work together to look for opportunities to add or delete sentences.

LEARNING OBJECTIVES

- Use strategies to revise a draft.
- Use word-reference resources.
- Identify synonyms.
- Work collaboratively.
- Improve writing skills.
- **Language** Acquire new vocabulary.
- **Language** Share information in cooperative groups.

MATERIALS   Online

Display and Engage *6.7*

Classroom materials *plastic baggies, colored and white index cards, markers, tape, thesaurus or dictionary (1 per group)*

Writer's Notebook *p. 6.9*

INSTRUCTIONAL VOCABULARY

- **synonym** word that means the same or almost the same as another word

TEACHER TIP

After the activity, collect the synonym bags and place them in a resource area for students to use in other writing.

Introduce the Revision Skill

- Explain that two important parts of revising content are adding details and replacing words that don't add anything to the writing.

- Tell students that asking questions is a good way to identify poor word choice. For example, *What boring or overused words have I used? Do my words appeal to the senses? How can I add energy to my writing?*

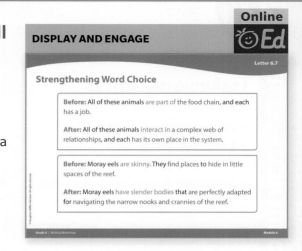

- Show **Display and Engage 6.7**. Read the first set of example sentences. Break down the changes with this model.

  THINK ALOUD *When I read the first example, the phrases* are part of, the food chain, *and* has a job *don't help me see, hear, or feel anything. They aren't very descriptive or interesting to me as a reader. The word* interact *is much more specific than* a part of. *A complex web of relationships gives me much more detail about how the animals are related.* Has a job *isn't as descriptive as* has its own place in the system.

- Invite students to add their own comments about the two sentences. Encourage students to think about how they might use these techniques to revise their letters and other writing.

- Read the second set of example sentences with students. Have students offer their ideas on why the second set is better.

Identify Synonyms

- Remind students that a **synonym** is a word having the same meaning or almost the same meaning as another word. Remind students they can use a thesaurus or dictionary to identify synonyms for words they would like to replace.

- Arrange students in groups of four. Provide each team with plastic baggies, colored and white index cards, markers, tape, and a thesaurus or dictionary. Tell students to select a word from their letters that is weak or needs replacing. Have them write the word on a colored index card and tape the card to a plastic baggie.

- Encourage students to think of a strong synonym for the word. Use a marker to print the synonym on a white index card. Place it in the bag. Then give the bag to the next member of the group who will look at the word and synonym and then identify and add another synonym to the bag. Continue until all members of the group have added a synonym to each bag.

- Point out that students now have four different synonyms they might use to strengthen their word choice.

Revise for Word Choice

- Have students use the strategy they just learned to revise their letters by strengthening word choice.

- Distribute **Writer's Notebook page 6.9** to students and review the items with students. Have them use the checklist to revise their drafts to improve word choice by adding, deleting, and rearranging ideas.

CORRESPONDENCE • LETTER

LEARNING OBJECTIVES

- Write correctly formed sentences.
- Apply correct punctuation.
- **Language** Recognize incorrect sentence structure.
- **Language** Recognize incorrect verb tense.

MATERIALS   Online

Anchor Chart W13: *Editing Checklist*

TARGETED GRAMMAR SUPPORT

You may want to have students use the following grammar minilessons as they edit their letters.

- **1.3.4 Review Fragments and Run-On Sentences,** p. W229
- **1.1.3 Subject-Verb Agreement,** p. W218
- **3.2.5 Using Verb Tenses Correctly,** p. W275

Introduce the Editing Skill

- Explain that once students have revised their draft for content, they are ready to check for other errors. Say: *This is the editing step in the writing process. Editing includes checking mechanics, such as grammar, capitalization, punctuation, and spelling. It's too difficult to check all those elements at the same time, so when I edit, I check them one at a time. I sometimes start with grammar. Then I make sure my verb tenses agree. Let's start by checking sentences to be sure they are complete.*

- As needed, revisit relevant grammar topics. Show students **Anchor Chart W13: Editing Checklist**.

Online ⊙Ed

ANCHOR CHART

EDITING CHECKLIST

CAPITALIZE
- the first word of a sentence
- proper nouns
- the pronoun "I"
- historical periods, events, and documents
- titles of books, stories, and essays
- languages and nationalities

PUNCTUATE
- **.** Periods end statements or commands.
- **,** Commas create a pause or join compound sentences.
- **?** Question marks end questions.
- **" "** Quotation marks show that someone is speaking.
- **!** Exclamation points show emotion or excitement.

SPELL CORRECTLY
Use a dictionary. ➔ Check spelling and meaning.   DICTIONARY

- Write the following paragraph on the board or on chart paper:

> A book about coral reefs. I learn that there are many different animals that live there. More information on this topic. Please told me where I can look to find more about it

- Tell students that they should begin by deciding whether each sentence is complete. Work through the paragraph one sentence at a time. Read the first group of words aloud. Ask: *Is this a complete sentence? Why or why not?* (No, it doesn't have a verb.) *How could you make it a complete sentence?* (Possible answer: Add I read *to the beginning of the sentence.*)

- Repeat with the rest of the paragraph. Ignore errors in verb tense at this point.

- Read the second sentence aloud. Ask: *What are the verbs in this sentence?* (learn, track) *Are both verbs the correct tense?* (Possible answer: No, learn *should be* learned *because it happened in the past.*)

- Repeat with the last sentence. Ask: *What are the verbs in this sentence?* (told, look, find) *Are they all in the correct tense?* (Possible answer: No, told *would have happened in the past.* Tell *is the correct tense.*)

- Ask students to find the punctuation error. (*The last sentence has no end punctuation.*) Correct the error, and remind students to check their punctuation.

Edit for Sentence Structure and Verb Tense

- Explain to students how to make the proofreading marks that delete a word or words and that insert a word or words.

- Have students work on editing their letters for complete sentences and verb tense.

- Circulate the room, monitoring progress and offering suggestions where needed.

LEARNING OBJECTIVES

- Use correct capitalization.
- Use correct punctuation.
- **Language** Increase understanding of English conventions.

MATERIALS
Online Ed

Anchor Chart W17: *Proofreading Marks*
Classroom materials *chart paper*
Display and Engage *6.4a–6.4c*

TARGETED GRAMMAR SUPPORT

You may want to have students use the following grammar minilessons as they edit their letters.

- **2.1.5 Using Proper Nouns,** p. W240
- **6.2.5 Using Punctuation Correctly,** p. W340

Review Proofreading Checklist

- Students will edit their letters for correct capitalization and punctuation. Say: *Formal letters contain several features with specific capitalization and punctuation rules.* Write these rules on the board or chart paper:

  CAPITALIZATION: The following should start with a capital letter:
  - the first word in a sentence
  - months of the year
  - the word Dear in the greeting
  - proper names (people's names, places, cities, states, streets)
  - titles (Mr., Mrs., Ms., Miss, Dr.)
  - the first word of the closing

  PUNCTUATION:
  - comma between the date and year
  - colon after greeting in a formal letter
  - punctuation ends every sentence (. ? !)
  - too many or too few commas

- Show **Display and Engage 6.4a**. Model editing the page by checking the capitalization against the rules you have written. Discuss the reasons for capital letters in the heading. Then move on to punctuation. Point out the placement of the commas, the period after the title *Mr.*, and the colon at the end of the greeting.

- Show **Display and Engage 6.4b**. Have volunteers explain why some words are capitalized. (*first words in sentences, proper names*) Point out end punctuation and why there is a comma after *topic*. (*compound sentence joined by a conjunction*)

- Finish reviewing the model for capitalization and punctuation with **Display and Engage 6.4c**.

Edit for Capitalization and Punctuation

- Use **Anchor Chart W17: Proofreading Marks** to review the specific marks used to edit capitalization and punctuation. Have students use the marks to edit their letters. Circulate the room, monitoring and offering feedback.

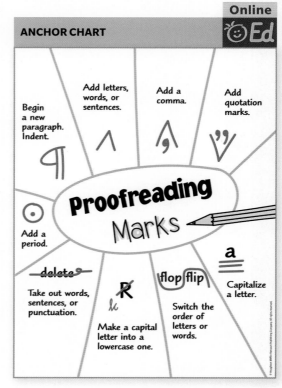

CORRESPONDENCE • LETTER WRITING

LEARNING OBJECTIVES

- Proofread writing for mechanics.
- **Language** Edit writing with peer support.

TARGETED GRAMMAR SUPPORT

You may want to have students refer to the following grammar minilessons as they edit their letters.

- **2.6.2 Pronouns and Homophones,** p. W262
- **1.3.3 Writing Complete Sentences,** p. W228
- **3.2.3 Consistent Use of Tenses,** p. W273

Introduce the Clocking Activity

- Tell students they will be proofreading each other's letters with the clocking activity. Review the clocking activity.

  » Students write their names on a sheet of blank paper and label it *Proofreading Page*. Students then write the following numbers and items to be checked.

  1. Spelling

  2. Capitalization

  3. Punctuation

  4. Complete Sentences

  5. Verb Tense

  » Students place the proofreading page on top of their letter draft.

  » Students sit in concentric circles and exchange letters and proofreading pages.

  » Teacher calls out a number to be checked. Students write their name next to that number as the proofreader/editor of that item. Students rapidly skim the page, locating and checking examples of the designated item.

  » Proofreaders do not correct items on the draft. If there are no errors in that item, the proofreader draws a smiley face or writes a positive comment next to that number. If the proofreader finds what he or she believes is an error, he or she writes the correction next to the number.

  » When all students are finished, the teacher calls out the second number to be checked. Students repeat the proofreading process.

  » You may wish to have students return the papers after several items. Students in the outer circle move one place to the right and again exchange papers, allowing several editors to read each letter.

  » When the editing process is complete, students return papers to the writer.

Integrate Proofreading Edits

- Have students use their proofreading pages to make any corrections that they agree need changing. Tell students that if they disagree with the proofreader's suggestion, they should discuss it with you.

- Circulate the room, answering questions when necessary. Encourage students to read through the entire letter one more time after they have completed their edits.

 ENGLISH LEARNER SUPPORT: Support Proofreading

SUBSTANTIAL

If students have trouble understanding the proofreading process, you may wish to learn key words in their home languages. For example, in Haitian Creole, *koreksyon* means *proofread*; in Spanish, *capitalización* means *capitalization*.

MODERATE

Explain to students that capitalization in English may not follow the same rules as students' home languages. For instance, in Spanish, months of the year are not capitalized.

LIGHT

Even advanced students usually have trouble with some part of proofreading. Encourage students to identify and work on areas they find challenging.

LEARNING OBJECTIVES
- Publish writing.
- Use technology to assist with writing.
- **Language** Demonstrate increased comprehension of English.

MATERIALS   Online

Display and Engage *6.3*
Writer's Notebook *p. 6.3*

TEACHER TIP

If you choose to send your students' letters to the experts they have chosen, help them write the addresses on the envelopes.

Prepare the Final Copy

- Explain that in this lesson, students will prepare and publish their letters. Point out that the word *publish* can mean different things depending on the type of writing produced and the reason for writing. In this case, *publishing* means writing and sending their letters to the experts of their choice.

- Encourage students to give their letters one last check before writing the final version. You may wish to review the writing prompt on **Display and Engage 6.3**. Suggest that students also review the rubric on **Writer's Notebook page 6.3**. Provide a sample checklist.

> a. I have the correct name, title, and address of the expert.
>
> b. I have followed all the steps of the writing prompt.
>
> c. My letter is polite, interesting, and easy to understand.

- Circulate among students as they check their drafts. If any students are still missing a correct name and address for the expert they have chosen, help them locate and record the information.

- After students have completed their final check, encourage them to make a clean copy of their final edited draft.

  THINK ALOUD *After I edit and proofread my draft, I often find that it isn't easy to read because of all the marks and changes. I like to make a clean copy of the edited draft so that I won't make any mistakes when I write the final copy.*

Publish Writing

- Distribute stationery and envelopes to students. You may wish to use lined stationery to help students keep the lines in their letter equally spaced.

- Remind students to use their best handwriting as they write their letters. *Start each line directly under the previous line. Don't forget to indent the first line of each paragraph.*

- If computers are available, some students may prefer typing their letters. Model setting the tabs and margins for a formal letter before they begin typing.

- Have students prepare two final copies—one to send and one to keep.

- Model the placement of addresses on the envelope. Then have students address their envelopes. Demonstrate how to fold the stationery to fit the envelope. Then have students each place one copy of their letters in their addressed envelopes.

LEARNING OBJECTIVES

- Share writing.
- Hold a collaborative discussion.
- **Language** Ask and answer questions using academic language.

MATERIALS   Online Ed

Writer's Notebook *pp. 6.2, 6.10*

 LEARNING MINDSET:
Wonder

Review Remind students that wonder leads to asking questions. *The questions you asked led you to research and learn more about something that interested you. Questions also helped you strengthen your writing by focusing on what needed revision. What more would you like to know about natural wonders?* Encourage students to think about ways in which being curious about natural wonders has helped them expand how they think about their world.

Share Writing

- Tell students that they will share their finished letters with classmates.

- Have students form groups of four or five and sit in a circle so that they can easily see and hear others.

- Have students take turns reading their letters aloud.

- When a student has finished reading, encourage listeners to ask the presenter questions about his or her letter. Encourage the speaker to respond to each question. Remind students to make eye contact with one another as they discuss their letters.

Reflect on Writing

- Have students turn to the goals they set at the beginning of this Writing Workshop on **Writer's Notebook page 6.2** or in their notebooks. Then ask students to complete the goal evaluation on **Writer's Notebook page 6.10**. As part of this goal evaluation exercise, encourage students to reflect on their goals and then Turn and Talk with a partner about how they did or didn't meet their goals. Encourage students to take notes about what they would like to improve in their next writing assignment.

- As a class, have an informal discussion of this writing assignment. Encourage students to think about and express their feelings about the following topics:

> - How did you feel about the assignment at the beginning?
> - Did your feelings change as you researched your topic and began drafting the letter?
> - What did you like most about the assignment? Why?
> - What did you like least? Why?
> - What was the easiest part of the assignment? What was the most difficult part?
> - What, if anything, will you do differently in your next writing assignment? Why?

 ENGLISH LEARNER SUPPORT: Facilitate Discussion

SUBSTANTIAL
Pair students who have similar language abilities. Allow them to read their letters to each other instead of to the entire group.

MODERATE
Pair students who have similar language abilities. Allow them to practice reading their letters to each other before reading them to the entire group.

LIGHT
Encourage students to discuss not only what they will do differently in their next writing assignment, but also whether they have mastered that particular skill in their home language.

NARRATIVE

Imaginative Story

FOCUS STATEMENT Imaginative stories can make us laugh and teach us a lesson.

FOCAL TEXT

The Luck of the Loch Ness Monster: A Tale of Picky Eating

Author: Alice Weaver Flaherty

Illustrator: Scott Magoon

Summary: A funny tall tale that tells how the Loch Ness Monster grew to be so big.

WRITING PROMPT

READ this sentence: *Imaginative stories and traditional tales can explain why things are the way they are.*

THINK about an interesting natural occurrence or animal.

WRITE an imaginative story that explains how that thing came to be. Tell the story in order and use descriptive words or phrases.

LESSONS

1 **Introducing the Focal Text**

2 **Vocabulary**

3 **Prewriting I: Preparing to Write**

4 **Prewriting II: Types of Imaginative Literature**

5 **Prewriting III: Plotting Events**

6 **Drafting I: Beginning the Draft**

7 **Drafting II: Integrating Narrative Elements**

8 **Drafting III: Completing the Draft**

9 **Revising I: Organizing Events**

10 **Revising II: Conferencing**

11 **Revising III: Descriptive Language**

12 **Revising IV: Integrating Strong Verbs**

13 **Editing I: Peer Proofreading**

14 **Publishing**

15 **Sharing**

LEARNING MINDSET: Self-Reflection

Display **Anchor Chart 31: My Learning Mindset** throughout the year. Refer to it to introduce Self-Reflection and to reinforce the skills you introduced in previous modules.

NARRATIVE • IMAGINATIVE STORY

LEARNING OBJECTIVES

- Establish a purpose for reading.
- Make and describe personal connections to sources.
- Explain the author's use of text structure in a literary text.
- Describe how the language, setting, and characters contribute to a story's plot.
- Refer to text details to explain what the text says explicitly and to make inferences.
- Determine the lesson or theme of a story.
- **Language** Write about imaginative stories by using sentence frames.
- **Language** Describe the features of imaginative stories by using visual support.

MATERIALS Online Ed

Display and Engage *7.1*

Focal Text *The Luck of the Loch Ness Monster*

INSTRUCTIONAL VOCABULARY

- **narrative** a story
- **narrator** the person who tells a story
- **dialogue** the words that characters in a story or drama say aloud to each other

Priming the Students

Explore the Topic

- Establish a purpose for reading by explaining to students that in this module, they will examine how imaginative stories can make us laugh and teach us a lesson.

- Point out that for centuries, people have used stories to teach lessons. Through their characters, settings, and plot, these stories have conveyed important teachings to the audience in an entertaining way.

- To help students make connections to this topic, have them think about other examples of traditional tales or imaginative fiction, such as "The Tortoise and the Hare" or "The Boy Who Cried Wolf," that have taught them lessons. Have volunteers briefly summarize the characters, setting, and plot of the stories. Then ask follow-up questions: *What lesson does the story teach? How does the outcome of the story reflect this lesson?*

- Draw a t-chart on the board or on chart paper. Title the chart *Stories with Lessons*. Label the left column *Title*. Write the story titles in this column.

- Label the right column *Lesson.* Describe the lesson each story teaches.

- Ask: *Why do you think the author used a story to teach this lesson?* Model thinking about how a story's text structure can help authors to teach readers a lesson:

  THINK ALOUD *When I first read "Cinderella," I remember thinking how happy I was that the prince fell in love with Cinderella. Even though her stepsisters and stepmother treated her unkindly throughout the story, Cinderella remained a nice person. Her kindness was rewarded at the end of the story, while the meanness of her stepsisters and stepmother was not. By having readers sympathize with the character of Cinderella throughout the story, the author helps us see the value of being a good person and the positive results it can bring.*

Discuss the Focus Statement

- Show **Display and Engage 7.1**. Read the Focus Statement with students. Have students write a short response to the statement and share it with the class.

Online Ed

DISPLAY AND ENGAGE

Imaginative Story 7.1

Focus Statement

Imaginative stories can make us laugh and teach us a lesson.

ENGLISH LEARNER SUPPORT: Scaffold Writing

SUBSTANTIAL

Provide sentence frames to help students respond to the Focus Statement: *Imaginative stories include _____ that make us laugh. They use _____ to teach us a lesson.*

MODERATE

Provide sentence frames to aid students' responses to the Focus Statement: *Imaginative stories can make us laugh by _____. They teach us a lesson by _____.*

LIGHT

Have students use a Think-Pair-Share routine to discuss their responses to the Focus Statement. Have students first think about the statement before discussing their thoughts with a partner. Then have pairs share their written responses with the class.

Priming the Text

Prepare to Read

- Have students think about some features of imaginative stories. Ask volunteers to share their ideas. Then write their suggestions on the board or on chart paper.

The Luck of the Loch Ness Monster

- Flip through *The Luck of the Loch Ness Monster* with students. Give students time to look at the pictures. Ask: *What imaginative things do you see in the pictures?* (*an animal that looks like a monster; buildings that look like castles*)

- Show the cover of *The Luck of the Loch Ness Monster* and discuss the title of the book. As a class, use either the Internet or a reference text to determine what the Loch Ness Monster is.

- Ensure that students understand the meaning of *loch* by explaining that it is the Scottish word for *lake*.

- Point out the subtitle: *A Tale of Picky Eating*. Have students make predictions about how this subtitle might relate to the story.

Engage and Respond

- Have students Turn and Talk to a partner. Ask them to discuss whether they think *The Luck of the Loch Ness Monster* is going to be a serious story or a funny story and why.

ENGLISH LEARNER SUPPORT: Facilitate Discussion

SUBSTANTIAL
When identifying imaginative things in the book's pictures, have students answer yes/no questions, such as *Do you see something that looks like a monster?* Then have students point to the image.

MODERATE
Provide a sentence stem to help students identify an imaginative story's features: *Some features of imaginative stories are _____.*

LIGHT
Allow students additional time, as necessary, to respond to the discussion items.

LEARNING MINDSET:
Self-Reflection

Introduce Explain the meaning of self-reflection to students. *Self-reflection means reflecting on your work and asking yourself how to make it better. By practicing self-reflection when you read and write, you can catch mistakes and learn new things. In* The Luck of the Loch Ness, *you'll discover how a "monster" reflects on itself and realizes, to its great surprise, just how much it has changed over time.* Tell students that when they are reading and writing, they should pay close attention to the material to ensure they are not missing anything.

 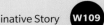

The Read

Read the Focal Text

- As you read *The Luck of the Loch Ness Monster*, allow volunteers to read aloud the parts of the story's narrator and characters. Since most of the story consists of narration, have volunteers take turns as the narrator. Discuss the meanings of **narrative** (a story) and **narrator** (the person who tells a story) before beginning. Add these words to the class Instructional Vocabulary list, and have students add the words and their own definitions to their glossaries.

- Stop at the following points to discuss the story's text features.

  » Read through page 9. Ask: *What is the setting of the story? (a cruise ship on the sea) How does this setting affect the story's plot? (Katerina-Elizabeth throws her oatmeal off of the ship and into the sea. A sea worm eats it.)*

  » Read pages 20 and 21. Ask: *Why is the worm crying? (It's upset that Katerina-Elizabeth got off of the ship. Now that she's gone, it won't get oatmeal from her.)*

  » Read page 23. Point out the **dialogue**, or the words a character says aloud, that appears on the page. Explain that the quotation marks help set off the character's words. The dialogue tag *she shouted* tells who is saying the words and how the character is saying them. Ask: *Why do you think this character shouts instead of just speaking? (She's probably surprised by the worm and maybe is also afraid of what she thinks is a monster.)*

  » Read page 24. Ask: *What funny descriptions does the author use to explain changes to the worm's appearance? (The author describes the worm as "thick as an elephant's belly and as long as the main hall of an elementary school.") What does this tell you about the worm's size? (It's really big.)*

  » Read page 32. Ask: *What lesson or theme does the story convey about picky eaters? (You can still grow up to be a happy person even if you're a picky eater.)*

- Finish reading the book with students. Have students explain how the end of the book relates to events at the beginning.

Engage and Respond

- Have students write two or three sentences that answer this question: *Why do you think the monster kisses Katerina-Elizabeth at the end of the book?* Have students share their responses with a partner.

LEARNING OBJECTIVES

- Acquire and use academic words and phrases.
- Use context to determine a word's meaning.
- Use print or digital resources to determine a word's meaning.
- **Language** Discuss vocabulary words by using visual support

MATERIALS   Online

Focal Text *The Luck of the Loch Ness Monster*

Writer's Notebook *p. 7.1*

Review the Focal Text

- Review the first few pages of *The Luck of the Loch Ness Monster* with students. Point out that the text includes many descriptive words and funny comparisons to help readers imagine the story's events.

- Continue paging through *The Luck of the Loch Ness Monster* and have students identify additional words they find interesting, such as those below. Pause to discuss why the words are interesting. Then have students add them to their Word Bank on **Writer's Notebook page 7.1**.

gooey (p. 6)	hurled (p. 22)	imposing (p. 24)
stunted (p. 6)	thatched (p. 22)	suet (p. 26)
gobbled (p. 9)	plowing (p. 23)	flocked (p. 28)

- Choose words from the list above and identify synonyms for the words, such as the following: *gobbled/ate; hurled/threw; plowing/moving; flocked/gathered.*

- To help students understand the differences between words with similar meanings, use this model:

  The words big, huge, gigantic, *and* gargantuan *are all similar words. Each describes something or someone as very large. But the words refer to largeness in different degrees.* Huge *describes something or someone as even bigger than* big. Gigantic *describes something or someone as bigger than* huge. *And* gargantuan *describes something or someone as bigger than* gigantic.

- Explain the difference between each word from the story and its synonym.

  » Gobbled *means* ate quickly and noisily.

  » Hurled *means* threw with a lot of force.

  » Plowing *means* forcibly moving.

  » Flocked *means* gathered in a large group.

- Have students use the story's context to explain why the author might have chosen to use these words instead of other synonyms.

- Have pairs look up the meanings of the remaining words in their Word Bank using a dictionary or other resource.

Engage and Respond

- Have students write a few sentences explaining which new word from their Word Bank they would most likely use in their own writing, and why.

 ENGLISH LEARNER SUPPORT: Support Discussion

SUBSTANTIAL
When explaining the differences between words and their synonyms, use gestures to act out the words' meanings.

MODERATE
Support students' understanding of new vocabulary words by using pictures in the text to convey the words' meanings.

LIGHT
Have students work in pairs to use context to determine why the author might have chosen certain words instead of their synonyms.

NARRATIVE • IMAGINATIVE STORY

LEARNING OBJECTIVES

- Engage in writing as a process.
- Use prewriting strategies to plan the first draft of an imaginative story.
- Use guidance from adults during the planning process.
- **Language** Discuss the writing model using teacher and peer support.

MATERIALS   Online

Display and Engage *7.2, 7.3a–d*
Writer's Notebook *pp. 7.2, 7.3, 7.4, 7.5*

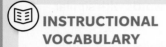 **INSTRUCTIONAL VOCABULARY**

- **character** a person or animal in a story
- **setting** where or when a story takes place

Discuss the Writing Prompt

- Tell students that in this module, they will write a type of text known as an imaginative story. Explain that an imaginative story includes interesting and often unrealistic characters, settings, and events. Show **Display and Engage 7.2** and read the Writing Prompt together. Note the tips.

- Distribute **Writer's Notebook page 7.2**. Discuss the different expectations of the rubric. Remind students to use the rubric as a resource while drafting and revising.

Review the Model

- Show **Display and Engage 7.3a–d** and distribute **Writer's Notebook pages 7.3 and 7.4**. Read the model with students. Have them identify the beginning, middle, and end. Encourage students to mark the model's organizational structure in different colors on the page.

- Have students first look closely at the model's beginning. Have them identify the story's main **character** (a person or animal in a story) and **setting** (where or when a story takes place). Add these words to the class Instructional Vocabulary list, and have students add the words and their definitions to their glossaries.

- Next, review the middle of the story. Have students summarize the main events.

- Finally, have students discuss how the ending wraps up the story's events. Also have students identify the event in nature the story helps to explain.

Set Goals for Writing

- Have students consider the goals they would like to set for their imaginative stories. Then have them add these goals to the list on **Writer's Notebook page 7.5** or write them in their own notebooks.

🗨 ENGLISH LEARNER SUPPORT: Support Discussion

SUBSTANTIAL
As you review the model with students, use gestures to support students' understanding of the story's events.

MODERATE
Have students discuss features of the model with partners before sharing ideas with the class.

LIGHT
Give students extra time to answer questions about the model.

LEARNING OBJECTIVES

- Plan an imaginative story.
- Narrow the topic of the story.
- Select an audience and purpose for the story.
- Use the guidance of peers and adults to assist in the planning process.
- **Language** Describe writing plans by using the vocabulary words *setting* and *characters*.

MATERIALS

Online Ed

Display and Engage *7.4*

Anchor Chart W3: *Narrative Elements*

Writer's Notebook, *p. 7.6*

Discuss Types of Imaginative Literature

- Show **Display and Engage 7.4** and together discuss the different types of imaginative literature.

- Ask: *Have you read any fables, myths, tall tales, or legends? Tell me about them.* (*Responses may vary.*) If students have trouble naming examples of imaginative literature, provide them with some examples they may already be familiar with.

- Next, have students choose the type of story they would like to write. Remind them that their story needs to tell how a natural occurrence or an animal came to exist.

Review Features of Narratives

- Show **Anchor Chart W3: Elements of a Narrative** and read the points with students. Have students discuss what they liked about previous narratives they have read. Write their ideas on the board.

Begin Prewriting

- Have students start planning their writing by choosing their story's setting and characters. Instruct students to add this information to **Writer's Notebook page 7.6**, along with the type of story they have chosen to write.

- Remind students to consider audience and purpose when planning their writing. Ask: *Who is your audience? Are you writing to inform, entertain, learn, or persuade?* For those students who have difficulty, form a small group and review how to determine their audience and purpose before writing.

 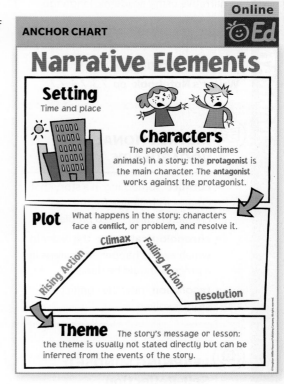
ENGLISH LEARNER SUPPORT: Scaffold Writing

SUBSTANTIAL

To assist students with planning their stories, provide some examples of possible settings and characters on a word wall.

MODERATE

Provide sentence frames to help students with their planning: *My setting will be _____. My main characters will be _____.*

LIGHT

Pair students to discuss their ideas before having them independently complete their writing plans.

NARRATIVE • IMAGINATIVE STORY

LEARNING OBJECTIVES

- Describe in depth the characters, setting, and events in a story.
- Plan the first draft of an imaginative story.
- Use guidance from adults during the planning process.
- Describe writing plans by using graphic organizers.
- **Language** Discuss elements of a narrative using academic language.

MATERIALS   Online

Display and Engage *7.3a-b*
Writer's Notebook *pp. 7.3, 7.4, 7.7*

INSTRUCTIONAL VOCABULARY

- **conflict** something in a story that creates a challenge for the characters; also called *problem*
- **chronological order** the order in which events happened or steps in a process should be done
- **resolution** how the conflict in a story is solved

LEARNING MINDSET: Self-Reflection

Normalize Acknowledge that students may find planning their story challenging, and that this is a normal response. Say: *As you plan your story, you may find it difficult to think of new ideas or decide how you're going to tie your ideas together. This is a normal response to a challenging assignment. If you need to, take a break from your planning and then try again later.*

Introduce Conflict

- Show the model on **Display and Engage 7.3a** and distribute **Writer's Notebook page 7.3**. Review the model's beginning. Ask: *What problem does Julia have with the village she lives in?* (*It has no colors other than black, white, and gray. It is depressing.*)

- Explain to students that this problem is called the story's **conflict**—the main challenge the character faces in a story. An author will usually introduce the conflict early in a story. The story's events then gradually lead toward a solution to this conflict.

Discuss Chronological Order

- Explain that authors typically present a story's events in **chronological order**, or the order in which events happen in the story. Tell students they will use chronological order in their own stories to help readers clearly follow what's happening.

- Return to the model, and review the second paragraph on **Display and Engage 7.3b**. Ask: *What is the first thing Julia does?* (*She walks through the village.*) *What happens next?* (*She passes the house of an old woman, and the woman motions for her to come over.*)

- Reiterate that this series of events is an example of chronological order. The author describes the events in the order in which they happen. Then continue reviewing the model with students, having them identify the order of the events.

Examine Resolution

- Explain to students that a story's **resolution** is how it ends or how the conflict is solved.

- Have students review the model's ending on **Writer's Notebook page 7.4**. Remind students that the conflict is that the village has very few colors, which depresses Julia.

- Ask: *How is this conflict solved at the end of the story?* (*Julia uses her finger to draw a colorful rainbow in the sky.*)

- Add *conflict, chronological order,* and *resolution* to the class Instructional Vocabulary list, and encourage students to add the words and definitions to their glossaries.

Continue Prewriting

- To help students determine the order of events in their own stories, provide the graphic organizer flow chart on **Writer's Notebook page 7.7**. Remind students that the events in their story should flow from the conflict and lead to the resolution. Make sure students understand that their stories can have fewer or more events than are listed in the chart.

LEARNING OBJECTIVES

- Compose an informational free write featuring a topic sentence.
- Develop a first draft by organizing its structure and developing an engaging idea.
- Write in a short time frame.
- **Language** Compose a free write by using language supports such as graphic organizers and sentence stems.

MATERIALS   Online

Display and Engage *7.5*

Writer's Notebook *pp. 7.6, 7.7, 7.8*

Prepare to Draft

- As students prepare to begin their first drafts, have them take part in a freewrite to spur their thoughts about their story. Explain the strategy to students:

Freewriting involves writing whatever ideas you have in your head. You don't have to think about spelling or punctuation while you're freewriting. The main point is just to get some of your ideas down on paper. Then, later on, you can use these ideas to help you structure the organization of your first draft.

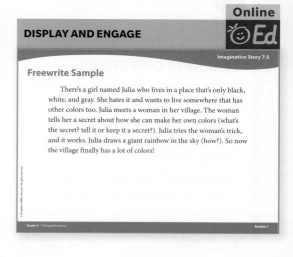

Online

DISPLAY AND ENGAGE

Imaginative Story 7.5

Freewrite Sample

There's a girl named Julia who lives in a place that's only black, white, and gray. She hates it and wants to live somewhere that has other colors too. Julia meets a woman in her village. The woman tells her a secret about how she can make her own colors (what's the secret? tell it or keep it a secret?). Julia tries the woman's trick, and it works. Julia draws a giant rainbow in the sky (how?). So now the village finally has a lot of colors!

Grade 4 | Writing Workshop   Module 7

- Show **Display and Engage 7.5** to introduce a freewrite. Read the example with the class. Point out that the writer summarized her ideas about the story and even jotted down questions to herself as she wrote.

- Explain out that the freewrite is a quick, informal piece of writing. The writer does not get bogged down in details or specifics about the story. Instead, she gives a simple summary that starts with a topic sentence, refers only to the story's main events, and then briefly reveals how the story ends.

- Distribute **Writer's Notebook page 7.8**. Have students spend some time freewriting a summary of their own stories, using the sample freewrite as a model.

- Have students begin their freewrite paragraph with a simple topic sentence that identifies their story's main characters and conflict. Then have them briefly summarize the rest of the story. They can include questions to themselves about points they have not yet figured out.

- Remind students not to worry about their spelling and punctuation as they free write.

- Give students a time limit, such as five or ten minutes. Then have volunteers share their writing with the class.

Begin to Draft

- Have students begin to draft their imaginative stories, using their freewrites and the notes and graphic organizers from **Writer's Notebook pages 7.6** and **7.7**.

 ENGLISH LEARNER SUPPORT: Support Discussion

SUBSTANTIAL

Have students work in pairs to review their prewriting materials and discuss their plans before they begin their freewrite.

MODERATE

Provide students with a sentence frame for the topic sentence of their freewrite: *I'm going to write about _____.*

LIGHT

Have students read their freewrites silently to themselves before sharing them with the class.

NARRATIVE • IMAGINATIVE STORY

LEARNING OBJECTIVES

- Examine and identify types of conflict in literary texts.
- Engage in writing as a process.
- Compose the first draft of an imaginative story.
- **Language** Express ideas about literary texts by using the vocabulary word *conflict*.

MATERIALS   Online Ed

Anchor Chart W5: *Types of Conflict*

Focal Text *The Luck of the Loch Ness Monster*

Display and Engage *7.3a*

Writer's Notebook *pp. 7.6, 7.7, 7.8*

 LEARNING MINDSET: Self-Reflection

Apply As students continue working on their first drafts, have them think about how they can make improvements to their writing. Say: *As you continue writing your story, look for mistakes you may have made along the way or parts of the story you might need to make clearer. Then think about how you can make improvements. Remember that mistakes give us an opportunity to make our work even better.*

Introduce the Skill

- Display **Anchor Chart W5: Types of Conflict** and read the points with students. Discuss each type of conflict, clarifying meaning as necessary.

- Have students think about and identify different ways a story can reflect each type of conflict. Ask: *What are some ways a character can be in conflict with another person? With something in nature? With other people? With himself or herself?* (*Responses may vary.*)

- Return to *The Luck of the Loch Ness Monster*. Ask: *What is the problem, or conflict, Katerina-Elizabeth experiences in the story?* (*Her parents want her to eat oatmeal, but she doesn't want to.*) Have students identify text evidence that tells them this. Then ask: *Which type of conflict is this?* (*conflict with others*)

- Let students know that stories can feature multiple types of conflict, but one is usually emphasized more than others. The main conflict is what drives the story's events.

- Show **Display and Engage 7.3a** to return to the imaginative story model. Review the story's conflict with students: Julia lives in a village that has few colors, and this depresses her. Ask: *Which type of conflict is this?* (*conflict with nature*)

- Have students review their free writes on **Writer's Notebook page 7.8**, their notes and graphic organizers on **Writer's Notebook pages 7.6** and **7.7**, and the first drafts they have started. Then have volunteers identify the type of conflict their story features. Ask students to explain their thoughts.

Continue to Draft

- Have students continue writing their first drafts. Circulate the room, offering assistance to students as needed.

 ENGLISH LEARNER SUPPORT: Support Discussion

ALL LEVELS Give students extra time to respond to the discussion questions.

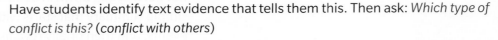

ANCHOR CHART

Online Ed

Types of Conflict

Character vs. Character

Two or more characters have a problem.

Character vs. Self

A character faces an inner struggle.

Character vs. Nature

A character faces the forces of nature.

Character vs. Society

A character struggles against society's rules.

Review a Narrative's Ending

- To help students organize and develop the structure of their drafts, review the characteristics of a narrative's ending. Say: *A narrative's ending should reveal the story's resolution by telling how the conflict in the story has been solved. An ending should also leave the reader satisfied, not confused about what happened in the story.*

- Return to *The Luck of the Loch Ness Monster*. Remind students of the story's conflict: Katerina-Elizabeth's parents want her to eat oatmeal, but she doesn't want to eat it.

- Reread the story from page 32 to the end. Ask: *Does the story's ending resolve this conflict?* (yes) *How?* (*It says that Katerina-Elizabeth "lived happily ever after" in spite of her parents' insistence that she eat oatmeal.*)

- Discuss with students whether they find this ending satisfying, and why.

Examine the Writing Model

- Show **Display and Engage 7.3d**. Review the model's conflict and resolution. Say: *Julia lives in a village that has few colors, and this depresses her. At the end, she uses her finger to draw a rainbow in the sky.*

- Ask: *How does this ending resolve the story's conflict?* (*By drawing a rainbow, Julia adds a lot of color to her village.*)

- Discuss with students whether they find this ending satisfying, and why.

Continue to Draft

- Have students continue writing their first drafts. Circulate the room, offering assistance to students as needed. As you circulate, group students who need support on similar grammar topics. Use the grammar minilessons or the students' own writing to provide targeted review and support.

 ENGLISH LEARNER SUPPORT: Facilitate Discussion

SUBSTANTIAL

Rephrase questions to allow yes/no responses from students, such as by asking: *Is Katerina-Elizabeth happy at the end of the story?*

MODERATE

Students may not understand what a "satisfying" story ending is. Recast the question, such as by asking *Is the ending clear to you? Is this a good ending?*

LIGHT

Provide a sentence frame for students to use when discussing the story and writing model: *I think this ending is/is not satisfying because _____.*

NARRATIVE • IMAGINATIVE STORY

LEARNING OBJECTIVES

- Organize and develop the structure of a first draft.
- Use transition words to manage a sequence of events.
- Revise a literary text to improve its organization and clarity of content.
- **Language** Revise writing by using transition words.

MATERIALS Online

Display and Engage *7.3b–d*
Writer's Notebook *pp. 7.3, 7.4*

📖 INSTRUCTIONAL VOCABULARY

- **transition word** word that links ideas together

Review Organization

- Write the following events from the writing model on the board. List them in the order shown below.

  > 1. The old woman tells Julia a secret.
  >
  > 2. The woman asks Julia what it is that bothers her.
  >
  > 3. Julia runs up a hill and draws a rainbow in the sky with her finger.
  >
  > 4. Julia walks through the village.
  >
  > 5. The old woman motions to Julia.
  >
  > 6. Julia says that she thinks the village's colors are dull.

- Discuss with students whether this sequence of events would make sense in a story. Ask: *Do you think an audience would like to read a story with the events organized in this way? Why not?* (*No, it would be confusing.*)

- Emphasize to students the importance of having their story's events ordered in a way that makes sense.

Introduce Transition Words

- Explain to students that **transition words** are words that link ideas together. One reason writers use transition words is to help readers follow the sequence of events in a text.

- Provide some examples of transition words that help signal a sequence of events, such as *afterwards, before, finally, next,* and *then.*

- Show **Display and Engage 7.3b–d** and have students turn to **Writer's Notebook pages 7.3** and **7.4**. Have students circle transition words in the writing model that tell when events happened, such as *eventually, when, immediately, first,* and *then.*

- Add the phrase *transition word* to the class Instructional Vocabulary list. Have students add the phrase and definition to their glossaries.

Revise for Organization

- Have students revisit their drafts and add transitions words to clarify the sequence of events.

LEARNING OBJECTIVES

- Pose and respond to questions.
- Engage in writing as a process.
- Revise drafts for clarity of content, with support from peers and adults.
- **Language** Express opinions by using the vocabulary words *conflict*, *setting*, and *characters*.

MATERIALS   Online

Anchor Chart W3: *Narrative Elements*
Writer's Notebook pp. 7.2, 7.9

Small Group Conferences

- Review **Anchor Chart W3: Narrative Elements** and the rubric on **Writer's Notebook page 7.2**. Remind students that their stories should include these elements.

- Next, tell students that it is time to read their classmates' writing and provide feedback.

  » Divide the class into small groups of four or five.

  » Writers will read, pause, and then read again.

  » Listeners should listen. Upon the second reading, they will take notes, including identifying which emotions—such as sadness, happiness, curiosity, or fear—they feel at different points in the story.

  » After each reading, the group comments, suggests, advises, and discusses by using **Writer's Notebook page 7.9**.

Reflect

- Debrief with the class. Discuss students' responses to the following questions.

  - What feedback kept coming up in your groups?
  - What were the best things your group members did in their stories?
  - How might writers do a better job of exciting readers' emotions?
  - What have you learned about writing stories?

Continue to Revise

- Have students continue to revise, using the feedback they gained in the small group conferences and the information they learned from the debriefing.

 ENGLISH LEARNER SUPPORT: Elicit Participation

SUBSTANTIAL
Before having students break for their conferences, choral read students' stories with them to make them more comfortable with reading aloud.

MODERATE
Have partners practice reading their stories to each other before reading them to their group.

LIGHT
Allow students to read quietly to themselves before reading their stories to their group.

NARRATIVE • IMAGINATIVE STORY

LEARNING OBJECTIVES

- Utilize elements of style, such as word choice.
- Choose words to convey ideas precisely.
- Revise drafts to provide clarity.
- Use the support of peers and adults to revise writing.
- **Language** Edit writing by using adverbs.

MATERIALS   Online

Anchor Chart W14: *Improving Word Choice*

INSTRUCTIONAL VOCABULARY

- **adverb** a word that describes a verb or an adjective

TARGETED GRAMMAR SUPPORT

You may want to consult the following grammar minilessons to review key revising topics.

- **4.2.1 Adverbs,** p. W301
- **4.2.2 Adverbs of Frequency and Intensity,** p. W302
- **4.2.3 Adverbs in Different Parts of Sentences,** p. W303

Introduce Descriptive Language

- Display **Anchor Chart W14: Improving Word Choice** and review the items on the chart.

- Explain to students the importance of a writer's word choice. Say: *The words a writer uses to describe his or her settings, characters, and events can determine whether a story is boring or exciting for the reader.*

- Tell students that one way to make a sentence more precise and vivid is to add an **adverb**, a word that describes a verb or an adjective. Adverbs modify words by telling *when, where, how,* and *to what extent.*

- Write a definition for *adverb* on the class Instructional Vocabulary list. Have students write a definition in their own glossaries if they have not already.

Review Forming Adverbs

- Explain to students that most adverbs end in *-ly.* Students can add these letters to the ends of many adjectives to turn them into adverbs.

- To demonstrate this, write the following examples on the board. Have students help explain the difference between each adjective and adverb by identifying the noun and verb each modifies.

> The <u>quiet</u> baby slept in its crib. (adjective)
>
> The baby slept <u>quietly</u> in its crib. (adverb)
>
> The belt was <u>tight</u> around my waist. (adjective)
>
> I <u>tightly</u> pulled the belt around my waist. (adverb)

- Clarify that not all adverbs end in *-ly.* Say: *Words like* soon, here, well, *and* very *are also adverbs because they tell* when, where, how, *and* to what extent.

Revise for Descriptive Language

- Have students revise their writing by adding adverbs and other descriptive language.

- As students revise, suggest they first identify verbs and adjectives and then determine whether they could use additional modifying.

- Circulate the room and assist students with revising. If students need help with a specific grammar topic, do a direct teach.

 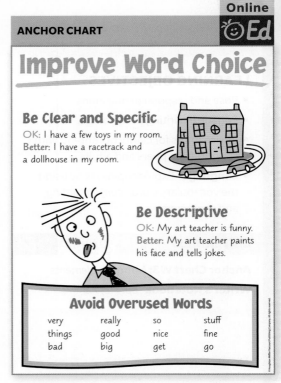

LEARNING OBJECTIVES

- Utilize elements of style, such as word choice.
- Choose words to convey ideas precisely.
- Revise drafts to provide clarity.
- Use the support of peers and adults to revise writing.
- **Language** Edit using action verbs.

TARGETED GRAMMAR SUPPORT

You may want to consult the following grammar minilessons to review key revising topics.

- **3.1.1 Action Verbs,** p. W266
- **3.1.3 Linking Verbs,** p. W268

 INSTRUCTIONAL VOCABULARY

- **action verb** a verb that tells what its subject does

 LEARNING MINDSET: Self-Reflection

Review Remind students about the importance of self-reflection. Say: *Think back to how self-reflection enabled you to make improvements to your writing. How did doing something differently in your writing allow you to succeed?*

Review Verbs

- Review with students the different forms of the verb *to be* by writing them on the board.

be	are	been
am	was	being
is	were	

- Explain that these verbs can act as either linking verbs or helping verbs. Then point out that replacing a *to be* verb with an **action verb**, or a verb that tells what its subject does, often has a greater impact on the reader because it is stronger and more interesting.

- Provide students with examples that demonstrate how to replace linking verbs with action verbs.

> Kyle was afraid of the dark. (linking verb)
>
> Kyle feared the dark. (action verb)
>
> Mika is happy about her new pet. (linking verb)
>
> Mika adores her new pet. (action verb)

- Ask volunteers to suggest other action verbs they could use to replace the linking verbs in the example sentences.

- Add the phrase *action verb* to the class Instructional Vocabulary list. Have students add the phrase and definition to their glossaries.

Revise for Stronger Verbs

- Have students revise their stories by replacing weak *to be* verbs with stronger action verbs.

 ENGLISH LEARNER SUPPORT: Scaffold Revision

SUBSTANTIAL
Assist students by circling linking verbs in their writing and discussing suggestions about action verbs they can use to replace them.

MODERATE
Have students circle linking verbs in their writing and discuss with a partner action verbs they might use to replace them.

LIGHT
Have partners work together to replace the verbs in their stories with stronger ones.

NARRATIVE • IMAGINATIVE STORY

LEARNING OBJECTIVES

- Edit drafts to check for elements of an imaginative story.
- Edit drafts to maintain complete sentences and subject-verb agreement.
- Edit drafts to ensure correct capitalization and punctuation.
- Work respectfully with others.
- **Language** Edit writing by employing proofreading marks.
- **Language** Edit writing by correcting grammar, usage, and spelling errors in a draft.

MATERIALS   Online

Anchor Chart W13: *Editing Checklist*
Anchor Chart W17: *Proofreading Marks*
Display and Engage 7.6

TARGETED GRAMMAR SUPPORT

You may want to consult the following grammar minilessons to review key editing topics.

- **2.1.3 Capitalizing Languages, People's Names, and Nationalities,** p. W238
- **6.1.1 Quotation Marks with Direct Speech,** p. W331
- **6.2.1 End of Sentence Punctuation,** p. W336
- **6.3.1 Commas with Direct Speech and Names,** p. W341

Review Checklists

- Display **Anchor Chart W13: Editing Checklist** and **Anchor Chart W17: Proofreading Marks** and review the items on each checklist.
- As needed, revisit grammar topics to which students may need additional review or practice.

Use the Clocking Activity

- Review the rules for clocking.

  » Students form concentric circles or sit opposite each other in rows. As students receive a peer's paper, they become that paper's editor.

  » Call out what item is to be checked by the editor: spelling, capital letters, use of quotation marks, or other areas of focus.

  » You may also want the students to move after a couple of items so that each student's paper is read by several editors.

  » No marks are made on the actual paper. All papers should have an editing page with the writer's name at the top.

  » Each editor places his or her name next to the number in turn and writes the concept to be checked.

  » When the editing process is completed, the students take their editing page and make any corrections. If there is a problem, they may discuss it with their editor or the teacher.

- Show **Display and Engage 7.6** and discuss the suggestions for editing an imaginative story.

Edit Writing

- Have students do a final pass through their imaginative stories, integrating the notes from the clocking activity into their own writing.

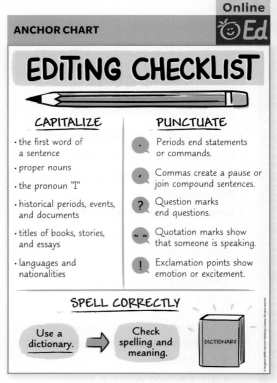

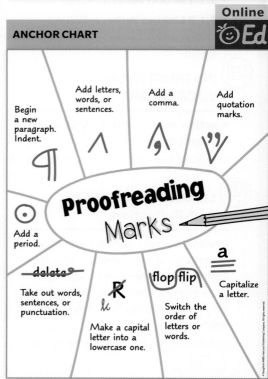

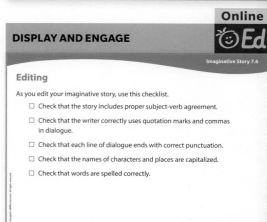

LEARNING OBJECTIVES

- Publish written works as part of the writing process.
- Use technology to produce and publish writing.
- **Language** Narrate a story aloud by using details.

MATERIALS   Online

Focal Text *The Luck of the Loch Ness Monster*

Writer's Notebook *pp. 7.5, 7.10*

Prepare the Final Copy

- Flip through *The Luck of the Loch Ness Monster* with students, briefly discussing how the author uses illustrations to help convey the story's events.
- Tell students to consider different ways to publish their stories. Provide a few examples:

  > a. They could produce neat, handwritten copies of their stories.
  >
  > b. They could use a word-processing program to type their stories.
  >
  > c. They could include hand-drawn illustrations to accompany the text.
  >
  > d. They could use a graphic design program to produce images for their stories.

Publish Writing

- Have student pairs work together to plan their final copies. Circulate the room and give tips to students.
- Have students work on the final copy and decide how they are going to publish it.
- Then have students turn to **Writer's Notebook page 7.5** and revisit the goals they set before they began writing. Have them Turn and Talk with a partner about their goals and take notes about what goals they might set for the next writing assignment. Then have students write a brief self-evaluation on **Writer's Notebook page 7.10**.

 ENGLISH LEARNER SUPPORT: Elicit Participation

SUBSTANTIAL

Help students determine which points in their stories might benefit from the use of illustrations as they read aloud.

MODERATE

Allow partners to practice reading their stories to each other before reading them to the class.

LIGHT

Have students practice reading their stories silently to themselves before they read them to the class.

Share Writing

- Divide the class into groups of three or four. Have students share their imaginative stories with their groups.

- Remind them to vary their pacing and expression to reflect the events in their stories.

- Encourage students to incorporate illustrations, gestures, or props into their readings.

- Remind students to have fun and think like a storyteller as they read.

- Instruct group members to listen actively to the reader. After members of each group have shared their stories, have students answer these questions:

> 1. What did you learn from the stories?
>
> 2. What did you enjoy most about the stories?
>
> 3. How were the topics of the group's stories similar or different?

Engage and Respond

- Conclude with an informal debriefing about how students felt about writing a story and whether they would like to write one again in the future.

 ENGLISH LEARNER SUPPORT: Support Discussion

SUBSTANTIAL
Rephrase the discussion questions to allow for yes/no answers, such as by asking, *"Did the stories have similar characters?"*

MODERATE
Provide sentence frames for students' responses, such as the following: *I learned _____. I really enjoyed _____. The topics were similar/different in these ways: _____.*

LIGHT
Give students extra time to respond to the questions.

Opinion Essay

FOCUS STATEMENT We should all try something new.

FOCAL TEXT

It's Disgusting and We Ate It! True Food Facts from Around the World and Throughout History

Author: James Solheim

Illustrator: Eric Brace

Summary: Facts about weird and interesting food from around the world.

WRITING PROMPT

READ the following sentence: *We should all try something new.*

THINK about a food that people may not like.

WRITE an opinion essay about why people should try that food. Use persuasive language and issue a call to action.

LESSONS

1. **Introducing the Focal Text**

2. **Vocabulary**

3. **Prewriting I: Preparing to Write**

4. **Prewriting II: Establishing an Opinion**

5. **Prewriting III: Organizing Reasons**

6. **Drafting I: Beginning the Draft**

7. **Drafting II: Integrating Persuasive Elements**

8. **Drafting III: Completing the Draft**

9. **Revising I: Combining Sentences**

10. **Revising II: Conferencing**

11. **Revising III: Connecting Ideas**

12. **Editing I: Proofreading for Mechanics**

13. **Editing II: Peer Proofreading**

14. **Publishing**

15. **Sharing**

LEARNING MINDSET: Planning Ahead

Display <u>Anchor Chart 31: My Learning Mindset</u> throughout the year. Refer to it to introduce Planning Ahead and to reinforce the skills you introduced in previous modules.

LEARNING OBJECTIVES

- Make connections to the topic and theme.
- Identify central ideas.
- **Language** Describe personal connections to an informational text.
- **Language** Explain author's use of text features.

MATERIALS Online

Focal Text *It's Disgusting and We Ate It!*
Writer's Notebook *p. 8.1*
Display and Engage *8.1*

Priming the Student

Explore the Topic

- Tell students that, in this module, they will read about unusual and surprising foods from around the world.

- Guide a discussion about students' favorite foods. Ask: *Who makes it? Do you eat it on special occasions? What are the ingredients? Do you know how to make it?*

- Have students describe the dish. Prompt them to share what the dish looks like, smells like, and tastes like. Record interesting and descriptive words that students use on chart paper. Encourage students to add the words to the Word Bank on **Writer's Notebook page 8.1** or to create a Word Bank in their own notebooks. Model this discussion in a Think Aloud.

  THINK ALOUD *One of my favorite foods is the baklava my grandma always had for dessert on the holidays. She got it from a deli in town. It was cut into triangles and spread out on my grandma's holiday platter. There was always honey running down the sides of every piece, making my fingers sticky. The crust was flaky and sweet. I took small bites to make each piece last. I let the honey and filling sit on my tongue, dissolving slowly. The filling was rich, and the chopped walnuts felt grainy on my tongue.*

- Show the cover of *It's Disgusting and We Ate It!* Ask: *What are they eating?* (*frogs and bugs*) Invite students to talk about unusual foods they have tried or foods that they really don't like. Have students describe their least favorite foods. Note any descriptive language students use and add it to the chart.

Discuss the Focus Statement

- Project **Display and Engage 8.1**. Read the focus statement with students. Have them write a few sentences in their notebooks describing a new food they tried recently or would like to try.

DISPLAY AND ENGAGE

Online Ed

Opinion Essay 8.1

Focus Statement

We should all try something new.

Priming the Text

Prepare to Read

- Review the descriptive words that students used as they discussed their most and least favorite foods. Connect the discussion to the focus statement. Ask: *Do you remember the first time you had your favorite food? Did you know it would be your favorite?*

It's Disgusting and We Ate It!

- Show the cover of *It's Disgusting and We Ate It!* again. Explain that *It's Disgusting and We Ate It!* is about the food people have eaten throughout history around the world. *Some of the food might not be something we'd ever think to eat, but, at one time or place, it could have been someone's favorite food!*

- Read the book's subtitle: *True Food Facts from Around the World and Throughout History.* Explain that this is an informational text. *Even though the book is comically illustrated, the information in it is factually true.*

- Show the inside front cover. Ask: *What does this picture show?* Guide students to recognize that this is a map of the world that shows where different types of food have been eaten.

- Read a few of the stranger captions from the inside front cover, such as green ant juice, and ask if students have ever eaten that food. Then ask if they would be willing to try it.

- Conduct a book walk, going through the book page by page. Point out the illustrations, headings, charts, and poems as you move through the text. Pause occasionally to read the speech-bubbles with the illustrations.

- Encourage students to make predictions or ask questions about what the illustrations show. For example, on page 6, ask: *Why might someone tell you to "close your eyes" when you eat something?*

Engage and Respond

- Have students Turn and Talk to a partner. Have them discuss what the people in the illustrations are eating and whether students would want to try that food for themselves.

 ENGLISH LEARNER SUPPORT: Conceptual Support

SUBSTANTIAL
Provide one-on-one support for students regarding any questions about food names or book structure concepts that need to be clarified during your book walk.

MODERATE
Have students work in pairs to identify what is pictured in the focal text. Allow students to share with their partners what unusual foods they enjoy or do not want to try.

LIGHT
Circulate among the students during the Turn and Talk to monitor for any breakdown of discussions between students. Aid students in illustration identification if necessary, writing the food's name on the board.

 LEARNING MINDSET: Planning Ahead

Introduce Throughout the module, students will be working on writing an opinion essay about why people should try a particular food. Say: *If we plan ahead, our task will be much easier.* Discuss setting goals with students. *Meeting each goal will get us one step to completing our opinion essay.* Make a list of suggested goals, such as deadlines for each important step of the writing phase, brought up in this discussion.

ARGUMENT • OPINION ESSAY

The Read

Read the Focal Text

- As you read *It's Disgusting and We Ate It!*, discuss text features and the organization of the text.

  » Read the Contents page. Point out the three sections of the book. Ask: *Why do you think Section Three refers to "your fridge"? How do you think the ideas in the book will be organized?*

  » Note the different sizes of headings on page 6. Guide students to recognize that the heading "Frog Legs" is smaller because it is a part of Part One, which is bigger.

  » As you move through the text, point out that the parentheses beneath some of the headings tell where those dishes came from.

  » Discuss the purpose of the illustrations throughout the book. Say: *Many informational texts will include photographs to provide more information. These illustrations are silly and fun. They are meant to entertain readers as they learn new things.*

- Have students study the illustrations on page 5 and then compare and contrast what they see with what they consider a typical lunch.

- Conduct a choral read of the poems in Part One with students. Then invite volunteers to recite a line or two of each poem using gestures and an appropriate tone of voice to enhance the recitation.

Engage and Respond

- Have partners choose two different dishes from Part One and then discuss which dish is the most unappetizing and why.

 ENGLISH LEARNER SUPPORT: Language Support

ALL LEVELS Support students' understanding of unfamiliar language and idioms throughout the text by rephrasing text or offering definitions and explanations as appropriate.

LEARNING OBJECTIVES

- Read and understand domain-specific vocabulary.
- Identify synonyms and antonyms.
- **Language** Describe relationships between words.

MATERIALS   Online

Focal Text *It's Disgusting and We Ate It!*

Writer's Notebook *p. 8.1*

Display and Engage *8.2*

Review the Focal Text

- Guide students to add words to the Word Bank on **Writer's Notebook page 8.1** or to their glossary in their own notebooks. Re-read Part One of *It's Disgusting and We Ate It!*, stopping after each page to allow students the opportunity to add words from the page to their Word Banks. Students may choose some of the following words:

disgusting	adventurous	juicy
wildest	slimy	freaky
squirmy	delightful	dangerous
steaming	horrid	tender

- Create a T-chart on chart paper or on the board. Label the T-chart with the word *disgusting*. Label the first column *Synonyms* and label the second column *Antonyms*. Make sure students understand both terms and their meanings. Suggest a few sample words and ask students to volunteer antonyms and synonyms for each example word to evaluate student understanding.

- Guide students to use appropriate resources, such as a dictionary and a thesaurus, as they work together to add synonyms and antonyms of the word *disgusting* to the chart. Then show **Display and Engage 8.2**. Walk students through the thesaurus entry for the word *disgusting* and the list of synonyms and antonyms. Invite students to provide any other synonyms and antonyms of *disgusting* that they might know.

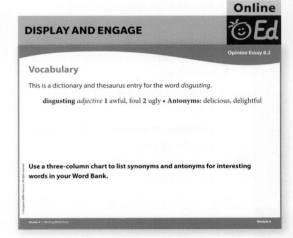

Engage and Respond

- Have partners work together to create their own three-column chart with the headings *Word*, *Synonyms*, and *Antonyms*. Have students list adjectives and verbs in the first column and add synonyms and antonyms in the other two columns.

ARGUMENT • OPINION ESSAY

LEARNING OBJECTIVES

• Identify task, audience, and purpose.
• Set goals for writing.
• **Language** Discuss writing tasks with academic language.

MATERIALS   Online Ed

Display and Engage 8.3
Writer's Notebook pp. 8.2, 8.3
Anchor Chart W8: *Parts of an Argument*

 INSTRUCTIONAL VOCABULARY

• **opinion** an idea or belief that cannot be proven
• **argument** a type of writing that tries to persuade readers to think a certain way
• **facts** information that can be proven
• **reasons** statements or facts that explain an idea
• **support** explain or give evidence for an idea

Discuss the Writing Prompt

• Tell students that in this module they will write an **opinion** essay. Explain that an opinion essay is a type of **argument** that gives **facts** and **reasons** to **support** an idea or belief. Add these terms to the class Instructional Vocabulary list and have students add them to their own glossaries.

• Show **Display and Engage 8.3** and read the Writing Prompt together. Note the tips.

• Distribute **Writer's Notebook page 8.2**. Explain that the rubric can help students understand the features and what is expected of a strong opinion essay. Discuss the different expectations of the rubric. Remind students they should use this rubric as a resource while drafting and revising.

• Display **Anchor Chart W8: Parts of an Argument** and read the points with students. Talk about the task of writing an opinion essay. Conduct a group discussion around these questions: *Why might someone not want to try a new food? What are some ways to convince people to try something new?* Connect these questions to the idea of writing to persuade an audience.

Set Goals for Writing

• Prompt students to think about their past writings and what they would like to improve. Have them consider goals for their opinion essay. Tell students to create a set of goals by adding their own goals to the list provided on **Writer's Notebook page 8.3** or in their own notebooks.

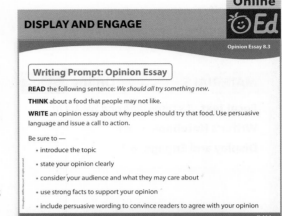

Online Ed

DISPLAY AND ENGAGE

Opinion Essay 8.3

Writing Prompt: Opinion Essay

READ the following sentence: *We should all try something new.*
THINK about a food that people may not like.
WRITE an opinion essay about why people should try that food. Use persuasive language and issue a call to action.

Be sure to —
• introduce the topic
• state your opinion clearly
• consider your audience and what they may care about
• use strong facts to support your opinion
• include persuasive wording to convince readers to agree with your opinion

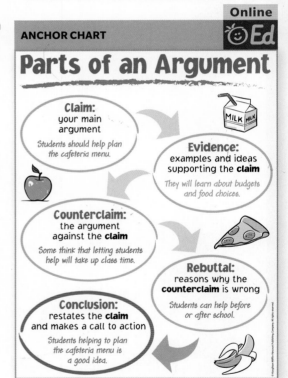

Online Ed

ANCHOR CHART

Parts of an Argument

Claim: your main argument
Students should help plan the cafeteria menu.

Evidence: examples and ideas supporting the **claim**
They will learn about budgets and food choices.

Counterclaim: the argument against the **claim**
Some think that letting students help will take up class time.

Rebuttal: reasons why the **counterclaim** is wrong
Students can help before or after school.

Conclusion: restates the **claim** and makes a call to action
Students helping to plan the cafeteria menu is a good idea.

LEARNING OBJECTIVES

- Consider opinions and topics for opinion essay.
- Use prewriting strategies.
- **Language** Discuss experiences.

MATERIALS
Online

Display and Engage 8.4a–8.4c
Writer's Notebook pp. 8.4, 8.5

LEARNING MINDSET:
Planning Ahead

Apply Tell students that, as they brainstorm their topic, they should plan ahead for the next steps in the writing process. Say: *Consider that you will have to develop the topic of your choice into an essay. Make sure that you have plenty to say about the topic you choose. If you feel strongly about a topic, you will likely have a lot to say about it.* Have students jot down notes about the reasons they think what they do about the topics they consider. The more notes next to a topic idea, the stronger that topic choice probably is.

TEACHER TIP

The discussion surrounding foods that people may not like has the potential to become sensitive, pitting opinions of different cultural groups against each other. Carefully guide discussion to validate all tastes and preferences, emphasizing the focus statement of trying something new.

Choose a Topic

- Show **Display and Engage 8.4a–8.4c** and distribute **Writer's Notebook page 8.4**. Read through the model and point out the introduction, body, and the conclusion.

- Have students underline the topic and circle the opinion statement. Ask: *What does the author think about sardines? What does the author assume the reader thinks about sardines? How do you know?*

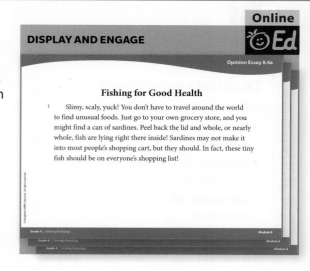

DISPLAY AND ENGAGE
Online Ed
Opinion Essay 8.4a

Fishing for Good Health

1   Slimy, scaly, yuck! You don't have to travel around the world to find unusual foods. Just go to your own grocery store, and you might find a can of sardines. Peel back the lid and whole, or nearly whole, fish are lying right there inside! Sardines may not make it into most people's shopping cart, but they should. In fact, these tiny fish should be on everyone's shopping list!

- Remind students of the favorite dishes they discussed in Lesson 1. Guide a discussion about those dishes and other dishes that students are familiar with. Ask questions such as:

  » *Do you think other people like the same kind of food you do?*

  » *What is a food you don't think you would ever try?*

  » *What would convince you to try something new?*

- Distribute **Writer's Notebook page 8.5** and have students add their ideas to the idea web.

- Have partners share their idea webs and discuss which foods they would be most interested in reading about.

- Model choosing a topic through a Think Aloud.

  THINK ALOUD *I want my audience to be interested in what I'm writing about. One time I went to a restaurant, and they served us sardines. The sardines were still in a can! Suddenly there were fish sitting on the table. I thought it was gross. The waiter showed us how to eat them, though, with crackers and cheese. It was strange but good. I recently learned that sardines are healthful for you. I don't think a lot of people know this. I think they might be interested.*

- Have students highlight the topic in their idea web that they will write about.

- Review the writing prompt. Then, guide students to write an opinion about the food they chose, responding to the prompt.

 ENGLISH LEARNER SUPPORT: Facilitate Discussion

SUBSTANTIAL
Have pairs with shared home languages discuss familiar dishes and brainstorm topics in that language.

MODERATE
Provide a selection of realia, such as menus or pictures of different dishes, to help support students' conversations.

LIGHT
Rephrase student descriptions as necessary and provide vocabulary for dishes under discussion.

LEARNING OBJECTIVES

- Gather relevant information.
- Identify reasons and supporting evidence.
- Organize reasons and supporting evidence text.
- **Language** Explain reasons using transitions.

MATERIALS   Online Ed

Display and Engage 8.4a–8.4c, 8.5

Writer's Notebook p. 8.6

 INSTRUCTIONAL VOCABULARY

- **opinion** an idea or belief that cannot be proven
- **transition words** words that connect ideas

Develop Support

- Return to the model and direct students' attention to the body of the essay.

- Have partners work together to reread the body of the model and find three reasons that support the author's **opinion**.

- Show **Display and Engage 8.5** and read the examples. Lead students to identify the reasons that were included in the essay. Ask: *Why were these reasons chosen for the essay?* Guide students to recognize that the reasons that weren't included were not as strong as the reasons that were included. Point out that the reasons are strong because they can be supported by specific facts and details.

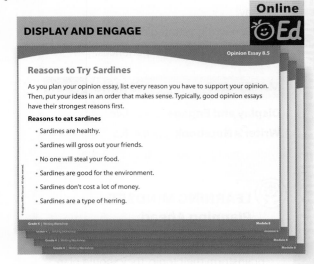

Online Ed

DISPLAY AND ENGAGE

Opinion Essay 8.5

Reasons to Try Sardines

As you plan your opinion essay, list every reason you have to support your opinion. Then, put your ideas in an order that makes sense. Typically, good opinion essays have their strongest reasons first.

Reasons to eat sardines

- Sardines are healthy.
- Sardines will gross out your friends.
- No one will steal your food.
- Sardines are good for the environment.
- Sardines don't cost a lot of money.
- Sardines are a type of herring.

- Distribute **Writer's Notebook page 8.6** and explain that students will organize their essay by developing reasons to support their opinion using the Idea-Support Map.

- Draw an Idea-Support Map on the board and complete it using the ideas from the model.

Everyone should eat sardines.		
Sardines are healthy.	Sardine fishing is good for the environment.	Sardines are inexpensive.

- Have students complete their Idea-Support Map. Circulate through the room offering prompts and suggestions such as: *What is an example of this?*

Connect Ideas

- Explain that writers connect ideas in an essay using **transition words**. Write a list of transition words on the board.

and	or	but
because	though	besides
since	finally	when

- Say: *The most common transition words are and, or, but, and because.* Point out how each transition word is used, either adding to an idea, explaining an idea, contrasting an idea, or showing cause. Refer to **Display and Engage 8.4a–8.4c**. Allow students to find sentences from the model that contain transition words.

ARGUMENT • OPINION ESSAY

LEARNING OBJECTIVES
- Develop an initial draft.
- Organize ideas to support an opinion.
- **Language** Express opinions in writing.

MATERIALS Online

Anchor Chart W8: *Parts of an Argument*
Writer's Notebook pp. 8.2, 8.4
Display and Engage 8.4a–8.4c

Prepare to Draft

- Remind students that they will develop their ideas into an opinion essay. Tell them that the purpose of an opinion essay is to persuade readers to think a certain way or to take a specific action.

- Display **Anchor Chart W8: Parts of an Argument** and read the elements of an argument, making sure students understand each point.

- Revisit the rubric for the opinion essay on **Writer's Notebook page 8.2**. Review any terms students may be unfamiliar with as you review each point with the class.

- Show **Display and Engage 8.4a–8.4c** or distribute **Writer's Notebook page 8.4** again. Draw students' attention to the first sentence of the introduction. Ask: *How does the author get readers' attention?*

- Explore the model's introduction with students. Point out the way that the author introduces the topic and leads into the opinion statement.

- Reread the conclusion of the model. Ask: *Why does the author say that people may not like sardines? How does the author try to convince people to try sardines anyway?*

Begin to Draft

- Write the following reminders on the board as students begin to draft:

  1. Get readers' attention with an interesting question or surprising, attention-grabbing statement.

  2. Tell specifically how the food looks, sounds, feels, tastes, and smells.

  3. Include explanations, facts, and details that strongly support your opinion.

- Remind students that they have their reasons and supporting reasons recorded. Students should refer back to their reasons as they draft their essay.

 ENGLISH LEARNER SUPPORT: Scaffold Writing

ALL LEVELS Allow students to record their ideas in a list. Then work with them to craft the items on their list into sentences using frames such as the following: *People may not like _____ because _____. However, _____.*

ARGUMENT • OPINION ESSAY

LEARNING OBJECTIVES

- Develop an engaging idea in writing.
- Draft an opinion essay supported with reasons.
- Connect ideas in writing.
- Write to persuade.
- **Language** Use transition words to connect ideas.

MATERIALS   Online

Display and Engage 8.4a–8.4c, 8.6
Writer's Notebook p. 8.4

INSTRUCTIONAL VOCABULARY

- **reasons** statements or facts that explain an idea
- **support** information that helps explain an idea
- **transition words** words that connect ideas

LEARNING MINDSET: Planning Ahead

Review Encourage students to continue planning ahead as they move through the writing process. Have them set goals for themselves. Say: *Set a goal to include two details or examples for each reason you include in your essay.* Tell students that once they reach their goal, they will be able to move on to the next reason with a sense of accomplishment.

Introduce the Skill

- Review the importance of providing **reasons** in **support** of an opinion. Say: *Reasons explain why. If you can tell your reader why you think something is true, there is a better chance of persuading your reader to agree with your opinion.*

- Remind students that a strong essay clearly connects ideas. Point out that transition words connect opinions and reasons so readers can understand the author's main ideas.

- Show **Display and Engage 8.4a–8.4c** or pass out **Writer's Notebook page 8.4** again as you return to the model. Point out the transition phrase *In fact* in the last sentence of the first paragraph.

- Explain that *in fact* provides emphasis for the idea that came before it in the model. Tell students that this transition phrase is used to introduce an example or other supporting evidence.

- Work through the rest of the model with students, calling out the following **transition words**:

  » *though*, paragraph 2, sentence 4

  » *besides*, paragraph 3, sentence 1

  » *so*, paragraph 3, sentence 2

  » *since*, paragraph 3, sentence 3

  » *finally*, paragraph 4, sentence 1

  » *when*, paragraph 4, sentence 3

  » *but*, paragraph 5, sentence 1

- Invite volunteers to identify the ideas that the transition words connect.

- Show **Display and Engage 8.6** and read the categories, explanations, and example transition words.

- Write the following example on the board. Have students identify each transition word or phrase, the idea it connects, and the kind of connection.

Online ⊙Ed

DISPLAY AND ENGAGE

Opinion Essay 8.6

Transition Words

Transition words show the connections between different ideas in writing.

Type of Connection	Transition Words
additional ideas	and, additionally, also, too
contrasting ideas	but, even though, although, despite
causes	since, because, because of, for this reason
examples	for example, including, for instance
sequence	first, then, next, finally

As you draft your opinion essay, look for places to use transition words to show how your ideas are connected.

Grade 4 | Writing Workshop
Module 8

> Some people seek out new and interesting foods.
>
> Despite this, most people prefer foods that are familiar.
>
> Because of this, many familiar foods are called "comfort foods."

Apply the Skill

- Tell students to think about the ideas in their opinion essays. Have them make a plan to connect their ideas using appropriate transition words or phrases. Then have them continue to draft.

ARGUMENT • OPINION ESSAY

LEARNING OBJECTIVES

- Recognize features of argumentative writing.
- Identify calls to action in persuasive texts.
- Develop drafts of persuasive writing.
- **Language** Write a call to action.

MATERIALS
Online Ed

Display and Engage 8.4c, 8.7

Writer's Notebook pp. 8.4, 8.6

 **INSTRUCTIONAL VOCABULARY**

- **call to action** words that urge a reader to do, think, or believe something

TARGETED GRAMMAR SUPPORT

You may want to consult the following grammar minilessons to review key editing topics.

- **1.2.3 Identify Kinds of Sentences,** p. W223
- **4.6.1 Prepositions,** p. W321
- **4.6.2 Prepositional Phrases,** p. W322

Introduce the Skill

- Show the model's conclusion again by using **Display and Engage 8.4c** and **Writer's Notebook page 8.4**. Ask: *What does the author tell the reader to do? Why does the author include this last line?* Explain that this is known as a **call to action**.

- Guide students to make the connection between the call to action and the purpose of an opinion essay: to persuade readers to do something or believe something.

- Say: *You are writing to convince readers to try a food they may not like. That is your purpose. Think about how you can conclude your essay with a call to action that helps achieve your purpose.*

- Show **Display and Engage 8.7** and read the examples of calls to action. Discuss as a class which sentences are the strongest, most persuasive statements.

- Have partners work together to craft their calls to action. Encourage them to be creative with their language to make the call to action appealing to readers. Say: *The call to action is your last chance to convince your reader. Think about what might convince you. You should also consider the reasons and support you provided earlier in your essay. How can your call to action relate to the information you provided?*

> **Online** Ed
>
> **DISPLAY AND ENGAGE**
> Opinion Essay 8.7
>
> **Call to Action**
>
> A good **call to action** tells readers what you want them to do, think, or believe. These are different examples of calls to action that might be in an opinion essay.
> - Eat more broccoli.
> - Try something new. You might like it.
> - Get your health on track by choosing tasty tomatoes!
> - Dare to be different—next time you eat out, order the snails.
> - You might want to try goat milk some day.
>
> As you draft your opinion essay, write a call to action that is memorable and speaks directly to the reader.
>
> Grade 4 | Writing Workshop   Module 8

- When pairs finish, invite them to share their calls to action with the class. Then, display the calls to action on the board.

Circulate the Room

- Have students continue working on their drafts.

- Remind them to use their Idea-Support Map on **Writer's Notebook page 8.6** to make sure they include all of their reasons to support their opinion.

- As needed, offer assistance to students as you circulate the room.

- As you circulate, group students who need support on similar grammar topics. Use grammar minilessons or the students' own writing to provide targeted review and support.

EL **ENGLISH LEARNER SUPPORT: Scaffold Writing**

SUBSTANTIAL
Provide a list of templates for a call to action and allow students to choose one. For example: *Try it! Take a bite! Pick up your fork and enjoy! Be brave, try something new today!*

MODERATE
Work with students to brainstorm ways to invite someone to eat something. Prompt students to offer serious and silly responses. Record their responses and have them choose one from the list.

LIGHT
Have partners use a thesaurus to aid them in finding different ways of phrasing their calls to action.

LEARNING OBJECTIVES
- Revise writing by combining sentences.
- Relate ideas using conjunctions.
- **Language** Combine sentences to relate ideas.

MATERIALS   Online

Display and Engage 8.8

 INSTRUCTIONAL VOCABULARY

- **independent clause** a clause that is a complete sentence on its own
- **dependent clause** a clause that is not a complete sentence on its own and is connected to an independent clause in a sentence
- **subordinating conjunction** a word or phrase that links a dependent clause to an independent clause

TARGETED GRAMMAR SUPPORT

You may want to consult the following grammar minilessons to review key editing topics.

- **1.2.3 Identify Kinds of Sentences,** p. W223
- **1.4.1 Compound Sentences,** p. W231
- **1.4.2 Complex Sentences,** p. W232
- **1.4.3 Commas in Compound Sentences,** p. W233

Introduce the Revision Skill

- Tell students that good writers look for opportunities to combine sentences to help readers better understand their writing and see how ideas are related. Explain that writers combine sentences to connect their ideas, to keep readers engaged, and to make sure the language they use flows smoothly from one idea to the next.

- Remind students that complex sentences can be made by combining **independent clauses**, which can stand alone as sentences, and **dependent clauses**. Tell students that these clauses can be combined using a **subordinating conjunction,** such as *if* or *because*. Review: *A dependent clause cannot stand on its own as a complete sentence. By itself, a dependent clause would be a sentence fragment.*

- Provide examples of dependent clauses:
  » *Where we go to school*
  » *If they want to be healthy*
  » *Although I like strawberries*

- Write the following sentences on the board.

  > Some people do not like spinach. Spinach is an important part of a balanced diet.

- Model how to combine the sentences.

  THINK ALOUD *These sentences are both short, simple sentences. They do not seem related, but they are both about spinach. I consider that these ideas can be contrasted. I can combine these sentences by making the first sentence into a dependent clause with the subordinating conjunction* although: "Although some people do not like spinach, it is an important part of a balanced diet."

- Show **Display and Engage 8.8**. Discuss how each pair of sentences has been combined by adding a subordinating conjunction. Discuss how each complex sentence shows the connection between words.

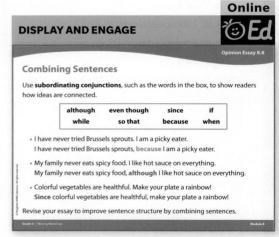

- Have student pairs work together to page through classroom library books and identify complex sentences. Have them share the most interesting sentences they have found.

Revise by Combining Sentences

- Have students revisit their own writing to combine sentences. Remind them to think about how the ideas are connected and combine their sentences in ways to make those connections clear to readers.

- As you circulate, group students who need support on similar grammar topics. Use the grammar minilessons or the students' own writing to provide targeted review and support.

LEARNING OBJECTIVES

- Conduct peer conferences to strengthen writing.
- Identify reasons and support in persuasive texts.
- Revise writing based on peer feedback.
- **Language** Share opinions in a collaborative activity.

MATERIALS   Online  Ed

Writer's Notebook *p. 8.7*

LEARNING MINDSET:
Planning Ahead

Review Remind students that it's helpful to set goals for the completion of a project. Guide them to make a calendar for when the next steps of the writing process will be completed. Circle the day when their opinion essays will be final and ready for publishing. Preview the publishing options in Lesson 14 with students and encourage them to begin thinking about what they might need for each option. Review that planning ahead like this means that students will have plenty of time to complete tasks and give their best effort.

Small Group Conferences

- Distribute **Writer's Notebook page 8.7**. Discuss the revision checklist with students. Explain that the checklist will be used to guide their small-group conferences and to help students identify the strengths of their essays.

- Prepare students to provide feedback on each other's writing.

  » Divide the class into pairs for a highlighting strategy activity, reminding students to bring a highlighter or colored marker along with a pen.

  » Direct writers to give their Writer's Notebook page to their partner.

  » Then have writers read their essay, pause, and then read it again.

  » After the first reading, tell listeners to make notes beside each checklist item.

  » During the second reading, have listeners jot down strong reasons and support they hear in the essay.

  » Then have listeners share their feedback with the writers.

  » Make sure writers highlight these reasons and support on their papers.

- Next have writers and listeners switch roles and repeat the process.

- After the conferences, have writers review the checklist to make sure their feedback is clear and complete.

Continue to Revise

- Have students return to their opinion essays and continue to revise. Have them review their reasons and support for strength and make sure to include any items that were missing or weak as noted on the checklist.

 ENGLISH LEARNER SUPPORT: Facilitate Discussion

SUBSTANTIAL

During the peer conference, provide copies of each writer's essay for both students to follow along with and point to during conferencing.

MODERATE

Provide this sentence frame for students to use during the conferencing: *One reason that was strong was _____ .*

LIGHT

Have students explain why they thought a reason was strong during the peer conference using this sentence frame: *I thought this reason was strong because _____.*

ARGUMENT • OPINION ESSAY

LEARNING OBJECTIVES

- Revise drafts to clearly connect ideas.
- Use transition words to strengthen writing.
- **Language** Share examples in whole-group settings.

MATERIALS   Online

Display and Engage 8.6

TEACHER TIP

To help students better understand transitions, have pairs of students look through classroom library books and find examples of the transitions on **Display and Engage 8.6**. Have them identify how the transition functions to connect the ideas in the text.

Review the Skill

- Remind students that they practiced connecting ideas in Lesson 7 earlier in this module.
- Revisit **Display and Engage 8.6** and have volunteers offer example sentences using one of the transition words or phrases from each category.
- Point out that transition words and phrases can be used at the beginning of a sentence, in the middle of a sentence, or even at the end of a sentence. Write the following examples of transition word placement on the board.

> Additionally, trying unfamiliar foods can provide a wider variety of vitamins in your diet.
>
> Trying unfamiliar foods can provide a wider variety of vitamins to your diet as well.
>
> Trying unfamiliar foods, however, can provide a wider variety of vitamins in your diet.

- Have volunteers underline the transition word or phrase in each sentence. (*additionally, as well, however*)
- Point out that not every transition word can be used in every position in a sentence. Read the sentence again with the transition words in different places in the sentence and have students decide whether or not each variation sounds natural or makes sense.
- Have students circle the commas and note their placement in the examples written on the board. Explain: *Commas are often used with transition words. They go after, around, or before a transition word depending on its placement in a sentence.*
- Note that some transitions, like the phrase *as well*, do not require commas.
- Encourage students to read their drafts and note transition words or phrases they have used. Ask volunteers to share the examples of transition words or phrases from their drafts.

Revise for Transitions

- Have students review and revise their essays to link their reasons to their opinion using transition words and phrases correctly. Remind them to pay attention to where the transition word or phrase is in the sentence and to determine if the addition of commas is necessary.

ARGUMENT • OPINION ESSAY

LEARNING OBJECTIVES

- **Language** Proofread writing for spelling.
- **Language** Edit writing for capitalization, punctuation, and mechanics.

MATERIALS   Online ⊙Ed

Anchor Chart W13: *Editing Checklist*

TEACHER TIP

Tell students that it is sometimes easier to spot mistakes in our writing when we read it out loud. Encourage students to read their essays out loud to a partner or even quietly to themselves as they proofread.

TARGETED GRAMMAR SUPPORT

You may want to consult the following grammar minilessons to review key editing topics.

- **1.4.1 Compound Sentences,** p. W231
- **1.4.2 Complex Sentences,** p. W 232
- **4.5.1 Making Comparisons,** p. W316
- **7.1.4 Frequently Confused Words,** p. W354
- **7.3.1 Spelling Homophones,** p. W361

Review Proofreading Checklist

- Display **Anchor Chart W13: Editing Checklist**.

- Review the items on the Editing Checklist. Review how to use proofreading marks. Discuss any points that seem unclear to students.

- As needed, revisit grammar topics on which students may need additional review or practice.

Proofread Writing

- Discuss with students the importance of proofreading for mechanics. Emphasize that mistakes in capitalization, punctuation, and spelling can interfere with the meaning of the essay for the reader and lead to misunderstandings.

- Have students independently edit their writing for spelling, punctuation, and grammar.

- Circulate the room and provide assistance, as needed.

- As you circulate, group students who need support on similar grammar topics. Use the grammar minilessons or the students' own writing to provide targeted review and support.

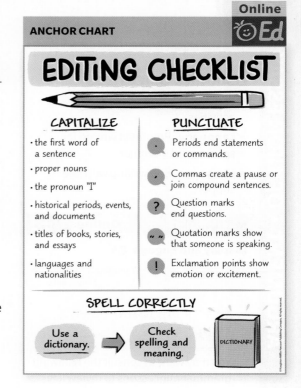

ANCHOR CHART   Online ⊙Ed

EDITING CHECKLIST

CAPITALIZE
- the first word of a sentence
- proper nouns
- the pronoun "I"
- historical periods, events, and documents
- titles of books, stories, and essays
- languages and nationalities

PUNCTUATE
- . Periods end statements or commands.
- , Commas create a pause or join compound sentences.
- ? Question marks end questions.
- " " Quotation marks show that someone is speaking.
- ! Exclamation points show emotion or excitement.

SPELL CORRECTLY
Use a dictionary. → Check spelling and meaning.   DICTIONARY

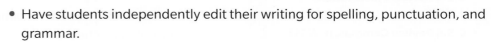

EL **ENGLISH LEARNER SUPPORT: Proofreading Support**

SUBSTANTIAL
Use proofreading marks to identify mechanical and usage errors for students. Then have students work to correct the errors, such as by looking up the correct spelling of a word in the dictionary.

MODERATE
Underline or highlight sentences that contain mechanical or usage errors. Then have students identify the error and correct it using proofreading marks.

LIGHT
Have students highlight sentences that they think may have an error, and then verify the mechanics or usage in reference materials such as a dictionary, style guide, or grammar book.

LEARNING OBJECTIVES

- Participate in shared learning activities.
- **Language** Proofread writing for spelling and grammar.
- **Language** Edit writing with peer support.

MATERIALS	Online

Display and Engage 8.9

TARGETED GRAMMAR SUPPORT

You may want to consult the following grammar minilessons to review key editing topics.

- **6.2.4 Review Punctuation,** p. W339
- **6.3.4 Review Commas,** p. W344
- **6.4.4 Review Proper Mechanics,** p. W349

Use the Clocking Activity

- Tell students that they will use the clocking activity to proofread each other's opinion essay.

- Show **Display and Engage 8.9** and discuss the proofreading checklist for an opinion essay. Confirm that students understand each item before moving on to the clocking activity.

- Review the rules for clocking.

  » Students form concentric circles or sit opposite each other in rows. As students receive a peer's paper, they become that paper's editor.

  » Call out an item to be checked by the editor using **Display and Engage 8.9**.

  » You may also want the students to rotate after a couple of items so that each student's paper is read by several editors.

  » Tell students that no marks are made on the actual paper. All comments should be made on the editing paper with the writer's name at the top.

  » Have each editor place his or her name next to the number in turn and write the concept to be checked.

  » When the editing process is completed, direct the writers to study their editing page and decide on any corrections they feel are necessary. If there is a problem or concern, allow students to discuss it with you or their editor.

Edit Writing

- Have students do a final pass through their opinion essays, integrating the notes from the clocking activity into their own writing.

🗨 ENGLISH LEARNER SUPPORT: Scaffold Writing

ALL LEVELS Arrange students for the clocking activity in such a way that higher proficiency students are editors for more difficult tasks, such as grammar and usage checks, while lower proficiency students are given more mechanical analysis, such as punctuation and capitalization checks.

Online

DISPLAY AND ENGAGE

Opinion Essay 8.9

Proofreading Checklist

As you edit your opinion essay, use this checklist.

- ☐ Check that there is a name on the paper.
- ☐ Check that all words are spelled correctly.
- ☐ Check for the use of correctly-formed complex sentences that connect dependent and independent clauses.
- ☐ Check that commas are used correctly.
- ☐ Check that each sentence ends with the proper punctuation.
- ☐ Check that all proper nouns and the beginnings of sentences are capitalized.

Grade 4 | Writing Workshop   Module 8

LESSON 14

PUBLISHING

LEARNING OBJECTIVES

- Publish writing.
- Use technology to assist with writing.
- Use visuals to enhance writing.
- **Language** Use academic language in collaborative discussions.

MATERIALS Online

Focal Text *It's Disgusting and We Ate it!*
Writer's Notebook p. 8.8

TEACHER TIP

Make color copies of pages from the focal text to serve as inspiration for students as they prepare final drafts.

Prepare the Final Copy

- Revisit the focal text *It's Disgusting and We Ate it!* Flip through several interior pages. Point out the way that the illustrations relate to the information given in the text. Pause to read one of the short poems.

- Prompt students: *If your essay was part of this book, what would the illustration for the food you chose look like? What would the poem be about?* Have students think about these questions as they prepare the final copy of their essays.

- Tell students that there are different ways they can publish their essays. Provide a few examples, such as the following:

  a. a short, fun poem as an introduction to the essay

  b. an illustration of the essay in the style of the focal text's illustrations

  c. a recipe for the food, attached to the end of the essay

  d. a book of essays compiled and organized according to the food's country of origin, as in the focal text

Publish Writing

- Have student pairs work together to plan their final copies. Circulate the room and give tips to students as needed.

- Have students work on the final copy and decide on their plan for publishing it. Encourage students to consider all of the options suggested for publishing, as well as any they may come up with on their own. Advise students to let the tone and nature of their essay help lead them to the option that best presents their essay.

Reflect on Writing

- Say: *Think about your opinion essay writing. Consider the steps you took in the writing process and the changes you made to your essay throughout it. What did you learn along the way?*

- Hand out **Writer's Notebook page 8.8** and allow time for students to think about and answer the questions.

EL ENGLISH LEARNER SUPPORT: Elicit Participation

SUBSTANTIAL
Provide sentence frames as students reflect on their writing. *I wrote about _____. I learned _____. What I liked most was _____. What I liked least was _____.*

MODERATE
Provide sentence frames as students reflect on their writing. *I learned that an opinion essay _____. Something that challenged me was _____.*

LIGHT
Provide sentence frames as students reflect on their writing: *One thing I learned about writing an opinion essay _____, The part of the writing process that helped me the most was _____ because _____.*

LEARNING OBJECTIVES

- Share writing.
- Conduct a self-evaluation.
- **Language** Ask and answer questions in collaborative settings.

MATERIALS	Online

Writer's Notebook *pp. 8.3, 8.9*

Share Writing

- Discuss with students tips for presenting their opinion essays. Write the following on the board.

> Stand up straight.
>
> Speak clearly.
>
> Make eye-contact with the audience.
>
> Read at an appropriate pace and volume.
>
> Change your tone of voice for questions or exclamations.

- Invite students to add their own tips to the list. Then have students share their opinion essays by reading them aloud.

- Encourage students to listen carefully and think about the reasons the writer provides. Invite them to ask questions about the essay when the writer is done reading.

- Take a quick poll of the audience: *Were you convinced?* Then have volunteers explain why they were or weren't convinced to try the food described in the essay.

Engage and Respond

- Conclude with an informal debriefing about whether students felt they successfully persuaded the audience to agree with their opinion.

- Have students turn to **Writer's Notebook page 8.3** and revisit the goals they set before they began writing. Have them Turn and Talk with a partner about how they feel they met their goals and take notes about what goals they might set for the next writing assignment.

- Prompt students to use what they discussed to complete the self-evaluation on **Writer's Notebook page 8.9**.

Research Report

FOCUS STATEMENT Understanding our world helps us protect it.

FOCAL TEXT

The Case of the Vanishing Honeybees: A Scientific Mystery

Author: Sandra Markle

Summary: An exploration into the science and history of honeybee population decline.

√ Mar 10 2023

WRITING PROMPT

READ this sentence: *Understanding our world helps us protect it.*

THINK about an endangered plant or animal.

WRITE a research report about that plant or animal. Conduct research, provide facts and details, and explain why the plant or animal should be protected.

·········· LESSONS ··········

LEARNING MINDSET:
Grit

Display **Anchor Chart 31: My Learning Mindset** throughout the year. Refer to it to introduce Grit and to reinforce the skills you introduced in previous modules.

INFORMATIONAL WRITING • RESEARCH REPORT

LEARNING OBJECTIVES

- Brainstorm words and phrases on a topic.
- Use background knowledge to prepare to read.
- Make personal connections to ideas.
- Read informational text with purpose and understanding.
- Analyze an informational text for author's craft.
- **Language** Discuss features of text with academic language.
- **Language** Speak using content-area vocabulary.

MATERIALS   Online

Classroom Materials *pictures of scientists and researchers at work*

Writer's Notebook *p. 9.1*

Display and Engage *9.1*

Focal Text *The Case of the Vanishing Honeybees*

Priming the Students

Explore the Topic

- Tell students that, in this module, they will investigate a real-life mystery about honeybees and learn how scientists are trying to solve it.

- Ask volunteers to tell something they know about mysteries. Ask follow-up questions, such as: *Have you ever solved a mystery? How did you do it? Why might you want to solve a mystery? Why might it be important to solve the mystery?*

- Model thinking about solving a mystery.

  THINK ALOUD *I remember when some of the vegetables in my family's garden were partly eaten. I didn't know what happened, and I wanted to solve the mystery. First, I looked for clues like footprints in the garden. Next, I made a list of all of the animals I had seen in the yard. Then, I read about the foods those animals eat. Finally, I watched the garden carefully, and one morning I solved the mystery. A rabbit was eating our lettuce and carrots! I was glad I solved the mystery.*

- Point out that all scientists are like detectives: they have a desire to learn, ask questions, and find solutions to mysteries about our world. Show students pictures of scientists and researchers at work in labs and in the field. As you look at the pictures, have students describe what they are seeing. List interesting words and ideas on the board or on chart paper under the title *Solving Scientific Mysteries*.

- Encourage students to add these words and phrases to the Word Bank on **Writer's Notebook page 9.1** or in their own notebooks as a resource for writing. Explain to students that writing things down will help them remember the ideas they discuss.

Discuss the Focus Statement

- Show **Display and Engage 9.1**. Read the Focus Statement with students. Have students discuss the statement with a partner, explaining their thoughts about it. Have students share their responses in small groups.

DISPLAY AND ENGAGE   Online

Research Report 9.1

Focus Statement

Understanding our world helps us protect it.

Grade 4 | Writing Workshop   Module 9

 ENGLISH LEARNER SUPPORT: Facilitate Discussion

ALL LEVELS If students have difficulty describing a mystery, give them a few examples. Then supply sentence frames to support students in sharing their responses.

Priming the Text

Prepare to Read

- Show the cover of *The Case of the Vanishing Honeybees*. Explain that detectives use the word *case* to refer to a problem they want to solve. Then have students think about what it means if something *vanishes*. (*It disappears and no one knows where it is.*) Write the words *case* and *vanishing* on the board. Have students add them and other interesting words and phrases to the Word Bank on **Writer's Notebook page 9.1** or in their own notebooks.

The Case of the Vanishing Honeybees

- Point out that the book you will be reading is an **informational text**. It will provide detailed information about honeybees as well as the mystery connected to them. Begin a class Instructional Vocabulary list and have students create a glossary section in the back of their notebooks. Add the term *informational text* to the class list and have students add the term and its definition to their glossaries.

- Display the contents page and read the chapter titles. Ask: *Why do you think two of the titles end with question marks?* (*because the author doesn't know the answers; because the author hasn't solved the mystery yet*)

- Point out the smaller print at the bottom of the contents page, beginning with "Author's Note." Explain that these features in the back of the book give additional factual information about honeybees.

  Ask: *Why might the author have included these additional pages at the end of the book?* (*to help the reader learn more about honeybees; to add information about honeybees that might help the reader solve the mystery*)

- Page through the book with students, pointing out the illustrations, photographs, diagrams, headings, and other text features. Have students describe what they see. Give them ample time to make observations and become familiar with the text. Take notes on the board or on chart paper.

- Point out the **glossary** on page 46. Discuss what a glossary is (the section of a book that gives the pronunciation and meaning of key terms in the book) and have students add a definition for it in their Instructional Vocabulary glossaries.

- Have students look at page 47. Explain that *digging deeper* means looking for more information. Point out that the page is divided into a section for books and a section for websites. Ask students why the author might have included this page. (*to make it easy for readers to find more information*)

Engage and Respond

- Have students Turn and Talk to a partner about what they want to learn by reading *The Case of the Vanishing Honeybees*, and why.

**LEARNING MINDSET:
Grit**

Introduce Explain to students that having grit means a person doesn't give up when something is challenging. Say: *Solving a mystery can take time, concentration, and a lot of work. Sometimes what you thought might be the answer may not be the solution. You must keep searching. The challenge involved in solving a mystery is a part of learning. You'll learn in* The Case of the Vanishing Honeybees *that scientists had to gather a lot of information and conduct a lot of research before they could solve the mystery.* Tell students that if they encounter challenges when they are conducting research they should think about the hard work and dedication of scientists. Dead ends and setbacks do not stop them from searching for answers and discovering solutions.

**INSTRUCTIONAL
VOCABULARY**

- **informational text** writing that presents factual information to expand a reader's knowledge
- **glossary** an alphabetical list of words and their meanings in the back of a book

The Read

Read the Focal Text

- Remind students that the text describes a mystery about honeybees. As you read *The Case of the Vanishing Honeybees*, stop at these points to discuss the content and the mystery-solving aspect of the text.

  » Read pages 4 and 5. Point out that the story begins by introducing the mystery. Ask: *What is the mystery?* (*Thousands of worker bees were missing.*)

  » Read the title on page 6. Then read the text. Ask: *Why are we in trouble if the honeybees are in trouble?* (*Honeybees pollinate many fruits and vegetables. Without the bees, those fruits and vegetables won't grow.*)

  » Read page 7. Point out the diagram to students and then have them explain what it shows. (*the reproductive parts of a flower*)

  » Read pages 8 and 9. After each page, stop and ask students what interesting words, sentences, or ideas they heard. Encourage them to add words and ideas to their Word Banks.

  » Read the caption on page 10. Explain that looking for signs is one way the beekeepers tried to solve the mystery.

  » Read page 11. Ask: *What does* join forces *mean?* (*to work together*) *Why was it a good idea for the scientists to join forces?* (*They could share information and possibly solve the mystery faster.*)

- Continue reading *The Case of the Vanishing Honeybees* with students as time permits. Discuss how the author describes the mystery and the attempts to solve it.

- Have students write interesting words and phrases related to the mystery in their Word Banks on **Writer's Notebook page 9.1** or in their own notebooks.

Engage and Respond

- Have students write three or four sentences about what they found most interesting in *The Case of the Vanishing Honeybees* and what they would like to know more about. Have students share their ideas with a partner.

 ENGLISH LEARNER SUPPORT: Elicit Participation

SUBSTANTIAL

Rephrase questions to allow for *yes/no* answers: *Did Dave Hackenberg find dead bees on the ground? Do bees pollinate many fruits and vegetables?*

MODERATE

Have students use a Think-Pair-Share routine. Allow them to think individually about their answers to the questions about the text. Then have pairs discuss their answers with each other before sharing them with the class.

LIGHT

Encourage students to take notes about the mystery as well as the factual information as you read. Have them refer to these notes for assistance as they respond to questions.

TEACHER TIP

Explain to students that the photographs in the book show the bees much larger than they really are. The photographer did this to make it easier for the reader to understand what the bees look like and how they live and work.

LEARNING OBJECTIVES

- Read and understand domain-specific vocabulary.
- Use context to determine meaning.
- Use print or digital resources to determine a word's meaning.
- **Language** Categorize words.
- **Language** Use strategies to learn domain-specific vocabulary.

MATERIALS   Online

Focal Text *The Case of the Vanishing Honeybees*

Writer's Notebook *p. 9.1*

Display and Engage *9.2*

Review the Focal Text

- Review the pages in *The Case of the Vanishing Honeybees* that you read aloud. Point out that the text is rich with vocabulary words related to honeybees, scientific inquiry, and solving the honeybee mystery.

- Page through *The Case of the Vanishing Honeybees* and have students identify additional words and phrases, such as the words below, that they find interesting. Pause to discuss why the words are interesting, and have students add them to their Word Banks on **Writer's Notebook page 9.1**.

beehives, p. 4	partnership, p. 9	overworked, p. 18
pollinate, p. 6	signs, p. 10	rent, p. 18
nectar, p. 7	metamorphosis, p. 12	researcher, p. 26
burrow, p. 7	habitat, p. 16	pesticides, p. 28

- Have students define the words on their lists using a print dictionary, the glossary in the back of *The Case of the Vanishing Honeybees*, or an online dictionary.

- Have students reread the sentences containing the words *rent* and *overworked* on page 18 of *The Case of the Vanishing Honeybees*. Then ask students what the words have in common. (*They are clues to the mystery*.)

- Ask students to identify three general science-related words, for example, *metamorphosis, habitat*, and *researcher*. Have them locate the words in the text and reread the sentences that contain them.

- Show **Display and Engage 9.2**. Read the directions with students. Then have students form pairs to organize the words in their Word Banks on **Writer's Notebook page 9.1**.

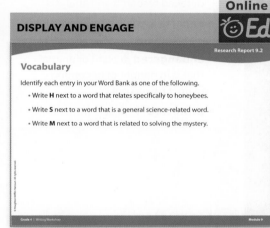

Online Ed

DISPLAY AND ENGAGE

Research Report 9.2

Vocabulary

Identify each entry in your Word Bank as one of the following.

- Write **H** next to a word that relates specifically to honeybees.
- Write **S** next to a word that is a general science-related word.
- Write **M** next to a word that is related to solving the mystery.

Engage and Respond

- Have students choose one of the entries from their Word Banks and write a few sentences explaining why they find their choice interesting.

 ENGLISH LEARNER SUPPORT: Build Vocabulary

SUBSTANTIAL

Help students categorize the words by giving them a choice of two options. For example, ask: *Is the word beehive related to bees or is it a general science word?* (*related to bees*)

MODERATE

Provide sentence frames for students to use as they categorize the words. *The word _____ is a _____ word because _____.*

LIGHT

Have student pairs explain their choice of categories to each other.

LEARNING OBJECTIVES

- Understand features of a research report.
- Set goals for writing.
- Create a research plan.
- **Language** Discuss writing tasks with academic language.

MATERIALS   Online Ed

Display and Engage *9.3*

Anchor Chart W7: *Elements of Informational Text*

Writer's Notebook *pp. 9.2, 9.3, 9.4*

 INSTRUCTIONAL VOCABULARY

- **research report** informational text written after conducting detailed research and analysis
- **experts** people who know a lot about a topic
- **endangered** a plant or animal that is in danger of becoming extinct (dying out)
- **protected** kept safe from harm

TEACHER TIP

Add the instructional vocabulary terms **research report** and **experts** to your class Instructional Vocabulary list. Have students add the terms and definitions to their glossaries.

Discuss the Writing Prompt

- Tell students that they will write a research report. Show **Display and Engage 9.3** and read the writing prompt together.

- Explain that a **research report** is a kind of nonfiction writing. The writer researches the topic by carefully reading and studying the work of **experts** who have written about the topic. Then the writer retells the information in his or her own words.

- Display **Anchor Chart W7: Elements of Informational Text** . Explain that in a research report, a writer researches facts and details about a topic. A writer may also use direct quotes from experts. Talk about different research reports students have read, and have them note the features they liked about those texts.

Set Goals for Writing

- Distribute **Writer's Notebook page 9.2**. Discuss the different expectations of the rubric. Tell students they can use this rubric as a resource while drafting and revising their own research reports.

- Have students think about the goals they would like to set for their research reports. Then have them set their goals by writing them on **Writer's Notebook page 9.3** or in their own notebooks.

Choose a Topic and Research Question

- Tell students that the first step in creating their research report is to choose a topic. The second is to form a research question.

- Distribute **Writer's Notebook page 9.4**. Review the words *endangered* and *protected* with students. Then discuss the plants and animals on the list.

- Model how to choose a topic and craft a research question.
  THINK ALOUD *First, I look at the lists of endangered plants and animals to see which one I might want to write about. I saw a Texas horned lizard at a wildlife museum. I would like to learn more about it, so I'll choose that for my topic. The main thing I want to know about the animal is why it should be protected, so I'll make that my research question:* Why should the Texas horned lizard be protected?

- After students have chosen a topic, have them write their research question.

LEARNING OBJECTIVES

- Understand features of a research report.
- Create a research plan.
- Identify primary and secondary research sources.
- **Language** Describe and explain a research topic.
- **Language** Discuss writing tasks with academic language.

MATERIALS Online

Anchor Chart W2: *Research Sources*
Display and Engage *9.4*
Writer's Notebook *p. 9.5*

INSTRUCTIONAL VOCABULARY

- **primary source** an original document, interview, or information from someone who has witnessed an event
- **secondary source** books, articles, or reports based on research someone else did

LEARNING MINDSET: Grit

Model: Tell students that sometimes we think something is too hard to do, but then we find out we can do it. Say: *I'm having trouble finding resources for my topic. I looked at books on a few shelves in the library, but I didn't find much. Then I used the online catalog and searched for my topic, and I found several resources. I felt better after I did that. I'm glad I didn't give up.*

Identify Sources

- Tell students that before they begin writing their reports, they need to do research. Show and discuss **Anchor Chart W2: Research Sources**. Have students share any experiences with or knowledge of the sources. Brainstorm additional research sources, and write them on the board.

- Show **Display and Engage 9.4**. Explain that there are two types of sources: **primary sources** and **secondary sources**. Read the descriptions on the chart.

- Explain the difference between primary and secondary sources:
  THINK ALOUD *I'm going to write about the Texas horned lizard. When I was at a wildlife museum recently, I took pictures and made notes about these lizards. These items are primary sources because they are firsthand knowledge. Later on, I got a library book about the lizards. This is a secondary source because they were written after the event or time period. Both sources have valuable information I can use.*

- Discuss whether each source on the Anchor Chart is a primary or a secondary source. Ask students how they know.

Create a Research Plan

- Have students turn to **Writer's Notebook page 9.5** or use their own notebooks to create a research plan.

- If possible, take students to the library or computer lab to look for additional sources. After this, have students add any additional sources they might want to consult to their research plans.

ANCHOR CHART

Research is using sources to find information.

CHICAGO DAILY — OCTOBER 9, 1871 — Chicago Is Burning

Great Fires in History

A **primary source** gives direct information about a topic.

A **secondary source** uses information from primary sources.

Good Sources ✓
- nonfiction books
- print or online magazines or newspapers
- respected websites

Avoid Plagiarism ✗
- Always list the sources you used for your ideas and information.
- Put the information you find in your own words.

DISPLAY AND ENGAGE Online

Research Report 9.4

Primary and Secondary Sources

A primary source is one that was written or occurred at the time of the event. It gives direct, first-hand knowledge of the topic. A secondary source is one that summarizes or describes a primary source. It was not written at the time of the event, but at a later time. As you research, make sure to use both kinds of resources.

Primary Sources	Secondary Sources
speeches	magazine articles
autobiographies	web pages
newspaper articles	encyclopedia entries
photographs and videos	other reference books
emails	textbooks
historical records	other books, including biographies

Grade 4 | Writing Workshop   Module 9

ENGLISH LEARNER SUPPORT: Tiered Support

SUBSTANTIAL
Show students examples of primary and secondary sources and explain how they are classified. Then show them again one at a time and ask students to say *primary source* or *secondary source*.

MODERATE
Provide sentence frames to facilitate identification of primary and secondary sources. For example: *I know this is a primary source because _____. This is a secondary source because _____.*

LIGHT
Have pairs of students explain to each other how they identify primary and secondary sources.

INFORMATIONAL TEXT • RESEARCH REPORT

LEARNING OBJECTIVES

- Gather sources.
- Evaluate sources.
- **Language** Describe and explain sources.
- **Language** Discuss writing tasks with academic language.

MATERIALS   Online Ed

Classroom Materials *a variety of research sources on endangered plants or animals*

Display and Engage *9.5*

Writer's Notebook *p. 9.5*

INSTRUCTIONAL VOCABULARY

- **evaluate** to decide what is most important to know

LEARNING MINDSET: Grit

Normalize Explain to students that it is normal to look at many possible sources before settling on the ones to use for a research report. Say: *Determining which sources to use for a research report is not an easy task. Both the school and the community library have many excellent books, videos, and encyclopedia articles to choose from. When you do an online search, you find a lot of information. It takes time to sort through all of these sources.* Tell students that researchers of all ages go through a similar process. Remind them that learning to do research now will help them with all of their future research.

Evaluate Sources

- Prior to the start of class, gather a variety of research sources related to the topic of endangered animals or plants. Make sure to have several good sources as well as some that are not relevant or credible. The model research report will discuss the Texas horned lizard, so you may want to gather sources on that topic.

- Show each of the sources to students. Read aloud the title and browse through the source. Invite students to comment on each source.

- Tell students that not all research sources they find will be useful or helpful to them. Tell them that they must **evaluate** the source. Explain that when they evaluate it, they look at it carefully to decide whether or not there is important information they can use in their report. Add the term *evaluate* to the class Instructional Vocabulary list and have students add it to their glossaries.

- Show **Display and Engage 9.5**. Read each question. Tell students they can use the questions as they evaluate their research sources.

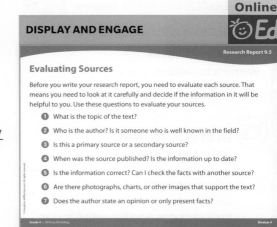

- Model using the questions on **Display and Engage 9.5** to evaluate two of the sources you assembled (e.g., a book about endangered animals written recently by a scientist and a blog post written by a student).

- Divide the class into small groups. Give each group one of the sources you have gathered. Have them use the questions on **Display and Engage 9.5** to evaluate the source. Tell students to write the answers to their questions on a piece of paper. Allow time for each group to present their evaluation to the class.

- Have students gather the sources they have identified in their research plan on **Writer's Notebook page 9.5**. Tell them to use the questions on **Display and Engage 9.5** to evaluate the sources. Tell them to put a plus sign (+) next to the name of each source they plan to use, and a minus (-) sign next to the ones they won't use.

 ENGLISH LEARNER SUPPORT: Support Comprehension

SUBSTANTIAL

Ask *yes/no* questions to help students choose their resources. For example: *Does this book have information about your topic? Does this Website have helpful pictures? Is this encyclopedia article easy to read?*

MODERATE

Suggest that pairs of students choose the same topic and evaluate their sources together. Have them use sentence frames to discuss their work: *I think this book is helpful because _____. / I am not going to use this source because it _____.*

LIGHT

Have students evaluate their sources independently. Then arrange them in small groups to review and discuss their decisions. Encourage students to offer each other constructive feedback. For example: *I agree that this book is useful because _____. I disagree about this Website because _____.*

INFORMATIONAL TEXT • RESEARCH REPORT

LEARNING OBJECTIVES

- Gather and evaluate resources.
- Take notes and organize ideas for writing.
- Identify details.
- **Language** Describe and explain resources.
- **Language** Discuss writing tasks with academic language.

MATERIALS   Online

Display and Engage *9.6a–b*
Writer's Notebook *p. 9.6*

 INSTRUCTIONAL VOCABULARY

- **notes** written information about a topic

Take Notes

- Remind students that before they begin writing their reports, they must do research. When they do research, they need to take **notes** on what they read. Explain that when they take notes, they write down important words and phrases from the text they are reading. They may also write down a few important sentences.

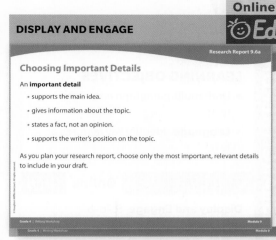

- Read the statements on **Display and Engage 9.6a**. Explain that useful information is related to the topic the student has chosen to write about. It may give details about what the animal or plant looks like or where it lives. The information will help students support their position about why the plant or animal needs to be protected.

- Model using the instructions and sample passage on **Display and Engage 9.6a–b** to show how to note relevant details.

  THINK ALOUD *I found a website about the Texas horned lizard. First, I write the name of the website and the URL, or web address, at the top of my note-taking page. That way I'll know where I found the information. Next, I read the text one time. Then I read it again and take notes. I write the words "phrynosoma cornutum" because that's the lizard's scientific name. I see the phrase "cute critter" in the second sentence. This phrase expresses the writer's opinion about the reptile. It's not a fact, so I won't include it. The text also says it's a reptile with scales and claws, and that the babies are born on land. These are important details, so I will write them down. Then I read that it's the official state reptile of Texas. That will be important when I tell why the lizard should be protected, so I'll write that down as well. Next I read that the sea turtle was made the second state reptile in 2013. That information is interesting but not related to my topic, so I won't add it to my notes.*

- Show students **Writer's Notebook page 9.6**. Tell them to use the suggestions on **Display and Engage 9.6a** as they take notes on the Writer's Notebook page or in their own notebooks. Students may create their own note cards if needed.

- Circulate the room as students work. As necessary, guide individuals to decide if the information they have is relevant to their topic or not.

 ENGLISH LEARNER SUPPORT: Facilitate Discussion

SUBSTANTIAL
Ask *yes/no* questions to help students choose their resources. For example: *Does this book have information about your topic? Does this website have helpful pictures? Is this article easy to read?*

MODERATE
Suggest that pairs of students choose the same topic and evaluate their sources together. Have them use sentence frames to discuss their work: *I think this book is helpful because _____. I am/am not going to use this source because it _____.*

LIGHT
Have students evaluate their sources independently. Then arrange them in small groups to discuss their decisions. Encourage students to offer each other constructive feedback. For example: *I agree that this book is useful because _____. I disagree with this Website because _____.*

LEARNING OBJECTIVES

- Draft multi-paragraph informative texts.
- **Language** Identify key features of text.

MATERIALS Online

Display and Engage 9.7a–b
Writer's Notebook p. 9.7

Prepare to Draft

- As students prepare to begin drafting, explain that they should include the facts from their notes in their reports, but that they need to use their own words to avoid plagiarism. Tell students to take care not to make their report read like a boring list.

- Let students know you will be sharing a model report about the endangered Texas horned lizard. Point out how boring this report would be if it started with something like this: *The Texas horned lizard is a reptile. It has scales. It has claws. It lives in Texas. It is the official state lizard. The Texas horned lizard should be protected.*

- Ask: *Why does that opening sound boring?* Guide students to see that it's just a list of facts. Each sentence starts the same way and is about the same length, so they all sound the same. The sentences have no personality. Help students realize that facts alone do not make a good research report. It's the way the facts are written and the way they support the main idea that makes the reader want to continue.

- Show **Display and Engage 9.7a–b** and distribute **Writer's Notebook page 9.7**. Read the model report with students.

- Next, work with students to mark the model research report's text structure in different colors. Have students identify and draw a red box around the topic and the main idea. Have students draw a green circle around each supporting detail in the body. Ask students to underline the specific words and phrases in blue.

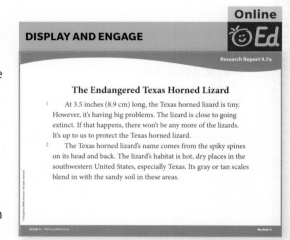

- Review with students how analyzing the model will help them as they begin to draft their research report.

Begin to Draft

- Have students begin to draft their research reports using the notes and graphic organizers from prewriting.

- Tell students to think about how they would describe the plant or animal to a friend, and how they would explain why it needs to be protected. Tell them to use an engaged voice in their writing. Remind students to vary their sentences to keep the writing interesting.

- Suggest that students write the body first, so they will know how to introduce it. Tell them that after they write the body, they should go back and write the introduction. Write these tips on the board:

  » Body:

    » State your topic and main idea in the first few sentences of each paragraph.

    » Follow the main idea with supporting details.

    » Include specific words/phrases to make your writing interesting.

  » Introduction:

    » Tell the topic of your report.

    » Write a statement that the plant/animal should be protected.

- Circulate the room as students work and offer assistance as needed.

LEARNING OBJECTIVES

- Find and use research in informational writing.
- Correctly quote from sources.
- **Language** Use commas and quotation marks correctly.

MATERIALS   Online

Display and Engage 9.8a, 9.8b

Focal Text *The Case of the Vanishing Honeybees*

Writer's Notebook *p. 9.7*

INSTRUCTIONAL VOCABULARY

- **quotation** the exact words a person says
- **plagiarism** copying someone else's work without giving credit

TEACHER TIP

Add the terms *quotation* and *plagiarism* to the class Instructional Vocabulary list and have students add the words and their definitions to their glossaries.

Using Quotations

- Discuss with students that **quotations** are useful in research reports because they give the reader the best and most accurate information. Using quotations from an expert also gives the writer and the report authority.

- Show **Display and Engage 9.8a**. Read each of the rules about formatting quotations. Read the sample sentences and ask students to explain how the formatting for each quotation works.

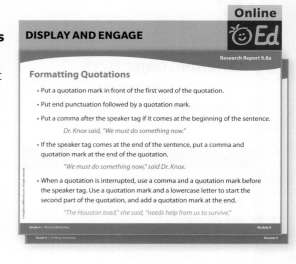

DISPLAY AND ENGAGE

Research Report 9.8a

Formatting Quotations

- Put a quotation mark in front of the first word of the quotation.
- Put end punctuation followed by a quotation mark.
- Put a comma after the speaker tag if it comes at the beginning of the sentence.
  Dr. Knox said, "We must do something now."
- If the speaker tag comes at the end of the sentence, put a comma and quotation mark at the end of the quotation.
  "We must do something now," said Dr. Knox.
- When a quotation is interrupted, use a comma and a quotation mark before the speaker tag. Use a quotation mark and a lowercase letter to start the second part of the quotation, and add a quotation mark at the end.
  "The Houston toad," she said, "needs help from us to survive."

- Turn to page 16 of *The Case of the Vanishing Honeybees*.

- Read aloud the quotation by Jeff Pettis in the middle of the page. Explain that the initial quotation marks signal the beginning of the quotation. Point to the speaker tag and explain that it tells who is speaking. Point to the second part of the first sentence and explain that the quotation marks show that the speaker is still talking. Explain that the next sentence is also part of the long quotation. Point out the end quotation marks.

- Look through the book with students to find additional quotations. Have students tell which formatting style is used in each quotation. Encourage students to refer to **Display and Engage 9.8a** as necessary.

- Have students examine the model on **Writer's Notebook page 9.7**. Use a Think Aloud to explain how you formatted a quotation in the model.

  THINK ALOUD *I read a report by a scientist named Dr. Nelson. I thought some of her words were important to include just as they were, so I used a direct quotation. I began with a speaker tag followed by a comma, then the quotation. I ended the sentence with a period and the end quotation marks. I double-checked my reference source to make sure I had her exact words.*

- Show **Display and Engage 9.8b**. Caution students that when they use a direct quotation, they must give the name of the original speaker. Explain that using someone else's words or work without crediting them is called **plagiarism**, and it is not permitted in any type of writing.

- Work with students to look through their sources and find a useful quotation. Have them add the quotation to their draft.

- Have volunteers offer examples of the quotes they used. Write a few of them on the board and work with the class to check the formatting. Have volunteers explain why they used quotations and how they knew what kind of formatting to use.

Continue to Draft

- Have students continue drafting. Circulate the room as students work.

LEARNING OBJECTIVES
- Develop a bibliography.
- **Language** Use punctuation correctly.

MATERIALS
Online Ed

Display and Engage 9.9

Focal Text *The Case of the Vanishing Honeybees*

INSTRUCTIONAL VOCABULARY

- **bibliography** a list of sources referred to in a text, usually included at the end of that text

LEARNING MINDSET: Grit

Review Remind students about the importance of grit. Say: *Creating a bibliography may seem like hard work. There are a lot of little details to pay attention to, and all of them are important. Each part of the bibliography has to be done correctly. You have already shown that you have grit because you chose a topic, gathered sources, and started a draft. You can keep going now.*

Introduce the Skill

- Explain to students that a **bibliography** is a list of sources referred to in a text, usually included at the end of that text. It can consist of any combination of books, magazine articles, Internet sources, and interviews. Each source is listed separately and is called an *entry*. Add *bibliography* to the class Instructional Vocabulary list and have students add the word and their definition to their glossaries.

- Point out that, similar to quotations, a bibliography entry has a certain format.

- Show **Display and Engage 9.9**. Explain that this is what the entry for *The Case of the Vanishing Honeybees* would look like in a bibliography. Read each of the rules about formatting a bibliography. Then point to each example and ask students to explain the formatting.

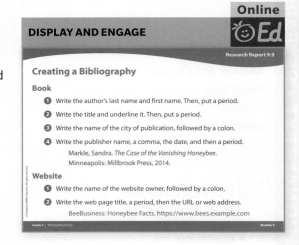

- Show students the bibliography on page 47 of *The Case of the Vanishing Honeybees*. Point out that the bibliography is divided into two sections, one for books and one for websites.

- Read each entry with students. Have them point out the features of the formatting. Explain that even though parts of the entry are not complete sentences, they still require a period. Point out that for their bibliographies, they do not have to include the summary sentence shown in these entries.

- Write the following sample entries on the board:

  » Archer, Melanie. <u>All Kinds of Lizards</u>. New York: Franzen Press, 2017.

  » LearnAboutIt: Lizards of Texas. https://www.learnlizards.example.com

- Then use a Think Aloud to explain how you formatted one book and one website for your model research report.

  THINK ALOUD *I arranged all of my source books in alphabetical order according to the author's last name. Then I made my first entry. I wrote down the author's last name, then the first name. Then I wrote a period. Next I wrote the title of the book and underlined it, followed by a period. Then I looked at the copyright page in the front of the book to find the rest of the information. I wrote the name of the city where the book was published, followed by a colon. Next I put the name of the publishing company, followed by a comma, and the year of publication.*

  I also wrote information for one of the websites. First I wrote the name of the website owner. Then I wrote the title of the page, and last I put the URL, or web address.

- Use some of the students' source books and websites to practice formatting entries for a bibliography. Write the examples on the board.

- Have students create their own bibliographies.

Continue to Draft

- Have students continue drafting. Circulate the room as students work. Offer assistance as needed.

LEARNING OBJECTIVES

- Draft a research report.
- **Language** Review key grammar topics.

MATERIALS   Online

Focal Text *The Case of the Vanishing Honeybees*

Display and Engage 9.7b

Writer's Notebook p. 9.7

INSTRUCTIONAL VOCABULARY

- **conclusion** a statement you make or an idea you have about a text based on thinking about the information in the text

TARGETED GRAMMAR SUPPORT

You may want to consult the following grammar minilessons to review key editing topics.

- **2.1.4 Review Proper Nouns,** p. W239
- **3.1.1 Action Verbs,** p. W266
- **4.1.1 Adjectives,** p. W296

Introduce the Skill

- Explain to students that a **conclusion** is a statement you make or an idea you have about a text based on thinking about the information in the text. Add the term to your class Instructional Vocabulary list and have students add it to their glossaries. Tell students that the conclusion comes at the end of their research report. Stress that the conclusion sums up the main idea and supporting details in the report. It does not state any new main idea or details.

- Revisit page 42 of *The Case of the Vanishing Honeybees*. Tell students the author ends the book with a strong conclusion. Ask students to listen for the conclusion as you read the page aloud. Explain that it is a strong conclusion because it restates the main idea that the case is not yet solved.

- Show **Display and Engage 9.7b** and have students follow along by looking at the model on **Writer's Notebook page 9.7**. Read the concluding paragraph of the model report with students. Have them identify the topic/main idea and the strong words and phrases. Discuss why the conclusion is strong.

  THINK ALOUD *This conclusion is strong because it summarizes the most important details. It ends by restating that the Texas horned lizard should be protected. The conclusion does not give any new information.*

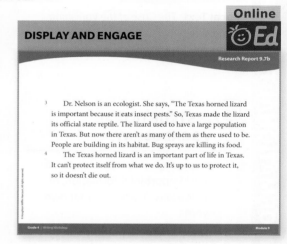

Online

DISPLAY AND ENGAGE

Research Report 9.7b

3   Dr. Nelson is an ecologist. She says, "The Texas horned lizard is important because it eats insect pests." So, Texas made the lizard its official state reptile. The lizard used to have a large population in Texas. But now there aren't as many of them as there used to be. People are building in its habitat. Bug sprays are killing its food.

4   The Texas horned lizard is an important part of life in Texas. It can't protect itself from what we do. It's up to us to protect it, so it doesn't die out.

Grade 4 | Writing Workshop   Module 9

Circulate the Room

- Remind students to continue to use their research sources and their planning notes. Remind them to write their facts in an interesting way.

- Have students continue to spend time writing their papers.

- Circulate the room as students work. Group students who need support on similar grammar topics. Use the grammar minilessons or the students' own writing to provide targeted review and support.

 ENGLISH LEARNER SUPPORT: Discuss Language Structures

SUBSTANTIAL

Review common and proper nouns with students. Make a T-chart on the board and label the columns *Common Nouns* and *Proper Nouns*. Invite students to write nouns from their research reports in the correct columns. Review the chart with the group. Use the following sentence frames if students need to move a noun to the other column: *This is a proper noun because _____. This is a common noun because _____.*

MODERATE

Pair students and have them read their research reports together. Then have them find at least two places where they can add adjectives. Tell them to make the additions and then discuss why their writing now sounds more exciting.

LIGHT

Have students review their writing in pairs and identify any tricky grammar points. Tell them to work together to correct any errors. Assist as necessary.

INFORMATIONAL TEXT • RESEARCH REPORT

LEARNING OBJECTIVES

- Correctly quote from sources.
- Identify main idea and important details.
- **Language** Use commas and quotation marks correctly.
- **Language** Summarize a source.

MATERIALS Online Ed

Focal Text *The Case of the Vanishing Honeybees*

Display and Engage *9.8*

INSTRUCTIONAL VOCABULARY

- **summary** a restatement of the most important information, or main ideas, in a text in your own words

- **paraphrase** to put someone else's ideas in your own words

TARGETED GRAMMAR SUPPORT

You may want to consult the following grammar minilessons to review key editing topics.

- **6.1.3 Quotations from Text,** p. W333
- **6.1.5 Using Quotations,** p. W335
- **7.2.1 Abbreviations for People and Places,** p. W356

Introduce the Revision Skill

- Tell students an important part of revising is making sure they have summarized the information from their sources. Explain that when they summarize, they include the main ideas and most relevant or important details.

- Also tell students that when they develop a **summary**, they need to **paraphrase**, or give the information from the source in their own words. Remind them that they discussed plagiarism in Lesson 8, and that if they correctly paraphrase in their summary, they will not be in danger of plagiarizing. Add the terms *summary* and *paraphrase* to the class Instructional Vocabulary list and have students add them and their definitions to their glossaries.

- Tell students to listen for the main idea and most important details as you read aloud page 22 of *The Case of the Vanishing Honeybees*.

- After you finish reading, ask students to tell you the main idea and most important details. Write them on the board and read them aloud. Then use a Think Aloud to model how to summarize and paraphrase. Write your paraphrased summary as you say it.

  THINK ALOUD *The main idea is that cell phones are not causing CCD. The details are that some people thought the wireless communication interfered with the bees' navigation. Cell phones and recorders were put inside five beehives. The bees made swarming sounds, but they didn't swarm. A scientist said cell phones would not be that close to bees, so the test was not realistic.*

  Now I'll paraphrase the main idea and details:

  > By doing an experiment, scientists proved that cell phones did not cause CCD. They used cell phones and audio recorders inside hives. When they turned on the music on the cell phones, the recorders picked up the usual swarming sounds. But, the bees stayed in the hive instead of leaving. This proved to the scientists that the cell phones didn't make the bees do anything different.

- To help with paraphrasing, suggest that students use a print or an online thesaurus to help them find words that are similar in meaning to those in their source texts.

Revisit Formatting Quotation Marks

- Show **Display and Engage 9.8** and review the rules for using quotation marks.

- Write a few quotations from *The Case of the Vanishing Honeybees* or from students' work. Have students correctly format them and explain what they did.

Revise for Quotations and Summaries

- Have students return to their writing to make sure they have summarized the information from their sources. Tell them to check that their summaries have been paraphrased, not plagiarized.

- Then have students check that they have used quotations correctly.

LEARNING OBJECTIVES

- Revise a research report.
- **Language** Discuss writing in small group conferences.

MATERIALS Online

Display and Engage 9.10

 LEARNING MINDSET: Grit

Normalize Tell students that it is normal to revise a piece of writing. Say: *Writing is rarely perfect on the first draft. Many writers, even famous ones, revise several times. It's the sign of a good writer to keep going until you are satisfied that the work is your best effort.*

Small Group Conference

- Tell students that it is time to read their classmates' writing and provide feedback. Explain that they will revise their drafts based on what they learn during the peer conference.

- Show **Display and Engage 9.10**. Tell students these questions will help them provide useful feedback. Read the list with students. Encourage them to ask questions about anything they don't understand.

- Divide students into groups of four or five. Tell them they will each take a turn reading while the others listen and take notes. Everyone in the group will get a turn.

- Tell students the reader will read his or her research report once while the listeners listen. Then the reader will read a second time and the listeners will take notes.

- Explain that the notes should refer to the questions on the list. Students should write something from the list that they liked in the writing. They should also write something that they either didn't understand, that they think could be explained better, or that they want to know more about.

- Debrief with the class. Discuss students' response to the following questions.

What have you learned about writing a research report?

How did peer conferencing help you improve your writing?

What suggestion do you have to improve the peer conferencing process for the next writing assignment?

Continue to Revise

- Have students revise their drafts, using the feedback they gained in small group conferences.

 ENGLISH LEARNER SUPPORT: Elicit Participation

SUBSTANTIAL
Work with students individually to identify examples in their writing that are referred to on the revising list. Have students choose one or two items to revise.

MODERATE
Supply sentence frames for students to use during the conferencing: *I liked it when you said _____. I didn't understand _____. I would like to know more about _____.*

LIGHT
Have partners explain to each other how using the peer conferencing process and the revising list helped them improve their writing. Provide sentence frames: *The peer conferencing helped me _____ because it _____. The revising checklist was helpful because _____.*

LEARNING OBJECTIVES

- Proofread writing for correct formatting of bibliography.
- Proofread writing for correct formatting of quotations.
- **Language** Proofread writing for grammar, usage, and mechanics.
- **Language** Edit writing with peer support.

MATERIALS   Online 📙 Ed

Anchor Chart W17: *Proofreading Marks*
Display and Engage *9.11*

TARGETED GRAMMAR SUPPORT

You may want to consult the following grammar minilessons to review key editing topics.

- **1.1.3 Subject-Verb Agreement,** p. W218
- **6.2.4 Review Punctuation,** p. W339
- **6.4.4 Review Proper Mechanics,** p. W349

Clocking Activity

- Review the rules for clocking.
- Students form concentric circles or sit opposite each other in rows. As students receive a peer's paper they become that paper's editor.
- Call out the item to be checked by the editor.
- Remind student editors that they do not make marks on the actual paper. Instead, the student editors put their comments on an editing page.
- The editor writes their name and the concept to be checked.
- When the editing process is completed, the students take the editing page and make corrections.
- If there is a problem, students discuss it with their teacher or the editor.

Review Proofreading Checklist

- Show **Anchor Chart W17: Proofreading Marks** and review with students how to mark up a text.
- Show **Display and Engage 9.11**. Review the proofreading checklist with students.
- Remind students to punctuate quotations correctly and state the name of the speaker accurately.
- Remind students to include all of their research sources in their bibliographies.

Edit Writing

- Have students do a final pass through their research reports, integrating the notes from the clocking and proofreading activities into their writing.

ANCHOR CHART   Online 📙 Ed

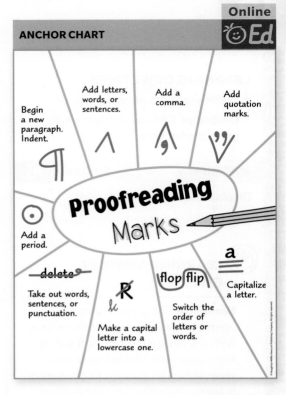

DISPLAY AND ENGAGE   Online 📙 Ed

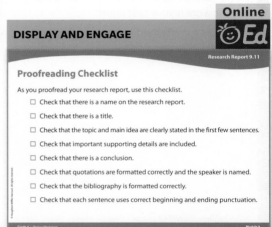

📣 ENGLISH LEARNER SUPPORT: Scaffold Proofreading

SUBSTANTIAL

Work with students as they edit. Use prompts to help them identify the items on the checklist. For example: *Point to the title. Point to a quotation. Point to the conclusion.*

MODERATE

Pair students and allow them to work as an editorial team. Have them use sentence frames as they discuss their editing: *The title is _____. The details are _____. The quotation is _____.*

LIGHT

As students proofread, ask them to share how proofreading other students' papers helps them proofread their own work.

LEARNING OBJECTIVES

- Proofread writing for correct formatting of bibliography.
- Proofread writing for correct formatting of quotations.
- **Language** Proofread writing for grammar, usage, and mechanics.
- **Language** Edit writing with peer support.

MATERIALS
Online

Display and Engage *9.9*
Writer's Notebook *p. 9.8*

Complete the Bibliography

- Show **Display and Engage 9.9**. Review with students the correct way to format a bibliographical entry.

- Remind students to check each of their research sources and make sure they have entered it in their bibliography.

- Allow time for students to complete their bibliographies.

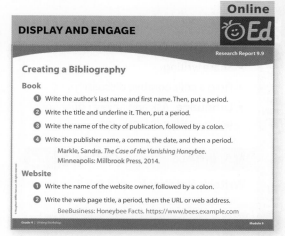

Reflect on the Process

- Tell students they will pause for a few minutes before publishing their writing to reflect on what they did in the module.

- Have students turn to **Writer's Notebook page 9.8**. Point out the reflection questions and read them with students. Tell them they should spend several minutes completing the page.

Publish Writing

- Discuss with students the different publishing options they have available. Remind them that a research report is meant to be shared with others. Provide a few examples of possible publishing options.

> 1. Print two copies of each student's research report and collect them in binders. Put one copy in the classroom library and one in the school media center.
>
> 2. Upload copies of their research reports to the class or school website.
>
> 3. Group similar research reports. Have each group make a video documentary and show it to other classes. Groups may also take turns taking it home to show families.

- Have students spend the rest of the time deciding how they will publish their writing.

LEARNING OBJECTIVES

- Share writing.
- Hold a collaborative discussion.
- **Language** Ask and answer questions using academic language.

MATERIALS   Online

Writer's Notebook *pp. 9.3, 9.9*

Share Writing

- Before students begin sharing their research reports, discuss the best ways to listen to a report that has details, facts, and possibly some scientific language.

- Suggest that students take brief notes in their notebooks as they listen, or take a few minutes after the presentation to write a few notes.

- Remind students that they will have the opportunity to ask questions after each report. Suggest that they may want to jot down questions in their Writer's Notebooks as they listen.

- Have students share their research reports. They can either read them aloud, or, if they have created a video, they can show it.

- Allow time after each research report for students to ask questions. Remind students to ask questions that are based on the research report and to speak in a respectful way. Point out that they are not offering criticism but trying to get a better understanding of the topic. Encourage the presenter to answer with details from their report or from their research.

Engage and Respond

- Conclude with an informal debriefing about doing research, writing a research report, formatting a bibliography, and presenting research to the class.

- Have students turn to **Writer's Notebook page 9.9** or the list of goals they set at the beginning of this Writing Workshop. Ask them to revisit the goals they set before writing on **Writer's Notebook page 9.3**. Then have them Turn and Talk with a partner about their goals. Encourage them to write how they met their goals, and goals they might set for their next writing assignment.

EL ENGLISH LEARNER SUPPORT: Elicit Participation

ALL LEVELS Before they share their research reports with the class, allow students to make an audio recording of their report. Have them listen to the recording and take notes about areas they want to improve. Then have them make a second recording, listen, and note their progress. They may want to read along with this recording several times before they give their report to the class.

Expository Essay

FOCUS STATEMENT Discoveries, big or small, personal or from others, are exciting.

FOCAL TEXT

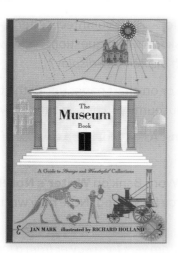

The Museum Book: A Guide to Strange and Wonderful Collections

Author: Jan Mark

Illustrator: Richard Holland

Summary: A history and exploration of museums.

WRITING PROMPT

READ the following sentence: *Museums are full of fascinating discoveries.*

THINK about a discovery someone has made that is featured in a museum.

WRITE about that discovery. Describe the discovery and explain how it was used, what it is, when it existed, what it did, and why it's in a museum.

LESSONS

1. **Introducing the Focal Text**

2. **Vocabulary**

3. **Prewriting I: Preparing to Write**

4. **Prewriting II: Conducting Research**

5. **Drafting I: Beginning the Draft**

6. **Drafting II: Integrating the Research**

7. **Drafting III: Completing the Draft**

8. **Revising I: Varying Sentence Length**

9. **Revising II: Conferencing**

10. **Revising III: Adding Transitions**

11. **Revising IV: The Central Idea**

12. **Editing I: Spelling and Mechanics**

13. **Editing II: Peer Proofreading**

14. **Publishing**

15. **Sharing**

LEARNING MINDSET:
Problem Solving

Display **Anchor Chart 31: My Learning Mindset** throughout the year. Refer to it to introduce Problem Solving and to reinforce the skills you introduced in previous modules.

LEARNING OBJECTIVES

- Brainstorm words and phrases on a topic.
- Use background knowledge to prepare to read.
- Discuss genre features of informative text.
- Discuss an author's audience and purpose.
- Read informational text with purpose and understanding.
- Analyze an informational text for author's craft.
- **Language** Share personal experiences orally to build background.

MATERIALS   Online

Writer's Notebook *p. 10.1*

Display and Engage *10.1*

Focal Text *The Museum Book*

 INSTRUCTIONAL VOCABULARY

- **glossary** the section of a book that gives the pronunciation and meaning of a word
- **index** the section of a book that shows the page number of different topics in the book
- **allusion** a reference to another person, place, thing, event, or literary work

Priming the Students

Explore the Topic

- Tell students that in this module, they will investigate discoveries made by researchers, explorers, and others.

- Point out that one of the best places to look at the discoveries of others is in a museum. Essentially, a museum houses the discoveries people have made over time.

- Ask students if they have visited a museum before. Have volunteers offer specific features of the museum, including exhibits. Ask follow-up questions: *How were the exhibits arranged? What was featured along with the items on display?*

- List appropriate words and ideas on the board or on chart paper under the title *Museums We Have Visited*. Add the names of museums you have visited as well.

- Point out that there are many kinds of museums. Ask: *What is the purpose of a museum?*

- Encourage students to add these ideas to the Word Bank on **Writer's Notebook page 10.1** or their own notebooks as a resource for writing. Note how writing things down extends memory.

- Ask: *What might it feel like to look at something from very far away or from a long time ago?* Model thinking about a display:

  THINK ALOUD *I remember when I went to the National Gallery in Washington, DC, to the King Tut Exhibit. I couldn't believe all the fine jewelry the ancient Egyptians had crafted with gold, precious stones, and turquoise. What discoveries they made! And then I was astonished by their discovery of how to preserve people as mummies.*

- Show students brochures from museums or show websites for different museums. As you look at the pictures, have students describe what they are seeing. Add interesting words and phrases to the list on the board and have students add them to their Word Banks.

> **Online**
>
> **DISPLAY AND ENGAGE**
>
> Expository Essay 10.1
>
> **Focus Statement**
>
> Discoveries, big or small, personal or from others, are exciting.
>
> Grade 4 | Writing Workshop   Module 10

Discuss the Focus Statement

Show **Display and Engage 10.1**. Read the Focus Statement with students. Have students write a few sentences that share their thoughts about the Focus Statement.

 ENGLISH LEARNER SUPPORT: Support Discussion

SUBSTANTIAL
Offer sentence frames to support volunteers in sharing their experiences.

MODERATE
Ask volunteers to share words and phrases about their museum visits to add to the board.

LIGHT
Ask volunteers to share the purpose of the museums they visited. Supply this frame: *At _____, people learn about _____.*

Priming the Text

Prepare to Read

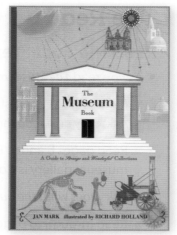

The Museum Book

- Show the cover of *The Museum Book*. Point out the subtitle: *A Guide to Strange and Wonderful Collections*. Talk about why books have subtitles. (*to tell more about what the book is about; to entice readers*)

- Point out that this book is an informational text and will give detailed information about a topic. Page through the book with students and discuss its organization, pointing out chapters, headings, words with definitions, and captions.

- Ask: *Why might the author have included these text features?* (*to help readers know what each section is about; to help readers better understand the text*)

- Write the words *guide, strange*, and *wonderful* on the board. Discuss their meanings. Have students add them to their Word Banks.

- Have students think about the difference between the meanings of *strange* and *wonderful*.

- Ask: *What might be something strange you might see in a museum? What might be something wonderful?*

- Page through the book with students and have them describe what they see. Give ample time for students to make observations and become familiar with the text. Take notes on the board or chart paper.

- Point out the typewriter and old building on the dedication page. Note that the typewriter shows up again at the end of the book on p. 52.

- Ask: *Why would the author and illustrator start and end with all those old-time buildings and objects?* (*to indicate to readers that the things discussed in the book are old*)

- Discuss what a **glossary** (p. 50) is with students, and have them add a definition for it to their Instructional Vocabulary glossaries.

- Show the **index** on p. 52. Talk about the function of an index in a book. Then discuss the difference between a glossary and an index. Have students add *index* to their glossaries.

Engage and Respond

- Have students Turn and Talk to a partner. Have them tell what they want to learn by reading *The Museum Book*, and why.

**LEARNING MINDSET:
Problem Solving**

Introduce Explain to students that it's normal to have to try several different ways to solve a problem. *Many discoveries are the result of someone uncovering a problem and then working hard to find a solution. You'll learn in* The Museum Book *how many collectors and museum curators ran into problems when deciding how to store and display their collections. They thought hard about how to best solve their problems, and then worked towards a solution.* Tell students that when they encounter a problem while writing, they should keep these collectors and curators in mind: *Think hard about how to best solve your problems and try different things to solve them.*

The Read

Read the Focal Text

- As you read *The Museum Book*, stop at these points to discuss text features.

  » Read page 7. Use a stage whisper as you read the last sentence on that page. Ask: *Why did I read that with a whisper?*

  » Read pages 8 and 9. Point out that the author is describing how different a museum gallery is from other types of buildings.

  » Ask: *Does what the author described sound like a zoo? Why or why not?*

  » Read through to page 12. Ask: *Why did the author include this dialogue with the guide?*

- Point out the many museum objects and people mentioned in this first chapter, such as *Queen Elizabeth I, totem poles,* and *a Viking ship.*

- In their Instructional Vocabulary glossaries, have students define **allusion** as *a reference to another person, place, thing, event, or literary work.* Point out that an allusion can be stated *(She is like Cinderella around animals.)* or it can be implied *(He is right out of a fairy tale.)*. Add the word **allusion** to the class Instructional Vocabulary list.

- Make certain students understand that allusions deepen our understanding because our minds automatically add the information from the allusion to its new context.

- Continue to read *The Museum Book* with students. Have students note any time they hear an interesting word, sentence, or idea. Have them write interesting words and phrases in their Word Banks.

- Continue reading as time permits.

Engage and Respond

- Have students write two or three sentences that answer the questions, *Did the author of The Museum Book keep readers interested? How?* Have students share their ideas with a partner.

 ENGLISH LEARNER SUPPORT: Elicit Participation

SUBSTANTIAL

To help students write sentences for the Engage and Respond activity, ask students to share what they found interesting in *The Museum Book*. Students may point, answer in simple words or phrases, or respond in their home language.

MODERATE

Supply this sentence frame: *The author of The Museum Book kept readers interested by _____.*

LIGHT

If possible, allow additional time for students to recite their sentences before sharing ideas with a partner.

LEARNING OBJECTIVES

- Read and understand domain-specific vocabulary.
- **Language** Explain meaning of domain-specific vocabulary.
- **Language** Label parts of speech.

MATERIALS
Online

Focal Text *The Museum Book*
Writer's Notebook *p. 10.1*
Display and Engage 10.2

TEACHER TIP

Encourage students to include the page number from *The Museum Book* if the Word Bank word is illustrated there. If it is not illustrated, suggest that they draw a picture to go with the word.

Review the Focal Text

- Review with students the first chapter of *The Museum Book*. Explain that it is rich with vocabulary and allusions.

- Have students return to the Word Bank on **Writer's Notebook page 10.1** or in their own notebooks. Page through *The Museum Book* and have students identify additional words and phrases, such as the words below, that they find interesting. Pause to discuss why each is interesting, and have students add the words to their Word Banks.

museum	locomotive	Viking ship
temple	engine	pandas
mosque	Queen Elizabeth I	whales
church	diamonds	dinosaurs
furniture	meteorites	tsar

- Show **Display and Engage 10.2**. Read the directions with students. Have students form pairs to identify each entry in the Word Bank.

- Have students look up the words on their lists using a dictionary or other resource.

- Then have students take one of the common nouns and change it to an adjective by putting it in a sentence. Model with this example: *We went to buy pottery at the pottery store.* Have students share their sentences with a partner.

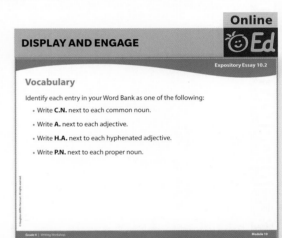

DISPLAY AND ENGAGE
Online

Expository Essay 10.2

Vocabulary

Identify each entry in your Word Bank as one of the following:
- Write **C.N.** next to each common noun.
- Write **A.** next to each adjective.
- Write **H.A.** next to each hyphenated adjective.
- Write **P.N.** next to each proper noun.

- Ask students what *Diplodocus, Tyrannosaurus rex,* and *dodo* have in common. *(all extinct)*

- Ask students what Queen Elizabeth I and Peter the Great have in common. *(rulers, all dead)*

Engage and Respond

- Have students choose one word from the Word Bank and write a few sentences explaining why they find the word interesting.

 ENGLISH LEARNER SUPPORT: Elicit Participation

SUBSTANTIAL
Allow students to explain the chosen word orally to a partner.

MODERATE
Provide sentence frames for students. *I think _____ is interesting because _____.*

LIGHT
Have student pairs discuss their chosen words aloud before writing down their thoughts.

INFORMATIONAL TEXT • EXPOSITORY ESSAY

LEARNING OBJECTIVES

- Understand features of informative writing.
- Set goals for writing.
- Use multiple prewriting strategies to plan writing.
- **Language** Discuss goals for writing.

MATERIALS Online ⊙Ed

Anchor Chart W5: *Informational Text*
Display and Engage *10.3*
Writer's Notebook *pp. 10.2–10.3*

TEACHER TIP

Model setting goals for writing expository essays. For example, encourage students to include three new facts about the topic and use both a print source and an online source to find information.

Review the Writing Process

- Tell students they will write an expository essay. Review the steps of the writing process. Point out that good writers take care to complete each step before moving to the next step and that sometimes writers discover they need to return to an earlier step.

- Display **Anchor Chart W5: Informational Text** and read the points with students. Talk about different informational texts students have read. Have them note features they liked about those texts. Write their ideas on the board.

- Show **Display and Engage 10.3** and read the Writing Prompt together. Note the tips.

- Distribute **Writer's Notebook page 10.2**. Discuss the different expectations of the rubric. Remind students they can use this rubric as a resource while drafting and revising.

Set Goals for Writing

- Point out that good writers think about what they want to improve with each new piece they write. Have students think about what goals they would like to set for their expository essays. Have them set their goals by adding to the list on **Writer's Notebook page 10.3** or writing goals in their own notebooks.

Informational Text

Introduction
- hooks the readers
- includes the central idea

Body
- supports the central idea with facts and details
- gives reasons and examples
- uses an organizational strategy

Conclusion
- restates the central idea
- leaves readers with a thought

Purpose
Informational texts often
- describe things, people, or events
- show sequence
- compare things
- show cause and effect
- show a problem and its solution

Expository Essay 10.3

Writing Prompt: Expository Essay

READ the following sentence: *Museums are full of fascinating discoveries.*

THINK about a discovery someone has made that is featured in a museum.

WRITE about that discovery. Describe the discovery and explain how it was used, what it is, when it existed, what it did, and why it's in a museum.

Be sure to —
- clearly state your central idea
- develop your writing in detail
- choose your words carefully
- use correct spelling, capitalization, punctuation, grammar, and sentences

Grade 4 | Writing Workshop   Module 10

 ENGLISH LEARNER SUPPORT: Facilitate Discussion

SUBSTANTIAL
Review students' last piece of writing with them. Talk about different goals they can work toward with the new piece. Write these goals for students and have students copy the goals into their Writer's Notebooks.

MODERATE
Discuss students' writing goals. Provide sentence frames to write the goals as needed.

LIGHT
Have student pairs discuss their writing goals before writing them down.

INFORMATIONAL TEXT • EXPOSITORY ESSAY

LEARNING OBJECTIVES

- Use multiple prewriting strategies to plan writing.
- Conduct research for writing.
- **Language** Discuss writing tasks using academic language.

MATERIALS   Online

Display and Engage *10.3*

Writer's Notebook *pp. 10.4–10.6*

TEACHER TIP

For the essay topic, you may want to cut the topics on the Writer's Notebook page into strips. Place the strips into a hat or box and have students draw randomly.

Discuss the Writing Prompt

- Show **Display and Engage 10.3** and read the Writing Prompt together. Note the tips.

- Distribute **Writer's Notebook page 10.4**. Tell students that these are the topics they can choose from to write their expository essays. Have students choose one of the topics and write what they already know about the topic. Allow students to choose their own topics if they wish.

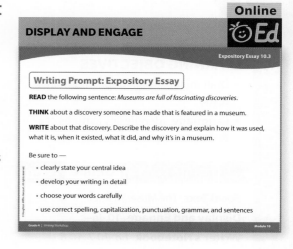

- Explain to students that after they have chosen a topic, they should identify their audience and purpose for writing. Distribute **Writer's Notebook page 10.5** and have them identify their audience and purpose.

Conduct Research

- Tell students they are going to conduct research.

- Model how to begin research by doing an Internet search. Use your own search as a model. Use this model for a search on the dodo bird:

  THINK ALOUD *I did a search for* dodo bird *and found lots of interesting information, so I took notes. Remember, writing extends our memory. I didn't just copy what was on the Internet because I want to use my own words. So I jotted down facts, details, and examples to refer to when I begin writing. Here is a sample of what I wrote down:*

  » *The dodo was a flightless bird. It was about three feet tall.*

  » *It lived on the island of Mauritius.*

  » *It went extinct in 1662.*

- Depending upon resources, take students to the library or computer lab or work out a schedule for students to use the classroom library and technology.

- Demonstrate how to do an Internet search for topics by name and how to look up topics in books using the index and table of contents.

- Together with students, check available databases.

- Show students the URL on a website and explain its function. Tell students to copy each URL into their notes so they can easily refer to the website later on.

Begin Prewriting

- Have students begin to plan their writing by conducting research about their topics. Have them take notes on **Writer's Notebook page 10.6** or on index cards.

INFORMATIONAL TEXT • EXPOSITORY ESSAY

LEARNING OBJECTIVES

- Draft multiple-paragraph informative texts.
- **Language** Identify key features of a text.

MATERIALS   Online

Focal Text *The Museum Book*

Display and Engage *10.4a–c*

Writer's Notebook *pp. 10.7, 10.8*

Classroom materials *crayons or colored pencils*

Prepare to Draft

- As students move from their notes to their drafts, discuss ways to make their expository essays more interesting. Display the following items on the board, and have students write them in their notebooks:

  - the odd museum object itself
  - the facts you found in your research
  - the way you write those facts

- Point out how boring *The Museum Book* would be if it said something like this in that first chapter:

  THINK ALOUD *A museum is a place that holds interesting things like steam locomotives, Viking ships, rocks, totem poles, stuffed fish, stuffed animals, Roman pottery, a real airplane, two-headed sheep, teeth, World War I tanks, and lots of old stuff.*

- Ask: *Why would that be boring?*

- Tell students that a simple list isn't interesting and this is where the craft of writing comes in. Good writers craft the information to make it interesting to the reader.

- Distribute **Writer's Notebook page 10.7**. Review how to organize ideas and research into the graphic organizer.

- Return to the opening of Chapter One of *The Museum Book* (p. 7), and ask the students how Jan Mark, the author, made it interesting to read.

- Show **Display and Engage 10.4a, 10.4b, and 10.4c** and distribute **Writer's Notebook page 10.8**. Read through the model essay with the students as they identify the introduction, the body, and the conclusion. Encourage them to mark the essay's text structure in different colors.

- Have students identify the hook and the central idea. Have them draw a red box around the central idea.

Online 🍎Ed

DISPLAY AND ENGAGE

Expository Essay 10.4a

The Extinct Dodo Bird

Imagine arriving on a tropical island, one that not many humans have ever seen. After a long voyage, it might feel great to be on land. Imagine looking around—and seeing big fluffy birds, nearly as tall as you! In the early sixteenth century, Portuguese sailors had this very experience as they laid eyes on the dodo bird. Sadly, dodo birds are extinct today, but they still fascinate people.

- Go to the body of the model essay. Ask students to find a definition, details, description, facts, and examples. Have them explain how the new fact in the conclusion is connected to the entire essay.

Begin to Draft

- Have students begin to draft their expository essays using the notes and graphic organizers from their notebooks.

- Circulate and offer assistance as needed.

LEARNING OBJECTIVES

- Find and use research in expository writing.
- Correctly quote from sources.
- **Language** Use commas and quotation marks correctly.

MATERIALS   Online

Focal Text *The Museum Book*

Display and Engage *10.4a–10.4c*

INSTRUCTIONAL VOCABULARY

- **internal documentation** a note in text showing the source that a quote or specific piece of information comes from

Introduce the Skill

- Turn to page 17 of *The Museum Book* and read it with students. Point out that although it is part of Chapter Two, it can stand alone as an expository essay.

- Help students draw the conclusion that if this is how published writers write essays, they should follow the model.

- Instruct students about how to incorporate resources into their papers. Again use the model on **Display and Engage 10.4a, 10.4b, 10.4c** as a mentor text.

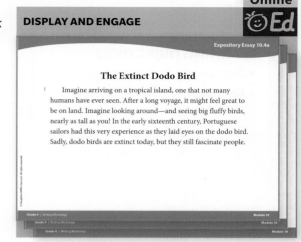

- Call students' attention to this sentence: *"The birds were first seen by Portuguese sailors in about 1507 ('History of the Dodo Bird')."*

- Point out that since this sentence contains a date, it is directly quoted from a reputable source: an encyclopedia. The reader knows where it comes from and that it wasn't made up. The reader can locate the source to read more about the topic.

- Explain the steps of integrating research.

  1. *If I use direct words or a statistic or fact for my paper from something I am reading, I put that in quotation marks. (It is like a person is telling you.)*

  2. *Then I add an open parenthesis.*

  3. *I write the source of the quotation after the open parenthesis by writing the last name of the author followed by the first name or initials and a period. Then I write the title of the book. I underline it or put it in italics.*

  4. *If my source is an article, I do the same thing, but I put the title in quotation marks.*

  5. *If my source is a website, I write the name of the website, the date I got the information, the URL, and the author's name if it is available.*

  6. *I close the parenthesis and write a period or continue the sentence.*

- Give students several examples.

- Give students a few sources to practice with. Tell them this is called **internal documentation**. Add that term to the class Instructional Vocabulary list and have students write it in their glossaries.

Continue to Draft

- Circulate the room, offering assistance to students as needed.

- If time allows, ask for volunteers who have used internal documentation. Have these volunteers explain why they used the piece of information and point out the different parts of the documentation.

INFORMATIONAL TEXT • EXPOSITORY ESSAY

LEARNING OBJECTIVES

- Draft an expository essay.
- **Language** Review key grammar topics.

TARGETED GRAMMAR SUPPORT

You may want to consult the following grammar minilessons to review key topics.

- **2.1.5 Using Proper Nouns,** p. W240
- **4.1.5 Using Adjectives,** p. W300
- **4.2.5 Using Adverbs,** p. W305

LEARNING MINDSET: Problem Solving

Normalize Explain to students that it's normal to have to try different things when completing a writing task. *Sometimes an idea you are writing about just doesn't work or it doesn't make sense. A key part of drafting is experimenting, so don't worry if something doesn't work. Try rewriting your idea or ask a partner for help.* As you circulate the room, encourage students to try rewriting sentences or ideas to see if a different wording sounds better. Give praise freely.

Circulate the Room

- Remind students that they can continue to use different resources, including their prewriting notes, dictionaries, and the Internet, to assist them with their writing.

- Explain to students that they should keep the structure of their essays in mind as they write. Tell them they should write an engaging introduction, a body with examples that support the central idea, and a conclusion that wraps up the essay.

- Have students continue to spend time writing their essays.

- Circulate the room, offering assistance and praise. When giving praise, use concrete examples of what the student has done correctly. For example: *Your hook really grabs my attention. You use concrete details to describe the topic.*

- As you circulate, group students who need support on similar grammar topics. Use the grammar minilessons or the students' own writing to provide targeted review and support.

 ENGLISH LEARNER SUPPORT: Discuss Language Structures

SUBSTANTIAL
Share examples of sentences that contain a grammar point students need to practice. Have students copy one or two of the sentences to provide exposure to the grammar point.

MODERATE
Provide sentences with blanks where grammar points are emphasized. Have students work together to complete the sentences. Ensure students have used grammar correctly and discuss changes if needed.

LIGHT
Have students review their writing for grammar points that have been especially tricky for them.

REVISING I: VARYING SENTENCE LENGTH

LEARNING OBJECTIVES

- Revise drafts to improve sentence structure by combining sentences.
- **Language** Apply knowledge of sentence structure to writing.
- **Language** Use different sentence lengths.

MATERIALS	Online Ed

Focal Text *The Museum Book, pp. 30–31*

Introduce the Revision Skill

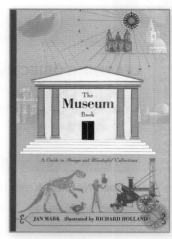

The Museum Book

- Tell students that an important part of revising is looking at the lengths of their sentences. Point out that good writers use sentences of different lengths to keep readers engaged. Turn to *The Museum Book* pp. 30–31 and read the first paragraph. Read in a monotone voice for several seconds.

- Ask students how boring it would be to listen to a speaker talking in just a single, flat tone. Tell them that is like a paper written with all the same length sentences. It is visually boring.

- Write the word *sentence* on the board. Say the word aloud so it sounds like *SENSE-TICE*. Use this model:

  THINK ALOUD *The word* sense *seems to have been born around 1200, when it meant* a statement of authority. *In the 1400s, the meaning changed to* a verdict or a decision in court. *But by the 1500s, it meant* meaning or, *specifically,* meaning expressed in words. *The word comes to us from the Latin but moved into late Middle English and now is part of modern English grammar.*

- Write the following sentence and read it aloud: *A sentence makes sense.* Point out that to make sense, sentences must have at least a subject and a verb; someone or something is doing something. Everything else in the sentence expands or clarifies these two things. Point out that another word for making sense is *coherenc.*

- Explain that, like boxes of cereal, sentences come in a variety of sizes and fit a variety of tastes.

- Some are the family-size sentences—long ones with lots of things embedded.

- Some are the mini-size sentences—short, maybe even one or two words.

- Display these sentences: *Dogs bark. Dogs bark at the postman when he knocks on the door. Dogs bark at the postman when he knocks on the door, but they also bark a welcome bark when their owners come home.*

- Explain that good writers vary their sentence lengths as a way to keep their readers interested. Discuss how each sentence adds more information about the basic action of the first sentence.

Revise for Sentence Structure

- Have students revisit their drafts to vary sentence length. Remind them to look for opportunities to revise their sentences by shortening or combining sentences for clarity and coherence.

 ENGLISH LEARNER SUPPORT: Scaffold Revision

SUBSTANTIAL
Work with students individually to orally add details to their simple sentences. Transcribe their longer sentences, and read them aloud with students.

MODERATE
Have student pairs work together to combine sentences.

LIGHT
As students revise, ask them to share how they improved the variety of sentence lengths in their writing.

INFORMATIONAL TEXT • EXPOSITORY ESSAY

LEARNING OBJECTIVES
- Revise an expository essay.
- **Language** Discuss writing in small group conferences.

MATERIALS   Online Ed

Writer's Notebook pp. 10.9–10.10
Display and Engage 10.5

LEARNING MINDSET:
Problem Solving

Apply Tell students that when they think they have solved a problem with their writing, they should check to be sure the solution has worked. Tell them it is okay to make changes if they notice something wrong or discover a better solution. Remind them that revising is a kind of problem solving.

Small Group Conferences

- Have students turn to **Writer's Notebook page 10.9**, and review the sentence starters. Then turn to **Writer's Notebook page 10.10**. Point out the revision checklist and read it with students. Tell them they will use this checklist to guide their small group conferences.

- Tell students that it is time to read their classmates' writing and provide feedback.

  » Divide the class into small groups of four or five.

  » Writers read aloud, pause, and then read again.

  » Listeners listen. Upon the second reading, they take notes—a word or a phrase—to help them remember anything they may wish to comment upon.

- After the reading, the group comments, suggests, and discusses by using **Display and Engage 10.5**.

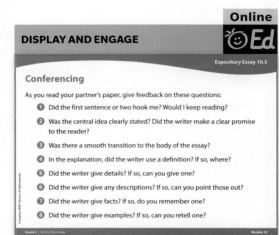

Online Ed

DISPLAY AND ENGAGE

Expository Essay 10.5

Conferencing

As you read your partner's paper, give feedback on these questions:

1. Did the first sentence or two hook me? Would I keep reading?
2. Was the central idea clearly stated? Did the writer make a clear promise to the reader?
3. Was there a smooth transition to the body of the essay?
4. In the explanation, did the writer use a definition? If so, where?
5. Did the writer give details? If so, can you give one?
6. Did the writer give any descriptions? If so, can you point those out?
7. Did the writer give facts? If so, do you remember one?
8. Did the writer give examples? If so, can you retell one?

Grade 4 | Writing Workshop   Module 10

- Debrief with the class. Discuss students' responses to the following questions.

  - What have you learned about writing essays?

  - How is writing an expository essay different than writing a personal narrative?

  - Which do you like writing more? Why?

Continue to Revise

- Have students continue to revise, using the feedback they gained in the small group conferences.

 ENGLISH LEARNER SUPPORT: Elicit Participation

SUBSTANTIAL
If necessary, rephrase questions so students can respond in single words or short phrases.

MODERATE
Supply sentence frames such as *I learned _____ about writing essays. I like writing _____.*

LIGHT
Challenge students to use this sentence frame: *Writing an expository essay is different than writing a personal narrative because _____.*

LEARNING OBJECTIVES

- Revise writing to link ideas.
- **Language** Use conjunctions to link sentences.
- **Language** Combine sentences.

MATERIALS
Online Ed

Display and Engage *10.4a–c*

Classroom materials *crayons or colored pencils*

 INSTRUCTIONAL VOCABULARY

- **transition word** a word that connects ideas

TARGETED GRAMMAR SUPPORT

You may want to consult the following grammar minilessons to review key grammar topics.

- **1.4.1 Compound Sentences,** p. W231
- **1.4.2 Complex Sentences,** p. W232
- **3.2.2 Helping Verbs and Past Participles,** p. W272

Introduce the Revision Skill

- Point out that an important part of revising is adding transition words to writing. **Transition words** help readers clearly understand how ideas are linked in writing.

- Have students write a definition for *transition word* in their Instructional Vocabulary glossaries if they have not already.

- Revisit the model on **Display and Engage 10.4**.

- Have students point out different transition words in the model. Have students underline the transition words in yellow.

- Discuss how the words make the model expository essay stronger.

- Point out that as they revise their papers for organization, students may discover that they want to combine sentences using transition words.

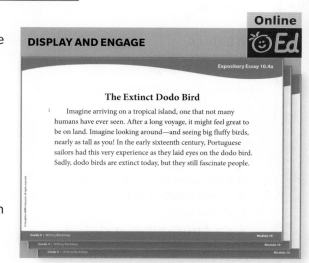

Online Ed

DISPLAY AND ENGAGE

Expository Essay 10.4a

The Extinct Dodo Bird

Imagine arriving on a tropical island, one that not many humans have ever seen. After a long voyage, it might feel great to be on land. Imagine looking around—and seeing big fluffy birds, nearly as tall as you! In the early sixteenth century, Portuguese sailors had this very experience as they laid eyes on the dodo bird. Sadly, dodo birds are extinct today, but they still fascinate people.

Revise for Organization

- Have students revise for transition words.

- Circulate the room and assist students with revising. If students need help with a specific grammar topic, do a direct teach.

- As you circulate, group students who need support on similar grammar topics. Use the grammar minilessons or the students' own writing to provide targeted review and support.

 ENGLISH LEARNER SUPPORT: Scaffold Revision

SUBSTANTIAL
Guide students to find one place in their writing where a conjunction could link ideas.

MODERATE
Encourage students to highlight or underline transition words in their writing. Remind them to look for the transition words the group discussed.

LIGHT
As you circulate, ask students to share their strongest examples of transition words. Guide revision as needed.

INFORMATIONAL TEXT • EXPOSITORY ESSAY

LEARNING OBJECTIVES

- Revise writing for ideas.
- Use a strong topic sentence.
- **Language** Write correctly formed sentences.

MATERIALS   Online

Display and Engage 10.6

TARGETED GRAMMAR SUPPORT

You may want to consult the following grammar minilessons to review key grammar topics.

- **1.2.5 Using Different Kinds of Sentences,** p. W225
- **3.1.1 Action Verbs,** p. W266

Introduce the Revision Skill

- Explain that all expository essays must have a central idea, and it must be stated early in the paper.

- Teach *promise* as the kid-friendly synonym for *central idea*. Explain that the central idea is the writer's promise to the reader.

- Show **Display and Engage 10.6**. Read together the *Five Do's and Don't's* for writing a good central idea. Explain to students that if they learn and use these, they will have an easier time revising their expository essays.

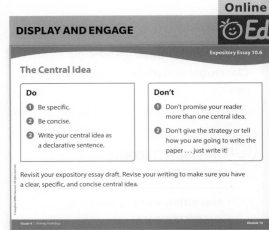

- Have students write these do's and don'ts on their own paper to use as a resource later.

- Use the focal text as an example. Write *I am going to explain about museums* on the board. Say: *Suppose Jan Mark had written: I am going to explain about museums. Does that topic sentence fit the do's we just talked about?*

- Point out how the extra words, such as *am going to explain*, make the writing weaker. Explain that these words are extra and unnecessary because expository writing is supposed to explain and readers expect to read an explanation. Note that those extra words just take up space and weaken the writing.

  THINK ALOUD   *To review, to write a central idea, you must make sure you are specific, concise, and make a statement. You shouldn't try to promise two or more things or tell how you are going to write the paper.*

Revise for Ideas

- Have students revise the central idea according to the criteria.

- As you circulate, group students who need support on similar grammar topics. Use the grammar minilessons or the students' own writing to provide targeted review and support.

 ENGLISH LEARNER SUPPORT: Scaffold Revision

SUBSTANTIAL
Read students' writing aloud, sentence by sentence. Discuss whether each sentence shows the intended meaning. If not, work together to revise to focus the ideas.

MODERATE
Have students form pairs. Have one student read the other's essay aloud, pausing after each sentence to discuss whether the writer's intended meaning is clear. If not, the pair should revise the sentence before continuing.

LIGHT
Have students use the five *Do's* and *Don't's* to analyze their own essays. Encourage students to read through their writing, focusing on one *do* or *don't* at a time.

INFORMATIONAL TEXT • EXPOSITORY ESSAY

LEARNING OBJECTIVES

- **Language** Proofread writing for spelling.
- **Language** Edit writing for capitalization, punctuation, and mechanics.

MATERIALS

Online

Anchor Chart W13: *Editing Checklist*

TARGETED GRAMMAR SUPPORT

You may want to consult the following grammar minilessons to review key grammar topics.

- **2.3.3 Pronoun-Antecedent Agreement,** p. W248
- **6.2.1 End of Sentence Punctuation,** p. W336
- **6.1.5 Using Quotations,** p. W335

Review Proofreading Checklist

- Revisit **Anchor Chart W13: Editing Checklist**.
- Review the items on the Editing Checklist. Review how to use proofreading marks.
- As needed, revisit grammar topics on which students may need additional review or practice.

Proofread Writing

- Have students independently edit their writing for spelling, mechanics, punctuation, and grammar.
- Circulate the room and provide assistance as needed.
- As you circulate, group students who need support on similar grammar topics. Use the grammar minilessons or the students' own writing to provide targeted review and support.

ANCHOR CHART Online

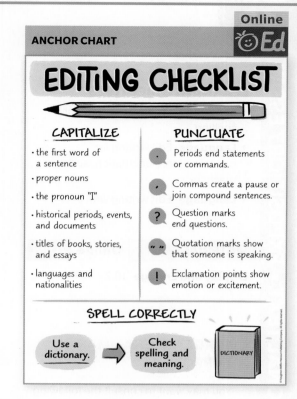

 ENGLISH LEARNER SUPPORT: Support Editing

ALL LEVELS Review students' writing with them. As you encounter a grammatical error, write on a separate piece of paper a sentence with the same grammatical error using different words. Discuss the grammatical error with students, and guide them to correct the same mistake in their own writing.

LEARNING OBJECTIVES

- **Language** Proofread writing for spelling.
- **Language** Edit writing for capitalization, punctuation, and mechanics.
- **Language** Edit writing with peer support.

MATERIALS   Online

Display and Engage *10.7*

TARGETED GRAMMAR SUPPORT

You may want to consult the following grammar minilessons to review key editing topics.

- **6.4.1 Capitalization and Writing Titles,** p. W346
- **6.2.4 Review Punctuation,** p. W339
- **1.2.3 Four Kinds of Sentences,** p. W223

Clocking Activity

- Review the rules for clocking.

  » Students form concentric circles or sit opposite each other in rows, hence the term clocking. In rows it is called digital clocking. As students receive a peer's paper, they become that paper's editor.

  » Call out what item is to be checked by the editor: spelling, its/it's, capital letters, and so forth.

  » You may also want the students to move after a couple of items so each student's paper is read by several editors.

  » No marks are made on the actual paper. All papers should have an editing page with their name at the top.

  » Each editor places his or her name next to the number in turn and writes the concept to be checked.

  » When the editing process is completed, the students take their editing page and make any corrections. If there is a problem, they may discuss it with their editor or the teacher.

- Show **Display and Engage 10.7** and discuss the checklist for editing an expository essay.

DISPLAY AND ENGAGE   Online

Expository Essay 10.7

Editing Checklist

Use this checklist as you edit your expository essay.

- ☐ Check that there is a name on the paper.
- ☐ Check that all the subjects and verbs agree.
- ☐ Check that every sentence has the correct punctuation.
- ☐ Check that every research citation is formatted correctly.
- ☐ Check that each sentence begins with a capital letter.
- ☐ Check that every compound sentence has a coordinating conjunction and a comma.

Grade 4 | Writing Workshop   Module 10

Edit Writing

- Have students do a final pass through their expository essays, integrating the notes from the clocking activity into their own writing.

- As you circulate, group students who need support on similar grammar topics. Use the grammar minilessons or the students' own writing to provide targeted review and support.

LESSON 14 — PUBLISHING

LEARNING OBJECTIVES
- Publish writing.
- Use technology to assist with writing.

MATERIALS Online Ed

Focal Text *The Museum Book*, p. 17

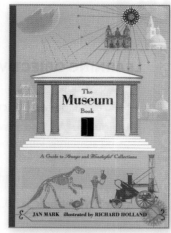

The Museum Book

Prepare the Final Copy

- Return to page 17 of *The Museum Book*. Suggest that if ideas *come from the Muses*, as the text says, and that the muses took care of the different kinds of ideas, such as *history, music, comedy*, and *poetry*, a good topic for an expository essay could have been about one or more of these Muses.

- Tell students that the content of their expository essays will give them ideas on interesting ways to publish their papers. Provide a few examples for an essay about one of the Muses:

> a. They could add a page of poetry as a prologue or epilogue for the topic.
>
> b. They could play background music that would go with the topic.
>
> c. They could capture the topic through dance—on a video perhaps.
>
> d. They could write something funny to introduce the topic.
>
> e. They could bring in something historical to enhance the essay.

Publish Writing

- Discuss with students the different publishing options they have available.

- Have student pairs work together to plan their final copies. Circulate the room and give tips to students.

- Have students spend the remainder of the time preparing the final copy and creating the publishing format.

TEACHER TIP

Group students according to their choices for the essay about one of the Muses. Have the group create a sample that they can refer to as they work.

LESSON 15

LEARNING OBJECTIVES

- Share writing.
- Hold a collaborative discussion.
- **Language** Ask and answer questions using academic language.

MATERIALS	Online

Writer's Notebook *p. 10.11*

 LEARNING MINDSET:
Problem Solving

Review Remind students that problem solving means figuring out how to resolve issues when they arise. *Sometimes you have lots of time to think about a plan. In other instances, you have to be ready to solve a problem as soon as it comes up, such as if something goes wrong when you are presenting to a group.* Encourage students to think about what problems might arise during their presentations and think about how they might solve those problems.

Share Writing

- Have students share their expository essays by reading them aloud. Have them discuss ideas they had for publishing and presenting that they gleaned from the Muses.

- Encourage students to ask the presenter questions about the presentation. Remind students of the rules of asking questions. Encourage the speaker to answer with details he or she learned from research.

Engage and Respond

- Conclude with an informal debriefing about how students felt about doing research, incorporating it, and presenting it.

- Have students turn to **Writer's Notebook page 10.11** or the list of goals they set at the beginning of this Writing Workshop. Have them revisit the goals they set before writing. Have them Turn and Talk with a partner about how they feel they met their goals and take notes about what goals they might set for the next writing assignment.

 ENGLISH LEARNER SUPPORT: Support Presenting

ALL LEVELS Work with students who may be intimidated by presenting. Assist them with pronouncing difficult words and speaking fluently. Model presenting by using the model essay as a guide.

Poem

FOCUS STATEMENT Poetry is both delightful and magical.

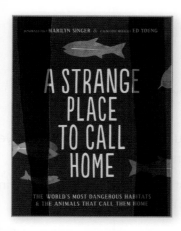

FOCAL TEXT

A Strange Place to Call Home: The World's Most Dangerous Habitats & the Animals that Call Them Home

Author: Marilyn Singer

Illustrator: Ed Young

Summary: A collection of poems, featuring many different forms, that tells about different animals and the extreme habitats in which they live.

WRITING PROMPT

READ the following sentence: *Poetry is both delightful and magical.*

THINK about a topic that you find interesting.

WRITE a series of poems on that topic using several different forms.

LESSONS

1. **Introducing the Focal Text**

2. **Vocabulary**

3. **Prewriting I: Limericks**

4. **Prewriting II: Riddle Poems**

5. **Prewriting III: Haiku and Tanka**

6. **Prewriting IV: Odes**

7. **Prewriting V: Couplets, Tercets, and Quatrains**

8. **Drafting I: Beginning the Draft**

9. **Drafting II: Sensory Language**

10. **Drafting III: Completing the Draft**

11. **Revising I: Revising Poetry**

12. **Revising II: Conferencing**

13. **Editing I: Peer Proofreading**

14. **Publishing**

15. **Sharing**

LEARNING MINDSET: Curiosity

Display **Anchor Chart 31: My Learning Mindset** throughout the year. Refer to it to introduce Curiosity and to reinforce the skills you introduced in previous modules.

LEARNING OBJECTIVES

- Establish purpose for reading.
- Explain use of text structure.
- **Language** Express thoughts on poetry.
- **Language** Speak using content-area vocabulary.

MATERIALS   Online

Focal Text *A Strange Place to Call Home*
Display and Engage 11.1, 11.2
Anchor Chart W10: *Elements of Poetry*
Writer's Notebook *p. 11.1*

 INSTRUCTIONAL VOCABULARY

- **poetry** a form of literature that uses rhythmic elements and often rhyme to express feelings and ideas
- **figurative language** words or expressions used in a way that means something different from their dictionary definitions
- **stanza** a group of lines that forms part of a poem

Priming the Students

Explore the Topic

- Tell students that in this module they will be exploring different types of poetry.

- Write the word **poetry** on the board. Invite students to share their definitions of poetry, and write their ideas on the board or chart paper.

- Use the following questions to discuss poetry. Help students connect with what they already know about the genre.

  - What makes poetry different from prose?
  - How do you feel about poetry?
  - Where did your feelings about poetry come from?

- Ask: *Have any of you ever written a poem?* Encourage students who answer yes to explain why and when, the title of the poem, and what it was about.

- Ask: *Does anyone have a favorite poem?* Invite students to elaborate by sharing the title of the poem, what it is about, and why it is a favorite.

- If you wish, share your feelings about poetry. For example: *I love poems that make me see or think about something in a different way. But sometimes poets get carried away, and I have no idea what they're talking about!*

- Explain that poetry uses rhythm and sometimes rhyme to express feelings and ideas. Add *poetry* to the class Instructional Vocabulary list, and have students add it to their personal lists.

DISPLAY AND ENGAGE   Online   Poem 11.1

Focus Statement

Poetry is both delightful and magical.

Grade 4 | Writing Workshop   Module 11

Discuss the Focus Statement

- Show **Display and Engage 11.1**. Read the focus statement with students. Explain that *magical* in this context means "apart from everyday life." Say: *Some synonyms for* delightful *include* pleasant, wonderful, *or* amusing. Invite students to share examples of how poems can be delightful and/or magical. Encourage students to explain their ideas.

- Have students work in small groups to share their thoughts about the focus statement. Then invite students to write a few sentences that reflect their thoughts about it.

 ENGLISH LEARNER SUPPORT: Facilitate Discussion

ALL LEVELS Ask students: *Do you know a poem in your home language? Could you share it with us?* See if students can loosely translate the meanings of the poems they share. Elicit how they feel when they are reciting or reading a poem as opposed to a story. There are also bilingual collections of poems in English with translations in other languages that you can share with students.

Priming the Text

Prepare to Read

- Show the cover of *A Strange Place to Call Home*. Read the title and subtitle. Remind students that a habitat is an animal's natural environment. Ask: *What might make a habitat dangerous? (Possible answers: temperature, food sources, predators)*

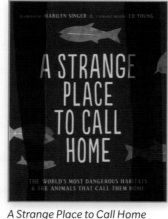

A Strange Place to Call Home

- Tell students that *A Strange Place to Call Home* is a collection of poems about animals and where they live. Ask: *Do you think the animals that live in dangerous habitats think their home is a strange place? Why or why not?* Accept all reasonable answers.

- Explain that the word *perspective* refers to a point of view, or a way of looking at something. Hold up a color photograph of a large animal, such as a lion, elephant, or giraffe. Tell students to quickly write the first three words they think of. Invite several volunteers to read their words. Point out that everyone saw the same picture, but they had different perspectives, or ways of thinking. Say: *Poetry helps us think about ordinary things from different perspectives, or points of view.*

- Go to the page with the heading "About Poetry Forms" at the end of the book. Read the page with students. Ask: *Why might a collection of different types of poems be more interesting to a reader? (Possible answer: Poems that are all alike would be boring.)*

- Display **Anchor Chart W10: Elements of Poetry**. Read the chart with students. Tell students that they will learn more about these elements as they work through this module. Invite them to watch for these elements in the poems in *A Strange Place to Call Home*.

Engage and Respond

- Explain that *A Strange Place to Call Home* combines information about animals and about poetry. Have students Turn and Talk to a partner about what they hope to learn by reading *A Strange Place to Call Home*.

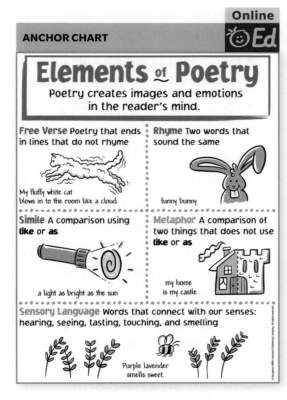

ANCHOR CHART Online Ed.

Elements of Poetry
Poetry creates images and emotions in the reader's mind.

Free Verse Poetry that ends in lines that do not rhyme

My fluffy white cat blows in to the room like a cloud

Rhyme Two words that sound the same

funny bunny

Simile A comparison using **like** or **as**

a light as bright as the sun

Metaphor A comparison of two things that does not use **like** or **as**

my home is my castle

Sensory Language Words that connect with our senses: hearing, seeing, tasting, touching, and smelling

Purple lavender smells sweet.

The Read

Read the Focal Text

- As you read poems from *A Strange Place to Call Home,* encourage students to think about these questions.

> What do you like about the poem?
>
> What don't you like?
>
> How does the author use words to create pictures?
>
> What is the main idea of the poem?

- Show **Display and Engage 11.2**. Explain that **figurative language** is important in poetry because it creates feelings and images. Discuss the types of figurative language. Encourage students to look for examples in the poems of *A Strange Place to Call Home.*

Online Ed

DISPLAY AND ENGAGE

Poem 11.2

Figurative Language

Figurative Language: words or expressions used in a way that means something different from their dictionary definitions

Types of figurative language

Simile: uses the word *like* or *as* to compare two unlike things
  Example: My feet were as cold as ice.

Metaphor: compares two unlike things by saying one is the other
  Example: She is a busy bee.

Personification: gives human qualities to objects or animals
  Example: The leaves danced in the wind.

Hyperbole: an exaggeration
  Example: I have a million things to do!

Grade 4 | Writing Workshop   Module 11

- After each poem, have students share their responses to the questions above. Point out **stanzas** (groups of lines that form parts of poems), lines that rhyme, and figurative language.

- Encourage students to write down any interesting or descriptive words or phrases from the poems on **Writer's Notebook page 11.1** or in their notebooks.

- Focus on the following poems.

  » "Frozen Solid": Ask: *Why do so many lines start with "If"? (These are all places that worms can live.)* Invite students to explain what the last two lines mean.

  » "Salt of the Earth": Encourage students to think about the rhyme pattern.

  » "On the Rocks": Display a picture of a limpet showing the suction cup. Ask: *In the second to the last line, what does "its thing" mean? (what the limpet does well)*

  » "A Bird in the Water": Say: *Notice how the author strings together images to help us visualize the tiny bird.* Explain that poems don't need complete sentences because they capture a feeling or an experience rather than tell a story or inform.

- Add *stanza, figurative language,* and the types of figurative language to the class Instructional Vocabulary list, and have students add the terms to their lists.

Engage and Respond

- Tell students to write two or three sentences about how the poems made them think differently about the animals and about poetry. Have partners share ideas.

 ENGLISH LEARNER SUPPORT: Support Comprehension

ALL LEVELS Explicitly explain the meaning of figurative expressions, and give cultural context if needed. Drawings can be helpful for beginners.

TEACHER TIP

Remember that this lesson is introductory. Students need to feel comfortable with poems, so make it fun, interesting, and challenging just to listen. As you read each poem, use the punctuation, rather than the ends of lines, to determine pauses. Discuss why you did this. Help students note the stanzas and rhyming lines.

LEARNING OBJECTIVES

- Read and understand domain-specific vocabulary.
- Identify and use sensory language.
- Use word-reference materials.
- Use word parts to clarify meaning.
- **Language** Use strategies to learn new language.
- **Language** Use sensory language.

MATERIALS Online Ed

Classroom Materials object hidden under a box

Focal Text *A Strange Place to Call Home*

Writer's Notebook *p. 11.1*

Choose Words and Phrases

- To begin the lesson, say: *Remember that poetry creates an experience for the reader rather than giving information or telling a story.* Have something unusual for the classroom—a bouquet of flowers, for example—hidden under a box on your desk. Tell students that when you lift the box they should focus on the object you reveal.

  » Lift the box, count silently to ten, and then replace the box.

  » Have students quickly write words and phrases related to the object.

  » Then ask: *How might you combine those words and phrases with other words to capture your experience of seeing the object?*

- Print the word *penguins* on the board or chart paper and have students write the word on **Writer's Notebook page 11.1** or in their notebooks. Ask: *What words or phrases come to mind when you think about penguins?* Add students' ideas to the list. Then refer to the poem "Think Cold" in *A Strange Place to Call Home*. Explain that you will work together to create a Penguin Word Bank.

- Model adding words to the Word Bank by pulling sensory words and phrases from the poem to add to the Word Bank. Add the underlined words and phrases to the list of student words.

  THINK ALOUD *When I think of penguins, I see <u>black and white birds</u> that <u>waddle</u> around on the <u>ice</u>. I "think <u>cold</u>." But the poem is about penguins who live where there is no ice. The words <u>dig burrows with bills and legs</u> and <u>scorching sun</u> help me see and feel the penguins' environment.*

- Have students use the context of the poem and/or a dictionary to figure out the meanings of words such as *floes, burrow, clutch,* and *arid.*

- Display and read aloud the information on Humboldt penguins in the back of the book. Encourage students to add more words from this research to the Word Bank. Remind students that a list of words and phrases can be a great resource as they write.

Engage and Respond

- Divide the class into five groups. Have each group choose a different poem from *A Strange Place to Call Home*.

- Have groups create a list of words and phrases related to their animal. Tell students to choose sensory words or phrases that create a mental image of the animal or its habitat. Encourage them to use the description in the back of the book and to do some research on the animal to find more information.

 ENGLISH LEARNER SUPPORT: Build Vocabulary

SUBSTANTIAL
With students, pantomime words such as *cold* and *waddle* and point to pictures that illustrate other words.

MODERATE
Tell partners to work together to include in their notebooks brief definitions or drawings that illustrate the meanings of words they select.

LIGHT
Encourage students to use the words and phrases they are selecting in complete sentences that demonstrate their meaning.

Focus on Structure

- Refer to the poem "Salt of the Earth" from *A Strange Place to Call Home*.

- Explain that a **rhyme scheme** is the pattern of rhyming words at the end of lines. Ask: *Which lines rhyme in the first stanza? (the first and third lines)* Say: *If I use the letters A, B, C, and so on, to mark rhyming lines, the rhyme scheme for the poem is ABA.*

- Read the first stanza, stressing the **meter**, or rhythm: "*This HARSH and SALTy land (pause) it's NOT a PLACE to MOCK (pause) FlaMINgoes FIND it GRAND.*" Say: *The meter is the pattern of stressed and unstressed syllables. Meter is like the beat of a song.*

Focus on Limericks

- Limericks are a nonthreatening way to begin writing poetry because they are funny. Show **Display and Engage 11.3a**. Read the definition of a **limerick** and discuss its features. Then read the limerick on **Display and Engage 11.3b** aloud as students follow on **Writer's Notebook page 11.2**.

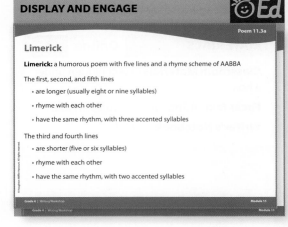

DISPLAY AND ENGAGE   Online

Poem 11.3a

Limerick

Limerick: a humorous poem with five lines and a rhyme scheme of AABBA

The first, second, and fifth lines
- are longer (usually eight or nine syllables)
- rhyme with each other
- have the same rhythm, with three accented syllables

The third and fourth lines
- are shorter (five or six syllables)
- rhyme with each other
- have the same rhythm, with two accented syllables

- Check the rhyme scheme against the features of the limerick on the Display and Engage page. Say: *The words* tree, knee, *and* glee *rhyme. So the first, second, and fifth lines rhyme. The third and fourth lines end in the words* return *and* learn, *and they rhyme. So the rhyme scheme is AABBA.*

- Have students highlight the rhyming words with different colored markers.

- Reread the limerick, emphasizing the meter. Encourage students to underline the stressed syllables. Ask: *How many syllables are stressed in the first line? (3) the second line? (3)*

- Have students identify the stressed syllables in the last three lines.

- Work with students to write a limerick. Write on the board: *There was a fourth grader named _____.* Agree on a one-syllable name to complete the line.

  » Have students list as many rhyming words as they can for the name and then write a second line that ends with one of those rhyming words.

  » Ask students to suggest what might happen to the person in the next two lines. Write a suggestion for the third line.

  » Have students list as many rhyming words as they can for the last word of the third line and then write a suggested fourth line that ends with a rhyming word.

  » Remind students the last line must rhyme with the first two. Write a suggested fifth line.

  » Check the rhyme scheme and meter with students, revising as necessary.

- Add *rhyme scheme, meter,* and *limerick* to the class Instructional Vocabulary list, and have students add the terms to their own lists.

Write a Limerick

- Have students use **Writer's Notebook page 11.2** to write their own limericks.

LEARNING OBJECTIVES

- Understand the structure of a riddle.
- Write a riddle.
- **Language** Adapt spoken language to write poetry.

MATERIALS   Online Ed

Display and Engage *11.4*

Writer's Notebook *p. 11.3*

INSTRUCTIONAL VOCABULARY

- **riddle** a poem that cleverly describes a person, place, thing, or idea without naming it. The reader is supposed to guess what the riddle is describing.
- **homophone** a word that sounds the same, but has a different meaning and/or spelling, as another word

Focus on Riddle Poems

- Share with students the history of **riddles**. Explain that many people think riddles are simply for fun, but they have a long history that goes back to Greek writers and artists 2,500 years ago. Tell students that many writers and poets over the centuries have written fun, interesting, and thought-provoking riddles.

- Show **Display and Engage 11.4** and read the definition of a riddle poem. Then read the model aloud as students follow on **Writer's Notebook page 11.3**. Ask: *What do you think the answer is?* (*a pencil sharpener*) As students respond, have them explain how they reached their answers.

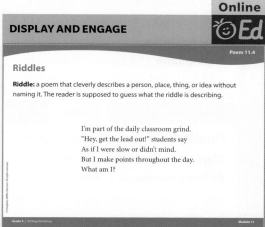

- Ask: *What is the rhyme scheme for the riddle?* (*ABAB*) Have students highlight and label the rhyme scheme and underline the stressed syllables in each line to show meter.

- Invite students to share their favorite riddles with the class.

- Tell students that riddles sometimes use **homophones** that surprise the reader. Review the definition of homophones—words that sound the same, but have different meanings and/or spellings.

- Share the following riddle with students. Read the riddle aloud first, and then write it on the board or chart paper.

> What is black and white and read all over?

- Model breaking down the riddle, noting the homophone.

   THINK ALOUD *The riddle begins by asking what is black and white. That could be a lot of things—from a skunk to a penguin to the page in a book! Then the riddle says that the thing is "read all over." The word* read *(r-e-a-d) is a homophone for the color name* red, *but it means something entirely different. If the object is read, it must have printed words. A black and white object with print could be either a newspaper or a book.*

- Add *riddle* and *homophone* to the class Instructional Vocabulary list, and have students add the terms to the lists in their notebooks.

Write a Riddle Poem

- Give students time to write their own riddle poems using **Writer's Notebook page 11.3**. Remind students to include a rhyme scheme in their poem. Challenge them to include a homophone.

- Invite students to share their riddles in small groups.

LEARNING OBJECTIVES

- Understand the structure of a haiku.
- Understand the structure of a tanka.
- Write a haiku.
- Write a tanka.
- **Language** Use spoken language to write poetry.

MATERIALS   Online

Focal Text *A Strange Place to Call Home*

Display and Engage *11.5a–b*

Writer's Notebook *p. 11.4*

INSTRUCTIONAL VOCABULARY

- **haiku** a three-line poem with 17 syllables—5 in the first line, 7 in the second line, and 5 in the third line
- **tanka** a haiku with two additional 7-syllable lines at the end

TEACHER TIP

If it is feasible in your location, you may wish to take students outside to encourage more thoughts about nature. Encourage students to write their ideas in a notebook as they observe natural phenomena.

Focus on Haiku

- Introduce the **haiku** as a form of poetry that originated in Japan. Explain that a haiku typically describes something simple yet beautiful in nature. Tell students that haiku contests are held in Japan.

- Show **Display and Engage 11.5a** and read the definition of a haiku. Display the poem "Dry as Dust" from *A Strange Place to Call Home*. Have students count the syllables to show that it is a haiku. Point out that a haiku doesn't require a rhyme scheme or meter. Read the model haiku, with students following along on **Writer's Notebook page 11.4**. Have students count the syllables in the model haiku.

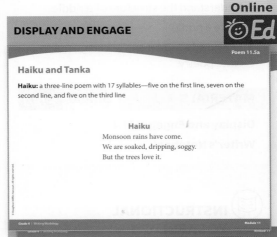

- Ask: *What other things in nature could you describe in a haiku?* As students respond, write their ideas on the board. Work with students to select one topic.

- Write a class haiku. Agree on a topic. As students suggest words or phrases, write them on the board or chart paper. Continue to revise the lines until the poem fits the haiku form. Write the completed haiku on the board or paper.

Focus on Tanka

- Show **Display and Engage 11.5b** and read the definition of a **tanka**. Read the tanka model aloud as students follow on **Writer's Notebook page 11.4**. Ask: *What is the purpose of the last two lines? (They add to the description of the trees in the haiku.)* Count the syllables in each of the last two lines.

- Return to the class haiku, and brainstorm ideas for the last two lines. Write students' ideas on the board and revise the lines until the poem fits the tanka form.

- Add *haiku* and *tanka* to the class Instructional Vocabulary list, and have students add the terms to the lists in their notebooks.

Write a Haiku and Tanka

- Invite students to write a haiku about a topic of their own choosing using **Writer's Notebook page 11.4**. Then have them add two lines to create a tanka.

- When students are finished, encourage them to share their poems with a partner.

 ENGLISH LEARNER SUPPORT: Scaffold Writing

SUBSTANTIAL

Draw lines between the syllables and read the models aloud, pointing to each syllable. Help students do the same for their own poems.

MODERATE

Tell students to draw lines between the syllables of their poems and read their poems aloud to ensure they have the correct number. Assist if necessary.

LIGHT

Tell students to think of synonyms for words they wish to use to help them select words with the correct number of syllables.

LEARNING OBJECTIVES

- Understand the structure of an ode.
- Write an ode.
- **Language** Adapt spoken language to write poetry.

MATERIALS   Online

Display and Engage *11.6a–b*

Writer's Notebook *p. 11.5*

 INSTRUCTIONAL VOCABULARY

- **ode** a poem that celebrates or praises a person, place, thing, or idea

Focus on Odes

- Tell students that in this lesson they will read and write another form of poetry called an **ode**.

- Show **Display and Engage 11.6a**. Read the definition and features of an ode. Read the model on **Display and Engage 11.6b** as students follow on **Writer's Notebook page 11.5**. Ask: *What does the ode express feelings about? (the weekend)* Explain that an ode can celebrate anything from aardvarks to zeroes.

- Analyze the structure of the model. Point out examples of simile (*"Like a ball of happiness"*), metaphor (*"A break in the storm"*), and personification (*"you tempt and tease"*).

- Have students brainstorm topics for an ode. List them on the board, and allow the class to vote to choose one topic. Guide practice by working with students to generate ideas for a class ode to the topic. Write guiding questions such as:

> What do you see, hear, feel, (smell or taste), when you think about _____?
>
> What action words describe _____?
>
> What figurative language can you use to describe _____?

- Write students' ideas on the board. Then invite students to write lines for the ode on the board. Keep revising until the class is satisfied with the ode.

- Add *ode* and its definition to the class Instructional Vocabulary list, and have students add it to their own lists.

Write an Ode

- Invite students to think of something they could celebrate in an ode. Have them jot down ideas using **Writer's Notebook page 11.5** or their notebooks before selecting one idea as their topic.

- Allow sufficient time for students to develop and write their odes.

- Invite students to share their odes with a partner.

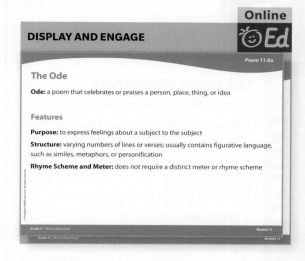

(EL) ENGLISH LEARNER SUPPORT: Scaffold Writing

SUBSTANTIAL

Provide simple frames of an ode for students to complete, such as *Oh _____. How _____ you are. You make me feel _____. You are like _____.*

MODERATE

Provide more complex frames to guide students, such as *When I think of you, I (see, hear, feel) _____. You are as _____ as _____.*

LIGHT

Encourage students to jot down words related to their topic in the categories of sensory words, action verbs, and figurative language. Provide and demonstrate how to use a thesaurus.

LEARNING OBJECTIVES

- Understand the structures of poems.
- Analyze rhyme and meter in poetry forms.
- Compare and contrast poem structures.
- Write a couplet, tercet, and quatrain.
- **Language** Adapt spoken language to write poetry.

MATERIALS   Online

Display and Engage *11.7 a–b*
Writer's Notebook *p. 11.6*

 INSTRUCTIONAL VOCABULARY

- **couplet** a two-line poem that rhymes.
- **tercet** a couplet with one added line that rhymes
- **quatrain** a four-line poem with a specific rhyme scheme

Review Rhyme and Meter

- Write the following familiar poem on the board, and read it aloud.

> Twinkle, twinkle, little star,
>
> How I wonder what you are.
>
> Up above the world so high,
>
> Like a diamond in the sky.

- Review rhyme scheme. Ask: *Which words in the poem rhyme?* (*star/are, high/sky*) Say: *Remember that we mark the end of a line of poetry with A, B, C, and so forth, depending on the rhyme. So the rhyme scheme for this poem is AABB.*

- Read the poem again, stressing the meter. Clap (loud, soft, loud, soft) to the first line. Have students read and clap to match the meter of the rest of the poem.

Focus on Couplets, Tercets, and Quatrains

- Show **Display and Engage 11.7a** and have students follow on **Writer's Notebook page 11.6**. Read the definition of a **couplet**. As you read the couplet, match your tone to the meaning of the line to demonstrate that the tone can change even when the meter remains the same.

- Read the definition of **tercet** and the model. Point out the AAA rhyme scheme.

- Show **Display and Engage 11.7b**. Read the definition of **quatrain**. Explain that couplets can stand on their own as poems, or they can be combined to form quatrains. Read the three quatrains. Ask: *How do the rhyme schemes differ?* (*"Humpty Dumpty" is AABB. "Mary Had a Little Lamb" is ABCB. "Sleep" is AAAA.*)

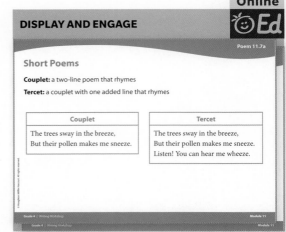

Online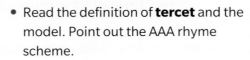

DISPLAY AND ENGAGE

Poem 11.7a

Short Poems

Couplet: a two-line poem that rhymes
Tercet: a couplet with one added line that rhymes

Couplet	Tercet
The trees sway in the breeze, But their pollen makes me sneeze.	The trees sway in the breeze, But their pollen makes me sneeze. Listen! You can hear me wheeze.

Grade 4 | Writing Workshop   Module 11

- Explain that the easiest way to start a short poem is to make lists of rhyming words. Model how to move through the alphabet with a sound to find words, such as *at, bat, cat, fat, hat, mat, pat.*

- Work with students to write a couplet on the board. Add a third rhyming line to create a tercet. Then write a new quatrain. Guide students to analyze their work for rhyme scheme and meter.

- Add *couplet*, *tercet*, and *quatrain* and their definitions to the class Instructional Vocabulary list, and have students add the terms and definitions to their own lists.

Write Poems

- Give students time to write several couplets using **Writer's Notebook page 11.6**. Challenge them to use different rhyme schemes and meters. Then have them add a line to one couplet to turn it into a tercet. Finally, have them write a quatrain.

LEARNING OBJECTIVES

- Draft a series of poems.
- Write poetry in different forms.
- Use features of poetry correctly.
- **Language** Write poetry using new basic/content-based vocabulary.

MATERIALS   Online

Display and Engage 11.8

Writer's Notebook *pp. 11.7, 11.8, 11.9*

 LEARNING MINDSET: Curiosity

Normalize Remind students that good writers aren't afraid to take risks. They try to stretch their limits by wondering how else they might accomplish a task. Say: *Being curious and playful as you write your poems can give you new ideas you might not have thought of if you concentrate only on finishing the assignment.* Being curious opens a learner's mind to new and exciting possibilities.

Prepare to Draft

- Tell students they will begin writing poems to a prompt.

- Show **Display and Engage 11.8** and read the prompt. Write the key parts of the prompt on the board or on chart paper.

  » Choose a topic you find interesting.

  » Write a series of poems on that topic.

  » Use different forms of poetry.

- Model using the prompt to decide on a topic.

  THINK ALOUD *I've already written a limerick about a boy and a bee in a tree, and a haiku and tanka about rain and trees. I like my ode about weekends, but I'm not sure it would work in other forms. I think writing about animals would be more interesting. I'll try writing three or four different types of poems about animals.*

- Refer students to **Writer's Notebook page 11.7**. Discuss the features described in the rubric with students. Suggest that students use this rubric as a resource as they write.

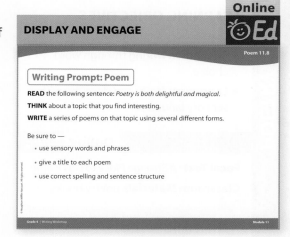

Set Goals for Writing

- Remind students that effective writers set goals before writing. They think about their previous writing and what they would like to improve. Ask students to think about what goals they would like to set for their series of poems and to add those goals to the list on **Writer's Notebook page 11.8** or in their own notebooks.

Begin to Draft

- Have students begin to draft their series of poems, using their Word Bank, their prewriting notes, the rubric, and the poems they have already written. Explain that they can begin with something they've already written and add poems in other forms on the same topic, or they can start over with a new topic.

- Suggest students use the graphic organizer on **Writer's Notebook page 11.9** to help organize their ideas.

 ENGLISH LEARNER SUPPORT: Scaffold Writing

SUBSTANTIAL

Let students begin by drawing a picture of their topic. Encourage them to draw other images around the topic that represent what they see, hear, or feel. Then help them label each picture with words or phrases they can use to write their poems.

MODERATE

Before students write, suggest that they brainstorm words and phrases in a word web around their chosen topic. Assist if necessary.

LIGHT

To help students create meter in their poems, suggest they say words and poem lines "aloud in their heads" to hear the stresses. Demonstrate how to use a dictionary pronunciation respelling to determine accented syllables if they are unsure.

POETRY · POEM

LEARNING OBJECTIVES

- Use sensory language.
- Strengthen writing through word choice.
- **Language** Write and describe with sensory language.

MATERIALS Online Ed

Focal Text *A Strange Place to Call Home*
Classroom Materials poetry books

 INSTRUCTIONAL VOCABULARY

- **sensory language** words that describe sights, sounds, smells, touches, and tastes to help the reader create a mental picture

TEACHER TIP

For extra practice, invite students to follow your model. Tell them to think about a familiar object and complete the sentence frames on paper as they think about the object. Then have students share their sensory descriptions in small groups as other group members try to guess what the object is.

Focus on Sensory Language

- Remind students that good poetry shares an experience of a person, place, thing, activity, or idea. Point out that what we experience comes through our senses.

- Write the following sentence frames on the board or chart paper.

> I see _____.
>
> I hear _____.
>
> I smell _____.
>
> I feel _____.
>
> I taste _____.

- Model thinking about a familiar object and completing the sentence frames.
  THINK ALOUD *I see different sized pieces of wood in a pile. The wood feels rough and hard. I see a red, orange, and yellow glow around the pile. I hear snapping and crackling. I smell smoke. I feel warmth.*

- Have students guess the object that you are describing. *(a campfire)*

- Explain that you used **sensory language**—words that create a mental picture by describing sights, sounds, smells, touches, and tastes —to describe the fire.

- Divide the class into five groups. Assign one of the senses to each group. Have students revisit the focal text, the model poems, and other poetry books in the classroom library to find examples of sensory language related to their group's sense. Tell each group to record their examples on a sheet of chart paper. Point out that the taste and smell groups may not find as many examples.

- When they are finished, have groups post their sensory word/phrase lists around the room. Invite members of each group to share what they found. Have the class brainstorm other words to add to each list.

- Add *sensory language* to the class Instructional Vocabulary list, and have students add the term and its definition to their individual lists.

Continue to Draft

- Have students return to their writing, focusing on adding more sensory language to their drafts. Suggest they use the sensory word charts as a resource.

 ENGLISH LEARNER SUPPORT: Build Vocabulary

SUBSTANTIAL
Have students draw the topic of their poem. Work with them to create a word bank they may draw from for sensory language describing their topic.

MODERATE
Have students create their own word bank to describe their topic by completing the *I see . . . I hear . . . I smell . . . I feel . . . I taste . . .* sentence frames.

LIGHT
Have students discuss their topics with a partner. Partners can offer suggestions for more sensory language to use.

LEARNING OBJECTIVES

- Complete a draft of a series of poems.
- Use rules of poetic forms correctly.
- **Language** Write poetry using new vocabulary and learned forms.

MATERIALS

Online

Anchor Chart W10: *Elements of Poetry*
Display and Engage *11.3–11.7*

Focus on Elements and Forms of Poetry

- Revisit **Anchor Chart W10: Elements of Poetry** to review the elements of poetry. It might also be helpful to use **Display and Engage 11.3–11.7** to review the features of each type of poetry.

Continue to Draft

- Give students plenty of time to complete their series of poems, making sure that each poem conforms to the rules of that form and uses as much sensory and figurative language as possible.

- Encourage students to share their poems with a partner to get feedback before completing their drafts.

- Suggest that students write each poem in their series on a separate sheet of paper so that they have room to revise in the next lessons.

ANCHOR CHART Online

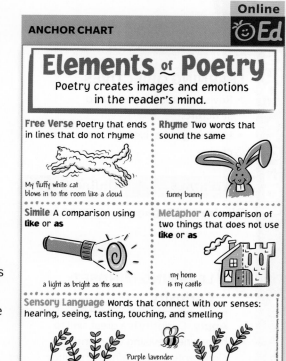

Elements of Poetry
Poetry creates images and emotions in the reader's mind.

Free Verse Poetry that ends in lines that do not rhyme
My fluffy white cat blows in to the room like a cloud

Rhyme Two words that sound the same
funny bunny

Simile A comparison using **like** or **as**
a light as bright as the sun

Metaphor A comparison of two things that does not use **like** or **as**
my home is my castle

Sensory Language Words that connect with our senses: hearing, seeing, tasting, touching, and smelling
Purple lavender smells sweet.

 ENGLISH LEARNER SUPPORT: Scaffold Writing

SUBSTANTIAL
Work with students individually to add figurative language to their writing. Write their ideas, and read them aloud with students.

MODERATE
Have students share poems with a partner and use their partner's feedback to add sensory and figurative language.

LIGHT
As students complete their drafts, ask them to share how they included figurative language in their poems.

POETRY • POEM

LEARNING OBJECTIVES

- Revise poems for clarity and structure.
- **Language** Revise to improve word choice.

MATERIALS   Online

Display and Engage *p. 11.9 a–11.9b*

LEARNING MINDSET: Curiosity

Apply Curiosity is a great skill to have when revising your writing. *Good writers aren't afraid to change what they've written if the changes make the writing more fun, interesting, or effective. They figure out what to change by asking questions about what they've already written.* Encourage students to ask ,"What would happen if..." questions as they revise their poems.

TARGETED GRAMMAR SUPPORT

You may want to have students refer to the following grammar minilesson as they revise their poems.

- **3.1.1 Action Verbs,** p. W266

Introduce the Revision Skill

- Tell students they will begin to revise their poetry. Explain that *revising* means "looking again." Say: *You shift from creating to asking yourself questions such as, "Does this say what I want it to say?" and "How can I make this more fun or more interesting?"*

- Show **Display and Engage 11.9a–b**. Read the title. If students aren't familiar with the idiom "nuts and bolts," explain that it refers to the basic parts of something. In poetry, this refers to the structure and features of a type of poem. Explain that these are steps a poet might use to revise the "basics" of poetry. Have students take notes in their notebooks as you read and discuss each point.

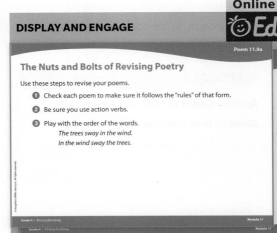

Online

DISPLAY AND ENGAGE

Poem 11.9a

The Nuts and Bolts of Revising Poetry

Use these steps to revise your poems.

1. Check each poem to make sure it follows the "rules" of that form.
2. Be sure you use action verbs.
3. Play with the order of the words.
   The trees sway in the wind.
   In the wind sway the trees.

» **First point:** Tell students to check the "rules" for each type of poem they wrote. For example, a haiku must have three lines with five syllables on the first line, seven on the second line, and five on the third line. Remind students that some poems have rules for rhyme scheme and meter, while other forms, such as the ode, do not.

» **Second point:** Write these two sentences on the board and ask students to compare/contrast how the two verbs make them feel:

- She is happy.
- She beams with happiness.

» **Third point:** Say: *In this step, think about whether you can make a line stronger or more interesting by moving the parts around.* Ask students to compare/contrast the sentences in the example.

» **Fourth point:** Discuss the difference between *general* and *precise* and the examples. Suggest that students read through their poems and ask themselves which general words they could change to precise words to help the reader share their sensory experience.

» **Fifth point:** Encourage students to think about the feeling they are trying to share with the reader. When they think of the subject of the poem, do they feel joy? wonder? surprise? amazement? Tell students to ask themselves whether each word, phrase, and line of their poem contributes to that feeling.

Revise the "Nuts and Bolts"

- Give students time to revise their poems using the steps. If students need help with a particular task, ask questions that will draw out their thinking.

- As you circulate, group students who need support on similar grammar topics. Use the grammar minilesson or the students' own writing to provide targeted review and support.

LEARNING OBJECTIVES

- Work collaboratively to improve writing.
- **Language** Express opinions about revising.

MATERIALS Online **Ed**

Writer's Notebook *p. 11.10*

Small Group Conferences: Pointing

- Say: *In this lesson, we will divide into conferencing groups. You'll read your poems to one another and share what you liked about the poems.* Refer students to **Writer's Notebook page 11.10**. Read the list of questions, and remind students to think about them as they listen to the poems.

- Explain: *When I listen to a poem, I sometimes close my eyes so I can focus on the words instead of being distracted by what I see. I make mental pictures of what the poem is saying. After the poem is finished, I can look back and remember which pictures were the most vivid or the most fun.*

- Divide students into small groups. Review the steps group members should take during this conferencing:

  » Take turns reading your series of poems clearly and with expression.

  » Pause for a few seconds, and then read the poems again.

  » After the second reading, listeners should jot down words, phrases, images, or anything else that jumped out as they heard the poems.

  » Listeners then share what they liked with the poet. The poet may wish to write down comments to use in revising.

- Debrief with the class. Focus on how students can use the peer review to improve their writing. Write the following questions on the board, and lead a discussion with students about their experiences.

> - In what ways was reading your poems to others helpful?
> - What did you learn about your group members as they shared their poems?
> - How will this process help you revise your poems?

Continue to Revise

- Have students continue revising their poems using the feedback they gained in the small group conferences.

 ENGLISH LEARNER SUPPORT: Support Speaking

ALL LEVELS Provide an opportunity for students to practice reading their poems to you or to a partner before they read aloud to the small group.

LEARNING OBJECTIVES

- Proofread writing for mechanics, grammar, and conventions.
- **Language** Edit writing with peer support.

MATERIALS   Online

Anchor Chart W13: *Editing Checklist*

TARGETED GRAMMAR SUPPORT

You may want to have students refer to the following grammar minilessons as they edit their poems.

- **1.1.3 Subject-Verb Agreement,** p. W218
- **7.3.5 Connect to Writing: Using Correct Spelling,** p. W365

Peer Proofreading

- Display <u>**Anchor Chart W13: Editing Checklist**</u> and read the items with students. Review how to use proofreading marks to edit spelling, grammar, and usage.

- Tell students that they will be proofreading the poems of a classmate.

- Remind students that when they proofread a peer's writing, they should mark grammar or usage mistakes so the writer can fix them on the final copy. For example, if a verb doesn't agree with the subject, they should circle the verb and indicate that there is a problem by writing *agreement* above it.

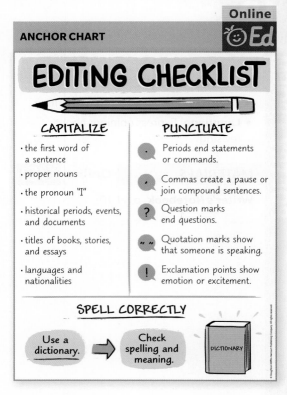

ANCHOR CHART

- Remind students that incomplete sentences are often acceptable in poetry. If proofreaders see something they question, they should point it out rather than marking it wrong.

- Have student partners exchange papers and proofread, using the editing checklist on the Anchor Chart.

- Have students return papers to the writer when editing is complete.

Integrate Proofreading Edits

- Have students make any corrections that they agree need changing. If a student disagrees with the proofreader's suggestion, discuss the need for correction with the partners.

- As you circulate, group students who need support on similar grammar topics. Use the grammar minilessons or the students' own writing to provide targeted review and support.

- Encourage students to read their poems one more time after they have completed their edits.

 ENGLISH LEARNER SUPPORT: Support Editing

SUBSTANTIAL

Share sample sentences that contain a grammar point or spelling issue that students need to practice. Have students copy a few of the sentences to provide practice and then proofread/edit their poems for this issue.

MODERATE

Provide sentences with blanks where grammar choices need to be made. Have students work together to complete the sentences. Ensure students have used grammar correctly and discuss changes if needed. Then have students proofread/edit their poems for this issue.

LIGHT

Have students review their writing for English grammar, usage, or spelling points that have been problematic for them.

LEARNING OBJECTIVES

- Publish writing.
- **Language** Demonstrate increased comprehension of English in order to publish writing.

MATERIALS   Online Ed

Focal Text *A Strange Place to Call Home*
Writer's Notebook *p. 11.11*

TEACHER TIP

After students finalize their published poems, you may wish to create a class anthology. Invite students to submit their favorite poems.

Think About Ways to Publish

- Revisit the focal text and discuss the unique illustrations. Point out that some of them appear to be collages made with torn paper or other materials. Show the poem "Think Heat" and point out how the fur texture and bright faces of the monkeys help bring the poem to life.

- Next, show the pages for "Salt of the Earth" and "A Fish in the Air." Say: *I notice that the images don't look like the real animals. They just suggest their parts, similar to the way the poems suggest certain features of the animals. The illustrations and the poems have the same feeling.*

- Explain that in this lesson, students will prepare and publish their poems. Encourage students to think about how they might add illustrations to bring their poems to life.

- Say: *There are many ways you might choose to publish your poems.* Write the following on the board:

> - Type the poems on separate pages and add graphics.
> - Write each poem on art paper. Add illustrations. Create a book by tying the sheets together with yarn or string.
> - Write and illustrate each poem on poster board.
> - Create a multimedia presentation with music and pictures to accompany the poems.

Publish Writing

- Give students plenty of time to publish their poems using their chosen method. You may wish to provide art materials that students can use when publishing their poems.

Revisit Goals

- Have students use **Writer's Notebook page 11.11** to revisit their goals and reflect on what they did well and what they might want to work on in their next piece of writing.

LEARNING OBJECTIVES

- Share writing.
- Hold a collaborative discussion.
- **Language** Share poetry.
- **Language** Ask and answer questions using academic language.

MATERIALS   Online

Focal Text *A Strange Place to Call Home*

 LEARNING MINDSET:
Curiosity

Review Remind students that curiosity leads to asking questions. Say: *The questions you asked led you to think about how you could stretch your abilities as you wrote your poems. Questions also helped you strengthen your writing by focusing on what needed revision.* Encourage students to think about ways in which being curious about poetry has helped them expand their thinking.

Share Writing

- Tell students they will share their finished poems with classmates.
- Ask students to select their favorite poem.
- Model reading one of the poems in *A Strange Place to Call Home* with expression, and encourage students to use expression in their readings.
- Give students time to practice reading their poem to a partner, and encourage partners to give feedback to each other.
- After practice, have students take turns reading their poems to the class.
- When a student has finished reading, encourage listeners to ask the presenter questions about the poem and the speaker to respond to each question. Remind students to make eye contact with one another as they discuss their poems.

Reflect on Writing

- As a class, hold an informal discussion of this writing assignment. Encourage students to think about and express their feelings about the following topics. Ask these questions, or write them on the board.

> - How did you feel about the assignment at the beginning?
> - Did your feelings about poetry change as you learned about different forms of poetry or as you began writing your own poems?
> - What did you like most about the assignment? Why?
> - What did you like least? Why?
> - What was the easiest part of the assignment? What was the most difficult part?

 ENGLISH LEARNER SUPPORT: Support Speaking

ALL LEVELS Allow students to choose partners with whom they feel most comfortable to practice reading their poems.

Editorial

FOCUS STATEMENT   Even small choices can lead to big change.

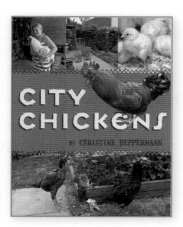

FOCAL TEXT

City Chickens

Author: Christine Heppermann

Summary: A family sets up a rescue for homeless chickens in Minnesota.

WRITING PROMPT

READ the following sentence: *Even small choices can lead to big change.*

THINK about a change you'd like to see in your school.

WRITE an editorial explaining what you would like to see changed and why. Use reasons and facts to support your opinion.

LESSONS

<table>
<tr><td>

1. **Introducing the Focal Text**

2. **Vocabulary**

3. **Prewriting I: Preparing to Write**

4. **Prewriting II: Establishing an Opinion**

5. **Prewriting III: Choosing Support**

6. **Drafting I: Beginning the Draft**

7. **Drafting II: Integrating Argumentative Elements**

8. **Drafting III: Completing the Draft**

9. **Revising I: Choosing Good Reasons**

10. **Revising II: Conferencing**

11. **Revising III: Punctuation for Effect**

</td><td>

12. **Editing I: Spelling and Mechanics**

13. **Editing II: Peer Proofreading**

14. **Publishing**

15. **Sharing**

</td></tr>
</table>

LEARNING MINDSET:
Perseverance

Display <u>Anchor Chart 31: My Learning Mindset</u> throughout the year. Refer to it to introduce Perseverance and to reinforce the skills you introduced in previous modules.

ARGUMENT • EDITORIAL

LEARNING OBJECTIVES

- Brainstorm words and phrases on a topic.
- Use background knowledge to prepare to read.
- Discuss genre features of informative text.
- Read informational text with purpose and understanding.
- Analyze an informational text for author's craft.
- **Language** Discuss features of text with academic language.

MATERIALS   Online

Display and Engage *12.1*
Focal Text *City Chickens*

TEACHER TIP

Preview *City Chickens* before reading it aloud. Some of the incidents mentioned in it may be disturbing to students.

Priming the Students

Explore the Topic

- Tell students that in this module they will learn about an unusual choice made by a married couple in Minneapolis, Minnesota. They will also write to support a new choice for their school community.

- Point out that students make choices every day. Some of the choices have few consequences, like which type of cereal they choose to have for breakfast. Other choices are more significant.

    THINK ALOUD *Sometimes a choice can have negative consequences. For example, imagine you decided to ignore your alarm clock one morning. That choice made you miss the school bus.*

    » *Because you missed the bus, your mother had to drive you to school. Because she drove you, she was late to work.*

    » *Because she was late to work, she had to stay later to make up the time. Because she had to stay later, she could not get to your baseball game.*

    » *You hit a home run at the game, but she missed seeing it, which made both of you sad.*

    » *How would the day have been different if you had gotten up on time?*

- Suggest another scenario where a deliberate choice leads to a positive result.

    THINK ALOUD *Sometimes a choice can have positive effects. For example, suppose one of the comments on a piece of your writing is that you need to work on your spelling because the misspellings are distracting your reader.*

    » *You decide that the comment makes sense. You pay attention to spelling patterns in words. You work hard to improve your spelling.*

    » *On your next writing assignment, you pay attention to the spelling. When you have questions, you ask for help. You use the spell-check program on the computer, but you also watch for the kinds of errors that spelling programs can't find.*

    » *When this assignment is returned, you get a comment, "Wow, now your reader can stay on track with your message! Thanks for choosing to be a more careful speller!"*

    » *How would you feel about your choice?*

- Conclude the discussion by writing *choice = cause* on the board. Point out that choices are causes that can start a chain of effects, or results, in your life or in your community.

Discuss the Focus Statement

- Show **Display and Engage 12.1**. Read the Focus Statement with students. Have students write and share some examples of small choices that can make a big difference.

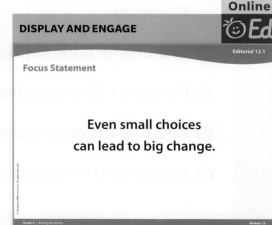

DISPLAY AND ENGAGE   Online

Editorial 12.1

Focus Statement

Even small choices can lead to big change.

Priming the Text

Prepare to Read

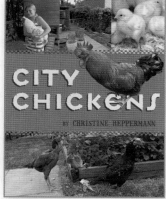

City Chickens

- Show the cover of *City Chickens*. Point out the photographs on the cover. Ask: *If this book is illustrated with photographs, what does that tell you about the story in it? (It is more likely to be about a real subject, or to be nonfiction.)*

- Point out that this book is an **informational text** and will share detailed information about a topic. Have students add the term *informational text* to their glossaries. Add it to the class Instructional Vocabulary list as well. Then page through the book with students, pointing out chapter headings, photographs, and captions.

- Call attention to the features at the end of the book, beginning on page 48. Say: *I see some unusual additions to this book.*

  » *"Mary's Art" shows paintings of chickens, so I think Mary is an important person in this book.*

  » *It's not unusual to have an author's note in a book. I see that the first line of the note begins, "My first visit to Chicken Run Rescue, in the fall of 2007. . ." This tells me that the book is about a real place.*

  » *The next extra feature at the back of the book is called "How to Care for City Chickens." That tells me that the author wants people to know that they can care for chickens in their neighborhoods, which is really interesting to me. I wonder if I would want to do that.*

  » *On the next page, "For Educators," tells me that the author wants teachers to know something more about school programs that hatch chicks.*

  » *The last feature, "Author's Sources," shows me that the author did research for this book. That tells me that she used facts and wants her readers to have a chance to learn more about the subject.*

- Page through the book with students and have them describe what they see. Give ample time for students to make observations and become familiar with the text.

Engage and Respond

- Have students Turn and Talk to a partner. Have them tell what they want to learn by reading *City Chickens* and why.

 ENGLISH LEARNER SUPPORT: Facilitate Language Connections

ALL LEVELS As you discuss *informational text,* point out that the word *information* has a cognate in several languages:

- Spanish: *información*
- Portuguese: *informação*
- Italian: *informazioni*
- French: *information*

 LEARNING MINDSET:
Perseverance

Introduce Throughout the focal text, students will encounter examples of perseverance in the ways that Mary and Bert handle challenging situations with the chickens. Discuss with students the meaning of the word *perseverance*. Tell students that few problems are solved on the first attempt and that developing perseverance will help them persist until a problem is resolved. Give feedback when you notice that a student is demonstrating perseverance. Say: *I notice that you are working hard to understand the lesson. I admire your perseverance. Good for you for sticking with it!*

INSTRUCTIONAL VOCABULARY

- **informational text** writing that shares detailed information about a topic

ARGUMENT • EDITORIAL

The Read

Read the Focal Text

- As you read *City Chickens*, stop at these points to discuss the text features.

  » Ask: *Look at the curling type on page 2. What attitude does that share with the reader?* (*humor or lightheartedness*)

  » Point out the red printing on page 4. Read the sentences aloud. Ask: *Why would the author want to call attention to these sentences?* (*to show that they share important information*)

  » Discuss the content of the sentences. Ask: *Do the red sentences on page 4 describe what you see in a normal house? Why or why not?* (*The names of the places are the same as in a normal house, but having chickens in these places and what the chickens are doing is not normal.*)

  » Point out the pictures on pages 5, 6, and 7 and read the red type at the top of page 8. Ask: *What is the overall message from these photographs and words?* (*Chickens are lovable, and Mary loves them.*)

  » Call attention to the photograph on page 10. Ask: *How does this picture contrast with the earlier pictures of chickens?* (*It shows a rooster that is injured, not happy and healthy like the earlier pictures.*)

  » As you get to the white type on page 11, read it slowly. Ask: *Why would these sentences be emphasized?* (*They make an important statement about how chickens are treated.*) *What do these words tell you about Mary?* (*She has thought a lot about chickens and how they are treated.*)

Engage and Respond

- Revisit the Focus Statement: *Even small choices can lead to big change.* Then have students write two or three sentences that answer this question: *How might the small choice of visiting the county fair have led to a big change in Mary's life?* (*She saw a mistreated miniature pony there, and she never forgot it. It could have influenced her concern and care for animals later in her life.*)

EL ENGLISH LEARNER SUPPORT: Facilitate Comprehension

ALL LEVELS You may want to clarify the parts of speech of some words in the book. For example, students will likely think of the word *city* as a noun. However, in the title of the book for this module, it is used as an adjective that describes the chickens (city chickens, or chickens that live in a city). Similarly, in the name of the rescue agency, *Chicken Run Rescue*, the word *run* is not a verb but is rather a noun that refers to an enclosed place where animals can roam freely—a chicken run.

ARGUMENT • EDITORIAL

LEARNING OBJECTIVES

- Use context to understand domain-specific vocabulary.
- Use resources to determine meaning and find synonyms.
- **Language** Explain meaning of domain-specific vocabulary.

MATERIALS   Online

Focal Text *City Chickens*

Display and Engage *12.2*

Writer's Notebook *p.12.1*

Review the Focal Text

- Review with students up to page 13 in *City Chickens*. Explain that the author uses descriptive language, especially verbs, to convey meaning.

- Turn to the first page of the text. Read aloud the first four sentences. Ask: *Which words in these sentences show action?* (*the verbs* roars, howls, swish, *and* crows) Explain that the author probably chose these words for their descriptive qualities.

- Show **Display and Engage 12.2**. Have students copy the chart into the Word Bank on **Writer's Notebook page 12.1** or in their own notebooks. Then, as a group, explore synonyms for each verb that are consistent with its meaning in the sentence. As students suggest words, write them on the board and have students note them in their charts. (*roars: speeds, moves, rumbles, thunders; howls: barks, cries, bays; swish: taps, hits, rustles, whooshes; crows: squawks, cries, calls*)

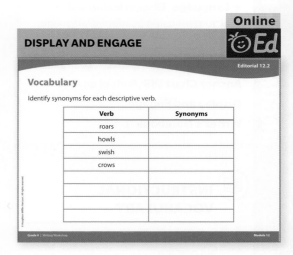

- Next, divide the class into small groups. Tell students to read page 25 in *City Chickens*. Direct them to list the verbs on the page in their charts in the Word Bank (*probes, bobs, clucks, race, topples*). Challenge each group to write synonyms for each verb. Allow them to use an online or print thesaurus. Have students vote on the best synonym for each word.

- Have each group report their choices. Discuss how the author must have sought just the right word for each action. Point out that writers use the most descriptive, vivid word choices to

  » paint a picture for the reader.

  » make the meaning clear to the reader.

  » keep the reader interested.

- Allow students to peruse *City Chickens* to find other verbs or other highly descriptive words and add them to their Word Bank.

Engage and Respond

- Have students choose one favorite word from their Word Banks and write a few sentences explaining why they chose it. Then tell students to write an original sentence using that word choice.

LESSON 3

ARGUMENT · EDITORIAL

LEARNING OBJECTIVES

- Discuss elements of an argument.
- Discuss the writing prompt.
- Consider topics for an editorial.
- **Language** Discuss features of an argument using academic language.

MATERIALS   Online

Anchor Chart W8: *Parts of an Argument*

Display and Engage *12.3*

Writer's Notebook *p.12.2*

INSTRUCTIONAL VOCABULARY

- **editorial** an article that expresses an opinion
- **argument** writing that makes a statement and supports it in order to convince readers
- **claim** the main argument
- **opinion** a belief
- **reason** a statement that explains an opinion
- **fact** a statement that can be proven

TEACHER TIP

Look for editorials about issues that will interest your students in your local newspaper, or encourage students to look for editorials and share them with the class.

Review the Writing Process

- Review the steps in the writing process. Point out that good writers take care to complete each step before moving to the next one. Note that sometimes even the best writers discover that they need to return to an earlier step.

- Display **Anchor Chart W8: Parts of an Argument**. Use it as you discuss terms relating to argument writing.

- Tell students that in this module they will write an **editorial**, an article for a school newspaper or other publication. Familiarize students with the following terms.

  » Editorials are a form of writing called **argument**, meaning that an editorial makes a statement of opinion and supports it with facts and reasons in order to convince readers. The main argument is called a **claim**.

  » Editorials state an **opinion**, or a person's belief, and support the opinion with **reasons**, statements that explain the opinion.

  » Opinions can also be supported with **facts**, or statements that can be proven.

- Write these terms on the class Instructional Vocabulary list and have students add them to their glossaries.

Read the Prompt

- Show **Display and Engage 12.3**. Discuss the prompt with students and remind them that they will have guidance throughout the writing process. Suggest that students begin thinking about issues or possible changes in their school about which they have strong opinions.

- Distribute **Writer's Notebook page 12.2**. Discuss the different expectations of the rubric. Remind students that they should use the rubric to guide their drafting and revising.

ANCHOR CHART   Online

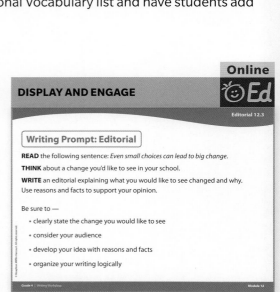

DISPLAY AND ENGAGE   Online

Editorial 12.3

Writing Prompt: Editorial

READ the following sentence: *Even small choices can lead to big change.*

THINK about a change you'd like to see in your school.

WRITE an editorial explaining what you would like to see changed and why. Use reasons and facts to support your opinion.

Be sure to —

- clearly state the change you would like to see
- consider your audience
- develop your idea with reasons and facts
- organize your writing logically

Grade 4 | Writing Workshop   Module 12

LEARNING OBJECTIVES

- Discuss features of an editorial.
- Narrow the topic for an editorial.
- Set goals for writing.
- Plan the first draft of an editorial.
- **Language** Discuss the features of editorials using academic language.

MATERIALS   Online

Display and Engage *12.4a–12.4b*

Classroom materials *editorials from school or community publications (optional)*

Writer's Notebook *pp.12.3, 12.4*

TEACHER TIP

As you brainstorm topics with students, be careful about mentioning or supporting topics that could be sensitive or problematic in your school or community.

Discuss the Purpose and Features of an Editorial

- Remind students that they will be writing an editorial about an issue in their school.

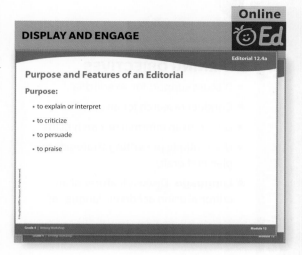

- Show **Display and Engage 12.4a–12.4b**. Discuss the purposes of editorials and remind students that the prompt calls for an editorial about a change or issue in their school.

- Discuss the features of an editorial. Point out that the structure of an editorial is similar to that of a persuasive essay. The audience, however, is the readers of a publication. Ask: *What sort of publication would have an editorial about an issue in our school? (the school newspaper, a community newspaper, the school website)* If you have example editorials from such publications, share them with students.

- Model a possible topic for students:

  THINK ALOUD *I am thinking I want to encourage kids at school to care for animals. City Chickens put me in a mood to write about birds, so that will be my topic.*

  » *We could put up bird feeders. I think I'll investigate that. I will need to find out where the feeders could go, how much the feeders and food will cost, and whether the school can afford them.*

  » *I need to consider how others in the school might feel about birds and attracting them with bird feeders. Who might object to bird feeders?*

- As a group, brainstorm editorial ideas. Record the ideas on a large sheet of paper. Say: *Remember that if someone is arguing in favor of something, there may be good reasons for the opposite opinion. Two people could write editorials on the same subject that are completely opposite!*

- When there is an adequate supply of possible topics, end the brainstorming session and have students turn to **Writer's Notebook page 12.3**. Allow time for students to carefully consider topics before they fill out the planning sheet.

- Then have students record their goals for their editorials on **Writer's Notebook page 12.4**.

EL **ENGLISH LEARNER SUPPORT: Planning Support**

SUBSTANTIAL
Discuss goals for students' editorials. Write these goals for students, and have students copy their goals into their Writer's Notebook.

MODERATE
Discuss students' writing goals. Provide sentence frames to write their goals, as needed.

LIGHT
Have student pairs discuss their writing goals before writing them.

LEARNING OBJECTIVES

- Discuss support for an editorial.
- Conduct research for an editorial.
- Generate an informal research plan.
- Use multiple prewriting strategies to plan first draft.
- **Language** Discuss features of an editorial using academic language.

MATERIALS   Online

Display and Engage 12.5a–12.5b

Writer's Notebook pp. 12.5, 12.6

TEACHER TIP

You may want to invite your principal into your classroom to answer students' questions about possible changes they are writing about. This may be easier on your principal than meeting with students individually!

 LEARNING MINDSET: Perseverance

Apply Point out to students that many worthwhile changes or tasks can be challenging or difficult at times. Provide encouragement. Say: *You may be thinking that you can't come up with any sources of information, or that your ideas just aren't coming together. Be patient and keep working on the task. Small steps will get you to your goal!*

Discuss the Model

- Show the model on **Display and Engage 12.5a–12.5b** and allow students to follow along with **Writer's Notebook page 12.5**. Ask volunteers to read the editorial aloud.

- Have students use markers or crayons to annotate their copies of the model as you mark on the projected copy.

  THINK ALOUD *I want to see what the writer included in this editorial.*

  » *Where is the claim stated?* (*end of the first paragraph*) *I'll mark that in green.*

  » *What does the writer tell about in the first sentence of the second paragraph?* (*reasons against the bird feeder*) *Does the writer just give up because there are objections?* (*No, the writer gives answers to the objections.*) *I'll mark the reasons against in blue and the responses in red.*

  » *What happens in the third paragraph?* (*The writer further supports the idea.*) *This is more support, so I'll underline it in red.*

- Note to students that the concluding paragraph repeats and reinforces the opinion that is introduced in the first paragraph.

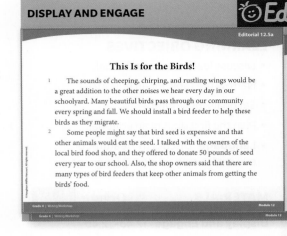

Conduct Research

- Point out that because the editorial is about school, most of the research may consist of talking to people associated with the school. Library research may also be appropriate.

- Information sources for an editorial will also depend on the topic. Have students work in groups using **Writer's Notebook page 12.6** to generate an informal research plan and identify the best sources of information. Circulate and give advice as needed.

- Have students work to determine the best sources for their individual topics, and encourage them to develop their research questions and to begin their research.

EL **ENGLISH LEARNER SUPPORT: Research Support**

SUBSTANTIAL

Help students frame research questions.

MODERATE

Provide sentence frames that will lead to research questions: *Our school needs _____ in order to _____. _____ should support this idea because _____.*

LIGHT

Have students work together to develop research questions.

LEARNING OBJECTIVES

- Develop drafts by developing an engaging idea.
- Develop drafts by organizing with purposeful structure.
- **Language** Discuss features of editorials with academic language.

MATERIALS   Online

Display and Engage *12.5a, 12.6*
Anchor Chart W6: *5+1 Ways to Start a Story*
Classroom materials *yellow, pink, and blue index cards*

 ### INSTRUCTIONAL VOCABULARY

- **counterclaim** an argument against a writer's claim
- **rebuttal** reasons why a counterclaim is wrong

TEACHER TIP

If students have difficulty constructing the hook for their introductions, tell them that they can write the introduction after the body is complete. Sometimes an idea will come to them as they write.

Discuss Introductions

- As students research, discuss ways to make their editorials more interesting.

- Project **Display and Engage 12.6**. Read aloud the first introductory sentence. Ask: *Would this sentence make you want to read more? Why or why not?* As you read the rest of the introductory sentences, elicit that these introductions aren't engaging for readers.

- Project **Display and Engage 12.5a**. Read aloud the model's introduction. Point out that, as in *City Chickens*, the model's opening helps readers hear the birds. Then the writer connects the sounds to the main point.

- Display **Anchor Chart W6: 5+1 Ways to Start a Story**. Before reviewing the ideas with students, point out that these fiction-writing openers can be adapted for editorials. Discuss other ideas students have for hooking readers.

Organize Research

- Have students take out their research and other planning notes.

- Ask students to circle two or three strong arguments that support their claim. Then have them circle one or two arguments against their main claim.

- Point out that good editorial writers bring up the arguments against their claims, called **counterclaims**, and explain why those arguments are wrong. This explanation is called a **rebuttal**.

- Tell students as they draft, they should plan on including a counterclaim or two with rebuttal to strengthen their editorials. Point out that acknowledging and rebutting an opposing viewpoint about their argument tells readers that they truly understand the topic.

- Distribute three colors of index cards. Have students write arguments supporting their main idea on pink cards, arguments against their main idea on blue cards, and information for the introduction and conclusion on yellow cards.

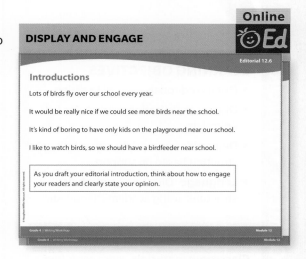

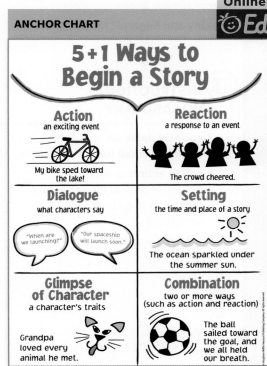

ARGUMENT • EDITORIAL

LEARNING OBJECTIVES

- Discuss editorials as a call to action.
- Discuss organizational structures for editorials.
- Determine appropriate organizational structure based on support.
- **Language** Discuss organizational structures using academic language.

MATERIALS   Online Ed

Classroom materials *index cards from previous lesson, large sheet of paper*

Display and Engage *12.5a-12.5b*

INSTRUCTIONAL VOCABULARY

- **counterclaim** an opposing argument about the author's claim
- **call to action** a statement in arguments where the writer asks the reader to do or think something

TEACHER TIP

The organizational patterns presented in this lesson are not the only possible patterns, but they are easily understood by students. If students want to try other patterns, allow them to do so.

Discuss Organizational Patterns

- Tell students that organizational patterns can help them present their arguments in a way that makes readers want to act.

- Have students take out their colored index cards. Provide time to write new cards if necessary. Say: *Today we will talk about organizing your editorial.*

- Have students select several pink cards that best support their position. Have students number the cards, with 1 being the best support, 2 the next best, and so on.

- Have students choose the blue cards with the strongest arguments against their main point, and then number the best opposition 1, the next best 2, and so on.

- Explain that students will be rearranging the cards to learn about organizational patterns.

- Write **counterclaim** on the left half of a large sheet of paper. Say: *A counterclaim is an opposing argument about your claim. This pattern introduces a counterclaim then offers a rebuttal to show why your opinion is the stronger argument.* To illustrate this pattern, tape cards to the paper in this order:

  1. The yellow introduction card.

  2. The strongest point against your position (a blue card). The writer will need to supply evidence to defeat the counterclaim.

  3. The rebuttal, or the strongest point supporting your position (a pink card).

  4. The yellow conclusion card.

- Write *Two Reasons* on the right half of the same paper. Say: *This is another organizational pattern. This one is simple: your argument is supported by two strong reasons.* To illustrate this pattern, tape cards to the paper in this order:

  1. The yellow introduction card.

  2. The first point supporting your position (a pink card).

  3. The rebuttal, or the second point supporting your position (a pink card).

  4. The yellow conclusion card.

- Point out that the Two Reasons pattern does not include arguments against the position.

- Project **Display and Engage 12.5a-12.5b**. Ask: *Which pattern of organization did this writer use?* (*counterclaim and rebuttal*)

- Allow time for students to determine which organizational pattern they want to use and to continue drafting their editorials.

- Point out that editorials often include a **call to action**, meaning that they are meant to inspire readers to do or think something. Have students add *call to action* to their glossaries. You may also want to add the term to your class Instructional Vocabulary list.

- Ask: *What do you want the readers of your editorial to do or think? This is your call to action. Wrap up your editorial by directly telling your readers what you what them to do or think!*

- Have students add a call to action to their editorials.

ARGUMENT • EDITORIAL

LEARNING OBJECTIVES

- Discuss differences between formal and informal language.
- Discuss effects of formal language.
- **Language** Discuss types of language using academic terms.

MATERIALS   Online

Display and Engage *12.7*

INSTRUCTIONAL VOCABULARY

- **formal language** a style of speaking or writing that follows the rules of proper English
- **informal language** a relaxed style of speaking or writing that you use with people you know, like friends and family

---

TEACHER TIP

Point out that formal language can sound almost humorous if it is taken to an extreme. Have some fun with exaggerating formal language.

Introduce the Skill

- Begin by formally addressing the students: *Students, today we shall endeavor to discuss the finer points of formal and informal language.* After continuing with a few more formal sentences, ask: *What was unusual about the way I was talking?* Elicit from students that your speech was more formal than usual.

- Point out that **formal language** strictly follows grammar rules and uses more specific, higher-level vocabulary, while **informal language** is not strictly bound by grammar and uses more casual words. Record these terms in the class Instructional Vocabulary list and remind students to add them to their glossaries.

- Project **Display and Engage 12.7**. Use the example to illustrate the differences between the types of language. As a class, construct formal alternatives for the remaining sentences. (*Possible responses: Would you like to go to a movie? I did not do anything to your book. I am very tired of such cold and rainy weather.*)

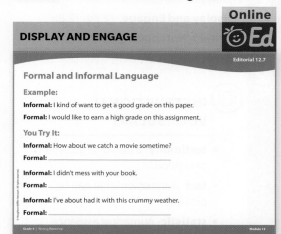

DISPLAY AND ENGAGE   Online

Editorial 12.7

Formal and Informal Language

Example:

Informal: I kind of want to get a good grade on this paper.

Formal: I would like to earn a high grade on this assignment.

You Try It:

Informal: How about we catch a movie sometime?

Formal: _____

Informal: I didn't mess with your book.

Formal: _____

Informal: I've about had it with this crummy weather.

Formal: _____

Grade 4 | Writing Workshop   Module 12

- Elicit from students that formal language does not use contractions or slang and uses complete sentences.
  Ask: *Which type of language has more authority, or believability?* (*formal*) *Which type of language should you use in your editorial?* (*formal*)

- Point out that most forms of writing should use relatively formal language; however, in everyday speech, informal language is acceptable.

- Encourage students to continue drafting their editorials, incorporating formal language as they write.

 ENGLISH LEARNER SUPPORT: Scaffold Writing

SUBSTANTIAL

Select a sentence from the student's writing and work with the student to identify the elements of informal language. Help the student revise the sentence using a more formal tone, and then mark other instances for the student to correct. Allow the student to consult you as needed.

MODERATE

Underline sentences from the students' writing that contain informal language. Provide a model for revision and then have students independently work, consulting you as necessary.

LIGHT

Have students work in pairs to identify informal language and revise those targeted sentences with more formal language.

ARGUMENT • EDITORIAL

LEARNING OBJECTIVES

- Discuss types of support.
- Identify relevant information.
- **Language** Discuss types and quality of support using academic language.

MATERIALS   Online

Display and Engage *12.8a–12.8b*

Writer's Notebook *p. 12.7*

INSTRUCTIONAL VOCABULARY

- **testimony** a personal statement of support
- **fact** a statement that can be proven
- **statistic** numerical evidence
- **survey** the answers to questions, usually reported as statistics
- **quotation** the exact words from a source
- **relevant** relates to the topic
- **current** recent
- **reliable** from a qualified source that can be trusted

TEACHER TIP

Some types of evidence may overlap; for example, a statistic is also a fact. Don't be overly concerned about the definitions as long as students understand the general concept of types of support and what makes for good supporting statements.

Introduce the Revision Skill

- Point out to students that an opinion is not enough to convince readers. Opinions need to be supported with **reliable** information before readers can be persuaded and inspired to act.

- Project **Display and Engage 12.8a–12.8b**. With students, work through the different kinds of support and qualities of good information. At an appropriate moment, add new terms to the class Instructional Vocabulary list and have students add terms to their glossaries.

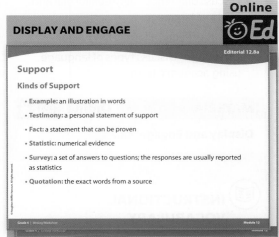

- As a class, work on **Writer's Notebook page 12.7**. This activity will help students learn to evaluate different sources of information. Discuss using support wisely and fairly.

- Point out that if students have concerns about the quality of their support, they should:

  » remove support that isn't **relevant.**

  » strengthen weak support.

  » find additional support.

- Also point out that students will need to have at least two major points of support, so they should identify and use the points for which they have the strongest, most reliable information.

Revise for Support

- Have students evaluate and revise their drafts for support.

 ENGLISH LEARNER SUPPORT: Evaluating Support

SUBSTANTIAL

Work with students individually to evaluate their use of support one point at a time. Ask yes/no questions to prompt students' thinking, such as: *Is this support current?*

MODERATE

Review students' editorials. Indicate a section of each student's editorial that requires additional support. Work with students to determine which type of support would be most useful; then have the students do additional research.

LIGHT

As students revise, have them talk with a partner about the strength of their sources and supportive information. Encourage students to provide feedback to their partners.

LESSON 10

REVISING II: CONFERENCING

LEARNING OBJECTIVES

- Review elements of an argument.
- Engage in a conference with a peer.
- Revise a draft of an editorial.
- **Language** Discuss writing using academic language.

MATERIALS   Online *Ed*

Anchor Chart W8: *Parts of an Argument*

Writer's Notebook *p. 12.8*

LEARNING MINDSET:
Perseverance

Apply Explain to students that sometimes persevering may mean that they try something new or redo something they thought was finished. After their conferences, they may find that they need to find other support or reorganize their editorials. Say: *To persevere, you need to keep focusing on what will make for a good final written product. Going back to an earlier step is not a defeat but the perseverance of sticking with a job until it is done well.*

Review Partner's Editorial

- Revisit **Anchor Chart W8: Parts of an Argument**. Remind students that incorporating these elements will make their editorials stronger and more persuasive.

- Distribute **Writer's Notebook page 12.8**. Point out the conferencing list and read it aloud with students. Tell them that they will use this list to guide their conferencing work with a partner.

- Pair students with a partner to give each other feedback on their editorials.

  » Make sure each student has a partner.

  » Instruct one partner to read his or her editorial aloud, pause, and then read it again.

  » Then have the other partner listen and jot down notes about the editorial on the conferencing sheet.

  » After both editorials have been read, allow partners to share their observations of each other's work.

- If time permits, consider having students switch partners to receive additional feedback on their editorials. Make additional conferencing sheets available or have students write their comments in their partner's notebook.

Continue to Revise

- Have students continue to revise, using the feedback they received from peers.

 ENGLISH LEARNER SUPPORT: Conferencing Support

SUBSTANTIAL

If necessary, rephrase the questions from **Writer's Notebook page 12.8** so students can respond in single words or short phrases.

MODERATE

Supply sentence frames for students such as: *The introduction is interesting because* _____.

LIGHT

Challenge students to use this sentence frame: *The feedback I received from my partner was useful because* _____. Then have students volunteer specific changes they will make to their editorials as a result of suggestions by their peers.

ARGUMENT • EDITORIAL

LEARNING OBJECTIVES

- Discuss sentence types.
- Revise writing.
- **Language** Discuss different types of punctuation.
- **Language** Choose punctuation for effect.

MATERIALS   Online

Display and Engage *12.9*

INSTRUCTIONAL VOCABULARY

- **dash** a punctuation mark that indicates a pause; it is used to set a group of words off from the rest of a sentence
- **ellipsis** a punctuation mark made up of three periods; it is used to show a pause or an omission of words from a quotation that is not needed for meaning.

TARGETED GRAMMAR SUPPORT

You may want to consult the following grammar minilessons to review key editing topics.

- **1.2.1 Declarative and Interrogative Sentences,** p. W221
- **1.2.2 Imperative and Exclamatory Sentences,** p. W222
- **6.2.1 End of Sentence Punctuation,** p. W336

Introduce the Revision Skill

- Point out to students that they can use different sentence types and punctuation to create specific effects and to make their editorials more interesting for readers.

- Project **Display and Engage 12.9**. Read aloud the first example, and say: *An editorial can sound boring if all the sentences are declarative. Declarative sentences make a statement and end with a period. Try changing a simple declarative sentence into an interrogative sentence that asks a question to make your readers want to consider and answer it.*

  DISPLAY AND ENGAGE   Online

  Editorial 12.9

  Punctuation for Effect

  1. **Question mark:** shows curiosity or invites the reader to consider an idea
     Example: Don't you think our school needs a bird feeder?

  2. **Exclamation point:** shows enthusiasm and adds excitement
     Example: The support from our community has been amazing!

  3. **Dash:** sets words apart; shows a longer pause than a comma; adds emphasis
     Example: A bird feeder—even a small one—would benefit us.

  4. **Ellipsis:** suggests a pause or an omission of words in a quotation
     Example: The principal said, "The bird feeder is one idea . . . ."

  Grade 4 | Writing Workshop   Module 12

- Read aloud the second example and remind students that exclamatory sentences can add a feeling of excitement to a piece of writing. Caution students to use exclamation points sparingly so the effect is not muted.

- Read aloud the third example and say: *A **dash** is a long hyphen, and it shows a pause. Dashes can also break up a sentence to draw attention to an idea.*

- Read aloud the fourth example and say: *An **ellipsis** is a set of three periods. This punctuation mark can show that unnecessary words are intentionally left out of a quotation or that there is a pause in the sentence.* Note to students that the plural form of the word *ellipsis* is *ellipses*.

Revise for Effect

- Challenge students to find places in their editorial where they can vary their sentence types or change punctuation for effect.

- As students continue to revise, walk among them offering assistance.

 ENGLISH LEARNER SUPPORT: Scaffold Revision

SUBSTANTIAL

Guide students to find one or two places in their writing where punctuation marks could be varied for more effective sentences.

MODERATE

Encourage students to highlight or underline punctuation marks in their writing. If there is little variation, have them consider where they might vary punctuation, using some of the punctuation marks from this lesson.

LIGHT

Have students select different types of sentences from their editorials and describe appropriate punctuation choices.

LEARNING OBJECTIVES

- **Language** Proofread writing for spelling.
- **Language** Edit writing for grammar and mechanics.

MATERIALS
Online **Ed**

Anchor Chart W17: *Proofreading Marks*

TARGETED GRAMMAR SUPPORT

You may want to consult the following grammar minilessons to review key editing topics.

- **1.2.4 Review Kinds of Sentences,** p. W224
- **2.1.3 Capitalizing Languages, People's Names, and Nationalities,** p. W238
- **6.4.2 End Punctuation,** p. W347

Review Proofreading Chart

- Remind students that they just increased the power of their writing by revising their punctuation marks. Point out that mistakes in grammar, mechanics, and spelling will diminish the power of any writing because such mistakes distract readers.

- Display **Anchor Chart W17: Proofreading Marks**. Review the proofreading marks with students.

Proofread Writing

- Have students independently edit their writing for spelling, mechanics, punctuation, and grammar.

- Circulate the room and provide assistance, as needed.

- As you circulate, group students who need support on similar grammar topics. Use the grammar minilessons or the students' own writing to provide targeted instruction, review, and support.

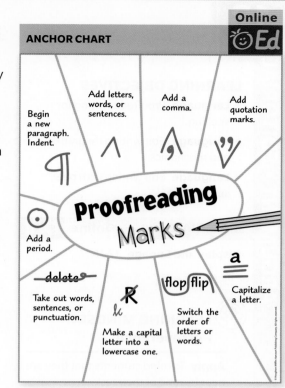

ANCHOR CHART · Online **Ed**

 ENGLISH LEARNER SUPPORT: Editing Support

ALL LEVELS Review students' writing with them. As you encounter a grammatical error, write a different sentence that contains the same grammatical error on another sheet of paper. Discuss the grammatical error with students and guide them to correct the same mistake in their own writing.

ARGUMENT • EDITORIAL

LEARNING OBJECTIVES

- **Language** Proofread writing for spelling.
- **Language** Edit writing for grammar and mechanics.
- **Language** Edit writing with peer support.

MATERIALS   Online

Display and Engage 12.10

LEARNING MINDSET: Perseverance

Apply Remind students that they are near the end of their task. Congratulate them on their perseverance so far, and encourage them to continue working diligently to its completion. Say: *I think it's a great feeling when you know that you have kept at a task, even when it has been difficult. You are learning a lot about editorials, writing, and yourself!*

TARGETED GRAMMAR SUPPORT

You may want to consult the following grammar minilessons to review key editing topics.

- **1.1.3 Subject-Verb Agreement,** p. W218
- **1.2.3 Four Kinds of Sentences,** p. W223
- **3.3.4 Review Progressive Verb Tenses,** p. W279
- **6.1.4 Review Quotations,** p. W334

Use the Clocking Activity

- Show **Display and Engage 12.10** and discuss the items to be checked by editors. Keep the checklist visible during the clocking exercise.

- Review the rules for clocking.

  » Each writer prepares a cover page for his or her editorial. This page should have the writer's name at the top and be divided into several sections. Each section is labeled from 1–6, with each number corresponding to an editing task.

  » Students form concentric circles, hence the term *clocking*. Students in the inner circle trade papers with their classmates in the outer circle. As students receive a peer's editorial, they become that editorial's editor.

  » No marks are made on the actual editorial. Each editor writes his or her name in a specific section on the editing page and makes comments on each editing task.

  » Call out which item is to be checked by the editor: 1. features of an editorial; 2. variety of complete sentence types; 3. punctuation within sentences; 4. capitalization; 5. punctuation at the end of sentences, including question marks and exclamation points; and 6. other comments.

  » After pairs complete the first editing task, have students collect their editorials and move to another editor. Continue the process until the entire editing page is completed.

Edit Writing

- When the editing process is completed, have students return the editing page and editorial to the writer. Then have the writer use the editing page as a guide to make edits to the editorial.

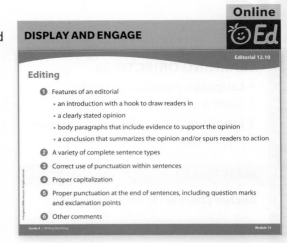

Online

DISPLAY AND ENGAGE

Editorial 12.10

Editing

1. Features of an editorial
   - an introduction with a hook to draw readers in
   - a clearly stated opinion
   - body paragraphs that include evidence to support the opinion
   - a conclusion that summarizes the opinion and/or spurs readers to action
2. A variety of complete sentence types
3. Correct use of punctuation within sentences
4. Proper capitalization
5. Proper punctuation at the end of sentences, including question marks and exclamation points
6. Other comments

Grade 4 | Writing Workshop   Module 12

 ENGLISH LEARNER SUPPORT: Language Structure

SUBSTANTIAL

Share sample sentences that contain a grammar convention that students need to understand and practice. Have students copy a few of the sentences to provide exposure to that specific grammar convention.

MODERATE

Provide sentences with blanks where grammar and punctuation choices need to be made. Have students work together to complete the sentences. Ensure students have used grammar and punctuation correctly and clarify with further instruction as necessary.

LIGHT

Have students review their writing for grammar conventions that have been especially tricky for them. Provide any clarification on specific grammar rules as needed.

ARGUMENT • EDITORIAL

LEARNING OBJECTIVES
- Write a title for the editorial.
- Publish writing.
- Use technology to assist with publishing.
- **Language** Discuss publishing using academic vocabulary.

MATERIALS   Online

Writer's Notebook *pp.12.4, 12.9*

TEACHER TIP

Before submitting any student work for any type of publication, check your school or district policies for publishing student work.

Prepare the Final Copy

- Allow time for last-minute changes as students work together in pairs to finalize their editorials.

- Have students write titles for their editorials and prepare a final copy.

- Circulate among the students and offer assistance as needed.

Discuss Publishing

- Tell students that the content of their editorials will give them hints about places where they can be published. Possibilities could include:

> a. sending the editorial to the school newspaper.
>
> b. sending the editorial to another community publication.
>
> a. posting the editorial on the school website.
>
> b. sending the editorial to the principal or school board.

- Have students confer about where and how they might publish their editorials.

Engage and Respond

- Have students read **Writer's Notebook page 12.9**. Then have students turn to **Writer's Notebook page 12.4** and revisit the goals they set before writing. Allow students to Turn and Talk with a partner about their goals. Have students take notes about the goals they might set for their next writing assignment.

LEARNING OBJECTIVES

- Share writing.
- Participate in a collaborative discussion.
- **Language** Discuss editorials using academic language.

Share Writing

- Have students share their editorials by reading them aloud. Have students discuss ideas they had for publishing during the last lesson.

- Encourage students to ask the presenters questions about their editorials. Remind students of the rules regarding asking questions and offering positive feedback. Encourage speakers to answer any questions with details they learned as they were writing.

Engage and Respond

- Conclude with an informal debriefing about how students felt about writing editorials. Ask the following questions:

  » *How did your attitude toward editorials change as you worked on this assignment?*

  » *What did you like best about writing your editorial?*

  » *What did you like least?*

  » *Describe your thoughts about publishing your editorial.*

  » *Do you think your editorial would persuade an audience? Why or why not?*

 ENGLISH LEARNER SUPPORT: Practice Reading

ALL LEVELS Allow time for students to practice reading their editorials aloud before they present their writing to the group. Have them rehearse their reading with you, another adult, a student partner, or by themselves.

Grammar Minilessons

GRAMMAR MINILESSONS • TOPICS AND SKILLS

Customize your grammar instruction to your classroom needs. These minilessons can be

- **INTEGRATED** Support the grammar instruction in the Writing Workshop revising and editing lessons.
- **DIFFERENTIATED** Deliver based on needs demonstrated in each student's writing.
- **SYSTEMATIC** Teach according to scope and sequence indicated in the weekly planners.

GRAMMAR MINILESSONS • TOPICS AND SKILLS

TOPIC 3 — VERBS

GRAMMAR MINILESSONS • TOPICS AND SKILLS

LEARNING OBJECTIVES

- **Language** Identify simple and complete subjects and predicates.
- **Language** Use the parts of a sentence correctly in writing and speaking.

MATERIALS Online

Display and Engage *Grammar 1.1.1a, 1.1.1b, 1.1.1c, 1.1.1d*

Printable *Grammar 1.1.1*

 INSTRUCTIONAL VOCABULARY

- **subject** the naming part of the sentence that tells who or what
- **predicate** the action part of the sentence that tells what the subject does or did
- **simple subject** is the main word that is the focus of the sentence
- **complete subject** all the words that tell who or what is doing the action
- **simple predicate** the main word that tells what the subject does or is
- **complete predicate** all the words that tell what the subject is or does

Connect and Teach

- Show **Display and Engage: Grammar 1.1.1a**. Explain that a **sentence** expresses a complete thought. Remind students that a sentence starts with a capital letter and ends with punctuation. Point out that every complete sentence has a **simple subject** and a **simple predicate**.

- Model identifying the simple subject and the simple predicate in this sentence: *Adventurous Katie swam in the ocean.*

  THINK ALOUD Katie *is the simple subject. I ask:* What is the main word that tells what the subject does or is? Katie swam. *So* swam *is the simple predicate.*

- Explain that a **complete subject** is all of the words about the subject. A **complete predicate** is all the words that tell what the subject does.

- Use the example to identify the complete subject and the complete predicate.

  THINK ALOUD *I look for words that tell about Katie. The complete subject is* Adventurous Katie. *I'll look for all the words that tell what the Katie did. The complete predicate is* swam in the ocean.

Engage and Apply

- Complete items 1–8 on **Display and Engage: Grammar 1.1.1c, Grammar 1.1.1d** with the students.

- Have students give complete sentences with simple subjects and predicates and then share the complete subject and predicate.

- Have students complete **Printable: Grammar 1.1.1** to review simple and complete subjects and predicates.

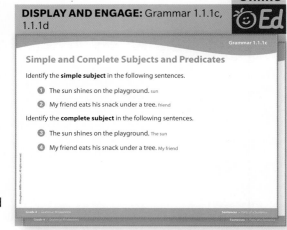

- Have students edit a writing draft to review simple and complete subjects and predicates.

 ENGLISH LEARNER SUPPORT: Scaffolded Practice

SUBSTANTIAL

Write: *Sarah bakes a cake.* Point out the subject and predicate, *Sarah, bakes.* Guide students to make sentences using *mixes the batter; Sarah; pours the batter; eats the cupcake.* Work together to identify the simple and complete subject and predicate for each sentence.

MODERATE

Have students copy two sentences from their reading. Have pairs identify the simple and complete subjects and predicates and share them with a partner.

LIGHT

Have students write two sentences and exchange them with a partner. Have them circle the complete subjects and underline the complete predicates, and then share the simple subjects and predicates.

LEARNING OBJECTIVES

- **Language** Identify compound subjects and predicates.
- **Language** Use the parts of a sentence correctly in speaking and writing.

MATERIALS

Online

Display and Engage *Grammar 1.1.2a, 1.1.2b*

Printable *Grammar 1.1.2*

 INSTRUCTIONAL VOCABULARY

- **simple subject** is the main word that is the focus of the sentence
- **complete subject** all the words that tell who or what is doing the action
- **compound subject** two or more subjects
- **simple predicate** the main word that tells what the subject does or is
- **complete predicate** all the words that tell what the subject is or does
- **compound predicate** a predicate with two or more actions

Connect and Teach

- Show **Display and Engage: Grammar 1.1.2a**. Review the definition of a **simple subject** and **predicate**. Explain that a **complete subject** is made up of all of the words that name the person or thing the sentence is about and that a **complete predicate** is made up of all the words that tell what the subject does or did.

- Explain that a sometimes there is more than one subject in a sentence. Explain that a **compound subject** is two or more subjects in a sentence. Explain that a **compound predicate** has two or more actions. A coordinating conjunction combines the subjects or predicates.

- Model identifying a compound subject using this sentence: *Hugo and Nancy knit socks and donate them to the community shelter.*

  THINK ALOUD *To identify a compound subject, I ask:* How many subjects are there? What word is used to combine the compound subject? *I see that* and *is used to combine the compound subject,* Hugo and Nancy. *I see two actions for the compound predicate,* knit *and* donate.

- Guide students to identify the complete subject and predicate in the sentence. *Hugo and Nancy; knit socks and donate them to the community shelter*

Engage and Apply

- Complete items 1–6 on **Display and Engage: Grammar 1.1.2b** with the students.

- Remind students that coordinating conjunctions like *and* can combine subjects and predicates.

- Have students complete **Printable: Grammar 1.1.2** to review compound subjects and predicates.

- Have students edit a writing draft to review compound subjects and predicates.

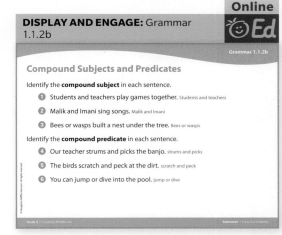

DISPLAY AND ENGAGE: Grammar 1.1.2a

Online ⊙Ed

Compound Subjects and Predicates

A **compound subject** is made up of two or more subjects joined by a coordinating conjunction such as *and* or *or*.

A **compound predicate** is made up of two or more predicates joined by a coordinating conjunction such as *and, or, but,* and *so.*

compound subject
Jan and Jules play board games.

compound predicate
Jan sorts and counts the game pieces.

DISPLAY AND ENGAGE: Grammar 1.1.2b

Online ⊙Ed

Compound Subjects and Predicates

Identify the **compound subject** in each sentence.
1. Students and teachers play games together. Students and teachers
2. Malik and Imani sing songs. Malik and Imani
3. Bees or wasps built a nest under the tree. Bees or wasps

Identify the **compound predicate** in each sentence.
4. Our teacher strums and picks the banjo. strums and picks
5. The birds scratch and peck at the dirt. scratch and peck
6. You can jump or dive into the pool. jump or dive

 ENGLISH LEARNER SUPPORT: Scaffolded Practice

ALL LEVELS Point out the difference between a phrase and a subject, predicate, and sentence.

- A phrase is a group of words. *the blue sky; a lost shoe*
- The subject tells who or what. It has a noun or a pronoun. *The brothers; Payton and Lia; They*
- The predicate is the action part. It always includes a verb. *run a race; read a book*
- A simple subject or simple predicate is simple because it is just one word. *Sasha dances.*
- A complete subject or predicate are all the words that tell about who does something and what they do. *Graceful Sasha dances in the ballet.*

Choose sentences from books to practice telling identifying phrases, subjects, predicates, and sentences.

LEARNING OBJECTIVES

- **Language** Form subject-verb agreement.
- **Language** Use the parts of a sentence correctly in speaking and writing.

MATERIALS
Online

Display and Engage *Grammar 1.1.3a, 1.1.3b*

Printable *Grammar 1.1.3*

INSTRUCTIONAL VOCABULARY

- **simple predicate** the main word that tells what the subject does or is
- **present tense** a verb that tells what is happening now

Connect and Teach

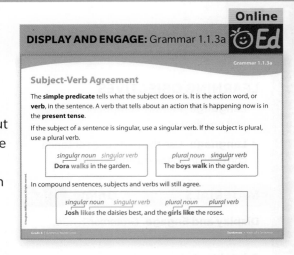

- Show **Display and Engage: Grammar 1.1.3a**.

- Remind students that **verbs** show action. A present-tense verb tells about an action happening now. A past-tense verb tells about an action that has happened in the past. Regular verbs in the past tense have the ending *-ed*. Verbs in the present tense have two forms. The correct form depends on what the **subject** of the sentence is.

- Add *-s* to the verb when the noun in the subject is singular, unless the subject is *I*.

- Do not add *-s* to the verb when the noun in the subject is plural.

- Model how to determine which present-tense form to use with these sentences: *Hana walk/walks home after school. The boys walk/walks home after school.*

  THINK ALOUD *To form verbs in the present tense, I ask:* Is the noun in the subject singular or plural? *In the first sentence,* walks *is correct because* Hana *is a singular noun. In the second sentence,* walk *is correct because* boys *is a plural noun.*

- Use the following examples to model subject-verb agreement.

  » *Ann dribbles the basketball.*
    Ann is the simple subject. Add *-s* to dribble because Ann is a singular noun.

  » *Ann and Frank dribble the basketballs.*
    Ann and Frank is the simple subject, but is also a compound subject. Do not add *-s* because Ann and Frank name more than one person, so it is a plural subject.

Engage and Apply

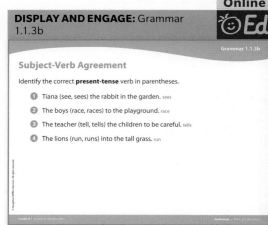

- Complete items 1–4 on **Display and Engage: Grammar 1.1.3b** with the students.

- Have students find examples of sentences with present-tense verbs and past-tense verbs. Have pairs identify if the nouns are singular or plural. Remind them to look for compound subjects.

- Have students complete **Printable: Grammar 1.1.3** to review subject-verb agreement.

- Have students edit a writing draft to review subject-verb agreement.

EL **ENGLISH LEARNER SUPPORT: Scaffolded Practice**

ALL LEVELS Write two lists: one of singular and plural subjects and one of singular and plural action verbs. Have students work in mixed-proficiency groups to match singular subjects to singular verbs and plural subjects to plural verbs. Then have partners choose two subjects and verbs from the lists and write sentences with subject-verb agreement.

LEARNING OBJECTIVES

- **Language** Review the parts of a sentence.
- **Language** Use the parts of a sentence correctly in speaking and writing.

MATERIALS   Online

Display and Engage *Grammar 1.1.4a, 1.1.4b, 1.1.4c, 1.1.4d*

Printable *Grammar 1.1.4*

 INSTRUCTIONAL VOCABULARY

- **subject** the naming part of the sentence that tells who or what
- **predicate** the action part of the sentence that tells what the subject does or did
- **simple subject** the main word that is the focus of the sentence
- **complete subject** all the words that tell who or what is doing the action
- **compound subject** two or more subjects
- **simple predicate** the main word that tells what the subject does or is
- **complete predicate** all the words that tell what the subject is or does
- **compound predicate** a predicate with two or more actions
- **present tense** a verb that tells what is happening now

Review Parts of a Sentence

- Show **Display and Engage: Grammar 1.1.4a, Grammar 1.1.4b,** and **Grammar 1.1.4c**. Review the types of subjects and predicates and how to form subject-verb agreement.

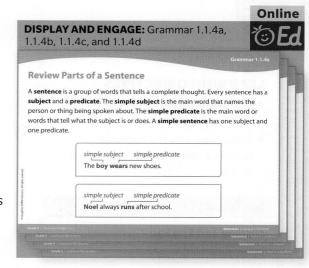

DISPLAY AND ENGAGE: Grammar 1.1.4a, 1.1.4b, 1.1.4c, and 1.1.4d

Review Parts of a Sentence

A **sentence** is a group of words that tells a complete thought. Every sentence has a **subject** and a **predicate**. The **simple subject** is the main word that names the person or thing being spoken about. The **simple predicate** is the main word or words that tell what the subject is or does. A **simple sentence** has one subject and one predicate.

> simple subject   simple predicate
> The **boy wears** new shoes.

> simple subject   simple predicate
> **Noel** always **runs** after school.

- The **simple subject** tells who does what in the sentence. The **complete subject** is made up of all the words that tell who or what is doing the action in the sentence. A **compound subject** is made up of two or more subjects joined by a conjunction such as *and* or *or*.

- The **simple predicate** tells what the subject does or did. The **complete predicate** is made up of all the words that tell what the subject does or did. A **compound predicate** is made up of two or more predicates joined by a **coordinating conjunction** such as *and, or, but,* and *so*.

- Have students complete **Display and Engage: Grammar 1.1.4d**.

- Write the following sentences on the board and ask students to identify the parts of the sentence.

  » *Frank plays volleyball.*
    Name the subject and predicate.
    Frank is the simple subject, *plays* is the simple predicate; *plays volleyball* is the complete predicate.
    Do the subject and verb agree?
    Frank is singular, so add *-s* to play.

  » *Frank and Jasper run and swim.*
    Name the subject and predicate.
    Frank and Jasper is the compound subject: *run and swim* is the compound predicate.
    Do the subject and verb agree?
    Frank and Jasper is plural so do not add *-s* to either verb.

- Have students complete **Printable: Grammar 1.1.4** to review the parts of a sentence.

- Have students edit a writing draft to review the parts of a sentence.

 ENGLISH LEARNER SUPPORT: Scaffolded Practice

ALL LEVELS Remind students that *simple* in this context means "the main part." Provide additional examples of simple subjects and predicates, such as *dog, girl, bear, went, reads,* and *growled.*

Students may omit the final *-s* from third-person present-tense regular verbs. They may say *he walk* instead of *he walks.* Guide students to complete these sentence frames using subject-verb agreement.

I _____ (run/runs) to the park. run

She _____ (run/runs) with me to the park. runs

SENTENCES • PARTS OF A SENTENCE

LEARNING OBJECTIVES

- **Language** Write sentences with subject-verb agreement.
- **Language** Use the parts of a sentence correctly in speaking and writing.

MATERIALS   Online

Display and Engage *Grammar 1.1.5*

Printable *Grammar 1.1.5*

INSTRUCTIONAL VOCABULARY

- **subject** the naming part of the sentence that tells who or what
- **present tense** a verb that tells what is happening now

Connect and Teach

- Tell students that sentences that flow together naturally are important in writing so that readers stay focused and interested.

- Explain that one part of revising is to combine sentences with coordinating conjunctions to create new sentences with compound subjects and predicates.

- Show **Display and Engage: Grammar 1.1.5**. Read aloud the information to review subjects and predicates and subject-verb agreement. Discuss the examples.

Engage and Apply

- Explain that combining subjects and predicates with a coordinating conjunction can lead to sentences that flow naturally.

- Guide students to combine these sentences using a compound subject.

  » *Sharks live near coral reefs. Eels live near coral reefs.*
    Sharks and eels live near coral reefs.

- Explain that you can add the coordinating conjunction *and* to combine the subjects to make a compound subject, *Sharks and eels*.

- Guide students to combine these sentences using a compound predicate.

  » *Fish swim around the coral reef. Fish hide around the coral reef.*
    Fish swim and hide around the coral reef.

- Explain that you can add the coordination conjunction *and* to make a compound predicate, *swim and hide*.

- Have students complete **Printable: Grammar 1.1.5** to review subject-verb agreement.

- Have students edit a writing draft to review subject-verb agreement.

DISPLAY AND ENGAGE: Grammar 1.1.5   Online

Connect to Writing: Using Sentences with Subject-Verb Agreement

In your writing, pay attention to the endings of the verbs you use. The correct form to use depends on what the subject of the sentence is. Always check the spelling of each verb ending.

Singular Subject	Plural Subject
singular noun add -s **Mr. Garza** eats fruit for breakfast.	plural noun do not add -s **Mr. Garza and Mrs. Garza** eat fruit for breakfast.
singular noun add -es **Mr. Garza** watches a new movie.	plural noun do not add -es **Mr. Garza and Mrs. Garza** watch a new movie.

ENGLISH LANGUAGE SUPPORT: Scaffolded Practice

SUBSTANTIAL

Write several simple sentences. Have a student circle the subjects. Then invite another student to underline the predicates. Repeat the process with sentences that contain compound subjects and predicates.

MODERATE

Using students' past writing, model how to combine subjects and predicates using coordinating conjunctions. Then share sentences that can be combined and work together to create a new sentence.

LIGHT

Have students work with a partner to write sentences of their own about characters or events in their reading. Have pairs identify the subjects and predicates.

LEARNING OBJECTIVES

- **Language** Identify declarative and interrogative sentences.
- **Language** Use the four kinds of sentences correctly in writing and speaking.

MATERIALS   Online

Display and Engage *Grammar 1.2.1a, 1.2.1b*

Printable *Grammar 1.2.1*

 INSTRUCTIONAL VOCABULARY

- **statement/declarative sentence** a sentence that tells something
- **question/interrogative sentence** a sentence that asks a question

Connect and Teach

- Show **Display and Engage: Grammar 1.2.1a**. Explain that a **declarative sentence** is a statement and ends with a period. Point out that an **interrogative sentence** asks a question, and it ends with a question mark. Also point out that both kinds of sentences begin with a capital letter.

- Model identifying the declarative and interrogative sentences in the following examples: *Abraham Lincoln had a sister. What is her name?*

  THINK ALOUD *To identify the kind of sentences, I ask:* Does the sentence make a statement? Does the sentence ask a question? *The first example is a statement that ends with a period. So it is a declarative sentence. The next example is question, and it ends with a question mark. So it is an interrogative sentence.*

Engage and Apply

- Complete items 1–5 on **Display and Engage: Grammar 1.2.1b** with the students.

- Ask students to describe the punctuation and capitalization in each sentence.

- Have students complete **Printable: Grammar 1.2.1** to review declarative and interrogatory sentences.

- Have students edit a writing draft to review declarative and interrogatory sentences.

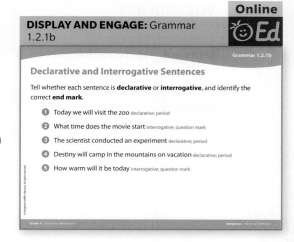

DISPLAY AND ENGAGE: Grammar 1.2.1a   Online

Grammar 1.2.1a

Declarative and Interrogative Sentences

A sentence that makes a statement is a **declarative sentence**. It ends with a period (.).

A sentence that asks a question is an **interrogative sentence**. It ends with a question mark (?).

Every sentence begins with a capital letter.

| **Declarative Sentence** |
| Manuel and his sister like the zoo. |

| **Interrogative Sentence** |
| Do you like the zoo? |

DISPLAY AND ENGAGE: Grammar 1.2.1b   Online

Grammar 1.2.1b

Declarative and Interrogative Sentences

Tell whether each sentence is **declarative** or **interrogative**, and identify the correct **end mark**.

1. Today we will visit the zoo declarative; period
2. What time does the movie start interrogative; question mark
3. The scientist conducted an experiment declarative; period
4. Destiny will camp in the mountains on vacation declarative; period
5. How warm will it be today interrogative; question mark

 ENGLISH LEARNER SUPPORT: Facilitate Language Connections

In Cantonese, Hmong, and Tagalog, the order of subject and verb may be the same in both questions and statements. Students may create constructions, such as, *When you will come back?* Provide practice and support with subject-verb inversion in questions that use helping verbs, for example, *When will you come back?*

Scaffolded Practice

SUBSTANTIAL

Choose declarative and interrogative sentences from a familiar story. Have students repeat the sentences after you. Write the sentences on the board. Have students listen to the difference of intonation between declarative and interrogative sentences to identify each sentence by type. Have students repeat the types after you.

MODERATE

Have students choose declarative and interrogative sentences from a familiar story and identify each. Ask volunteers to read them aloud, paying attention to the difference in intonation between declarative and interrogative sentences

LIGHT

Display different sentence types to talk about a topic or a story. Have students identify which sentences make a statement, ask a question, express strong feeling, or give a command. Have students come up with examples of different sentences as they discuss a topic or a story.

SENTENCES • KINDS OF SENTENCES

LEARNING OBJECTIVES

- **Language** Identify imperative and exclamatory sentences.
- **Language** Use the four kinds of sentences correctly in writing and speaking.

MATERIALS Online

Display and Engage *Grammar 1.2.2a, 1.2.2b*

Printable *Grammar 1.2.2*

 INSTRUCTIONAL VOCABULARY

- **command/imperative sentence** a sentence that gives a command
- **exclamation/exclamatory sentence** a sentence that shows strong feelings

Connect and Teach

- Show **Display and Engage: Grammar 1.2.2a**. Explain that an **imperative sentence** is a command and is punctuated with a period or an exclamation point.

- Point out that an **exclamatory sentence** shows strong feeling and ends with an exclamation point. Explain that the exclamation point is used for effect—to highlight a strong feeling.

- Model identifying the imperative and exclamatory sentences in the following examples: *Go to the park at ten o'clock. I can't wait to play soccer.*

  THINK ALOUD *To identify the kind of sentences, I ask:* Does the sentence give a command? Does the sentence show strong feeling? *The first sentence is a command. So it is an imperative sentence. This next sentence shows strong feeling and ends with an exclamation point. It is an exclamatory sentence.*

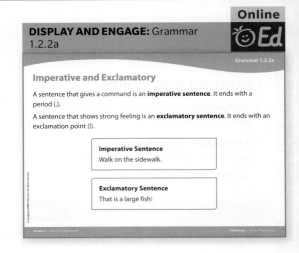

DISPLAY AND ENGAGE: Grammar 1.2.2a

Online Ed

Grammar 1.2.2a

Imperative and Exclamatory

A sentence that gives a command is an **imperative sentence**. It ends with a period (.).

A sentence that shows strong feeling is an **exclamatory sentence**. It ends with an exclamation point (!).

Imperative Sentence
Walk on the sidewalk.

Exclamatory Sentence
That is a large fish!

Engage and Apply

- Complete items 1–5 on **Display and Engage: Grammar 1.2.2b** with students.

- Have students give imperative and exclamatory sentences. Have them identify and explain the end punctuation for each sentence.

- Have students complete **Printable: Grammar 1.2.2** to review imperative and exclamatory sentences.

- Have students edit a writing draft to review imperative and exclamatory sentences.

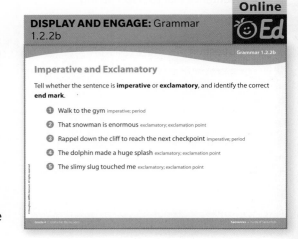

DISPLAY AND ENGAGE: Grammar 1.2.2b

Online Ed

Grammar 1.2.2b

Imperative and Exclamatory

Tell whether the sentence is **imperative** or **exclamatory**, and identify the correct **end mark**.

1. Walk to the gym imperative; period
2. That snowman is enormous exclamatory; exclamation point
3. Rappel down the cliff to reach the next checkpoint imperative; period
4. The dolphin made a huge splash exclamatory; exclamation point
5. The slimy slug touched me exclamatory; exclamation point

EL **ENGLISH LEARNER SUPPORT: Scaffolded Practice**

SUBSTANTIAL

Write an imperative and an exclamatory sentence without end punctuation:
Sit at the table.
I won the race!

Ask students which sentence tells someone what to do. Then ask which sentence has a strong feeling, such as excitement. Guide them to add a period to the imperative sentence and an exclamation point to the exclamatory sentence.

MODERATE

Say imperative sentences and have students follow the commands. Ask students to name the end punctuation that should be used. Then give exclamations and have students name the end punctuation. Have students repeat the exclamations with strong feeling.

LIGHT

Have students write two commands and two exclamations without end punctuation. Then have partners carry out the commands and repeat the sentences with feeling. As a group, talk about the end punctuation for each type of sentence.

LEARNING OBJECTIVES

- **Language** Identify the four kinds of sentences.
- **Language** Use the four kinds of sentences correctly in writing and speaking.

MATERIALS

Online Ed

Display and Engage *Grammar 1.2.3a, 1.2.3b, 1.2.3c*

Printable *Grammar 1.2.3*

INSTRUCTIONAL VOCABULARY

- **statement/declarative sentence** a sentence that tells something
- **question/interrogative sentence** a sentence that asks a question
- **command/imperative sentence** a sentence that gives a command
- **exclamation/exclamatory sentence** a sentence that shows strong feelings

Connect and Teach

- Show **Display and Engage: Grammar 1.2.3a**. Review with students the four kinds of sentences: **declarative**, **interrogative**, **imperative**, and **exclamatory**. Remind students that all sentences begin with a capital letter.

- Model how to identify kinds of sentences using the following example: *What time is the meeting tomorrow?*

  THINK ALOUD *To identify what kind of sentence this is, I ask:* What is the purpose of the sentence? What punctuation should be used? *The sentence ends with a question mark. Its purpose is to ask a question. So, this is an interrogative sentence.*

- Repeat the process above to guide students to identify the type of each of these sentences: *He was extremely excited about the team's win!* (expresses a strong feeling/ exclamatory) *I like dogs better than cats.* (tells about something/declarative) *Put on your coat.* (gives a command/imperative)

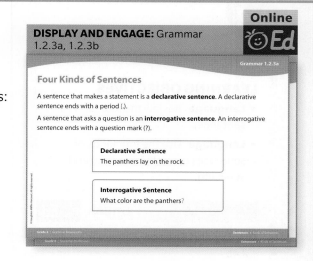

Engage and Apply

- Complete items 1–5 on **Display and Engage: Grammar 1.2.3c** with the students.

- Have students give examples of each type of sentence and explain the punctuation used.

- Have students complete **Printable: Grammar 1.2.3** to review the four kinds of sentences.

- Have students edit a writing draft to review the four kinds of sentences.

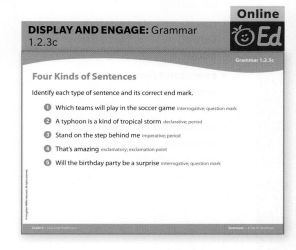

ENGLISH LEARNER SUPPORT: Scaffolded Practice

SUBSTANTIAL

Write examples of each kind of sentence. Point out the end punctuation and the purpose of each sentence. Guide students to identify each type of sentence and the punctuation.

He has an orange cat. declarative   *Read chapter two.* imperative
Did you talk to your sister? interrogative   *I was picked to sing in the show!* exclamatory

MODERATE

Have students identify which purpose matches each end punctuation. Then give examples of each type of sentence.

I like to eat apples every day. declarative   *Clean your room.* imperative
Can we see that movie? interrogative   *She is the fastest runner!* exclamatory

LIGHT

Have pairs write definitions of each type of sentence and why it is used. Then have them write examples of each sentence.

LEARNING OBJECTIVES

- **Language** Review the four kinds of sentences.

- **Language** Use the four kinds of sentences correctly in writing and speaking.

MATERIALS   Online 🍎Ed

Display and Engage *Grammar 1.2.4a, 1.2.4b*

Printable *Grammar 1.2.4*

INSTRUCTIONAL VOCABULARY

- **statement/declarative sentence** a sentence that tells something

- **question/interrogative sentence** a sentence that asks a question

- **command/imperative sentence** a sentence that gives a command

- **exclamation/exclamatory sentence** a sentence that shows strong feelings

Review Kinds of Sentences

- Show **Display and Engage: Grammar 1.2.4a**. Read the instruction to review the kinds of sentences. Then have students complete the activity on **Display and Engage: Grammar 1.2.4b**.

- Review the four kinds of sentences: declarative, interrogative, imperative, and exclamatory. Discuss the punctuation for each type. Remind students that the first word of each type of sentence is capitalized.

DISPLAY AND ENGAGE: Grammar 1.2.4a and 1.2.4b

Online 🍎Ed

Grammar 1.2.4a

Review Kinds of Sentences

There are four kinds of sentences:

- A sentence that makes a statement is a **declarative sentence**. It ends with a period.
- A sentence that asks a question is an **interrogative sentence**. It ends with a question mark.
- A sentence that gives a command is an **imperative sentence**. It ends with a period or exclamation point.
- A sentence that shows strong feeling is an **exclamatory sentence**. It ends with an exclamation point.

- Write the following sentences on the board. Have students identify the sentence type and its purpose.

  » *We visited my grandmother last night. declarative; tell something*

  » *Finish your homework before dinner. imperative; tell to do something*

  » *Does she have volleyball practice tomorrow? interrogative; ask something*

  » *I can't believe I won the science fair! exclamatory; tell with strong feeling*

- Then have students complete **Printable: Grammar 1.2.4** for more practice with sentence types.

- Have students create a four-column chart with the names of each kind of sentence across the top: declarative, interrogative, imperative, exclamatory. Have them note the end punctuation for each kind of sentence and its purpose. Have pairs find or write examples of each kind of sentence.

- Have students edit a writing draft using a variety of kinds of sentences.

EL **ENGLISH LEARNER SUPPORT: Facilitate Language Connections**

In Spanish, interrogative and exclamatory sentences have inverted question and exclamation points as beginning punctuation as well. Explain that in English, question and exclamation points are only needed at the ends of sentences.

Scaffolded Practice

ALL LEVELS Remind students that the punctuation at the end of a sentence can help them tell what type of sentence it is. Provide examples of each kind of sentence: *When is the next math test? Look at the schedule. The test is on Friday. Wow! That is really soon.*

Have students use the end punctuation to identify the kind of sentence.

LEARNING OBJECTIVES

- **Language** Use the four kinds of sentences to convey ideas.
- **Language** Use the four kinds of sentences correctly in writing and speaking.

MATERIALS   Online

Display and Engage *Grammar 1.2.5*

Printable *Grammar 1.2.5*

INSTRUCTIONAL VOCABULARY

- **statement/declarative sentence** a sentence that tells something
- **question/interrogative sentence** a sentence that asks a question
- **command/imperative sentence** a sentence that gives a command
- **exclamation/exclamatory sentence** a sentence that shows strong feelings

Connect and Teach

- Show **Display and Engage: Grammar 1.2.5**. Review how to identify and use the four kinds of sentences.

- Tell students that the use of different types of sentences will lend variety and interest to their writing, keeping readers focused and engaged.

- Remind students that checking for a mix of sentence types is an important part of revising.

DISPLAY AND ENGAGE: Grammar 1.2.5   Online Ed

Grammar 1.2.5

Connect to Writing: Using Different Kinds of Sentences

Avoid using too many declarative statements when you write. Turn some declarative statements into questions, imperatives, and exclamations. This will make your writing livelier and help to keep your readers' attention.

Declarative Statements	Four Kinds of Sentences
We watched the elephants play in the sand. They looked very happy. One elephant seemed to be afraid of the pond. Then one elephant sprayed me with water.	We watched the elephants play in the sand. They looked very happy! Was one elephant afraid of the pond? Then one elephant sprayed me with water!

Engage and Apply

- Display these sentences. Guide students to restate each statement as a question, a command, or an exclamation. Have them identify each type of sentence they create and explain the end punctuation. Also have them tell which words should be capitalized and why.

  » *Sarah rode her bike to school in the rain. declaratory*

  » *She got so wet! exclamatory*

  » *She has to change into dry clothes. imperative*

  » *Why would she ride her bike in the rain? interrogative*

- Have students complete **Printable: Grammar 1.2.5** to review the four kinds of sentences.

- Have students edit a writing draft to review the four kinds of sentences.

EL ENGLISH LEARNER SUPPORT: Support Revision

SUBSTANTIAL

Read aloud from students' past writing. Work together to determine if the writing has a variety of sentence types. Choose two declarative sentences and model how to revise them to interrogative, imperative, or exclamatory.

MODERATE

Read aloud from students' past writing. Work together to identify declarative sentences that can be revised to use a different sentence type. Discuss how it makes the writing more interesting. Choose sentences to revise and read aloud the improved writing together.

LIGHT

Have students share their writing with a partner. Have partners identify declarative sentences that can be revised to include a different sentence type. Ask volunteers to share how they would revise the declarative sentences.

LEARNING OBJECTIVES

- **Language** Identify sentence fragments.
- **Language** Use sentences correctly in speaking and writing.

MATERIALS
Online

Display and Engage *Grammar 1.3.1a, 1.3.1b*

Printable *Grammar 1.3.1*

 INSTRUCTIONAL VOCABULARY

- **sentence fragment** a group of words that does not tell a complete thought
- **subject** the part of a sentence that tells who or what is doing the action
- **predicate** the part of a sentence that tells what action is being done

Connect and Teach

- Show **Display and Engage: Grammar 1.3.1a**. Tell students that a **sentence fragment** is a group of words that does not tell a complete thought.

- Explain that fragments lack a **subject**, a **predicate**, or both.

  THINK ALOUD *Listen to this group of words:* Went to the baseball game. *When I read this group of words, I see that it does not tell a complete thought. It does not say who went to the game. I can correct this fragment by adding a subject to complete the thought:* My friends went to the baseball game.

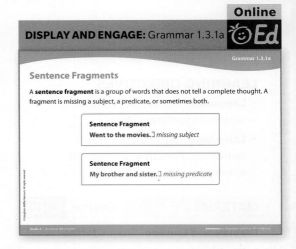

Engage and Apply

- Complete items 1–4 on **Display and Engage: Grammar 1.3.1b** with students.

- Write a variety of sentence fragments. Have students identify what is missing from each fragment and correct the error.

  » *The bird.* missing predicate

  » *Landed in the birdhouse.* missing subject

  » *Went sledding.* missing subject

  » *The boys.* missing predicate

- Have students complete **Printable: Grammar 1.3.1** to review sentence fragments.

- Have students edit a writing draft to correct any sentence fragments.

 ENGLISH LEARNER SUPPORT: Scaffolded Practice

ALL LEVELS Provide examples of fragments and complete sentences. Have students identify each and explain what is missing from the fragments. Have students make suggestions for correcting the fragments as they are able. Ask for different suggestions to show different options to correct each fragment.

Sarah went to the library. complete sentence
Ran down the street. fragment; missing the subject
The team. fragment: missing the predicate
Sarah went to the library. complete sentence
Ran down the street. fragment; missing the subject
The team. fragment; missing the predicate

LEARNING OBJECTIVES

- **Language** Identify run-on sentences.
- **Language** Use sentences correctly in speaking and writing.

MATERIALS   Online

Display and Engage Grammar 1.3.2a, 1.3.2b

Printable Grammar 1.3.2

 INSTRUCTIONAL VOCABULARY

- **run-on sentence** a sentence that has two complete thoughts, or sentences, that run into each other
- **comma splice** a comma incorrectly connecting two thoughts without a conjunction

Connect and Teach

- Show **Display and Engage: Grammar 1.3.2a**. Explain that a run-on sentence is a sentence that has two complete thoughts, or sentences, that run into each other without appropriate punctuation or a conjunction.

- Tell students that there are two ways to correct a run-on sentence: they can form two separate sentences by adding punctuation and a capital letter, or they can form a single compound sentence by adding a comma and a conjunction.

  THINK ALOUD *I read this sentence:* James wants a new shirt he is going to the store. *I see that it has two complete thoughts. I can correct this run-on by putting a period after shirt and starting the next sentence with a capital letter or by adding a comma and the word* so *after* shirt. James wants a new shirt. He is going to the store. James wants a new shirt, so he is going to the store.

- Explain that a comma alone cannot separate two independent clauses. This error is a type of run-on sentence called a **comma splice**. For example: *James bought a shirt, he bought a pair of pants.* Tell students that they should always use a coordinating conjunction or use a period or semicolon to separate the clauses. Work with students to revise the sentence. (*James bought a shirt, and he bought a pair of pants.*)

Engage and Apply

- Complete items 1–5 on **Display and Engage: Grammar 1.3.2b** with students.

- Have students produce two complete sentences, and then exchange them with partners, who will make sure neither sentence is a fragment or run-on.

- Have students complete **Printable: Grammar 1.3.2** to review run-on sentences.

- Have students edit a writing draft to correct any run-on sentences.

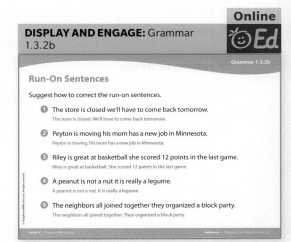

 ENGLISH LEARNER SUPPORT: Scaffolded Practice

ALL LEVELS Provide examples of run-on sentences for students to identify and correct.
Jason joined the soccer team. complete sentence
Jason loves soccer he joined the soccer team. run-on; Jason loves soccer, so he joined the soccer team.
The stadium is full I can't find a seat. run-on; The stadium is full. I can't find a seat.
Ask volunteers to share their corrected complete sentences.

LEARNING OBJECTIVES

- **Language** Write complete sentences.
- **Language** Use sentences correctly in speaking and writing.

MATERIALS   Online

Display and Engage *Grammar 1.3.3a, 1.3.3b*

Printable *Grammar 1.3.3*

INSTRUCTIONAL VOCABULARY

- **complete sentence** has a subject and predicate, and expresses one complete thought
- **subject** the part of a sentence that tells who or what is doing the action
- **predicate** the part of a sentence that tells what action is being done
- **comma splice** a comma incorrectly connecting two thoughts without a conjunction
- **fragment** a group of words that does not tell a complete thought
- **run-on sentence** a sentence that has two complete thoughts, or sentences, that run into each other

Connect and Teach

- Show **Display and Engage: Grammar 1.3.3a**. Review that a sentence tells a complete thought and has a **subject** and a **predicate**.

- Model how to correct the following **fragment** and **run-on sentence**: *Anna walked to the game Bill ran there. Found good seats.* Point out how to avoid a **comma splice**.

  THINK ALOUD *I can correct the run-on by adding a comma between* game and Bill. *Now that I read it aloud, I see I forgot to add a conjunction. If you add a comma but don't add a conjunction, you get a comma splice. To correct this error, I need to add a comma and the conjunction* and *between* game and Bill. Anna walked to the library, and Bill ran there. *The fragment needs a subject, so I'll add* They *before* found good seats *and make* found *lowercase.* Anne walked to the game, and Bill ran. They found good seats.

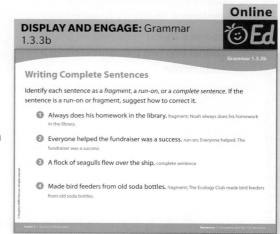

Engage and Apply

- Complete items 1–4 on **Display and Engage: Grammar 1.3.3b** with students.

- Write the following sentences on the board. Have students identify each as a fragment, run-on, or complete sentence, and orally correct each fragment or run-on.

  » *Mel likes fiction he wants to be a writer.* run-on; period after fiction; capitalize he

  » *On rainy days we go to the library.* complete sentence

  » *On weekends.* fragment; Sample answer: On weekends we read comics.

- Have students complete **Printable: Grammar 1.3.3** to review writing complete sentences.

- Have students edit a writing draft to review writing complete sentences.

 ENGLISH LEARNER SUPPORT: Scaffolded Practice

ALL LEVELS Review the difference between an incomplete and a complete sentence. Reinforce the difference by displaying the following word groups. Work with students to distinguish the complete sentences from the incomplete sentences. Ask students to identify what is missing and how to correct the incomplete sentences as they are able.

The cat in the window. incomplete sentence
The cat meows. complete sentence
Mom feeds the cat. complete sentence
Drinks water. incomplete sentence

LEARNING OBJECTIVES

- **Language** Identify sentence fragments and run-on sentences.
- **Language** Use sentences correctly in speaking and writing.

MATERIALS

Online

Display and Engage *Grammar 1.3.4a, 1.3.4b, 1.3.4c*

Printable *Grammar 1.3.4*

 INSTRUCTIONAL VOCABULARY

- **sentence fragment** a group of words that does not tell a complete thought
- **run-on sentence** a sentence that has two complete thoughts, or sentences, that run into each other
- **complete sentence** has a subject and predicate, and expresses one complete thought
- **subject** the part of a sentence that tells who or what is doing the action
- **predicate** the part of a sentence that tells what action is being done
- **comma splice** a comma incorrectly connecting two thoughts without a conjunction

Review Fragments and Run-On Sentences

- Show **Display and Engage: Grammar 1.3.4a** and then **1.3.4b**. Read aloud the instruction to review how to correct **fragments** and **run-on sentences**. Then have students complete the activity on **Display and Engage: Grammar 1.3.4c**.

DISPLAY AND ENGAGE: Grammar 1.3.4a, 1.3.4b, and 1.3.4c

Grammar 1.3.4a

Review Fragments and Run-On Sentences

A sentence tells a complete thought. It has a subject and a predicate. A group of words that does not tell a complete thought is called a **sentence fragment**.

Sentence Fragments	Corrected Sentences
Helped clean up the park.	The class helped clean up the park.
Makes us feel good.	Volunteering makes us feel good.

- Write these sentences on the board. Have students identify if the sentence is a run-on, fragment, or **comma splice**. Then have students share what to add to create a complete sentence.

  » *Scientists closely study.* fragment; add a predicate

  » *Read the chapter take careful notes.* run-on; add period after *chapter,* capitalize *take*

  » *Getting into bed very late.* fragment; add a subject

  » *He bakes a pie, she bakes a cake.* comma splice; add the conjunction *and* after the comma

- Have students complete **Printable: Grammar 1.3.4** to review fragments and run-on sentences.

- Have students edit a writing draft to review fragments and run-on sentences.

 ENGLISH LEARNER SUPPORT: Scaffolded Practice

ALL LEVELS Remind students that *fragment* means "piece or part." Provide additional examples of sentence fragments, such as *pool open; the boys were; went bowling.* Have students suggest ways to correct each fragment as they are able. complete sentences, such as *The pool is open now,* or *The boys went bowling.*

SENTENCES • FRAGMENTS AND RUN-ON SENTENCES

LEARNING OBJECTIVES

- **Language** Write using complete sentences.
- **Language** Use sentences correctly in speaking and writing.

MATERIALS   Online

Display and Engage *Grammar 1.3.5*

Printable *Grammar 1.3.5*

 INSTRUCTIONAL VOCABULARY

- **sentence fragment** a group of words that does not tell a complete thought
- **run-on sentence** a sentence that has two complete thoughts, or sentences, that run into each other
- **complete sentence** has a subject and predicate, and expresses one complete thought
- **comma splice** a comma incorrectly connecting two thoughts without a conjunction

Connect and Teach

- Explain that good writers use **complete sentences** to make their ideas clear. Using proper punctuation and capitalization makes their writing understandable for readers.

- Point out that an important part of revising is correcting **fragments**, **run-on sentences**, and **comma splices**.

- Show **Display and Engage: Grammar 1.3.5**. Read the sample sentences and review how to correct fragments, run-on sentences, and comma splices.

DISPLAY AND ENGAGE: Grammar 1.3.5

Online ⊙Ed

Grammar 1.3.5

Connect to Writing: Using Complete Sentences

When you write, you can fix a sentence fragment by adding the missing subject or predicate. To correct a run-on sentence or a comma splice, separate the two complete thoughts with a period.

Sentence Fragment	Run-On Sentence
Is almost out of whole grain muffins.	We are going to a museum on Friday there is a new dinosaur exhibit.
	We are going to a museum on Friday, there is a new dinosaur exhibit.
New, Complete Sentence	**New, Complete Sentences**
The café is almost out of whole grain muffins.	We are going to a museum on Friday. There is a new dinosaur exhibit.

Engage and Apply

- Display the following sentences. Guide students to correct the fragments, comma splices, and run-on sentences using the sample answers.

  » *To the store after lunch. Lupe walked to the store after lunch.*

  » *Felipe read books he listened to music. Add a period after books and capitalize he.*

  » *To go shopping. I like to go shopping.*

  » *The stores were closed, it was time to go home. Add so after comma.*

- Have students complete **Printable: Grammar 1.3.5** to review using complete sentences.

- Have students edit a writing draft to review using complete sentences.

 ENGLISH LEARNER SUPPORT: Support Revision

SUBSTANTIAL

Read aloud from students' writing, selecting fragments and run-ons for students to correct. Review that a fragment is an incomplete idea; it is missing a subject or a predicate. Review that a run-on is two complete thoughts in one sentence. Remind students that commas, conjunctions, and capitalizing letters can help correct sentences.

MODERATE

Read aloud from students' past writing. Working together, identify fragments, run-ons, and comma splices. Write corrections on the board and discuss how each was corrected.

LIGHT

Have students work in pairs to correct fragments, run-ons, and comma splices. Ask volunteers to share some of their correct sentences.

LEARNING OBJECTIVES

- **Language** Identify compound sentences.
- **Language** Use compound and complex sentences correctly in writing.

MATERIALS   Online

Display and Engage *Grammar 1.4.1a, 1.4.1b*

Printable *Grammar 1.4.1*

INSTRUCTIONAL VOCABULARY

- **comma** a mark that shows a pause in a sentence
- **compound sentence** a sentence that has two simple sentences joined by a comma and a connecting word, such as *and, or, but,* or *so*
- **coordinating conjunction** a word that connects other words or groups of words in a sentence

Connect and Teach

- Show **Display and Engage: Grammar 1.4.1a**. Discuss that a simple sentence has a subject and a predicate and is a complete thought.

- Explain that a **compound sentence** is made up of two simple sentences joined by a **coordinating conjunction**. A coordination conjunction is a conjunction, such as *and, but, or,* and *so.* Point out that in a compound sentence, a comma is used before the coordinating conjunction.

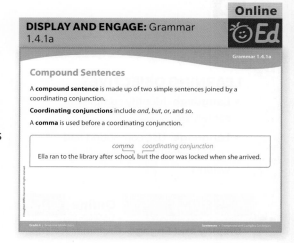

- Model identifying compound sentences by using the example sentence: *John packed his clothes, and he started thinking about summer camp.*

  THINK ALOUD *To identify a compound sentence, I ask:* Is the sentence made up of two simple sentences? Is one word a coordinating conjunction with a comma before it? *I see two simple sentences. The sentences are joined by the coordinating conjunction,* and. *I also see a comma before* and.

- *John packed his clothes, and he started thinking about summer camp.*

Engage and Apply

- Complete items 1–4 on **Display and Engage: Grammar 1.4.1b** with students.

- Have students complete **Printable: Grammar 1.4.1** to review compound sentences.

- Have students edit a writing draft to review compound sentences.

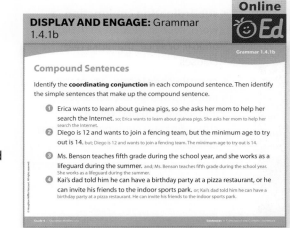

EL ENGLISH LEARNER SUPPORT: Scaffolded Practice

Explain that compound sentences are made up of two simple sentences that are joined by a conjunction and a comma.

SUBSTANTIAL

Write *I am cold. I don't like to wear sweaters.* Work with students to combine the sentences using a comma and the conjunction *but. I am cold, but I don't like to wear sweaters.*

MODERATE

Give student pairs a list of simple sentences. Have them create compound and complex sentences using conjunctions and commas.

I love snow.

It snows often in my town.

I don't like to feel cold.

It's fun to walk in the snow.

LIGHT

Have students write compound sentences about the selections they read. Have partners read each other's sentences and identify the conjunction and the sentence type.

LEARNING OBJECTIVES

- **Language** Identify complex sentences.
- **Language** Use compound and complex sentences correctly in writing.

MATERIALS   Online

Display and Engage *Grammar 1.4.2a, 1.4.2b*

Printable *Grammar 1.4.2*

INSTRUCTIONAL VOCABULARY

- **dependent clause** a group of words with both a subject and predicate that is not a complete sentence
- **subordinating conjunction** a word, such as *because, although, until, if,* or *since,* that links two clauses
- **complex sentence** a sentence made up of a simple sentence and a clause joined with a subordinating conjunction such as *because*

Connect and Teach

- Show **Display and Engage: Grammar 1.4.2a**. Explain that a **complex sentence** is made up of a **simple sentence** and a **dependent clause**. The two parts are joined by a **subordinating conjunction**, such as *because, although, until, if,* and *since*. If the conjunction begins the sentence, a comma is used after the first part of the sentence.

- Model identifying complex sentences by using this example sentence: *I need a new pair of sneakers because I have grown out of my old ones.*

  THINK ALOUD *I ask:* Is the sentence made up of a simple sentence and a dependent clause with a subordinating conjunction? *I see the simple sentence,* I need a new pair of sneakers *and the clause* because I have grown out of my old ones. Because *is a subordinating conjunction. It is in the middle of the sentence, so I don't use a comma.*

- Repeat the modeling with the following example sentence, pointing out the comma. *Since it is already late, we are not going to start watching the movie today.*

Engage and Apply

- Complete items 1–5 on **Display and Engage 1.4.2b** with students.

- Have students complete **Printable: Grammar 1.4.2** to review complex sentences.

- Have students edit a writing draft to review complex sentences.

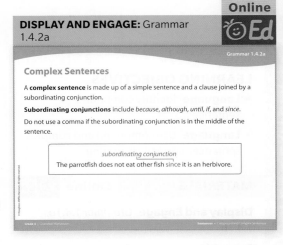

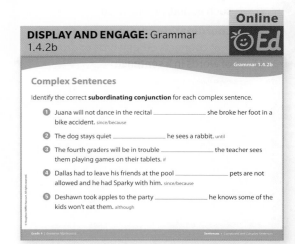

 ENGLISH LEARNER SUPPORT: Scaffolded Practice

ALL LEVELS Write *Ivan will read his book until dinner is ready.* Work with students to identify the following:

> simple sentence: *Ivan will read his book,* subordinating conjunction: *until,* words connected by the subordinating conjunction: *dinner is ready.*

> Help students understand that Ivan will read but will stop reading when dinner is ready.

> Write: *because, although, until, if, since.* Work together to select the conjunction that best completes each sentence. Point out commas in sentences beginning with subordinating conjunctions.

> Mr. Ramos rides a bike to work <u>because</u> he likes to exercise.
> <u>Although</u> the drums are her favorite instrument, Susan plays the trumpet in the band.
> You can watch TV <u>until</u> it is time to go to your grandfather's house.
> I walk the dog in the afternoon <u>since</u> I started working earlier in the day.
> <u>If</u> Alfred wants to play in the soccer game, he must finish his paper today.

LEARNING OBJECTIVES

- **Language** Use commas in a compound sentence.

- **Language** Use compound and complex sentences correctly in writing.

MATERIALS
Online **Ed**

Display and Engage *Grammar 1.4.3a, 1.4.3b*

Printable *Grammar 1.4.3*

 INSTRUCTIONAL VOCABULARY

- **comma** a mark that shows a pause in a sentence

- **compound sentence** a sentence that has two simple sentences joined by a comma and a connecting word, such as *and, or, but,* or *so*

- **coordinating conjunction** a word that connects other words or groups of words in a sentence

Connect and Teach

- Show **Display and Engage: Grammar 1.4.3a**. Review with students that in a **compound sentence**, a **comma** is used before the **coordinating conjunction**. Remind students that *and, or, but,* and *so* are coordinating conjunctions.

- Model the use of the comma in compound sentences in the example sentence: *Teva could help fix your bike, or she could tell you who to ask for help.*

  THINK ALOUD *To identify where to put the comma in this compound sentence, I ask:* Where is the coordinating conjunction? *I see the coordinating conjunction* or *before the word* she. *So, I know to place a comma before the conjunction in this compound sentence.*

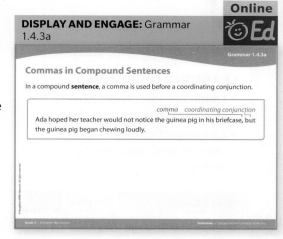

Engage and Apply

- Complete items 1–4 on **Display and Engage: Grammar 1.4.3b** with students.

- Ask students to give compound sentences. Write them on the board, leaving out the commas. Have students identify the coordinating conjunction in each compound sentence, and identify where to place the comma.

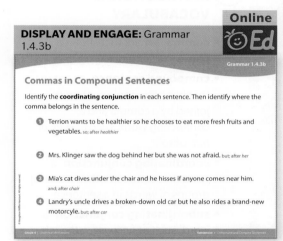

- Have students complete **Printable: Grammar 1.4.3** to review commas in compound sentences.

- Have students edit a writing draft to review commas in compound sentences.

 ENGLISH LEARNER SUPPORT: Facilitate Language Connections

Point out that in English, simple and compound sentences generally have the same word order and structure as Spanish sentences. Remind students that simply finding the word *and, but,* or *or* doesn't necessarily signify a compound sentence.

Scaffolded Practice

Present these sentences. Have students tell whether they are simple or compound sentences.

Ask Laura or Sarah for help with your homework. simple
Laura is great at math, and Sarah can help with English. compound
You can hand in your assignment today or tomorrow. simple
The teacher will grade it as soon as possible, but you might not get it back until next week. compound

SENTENCES • COMPOUND AND COMPLEX SENTENCES

LEARNING OBJECTIVES

- **Language** Identify and form compound and complex sentences.
- **Language** Use compound and complex sentences correctly in writing.

MATERIALS   Online Ed

Display and Engage *Grammar 1.4.4a, 1.4.4b, 1.4.4c*

Printable *Grammar 1.4.4*

 ### INSTRUCTIONAL VOCABULARY

- **comma** a mark that shows a pause in a sentence
- **compound sentence** a sentence that has two simple sentences joined by a comma and a connecting word, such as *and, or, but,* or *so*
- **coordinating conjunction** a word that connects other words or groups of words in a sentence
- **subordinating conjunction** a word, such as *because, although, until, if,* or *since,* that links two clauses
- **complex sentence** a sentence made up of a simple sentence and a clause joined with a subordinating conjunction such as *because*

Review Compound and Complex Sentences

- Show **Display and Engage: Grammar 1.4.4a** and then **1.4.4b**. Read the instruction and review the examples to review compound and complex sentences. Then have students work through the items on **Display and Engage: Grammar 1.4.4c**.

- Remind students that a **compound sentence** is made up of two simple sentences joined by a **comma** and a **conjunction**, such as *and, but, so,* or *or.* The comma is placed before the conjunction. A **complex sentence** is made up of a simple sentence and a **dependent clause** joined with a **subordinating conjunction**, such as *because.*

- Write the following sentences on the board. Have students identify each as a compound or complex sentence, and explain how the use of the comma is appropriate.

  » *The pond is frozen because it has been very cold outside. complex, no comma because subordinating conjunction is in the middle of the sentence*

  » *Since the temperature has been warming up, the pond is thawing. complex, comma after the dependent clause because it comes first*

  » *Water accumulates on the surface of the pond, and it is very slippery. compound, comma before coordinating conjunction*

  » *The kids go home before dark, and they drink hot chocolate to warm up. compound, comma before coordinating conjunction*

- Have students complete **Printable: Grammar 1.4.4** to review compound and complex sentences. Have students edit a writing draft to review compound and complex sentences.

DISPLAY AND ENGAGE: Grammar 1.4.4a, 1.4.4b, and 1.4.4c

Online Ed

> Grammar 1.4.4a
>
> **Review Compound and Complex Sentences**
>
> A **compound sentence** is made up of two simple sentences joined by a **coordinating conjunction**. The most common **coordinating conjunctions** are *and, but, or,* and *so.* Use a comma before a coordinating conjunction in a compound sentence.
>
> | Compound Sentence |
> |---|
> | *comma   coordinating conjunction* |
> | We had fun at the park today, so we will go back tomorrow. |

 ### ENGLISH LEARNER SUPPORT: Scaffolded Practice

ALL LEVELS The difference between coordinating and subordinating conjunctions can cause confusion for English language learners. Review with students the definition of each type of conjunction and its purpose in connecting words or groups of words. Give examples of each conjunction and discuss how it functions in a compound or complex sentence.

SUBSTANTIAL/MODERATE
Review coordinating conjunctions and subordinating conjunctions:
- coordinating conjunctions: *but, or, and, so*
- subordinating conjunctions: *until, although, if, since, because*

Write a compound and a complex sentence, omitting the comma. Work with students to place the comma and identify the type of conjunction.
Our class cleaned up the playground, and we repaired the broken swings.
Because of our hard work, everyone can enjoy the playground.

LIGHT
Have student pairs work together to write two examples of compound and complex sentences that require commas. Ask volunteers to share their sentences.

LEARNING OBJECTIVES

- **Language** Write using compound and complex sentences.
- **Language** Use compound and complex sentences correctly in writing.

MATERIALS   Online

Display and Engage *Grammar 1.4.5*

Printable *Grammar 1.4.5*

INSTRUCTIONAL VOCABULARY

- **comma** a mark that shows a pause in a sentence
- **compound sentence** a sentence that has two simple sentences joined by a comma and a connecting word, such as *and, or, but,* or *so*
- **coordinating conjunction** a word that connects other words or groups of words in a sentence
- **subordinating conjunction** a word, such as *because, although, until, if,* or *since,* that links two clauses
- **complex sentence** a sentence made up of a simple sentence and a clause joined with a subordinating conjunction such as *because*

Connect and Teach

- Explain that good writers use a variety of sentences, including **compound** and **complex sentences**, to make their writing interesting.

- Show **Display and Engage: Grammar 1.4.5**. Point out that an important part of revising is looking for short sentences that can be combined into compound or complex sentences. When combining sentences, it's important to check for the correct use of **commas** and **coordinating** and **subordinating conjunctions**.

Engage and Apply

- Have students complete the activity on **Display and Engage: Grammar 1.4.5**.

- Display the following pairs of sentences. Guide students to combine each pair to form a compound or complex sentence. Have them identify the type of sentence they form and explain the use of the comma as appropriate.

  » *Jill gathered her friends. She divided them into teams.*
  Jill gathered her friends, and she divided them into teams. compound; comma to separate the two simple sentences

  » *Jill was happy. Her friends were having fun.*
  Jill was happy because her friends were having fun. complex, no comma, subordinating conjunction in the middle of the sentence

  » *Nobody wanted to stop playing. They made plans to play tomorrow.*
  Because nobody wanted to stop playing, they made plans to play tomorrow. complex, comma after subordinating conjunction because it comes first

- Have students complete **Printable: Grammar 1.4.5** to review using compound and complex sentences.

- Have students edit a writing draft to review using compound and complex sentences.

 ENGLISH LEARNER SUPPORT: Support Revision

SUBSTANTIAL

Select short sentences from students' past writing. Model how to form a compound sentence, explaining that the comma and coordinating conjunction connects the two sentences to form one sentence. Then model how to create a complex sentence, using the subordinating conjunction to connect the simple sentences.

MODERATE

Select short sentences from students' past writing. Work together to revise the sentences into compound or complex sentences.

LIGHT

Have students review drafts of their writing. Have them work with a partner to identify examples of short sentences that can be revised into compound and complex sentences. Ask volunteers to share examples of their revisions.

NOUNS AND PRONOUNS • PROPER NOUNS

LEARNING OBJECTIVES

- **Language** Capitalize the names of historical events and documents.
- **Language** Use proper nouns correctly in speaking and writing.

MATERIALS
Online

Display and Engage *Grammar 2.1.1a, 2.1.1b*

Printable *Grammar 2.1.1*

 INSTRUCTIONAL VOCABULARY

- **common noun** a word that names a person, place, or thing
- **proper noun** a word that names a particular person, place, or thing and is capitalized
- **capital letter** a letter that comes at the beginning of a proper noun and is uppercase

Connect and Teach

- Show **Display and Engage: Grammar 2.1.1a**. Explain that a **common noun** does not name something specific, so it is not capitalized. A **proper noun** is a word that names a specfic person, place, or thing, so it begins with a **capital letter**. Names of historical events and documents are proper nouns and should be capitalized.

- Model identifying the proper nouns that name a historical event and document in the following examples: *Boston played a big part in the American Revolutionary War. The Stamp Act Congress created the Declaration of Rights and Grievances.*

  THINK ALOUD *To figure out which words to capitalize, I ask*: What words name a particular event or document? *In the first example,* Revolutionary War *names a particular historical event. So it is capitalized. In the next example,* Declaration of Rights and Grievances *names a historical document. So they are capitalized also.*

Engage and Apply

- Complete items 1–4 on **Display and Engage: Grammar 2.1.1b** with students.

- Have students scan their social studies textbook for examples of historical events and documents and discuss why each example is capitalized.

- Have students complete **Printable: Grammar 2.1.1** to review capitalizing historical events and documents.

- Have students edit a writing draft to review capitalizing proper nouns.

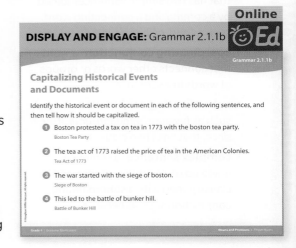

DISPLAY AND ENGAGE: Grammar 2.1.1a

Online Ed
Grammar 2.1.1a

Capitalizing Historical Events and Documents

Common nouns are nouns that name people, places, or things. They are not capitalized. **Proper nouns**, which name *particular* people, places, or things—such as historical periods, events, or documents—should always be capitalized.

historical event
Boston played a big part in the **American Revolutionary War**.

historical document
The Stamp Act Congress created the **Declaration of Rights and Grievances**.

DISPLAY AND ENGAGE: Grammar 2.1.1b

Online Ed
Grammar 2.1.1b

Capitalizing Historical Events and Documents

Identify the historical event or document in each of the following sentences, and then tell how it should be capitalized.

1 Boston protested a tax on tea in 1773 with the boston tea party.
Boston Tea Party

2 The tea act of 1773 raised the price of tea in the American Colonies.
Tea Act of 1773

3 The war started with the siege of boston.
Siege of Boston

4 This led to the battle of bunker hill.
Battle of Bunker Hill

 ENGLISH LEARNER SUPPORT: Facilitate Language Connections

Speakers of languages without alphabetic systems may need more practice starting proper nouns and sentences with capital letters. Provide practice sentences, such as *James sings in the choir. The name of the choir is The Riverdale Youth Voices.*

Scaffolded Practice

SUBSTANTIAL
Have students copy two sentences from their reading. Have them work in pairs to identify the common and proper nouns.

MODERATE
Write: *Jackson loved the snow, and he lived in the Rocky Mountains.* Have students underline the common nouns and capitalize the proper nouns.

LIGHT
Have students write two sentences of their own including some common and proper nouns. Then have them exchange papers with a partner. Tell them to circle the common nouns and underline the proper nouns.

LEARNING OBJECTIVES

- **Language** Capitalize titles.
- **Language** Use proper nouns correctly in speaking and writing.

MATERIALS   Online 😊 Ed

Display and Engage *Grammar 2.1.2a, 2.1.2b*

Printable *Grammar 2.1.2*

INSTRUCTIONAL VOCABULARY

- **common noun** a word that names a person, place, or thing
- **proper noun** a word that names a particular person, place, or thing and is capitalized
- **capital letter** a letter that comes at the beginning of a proper noun and is uppercase

Connect and Teach

- Show **Display and Engage: Grammar 2.1.2a**. Tell students that the titles of books, stories, and essays are **proper nouns**. Point out that each important word in a title should begin with a **capital letter**.

- Model identifying the title and which words to capitalize in the following example sentence: *Laura Ingalls Wilder wrote* Little House in the Big Woods.

  THINK ALOUD *I ask: Which words are part of a title? Little House in the Big Woods is the title of a book. Little, House, Big, and Woods are capitalized because they are important words in the title. The words* in *and* the *are not capitalized.*

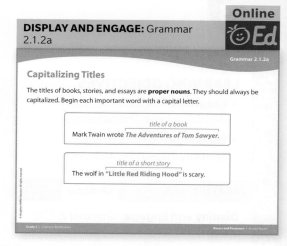

Engage and Apply

- Complete items 1–4 on **Display and Engage: Grammar 2.1.2b** with students.

- Have students name five books or stories that you can write on the board. Then have students explain which words in each title should be capitalized and why.

- Have students complete **Printable: Grammar 2.1.2** to review capitalizing titles.

- Have students edit a writing draft to review capitalizing titles.

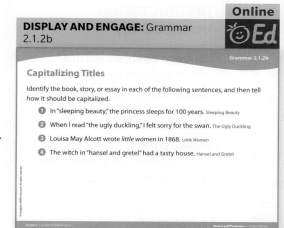

ENGLISH LEARNER SUPPORT: Scaffolded Practice

SUBSTANTIAL

Write the book title incorrectly: james and the giant peach. Explain that the important words tell about the book. Help students to identify the important words that should be capitalized.

MODERATE

Have students brainstorm a list of movie titles. Explain that movie titles are capitalized just like book titles. Ask students to tell which words should have capital letters and write the titles on the board.

LIGHT

Have students write a list of their favorite books and movies. Ask students to explain why certain words are capitalized and others are not. Ask: *Why are some words important?*

NOUNS AND PRONOUNS • PROPER NOUNS

LEARNING OBJECTIVES

- **Language** Capitalize languages, people's names, and nationalities.
- **Language** Use proper nouns correctly in speaking and writing.

MATERIALS   Online

Display and Engage *Grammar 2.1.3a, 2.1.3b*

Printable *Grammar 2.1.3*

 INSTRUCTIONAL VOCABULARY

- **common noun** a word that names a person, place, or thing
- **proper noun** a word that names a particular person, place, or thing and is capitalized
- **capital letter** a letter that comes at the beginning of a proper noun and is uppercase

Connect and Teach

- Show **Display and Engage: Grammar 2.1.3a**. Explain that **common nouns** are not specific, so they are not capitalized. Tell students that languages, people's names, and nationalities are **proper nouns**. They are specific. Explain that proper nouns should always be capitalized.

- Model identifying the proper nouns in the example sentence: *Mrs. Smith is French and learned to speak English.*

  THINK ALOUD *I ask:* What words name a language, person, or nationality? *I see that* Mrs. Smith *is capitalized. That's someone's name. The word* French *is capitalized. It is a nationality. The word* English *is also capitalized because it's a language.*

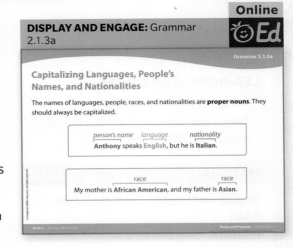

Engage and Apply

- Complete items 1–4 on **Display and Engage: Grammar 2.1.3b** with students. Have students explain their use of capitalization in the sentences.

- Work with students to create a list of languages, nationalities, and people's names they're familiar with. Write the list on the board. Have students explain why each one is capitalized.

- Have students complete **Printable: Grammar 2.1.3** to review capitalizing languages, people's names, and nationalities.

- Have students edit a writing draft to review capitalizing languages, people's names, and nationalities.

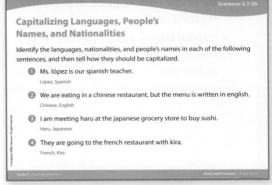

📣 ENGLISH LEARNER SUPPORT: Scaffolded Practice

SUBSTANTIAL

Write the following incorrectly: hindi, jamil. Tell students that these words are a language and a name, and that these are proper nouns that need capital letters. Ask students to help you capitalize each word. Then discuss which names a language and a name: Jamil is the boy's name. He speaks the Hindi language.

MODERATE

Create a three-column chart of languages, names, and nationalities. Have students identify which category each word belongs to and then capitalize the first letter.

LIGHT

Help students identify two countries and list the nationality, language, and common first name for a girl and a boy. Then have students write one sentence for each country using correct capitalization.

LEARNING OBJECTIVES

- **Language** Capitalize proper nouns.
- **Language** Use proper nouns correctly in speaking and writing.

MATERIALS — Online Ed

Display and Engage *Grammar 2.1.4a, 2.1.4b*

Printable *Grammar 2.1.4*

 INSTRUCTIONAL VOCABULARY

- **common noun** a word that names a person, place, or thing
- **proper noun** a word that names a particular person, place, or thing and is capitalized
- **capital letter** a letter that comes at the beginning of a proper noun and is uppercase

Review Proper Nouns

- Show **Display and Engage: Grammar 2.1.4a**. Read aloud the instruction to review capitalizing **proper nouns**. Then have students complete the activity on **Display and Engage: Grammar 2.1.4b**.

- Review with students that **common nouns** do not name something specific, so they are not capitalized. Proper nouns do name something specific, so they are capitalized.
Review the types of proper nouns: historical events and documents, titles, language, names, and nationalities. Explain that all of these are capitalized.

- Use the following chart to review each category.

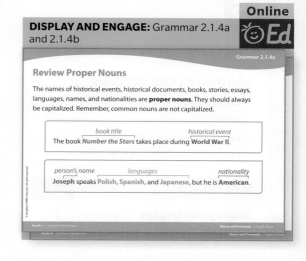

DISPLAY AND ENGAGE: Grammar 2.1.4a and 2.1.4b

Online 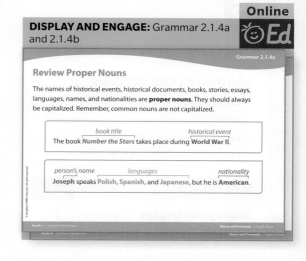Ed

Grammar 2.1.4a

Review Proper Nouns

The names of historical events, historical documents, books, stories, essays, languages, names, and nationalities are **proper nouns**. They should always be capitalized. Remember, common nouns are not capitalized.

book title — *historical event*
The book *Number the Stars* takes place during **World War II**.

person's name — *languages* — *nationality*
Joseph speaks **Polish**, **Spanish**, and **Japanese**, but he is **American**.

Capitalize Proper Nouns

historical events	War of 1812
historical documents	Declaration of Independence
titles	Where the Red Fern Grows
language	French
names	Julio, Julia
nationalities	Canadian, Japanese

- Have students complete **Printable: Grammar 2.1.4** to review proper nouns.

- Have students use the chart above and write examples of their own in each category. Have partners share their lists and discuss why each word is capitalized.

- Have students edit a writing draft to review proper nouns in each category: historical events and documents, titles, language, names, and nationalities.

 ENGLISH LEARNER SUPPORT: Scaffolded Practice

ALL LEVELS Review that a proper noun names a specific person, place, animal, or thing. The important words in a proper noun should be capitalized. Display the following sentences and have students identify each proper noun and its category.

Jim, Dora, and Jin live on the same street. (Jim, Dora, Jin; names)
She speaks Russian, Spanish, and English. (Russian, Spanish, English; languages)
Her parents are Chinese. (Chinese; nationality)

LEARNING OBJECTIVES

- **Language** Write proper nouns correctly.
- **Language** Use proper nouns correctly in speaking and writing.

MATERIALS Online Ed

Display and Engage *Grammar 2.1.5*

Printable *Grammar 2.1.5*

INSTRUCTIONAL VOCABULARY

- **common noun** a word that names a person, place, or thing
- **proper noun** a word that names a particular person, place, or thing and is capitalized
- **capital letter** a letter that comes at the beginning of a proper noun and is uppercase

Connect and Teach

- Show **Display and Engage: Grammar 2.1.5**. Tell students that the correct use of capital letters when using **proper nouns** makes their writing easier to understand. It also helps readers understand that the writer is referring to a particular person, place, event, or document.

- Explain that checking for correct capitalization is an important part of proofreading.

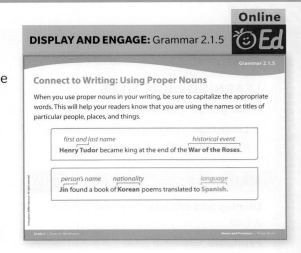

Engage and Apply

- Display the following sentences and have students rewrite them using correct capitalization.

  juan is mexican. Juan is Mexican.

  juan and his family speak spanish. Juan and his family speak Spanish.

  juan's parents, mr. and mrs.hernandez, are going to teach us to speak spanish.
  Juan's parents, Mr. and Mrs. Hernandez, are going to teach us to speak Spanish.

- Have students return to a piece of their writing. In pairs, have students look for proper nouns that need to be capitalized. Ask volunteers to share examples of proper nouns they capitalized.

- Have students complete **Printable: Grammar 2.1.5** to review using proper nouns.

- Share the following sentences and have students identify why words should be capitalized.

  The Battle of Gettysburg was an important point in the war. historical event

  Lucy and Gil are walking to the library. names

  We watched Brave last night. movie title

  My grandmother is American and Colombian. nationality

  Next year we will learn Spanish and Latin. languages

  The Treaty of Paris was signed in 1783. historical document

  The Museum Book is on sale today. book title

 ENGLISH LEARNER SUPPORT: Support Revision

SUBSTANTIAL

Read aloud students' writing, selecting sentences with proper nouns. Guide students to identify the proper nouns, explaining that proper nouns name particular things. Help students understand if the noun is a historical event or document, a title, a language, a name, or a nationality.

MODERATE

Have students return to a piece of their writing and work with a partner to identify all of the proper nouns. Then discuss as a group why the proper nouns are capitalized.

LIGHT

Have students work in pairs to find and correct capitalization of the proper nouns. Have volunteers explain why each word should be capitalized.

LEARNING OBJECTIVES

- **Language** Form possessive nouns.
- **Language** Use possessive nouns correctly in speaking and writing.

MATERIALS   Online

Display and Engage *Grammar 2.2.1a, 2.2.1b*

Printable *Grammar 2.2.1*

 **INSTRUCTIONAL VOCABULARY**

- **noun** a word that names a person, place, or thing
- **singular possessive noun** a noun that shows ownership
- **apostrophe** punctuation used to show possession

Connect and Teach

- Show **Display and Engage: Grammar 2.2.1a**. Explain that a **singular possessive noun** shows ownership of an object by one person or thing. Point out that adding **apostrophe** -*s* to a singular noun makes it possessive.

- Model identifying the singular possessive noun in the example: *the clam's shell.*

   THINK ALOUD *To identify the singular possessive noun, I ask:* What word shows ownership by one person or thing? *The word* clam's *shows ownership. The clam owns the shell.*

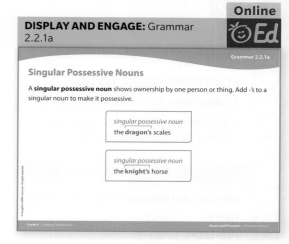

Engage and Apply

- Complete items 1–8 on **Display and Engage: Grammar 2.2.1b** with students.

- List the following words on the board. Work with students to make the possessive form by placing the apostrophes correctly.

   » *cat cat's*

   » *flower flower's*

   » *company company's*

- Have students complete **Printable: Grammar 2.2.1** to review singular possessive nouns.

- Have students edit a writing draft to review singular possessive nouns.

EL ENGLISH LEARNER SUPPORT: Facilitate Language Connections

Remind students that a noun names a person, place, thing, or animal. Review two types of nouns students have learned: singular and plural. Help students identify whether each noun below is a singular or plural noun.

girl singular: no final s   *lollipops plural: final s*   *cows plural: final s*
oven singular: no final s   *shoe singular: no final s*

Scaffolded Practice

SUBSTANTIAL

Write sentences such as *The car's tires were flat.* Have students read each sentence aloud and identify the possessive noun.
The carnival's rides were shut down. carnival's
The dog's collar was loose. dog's
The fan's blades were spinning. fan's

MODERATE

List several objects or people from students' reading. Have students write sentences by using each item with a possessive noun.

LIGHT

Have students write two of their own sentences about their reading using possessive nouns.

NOUNS AND PRONOUNS • POSSESSIVE NOUNS

LEARNING OBJECTIVES

- **Language** Form possessive nouns.
- **Language** Use possessive nouns correctly in speaking and writing.

MATERIALS   Online

Display and Engage *Grammar 2.2.2a, 2.2.2b*

Printable *Grammar 2.2.2*

INSTRUCTIONAL VOCABULARY

- **noun** a word that names a person, place, or thing
- **possessive noun** a noun that shows ownership
- **apostrophe** punctuation used to show possession
- **plural possessive noun** a plural noun that shows ownership

Connect and Teach

- Show **Display and Engage: Grammar 2.2.2a**. Explain that a **plural possessive noun** shows ownership by more than one person or thing.

- Explain that when a plural noun ends with *-s*, adding an **apostrophe** makes it possessive. However, for plural nouns that do not end in *-s*, such as *men* and *children*, add *-'s* to make the word possessive.

- Model identifying the plural possessive noun in the following example: *the foxes' ears.*

  THINK ALOUD *To identify the plural possessive noun, I ask:* What word shows ownership by more than one person or thing? *Foxes' is the plural possessive noun. It already ends in -s, so an apostrophe was added to make it possessive.*

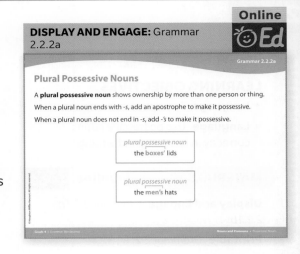

DISPLAY AND ENGAGE: Grammar 2.2.2a   Online Ed

Plural Possessive Nouns

A **plural possessive noun** shows ownership by more than one person or thing. When a plural noun ends with -s, add an apostrophe to make it possessive. When a plural noun does not end in -s, add -'s to make it possessive.

plural possessive noun
the boxes' lids

plural possessive noun
the men's hats

Engage and Apply

- Complete items 1–5 on **Display and Engage: Grammar 2.2.2b** with students.

- Write the following phrases on the board. Have students form the plural possessive form of each word with an *-s* by adding an apostrophe.
  mens shoes men's
  cows pasture cows'

- Have students complete **Printable: Grammar 2.2.2** to review plural possessive nouns.

- Have students edit a writing draft to review plural possessive nouns.

DISPLAY AND ENGAGE: Grammar 2.2.2b   Online Ed

Plural Possessive Nouns

Change each of the following phrases by using the *possessive* form of the underlined noun.

1. the walls of the buildings — the ___buildings'___ walls
2. the toys of the children — the ___children's___ toys
3. the fields of the farmers — the ___farmers'___ fields
4. the homes of their neighbors — their ___neighbors'___ homes
5. the honks of the geese — the ___geese's___ honks

ENGLISH LEARNER SUPPORT: Scaffolded Practice

SUBSTANTIAL

Review singular nouns and adding an *-'s* to form singular possessive nouns. Give examples of plural nouns. Add an apostrophe to form plural possessive nouns.

Singular: add -'s	Plural: add apostrophe
ship's	ships'
horse's	horses'
box's	boxes'

MODERATE

Brainstorm a list of plural nouns. Work together to create plural possessive nouns.

LIGHT

Have pairs create sentences using plural possessive nouns.

NOUNS AND PRONOUNS • POSSESSIVE NOUNS

LEARNING OBJECTIVES

- **Language** Form possessive nouns using apostrophes.
- **Language** Use possessive nouns correctly in speaking and writing.

MATERIALS
Online

Display and Engage *Grammar 2.2.3a, 2.2.3b*

Printable *Grammar 2.2.3*

INSTRUCTIONAL VOCABULARY

- **noun** a word that names a person, place, or thing
- **possessive noun** a noun that shows ownership
- **apostrophe** punctuation used to show possession
- **plural possessive** a plural noun that shows ownership

Connect and Teach

- Show **Display and Engage: Grammar 2.2.3a**. Review with students how to make singular nouns and plural nouns possessive.

- Give the following examples of how to make a singular noun possessive. Show the students a plural noun that ends in -s (plural), and a plural noun that does not end in -s (possessive).
  The dog's leash is hanging on the hook. Add -'s to *dog*.
  The women's tennis team is playing today. Add an apostrophe -s to *women*.
  The students' homework is due on Friday. Add an apostrophe after the -s.
  The fish's fins are blue. Add -'s to *fish*.

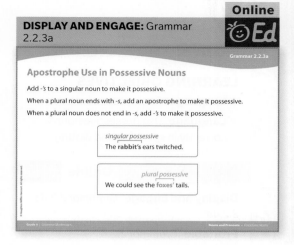

DISPLAY AND ENGAGE: Grammar 2.2.3a

Apostrophe Use in Possessive Nouns

Add -'s to a singular noun to make it possessive.

When a plural noun ends with -s, add an apostrophe to make it possessive.

When a plural noun does not end in -s, add -'s to make it possessive.

singular possessive
The **rabbit's** ears twitched.

plural possessive
We could see the **foxes'** tails.

Engage and Apply

- Complete items 1–6 on **Display and Engage: Grammar 2.2.3b** with students.

- Name several possessive nouns, and have students identify them as singular or plural. Then have students explain where the apostrophes should be placed.

  » *Karen's singular, 's*

  » *The students' plural, s'*

  » *The house's singular, 's*

  » *The planets' plural, s'*

- Have students complete **Printable: Grammar 2.2.3** to review apostrophe use in possessive nouns.

- Have students edit a writing draft to review apostrophe use in possessive nouns.

DISPLAY AND ENGAGE: Grammar 2.2.3b

Apostrophe Use in Possessive Nouns

Add the apostrophes correctly in the following possessive nouns.

1. The mans hat blew off. man's
2. All of the birds songs fell silent. birds'
3. The teams project won first prize. team's
4. The skaters costumes were gold. skaters'
5. The childrens eyes grew wide. children's
6. The three little pigs tails uncurled. pigs'

ENGLISH LEARNER SUPPORT: Scaffolded Practice

ALL LEVELS Remind students that an apostrophe in a possessive noun shows possession or ownership. Explain that possessive nouns show objects or other things that the noun possesses or owns. Brainstorm a list of things that students might own or possess. Remind students that ownership isn't limited to objects. Feelings and ideas can be owned. Write down students' ideas to show how to write the possessive forms.

LEARNING OBJECTIVES

- **Language** Form possessive nouns.
- **Language** Use possessive nouns correctly in speaking and writing.

MATERIALS   Online

Display and Engage *Grammar 2.2.4a, 2.2.4b*

Printable *Grammar 2.2.4*

INSTRUCTIONAL VOCABULARY

- **noun** a word that names a person, place, or thing
- **singular possessive noun** a noun that shows ownership
- **plural possessive noun** a plural noun that shows ownership
- **apostrophe** punctuation used to show possession

Review Possessive Nouns

- Show **Display and Engage: Grammar 2.2.4a**. Review forming **singular** and **plural possessive nouns** and discuss the examples. Then present **Display and Engage: Grammar 2.2.4b** and complete the activity with students.

- Remind students that possessive nouns show ownership, that the *-'s* is added to most singular nouns, and that an **apostrophe** is added at the end for most plural nouns.

- Have students correct the nouns in each phrase to form the possessive.

  » *the park flowers park's*

  » *the gardens gate gardens'*

  » *her teacher students teacher's*

  » *our dogs bowls dogs'*

  » *her oldest sons shoes son's*

- Have students complete **Printable: Grammar 2.2.4** to review possessive nouns.

- Have students edit a writing draft to review possessive nouns.

ENGLISH LEARNER SUPPORT: Scaffolded Practice

SUBSTANTIAL

Model using possessive nouns to create new sentences to help students understand the concept of possession.

the cat that belongs to my sister possessive noun: *my sister's cat*
a car that her neighbor owns possessive noun: *her neighbor's car*
the trophy that the team won possessive noun: *the team's trophy*
the books that the students read possessive noun: *the students' books*

MODERATE

Provide additional practice for students with these sentence frames.

The hat belongs to _____.
This is _____ jacket.

Have student pairs complete the sentence frames using the names of students and other classroom objects.

LIGHT

Have student pairs create sentences with possessive nouns using the names of students and other classroom objects. Have volunteers share their completed sentences.

LEARNING OBJECTIVES

- **Language** Write possessive nouns.
- **Language** Use possessive nouns correctly in speaking and writing.

MATERIALS   Online ⊙Ed

Display and Engage *Grammar 2.2.5*

Printable *Grammar 2.2.5*

INSTRUCTIONAL VOCABULARY

- **noun** a word that names a person, place, or thing
- **possessive noun** a noun that shows ownership
- **apostrophe** punctuation used to show possession
- **plural possessive noun** a plural noun that shows ownership

Connect and Teach

- Tell students that it is important to use **possessive nouns** as appropriate to ensure clarity in their writing. This helps the reader understand what is happening.

- Show **Display and Engage: Grammar 2.2.5**. Review forming possessive nouns and discuss the examples.

- Point out that an important part of revising is adding possessive nouns and checking that they are used correctly.

DISPLAY AND ENGAGE: Grammar 2.2.5   Online ⊙Ed

Grammar 2.2.5

Connect to Writing: Using Possessive Nouns

When you write, you can sometimes make a sentence clearer by adding a possessive noun to indicate ownership. Showing possession helps the reader better understand what is happening.

Unclear	Clear
We heard the voice, and we grinned and danced.	We heard the **singer's** voice, and we grinned and danced.

Engage and Apply

- Have students complete **Printable: Grammar 2.2.5** to review using possessive nouns.

- Have students review a piece of their writing and look for examples of possessive nouns. Have pairs revise nouns as needed or revise sentences to include possessive nouns for clarity.

- Display the following sentences. Guide students to use the correct possessive noun in each sentence.

  » *James shirt is blue. James'*

  » *The cellists instruments take up a lot of space. cellists'*

  » *The closets walls are white. closet's*

EL ENGLISH LEARNER SUPPORT: Scaffolded Practice

SUBSTANTIAL

Use photos and images to support the concept of possession. For example, show a picture of a girl with a dog and a boy with a horse. Write sentences and discuss what each noun owns. Ask students to identify the possessive noun.

The girl's brown dog barks at the neighbors. The dog belongs to the girl; girl's
The boy's white horse trots quickly around the field. The horse belongs to the boy; boy's

MODERATE

Working together, brainstorm a list of nouns, including names. Then brainstorm a list of things that can be owned or possessed. Create sentences with possessive nouns using the two lists.

LIGHT

Pairs can find examples of possessive nouns in their reading. Have pairs note the possessive noun and what was owned. Ask volunteers to share examples of each.

LEARNING OBJECTIVES

- **Language** Identify and use subject pronouns and object pronouns.
- **Language** Use pronouns correctly in speaking and writing.

MATERIALS Online

Display and Engage *Grammar 2.3.1a, 2.3.1b*

Printable *Grammar 2.3.1*

INSTRUCTIONAL VOCABULARY

- **pronoun** a word, such as *he, she,* or *they,* that takes the place of one or more nouns
- **subject pronoun** a type of pronoun that tells who or what does the action in the sentence
- **object pronoun** a type of pronoun that tells who or what receives the action of the verb

Connect and Teach

- Show **Display and Engage: Grammar 2.3.1a**. Explain that a **subject pronoun** tells who or what does the action of a sentence. An **object pronoun** tells who or what receives the action of the verb.

- Model identifying the subject and object pronouns in the following example sentences:
  We waited in line for the ride.
  We, subject pronoun
  Samir didn't want to wait for it.
  it, object pronoun

THINK ALOUD *To identify the subject pronoun, I ask:* What pronoun tells who or what does the action of the sentence? We *is the subject pronoun because it tells who watched. Then, for the second sentence, I ask:* What pronoun tells who or what receives the action of the verb? It *stands for the ride. The ride is what Samir did not want to wait for, so it is the object pronoun.*

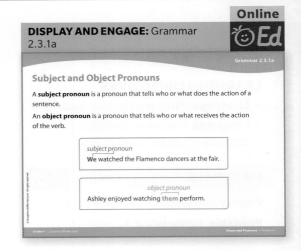

Engage and Apply

- Complete items 1–5 on **Display and Engage: Grammar 2.3.1b** with students.

- Together, generate sentences that include action verbs, and write the sentences on the board. Have students use and identify subject and object pronouns, as in the following:
  He skied down the mountain. subject, He
  John watched him. object, him

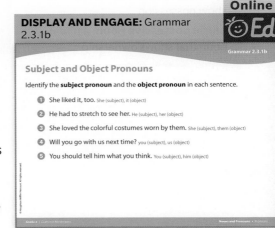

- Have students complete **Printable: Grammar 2.3.1** to review subject and object pronouns.

- Have students edit a writing draft to review subject and object pronouns.

 ENGLISH LEARNER SUPPORT: Facilitate Language Connections

In Spanish, speakers usually drop subject pronouns because the verb shows number. Have students practice including subject pronouns in sentences. For example, *What is it? It is her favorite dance. What does she like? She likes to paint.* Tell students that in English, we can drop the subject pronoun in commands, such as *Do your homework.*

Scaffolded Practice

ALL LEVELS Review that a pronoun takes the place of one or more nouns. Reinforce the difference between nouns and pronouns by displaying the following sentences. Work with students to distinguish nouns and pronouns.

She was a great cook. pronoun *she;* noun *cook*
The actors performed it. noun *actors;* pronoun *it*
He played the piano. pronoun *He;* noun *piano*

LEARNING OBJECTIVES

- **Language** Identify and use reflexive pronouns and demonstrative pronouns.
- **Language** Use pronouns correctly in speaking and writing.

MATERIALS Online

Display and Engage *Grammar 2.3.2a, 2.3.2b*

Printable *Grammar 2.3.2*

 INSTRUCTIONAL VOCABULARY

- **pronoun** a word, such as *he, she,* or *they,* that takes the place of one or more nouns
- **reflexive pronoun** a pronoun whose antecedent is the subject of the sentence
- **demonstrative pronoun** a pronoun, such as *this,* that talks about something nearby or far away

Connect and Teach

- Show **Display and Engage: Grammar 2.3.2a**. Explain that a **reflexive pronoun** ends in *-self* or *-selves* and is used when the subject of a sentence performs an action on itself. Then explain that a **demonstrative pronoun** is used to point out particular people or things. *This* is used to talk about one person or thing that is nearby; *these* is used to talk about more than one person or thing nearby. *That* is used to talk about one thing far away; *those* is used to talk about more than one person or thing far away.

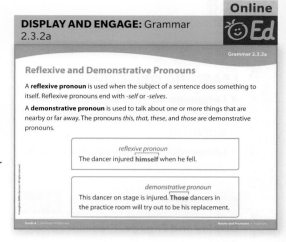

DISPLAY AND ENGAGE: Grammar 2.3.2a

Reflexive and Demonstrative Pronouns

A **reflexive pronoun** is used when the subject of a sentence does something to itself. Reflexive pronouns end with *-self* or *-selves*.

A **demonstrative pronoun** is used to talk about one or more things that are nearby or far away. The pronouns *this, that, these,* and *those* are demonstrative pronouns.

reflexive pronoun
The dancer injured **himself** when he fell.

demonstrative pronoun
This dancer on stage is injured. **Those** dancers in the practice room will try out to be his replacement.

- Model identifying the reflexive and demonstrative pronouns in the following sentences: *The pitcher injured herself when she slipped on the mound. These players will take over pitching for the rest of the game.*

  THINK ALOUD *To find the reflexive pronoun, I ask:* What pronoun tells that something happened to the subject? *The subject of the sentence is* pitcher. *The reflexive pronoun is* herself. *It tells that the pitcher got injured when she slipped. To find the demonstrative pronoun, I ask:* What pronoun points out a particular person or thing? *The word* players *is after the pronoun, so* these *is the demonstrative pronoun.*

Engage and Apply

- Complete items 1–6 on **Display and Engage: Grammar 2.3.2b** with students.

- Have students complete **Printable: Grammar 2.3.2** to review reflexive and demonstrative pronouns.

- Have students edit a writing draft to review reflexive and demonstrative pronouns.

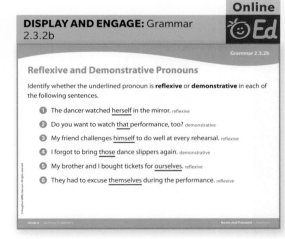

DISPLAY AND ENGAGE: Grammar 2.3.2b

Reflexive and Demonstrative Pronouns

Identify whether the underlined pronoun is **reflexive** or **demonstrative** in each of the following sentences.

1 The dancer watched herself in the mirror. reflexive
2 Do you want to watch that performance, too? demonstrative
3 My friend challenges himself to do well at every rehearsal. reflexive
4 I forgot to bring those dance slippers again. demonstrative
5 My brother and I bought tickets for ourselves. reflexive
6 They had to excuse themselves during the performance. reflexive

 ENGLISH LEARNER SUPPORT: Scaffolded Practice

SUBSTANTIAL

Write: *James loves basketball.* Guide students in saying a follow-up sentence, substituting pronouns for the nouns. Ask students to identify the types of pronouns.
Jean loves it, too. object pronoun
They play basketball. subject pronoun

MODERATE

Give partners sets of subject, object, reflexive, and demonstrative pronouns. Have them create complete sentence sets. Work together to identify the type of pronoun in sentences.

LIGHT

Have students write sentences about their reading using different types of pronouns. Remind them to make sure number and gender agree.

LEARNING OBJECTIVES

- **Language** Identify antecedents and understand pronoun-antecedent agreement.
- **Language** Use pronouns correctly in speaking and writing.

MATERIALS   Online ⊙Ed

Display and Engage *Grammar 2.3.3a, 2.3.3b*

Printable *Grammar 2.3.3*

INSTRUCTIONAL VOCABULARY

- **pronoun** a word, such as *he, she,* or *they,* that takes the place of one or more nouns
- **antecedent** the noun or pronoun that the pronoun replaces

Connect and Teach

- Show **Display and Engage: Grammar 2.3.3a**. Explain that an **antecedent** is the word or phrase a pronoun replaces. The antecedent may be in the same sentence, or it may fall in a previous sentence.

- Explain that when an antecedent is singular, the pronoun must also be singular. When an antecedent is plural, the pronoun must be plural.

- Model identifying the pronoun and antecedent in the example sentence: *Claire wants to be a scientist, so she studies hard in her science classes.*

  THINK ALOUD *To identify the pronoun, I look for a word that replaces a noun. To identify the antecedent, I look for the word that the pronoun replaces. In this case, the pronoun is* she, *and the antecedent is* Claire.

DISPLAY AND ENGAGE: Grammar 2.3.3a   Online ⊙Ed

Grammar 2.3.3a

Pronoun-Antecedent Agreement

An **antecedent** is the word or phrase a pronoun replaces.
A pronoun must always agree in number with the antecedent it replaces.

singular antecedent   singular pronoun
Rosa wants to be a dancer, so **she** is taking lessons.

plural antecedent   plural pronoun
Rosa and Cindy have dance lessons. **They** dance for an hour.

Engage and Apply

- Complete items 1–5 on **Display and Engage: Grammar 2.3.3b** with students.

- Use the sentence frame *I see _____* to name singular and plural items in the classroom. Have students respond *We see _____, too!* using the pronoun *it* or *them* as appropriate.

- Have students complete **Printable: Grammar 2.3.3** to review pronoun-antecedent agreement.

- Have students edit a writing draft to review pronoun-antecedent agreement.

DISPLAY AND ENGAGE: Grammar 2.3.3b   Online ⊙Ed

Grammar 2.3.3b

Pronoun-Antecedent Agreement

Identify a **pronoun** to complete each sentence. Identify the **antecedent** it replaces.

1. My sister hates ballet, but I like _____. it (pronoun); ballet (antecedent)
2. When my grandparents brought me a ballet DVD, I loved _____. it (pronoun); DVD (antecedent)
3. I should wear dance slippers, but _____ hurt my feet. they (pronoun); slippers (antecedent)
4. I'm not good at splits, but I am practicing _____. them (pronoun); splits (antecedent)
5. My grandmother says my grandfather was a beautiful ballet dancer when _____ was younger. he (pronoun); grandfather (antecedent)

ENGLISH LEARNER SUPPORT: Scaffolded Practice

SUBSTANTIAL

Write the sample sentences. Work together to help students understand the connection between antecedents and pronouns.

José works in a store. He works in the sports department. Antecedent: *José;* Pronoun: *He*
Natalia and Lee go to the store after school. They need a new basketball. Antecedent: *Natalia and Lee;* Pronoun: *They*

MODERATE

Have students brainstorm a list of singular and plural pronouns. Working together, write sentences, having students name the nouns that agree with the pronouns.

LIGHT

Have students write sentences using pronouns. With a partner, have students underline the antecedent and circle the pronoun, making sure pronouns agree with antecedents.

LEARNING OBJECTIVES

- **Language** Identify and use pronouns.
- **Language** Use pronouns correctly in speaking and writing.

MATERIALS   Online

Display and Engage *Grammar 2.3.4a, 2.3.4b, 2.3.4c*

Printable *Grammar 2.3.4*

INSTRUCTIONAL VOCABULARY

- **pronoun** a word, such as *he, she,* or *they,* that takes the place of one or more nouns
- **subject pronoun** a type of pronoun that tells who or what does the action in the sentence
- **object pronoun** a type of pronoun that tells who or what receives the action of the verb
- **reflexive pronoun** a pronoun whose antecedent is the subject of the sentence
- **demonstrative pronoun** a pronoun, such as *this,* that talks about something nearby or far away
- **antecedent** the noun or pronoun that the pronoun replaces

Review Pronouns

- Show **Display and Engage: Grammar 2.3.4a** and then **2.3.4b**. Read the instructions and walk through the examples to review the use of **subject**, **object**, **reflexive**, and **demonstrative pronouns**. Then have students complete the items on **Display and Engage: Grammar 2.3.4c**.

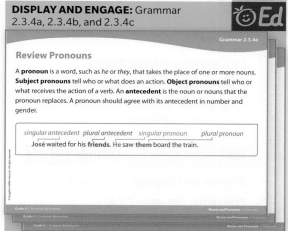

- Write the following sentences on the board. Have students identify the antecedent and its pronoun and determine if it agrees. Then guide students to share whether the pronoun is a subject or object pronoun.

  » *Pao and Darcy are partners on the science project. They made a working volcano.*
    antecedent *Pao and Darcy;* pronoun *They;* agreement *yes*
    What pronoun tells who or what did the action? *They* is the subject pronoun. They made the volcano.

  » *Ron made a sandwich for lunch. They enjoyed every bite of it!*
    antecedent *Ron;* pronoun *They;* agreement *no; should be singular, he*
    What pronoun tells who are what receives the action? *it* is the object pronoun. Ron enjoyed eating the sandwich, or *it*.

- Work together to identify the reflexive or demonstrative pronoun.

  » _____ *singers are practicing a song for the summer festival.* Demonstrative *These,* more than one singer

  » *The singers want to write a new song* _____ *for the show.* Reflexive, *themselves,* more than one singer

- Have students complete **Printable: Grammar 2.3.4** to review pronouns.

- Have students edit a writing draft to review pronouns.

 ENGLISH LEARNER SUPPORT: Scaffolded Practice

SUBSTANTIAL

Show a list of singular and plural pronouns. Explain that some pronouns are used for one person or thing and other pronouns are used for more than one person or thing.
Give examples of the pronouns in sentences, such as the following.

Josef, Mila, and Luz study after school. They go to Josef's house. They, more than one person

Luz asks her grandmother if she can study with Josef on Sunday. she, one person

MODERATE

Have pairs find three sentences with pronouns in classroom books. Have them note if the pronoun is a subject, object, reflexive, or demonstrative pronoun. Then have them note the antecedent and pronoun.

LIGHT

Have students write sentences with an example of each type of pronoun. Ask volunteers to share their sentences and identify how the pronoun is used.

LEARNING OBJECTIVES

- **Language** Write using pronouns.
- **Language** Use pronouns correctly in speaking and writing.

MATERIALS	Online

Display and Engage *Grammar 2.3.5*

Printable *Grammar 2.3.5*

INSTRUCTIONAL VOCABULARY

- **pronoun** a word, such as *he, she,* or *they,* that takes the place of one or more nouns
- **reflexive pronoun** a pronoun whose antecedent is the subject of the sentence
- **demonstrative pronoun** a pronoun, such as *this,* that talks about something nearby or far away
- **antecedent** the noun or pronoun that the pronoun replaces

Connect and Teach

- Tell students that good writers work to make their sentences flow smoothly. Explain that one way to do this is to use pronouns to combine sentences that have the same subject.

- Show **Display and Engage: Grammar 2.3.5**. Read the examples and point out how the pronouns help the writing flow and sound smoother.

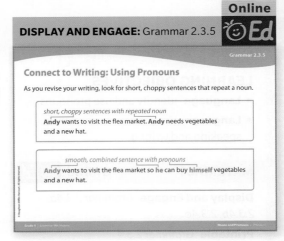

Engage and Apply

- Have students complete the activity on **Display and Engage: Grammar 2.3.5**.

- Display the following sentences. Guide students to combine them using a conjunction, a comma, and a pronoun.

  » *The playwrights had a meeting. The playwrights discussed the characters.*
  The playwrights had a meeting, and they discussed the characters.

- Display these sentence pairs. Have students use conjunctions and pronouns to combine them.

  » *A playwright named John was upset. He had to leave the meeting.*
  A playwright named John was upset, so he had to leave the meeting.

  » *The actors agreed that they needed the playwright. They didn't want John to be upset.*
  The actors agreed that they needed the playwright, but they didn't want John to be upset.

- Have students complete **Printable: Grammar 2.3.5** to review using pronouns.

- Have students edit a writing draft to review using pronouns.

ENGLISH LEARNER SUPPORT: Scaffolded Practice

SUBSTANTIAL

Write: *Viktor gave himself three days to learn the new song. That is when he wanted to play it on his guitar.*

Underline *himself* and remind students this is a reflexive pronoun. Underline *That* and explain it is a demonstrative pronoun. Have students identify the antecedents for each, *Viktor, three days*

MODERATE

Select sentences from students' past writing and work together to use pronouns to make the writing smoother and less choppy. Have students identify the types of pronouns used and whether they agree with the antecedent.

LIGHT

Have students say two sentences about their reading using different types of pronouns. Have students name the pronouns and the type of pronoun.

LEARNING OBJECTIVES

- **Language** Identify and use possessive pronouns.
- **Language** Use possessive nouns correctly in speaking and writing.

MATERIALS   Online

Display and Engage *Grammar 2.4.1a, 2.4.1b*

Printable *Grammar 2.4.1*

 **INSTRUCTIONAL VOCABULARY**

- **possessive pronoun** a pronoun that shows ownership, such as *mine, yours, his,* and *theirs*

Connect and Teach

- Show **Display and Engage: Grammar 2.4.1a**. Explain that a **possessive pronoun** shows ownership.

- Model using this sentence: *Sarah and Sarah's sister came over to play checkers.* Change to: *Sarah and her sister came over to play checkers.*

  THINK ALOUD *To determine whether to use a possessive pronoun, I ask:* Are there possessive nouns in the sentence? Do any of them need to be replaced to avoid repetition?

Engage and Apply

- Complete items 1–4 on **Display and Engage: Grammar 2.4.1b** with students.

- Have students complete **Printable: Grammar 2.4.1** to review possessive pronouns.

- Have students edit a writing draft to review possessive pronouns.

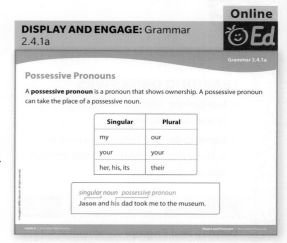

DISPLAY AND ENGAGE: Grammar 2.4.1a   Online Ed

Grammar 2.4.1a

Possessive Pronouns

A **possessive pronoun** is a pronoun that shows ownership. A possessive pronoun can take the place of a possessive noun.

Singular	Plural
my	our
your	your
her, his, its	their

singular noun   possessive pronoun
Jason and his dad took me to the museum.

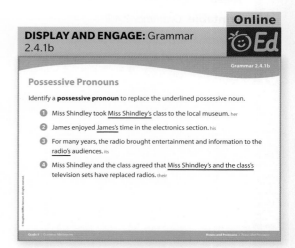

DISPLAY AND ENGAGE: Grammar 2.4.1b   Online Ed

Grammar 2.4.1b

Possessive Pronouns

Identify a **possessive pronoun** to replace the underlined possessive noun.

1. Miss Shindley took Miss Shindley's class to the local museum. her
2. James enjoyed James's time in the electronics section. his
3. For many years, the radio brought entertainment and information to the radio's audiences. its
4. Miss Shindley and the class agreed that Miss Shindley's and the class's television sets have replaced radios. their

 ENGLISH LEARNER SUPPORT: Facilitate Linguistic Connections

In Spanish, Cantonese, Vietnamese, Hmong, Haitian Creole, and Tagalog a prepositional phrase shows ownership. Speakers may say the dog of Tim for Tim's dog. Remind students to put the pronoun or noun first. Provide examples for practice, such as *This is the dog's bowl. This is his bowl.*

Scaffolded Practice

SUBSTANTIAL

Write: *A park is near our house.* Underline the possessive pronoun. *our*
Work with students to replace it with other possessive pronouns that make sense. *His, her, their*
Guide students to understand how the sentence's meaning changes with each one.

MODERATE

Have partners make a list of possessive pronouns and the nouns to which they refer. Have them take turns saying a sentence using one of the pronouns.

LIGHT

Have students write two sentences using possessive pronouns. Tell partners to switch papers and underline the pronouns.

LEARNING OBJECTIVES

- **Language** Identify and use possessive pronouns.
- **Language** Use possessive nouns with possessive pronouns correctly in speaking and writing.

MATERIALS   Online

Display and Engage *Grammar 2.4.2a, 2.4.2b*

Printable *Grammar 2.4.2*

Connect and Teach

- Show **Display and Engage: Grammar 2.4.2a**. Explain that some **possessive pronouns** are used before nouns and that others can stand alone.

- Model identifying the possessive pronoun that stands alone in the following sentences:
  That red jersey is mine. mine
  Those dirty sneakers are hers. hers

  THINK ALOUD *To determine* whether *the possessive pronoun stands alone, I ask:* Is the possessive pronoun followed by a noun? *The possessive pronoun,* mine, *is not followed by a noun.*

Engage and Apply

- Complete items 1–4 on **Display and Engage: Grammar 2.4.2b** with students.

- Advise the students to ask *Is the possessive pronoun followed by a noun?* to determine whether the possessive pronoun stands alone.

- Have students complete **Printable: Grammar 2.4.2** to review possessive pronouns.

- Have students edit a writing draft to review possessive pronouns.

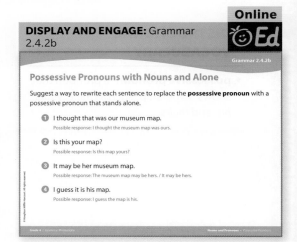

DISPLAY AND ENGAGE: Grammar 2.4.2a

Online Ed

Grammar 2.4.2a

Possessive Pronouns with Nouns and Alone

Some possessive pronouns are used **before nouns**, and others are used by themselves and stand alone.

These **possessive pronouns** can stand alone in a sentence: *mine, yours, his, hers, ours,* and *theirs.*

possessive pronoun used before noun
That is **my** museum map.

possessive pronoun that stands alone
That museum map is **mine**.

DISPLAY AND ENGAGE: Grammar 2.4.2b

Online Ed

Grammar 2.4.2b

Possessive Pronouns with Nouns and Alone

Suggest a way to rewrite each sentence to replace the **possessive pronoun** with a possessive pronoun that stands alone.

1. I thought that was our museum map.
   Possible response: I thought the museum map was ours.

2. Is this your map?
   Possible response: Is this map yours?

3. It may be her museum map.
   Possible response: The museum map may be hers. / It may be hers.

4. I guess it is his map.
   Possible response: I guess the map is his.

EL ENGLISH LEARNER SUPPORT: Scaffolded Practice

ALL LEVELS Ask students in mixed-proficiency groups to define a possessive pronoun and give an example of one. Then have them use that possessive pronoun in a sentence and identify the noun it refers to.

LEARNING OBJECTIVES

- **Language** Identify and use possessive pronouns.
- **Language** Use possessive nouns correctly in speaking and writing.

MATERIALS Online Ed

Display and Engage *Grammar 2.4.3a, 2.4.3b*

Printable *Grammar 2.4.3*

Connect and Teach

- Show **Display and Engage: Grammar 2.4.3a**. Review **possessive pronouns** and how to identify what they refer to in a sentence.

- Review the examples from the projectable and discuss whether the possessive pronoun stands alone.

  THINK ALOUD *To determine whether the possessive pronoun stands alone, I ask:* Is the possessive pronoun followed by a noun?

Engage and Apply

- Complete items 1–6 on **Display and Engage: Grammar 2.4.3b** with students.

- Write: *My aunt showed me which dinner was mine.*

- Work with students to identify the possessive pronoun followed by a noun. *My is a possessive pronoun followed by the noun aunt.*

- Work with students to find the possessive pronoun that stands alone.

- Ask: *What possessive pronoun is not followed by a noun? mine*

- Have students complete **Printable: Grammar 2.4.3** to review possessive pronouns.

- Have students edit a writing draft to review possessive pronouns.

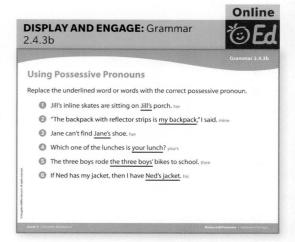

DISPLAY AND ENGAGE: Grammar 2.4.3a — Online Ed

Using Possessive Pronouns

Use a possessive pronoun to take the place of a possessive noun. Like a possessive noun, a possessive pronoun shows ownership. Some possessive pronouns are placed before nouns, while others stand alone.

> *possessive pronoun before a noun*
> Jeff left **his** backpack on the school bus.

> *possessive pronoun that stands alone*
> The red skates are **hers**.

DISPLAY AND ENGAGE: Grammar 2.4.3b — Online Ed

Using Possessive Pronouns

Replace the underlined word or words with the correct possessive pronoun.

1. Jill's inline skates are sitting on Jill's porch. *her*
2. "The backpack with reflector strips is my backpack," I said. *mine*
3. Jane can't find Jane's shoe. *her*
4. Which one of the lunches is your lunch? *yours*
5. The three boys rode the three boys' bikes to school. *their*
6. If Ned has my jacket, then I have Ned's jacket. *his*

 ENGLISH LEARNER SUPPORT: Scaffolded Practice

ALL LEVELS Provide additional practice with possessive pronouns by using sentence frames. For example, *Dr. Jones uses _____ stethoscope to listen to hearts. his*

LEARNING OBJECTIVES

- **Language** Identify and use possessive pronouns.
- **Language** Use possessive nouns correctly in speaking and writing.

MATERIALS   Online

Display and Engage *Grammar 2.4.4a, 2.4.4b*

Printable *Grammar 2.4.4*

Review Possessive Pronouns

- Show **Display and Engage: Grammar 2.4.4a**. Review possessive pronouns.

- Remind students that a **possessive pronoun** is a pronoun that shows ownership. A possessive pronoun can take the place of a possessive noun.

- Some possessive pronouns are used before nouns while others are used by themselves and stand alone. These possessive pronouns can stand alone in a sentence: *mine, yours, his, hers, theirs,* and *ours*

- Model using possessive pronouns in the following example sentences:
  Sally loves her new puppy. her
  Your sneakers look exactly like mine. mine

- Complete items 1–6 on **Display and Engage: Grammar 2.4.4b** with students.

- Write the following sentences and have students identify the possessive pronouns.
  Sarah is getting ready for her performance tonight. her
  Dennis is attending with his father. his

- Have students complete **Printable: Grammar 2.4.4** to review possessive pronouns.

- Have students edit a writing draft to review possessive pronouns.

DISPLAY AND ENGAGE: Grammar 2.4.4a and 2.4.4b

Online
Ed

Grammar 2.4.4a

Review Possessive Pronouns

A **possessive pronoun** shows ownership and takes the place of a possessive noun. Some possessive pronouns are placed before nouns, while others **stand alone**.

Possessive Pronouns	
Used Before Noun	**Stand Alone**
my, our	mine, ours
your	yours
his, her, its, their	his, hers, theirs

(EL) ENGLISH LEARNER SUPPORT: Scaffolded Practice

ALL LEVELS Provide additional practice with possessive pronouns by asking students to identify possessive pronouns in writing work they have handed in for other Language Arts assignments. Pair students in mixed-proficiency groups and have them identify the possessive pronouns in each other's work.

LEARNING OBJECTIVES

- **Language** Identify and use possessive pronouns.
- **Language** Use possessive pronouns correctly in speaking and writing.

MATERIALS   Online

Display and Engage *Grammar 2.4.5*
Printable *Grammar 2.4.5*

Connect and Teach

- Show **Display and Engage: Grammar 2.4.5**. Remind students that sentence fluency makes their writing clearer. Tell them to replace a repeated possessive noun with a possessive pronoun.

- Model replacing repeated possessive pronouns in the following sentences:
  Jill and Jill's friend went to the party together. Jill and her friend went to the party together.
  Sam and Sam's partner's piano duet was Thursday night. Sam and his partner's duet was Thursday night.

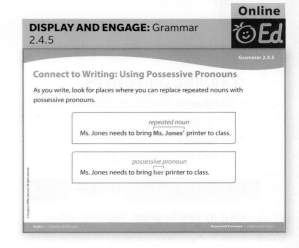

DISPLAY AND ENGAGE: Grammar 2.4.5

Connect to Writing: Using Possessive Pronouns

As you write, look for places where you can replace repeated nouns with possessive pronouns.

> *repeated noun*
> Ms. Jones needs to bring **Ms. Jones'** printer to class.

> *possessive pronoun*
> Ms. Jones needs to bring **her** printer to class.

Engage and Apply

- Have students write five interview questions for taking care of a pet. Then replace repeated possessive nouns with possessive pronouns.

- Have students complete **Printable: Grammar 2.4.5** to review possessive pronouns.

- Have students edit a writing draft to review possessive pronouns.

EL ENGLISH LEARNER SUPPORT: Scaffolded Practice

ALL LEVELS Provide additional practice with possessive pronouns by using sentence frames. For example, *The girl reads _____ book on the beach.* her

LEARNING OBJECTIVES

- **Language** Identify and use correct pronouns.
- **Language** Use and understand correct pronouns using *I* and *me*.

MATERIALS

Online Ed

Display and Engage *Grammar 2.5.1a, 2.5.1b*

Printable *Grammar 2.5.1*

 INSTRUCTIONAL VOCABULARY

- **subject pronoun** a type of pronoun that tells who or what does the action in the sentence
- **object pronoun** a type of pronoun that tells who or what receives the action of the verb

Connect and Teach

- Show **Display and Engage: Grammar 2.5.1a**. Explain that *I* is used as the subject of a sentence. *Me* is the object.

- Model using *I* and *me*: *Sally and I played together. Dennis played with Sally and me.*

  THINK ALOUD *When deciding whether to use* I *or* me *as the subject of a sentence, I ask: Is the pronoun the subject or the object of the sentence?* I *is used as the subject of a sentence.* Me *is the object.*

- Model using this sentence: *Sarah and Sarah's sister came over to play checkers.* Change to: *Sarah and her sister came over to play checkers.*

Engage and Apply

- Complete items 1–6 on **Display and Engage: Grammar 2.5.1b** with students.

- Have students complete **Printable: Grammar 2.5.1** to review using *I* and *me*.

- Have students edit a writing draft to review using *I* and *me*.

DISPLAY AND ENGAGE: Grammar 2.5.1a

Online Ed

Grammar 2.5.1a

Using *I* and *Me*

Use the pronoun *I* as the subject of a sentence. The pronoun *I* is always capitalized.

Use the pronoun *me* after action verbs and after prepositions such as *to, with, for,* or *at.*

When you talk about yourself and another person, always name yourself last.

> *use I as the subject of a sentence*
> Eileen and I learned so much!

> *use me after action verbs*
> James asked me to pick up the book.

DISPLAY AND ENGAGE: Grammar 2.5.1b

Online Ed

Grammar 2.5.1b

Using *I* and *Me*

Identify the correct word(s) in parentheses.

1. (Dominic and I, Dominic and me) wanted to save the forest. Dominic and I
2. Eileen told (I, me) what was happening to the forest. me
3. Carlos and (I, me) realized the deer had nowhere to go. I
4. Deer often visited (me and my family, my family and me). my family and me
5. My brother and (I, me) have seen them look for food. I
6. (Jack and me, Jack and I) watched the deer quietly through the window. Jack and I

 ENGLISH LEARNER SUPPORT: Facilitate Linguistic Connections

In Spanish, Cantonese, Vietnamese, Hmong, Haitian Creole, and Tagalog a prepositional phrase shows ownership. Speakers may say the *dog of Tim* for *Tim's dog*. Remind students to put the pronoun or noun first. Provide examples for practice such as *This is the dog's bowl. This is his bowl.*

Scaffolded Practice

SUBSTANTIAL

Write: *Brian sees a wolf. The wolf is eating his grass. Brian gets angry.* Then write *it, he,* and *his.* Guide students to rewrite the sentences, replacing the appropriate nouns with pronouns. *Brian sees a wolf. It is eating his grass. He gets angry.*

MODERATE

Write: *Brian sees many squirrels. Brian is angry at the squirrels.* Have partners replace the nouns with pronouns. Have students identify which are subject pronouns and which are object pronouns.

LIGHT

Have students write two sentences about deer using subject and object pronouns. Have partners share their sentences and identify subject and object pronouns.

LEARNING OBJECTIVES

- **Language** Identify and use correct pronouns.
- **Language** Use pronouns correctly in speaking and writing.

MATERIALS   Online

Display and Engage *Grammar 2.5.2a, 2.5.2b*

Printable *Grammar 2.5.2*

 **INSTRUCTIONAL VOCABULARY**

- **subject pronoun** a type of pronoun that tells who or what does the action in the sentence
- **object pronoun** a type of pronoun that tells who or what receives the action of the verb

Connect and Teach

- Show **Display and Engage: Grammar 2.5.2a**. Explain **subject pronouns** and **object pronouns** by using the projectable and discussing the example.

- Model using the following example sentence: *He talked to Sam and me.*

  THINK ALOUD *When choosing the correct pronoun, I ask: Does the pronoun tell who or what does the action? Or does it tell who or what is receiving the action? He does the action, and Sam, me follow the action and the word* to.

Engage and Apply

- Complete items 1–4 on **Display and Engage: Grammar 2.5.2b** with students.

- Have students complete **Printable: Grammar 2.5.2** to review using the right pronoun.

- Have students edit a writing draft to review using the right pronoun.

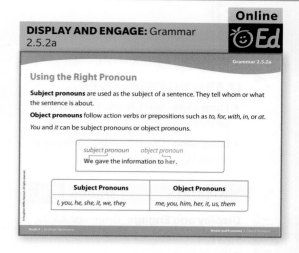

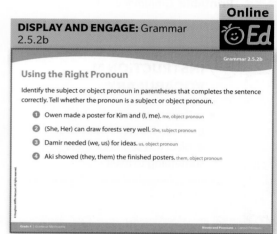

 ENGLISH LEARNER SUPPORT: Facilitate Linguistic Connections

Remind students that words in English do not follow Spanish rules about quantity. Provide these examples: *the bicycle belongs to Francis—her bicycle* (ownership by one owner); *the bicycles belong to Francis and Sam—their bicycles* (ownership by more than one owner).

Scaffolded Practice

ALL LEVELS Have students work in mixed-proficiency groups to correct their Reader's Notebook together. Have an Advanced/Advanced High student work with a Beginning/Intermediate student to correct any errors they make.

LEARNING OBJECTIVES

- **Language** Identify and use correct pronouns.
- **Language** Use pronouns correctly in speaking and writing.

MATERIALS Online

Display and Engage *Grammar 2.5.3a, 2.5.3b*

Printable *Grammar 2.5.3*

 INSTRUCTIONAL VOCABULARY

- **reflexive pronoun** a type of pronoun that tells when the subject of a sentence does something to itself

Connect and Teach

- Show **Display and Engage: Grammar 2.5.3a**. Tell students that a **reflexive pronoun** is used when the subject and object of a sentence are the same person/thing or people/things. A reflexive pronoun ends in *-self* or *-selves*.

- Display a list of reflexive pronouns *herself, himself, themselves, ourselves, myself.* Guide students to use each in a sentence.

    THINK ALOUD *To help me identify if a pronoun is reflexive I ask:* Does the pronoun tell that something happened to the subject and does it end in self or selves?

Engage and Apply

- Complete items 1–4 on **Display and Engage: Grammar 2.5.3b** with students.

- Write: *He made a sandwich for himself.* Guide students to identify the subject pronoun and to explain how it is used. *He is the subject; it tells who does the action.*
    Work with students to find the reflexive pronoun. *himself is the pronoun; it follows the word* for.

- Have students complete **Printable: Grammar 2.5.3** to review using reflexive pronouns.

- Have students edit a writing draft to review using reflexive pronouns.

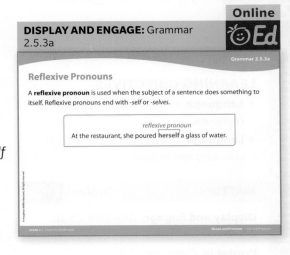

DISPLAY AND ENGAGE: Grammar
2.5.3a

Online Ed

Grammar 2.5.3a

Reflexive Pronouns

A **reflexive pronoun** is used when the subject of a sentence does something to itself. Reflexive pronouns end with *-self* or *-selves*.

reflexive pronoun
At the restaurant, she poured **herself** a glass of water.

DISPLAY AND ENGAGE: Grammar
2.5.3b

Online Ed

Grammar 2.5.3b

Reflexive Pronouns

Complete each sentence by adding a reflexive pronoun.

1. Anna and I baked _____ a cake. *ourselves*
2. Jim and John ate the cake by _____. *themselves*
3. Anna needed time by _____ to think about baking a new cake. *herself*
4. I decided that next time I'll bake a cake by _____. *myself*

 ENGLISH LEARNER SUPPORT: Facilitate Linguistic Connections

Review reflexive pronouns by displaying the following sentence frames. Work with students to choose the correct reflexive pronoun for each sentence.

Samantha painted the painting by _____. herself

Brad asked if he could go to the store by _____. himself

They wanted to go to the mall by _____. themselves

I was proud that I did the puzzle by _____. myself

NOUNS AND PRONOUNS • CORRECT PRONOUNS

LEARNING OBJECTIVES

- **Language**   Review correct pronouns.
- **Language**   Use correct pronouns in speaking and writing.

MATERIALS   Online

Display and Engage   *Grammar 2.5.4a, 2.5.4b*

Printable   *Grammar 2.5.4*

INSTRUCTIONAL VOCABULARY

- **subject pronoun**   a type of pronoun that tells who or what does the action in the sentence
- **object pronoun**   a type of pronoun that tells who or what receives the action of the verb
- **reflexive pronoun**   a type of pronoun that tells when the subject of a sentence does something to itself

Review Correct Pronouns

- Show **Display and Engage: Grammar 2.5.4a**. Review using the pronoun *I* as the subject of a sentence, and using the pronoun *me* after action verbs and after prepositions such as *to, with, for,* or *at*. Remind the students to name themselves last when talking about themselves and another person.

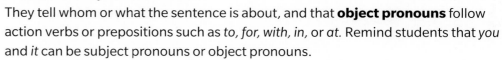

DISPLAY AND ENGAGE: Grammar 2.5.4a and 2.5.4b

Online Ed

Grammar 2.5.4a

Review: Correct Pronouns

Subject pronouns are used as the subject of a sentence. They tell whom or what the sentence is about. **Object pronouns** follow action verbs or prepositions. Use the pronoun *I* as the subject of a sentence and the pronoun *me* as the object.

subject pronoun
I walked to the restaurant.

object pronoun
Sally walked to the restaurant with me.

Use a **reflexive pronoun** when the subject does something to itself.

reflexive pronoun
Marco drove **himself** to the store.

- Review that **subject pronouns** are used as the subject of a sentence. They tell whom or what the sentence is about, and that **object pronouns** follow action verbs or prepositions such as *to, for, with, in,* or *at*. Remind students that *you* and *it* can be subject pronouns or object pronouns.

   THINK ALOUD   *To identify subject pronouns, I ask:* What pronoun tells who or what does the action of the sentence? *To identify object pronouns, I ask:* What pronoun tells who or what receives the action of the verb?

- Review that **reflexive pronouns** are used when the subject and object of a sentence are the same person/thing or people/things.

- Complete items 1–6 on **Display and Engage: Grammar 2.5.4b** with students.

- Have students complete **Printable: Grammar 2.5.4** to review correct pronouns.

- Have students edit a writing draft to review correct pronouns.

 ENGLISH LEARNER SUPPORT: Scaffolded Practice

ALL LEVELS   Have mixed-proficiency students work in pairs to review the drafts they edited and identify pronouns as either subject or object pronouns.

LEARNING OBJECTIVES

- **Language** Identify and use correct pronouns.
- **Language** Use pronouns correctly in speaking and writing.

MATERIALS   Online

Display and Engage *Grammar 2.5.5*

Printable *Grammar 2.5.5*

Connect and Teach

- Show **Display and Engage: Grammar 2.5.5**. Remind students that sentence fluency makes their writing clearer and easier to read. To avoid using a noun over and over, suggest that students replace it with a pronoun.

- Model using pronouns to avoid noun repetition with the following sentences:
  Sam studied hard for his math test. Sam wanted to get a high score.
  Sam studied hard for his math test. He wanted to get a high score.

Engage and Apply

- Have students replace the repeated nouns with pronouns. *Jim read books. Jim also reads magazines. Jim wanted to become a good reader. Jim read books. He also reads magazines. He wanted to become a good reader.*

- Have students complete **Printable: Grammar 2.5.5** to review using the correct pronoun in writing.

- Have students edit a writing draft to review using the correct pronoun in writing.

EL   ENGLISH LEARNER SUPPORT: Scaffolded Practice

ALL LEVELS Have mixed-proficiency students work in pairs to review books from the classroom library. Have them identify pronouns and explain whether they are subject or object pronouns, and whether the pronouns are reflexive.

Online Ed

DISPLAY AND ENGAGE: Grammar 2.5.5

Grammar 2.5.5

Connect to Writing: Using the Correct Pronouns

As you revise your writing, look for short, choppy sentences that repeat a noun. Try combining these sentences and replacing the noun with a pronoun.

short, choppy sentences with repeated nouns
Anna likes eating at the restaurant. Anna orders the lobster.

smooth combined sentence with pronouns
She likes eating at the restaurant, and she orders the lobster.

LEARNING OBJECTIVES

- **Language** Identify pronoun contractions.

- **Language** Use pronoun contractions and homophones in speaking and writing.

MATERIALS   Online

Display and Engage *Grammar 2.6.1a, 2.6.1b*

Printable *Grammar 2.6.1*

 INSTRUCTIONAL VOCABULARY

- **pronoun** a word that takes the place of a noun

- **contraction** a short way of writing two words, using an apostrophe to replace one or more letters

Connect and Teach

- Show **Display and Engage: Grammar 2.6.1a**. Explain that some **pronouns** can be combined with some verbs to form **contractions**.

- Model changing the pronoun and verb into a contraction: *I am excited for the fireworks tonight! I'm excited for the fireworks tonight!*

  THINK ALOUD *When deciding whether to use a pronoun contraction I ask: What two words can I combine to make a contraction? I and am make I'm.*

Engage and Apply

- Complete items 1–5 on **Display and Engage: Grammar 2.6.1b** with students.

- Have students complete **Printable: Grammar 2.6.1** to review pronoun contractions.

- Have students edit a writing draft to review pronoun contractions.

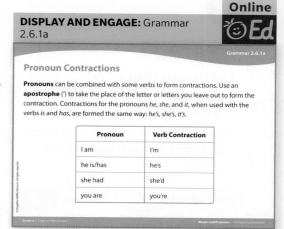

DISPLAY AND ENGAGE: Grammar 2.6.1a

Grammar 2.6.1a

Pronoun Contractions

Pronouns can be combined with some verbs to form contractions. Use an **apostrophe** (') to take the place of the letter or letters you leave out to form the contraction. Contractions for the pronouns *he*, *she*, and *it*, when used with the verbs *is* and *has*, are formed the same way: *he's, she's, it's.*

Pronoun	Verb Contraction
I am	I'm
he is/has	he's
she had	she'd
you are	you're

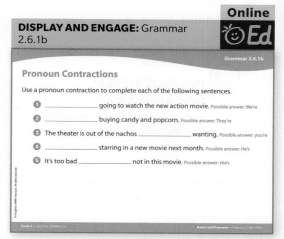

DISPLAY AND ENGAGE: Grammar 2.6.1b

Grammar 2.6.1b

Pronoun Contractions

Use a pronoun contraction to complete each of the following sentences.

1. _____ going to watch the new action movie. *Possible answer: We're*
2. _____ buying candy and popcorn. *Possible answer: They're*
3. The theater is out of the nachos _____ wanting. *Possible answer: you're*
4. _____ starring in a new movie next month. *Possible answer: He's*
5. It's too bad _____ not in this movie. *Possible answer: she's*

 ENGLISH LEARNER SUPPORT: Scaffolded Practice

SUBSTANTIAL

Write: *The frog is on the lily pad. The girl will go to the swamp. The kids are happy.* Then write *She, They, It.* Help students replace the nouns with pronouns. Then show them how to create contractions with each. *It is on the lily pad. She will go to the swamp. They are happy / It's on the lily pad. She'll go to the swamp. They're happy.*

MODERATE

Write: *The frog is on the lily pad. The girl will go to the swamp. The kids are happy.* Have students rewrite the sentences, replacing the nouns with pronouns. Then have partners work together to create contractions with the pronouns.
It is on the lily pad. She will go to the swamp. They are happy / It's on the lily pad. She'll go to the swamp. They're happy.

LIGHT

Have students write two sentences using pronouns. Then have them rewrite the sentences using contractions with their pronouns. Guide them as necessary.

NOUNS AND PRONOUNS • PRONOUN CONTRACTIONS

LEARNING OBJECTIVES

- **Language** Identify pronoun contractions and homophones.
- **Language** Use pronoun contractions and homophones in speaking and writing.

MATERIALS   Online Ed

Display and Engage *Grammar 2.6.2a, 2.6.2b*

Printable *Grammar 2.6.2*

 INSTRUCTIONAL VOCABULARY

- **homophones** words that sound the same but have different meanings and spellings

Connect and Teach

- Show **Display and Engage: Grammar 2.6.2a**. Explain that some pronoun contractions are **homophones**.

- Model identifying the homophones:
  They're hiking to the top of the mountain. They're
  I want to join their hike. their
  The trail starts over there. there
  THINK ALOUD *To use homophones properly, I can ask:* What sentence clues can I use to figure out the meaning and the correct spelling of the homophone? Does the sentence have a contraction?

Engage and Apply

- Complete items 1–4 on **Display and Engage: Grammar 2.6.2b** with students.

- Have students complete **Printable: Grammar 2.6.2** to review pronouns and homophones.

- Have students edit a writing draft to review pronouns and homophones.

 ENGLISH LEARNER SUPPORT: Scaffolded Practice

ALL LEVELS Review the difference between *its* and *it's*. Then have students use the correct form to complete each sentence frame.

_____ *time to go to school.* It's

The dog quickly drank _____ *water.* its

Although I disagree with it, _____ *still a good idea.* it's

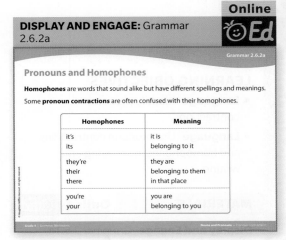

Online Ed

DISPLAY AND ENGAGE: Grammar 2.6.2a

Grammar 2.6.2a

Pronouns and Homophones

Homophones are words that sound alike but have different spellings and meanings. Some **pronoun contractions** are often confused with their homophones.

Homophones	Meaning
it's its	it is belonging to it
they're their there	they are belonging to them in that place
you're your	you are belonging to you

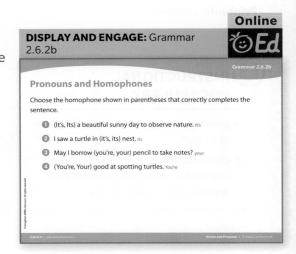

Online Ed

DISPLAY AND ENGAGE: Grammar 2.6.2b

Grammar 2.6.2b

Pronouns and Homophones

Choose the homophone shown in parentheses that correctly completes the sentence.

1. (It's, Its) a beautiful sunny day to observe nature. It's
2. I saw a turtle in (it's, its) nest. its
3. May I borrow (you're, your) pencil to take notes? your
4. (You're, Your) good at spotting turtles. You're

LEARNING OBJECTIVES

- **Language** Identify and use pronouns and homophones.
- **Language** Use pronoun contractions and homophones in speaking and writing.

MATERIALS Online

Display and Engage *Grammar 2.6.3a, 2.6.3b*

Printable *Grammar 2.6.3*

Connect and Teach

- Show **Display and Engage: Grammar 2.6.3a**. With students, review pronoun contractions and homophones.

- Review what a contraction is.
  THINK ALOUD *To identify a contraction I ask:* Is there a word with an apostrophe in the sentence? Which words are being combined?

Engage and Apply

- Complete items 1–5 on **Display and Engage: Grammar 2.6.3b** with students.

- Write this sentence on the board: *They've a report to complete and their own books to read.*

- Work with students to identify the contraction. Ask: *What is the contraction? They've What two words are combined to make the contraction? They and have*

- Work with students to find the homophone and identify its meaning. Ask: *What is the homophone? Their What does it mean? Belonging to them*

- Have students complete **Printable: Grammar 2.6.3** to review pronouns and homophones.

- Have students edit a writing draft to review pronouns and homophones.

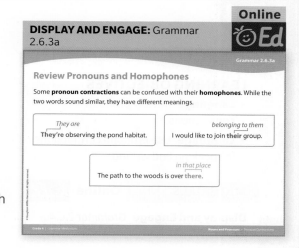

DISPLAY AND ENGAGE: Grammar 2.6.3a — Online

Review Pronouns and Homophones

Some **pronoun contractions** can be confused with their **homophones**. While the two words sound similar, they have different meanings.

They are
They're observing the pond habitat.

belonging to them
I would like to join their group.

in that place
The path to the woods is over there.

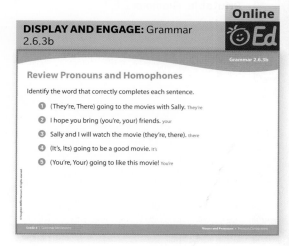

DISPLAY AND ENGAGE: Grammar 2.6.3b — Online

Review Pronouns and Homophones

Identify the word that correctly completes each sentence.

1. (They're, There) going to the movies with Sally. They're
2. I hope you bring (you're, your) friends. your
3. Sally and I will watch the movie (they're, there). there
4. (It's, Its) going to be a good movie. It's
5. (You're, Your) going to like this movie! You're

EL **ENGLISH LEARNER SUPPORT: Facilitating Linguistic Connections**

Many languages often omit subject pronouns from sentences, saying *is good* instead of *it is good*. Provide additional practice for students, making sure they include subject pronouns. For example, *What is she doing? She's singing. Who is that? She's a friend of mine.*

LEARNING OBJECTIVES

- **Language** Review pronoun contractions.
- **Language** Use pronoun contractions in speaking and writing.

MATERIALS Online

Display and Engage *Grammar 2.6.4a, 2.6.4b*

Printable *Grammar 2.6.4*

Review Pronoun Contractions

- Show **Display and Engage: Grammar 2.6.4a**. Review with students pronoun contractions and homophones.

- Remind students that pronouns can be combined with some verbs to form contractions and that they can use an **apostrophe** (') to take the place of the letter or letters they leave out to form the contraction.

- Review the following model sentences: *We'll go as soon as our bags our packed. They've already finished cleaning the kitchen. She's going to be the team captain.*

- Complete items 1–5 on **Display and Engage: Grammar 2.6.4b** with students.

- Have students complete **Printable: Grammar 2.6.4** to review pronoun contractions.

- Have students edit a writing draft to review pronoun contractions.

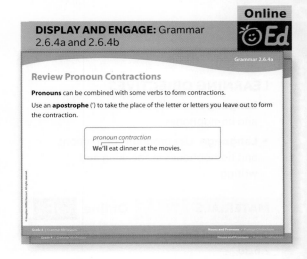

DISPLAY AND ENGAGE: Grammar 2.6.4a and 2.6.4b

Review Pronoun Contractions

Pronouns can be combined with some verbs to form contractions.
Use an **apostrophe** (') to take the place of the letter or letters you leave out to form the contraction.

> *pronoun contraction*
> **We'll** eat dinner at the movies.

EL ENGLISH LEARNER SUPPORT: Scaffolded Practice

ALL LEVELS Ask students to work in mixed-proficiency groups to identify pronoun contractions in classroom library books. Have them identify the contraction and the pronoun that is part of the contraction.

LEARNING OBJECTIVES

- **Language** Choose contractions and homophones to convey ideas in writing.
- **Language** Use pronoun contractions and homophones correctly in speaking and writing.

MATERIALS   Online

Display and Engage *Grammar 2.6.5*

Printable *Grammar 2.6.5*

Connect and Teach

- Show **Display and Engage: Grammar 2.6.5**. Review with students pronoun contractions and homophones.

- Discuss and correct the examples below:

  If your going to the beach, don't forget that its going to be very hot. Were going to need a beach umbrella. Tell Sam and Elisa to bring there sunscreen.

  *If **you're** going to the beach, don't forget that **it's** going to be very hot. **We're** going to need a beach umbrella. Tell Sam and Elisa to bring **their** sunscreen.*

Engage and Apply

- Have students write about a time when they completed a project. Have them include pronoun contractions and homophones. Then have partners proofread each other's work.

- Have students complete **Printable: Grammar 2.6.5** to review using pronoun contractions in writing.

- Have students edit a writing draft to review using pronoun contractions in writing.

 ENGLISH LEARNER SUPPORT: Scaffolded Practice

ALL LEVELS Ask students to work in mixed-proficiency groups to identify pronoun contractions and homophones in the drafts of other groups.

Online Ed

DISPLAY AND ENGAGE: Grammar 2.6.5

Grammar 2.6.5

Connect to Writing: Using Pronoun Contractions

As you edit your writing, check to see that you have used the correct form of frequently confused words. Rewrite any incorrect words so that your sentences make sense.

> **Incorrect**
> Their predicting heavy winds from here too the Rocky Mountains!

> **Correct**
> They're predicting heavy winds from here to the Rocky Mountains!

Grade 4 • Endeavor McClasseny   Nouns and Pronouns • Pronoun Contractions

ACTION VERBS

LEARNING OBJECTIVES

- **Language** Identify action verbs.
- **Language** Use verbs correctly in speaking and writing.

MATERIALS   Online ⓔEd

Display and Engage *Grammar 3.1.1a, 3.1.1b*

Printable *Grammar 3.1.1*

 INSTRUCTIONAL VOCABULARY

- **verb** word that shows action
- **action verb** a word that tells what a person or thing does

Connect and Teach

- Show **Display and Engage: Grammar 3.1.1a**. Explain that a **verb** shows action. An **action verb** tells what a person or thing does.

- Explain that a verb and its subject must agree in number. Tell students that when the subject of a sentence is a singular noun or *he, she,* or *it,* they should add an *-s* to most verbs. If the verb ends with *-s, -sh, -ch, -x,* or *-z,* they should add *-es.* If a subject ends in a consonant and *y,* they must change the *y* to *i* before adding *-es.*

- Model identifying the action verbs in the example sentences.

- Point out the subject-verb agreement in the examples.

Engage and Apply

- Complete items 1–10 on **Display and Engage 3.1.1b** with the students.

- Have students give sentences that contain action verbs. Write the sentences on the board. Have students identify each verb and explain why it is an action verb.

- Have students complete **Printable: Grammar 3.1.1** to review action verbs.

- Have students edit a writing draft to review action verbs.

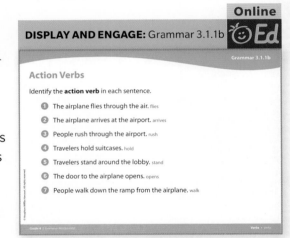

Online ⓔEd

DISPLAY AND ENGAGE: Grammar 3.1.1a

Action Verbs

A **verb** shows action. An **action verb** tells what a person or thing does.

> *action verb*
> The airplane **lands** on the runway.

> *action verb*
> People **stare** at their watches.

Online ⓔEd

DISPLAY AND ENGAGE: Grammar 3.1.1b

Action Verbs

Identify the **action verb** in each sentence.

1. The airplane flies through the air. flies
2. The airplane arrives at the airport. arrives
3. People rush through the airport. rush
4. Travelers hold suitcases. hold
5. Travelers stand around the lobby. stand
6. The door to the airplane opens. opens
7. People walk down the ramp from the airplane. walk

 ENGLISH LANGUAGE SUPPORT: Scaffolded Practice

Review the difference between verbs, nouns, and pronouns. Reinforce the difference by displaying the following words. Work with students to distinguish the verbs, nouns, and pronouns.

radio (noun) pushing (verb) I (pronoun) hearing (verb)

you (pronoun) sound (noun) landed (verb) seems (verb)

LEARNING OBJECTIVES

- **Language** Identify main and helping verbs.
- **Language** Use verbs correctly in speaking and writing.

MATERIALS
Online

Display and Engage *Grammar 3.1.2a, 3.1.2b*

Printable *Grammar 3.1.2*

INSTRUCTIONAL VOCABULARY

- **verb** word that shows action
- **main verb** the verb that tells the action when a verb is more than one word
- **helping verb** a verb that comes before a main verb and tells more about the action

Connect and Teach

- Show **Display and Engage: Grammar 3.1.2a**. Explain that some **verbs** are made up of more than one word. They contain a **main verb** and a **helping verb**. The main verb tells the action and is the most important verb. The helping verb comes before the main verb and tells more about the action. Helping verbs include *is, are, has, have, had, should, would, could, can,* and *may.*

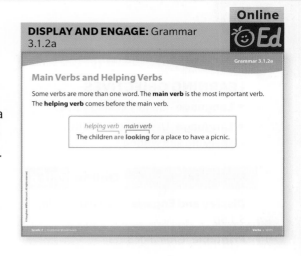

DISPLAY AND ENGAGE: Grammar 3.1.2a

Online

Main Verbs and Helping Verbs

Some verbs are more than one word. The **main verb** is the most important verb. The **helping verb** comes before the main verb.

helping verb main verb
The children are **looking** for a place to have a picnic.

- Model identifying the main verbs and helping verbs in the example sentence.

- Advise students to ask: *Which is the most important verb? Which verb comes before it?* to identify the main verbs and the helping verbs.

Engage and Apply

- Complete items 1–6 on **Display and Engage 3.1.2b** with the students.

- Ask students to give sentences that contain main verbs and helping verbs. Write the sentences on the board. Have students identify the main and helping verb in each sentence.

- Have students complete **Printable: Grammar 3.1.2** to review main verbs and helping verbs.

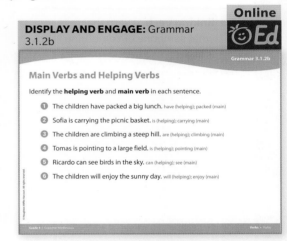

DISPLAY AND ENGAGE: Grammar 3.1.2b

Online

Main Verbs and Helping Verbs

Identify the **helping verb** and **main verb** in each sentence.

1. The children have packed a big lunch. have (helping); packed (main)
2. Sofia is carrying the picnic basket. is (helping); carrying (main)
3. The children are climbing a steep hill. are (helping); climbing (main)
4. Tomas is pointing to a large field. is (helping); pointing (main)
5. Ricardo can see birds in the sky. can (helping); see (main)
6. The children will enjoy the sunny day. will (helping); enjoy (main)

- Have students edit a writing draft to review main verbs and helping verbs.

 ENGLISH LANGUAGE SUPPORT: Scaffolded Practice

SUBSTANTIAL
Write *The man reports the story*. Ask students which word tells what the man does. Explain that *reports* is an action verb. Write *He is serious*. Ask students to tell what the verb is. Guide them to understand that *is* is a linking verb.

MODERATE
Write *The man reports the story. He is serious*. Ask students to tell what the verbs are. Have students make new sentences by changing just one word at a time. Remind them to change verbs and endings as necessary.

LIGHT
Have students write two sentences of their own using an action verb and a linking verb. Have partners trade papers and circle the verbs in each sentence. Have them label which is an action verb and which is a linking verb.

VERBS • VERBS

LEARNING OBJECTIVES

- **Language** Identify linking verbs.
- **Language** Use verbs correctly in speaking and writing.

MATERIALS   Online

Display and Engage *Grammar 3.1.3a, 3.1.3b*

Printable *Grammar 3.1.3*

 INSTRUCTIONAL VOCABULARY

- **linking verb** a verb that tells what someone or something is or is like

Connect and Teach

- Show **Display and Engage: Grammar 3.1.3a**. Explain that a **linking verb** tells what someone or something is or is like. Most linking verbs are forms of the verb *be*, such as *is, are*, and *were*. However, other words can be linking verbs, too. These words include *appear, become*, and *seem*.

- Explain that when using the verb *be*, students should use *am* with the subject *I*, and *is* or *was* with subjects that are singular.

- When subjects are plural, they should use *are* or *were*.

- Model identifying the linking verb in the example.

- Advise students to ask: *Which word tells what a person or thing is? Which word tells what a person or thing is like?* to identify linking verbs.

Engage and Apply

- Guide students to complete items 1–3 on **Display and Engage 3.1.3b**.

- Have students complete items 4–6 on their own.

- Ask students to give sentences that contain linking verbs and explain what the linking verb tells about the subject.

- Have students complete **Printable: Grammar 3.1.3** to review linking verbs.

- Have students edit a writing draft to review linking verbs.

Online

DISPLAY AND ENGAGE: Grammar 3.1.3a

Grammar 3.1.3a

Linking Verbs

A **linking verb** tells what someone or something is or is like.

Most linking verbs are forms of the verb *be*. The words *appear, become,* and *seem* can also be linking verbs.

> *linking verb*
> The students are eager to learn.

Grade 4 | Grammar Minilessons   Verbs • Verbs

Online

DISPLAY AND ENGAGE: Grammar 3.1.3b

Grammar 3.1.3b

Linking Verbs

Identify the **linking verb** in each sentence.

1. The teacher is ready to begin class. is
2. The students are quiet. are
3. Armando appears confident as he raises his hand. appears
4. Alicia thinks "I am smart because I know the answer." am
5. The teacher becomes happy when the students succeed. becomes
6. The students seem to enjoy learning. seem

Grade 4 | Grammar Minilessons   Verbs • Verbs

EL   **ENGLISH LEARNER SUPPORT: Facilitate Language Connections**

Some Spanish constructions use *have* where English uses *be*, as in *I have hunger* instead of *I am hungry* and *I have ten years* instead of *I am ten years old*. Provide extra practice and support for these differences.

Scaffolded Practice

ALL LEVELS Explain to students that in English, we use the verb *be* to tell what someone or something *is* or *was*. Guide students to use *be* in the following sentences and read them aloud together. *I _____ hungry.* am *Yesterday, I _____ thirsty.* was *Last night, I _____ tired, but I _____ not tired now.* was, am *I _____ ten years old.* am *Last year, I _____ nine years old.* was Change the pronouns to *we, you, he, she, they,* and *it* when applicable. Guide students to use the correct form of *be* to complete the sentences. Read aloud the new sentences.

LEARNING OBJECTIVES

- **Language** Identify action, main, helping, and linking verbs.
- **Language** Use verbs correctly in speaking and writing.

MATERIALS   Online

Display and Engage *Grammar 3.1.4a, 3.1.4b, 3.1.4c*

Printable *Grammar 3.1.4*

 **INSTRUCTIONAL VOCABULARY**

- **action verb** word that shows action, or what someone does
- **main verb** the verb that tells the action when a verb is more than one word
- **helping verb** a verb that comes before a main verb and tells more about the action
- **linking verb** a verb that tells what someone or something is or is like

Review Verbs

- Show **Display and Engage: Grammar 3.1.4a**. Review the following:

- An **action verb** is a word that tells what a person or thing does.

- The **main verb** is the most important verb. The **helping verb** comes before the main verb and helps to show the action.

- A **linking verb** tells what someone or something is or is like. Most linking verbs are forms of the verb *be*.

- Write these sentences on the board. Have students identify each verb and say whether it is an action verb, a main verb, a helping verb, or a linking verb:

  » *The fish jumped out of the water.* jumped: action verb

  » *The clouds were rolling in fast.* were: helping verb; rolling: main verb

  » *Thunder pounded and shook the sky.* pounded, shook: action verbs

  » *The storm was fierce, and people were seeking protection.* was: linking verb; were: helping verb; seeking: main verb

- Guide students to complete items 1–7 on **Display and Engage 3.1.4c**.

- Have students complete **Printable: Grammar 3.1.4** to review kinds of verbs.

- Have students edit a writing draft to review kinds of verbs.

DISPLAY AND ENGAGE: Grammar 3.1.4a, 3.1.4b

Online Ed

Review Verbs

A verb is a word that can show action. When a verb tells what people or things do, it is called an **action verb**. When a verb tells what someone or something is like, it is called a **linking verb**. Most linking verbs are forms of the verb *be*, such as *am, is, are, was,* and *were.*

action verb
The reporter **rushed** to the stadium.

linking verb
People **were** excited for the game.

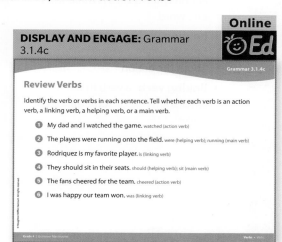

DISPLAY AND ENGAGE: Grammar 3.1.4c

Online Ed

Review Verbs

Identify the verb or verbs in each sentence. Tell whether each verb is an action verb, a linking verb, a helping verb, or a main verb.

1. My dad and I watched the game. watched (action verb)
2. The players were running onto the field. were (helping verb); running (main verb)
3. Rodriquez is my favorite player. is (linking verb)
4. They should sit in their seats. should (helping verb); sit (main verb)
5. The fans cheered for the team. cheered (action verb)
6. I was happy our team won. was (linking verb)

 ENGLISH LEARNER SUPPORT: Scaffolded Learning Practice

ALL LEVELS Write on the board: *Mr. Jones is our coach. He runs faster than all the other teachers.* Work with students to identify the verbs in the sentences and identify them as action or being verbs. *is: being; runs: action* Then have mixed proficiency partners write one sentence using an action verb and one sentence using a being verb.

VERBS • VERBS

LEARNING OBJECTIVES

- **Language** Choose strong verbs to convey ideas precisely.
- **Language** Use verbs correctly in speaking and writing.

MATERIALS   Online 🍎 *Ed*

Display and Engage *Grammar 3.1.5*
Printable *Grammar 3.1.5*

 INSTRUCTIONAL VOCABULARY

- **action verb** word that shows action, or what someone does
- **main verb** the verb that tells the action when a verb is more than one word
- **helping verb** a verb that comes before a main verb and tells more about the action
- **linking verb** a verb that tells what someone or something is or is like

Connect and Teach

- Show **Display and Engage: Grammar 3.1.5**.

- Remind students that careful word choice makes their writing clearer. Explain that good writers use precise verbs to make their writing lively and more interesting to readers.

- Point out that an important part of revising is replacing weak verbs with strong ones.

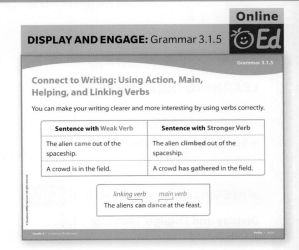

DISPLAY AND ENGAGE: Grammar 3.1.5

Online 🍎 *Ed*

Grammar 3.1.5

Connect to Writing: Using Action, Main, Helping, and Linking Verbs

You can make your writing clearer and more interesting by using verbs correctly.

Sentence with Weak Verb	Sentence with Stronger Verb
The alien came out of the spaceship.	The alien climbed out of the spaceship.
A crowd is in the field.	A crowd has gathered in the field.

linking verb   main verb
The aliens can dance at the feast.

Engage and Apply

- Display the following sentences. Guide students to identify each verb and then replace it with a stronger, more precise verb.

  » *The players are on the field.* are; sample answer: are practicing

  » *The storm lasted for hours.* lasted; sample answer: raged

  » *The players walked toward their opponents.* walked; sample answer: charged

  » *They had their protective uniforms.* had; sample answer: wore

- Remind students to use correct subject-verb agreement.

- Have students complete **Printable: Grammar 3.1.5** to review using action, main, helping, and linking verbs.

- Have students edit a writing draft to review using action, main, helping, and linking verbs.

 ENGLISH LANGUAGE SUPPORT: Scaffolded Practice

ALL LEVELS Have students name words that describe an action, or a verb. Discuss as a group what kind of action each one expresses (such as *doing* or *saying*). List these words on the board. Then use each in a sentence. Have students repeat chorally.

VERBS • VERB TENSES

LEARNING OBJECTIVES

- **Language** Introduce past, present, and future verb tenses.
- **Language** Use verb tenses correctly in speaking and writing.

MATERIALS   Online

Display and Engage *Grammar 3.2.1a, 3.2.1b*

Printable *Grammar 3.2.1*

INSTRUCTIONAL VOCABULARY

- **present tense** shows action that is happening now or that happens over and over
- **past tense** shows action that has already happened
- **future tense** shows action that will happen
- **regular verb** a verb whose past tense is formed by adding *-ed* to the present-tense first-person form

Connect and Teach

- Show **Display and Engage: Grammar 3.2.1a**. Explain that verb tenses tell when action takes place.

- Review with students that the **past tense** of many verbs is formed by adding *-ed* to the **present-tense** form. For example, *rained* is the past tense of *rain*. Explain that these verbs are **regular verbs**.

- Point out that the **future tense** is formed by placing *will* before the first-person, present-tense form of the verb.

- Model identifying the tenses in the example sentences: *My brother waits in line for movie tickets. My brother waited in line for movie tickets the other day. Tomorrow, my brother will wait in line for movie tickets.*

  THINK ALOUD *To identify the tense, I ask* When does the action take place? *In the first sentence, I know that the action,* waits, *is happening now, or in the present. In the second sentence, I see that the action,* waited, *took place in the past. In the third sentence, I see that the action,* will wait, *will take place tomorrow, in the future.*

- Explain that a verb and its subject must agree in number. Point out the subject-verb agreement in the example sentences.

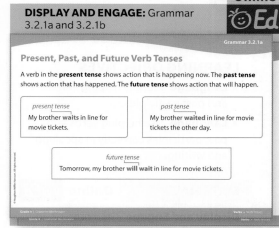

DISPLAY AND ENGAGE: Grammar 3.2.1a and 3.2.1b

Grammar 3.2.1a

Present, Past, and Future Verb Tenses

A verb in the **present tense** shows action that is happening now. The **past tense** shows action that has happened. The **future tense** shows action that will happen.

present tense
My brother **waits** in line for movie tickets.

past tense
My brother **waited** in line for movie tickets the other day.

future tense
Tomorrow, my brother **will wait** in line for movie tickets.

Engage and Apply

- Complete items 1–8 on **Display and Engage: Grammar 3.2.1b** with students.

- Have students complete **Printable: Grammar 3.2.1** for practice with past, present, and future tenses.

- Have students edit a writing draft using past, present, and future tenses of verbs.

 ENGLISH LEARNER SUPPORT: Scaffolded Practice

SUBSTANTIAL

Write: *We play cards every night* and *We played cards last night.* Have students identify the verb in each sentence. (*play, played*) Circle them. Then have students tell which sentence shows past tense. (*We played cards last night*).

MODERATE

Have students write *The bus stops at the corner.* Have them circle the verb and label the tense. (*stops, present*) Then have them write the sentence showing the other two verb tenses. (*The bus stopped at the corner.* past; *The bus will stop at the corner.* future)

LIGHT

Have students write a sentence about something that happened in a movie they saw. Have them write the three sentences, in three tenses, to tell about the action. Have them circle the verbs and label the verb tenses.

VERBS • VERB TENSES

LEARNING OBJECTIVES

- **Language** Identify helping verbs and past participles.
- **Language** Use helping verbs and past participles correctly in speaking and writing.

MATERIALS   Online

Display and Engage *Grammar 3.2.2a, 3.2.2b*

Printable *Grammar 3.2.2*

 INSTRUCTIONAL VOCABULARY

- **helping verb** a verb that comes before a main verb and tells more about the action
- **past participle** a verb form that can be used to form past tenses

Connect and Teach

- Show **Display and Engage: Grammar 3.2.2a**. Remind students that a **helping verb** can be added to a regular verb to tell more about the action.

- Review that the past tense of a regular verb is formed by adding *-ed* to the present form of the word and that this form of the verb is called the **past participle**. Explain that past participles are often used with helping verbs to show exactly when in the past an action took place.

- Model identifying the helping verb and past participle in the example sentences: *The actor has learned her lines. They have performed many plays.*

  THINK ALOUD *To identify the helping verb and past participle, I ask* Does the main verb end with *-ed*? Is it used with a helping verb? *In the first sentence, I see that* learned *ends in* -ed. *I also see that* has *comes before* learned. *So,* learned *is the past participle.*

- Repeat the modeling with the second example sentence.

Engage and Apply

- Complete items 1–6 on **Display and Engage: Grammar 3.2.2b** with students.

- Write the following sentence on the board: *All the restaurants have opened.* Have students identify the helping verb and past participle. (*have; opened*) Repeat with similar sentences.

- Have students complete **Printable: Grammar 3.2.2** for practice with helping verbs and past participles.

- Have students edit a writing draft using helping verbs and past participles.

Online

DISPLAY AND ENGAGE: Grammar 3.2.2a

Helping Verbs and Past Participles

The past tense of a regular verb is formed by adding *-ed* to its present form. When used with a helping verb, such as *has, have,* or *had,* it is called the **past participle**.

> *helping verb   past participle*
> The actor has learned her lines.

> *helping verb   past participle*
> They have performed many plays.

Online

DISPLAY AND ENGAGE: Grammar 3.2.2b

Helping Verbs and Past Participles

Identify the **helping verb** and **past participle** in each sentence.

1. The director had created new special effects. had (helping verb); created (past participle)
2. Thomas has talked to several directors. has (helping verb); talked (past participle)
3. I have worked on a movie. have (helping verb); worked (past participle)
4. The people in the audience have applauded. have (helping verb); applauded (past participle)
5. The filmmaker has completed the movie. has (helping verb); completed (past participle)
6. The reviewers have watched the movie several times. have (helping verb); watched (past participle)

 ENGLISH LEARNER SUPPORT: Facilitate Language Connections

In some languages, including Haitian Creole, Russian, Tagalog, and Vietnamese, the verb form using the helping verb *have* and the past participle (the present perfect) either does not exist or has a different function. You may create a visual timeline to show the meaning of the present perfect tense that illustrates the action having been done some time in the past, is continuing until the present, or has recently been completed.

Scaffolded Practice

Provide examples, such as *I have cleaned my room. She has played soccer for five years. We have finished our work.* Discuss how each sentence tells about an action in the past that may have happened a while ago, is still happening, or has recently been done. Make two columns and write in the first column *have* and *has,* and in the second column *visit, play, finish.* Provide practice using the correct forms of the helping verb *have* and the past participle with sentence frames: *I _____ _____ the museum. have visited People _____ _____ games for thousands of years. have played Ana _____ _____ her test and is reading now. has finished*

LEARNING OBJECTIVES

- **Language** Identify consistent verb tenses.

- **Language** Use verb tenses correctly in speaking and writing.

MATERIALS

Online

Display and Engage *Grammar 3.2.3a, 3.2.3b*

Printable *Grammar 3.2.3*

 INSTRUCTIONAL VOCABULARY

- **helping verb** a verb that comes before a main verb and tells more about the action

- **past participle** a verb form that can be used to form past tenses

Connect and Teach

- Show **Display and Engage: Grammar 3.2.3a**. Explain that in sentences that tell about events in one particular time, all the verbs should be in the same tense.

- Review that **helping verbs**, such as *has, have,* and *had,* when used with a **past participle**, show that something has already happened. *Will* shows what will happen in the future. Point out that the helping verb must agree with the subject of the sentence.

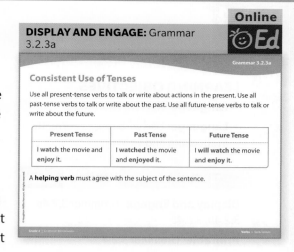

DISPLAY AND ENGAGE: Grammar 3.2.3a · Online Ed

Grammar 3.2.3a

Consistent Use of Tenses

Use all present-tense verbs to talk or write about actions in the present. Use all past-tense verbs to talk or write about the past. Use all future-tense verbs to talk or write about the future.

Present Tense	Past Tense	Future Tense
I **watch** the movie and enjoy it.	I **watched** the movie and **enjoyed** it.	I **will watch** the movie and **enjoy** it.

A **helping verb** must agree with the subject of the sentence.

- Use the example sentences to model the consistent use of tenses: *I buy a ticket and go inside. I watched the movies and enjoyed them. I will watch the movies and enjoy them.*

  THINK ALOUD *I ask,* Are the verbs telling about a particular time all in the same tense? *The first sentence tells about the present, so I use the present tense:* buy, go. *The second sentence tells about the past, so I use the past tense:* watched, enjoyed. *The third sentence tells about the future, so I use the future tense:* will watch.

Engage and Apply

- Complete items 1–5 in each section of **Display and Engage: Grammar 3.2.3b** with students.

- Write the following sentences on the board. *Next year, we will go camping. Then we got our camping badge.* Have students supply the correct tense for the second sentence. (*will get*) Repeat with similar sentence pairs.

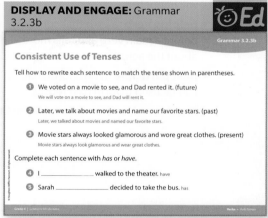

DISPLAY AND ENGAGE: Grammar 3.2.3b · Online Ed

Grammar 3.2.3b

Consistent Use of Tenses

Tell how to rewrite each sentence to match the tense shown in parentheses.

1 We voted on a movie to see, and Dad rented it. (future)
   We will vote on a movie to see, and Dad will rent it.

2 Later, we talk about movies and name our favorite stars. (past)
   Later, we talked about movies and named our favorite stars.

3 Movie stars always looked glamorous and wore great clothes. (present)
   Movie stars always look glamorous and wear great clothes.

Complete each sentence with *has* or *have.*

4 I _____ walked to the theater. have

5 Sarah _____ decided to take the bus. has

- Have students complete **Printable: Grammar 3.2.3** for practice with consistent use of tenses.

- Have students edit a writing draft using consistent verb tenses.

EL **ENGLISH LEARNER SUPPORT: Facilitate Language Connections**

Some languages, such as Cantonese and Korean, allow the use of the present tense for the future.

Scaffolded Practice

Provide practice with sentence frames, such as *I _____ after school. The families _____ next weekend. Anna _____ on vacation next summer.* Have students form the future tense by adding *will* to verbs. You may provide verbs or students may use their own verbs and activities. Beginning students may act out verbs or use their primary language as Intermediate or Advanced/Advanced High students supply the words.

LEARNING OBJECTIVES

- **Language** Review verb tenses.
- **Language** Use verb tenses correctly in speaking and writing.

MATERIALS
Online

Display and Engage *Grammar 3.2.4a, 3.2.4b, 3.2.4c*

Printable *Grammar 3.2.4*

 INSTRUCTIONAL VOCABULARY

- **present tense** shows action that is happening now or that happens over and over
- **past tense** shows action that has already happened
- **future tense** shows action that will happen
- **helping verb** a verb that comes before a main verb and tells more about the action
- **past participle** a verb form that can be used to form past tenses

Review Verb Tenses

- Show **Display and Engage: Grammar 3.2.4a**. Remind students that a verb in the **present tense** shows action that is happening now, a verb in the **past tense** shows action that has already happened, and a verb in the **future tense** shows action that will happen.

- Review with students that the past tense of many verbs is formed by adding *-ed* to the present form; for example, *walked* is the past tense of *walk*. Explain that these verbs are regular verbs.

- Point out that the future tense is formed by placing *will* before the present form of the verb.

- Write the following sentences on the board. Ask students to identify the verb and the verb tense.

  » *Jim will start preschool next year. start, future*

  » *Lucy attends preschool this year. attends, present*

  » *Jack finished preschool last year. finished, past*

- Remind students that a **helping verb** can be added to a regular verb to tell more about the action, and that **past participles** are often used with helping verbs to show exactly when in the past an action took place.

- Review that in sentences that tell about events in one particular time, all the verbs should be in the same tense.

- Complete items 1–5 on **Display and Engage: Grammar 3.2.4c** with students.

- Have students complete **Printable: Grammar 3.2.4** for practice with verb tenses.

- Have students edit a writing draft for correct use of verb tenses.

 ENGLISH LEARNER SUPPORT: Scaffolded Practice

ALL LEVELS Remind students to look for clue words in sentences to help them determine the tense, or when the action happened. Guide them to look for words such as *yesterday, tomorrow, always,* and *will.* Write sentences and have volunteers identify any clue words by circling them. Then have students identify the verb and verb tense. *I cooked dinner last week. We will go to the park after school. She writes stories in class. He has lived in the house for one year.*

VERBS • VERB TENSES

LEARNING OBJECTIVES

- **Language** Identify past, present, and future verb tenses; helping verbs and past participles; and consistent use of tenses.
- **Language** Use verb tenses correctly in speaking and writing.

MATERIALS   Online

Display and Engage *Grammar 3.2.5*
Printable *Grammar 3.2.5*

 INSTRUCTIONAL VOCABULARY

- **present tense** shows action that is happening now or that happens over and over
- **past tense** shows action that has already happened

Connect and Teach

- Show **Display and Engage: Grammar 3.2.5**. Explain that good writers use verb tenses correctly to make their writing clear and understandable for readers.
- Point out that an important part of revising is to make sure that all verbs are used correctly. In sentences about a particular time, verb tenses should be the same so that the reader understands when the action occurs.

DISPLAY AND ENGAGE: Grammar 3.2.5   Online **Ed**

Connect to Writing: Using Verb Tenses Correctly

When you write, be careful to use verb tenses correctly to show when events happened. Change tense only to show a change in time. Make sure your verbs agree with the subject and that you have formed the past tense correctly.

Incorrect Verb Agreement	Correct Verb Agreement
Hayley and I went to the movies. We watch *The Robot That Ate Chicago*. We knowed it would be scary, but we see it again tomorrow!	Hayley and I went to the movies. We watched *The Robot That Ate Chicago*. We knew it would be scary, but we will see it again tomorrow!

Engage and Apply

- Guide students to review **Display and Engage: Grammar 3.2.5**.
- Display the following paragraph. Have students identify the verbs and their tenses. *These days, movie theaters sell snacks. They also showed previews. Many viewers will enjoy the previews as much as the film. sell—present; showed—past; will enjoy—future*
- Work with students to revise the paragraph so that all the verbs are in the **present tense**. *sell; show; enjoy*
- Have partners rework the paragraph so that all the verbs are in the **past tense**. Point out that students need to delete the phrase *These days* or use a phrase such as *Years ago* to indicate past tense. *sold; showed; enjoyed*
- Have students complete **Printable: Grammar 3.2.5** for practice with using verb tenses correctly.
- Have students return to a draft of their writing. Have them work in pairs to check that they have used correct verb tenses.

ENGLISH LEARNER SUPPORT: Scaffolded Learning

Verbs in Cantonese, Haitian Creole, Hmong, Khmer, Korean, Tagalog, and Vietnamese do not change form to express tense. Students may omit tense markers. For example, they may say *he study in the library yesterday* instead of *he studied in the library yesterday*. Guide students to complete these sentence frames. *Sarah _____ (clap/clapped) during the performance yesterday. clapped We _____ (carry/carried) our books to school this morning. carried*

VERBS • PROGRESSIVE VERB TENSES

LEARNING OBJECTIVES

- **Language** Introduce the present progressive verb tense.
- **Language** Use the present progressive verb tense correctly in speaking and writing.

MATERIALS   Online ⊙Ed

Display and Engage *Grammar 3.3.1a, 3.3.1b*

Printable *Grammar 3.3.1*

INSTRUCTIONAL VOCABULARY

- **progressive verb tense** tells about an action that happens over a period of time
- **present progressive verb tense** tells about an action happening over a period of time in the present

Connect and Teach

- Show **Display and Engage: Grammar 3.3.1a**. Explain that the **progressive verb tense** tells about action that happens over a period of time.

- Explain that the **present progressive verb tense** tells about actions that are happening in the present and continuing. It is formed by using the present-tense form of *be* (*am/is/are*) and adding *-ing* to the present-tense form of the verb. Point out that *am, is,* or *are* must agree with the subject of the sentence.

- Model identifying and correctly using the present progressive verb tense in the example sentences: *Maggie is traveling to California by train. Her aunt and uncle are expecting her.*

  THINK ALOUD *I ask:* Is the action taking place over a period of time? Is it happening in the present? *I read* is traveling. Is *is a present-tense form of the verb* be. *It is used with the -ing form of* travel. *The action is taking place in the present. So,* is traveling *is the present progressive verb tense.*

- Repeat the modeling with the second example sentence.

Engage and Apply

- Complete items 1–6 on **Display and Engage: Grammar 3.3.1b** with students.

- Ask students to create sentences using the present progressive tense. Then, have them identify the verbs.

- Have students complete **Printable: Grammar 3.3.1** for practice with the present progressive verb tense.

- Have students edit a writing draft using the present progressive verb tense.

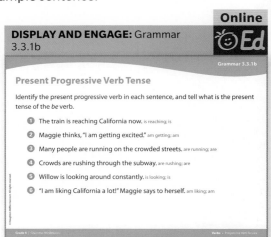

ENGLISH LEARNER SUPPORT: Scaffolded Practice

ALL LEVELS Review the present-tense forms of the verb *be* with students. Have students identify all the present-tense forms of *be* in these sentences. Have students identify the *-ing* form of the action. *Sean is traveling from New York.* is traveling *Jack and Liz are visiting my aunt and uncle.* are visiting *I am riding my bicycle this weekend.* am riding *Who is running in the hallway?* is running *Los Angeles is becoming my hometown.* is becoming *We are bringing food to your house.* are bringing *You are writing letters to your family.* are writing

LEARNING OBJECTIVES

- **Language** Introduce the past progressive verb tense.
- **Language** Use the past progressive verb tense correctly in speaking and writing.

MATERIALS
Online

Display and Engage Grammar 3.3.2a, 3.3.2b

Printable Grammar 3.3.2

 **INSTRUCTIONAL VOCABULARY**

- **progressive verb tense** tells about an action that happens over a period of time
- **past progressive verb tense** tells about an action that happened over a period of time in the past, but is no longer going on

Connect and Teach

- Show **Display and Engage: Grammar 3.3.2a**. Explain that the **past progressive verb tense** tells about actions that happened over a period of time in the past, but are no longer taking place.

- Tell students that the past progressive is formed by using the past-tense form of *be* (*was/were*) and adding *-ing* to the present-tense verb.

- Point out that *was* or *were* must agree with the subject of the sentence: *was* is used with singular subjects, and *were* is used with plural subjects.

- Model identifying and correctly using the past progressive in the example sentence: *Ben was walking to his aunt's home.*

  THINK ALOUD *To identify the past progressive tense, I ask:* Is the action taking place over a period of time? Is it happening in the past? *I read* was walking. Was *is the past-tense form of the verb* be. *It is used with the -ing form of* walk. *The action* was walking *is taking place in the past, but is not going on anymore. So,* was walking *is in the past progressive tense.*

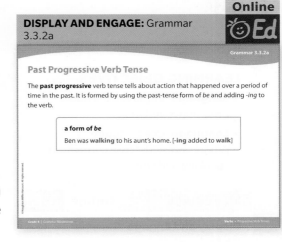

Engage and Apply

- Complete items 1–6 on **Display and Engage: Grammar 3.3.2b** with students.

- Write the following sentences on the board, and guide students in identifying the past progressive tense in each.

  » *Yesterday, I was working in the garden.* was working

  » *Last year, I was struggling with basic addition.* was struggling

- Ask students to create sentences using the past progressive tense. Then, have them identify the verbs.

- Have students complete **Printable: Grammar 3.3.2** for practice with the past progressive verb tense.

- Have students edit a writing draft using the past progressive verb tense.

 ENGLISH LEARNER SUPPORT: Scaffolded Practice

ALL LEVELS Review the past-tense forms of the verb *be* with students. Have students identify all the past-tense forms of *be* in these sentences. Have students identify the *-ing* form of the action.

Marta was listening to music. was listening
Laura and Karina were teaching my sister and brother. were teaching
I was swimming at the pool. was swimming
Who was buying all those cakes? was buying
We were dancing at the party. were dancing

LEARNING OBJECTIVES

- **Language** Introduce the future progressive verb tense.
- **Language** Use the future progressive verb tense correctly in speaking and writing.

MATERIALS Online

Display and Engage *Grammar 3.3.3a, 3.3.3b*

Printable *Grammar 3.3.3*

INSTRUCTIONAL VOCABULARY

- **progressive verb tense** tells about an action that happens over a period of time
- **future progressive verb tense** tells about an action that will happen over a period of time in the future

Connect and Teach

- Show **Display and Engage: Grammar 3.3.3a**. Explain that the **future progressive verb tense** tells about action that will happen over a period of time in the future.

- Tell students that the future progressive is formed by using *will be* and adding *-ing* to the verb. Point out that, like the present and past progressive verb tenses, *-ing* is added to the present-tense form of the verb.

- Model identifying and correctly using the future progressive verb tense with the example sentence: *Sarah will be returning to Colorado as often as possible.*

  THINK ALOUD *To identify the future progressive tense, I ask:* Is the action taking place over a period of time? Is it happening in the future? *I read* will be returning. Will be *is the future-tense form of the verb* be. *It is used with the* -ing *form of* return. *The action of returning will take place in the future. So,* will be returning *is in the future progressive tense.*

Engage and Apply

- Complete items 1–6 on **Display and Engage: Grammar 3.3.3b** with students.

- Write the following sentences on the board, and guide students in identifying the future progressive tense in each.

  » *I will be working on this model airplane for weeks.* will be working

  » *I will be attending camp this summer.* will be attending

- Ask students to create sentences using the future progressive tense. Then, have them identify the verbs.

- Have students complete **Printable: Grammar 3.3.3** for practice with the future progressive verb tense.

- Have students edit a writing draft using the future progressive verb tense.

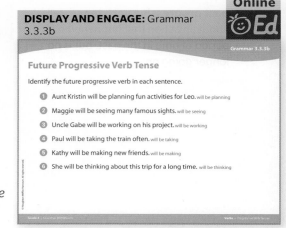
 ENGLISH LEARNER SUPPORT: Scaffolded Practice

ALL LEVELS Review the future-tense form of the verb *be* with students. Have students identify all the future-tense forms in these sentences. Have students identify the *-ing* form of the action.

Jin will be walking to the store this afternoon. will be walking
Sam and Maxim will be making the decorations for the party. will be making
I will be drawing pictures for my own book. will be drawing
Who will be climbing the wall next? will be climbing
The dog will be jumping on me when I get home. will be jumping
We will be sending the package after school. will be sending
You will be seeing the full moon tonight. will be seeing

LEARNING OBJECTIVES

- **Language** Review progressive verb tenses.
- **Language** Use progressive verb tenses correctly in speaking and writing.

MATERIALS   Online

Display and Engage *Grammar 3.3.4a, 3.3.4b, 3.3.4c*

Printable *Grammar 3.3.4*

INSTRUCTIONAL VOCABULARY

- **progressive verb tense** tells about an action that happens over a period of time

Review Progressive Verb Tenses

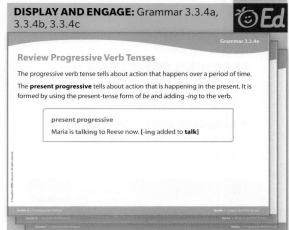

DISPLAY AND ENGAGE: Grammar 3.3.4a, 3.3.4b, 3.3.4c

Online Ed

Grammar 3.3.4a

Review Progressive Verb Tenses

The progressive verb tense tells about action that happens over a period of time.

The **present progressive** tells about action that is happening in the present. It is formed by using the present-tense form of *be* and adding -*ing* to the verb.

> present progressive
> Maria is **talking** to Reese now. [-*ing* added to **talk**]

- Show **Display and Engage: Grammar 3.3.4a** and then **Display and Engage: Grammar 3.3.4b**. Review that the tense of a verb tells when something happens. A **progressive verb tense** is used to tell about an action that happens over time.

- Progressive verb tenses are formed by using different forms of *be* and adding -*ing* to the present-tense form of the verb.

- Write the following sentences on the board, and have students identify each progressive verb. Also, have them tell whether the verb is present, past, or future progressive tense.

  » *I am going to the city.* am going; present progressive

  » *I was going to the city.* was going; past progressive

  » *I will be going to the city.* will be going; future progressive

- Review examples and complete items 1–4 on **Display and Engage: Grammar 3.3.4c** with students.

- Ask students to create sentences using a progressive verb tense. Then, have them identify the verbs.

- Have students complete **Printable: Grammar 3.3.4** for more practice with progressive verb tenses.

- Have students edit a writing draft using progressive verb tenses.

 ENGLISH LEARNER SUPPORT: Scaffolded Practice

SUBSTANTIAL

Write: *We are studying for our test now. We were studying for our test yesterday. We will be studying for our test tomorrow.* Work with students to circle each verb tense and identify when the action happened. *are studying—present; were studying—past; will be studying—future*

MODERATE

Have students write these sentences: *We are talking. We were talking. We will be talking.* Ask students to identify the time of action as *yesterday, today,* or *tomorrow.*

LIGHT

Have students write three sentences using each progressive verb tense. Have them exchange sentences with a partner and identify the verb tense in each.

LEARNING OBJECTIVES

- **Language** Identify and write progressive verb tenses.
- **Language** Use progressive verb tenses correctly in speaking and writing.

MATERIALS   Online

Display and Engage Grammar 3.3.5

Printable Grammar 3.3.5

 INSTRUCTIONAL VOCABULARY

- **progressive verb tense** tells about an action that happens over a period of time

Connect and Teach

- Show **Display and Engage: Grammar 3.3.5**. Explain that good writers use verb tenses and verb forms correctly to make their writing clear and help readers understand when events take place.

- Remind students that the **progressive verb tense** tells about an action that happens over a period of time.

- Point out that an important part of revising is checking for the correct verb tenses and verb forms. Also, point out that students should make sure that they use the same verb tense and verb form in each sentence that tells about actions that are taking place at the same point in time.

Engage and Apply

- Display the following sentences. Guide students in using progressive verb tenses to correct the sentences as necessary.

  » *In prehistoric times, dinosaurs are roaming the earth. were roaming*

  » *James studied dinosaurs now. is studying*

  » *Tomorrow, he is looking for food in the refrigerator. will be looking*

- Have students create sentences using the present, past, and future progressive verb tenses.

- Have students complete **Printable: Grammar 3.3.5** for more practice with using progressive verb tenses.

- Have students return to a draft of their writing using progressive verb tenses. Have them work in pairs to check that they have used progressive verb tenses correctly.

 ENGLISH LEARNER SUPPORT: Scaffolded Practice

ALL LEVELS Remind students to look closely at the form of the verb *be* to decide if a sentence is in the present progressive, past progressive, or future progressive. Write *Sara and Aunt Sofia are touring the city*. Underline the word *are*. Ask students if the verb *are* is in the present, past, or future tense. (*present*) In classroom books, have students look for sentences that include the present progressive, past progressive, and future progressive. Have students work with a partner to identify the verb tenses.

DISPLAY AND ENGAGE: Grammar 3.3.5

Online

Grammar 3.3.5

Connect to Writing: Using Progressive Verb Tenses

Good writers use verb tenses and verb forms correctly to make their writing clear and help readers understand when events take place.

The **present progressive** tells about action that is happening in the present and is formed by using the present-tense form of *be* and adding *-ing* to the verb.

The **past progressive** tells about action that happened over a period of time in the past. It is formed by using the past-tense form of *be* and adding *-ing* to the verb.

The **future progressive** tells about action that will happen over a period of time in the future. It is formed by using *will be* and adding *-ing* to the verb.

Grade 4 | Grammar Minilessons   Verbs • Progressive Verb Tenses

LEARNING OBJECTIVES

- **Language** Introduce modal auxiliaries to convey various conditions.
- **Language** Use modal auxiliaries correctly in speaking and writing.

MATERIALS   Online

Display and Engage *Grammar 3.4.1a, 3.4.1b*

Printable *Grammar 3.4.1*

 INSTRUCTIONAL VOCABULARY

- **helping verb** a verb that works with a main verb
- **modal auxiliary** a helping verb that shows how things could be or should be

Connect and Teach

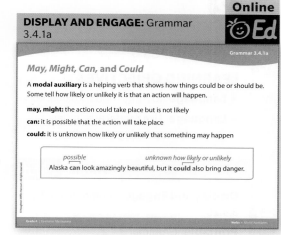

- Show **Display and Engage: Grammar 3.4.1a**. Remind students that a **helping verb** is a verb that comes before a main verb and tells more about the action. Explain that one type of helping verb is called a **modal auxiliary**. These verbs tell how things could be or should be. Some modal auxiliaries express certainty or lack of certainty that something will happen. Examples include *may, might, can,* and *could.* Point out that *will,* used to form the future tense, is also a modal auxiliary.

- Model identifying modal auxiliaries in the example sentence: *Alaska can look amazingly beautiful, but it could also bring danger.*

  THINK ALOUD *To identify a modal auxiliary, I ask:* Which word is a helping verb? Does it tell about the certainty of the action? *I read the helping verb* can. *It tells me that it is possible for Alaska to look beautiful. I also read the helping verb* could. *It tells me that it is unknown how likely or unlikely it is that Alaska will bring danger. So, both* can *and* could *are modal auxiliaries.*

Engage and Apply

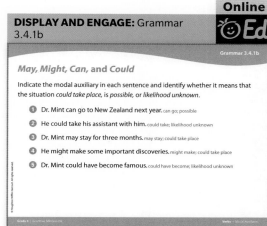

- Complete items 1–5 on **Display and Engage: Grammar 3.4.1b** with students.

- Write the following sentences on the board, and guide students in identifying the modal auxiliary in each.

  » *Sarah might go to the party. might*

  » *She could feel better by then. could*

- Ask students to create sentences using *may, might, can,* and *could* and explain how each affects the meaning of the sentence.

- Have students complete **Printable: Grammar 3.4.1** for practice with *may, might, can,* and *could.*

- Have students edit a writing draft using the modal auxiliaries *may, might, can,* and *could.*

 ENGLISH LEARNER SUPPORT: Scaffolded Practice

ALL LEVELS Write *may, might, can, could, should, must, would.* Discuss the different meanings of these modal auxiliaries. *May* and *might* tell about permission and possibility. *Can* and *could* tell about permission and possibility and ability. *Should* tells about advice or what makes sense. *Must* tells about certainty. Provide sentences with each modal auxiliary and discuss the meanings behind them. *We may have free time if we finish our work. You might want to check your work. Exercise can make us healthier. They could see the full moon from their window last night. I think we should get to the airport early. You must be happy that you won a prize!*

LEARNING OBJECTIVES

- **Language** Identify modal auxiliaries.
- **Language** Use modal auxiliaries correctly in speaking and writing.

MATERIALS   Online

Display and Engage *Grammar 3.4.2a, 3.4.2b*

Printable *Grammar 3.4.2*

 INSTRUCTIONAL VOCABULARY

- **modal auxiliary** a helping verb that shows how things could be or should be

Connect and Teach

- Show **Display and Engage: Grammar 3.4.2a**. Explain that *would, should,* and *must* are also **modal auxiliaries**. They express the feelings or opinion of the writer or speaker.

- Model identifying modal auxiliaries in the example sentences: *Alaska should be an industry-free zone. This land must be saved from air pollution.*

  THINK ALOUD *To identify the modal auxiliaries, I ask:* Which word is a helping verb? Does it express the writer's feelings or opinion? *First, I read the helping verb* should. *It tells me the writer is suggesting that Alaska be kept free of industry. The second helping verb I read is* must. *It tells me the writer feels that saving Alaska from pollution is very important. So, both* should *and* must *are modal auxiliaries because they express the writer's opinions and feelings.*

Engage and Apply

- Complete items 1–5 on **Display and Engage: Grammar 3.4.2b** with students.

- Write the following sentences on the board, and guide students in identifying the modal auxiliary in each.

  » *Sarah should go home. should*

  » *She must finish her homework. must*

- Ask students to create sentences using *would, should,* and *must*. Write the sentences on the board, and have students explain how each modal auxiliary affects the meaning of the sentence.

- Have students complete **Printable: Grammar 3.4.2** for practice with *would, should,* and *must.*

- Have students edit a writing draft using the modal auxiliaries *would, should,* and *must.*

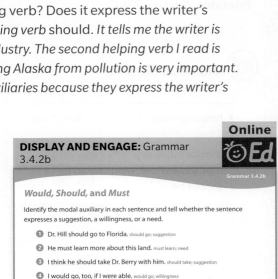

 ENGLISH LEARNER SUPPORT: Scaffolded Practice

SUBSTANTIAL

Write: *He will go to California next winter. He might go whale-watching.* Have students identify the modal auxiliaries and the main verbs. Ask *yes/no* questions to confirm students' understanding of the meanings of the verbs.

MODERATE

Write: *He will go to California next winter. He might go whale-watching.* Ask students which action is more likely to happen (the first). Repeat, using a variety of example sentences to show the meaning of modal auxiliaries.

LIGHT

Have student pairs write three sentences about a place they know, sentences that contain modal auxiliaries. Have students identify the modal auxiliary in each of the sentences and tell why it is used.

LEARNING OBJECTIVES

- **Language** Use modal auxiliaries to convey various conditions.
- **Language** Use modal auxiliaries correctly in speaking and writing.

MATERIALS   Online

Display and Engage *Grammar 3.4.3a, 3.4.3b*

Printable *Grammar 3.4.3*

INSTRUCTIONAL VOCABULARY

- **modal auxiliary** a helping verb that shows how things could be or should be

Connect and Teach

- Show **Display and Engage: Grammar 3.4.3a**. Remind students that **modal auxiliaries** show how things could be or should be. Point out that changing the modal auxiliary in a sentence can often change the meaning of the sentence.

- Model use of modal auxiliaries to express ideas clearly in the example sentences: *Teachers can help us learn about the world. Teachers must help us learn about the environment in order to protect it.*

  THINK ALOUD *To use modal auxiliaries effectively, I ask:* Which modal auxiliary helps express my idea clearly? *In the first sentence, I use the helping verb* can *because I want to say that it is possible for teachers to help us. In the second sentence, I use the modal auxiliary* must *because I feel that it is absolutely necessary for teachers to help us learn about the environment. I feel strongly about this.*

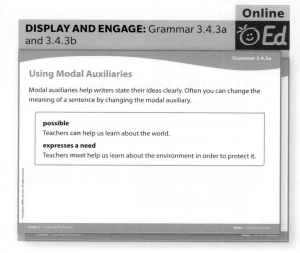

Engage and Apply

- Complete items 1–6 on **Display and Engage: Grammar 3.4.3b** with students.

- Write the following sentences on the board and guide students in identifying the modal auxiliary in each.

  » *You must wear warm clothes, a hat, and gloves.* must

  » *You could get sick if you fail to dress properly.* could

- Ask students to create sentences containing modal auxiliaries. Write the sentences on the board, and have students explain how each modal auxiliary affects the meaning of the sentence.

- Have students complete **Printable: Grammar 3.4.3** for practice with using modal auxiliaries.

- Have students use modal auxiliaries to edit a writing draft.

 ENGLISH LEARNER SUPPORT: Scaffolded Practice

SUBSTANTIAL

Write: *It will get dark soon. We should walk home now.* Have students identify the modal auxiliaries and the main verbs. Ask *yes/no* questions to confirm students' understanding of the meanings of the verbs.

MODERATE

Write: *It will get dark soon. We should walk home now.* Ask students which action expresses the writer's opinion or feeling (the second). Repeat, using different example sentences to show the meaning of modal auxiliaries.

LIGHT

Have student pairs write three sentences about actions, using modal auxiliaries to show that someone feels something should or must be done. Have students identify the modal auxiliary in each of the sentences and tell what it means and why it is used.

LEARNING OBJECTIVES

- **Language** Review modal auxiliaries.
- **Language** Use modal auxiliaries correctly in speaking and writing.

MATERIALS   Online *Ed*

Display and Engage *Grammar 3.4.4a, 3.4.4b, 3.4.4c*

Printable *Grammar 3.4.4*

 INSTRUCTIONAL VOCABULARY

- **modal auxiliary** a helping verb that shows how things could be or should be

Review Modal Auxiliaries

- Show **Display and Engage: Grammar 3.4.4a** and then **Display and Engage: Grammar 3.4.4b**. Remind students that **modal auxiliaries** can help writers express their ideas and make the meaning of a sentence clearer. Modal auxiliaries such as *may, can, could, might,* and *will* tell the reader how likely it is that something will happen. Modal auxiliaries such as *should, must,* and *would* help writers express their feelings or opinions.

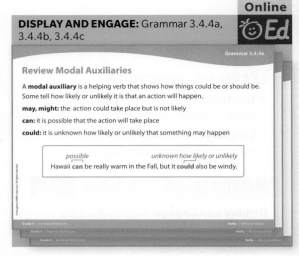

- Have students identify the modal auxiliaries in the following sentences and explain the meaning of each one.

  » *Jean might go to the conference tomorrow. might: It's possible but not definite that Jean will go to the conference.*

  » *Jack could be going, too. could: It's unknown how likely or unlikely it is that Jack will go with Jean.*

  » *That trail can be icy, so don't take it. can: It is possible the trail will be icy.*

  » *If you bike tomorrow, you must take the paved road. must: You have to take the paved road.*

  » *You should bring salt in case the paved road is icy, too. should: The speaker wants you to take salt with you.*

- Complete items 1–4 on **Display and Engage: Grammar 3.4.4c** with students.

- Have pairs use modal auxiliaries to discuss something that should be done during the school day, something that must be done during the school day, and something that could be done during the school day.

- Have students complete **Printable: Grammar 3.4.4** for more practice with modal auxiliaries.

- Have students edit a writing draft using modal auxiliaries.

 ENGLISH LEARNER SUPPORT: Scaffolded Practice

ALL LEVELS Provide additional practice with modal auxiliaries *can, might, should,* and *must.* Use sentence frames, such as *We _____ bring snacks on the hike.* Work with students to explain how each modal auxiliary changes the meaning of the sentence.

LEARNING OBJECTIVES

- **Language** Use modal auxiliaries to express ideas clearly in writing.

- **Language** Use modal auxiliaries correctly in speaking and writing.

MATERIALS   Online

Display and Engage *Grammar 3.4.5*

Printable *Grammar 3.4.5*

 **INSTRUCTIONAL VOCABULARY**

- **modal auxiliary** a helping verb that shows how things could be or should be

Connect and Teach

- Show **Display and Engage: Grammar 3.4.5**. Remind students that good writers use **modal auxiliaries** to make their ideas clear, to tell the reader how likely it is that something will happen, and to clearly express their feelings or opinions.

- Point out that an important part of revising is adding modal auxiliaries if they can make the writing clearer. Editing includes checking to see that modal auxiliaries are used correctly.

DISPLAY AND ENGAGE: Grammar 3.4.5

Online
Ed

Grammar 3.4.5

Connect to Writing: Using Modal Auxiliaries

A **modal auxiliary** is a helping verb that shows how things could be or should be. Some, such as *may, might, can,* and *could,* tell how likely or unlikely it is that an action will happen. Others, such as *would, should,* and *must,* express the opinions of the writer or speaker.

Modal auxiliaries make ideas clear, tell the reader how likely it is that something will happen, and clearly express the feelings or opinions of the writer. An important part of revising is adding modal auxiliaries if they can make the writing clearer.

Engage and Apply

- Display the following sentences. Guide students in identifying each modal auxiliary and discussing its meaning in the sentence.

  » *It could rain tomorrow. could*
  It is unknown how likely or unlikely it is that rain will occur.

  » *The sun might shine, though. might*
  It is possible that the sun could, but it is not likely that the sun will shine.

  » *You should bring your umbrella, just in case. should*
  An action is being suggested.

  » *You must be prepared for any weather. must*
  The action needs to happen.

- Ask students to create sentences containing modal auxiliaries. Write the sentences on the board, and have students explain how each modal auxiliary affects the meaning of the sentence.

- Have students complete **Printable: Grammar 3.4.5** for more practice with using modal auxiliaries in writing.

- Have students return to a draft of their writing. Encourage them to include modal auxiliaries to clarify the likelihood of events or actions and to clearly express their own feelings or opinions.

EL ENGLISH LEARNER SUPPORT: Scaffolded Practice

ALL LEVELS Write: *The scientists will make an important discovery.* Explain that *will* is a helping verb that shows that the action is going to happen in the future. Write the sentence again, replacing *will* with *might*. Explain that using *might* shows that an action could take place, but it is not certain. Then, rewrite the sentence again, this time, replacing *will* with *could*. Explain that *could* also tells us that it is unknown whether the action is going to happen. Have students rewrite the sentence three more times, using one of these modal auxiliaries each time: *can, should, would.* Encourage students to use their home languages to discuss how the meaning of the sentence changes, depending on the modal auxiliary in the sentence.

LEARNING OBJECTIVES

- **Language** Introduce irregular verbs.
- **Language** Use irregular verbs correctly in speaking and writing.

MATERIALS Online

Display and Engage *Grammar 3.5.1a, 3.5.1b*

Printable *Grammar 3.5.1*

 **INSTRUCTIONAL VOCABULARY**

irregular verb a verb that does not end in *-ed* in the past tense

Connect and Teach

- Show **Display and Engage: Grammar 3.5.1a**. Review with students that past tense is the form of a verb that tells about actions that happened in the past.

- Explain that an **irregular verb** is a verb that does not end with *-ed* to show past tense. Explain that the spelling of irregular verbs must be memorized.

- Model identifying the irregular verb in the example sentence: *Yesterday, Mom brought me a book about Rosa Parks.*

   THINK ALOUD *When I read the sentence, I see that it is about an action that happened in the past, but I don't see a verb that ends in -ed. I ask: Which word in the sentence is a verb that does not end in -ed? I can see that the past-tense verb, brought, does not end in -ed, so it must be an irregular verb.*

Engage and Apply

- Complete items 1–8 on **Display and Engage: Grammar 3.5.1b** with students.

- Ask partners to provide oral sentences that include irregular verbs. Write the sentences and guide students to identify each irregular verb; underline the verb as the student identifies it.

   » *Scientists knew about changes to the ecosystem. knew*

   » *Many animals left their habitats. left*

- Then, have students complete **Printable: Grammar 3.5.1** for more practice with irregular verbs.

- Have students edit a writing draft using irregular verbs.

DISPLAY AND ENGAGE: Grammar 3.5.1a

Online Ed

Grammar 3.5.1a

Irregular Verbs

Verbs that do not add *-ed* to show past action are called **irregular verbs**. The spellings of irregular verbs must be memorized.

> *irregular verb*
> Mom **brought** me a book about Rosa Parks.

> *irregular verb*
> I **thought** she was going to the store.

DISPLAY AND ENGAGE: Grammar 3.5.1b

Online Ed

Grammar 3.5.1b

Irregular Verbs

State the correct form of the verb in parentheses to show past action.

1. Sally _____ that it was raining outside. (think) thought
2. He _____ up a funny joke. (make) made
3. She _____ a rainbow kite. (fly) flew
4. The man _____ his friend a high five. (give) gave
5. The story _____ an unlikely turn. (take) took
6. The lightning bolt _____ the tree. (strike) struck
7. A loud cough _____ out of his mouth. (shoot) shot
8. The experiment _____ scientists a new view on flying. (give) gave

---

EL ENGLISH LEARNER SUPPORT: Facilitate Language Connections

Point out the cognates in the list above. Then, explain that irregular verbs do not follow spelling rules to show changes in tense. In Cantonese, Hmong, Vietnamese, Tagalog, and Haitian Creole, verbs do not change to show tense. Instead, adverbs or expressions of time indicate when an action has taken place. Help students learn the patterns used to indicate past, future, and past perfect. For example: *What is the past tense of see? What is the past tense of affect?*

Scaffolded Practice

SUBSTANTIAL/MODERATE

Write: *I wanted to help the environment. He thought so, too.* Circle the verb in each sentence. Guide students to say the present tense of each verb and to tell if it is regular or irregular.

LIGHT

Have students write one sentence using a regular past-tense verb and another sentence using an irregular past-tense verb. Have partners trade sentences and identify which is the regular and which is the irregular verb.

LESSON 3.5.2

THE VERB *BE*

LEARNING OBJECTIVES

- **Language** Introduce the verb *be*.
- **Language** Use the verb *be* correctly in speaking and writing.

MATERIALS Online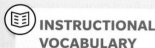

Display and Engage *Grammar 3.5.2a, 3.5.2b*

Printable *Grammar 3.5.2*

INSTRUCTIONAL VOCABULARY

be verb that tells what something is or is like

Connect and Teach

- Show **Display and Engage: Grammar 3.5.2a**. Explain that the verb *be* does not show action. It tells what someone or something is or is like. The verb *be* has special form, depending on tense and subject.

- Model identifying the correct form of the verb *be* in the example sentence: *Today's forecast is blue skies and sunshine.*

  THINK ALOUD *To identify the correct form of the verb* be, *I ask:* What is the subject? What is the tense? What form of *be* is correct? *The subject is* forecast, *a singular noun. The tense is* present. *The correct form of* be *is* is.

Engage and Apply

- Complete items 1–6 on **Display and Engage: Grammar 3.5.2b** with students.

- Write the following sentences on the board. Have students orally supply the correct form of the verb *be*.

  » *The weather (is, are) changing. is*

  » *Snow (was, were) falling all day. was*

- Then, have students complete **Printable: Grammar 3.5.2** for more practice with the special verb *be*.

- Have students edit a writing draft using the verb *be*.

EL ENGLISH LEARNER SUPPORT: Scaffolded Practice

ALL LEVELS Have students write: *I thought the clouds looked dark. Then I heard thunder. A storm was near.* Have students circle the verbs and label them as regular or irregular.

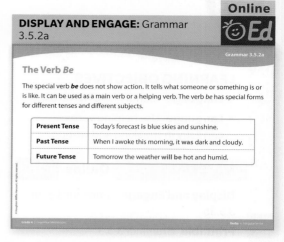

DISPLAY AND ENGAGE: Grammar 3.5.2a

Online Ed

Grammar 3.5.2a

The Verb *Be*

The special verb *be* does not show action. It tells what someone or something is or is like. It can be used as a main verb or a helping verb. The verb *be* has special forms for different tenses and different subjects.

Present Tense	Today's forecast is blue skies and sunshine.
Past Tense	When I awoke this morning, it was dark and cloudy.
Future Tense	Tomorrow the weather will be hot and humid.

DISPLAY AND ENGAGE: Grammar 3.5.2b

Online Ed

Grammar 3.5.2b

The Verb *Be*

Choose the correct form of the verb *be* to complete each sentence. Tell whether the verb is in the past, present, or future tense.

1. I _____ watching the news on the television. (am, is) am; present
2. The reporter _____ a woman named Amanda Brandt. (is, are) is; present
3. Rain _____ here later this week. (were, will be) will be; future
4. The clouds _____ in the sky this morning. (was, were) were; past
5. Raindrops _____ are falling on the ground. (is, are) are; present
6. That hail _____ very loud. (am, is) is; present

LEARNING OBJECTIVES

- **Language** Identify helping verbs.
- **Language** Use helping verbs correctly in speaking and writing.

MATERIALS   Online

Display and Engage *Grammar 3.5.3a, 3.5.3b*

Printable *Grammar 3.5.3*

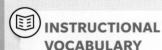 **INSTRUCTIONAL VOCABULARY**

helping verb verbs that come before a verb, such as *had, have,* and *has*

Connect and Teach

- Show **Display and Engage: Grammar 3.5.3a**. Review that most irregular verbs change spelling when they are used with **helping verbs**.

- Review some examples of helping verbs, such as *had, have,* and *has.*

- Using the example sentence, model identifying the correct past-tense spelling of *take* when used with a helping verb.

  THINK ALOUD *Take is an irregular verb, so its form changes to* took *when it is used in the past tense. When it is used with the helping verb* has, *the form changes again, this time to* taken: *Mr. Conroy has taken several trips.*

Engage and Apply

- Complete items 1–5 on **Display and Engage: Grammar 3.5.3b** with students.

- Write these sentences on the board. Have students supply the correct irregular verbs and helping verbs.

  » *The town (had grown, had grew) by a hundred people. had grown*

  » *No one (has done, has did) more work on the project. has done*

- Then, have students complete **Printable: Grammar 3.5.3** for more practice with helping verbs.

- Have students edit a writing draft using helping verbs.

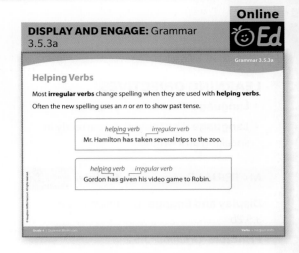

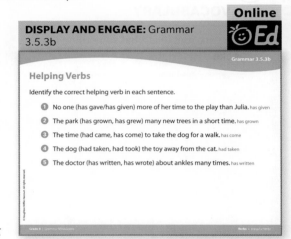

EL **ENGLISH LEARNER SUPPORT: Scaffolded Learning**

ALL LEVELS Ask students to work in mixed-proficiency groups and define the term *helping verb* and give examples: *I have seen the new movie. We have written some stories. She has taught math at another school.* Have students identify the helping verb and verb in each sentence. Make a chart to show which form of the helping verb *have* to use with *I, we,* and *she.* Continue to give example sentences with *you, he,* and *they.* Guide students to add these examples to the chart.

LEARNING OBJECTIVES

- **Language** Review irregular verbs.
- **Language** Use irregular verbs correctly in speaking and writing.

MATERIALS
Online

Display and Engage *Grammar 3.5.4a, 3.5.4b, 3.5.4c*

Printable *Grammar 3.5.4*

 INSTRUCTIONAL VOCABULARY

- **irregular verb** a verb that does not end in *-ed* in the past tense
- **be** verb that tells what something is or is like
- **helping verb** verbs that come before a verb, such as *had, have,* and *has*

Review Irregular Verbs

- Show **Display and Engage: Grammar 3.5.4a** and then **Display and Engage: Grammar 3.5.4b** to students. Remind students that the past tense of **irregular verbs** is not formed by adding *-ed* to a verb. Guide students to recall that the spelling of irregular verbs must be memorized.

- Ask students to recall that the verb **be** does not show action; instead, it tells what someone or something is like. Point out again that the correct form of *be* depends on the tense and subject.

- Remind students that most irregular verbs change form when they are used with **helping verbs**.

- Have students complete the activity on **Display and Engage: Grammar 3.5.4c**.

- Write three lists on the board: *Irregular Verbs, Helping Verbs,* and *Forms of the Verb Be.* Have small groups work together to write one sentence for each type of verb. Have volunteers share their sentences and work together to correct any errors in verb form.

- Then, have students complete **Printable: Grammar 3.5.4** for more practice with irregular verbs.

- Have students edit a writing draft using irregular verbs.

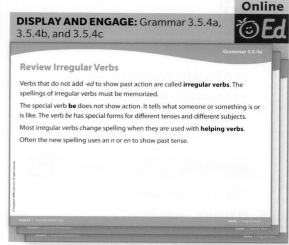

DISPLAY AND ENGAGE: Grammar 3.5.4a, 3.5.4b, and 3.5.4c

Online Ed

Grammar 3.5.4a

Review Irregular Verbs

Verbs that do not add *-ed* to show past action are called **irregular verbs**. The spellings of irregular verbs must be memorized.

The special verb **be** does not show action. It tells what someone or something is or is like. The verb *be* has special forms for different tenses and different subjects.

Most irregular verbs change spelling when they are used with **helping verbs**.

Often the new spelling uses an *n* or *en* to show past tense.

 ENGLISH LEARNER SUPPORT: Scaffolded Practice

ALL LEVELS Write the following sentences: *I take the bus. Yesterday I took the bus. Tomorrow I will take the bus.* Say each sentence aloud and have students repeat. Circle the form of *take* in each sentence. Explain that *take* is an irregular verb and has a different form depending on the tense that is used. Provide sentence frames for *take* that have time clues. *We _____ deep breaths to get focused. Yesterday we _____ deep breaths to get focused. Tomorrow we _____ deep breaths again.* Have students work with partners to complete each sentence frame.

VERBS · IRREGULAR VERBS

LEARNING OBJECTIVES

- **Language** Use irregular verbs.
- **Language** Use irregular verbs correctly in speaking and writing.

MATERIALS   Online

Display and Engage *Grammar 3.5.5*

Printable *Grammar 3.5.5*

 **INSTRUCTIONAL VOCABULARY**

- **irregular verb** a verb that does not end in *-ed* in the past tense
- **be** verb that tells what something is or is like
- **helping verb** verbs that come before a verb, such as *had*, *have*, and *has*

Connect and Teach

- Show **Display and Engage: Grammar 3.5.5**. Explain that good writers always use **irregular verbs** correctly to make their writing clear and understandable for readers.

- Point out that an important part of revising is to make sure that all verbs are used correctly so that the reader understands the action and can tell when it happened.

Engage and Apply

- Display the following sentences. Guide students to choose the correct irregular verbs and helping verbs.

  » *Last year, Jeff (grow, grew) his hair long.* grew

  » *The parents (have took, have taken) the vans to the science fair.* have taken

  » *Samantha (wear, wore) a red dress for her recital.* wore

- Remind students about using the verb *be* and using helping verbs. Have one group of students write sentences using forms of the verb *be*. Have another group of students write sentences using helping verbs. Have both groups gather into pairs and review the sentences, correcting any errors in verb form.

- Then, have students complete **Printable: Grammar 3.5.5** for more practice with irregular verbs.

- Have students edit a writing draft using irregular verbs.

(EL) ENGLISH LANGUAGE SUPPORT: Scaffolded Practice

ALL LEVELS Write: *She opened her umbrella. She held the umbrella.* Point to *opened* and remind students it is a regular verb. It uses *-ed*. Point to *held* and remind students that irregular verbs do not have an *-ed* ending. Write: *The teacher thought I ran very fast today.* Have students identify the irregular verbs. *thought, ran* Have students create their own sentences using irregular verbs. List some examples of irregular verbs that students can use.

Online

DISPLAY AND ENGAGE: Grammar 3.5.5

Grammar 3.5.5

Connect to Writing: Using Irregular Verbs

The use of an incorrect verb form can confuse your readers. When you proofread your writing, be sure you have used the correct forms of irregular verbs to show past action. Also be sure that you have used correct forms of the helping verbs *has*, *have*, and *had*.

Incorrect Verb Form	Correct Verb Form
The social studies teacher has **brung** a poster showing the locations of Revolutionary War battles. Yesterday, I **writed** an essay on the Battle of Yorktown.	The social studies teacher has **brought** a poster showing the locations of Revolutionary War battles. Yesterday, I **wrote** an essay on the Battle of Yorktown.

LEARNING OBJECTIVES

- **Language** Introduce present participles.
- **Language** Use present participles correctly in speaking and writing.

MATERIALS Online

Display and Engage *Grammar 3.6.1a, 3.6.1b*

Printable *Grammar 3.6.1*

INSTRUCTIONAL VOCABULARY

- **participle** a verb form that can be used as an adjective
- **present participle** a verb form that expresses present tense

Connect and Teach

- Show **Display and Engage: Grammar 3.6.1a**. Remind students that a **participle** is a verb form that can be used as an adjective. Explain that every verb has a **present participle** that ends in -*ing*.

- Explain that an irregular verb is a verb that does not end with -*ed* to show past tense. Explain that the spelling of irregular verbs must be memorized.

- Model identifying the present participle and the noun it describes in this sentence: *I watched the setting sun.*

  THINK ALOUD *To identify the present participle, I ask:* Which verb form ending in -*ing* describes a noun? Setting *ends in* -ing. *It describes the noun* sun.

Engage and Apply

- Complete items 1–6 on **Display and Engage: Grammar 3.6.1b** with students.

- List the following verbs on the board. Have students form the present participles. Then work together to use them to describe nouns, such as the *heating* sun and a *flooding* rain.
  heat heating
  flood flooding
  snap snapping
  crack cracking
  shout shouting
  jump jumping

- Then, have students complete **Printable: Grammar 3.6.1** for more practice with present participles.

- Have students edit a writing draft using present participles.

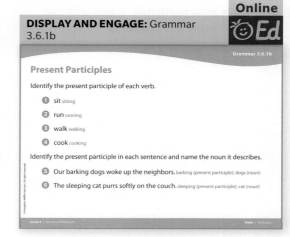

DISPLAY AND ENGAGE: Grammar 3.6.1a — Online

Present Participles

A **present participle** is a verb form that ends in -*ing*.

Verb	Present Participle
break	breaking
dance	dancing
dig	digging

A present participle can be used as an adjective.

present participle
I watched the **digging** crabs hide on the beach.

DISPLAY AND ENGAGE: Grammar 3.6.1b — Online

Present Participles

Identify the present participle of each verb.
1. sit sitting
2. run running
3. walk walking
4. cook cooking

Identify the present participle in each sentence and name the noun it describes.
5. Our barking dogs woke up the neighbors. barking (present participle); dogs (noun)
6. The sleeping cat purrs softly on the couch. sleeping (present participle); cat (noun)

ENGLISH LEARNER SUPPORT: Scaffolded Practice

ALL LEVELS Review present and past tense verb forms with students. Reinforce the difference by displaying the following sentences. Work with students to identify which are written in present tense and which are written in past tense.
The gophers hide. present
The princess washed her hair. past
He asks the others to help out. present
The sun set in the distance. past
Model identifying the present participle and the noun it describes in the example sentence:
I watched the setting sun.

LEARNING OBJECTIVES

- **Language** Introduce past participles.
- **Language** Use past participles correctly in speaking and writing.

MATERIALS   Online

Display and Engage *Grammar 3.6.2a, 3.6.2b*

Printable *Grammar 3.6.2*

 INSTRUCTIONAL VOCABULARY

- **past participle** a verb form that expresses past tense

Connect and Teach

- Show **Display and Engage: Grammar 3.6.2a**. Explain that every verb has a **past participle** that can be used as an adjective. Explain that most past participles end in -*d* or -*ed* and those that do not are irregular verbs and have special forms of the past participle.

- Model identifying the past participle and the noun it describes in this example sentence: *Bothered by mosquitoes, we moved inside.*

  THINK ALOUD *To identify the past participle, I ask:* Which verb form that tells about a past action modifies a noun? *For example: My puppy was dragging the chewed stick around the house.* Chewed *tells about a past action. It modifies, or describes, the noun* stick.

- Ask students to share sentences using the past participles *tied*, *cooked*, and *walked* as adjectives.

Engage and Apply

- Complete items 1–6 in each section on **Display and Engage: Grammar 3.6.2b** with students.

- List the following verbs on the board. Have students form the past participles. Then work together to use them to describe nouns, such as *heated pan* and *popped balloon.*

  burn burned
  straighten straightened
  chill chilled
  ruin ruined
  gain gained
  lose lost

- Then, have students complete **Printable: Grammar 3.6.2** for more practice with past participles.

- Have students edit a writing draft using past participles.

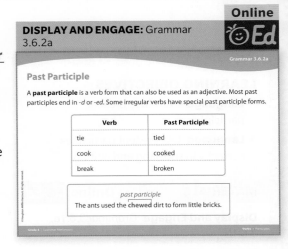

 ENGLISH LEARNER SUPPORT: Scaffolded Practice

SUBSTANTIAL

Write on the board, *The ants are digging. They are making tunnels.* Guide students to use *digging* as a participle to complete this sentence: *The _____ ants are making tunnels.*

MODERATE

Write the following sentences on the board and guide students to identify the participle in each sentence. *Discarded seeds sprout into new plants. Army ants form living bridges.*

LIGHT

Have partners work together to create sentences that describe nouns using the following past participle and present participle: *discarded, digging.*

LESSON 3.6.3 PARTICIPLE PHRASES

LEARNING OBJECTIVES

- **Language** Introduce participle phrases.
- **Language** Use participle phrases correctly in speaking and writing.

MATERIALS Online Ed

Display and Engage *Grammar 3.6.3a, 3.6.3b*

Printable *Grammar 3.6.3*

 INSTRUCTIONAL VOCABULARY

- **participle phrase** describes a noun

Connect and Teach

- Show **Display and Engage: Grammar 3.6.3a**. Explain that a **participle phrase** contains a participle and other words and can be used to describe a subject.

- Tell students that a participle phrase can be simply the participle or several words together, and it can have either a past or present participle.

- Model identifying the participle phrase and the subject it describes in the example sentence:
  Leaving their homes behind, the ants moved to a new field.

  THINK ALOUD *To identify participle phrases, I ask:* Which phrase contains a participle that tells about a subject? Leaving their homes *includes the participle* Leaving. *The phrase tells about the subject,* ants.

Engage and Apply

- Complete items 1–4 on **Display and Engage: Grammar 3.6.3b** with students.

- Work with students to identify the participle phrases in the following sentences.

  » *Working until the last minute, Jack finished his report.* **Working until the last minute**

  » *Watching carefully, the bird dove to grab a fish.* **Watching carefully**

- Then, have students complete **Printable: Grammar 3.6.3** for more practice with participle phrases.

- Have students edit a writing draft using participle phrases.

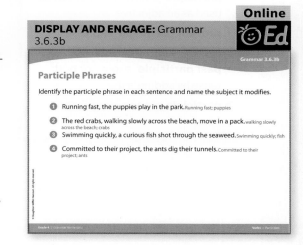

DISPLAY AND ENGAGE: Grammar 3.6.3a

Grammar 3.6.3a

Participle Phrases

A **participle phrase** contains a participle and other accompanying words. A participle phrase can be used to modify a subject.

participle phrase
Carrying the seaweed, the crabs made their way to the rock.

DISPLAY AND ENGAGE: Grammar 3.6.3b

Grammar 3.6.3b

Participle Phrases

Identify the participle phrase in each sentence and name the subject it modifies.

1. Running fast, the puppies play in the park. Running fast; puppies
2. The red crabs, walking slowly across the beach, move in a pack. walking slowly across the beach; crabs
3. Swimming quickly, a curious fish shot through the seaweed. Swimming quickly; fish
4. Committed to their project, the ants dig their tunnels. Committed to their project; ants

---

EL **ENGLISH LEARNER SUPPORT: Scaffolded Practice**

ALL LEVELS Invite students to work in mixed-proficiency groups to identify the participle in the following sentence: *Fearing a storm, Richard returned home early. Fearing* Then, have students work together to identify the participle phrase. *Fearing a storm.* Ask students who or what the subject is. Provide more sentences with participle phrases for students to practice, having students name the participle, the participle phrase, and the subject of each sentence.

LEARNING OBJECTIVES

- **Language** Review participles.
- **Language** Use participles correctly in speaking and writing.

MATERIALS   Online

Display and Engage *Grammar 3.6.4a, 3.6.4b, 3.6.4c*

Printable *Grammar 3.6.4*

INSTRUCTIONAL VOCABULARY

- **participle** a verb form that can be used as an adjective
- **present participle** expresses present tense by adding *-ing*
- **past participle** expresses past tense by adding *-ed*
- **participle phrase** describes a noun

Review Participles

- Show **Display and Engage: Grammar 3.6.4a** and then **Display and Engage: Grammar 3.6.4b**. Remind students that a **present participle** is a verb form that ends in *-ing*. Point out again that a present participle can be used as an adjective. Guide students in recalling that a **past participle** is a verb form that can also be used as an adjective. Ask students to recall that most past participles end in *-d* or *-ed*. Read aloud the sentences and review present and past participles and **participle phrase**.

- Have students complete the activity on **Display and Engage: Grammar 3.6.4c**.

- Have students complete **Printable: Grammar 3.6.4** for more practice with participles.

- Ask students to use the past participles in the examples—*breaking, running, locked,* and *broken*—in new sentences.

- Have students edit a writing draft using participles.

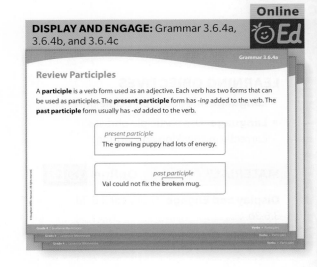

DISPLAY AND ENGAGE: Grammar 3.6.4a, 3.6.4b, and 3.6.4c

Grammar 3.6.4a

Review Participles

A **participle** is a verb form used as an adjective. Each verb has two forms that can be used as participles. The **present participle** form has *-ing* added to the verb. The **past participle** form usually has *-ed* added to the verb.

present participle
The growing puppy had lots of energy.

past participle
Val could not fix the **broken** mug.

 ENGLISH LEARNER SUPPORT: Scaffolded Practice

ALL LEVELS Remind students that sentences sometimes have many parts that work together to show action. Help students identify the complete verb in sentences, such as: *Plants have existed for millions of years. The plants had adapted to harsh conditions.*

LEARNING OBJECTIVES

- **Language** Identify participle phrases.
- **Language** Use participle phrases correctly in speaking and writing.

MATERIALS   Online

Display and Engage *Grammar 3.6.5*

Printable *Grammar 3.6.5*

 INSTRUCTIONAL VOCABULARY

- **participle** a verb form that can be used as an adjective
- **present participle** expresses present tense by adding -ing
- **past participle** expresses past tense by adding -ed
- **participle phrase** describes a noun

Connect and Teach

- Show and discuss examples on **Display and Engage: Grammar 3.6.5**. Tell students that good writers work to make their sentences flow smoothly. Explain that one way to do this is to use a **participle phrase** to combine two related sentences.

- Ask students to explain why the combined sentence is more effective than the two sentences standing alone. *The combined sentence is smoother and more interesting.*

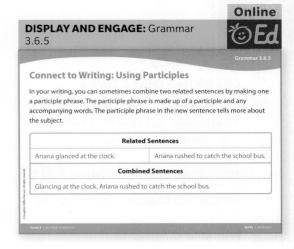

Engage and Apply

- Display the following sentences. Guide students to combine them using a participle phrase.
  The students studied shells at the beach. They gathered sand samples to examine later.
  Studying shells at the beach, the students gathered sand samples to examine later.

- Have students combine these sentences using a participle phrase.
  Kara was anxious about arriving late. She left an hour early.
  Anxious about arriving late, Kara left an hour early.

- Then, have students complete **Printable: Grammar 3.6.5** for more practice with participle phrases.

- Have students edit a writing draft using participle phrases.

 ENGLISH LEARNER SUPPORT: Scaffolded Practice

ALL LEVELS Write the following sentences: *The anthill absorbed the sun's rays. The anthill transferred the heat down into the nest.* Underline *absorbed* and *transferred*. Remind students that these are past tense verbs. Review the term *participle*. Write *absorbing* and *transferred*. Guide students to understand that *absorbing* is a present participle because it describes something that is happening now. *Transferred* is a past participle because the action happened in the past. Have students create noun phrases by using familiar actions, such as *The boy laughed/the laughing boy*, and *She locked the door/the locked door*. Using students' example phrases, demonstrate how to expand them into sentences. For example: *Placing it carefully, the ant moves its seed.* Have students add a participle phrase to help describe someone or something in their writing or to combine ideas.

LEARNING OBJECTIVES

- **Language** Introduce adjectives.
- **Language** Use adjectives correctly in speaking and writing.

MATERIALS   Online

Display and Engage *Grammar 4.1.1a, 4.1.1b*

Printable *Grammar 4.1.1*

INSTRUCTIONAL VOCABULARY

- **noun** a word that names a person, place, or thing
- **adjective** a word that gives information about a noun or pronoun

Connect and Teach

- Show **Display and Engage: Grammar 4.1.1a**. Remind students that a **noun** names a person, place, or thing. Explain that an **adjective** describes a noun or pronoun. Point out that adjectives often tell what kind, how many, or which one. Tell students that an adjective typically comes before the noun that it describes.

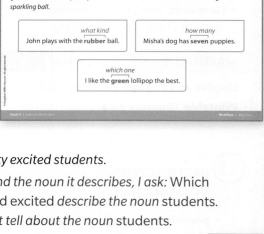

DISPLAY AND ENGAGE: Grammar 4.1.1a   Online

Adjectives

An **adjective** is a word that gives information about a noun or pronoun. An adjective can tell *what kind*, *which one*, or *how many*. Choose adjectives that give the exact description you intend. *Silver ball* has a different meaning than *sparkling ball*.

what kind	*how many*
John plays with the **rubber** ball.	Misha's dog has **seven** puppies.

which one
I like the **green** lollipop the best.

- Model identifying the adjectives and the noun described by the adjectives in the following sentence: *The bus carried fifty excited students.*

  THINK ALOUD *To identify the adjective and the noun it describes, I ask:* Which words describe a noun? *The words* fifty *and* excited *describe the noun* students. *So,* fifty *and* excited *must be adjectives that tell about the noun* students.

Engage and Apply

- Complete items 1–6 on **Display and Engage: Grammar 4.1.1b** with students.

- Work with students to identify adjectives that could describe the following nouns: *day, thunder, cat, bicycle.*

- Have students complete **Printable: Grammar 4.1.1** for practice with adjectives.

- Have students edit a writing draft using adjectives.

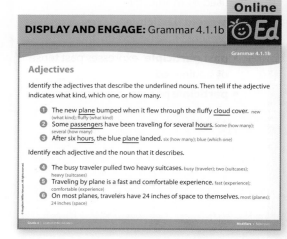

DISPLAY AND ENGAGE: Grammar 4.1.1b   Online

Adjectives

Identify the adjectives that describe the underlined nouns. Then tell if the adjective indicates what kind, which one, or how many.

1. The new plane bumped when it flew through the fluffy <u>cloud</u> cover. new (what kind); fluffy (what kind)
2. Some <u>passengers</u> have been traveling for several <u>hours</u>. Some (how many); several (how many)
3. After six <u>hours</u>, the blue <u>plane</u> landed. six (how many); blue (which one)

Identify each adjective and the noun that it describes.

4. The busy traveler pulled two heavy suitcases. busy (traveler); two (suitcases); heavy (suitcases)
5. Traveling by plane is a fast and comfortable experience. fast (experience); comfortable (experience)
6. On most planes, travelers have 24 inches of space to themselves. most (planes); 24 inches (space)

ENGLISH LEARNER SUPPORT: Scaffolded Practice

SUBSTANTIAL/MODERATE

Write: *The kids were _____ and _____.* Have students copy the sentence and work in groups to complete it with adjectives. Encourage students to use their first language to discuss adjectives they can use and then find English words that would work. Then have students read their sentences to the class.

LIGHT

Have students write two sentences using adjectives. Have them exchange sentences with a partner and underline the adjectives.

MODIFIERS • ADJECTIVES

LEARNING OBJECTIVES

- **Language** Introduce adjectives after *be*.
- **Language** Use adjectives after *be* correctly in speaking and writing.

MATERIALS   Online

Display and Engage *Grammar 4.1.2a, 4.1.2b*

Printable *Grammar 4.1.2*

INSTRUCTIONAL VOCABULARY

- **noun** a word that names a person, place, or thing
- **pronoun** a word that stands in for a noun, such as *he, she,* and *it*
- **adjective** a word that gives information about a noun or pronoun

Connect and Teach

- Show **Display and Engage: Grammar 4.1.2a**. Point out to students that **adjectives** do not always occur near the **noun** or **pronoun** they describe. Tell them the adjective can come after a form of the verb *be* in a sentence.

- Remind students that the verb *be* has special forms, such as *am/was, are/were,* and *is/was.*

- Model identifying the adjective and the noun it describes in this sentence: *The ice was slippery.*

  THINK ALOUD *To identify the adjective and the noun it describes, I ask:* What adjective follows a form of *be*? What word does it describe? *I see a form of the verb* be *in this sentence:* was. *The word after* was *is an adjective because it tells "what kind." So, it must describe the subject of the sentence,* ice.

Engage and Apply

- Complete items 1–4 on **Display and Engage: Grammar 4.1.2b** with students.

- Write the following sentence frames on the board. Have students suggest adjectives to describe the nouns. *The sky was _____ . bright, dark, stormy The boys are _____ all day. noisy, sleepy, busy*

- Have students complete **Printable: Grammar 4.1.2** for practice with adjectives after *be*.

- Have students edit a writing draft using adjectives after *Be*.

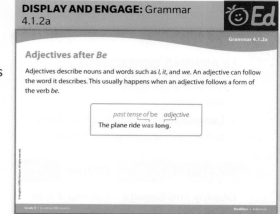

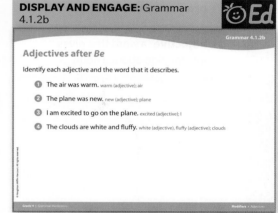

ENGLISH LEARNER SUPPORT: Scaffolded Practice

ALL LEVELS Reinforce the concept of nouns and adjectives by displaying the following sentences. Help students identify each adjective and the noun that each describes.

The playground was huge. adjective: huge; noun: playground

Thirty kids played on the huge playground. adjectives: thirty, huge; nouns: kids, playground

LEARNING OBJECTIVES

- **Language** Identify and use ordering adjectives.
- **Language** Use ordering adjectives correctly in speaking and writing.

MATERIALS   Online

Display and Engage *Grammar 4.1.3a, 4.1.3b*

Printable *Grammar 4.1.3*

INSTRUCTIONAL VOCABULARY

- **noun** a word that names a person, place, or thing
- **pronoun** a word that stands in for a noun, such as *he, she,* and *it*
- **adjective** a word that gives information about a noun

Connect and Teach

- Show **Display and Engage: Grammar 4.1.3a.** Review with students that an **adjective** describes a **noun** or **pronoun**.

- Adjectives often appear before the nouns they describe. Sometimes a writer uses more than one adjective to describe a noun. When this is done, the adjectives should be in a certain order. That order is generally number, opinion, size, shape, age, color, material, and purpose.

- Model ordering adjectives in this sentence: *There are fifteen ugly green frogs in the pond.*

  THINK ALOUD *To determine the correct way to order adjectives, I ask:* What's the right order for the adjectives? *This first adjective* (fifteen) *tells how many frogs are in the pond. The second adjective* (ugly) *is an opinion about the appearance of the frogs. The third adjective* (green) *tells the color of the frogs. These adjectives are in the correct order.*

Engage and Apply

- Complete items 1–3 on **Display and Engage: Grammar 4.1.3b** with students.

- Have students put the following adjectives describing rocks in the correct order: *purple, six, lovely.* Then have students use the adjectives in a sentence.

- Have students complete **Printable: Grammar 4.1.3** for practice with ordering adjectives.

- Have students edit a writing draft using ordering adjectives.

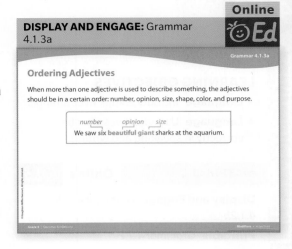

DISPLAY AND ENGAGE: Grammar 4.1.3a   **Online**

Grammar 4.1.3a

Ordering Adjectives

When more than one adjective is used to describe something, the adjectives should be in a certain order: number, opinion, size, shape, color, and purpose.

number   opinion   size
We saw six beautiful giant sharks at the aquarium.

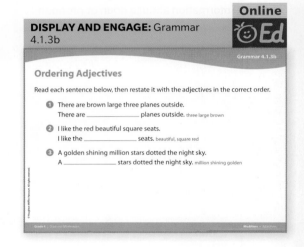

DISPLAY AND ENGAGE: Grammar 4.1.3b   **Online**

Grammar 4.1.3b

Ordering Adjectives

Read each sentence below, then restate it with the adjectives in the correct order.

1. There are brown large three planes outside.
   There are _____ planes outside. three large brown
2. I like the red beautiful square seats.
   I like the _____ seats. beautiful, square red
3. A golden shining million stars dotted the night sky.
   A _____ stars dotted the night sky. million shining golden

ENGLISH LEARNER SUPPORT: Facilitate Language Connections

In Spanish and Haitian Creole, adjectives commonly come after nouns. For example: *It was a storm scary.* Provide students with additional practice by giving them a list of sentences with the adjective omitted. Have them insert the adjective in the correct place.

Scaffolded Practice

ALL LEVELS Write: *The spotted cute two puppies are jumping up and down.* Read the sentence aloud and have students identify the adjectives. Remind students of the general order of adjectives: *number, opinion, size, shape, age, color, material,* and *purpose.* Work with students and have them determine the correct order of the adjectives. Write the improved sentence and read it aloud together.

LEARNING OBJECTIVES

- **Language** Review adjectives.
- **Language** Use adjectives correctly in speaking and writing.

MATERIALS Online

Display and Engage *Grammar 4.1.4a, 4.1.4b, 4.1.4c*

Printable *Grammar 4.1.4*

 INSTRUCTIONAL VOCABULARY

- **noun** a word that names a person, place, or thing
- **pronoun** a word that stands in for a noun, such as *he, she,* and *it*
- **adjective** a word that gives information about a noun

Review Adjectives

- Show **Display and Engage: Grammar 4.1.4a** and then **Grammar 4.1.4b**. Remind students that an **adjective** describes a **noun** or **pronoun**. When writers use more than one adjective to describe a noun, the adjectives should be in the proper order. This order is generally number, opinion, size, shape, age, color, material, and purpose. Have students complete the following sentences with appropriate adjectives in the correct order. Sample answers are provided.

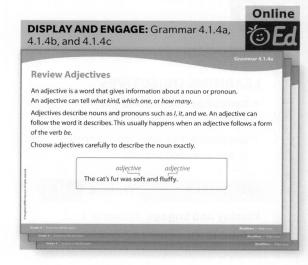

DISPLAY AND ENGAGE: Grammar 4.1.4a, 4.1.4b, and 4.1.4c

Grammar 4.1.4a

Review Adjectives

An adjective is a word that gives information about a noun or pronoun. An adjective can tell *what kind, which one,* or *how many.*

Adjectives describe nouns and pronouns such as *I, it,* and *we.* An adjective can follow the word it describes. This usually happens when an adjective follows a form of the verb *be.*

Choose adjectives carefully to describe the noun exactly.

> *adjective   adjective*
> The cat's fur was soft and fluffy.

» *I see _____ _____ shrubs. three, bushy*

» *That is a _____ _____ flower. tall, pink*

» *That is a _____ _____ camellia. beautiful, blooming*

» *Those are _____ _____ leaves. shiny, round*

» *This is a _____ _____ garden. compact, sunny*

- Have students complete the activity on **Display and Engage: Grammar 4.1.4c**.

- Then have students complete **Printable: Grammar 4.1.4** for more practice with adjectives.

- Have students edit a writing draft using adjectives.

 ENGLISH LEARNER SUPPORT: Facilitate Language Connections

Unlike English, Spanish adjectives change to agree with the noun they tell about in gender and number.

Scaffolded Practice

ALL LEVELS Have students practice placing adjectives. Provide the following sentences to model: *The dog is tired. The tree is shady. The dogs sleep under the shady tree. The tired dogs sleep under the shady tree.*

LEARNING OBJECTIVES

- **Language** Identify and use adjectives.
- **Language** Use adjectives correctly in speaking and writing.

MATERIALS   Online ⊙Ed

Display and Engage *Grammar 4.1.5*

Printable *Grammar 4.1.5*

INSTRUCTIONAL VOCABULARY

- **noun** a word that names a person, place, or thing
- **pronoun** a word that stands in for a noun, such as *he, she,* and *it*
- **adjective** a word that gives information about a noun

Connect and Teach

- Show **Display and Engage: Grammar 4.1.5**. Explain that good writers use adjectives to make their writing more interesting. Remind students that when they use more than one adjective to describe something, they must make sure the adjectives are in the correct order.

- Point out that an important part of revising is checking for the use of adjectives and making sure they are in the correct order.

- Explain that students should also look for opportunities to combine sentences using adjectives.

Engage and Apply

- Display the following sentences. Guide students in putting the adjectives in the correct order.

  » *Frank is a brown sweet puppy. sweet brown*

  » *He has light three spots on his face. three light*

  » *He has a curly short tail. short curly*

  » *He has a long pink wet tongue. long wet pink*

  » *We've had him for awesome two months. two awesome*

- Have students complete **Printable: Grammar 4.1.5** for practice with adjectives.

- Have students edit a writing draft using adjectives.

ⓔ ENGLISH LANGUAGE SUPPORT: Scaffolded Practice

ALL LEVELS Write: *The six horses are scared. The farmers lead the horses into the barn.* Guide students to combine the sentences. *The farmers lead the six scared horses into the barn.* Read aloud the new sentence together. Have students suggest more adjectives they can add. Read aloud the sentence with the added adjectives.

Online ⊙Ed

DISPLAY AND ENGAGE: Grammar 4.1.5

Grammar 4.1.5

Connect to Writing: Using Adjectives

To make writing flow smoothly, move adjectives to combine sentences. If two choppy sentences tell about the same noun, combine the sentences by moving the adjectives from one sentence and placing them before the noun in the other. Make sure the adjectives are in the correct order and choose exact adjectives.

Short, Choppy Sentences	
The fish swam in circles in the tank.	There were six colorful fish.

Longer, Smoother Sentence
The six colorful fish swam in circles in the tank.

Grade 4 | *Grammar Minilessons*   *Modifiers • Adjectives*

LEARNING OBJECTIVES

• **Language** Introduce adverbs.

• **Language** Use adverbs correctly in speaking and writing.

MATERIALS

Online

Display and Engage *Grammar 4.2.1a, 4.2.1b*

Printable *Grammar 4.2.1*

INSTRUCTIONAL VOCABULARY

• **adverb** word that describes a verb

Connect and Teach

• Show **Display and Engage: Grammar 4.2.1a**. Explain that an **adverb** tells something about a verb including *how, when,* and *where.* Point out that adverbs can appear before or after the verbs they modify. Tell students that an adverb that tells how usually ends in *-ly.*

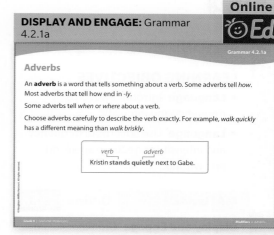

DISPLAY AND ENGAGE: Grammar 4.2.1a — Online Ed

Adverbs

An **adverb** is a word that tells something about a verb. Some adverbs tell *how.* Most adverbs that tell how end in *-ly.*

Some adverbs tell *when* or *where* about a verb.

Choose adverbs carefully to describe the verb exactly. For example, *walk quickly* has a different meaning than *walk briskly.*

> verb   adverb
> Kristin **stands quietly** next to Gabe.

• Model identifying the adverb and the verb it tells about in this sentence: *Pam waits patiently outside Art's house.*

THINK ALOUD *To identify the adverb and the verb it tells about, I ask:* What is the verb? *The action of the sentence is* waits. *Then I ask:* What word tells how about the verb? Patiently *tells how Pam waits.* Patiently *is the adverb.*

• Ask students to identify the adverb in the following sentence and to name the verb it modifies: *The dog waits quietly. adverb: quietly; verb: waits*

Engage and Apply

• Complete items 1–6 on **Display and Engage: Grammar 4.2.1b** with students.

• Write the following sentence on the board. Work with students to identify the verb and the adverb that tells how. *Peter waved excitedly at Stan. verb: waved; adverb: excitedly*

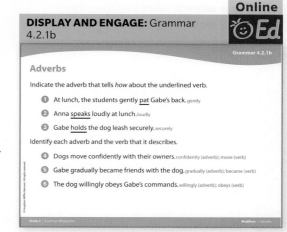

DISPLAY AND ENGAGE: Grammar 4.2.1b — Online Ed

Adverbs

Indicate the adverb that tells *how* about the underlined verb.

1. At lunch, the students gently pat Gabe's back. *gently*
2. Anna speaks loudly at lunch. *loudly*
3. Gabe holds the dog leash securely. *securely*

Identify each adverb and the verb that it describes.

4. Dogs move confidently with their owners. *confidently (adverb); move (verb)*
5. Gabe gradually became friends with the dog. *gradually (adverb); became (verb)*
6. The dog willingly obeys Gabe's commands. *willingly (adverb); obeys (verb)*

• Have students complete **Printable: Grammar 4.2.1** for practice with adverbs.

• Have students edit a writing draft using adverbs.

EL **ENGLISH LEARNER SUPPORT: Facilitate Language Connections**

In Cantonese, adverbs usually come before, rather than after, verbs. Speakers of Cantonese may carry over this practice to English, using phrases such as *slowly talk* rather than *talk slowly.* Provide additional practice placing adverbs after verbs. For example: *You should eat more slowly.*

Scaffolded Practice

SUBSTANTIAL

Write: *The turtles slept soundly and quietly. Sarah studied inside.* Have students read the sentences aloud. Circle the adverbs that tell *how.* *soundly, quietly* Underline the adverb that tells *where.* *inside* Guide students to understand the difference.

MODERATE

Have students use the following sentence frames to write complete sentences using adverbs: *The cats walked _____. Trainers work _____ to train them.*

LIGHT

Have students write two or three sentences using adverbs that tell *how, where,* or *when.* Have partners exchange papers and underline the adverbs.

LEARNING OBJECTIVES

- **Language** Introduce adverbs of frequency and intensity.
- **Language** Use adverbs of frequency and intensity correctly in speaking and writing.

MATERIALS   Online

Display and Engage *Grammar 4.2.2a, 4.2.2b*

Printable *Grammar 4.2.2*

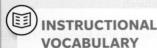 **INSTRUCTIONAL VOCABULARY**

- **adverb** word that describes a verb

Connect and Teach

- Show **Display and Engage: Grammar 4.2.2a**. Point out that an **adverb** of frequency can tell how often an action happens. An adverb of intensity can tell how much or to what degree an action happens.

- Model identifying the verb and then the adverb that tells how often in the example sentence: *My dog usually wakes at 6 a.m.*

  THINK ALOUD *To identify the adverb and the verb it tells about, I ask:* Which word is the verb? *Wakes is the action in the sentence.* Which word tells how often or how much? *The word* usually *tells how often my dog wakes at 6 a.m.*

- Ask a volunteer to read aloud the second example and identify the adverb and the verb it modifies. *adverb: a lot; verb: barks*

Engage and Apply

- Complete the items on **Display and Engage: Grammar 4.2.2b** with students.

- List the following verbs on the board: *go, write, hold.* Have students use each verb in an oral sentence with an adverb that tells how often or how much for each verb. Sample adverbs are provided.
  go usually
  write frequently
  hold never

- Have students complete **Printable: Grammar 4.2.2** for practice with adverbs of frequency and intensity.

- Have students edit a writing draft using adverbs of frequency and intensity.

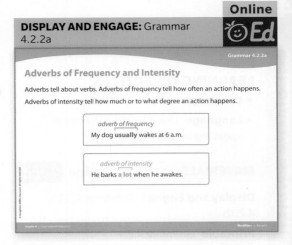

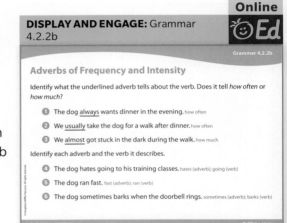

(EL) **ENGLISH LEARNER SUPPORT: Scaffolded Practice**

ALL LEVELS Reinforce the concept of verbs and adverbs by displaying the following sentences. Help students identify each adverb and the verb that the adverb describes.

The kittens grow quickly. adverb: quickly; verb: grow
The kitten willingly learns new skills. adverb: willingly; verb: learns
Jan brings the books back to Molly. adverb: back; verb: brings
The parents often avoid open spaces. adverb: often; verb: avoid

LEARNING OBJECTIVES

- **Language** Introduce adverbs in different parts of sentences.
- **Language** Use adverbs in different parts of sentences correctly in speaking and writing.

MATERIALS
Online

Display and Engage *Grammar 4.2.3a, 4.2.3b*

Printable *Grammar 4.2.3*

 **INSTRUCTIONAL VOCABULARY**

- **adverb** word that describes a verb

Connect and Teach

- Show **Display and Engage: Grammar 4.2.3a**. Explain that an **adverb** can be used at the beginning, middle, or end of a sentence.

- Model identifying the adverb in each example sentence: *Sometimes, the dog needs a nap. The dog eats dinner and quickly goes outside. I walk the dog proudly.*

  THINK ALOUD *To identify the adverb and where in the sentence it is used, I ask:* What is the adverb that tells about the verb? *In the first sentence,* Sometimes *is the adverb; in the second,* quickly; *and* proudly *in the third. Then I ask:* In what part of the sentence is the adverb? *In the first sentence, the adverb is in the beginning; in the second, in the middle.*

- Ask students to identify the adverb in the third sentence and tell where it is located. *proudly; end of sentence*

Engage and Apply

- Complete items 1–4 on **Display and Engage: Grammar 4.2.3b** with students.

- Have students say sentences that place adverbs at the beginning, middle, and end of the sentences.

- Have students complete **Printable: Grammar 4.2.3** for practice with adverbs in different parts of sentences.

- Have students edit a writing draft using adverbs in different parts of sentences.

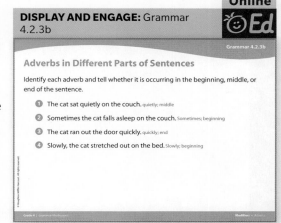

DISPLAY AND ENGAGE: Grammar 4.2.3a — Online Ed
Grammar 4.2.3a

Adverbs in Different Parts of Sentences

An adverb can be used anywhere in a sentence.
It can come at the beginning, middle, or end.

> **Beginning:** Sometimes the dog needs a nap.
> **Middle:** The dog eats dinner then quickly goes outside.
> **End:** I walk the dog proudly.

DISPLAY AND ENGAGE: Grammar 4.2.3b — Online Ed
Grammar 4.2.3b

Adverbs in Different Parts of Sentences

Identify each adverb and tell whether it is occurring in the beginning, middle, or end of the sentence.

1. The cat sat quietly on the couch. quietly; middle
2. Sometimes the cat falls asleep on the couch. Sometimes; beginning
3. The cat ran out the door quickly. quickly; end
4. Slowly, the cat stretched out on the bed. Slowly; beginning

 ENGLISH LEARNER SUPPORT: Scaffolded Practice

ALL LEVELS Have students work in mixed-proficiency groups to locate sentences in classroom library books that contain adverbs used in the beginning, middle, and end of sentences. Have students read aloud the sentences and identify the adverbs. Students may point to the adverbs while others say them aloud.

LEARNING OBJECTIVES

- **Language** Review adverbs.
- **Language** Use adverbs correctly in speaking and writing.

| MATERIALS | Online |

Display and Engage *Grammar 4.2.4a, 4.2.4b, 4.2.4c*

Printable *Grammar 4.2.4*

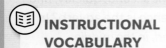 **INSTRUCTIONAL VOCABULARY**

- **adverb** word that describes a verb

Review Adverbs

- Remind students that an **adverb** is a word that modifies a verb. Guide students in recalling that adverbs of frequency can tell how often an action happens, and verbs of intensity can tell how much or to what degree an action happens. Ask students to recall that an adverb may be located at a variety of locations within a sentence.

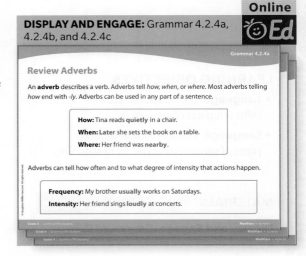

- Show **Display and Engage: Grammar 4.2.4a** and then **Display and Engage: Grammar 4.2.4b**. Read aloud the sentences to review adverbs. Work with students to identify the location of each adverb.

- Have students complete the activity on **Display and Engage: Grammar 4.2.4c**.

- Then have students complete **Printable: Grammar 4.2.4** for more practice with adverbs.

- Have students edit a writing draft using adverbs.

 ENGLISH LEARNER SUPPORT: Scaffolded Practice

ALL LEVELS Review with students that adverbs can describe how, how much, how often, or when something happens. Provide examples of each, such as *softly, neatly, never, always.* Have students in mixed-proficiency groups use the adverbs in sentences.

LEARNING OBJECTIVES

- **Language** Identify and use adverbs.
- **Language** Use adverbs correctly in speaking and writing.

MATERIALS
Online

Display and Engage *Grammar 4.2.5*

Printable *Grammar 4.2.5*

 **INSTRUCTIONAL VOCABULARY**

- **adverb** word that describes a verb

Connect and Teach

- Show **Display and Engage: Grammar 4.2.5**. Remind students that an **adverb** is a word that can modify a verb. Explain that precise adverbs tell readers exactly how, when, and where things happen.

- Point out that adverbs make writing more interesting and easier to understand.

Engage and Apply

- Display the following sentences. Have students identify the adverbs and decide if they tell how or how often something happens.

  » *The children enter the auditorium quietly.* quietly; how

  » *The teacher always says hello to them.* always; how often

  » *Frequently, the children practice singing.* Frequently; how often

- Have students complete **Printable: Grammar 4.2.5** for practice with adverbs.

- Have students edit a writing draft using adverbs.

 ENGLISH LEARNER SUPPORT: Scaffolded Practice

ALL LEVELS Make a chart for different kinds of adverbs: *when, where, how, how often, how much something happens.* Name adverbs the class has come across and have students tell in which category each adverb belongs. Have students work in groups to make sentences using the adverbs listed. Work together to discuss where in the sentence to place the adverbs.

DISPLAY AND ENGAGE: Grammar 4.2.5
Online **Ed**

Grammar 4.2.5

Connect to Writing: Using Adverbs

When you write, use precise adverbs to create clear pictures of how, when, where, and to what degree things happen. Precise adverbs also help make your writing more interesting and easier to understand.

Less Precise Adverbs	More Precise Adverbs
We often go to the lake during the summer.	We regularly go to the lake during the summer.
My cat meows for her dinner.	My cat cries loudly for her dinner.

Grade 4 | Grammar · hmhco.com

Modifiers · Adverbs

LEARNING OBJECTIVES

- **Language** Identify and use clauses.
- **Language** Use clauses correctly in speaking and writing.

MATERIALS
Online

Display and Engage *Grammar 4.3.1a, 4.3.1b*

Printable *Grammar 4.3.1*

INSTRUCTIONAL VOCABULARY

- **clause** group of words that has a subject and a predicate
- **independent clause** a clause that can stand alone as a complete sentence
- **dependent clause** a clause that cannot stand alone because it is not a complete sentence

Connect and Teach

- Show **Display and Engage: Grammar 4.3.1a**. Review that a **clause** is a group of words that has a subject and predicate, but may or may not stand alone. Explain that a clause that can stand alone is called an **independent clause**. It is a complete sentence. A clause that cannot stand alone is called a **dependent clause**. It is not a complete sentence. Explain that a dependent clause gives more information about the action in the sentence and starts with a transition word such as *before, since,* or *because.*

- Model identifying clauses in the following sentence: *Some bugs like to burrow in dirt when they get big enough.*

  THINK ALOUD *To identify clauses, I ask:* Which clauses can stand alone? Which clauses cannot stand alone? Some bugs like to burrow in dirt *contains a subject and a predicate and can stand alone. It is an independent clause.* When they get big enough *has a subject and a predicate, but it cannot stand alone. It needs the rest of the sentence to complete the thought, so it is a dependent clause.*

Engage and Apply

- Complete items 1–5 on **Display and Engage: Grammar 4.3.1b** with students.

- Ask students to say sentences that contain independent and dependent clauses. Write them on the board. Have students identify the clauses in each sentence.

- Have students complete **Printable: Grammar 4.3.1** for practice with clauses.

- Have students edit a writing draft using clauses.

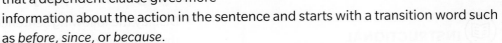
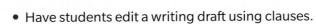
 ENGLISH LEARNER SUPPORT: Scaffolded Practice

SUBSTANTIAL/MODERATE

Give partners several written sentences containing independent and dependent clauses. Have them identify each type of clause. Remind students to look for transition words or words that signal more information will follow: *since, before, because.*

LIGHT

Display several dependent clauses. Have students discuss why each is not a complete sentence. Tell students to add an independent clause to each to form a complete sentence.

LEARNING OBJECTIVES

- **Language** Identify and use relative pronouns.
- **Language** Use relative pronouns correctly in speaking and writing.

MATERIALS   Online

Display and Engage Grammar 4.3.2a, 4.3.2b

Printable Grammar 4.3.2

 INSTRUCTIONAL VOCABULARY

- **relative pronoun** a type of pronoun used to introduce a dependent clause that gives more information about a noun

Connect and Teach

- Show **Display and Engage: Grammar 4.3.2a**. Explain that a **relative pronoun** follows a noun and introduces a dependent clause that tells about the noun. The pronoun refers to the noun it stands for. Examples of relative pronouns are *who, whom, whose, which,* and *that.*

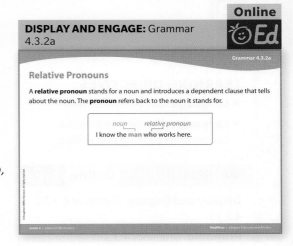

- Review the examples with students. Then model identifying the relative pronoun in the following sentence: *She is the woman who owns the farm.*

  THINK ALOUD *To find the relative pronoun, I ask:* Which word introduces a dependent clause that tells about the noun that comes before it? *The word* who *refers to the woman and introduces the dependent clause* who owns the farm. *That clause tells about the woman;* who *is the relative pronoun.*

Engage and Apply

- Complete items 1–4 on **Display and Engage: Grammar 4.3.2b** with students.

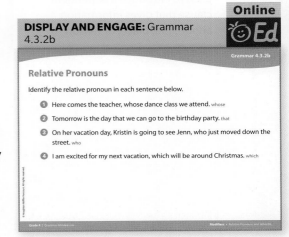

- Display sentences such as the following. Have students identify the relative pronouns and the clauses they introduce.

  That store sells popcorn, which is the city's most popular snack food. <u>which is the city's most popular snack food</u>

- Have students complete **Printable: Grammar 4.3.2** for practice with relative pronouns.

- Have students edit a writing draft using relative pronouns.

 ENGLISH LEARNER SUPPORT: Scaffolded Practice

ALL LEVELS Review the characteristics of complete sentences. Remind students that sentences have a subject that tells who or what and a predicate that tells about the action or state of being. Have students in mixed-proficiency groups tell which of the following is a complete sentence.

The bugs in the grass. not a sentence

She gestures to the kids. complete sentence

Rewrite the examples above as complete sentences or sentences with relative pronouns *who, whom, whose, which,* or *that. I like the bugs in the grass that are red with black spots. She gestures to the kids who need to stop at the corner.* Have students identify the relative pronouns in the sentences by pointing to or saying them. Have other students identify the dependent clauses that follow the relative pronoun by reading them aloud.

LEARNING OBJECTIVES

- **Language** Use relative adverbs.
- **Language** Use relative adverbs correctly in speaking and writing.

MATERIALS   Online

Display and Engage *Grammar 4.3.3a, 4.3.3b*

Printable *Grammar 4.3.3*

 INSTRUCTIONAL VOCABULARY

- **relative adverb** a type of adverb used to introduce a dependent clause that gives information about time, place, or reason

Connect and Teach

- Show **Display and Engage: Grammar 4.3.3a**. Explain that a **relative adverb** introduces a clause that tells about a place, a time, or a reason. Examples of relative adverbs are *where, when,* and *why*.

- Model identifying relative adverbs in the example: *The driveway is where we'll play hopscotch.*

  THINK ALOUD *To find the relative adverb, I ask:* Which word introduces a dependent clause that tells about a place, a time, or a reason? Where *is an adverb that introduces the dependent clause* where we'll play hopscotch. *The clause tells about a place:* the driveway.

- Ask students to share a new sentence to introduce a dependent clause with the relative pronoun *when*.

DISPLAY AND ENGAGE: Grammar
4.3.3a

Online ⊙ Ed

Relative Adverbs

A **relative adverb** introduces a dependent clause that tells about a place, a time, or a reason.

tells about a place (the garden)
This is the garden where we'll plant cucumbers.

Engage and Apply

- Complete items 1–5 on **Display and Engage: Grammar 4.3.3b** with students.

- Write sentences such as these on the board. Have students identify the relative adverbs and the clauses they introduce. *I remember last year, when this driveway was nothing but rocks.* when *this driveway was nothing but rocks We didn't know why we had flat tires on our bikes.* why *we had flat tires Now it's a place where we can ride and play.* where *we can ride and play*

DISPLAY AND ENGAGE: Grammar
4.3.3b

Online ⊙ Ed

Relative Adverbs

Identify the relative adverb in each sentence below.

1. I will never forget the day when I met my best friend. when
2. The library is a place where you can borrow books. where
3. I don't know why Ellie got so angry. why
4. Autumn is the time when the leaves fall off the trees. when
5. They grew flowers where there once were weeds. where

- Have students complete **Printable: Grammar 4.3.3** for practice with relative adverbs.

- Have students edit a writing draft by adding or revising relative adverbs.

 ENGLISH LEARNER SUPPORT: Scaffolded Practice

ALL LEVELS Provide students in mixed-proficiency groups with sentence frames with dependent clauses. Have students fill in the frame with a relative adverb, *where, when,* or *why,* to complete each sentence. For example, *We went to the park _____ there was a baseball field. We went to the park _____ it was a sunny day. We can see now _____ people like that park.* Guide students to understand which relative adverb fits best in each sentence.

LEARNING OBJECTIVES

- **Language** Review relative pronouns and adverbs.

- **Language** Use relative pronouns and adverbs correctly in speaking and writing.

MATERIALS   Online

Display and Engage *Grammar 4.3.4a, 4.3.4b, 4.3.4c*

Printable *Grammar 4.3.4*

 INSTRUCTIONAL VOCABULARY

- **relative adverb** a type of adverb used to introduce a dependent clause that gives information about time, place, or reason

- **relative pronoun** a type of pronoun used to introduce a dependent clause that gives more information about a noun

Review Relative Pronouns and Adverbs

- Review with students that adverbs are words that describe verbs. Adverbs can tell how, when, or where an action happens. Remind them that adverbs can come before or after the verbs they describe.

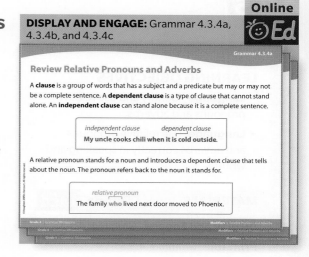

DISPLAY AND ENGAGE: Grammar 4.3.4a, 4.3.4b, and 4.3.4c

- Show **Display and Engage: Grammar 4.1.4a** and then **Grammar 4.1.4b**. Read aloud the information to review **relative pronouns** and **relative adverbs**. Then write the following sentences on a display surface, and ask students to orally identify the relative pronoun or adverb in each sentence: *There must be a reason why the ice won't melt.* why *The field where we'll play the game is muddy.* where *We have found someone who will help with the uniforms.* who

- Show **Display and Engage: Grammar 4.3.4c**, and ask students to complete the activity.

- Then have students complete **Printable: Grammar 4.3.4** for more practice with relative pronouns and adverbs.

- Have students edit a writing draft, adding or revising relative pronouns and adverbs.

MODIFIERS • RELATIVE PRONOUNS AND ADVERBS

LEARNING OBJECTIVES

- **Language** Identify and use relative pronouns and adverbs.
- **Language** Use relative pronouns and adverbs correctly in speaking and writing.

MATERIALS Online

Display and Engage *Grammar 4.3.5*

Printable *Grammar 4.3.5*

INSTRUCTIONAL VOCABULARY

- **clause** group of words that has a subject and a predicate
- **relative adverb** a type of adverb used to introduce a dependent clause that gives information about time, place, or reason
- **relative pronoun** a type of pronoun used to introduce a dependent clause that gives more information about a noun

Connect and Teach

- Show **Display and Engage: Grammar 4.3.5**. Explain that good writers combine **clauses** properly so that their writing is easy to follow and flows smoothly.

- Point out that an important part of revising is combining sentences and checking to see that **relative adverbs** and **relative pronouns** are used correctly.

DISPLAY AND ENGAGE: Grammar 4.3.5

Online **Ed**

Connect to Writing: Using Relative Pronouns and Adverbs

When you write, combine sentences using clauses to help clearly show how related ideas are connected. Use relative adverbs or pronouns, as appropriate.

Separate	Combined
I began reading the comic book. I took it out of the bag.	I began reading the comic book when I took it out of the bag.
Ella painted a huge portrait of her son. Ella is an artist.	Ella, who is an artist, painted a huge portrait of her son.

Engage and Apply

- Display the following sentences. Guide students to combine the short sentences, using relative adverbs and pronouns.

  » *That was the day. The new fish arrived.* *That was the day when the new fish arrived.*

  » *The fish were put in the large aquarium. They could swim all around.* *The fish were put in the large aquarium, where they could swim all around.*

  » *The fish hid under the coral arch. The coral arch provided safety.* *The fish hid under the coral arch, which provided safety.*

  » *Later, they swam to the surface. Their food was located there.* *Later, they swam to the surface, where their food was located.*

- Have students complete **Printable: Grammar 4.3.5** for practice with relative pronouns and adverbs.

- Have students edit a writing draft using relative pronouns and adverbs.

MODIFIERS • COMPARATIVE AND SUPERLATIVE ADJECTIVES AND ADVERBS

LEARNING OBJECTIVES

- **Language** Identify and use comparative forms of adjectives.
- **Language** Use comparative forms of adjectives correctly in speaking and writing.

MATERIALS   Online

Display and Engage *Grammar 4.4.1a, 4.4.1b*

Printable *Grammar 4.4.1*

INSTRUCTIONAL VOCABULARY

- **adjective** word that describes a noun
- **comparative** adjective or adverb that compares two persons, places, things, or actions

Connect and Teach

- Show **Display and Engage: Grammar 4.4.1a**. Remind students that an **adjective** describes a noun. Explain that a **comparative** adjective compares two persons, places, or things. Shorter comparative adjectives typically end in *-er*.

- Model using a comparative adjective correctly as shown in the example sentence: *A turtle is slower than a rabbit.*

THINK ALOUD *To decide if the comparative adjective is used correctly, I ask: Are there two persons, places, or things being compared? Yes. There are two things: a turtle and a rabbit. Then I ask: Does the adjective end in -er or use more? Yes. Slower ends in -er.*

Engage and Apply

- Complete items 1–7 on **Display and Engage: Grammar 4.4.1b** with students.

- Have students form the correct comparative adjective for each sentence.

- Have students complete **Printable: Grammar 4.4.1** for practice using comparative forms of adjectives.

- Have students edit a writing draft using comparative forms of adjectives.

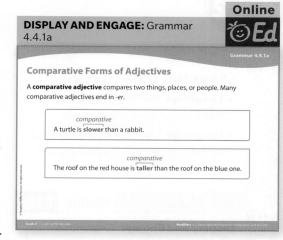
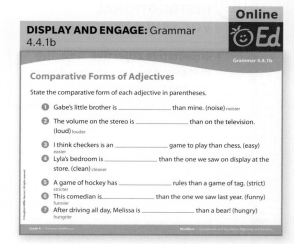
 ENGLISH LEARNER SUPPORT: Scaffolded Practice

ALL LEVELS Review that adjectives describe nouns. Reinforce identifying adjectives by displaying the following sentences. Have students identify the adjective in each sentence. Then ask students questions to guide them to tell which are comparative. *Are two things being compared in the sentence? Does the adjective end in -er or have the word* more *in front of it?*

The brown dog runs in the park. brown

The sugar is heavier than the flour. heavier; comparative

Fido is a stinky pet. stinky

His cage is cleaner than the box. cleaner; comparative

LESSON 4.4.2

SUPERLATIVE FORMS OF ADJECTIVES

LEARNING OBJECTIVES
- **Language** Identify and use superlative forms of adjectives.
- **Language** Use superlative forms of adjectives correctly in speaking and writing.

MATERIALS   Online ⊙Ed

Display and Engage *Grammar 4.4.2a, 4.4.2b*

Printable *Grammar 4.4.2*

INSTRUCTIONAL VOCABULARY

- **superlative adjective** adjective that expresses the extreme degree of comparison

Connect and Teach

- Show **Display and Engage: Grammar 4.4.2a**. Explain that a **superlative adjective** compares more than two persons, places, or things. Form the superlative adjective in a one-syllable word by adding -*est*. For adjectives that have two syllables, place the word *most* in front of the adjective.

- Model using a superlative adjective correctly as shown in this example sentence: *A snail is the slowest of them all.*

  THINK ALOUD *To decide if the superlative adjective is used correctly, I ask:* Are there more than two persons, places, or things being compared? *Yes, all animals are compared.* Does the adjective end in -*est* or use *most*? *Yes:* slowest *ends in* -est.

- Remind students that when using more than one adjective to describe a noun, they should appear in the following order: number, opinion, size, shape, color. Model how to correct the order of adjectives in this sentence: *The four largest ugliest toads slept in the tree hollow. The four ugliest, largest toads slept in the tree hollow.*

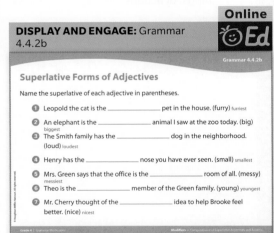

DISPLAY AND ENGAGE: Grammar 4.4.2a   Online ⊙Ed

Grammar 4.4.2a

Superlative Forms of Adjectives

A **superlative adjective** compares more than two things, places, or people. Many superlative adjectives end in -*est*.

| *superlative* |
| A snail is **slowest** of them all. |

| *superlative* |
| The dogs all run fast, but Spot is **fastest** of them all. |

Engage and Apply

- Complete items 1–7 on **Display and Engage: Grammar 4.4.2b** with students.

- Have students reorder the adjectives in the following sentence: *It was the greenest, prettiest, tallest mountain they had ever seen.* prettiest, tallest, greenest

- Have students complete **Printable: Grammar 4.4.2** for practice using superlative forms of adjectives.

- Have students edit a writing draft using superlative forms of adjectives.

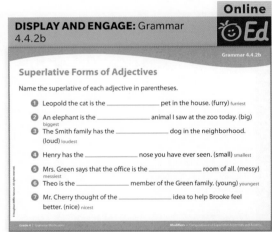

DISPLAY AND ENGAGE: Grammar 4.4.2b   Online ⊙Ed

Grammar 4.4.2b

Superlative Forms of Adjectives

Name the superlative of each adjective in parentheses.

1. Leopold the cat is the _____ pet in the house. (furry) furriest
2. An elephant is the _____ animal I saw at the zoo today. (big) biggest
3. The Smith family has the _____ dog in the neighborhood. (loud) loudest
4. Henry has the _____ nose you have ever seen. (small) smallest
5. Mrs. Green says that the office is the _____ room of all. (messy) messiest
6. Theo is the _____ member of the Green family. (young) youngest
7. Mr. Cherry thought of the _____ idea to help Brooke feel better. (nice) nicest

ENGLISH LEARNER SUPPORT: Scaffolded Practice

SUBSTANTIAL
Provide sentence frames with superlative adjectives. Have students identify names of classroom objects that correctly complete the sentence frames. *The _____ is the loudest object in the room. The _____ is the biggest book on the shelf. The _____ is the highest thing on the wall.*

MODERATE
Provide sentence frames. Have students name superlative adjectives that complete the sentence frames. *The pencil sharpener is the _____ object in the room. The dictionary is the _____ book on the shelf. The poster is the _____ thing on the wall.*

LIGHT
Have students write their own sentences, using comparative and superlative adjectives to compare classroom objects.

MODIFIERS • COMPARATIVE AND SUPERLATIVE ADJECTIVES AND ADVERBS

LEARNING OBJECTIVES

- **Language** Introduce comparative and superlative forms of adverbs.
- **Language** Use comparative and superlative forms of adverbs correctly in speaking and writing.

MATERIALS
Online

Display and Engage *Grammar 4.4.3a, 4.4.3b*

Printable *Grammar 4.4.3*

INSTRUCTIONAL VOCABULARY

- **adverb** word that modifies a verb
- **comparative adverb** a word that compares the action of two things
- **superlative adverb** a word that compares the action of more than two things; a word that expresses the extreme degree of comparison

Connect and Teach

- Show **Display and Engage: Grammar 4.4.3a**. Remind students that an **adverb** tells about a verb. It often ends with the letters *-ly*.

- A **comparative adverb** compares the action of two things. The word *more* is often used.

- A **superlative adverb** compares the action of more than two things. The word *most* is often used.

- Use the example sentences to model use of a comparative adverb and a superlative adverb. *A. J. walked <u>slowly</u>. Ty walked more <u>slowly</u> than A. J. Baby Beau walked <u>most slowly</u> of all.*

  THINK ALOUD *To decide if the adverb is used correctly, I ask:* Does the adverb end in -ly? *Yes,* slowly *ends in* -ly. *Is the word* more *or* most *added?* Yes, the first sentence uses more; the second uses most.

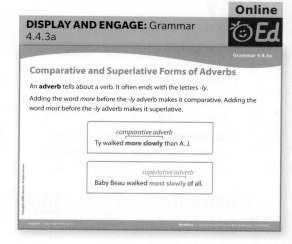

Engage and Apply

- Complete items 1–4 on **Display and Engage: Grammar 4.4.3b** with students.

- Have students complete **Printable: Grammar 4.4.3** for practice using comparative and superlative forms of adverbs.

- Have students edit a writing draft using comparative and superlative forms of adverbs.

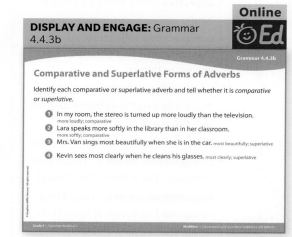

ENGLISH LEARNER SUPPORT: Scaffolded Practice

SUBSTANTIAL
Display sentences that compare actions. *The cat moves quickly across the yard. The squirrel moves more quickly than the cat. The bird moves the most quickly of the animals.* Have students identify by pointing to or naming the adverb, comparative adverb, and superlative adverb.

MODERATE
Display sentence frames to compare actions. *The cat moves _____ across the yard. The squirrel moves _____ _____ than the cat. The bird moves the _____ _____ of the animals.* Have students complete the sentence frames with an adverb, comparative adverb, and superlative adverb. Review how to form comparative and superlative adverbs by adding *more* or *most* in front of the adverb.

LIGHT
Have student pairs write sentences using comparative and superlative adverbs to compare animals or vehicles and say the completed sentences.

MODIFIERS • COMPARATIVE AND SUPERLATIVE ADJECTIVES AND ADVERBS

LEARNING OBJECTIVES

- **Language** Review comparative and superlative adjectives and adverbs.
- **Language** Use comparative and superlative adjectives and adverbs correctly in speaking and writing.

MATERIALS   Online

Display and Engage *Grammar 4.4.4a, 4.4.4b, 4.4.4c*

Printable *Grammar 4.4.4*

INSTRUCTIONAL VOCABULARY

- **adjective** word that describes a noun
- **comparative adjective** adjective that compares two persons, places, or things
- **superlative adjective** adjective that expresses the extreme degree of comparison
- **adverb** word that modifies a verb
- **comparative adverb** a word that compares the action of two things
- **superlative adverb** a word that compares the action of more than two things; a word that expresses the extreme degree of comparison

Review Comparative and Superlative Adjectives and Adverbs

- Show **Display and Engage: Grammar 4.4.4a** and then **Display and Engage: Grammar 4.4.4b**. Remind students that a **comparative adjective** compares two persons, places, or things. It is formed with the ending -*er* for most adjectives. A **superlative adjective** compares more than two persons, places, or things. It is formed with the ending -*est* for most adjectives.

- Review with students that the word *more* is used in forming the **comparative** form of most **adverbs**. The word *most* is used in forming the **superlative** form of most adverbs.

- Have students complete the activity on **Display and Engage: Grammar 4.4.4c**.

- Have students use comparative and superlative forms of *big, small, interesting,* and *slow* to compare classroom objects and school pets.

- Then have students complete **Printable: Grammar 4.4.4** for more practice with comparative and superlative adjectives and adverbs.

- Have students edit a writing draft using comparative and superlative adjectives and adverbs.

ENGLISH LEARNER SUPPORT: Scaffolded Practice

ALL LEVELS Remind students that adjectives describe nouns and that adverbs describe verbs, or action words. Have mixed-proficiency groups of students locate comparative and superlative adjectives and adverbs in classroom library books. Write examples that students find of comparative and superlative adjectives and adverbs. Brainstorm other nouns and verbs that can be described using the examples. Less proficient students may repeat the phrases after you. More proficient students may try using them in their own sentences.

LEARNING OBJECTIVES

- **Language** Identify and use comparative and superlative forms of adverbs.
- **Language** Use comparative and superlative forms of adverbs correctly in speaking and writing.

MATERIALS   Online

Display and Engage *Grammar 4.4.5*

Printable *Grammar 4.4.5*

INSTRUCTIONAL VOCABULARY

- **adjective** word that describes a noun
- **comparative adjective** adjective that compares two persons, places, or things
- **superlative adjective** adjective that expresses the extreme degree of comparison
- **adverb** word that modifies a verb
- **comparative adverb** a word that compares the action of two things
- **superlative adverb** a word that compares the action of more than two things; a word that expresses the extreme degree of comparison

Connect and Teach

- Remind students that comparative adjectives and adverbs compare two and that superlative adjectives and adverbs compare more than two.

- Show **Display and Engage: Grammar 4.4.5**. Tell students that it is important to express ideas clearly in their writing. This will make their writing precise, interesting, and clear to their readers.

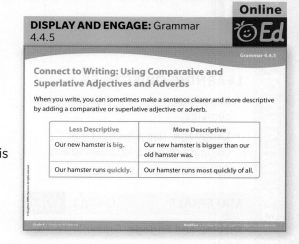

Connect to Writing: Using Comparative and Superlative Adjectives and Adverbs

When you write, you can sometimes make a sentence clearer and more descriptive by adding a comparative or superlative adjective or adverb.

Less Descriptive	More Descriptive
Our new hamster is big.	Our new hamster is bigger than our old hamster was.
Our hamster runs quickly.	Our hamster runs most quickly of all.

- Ask students to discuss ways to use **comparative** and **superlative** forms of **adjectives** and **adverbs** in their writing.

- As necessary, guide the discussion by pointing out ideas such as the following: *Comparative and superlative forms of adjectives and adverbs could be used to compare characters. They could be used to compare settings. They could be used to compare feelings.*

Engage and Apply

- Write this sentence on the board: *My hair is long.* Have students identify the adjective *long* and write a comparative and superlative sentence for it. *My hair is longer. My hair is the longest.*

- Repeat the process to form comparative and superlative adverbs in this sentence: *Ken jumps high. Ken jumps higher. Ken jumps the highest.*

- Have students complete **Printable: Grammar 4.4.5** for practice using comparative and superlative forms of adverbs.

- Have students edit a writing draft using comparative and superlative forms of adverbs.

ⓔ ENGLISH LEARNER SUPPORT: Scaffolded Practice

ALL LEVELS Review comparative and superlative adjectives in mixed-proficiency student pairs. Have students choose three classroom objects and compare them using comparative and superlative adjectives. Review comparative and superlative adverbs. Have students choose three actions and compare them using comparative and superlative adjectives. Circulate and provide corrective feedback.

LEARNING OBJECTIVES

- **Language** Introduce adjectives that compare.
- **Language** Use adjectives that compare correctly in speaking and writing.

MATERIALS　　　Online Ed

Display and Engage *Grammar 4.5.1a, 4.5.1b*

Printable *Grammar 4.5.1*

 INSTRUCTIONAL VOCABULARY

- **adjectives** words used to describe a person, place, or thing
- **compare** to examine the differences and/or similarities between people, places, or things
- **comparison** the act of looking at things to see how they are similar or different

Connect and Teach

- Show **Display and Engage: Grammar 4.5.1a**. Explain that **adjectives** can be used to **compare** two or more things in a sentence. A **comparison** is the act of looking at things to see how they are similar or different.

- Model adding *-er* and *-est* to adjectives in these sentences: *Logan is shorter than Bob. Molly is the shortest of everyone.*

THINK ALOUD *To determine whether to add -er or -est, I ask: How many persons, places, or things are being compared in the sentence? Logan is only compared to Bob, so -er is used. Molly is compared to everyone, so -est is used.*

Engage and Apply

- Complete items 1–4 on **Display and Engage: Grammar 4.5.1b** with students.

- Have students use the Think Aloud activity you modeled to guide them in identifying the adjective ending to use.

- Have students complete **Printable: Grammar 4.5.1** for practice with adjectives that compare.

- Have students edit a writing draft using adjectives that compare.

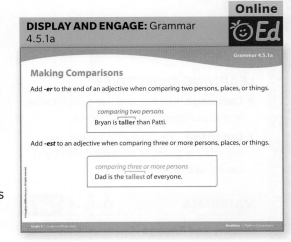

DISPLAY AND ENGAGE: Grammar 4.5.1a　　Online Ed

Grammar 4.5.1a

Making Comparisons

Add *-er* to the end of an adjective when comparing two persons, places, or things.

> *comparing two persons*
> Bryan is **taller** than Patti.

Add *-est* to an adjective when comparing three or more persons, places, or things.

> *comparing three or more persons*
> Dad is the **tallest** of everyone.

Grade 4 | Grammar Minilessons　　Modifiers • Making Comparisons

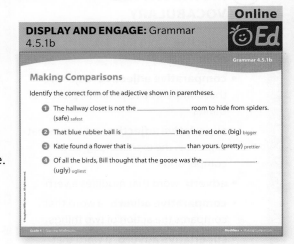

DISPLAY AND ENGAGE: Grammar 4.5.1b　　Online Ed

Grammar 4.5.1b

Making Comparisons

Identify the correct form of the adjective shown in parentheses.

1. The hallway closet is not the _____ room to hide from spiders. (safe) safest
2. That blue rubber ball is _____ than the red one. (big) bigger
3. Katie found a flower that is _____ than yours. (pretty) prettier
4. Of all the birds, Bill thought that the goose was the _____. (ugly) ugliest

Grade 4 | Grammar Minilessons　　Modifiers • Making Comparisons

EL **ENGLISH LEARNER SUPPORT: Scaffolded Practice**

SUBSTANTIAL

Draw two vertical lines on the board. Make one taller than the other. Have students point to the line that is shorter, and then have them complete this sentence: *This line is _____.* Repeat with students with the word *straightest*.

MODERATE

Have partners find two and three objects to compare by adding *-er* and *-est* to words. Tell them to use the words in a sentence that compares the objects. Have partners check the sentences.

LIGHT

Have students write sentences comparing two and three objects by adding *-er* and *-est* to words. Then have partners check the sentences.

LEARNING OBJECTIVES

- **Language** Use *more* and *most* in making comparisons.
- **Language** Use *more* and *most* correctly in speaking and writing.

MATERIALS   Online

Display and Engage *Grammar 4.5.2a, 4.5.2b*

Printable *Grammar 4.5.2*

INSTRUCTIONAL VOCABULARY

- **adjectives** words used to describe a person, place, or thing
- **compare** to examine the differences and/or similarities between people, places, or things
- **comparison** the act of looking at things to see how they are similar or different

Connect and Teach

- Show **Display and Engage: Grammar 4.5.2a**. With long **adjectives**, use *more* to **compare** two. Use *most* to compare three or more.

- Model using this sentence: *Learning about arachnids is more interesting than learning about amphibians.*

  THINK ALOUD *To decide whether to use* more *or* most, *I ask: How many persons, places, or things are being compared? In this sentence, only two things are being compared: arachnids and amphibians. So, the word* more *is used to compare them.*

- Ask students to use the examples on **Display and Engage: Grammar 4.5.2a** to explain why *more interesting* is used in the first sentence and *most interesting* is used in the second sentence. *In the first sentence, two animals are being compared. In the second sentence, more than two animals are being compared.*

Engage and Apply

- Complete items 1–4 on **Display and Engage: Grammar 4.5.2b** with students.

- Have students use the Think Aloud activity you modeled earlier to help determine if *more* or *most* should be used.

- Have students complete **Printable: Grammar 4.5.2** for practice with **comparisons** using *more* and *most*.

- Have students edit a writing draft using comparisons with *more* and *most*.

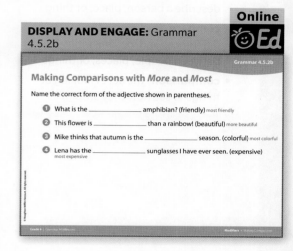

ENGLISH LEARNER SUPPORT: Facilitate Language Connections

Point out that items are compared in English in much the same way as they are compared in Spanish. Provide these examples:

Spanish: *más importante que como*
English: *more important than*
Spanish: *menos importante que*
English: *less important than*

Scaffolded Practice

ALL LEVELS Provide a sentence frame. *This holiday was _____ _____ than regular days.* Choose a specific holiday to discuss possible adjectives, such as *more festive, more fun, more serious, more celebrated*. Encourage students to talk about other holidays and other adjectives they can use to describe them. Allow students to use their primary language to discuss holidays and to provide a bridge to learning the English words for concepts they already know in their primary language.

MODIFIERS • MAKING COMPARISONS

LEARNING OBJECTIVES

- **Language** Identify and use *more* and *most* in making comparisons.
- **Language** Use *more* and *most* correctly in speaking and writing.

MATERIALS Online Ed

Display and Engage *Grammar 4.5.3a, 4.5.3b*

Printable *Grammar 4.5.3*

INSTRUCTIONAL VOCABULARY

- **adjectives** words used to describe a person, place, or thing
- **compare** to examine the differences and/or similarities between people, places, or things
- **comparison** the act of looking at things to see how they are similar

---

Connect and Teach

- Show **Display and Engage: Grammar 4.5.3a**. Explain that some **adjectives** change forms when used to **compare** things: *good, better, best, worse, worst.*

- Model comparing with forms of *good* and *bad*: *What is the best weather for swimming?*
  THINK ALOUD *To decide whether to use* good *or* bad, *I ask:* How many persons, places, or things are being compared? *All of the weather is being compared. That's more than two, so* best *is used.*

- Ask students to correctly compare with a form of *bad* in the following sentences and to explain why they chose the form of *bad* that they selected: *The weather is _____ today than it was yesterday.* worse *(compares two things; weather yesterday and weather today)* This is the _____ weather we have had in the past three months. worst *(compares more than two things; weather today and weather in many months)*

Engage and Apply

- Complete items 1–4 on **Display and Engage: Grammar 4.5.3b** with students.

- Have students find the adjective and tell how many things are being compared. *My headache is better today than it was yesterday.* better

- Have students explain why *better* is correct. *Two things are being compared.*

- Have students complete **Printable: Grammar 4.5.3** for practice comparing with *good* and *bad*.

- Have students edit a writing draft using **comparisons** with *good* and *bad*.

DISPLAY AND ENGAGE: Grammar 4.5.3a Online Ed

Grammar 4.5.3a

Comparing with *Good* and *Bad*

Change the forms of the adjectives *good* and *bad* when you make comparisons.

Change *good* to *better* when comparing two things. Change *good* to *best* when comparing three or more things.

Change *bad* to *worse* when comparing two things. Change *bad* to *worst* when comparing three or more things.

one	good, bad
two	better, worse
three or more	best, worst

DISPLAY AND ENGAGE: Grammar 4.5.3b Online Ed

Grammar 4.5.3b

Comparing with *Good* and *Bad*

State the correct form of the adjective shown in parentheses.

❶ Jen thinks the _____ dog of all is the German Shepherd. (good) best

❷ The _____ time of the day is the morning. (bad) worst

❸ Daniel thinks the study of amphibians is _____ than the study of mammals. (good) better

❹ The rainfall is _____ this year than it was last year. (bad) worse

---

ⓔ ENGLISH LEARNER SUPPORT: Scaffolded Practice

ALL LEVELS Provide practice using the comparative and superlative forms of *good*. Have students draw pictures of good, better, and best things that they would like to happen. Suggest the pictures show a person showing different degrees of happiness or excitement to reflect each situation. Have students fill in sentence frames with *good, better,* or *best. It is good when _____. It is better when _____. It is best when _____!* Have students share their pictures and read their sentences aloud. Allow less proficient students to use their primary language to communicate what they would like to write and have more proficient students help them fill in the sentence frames. Provide guidance as needed.

LEARNING OBJECTIVES

- **Language** Review identifying and using comparisons.
- **Language** Review using comparisons correctly in speaking and writing.

MATERIALS   Online

Display and Engage *Grammar 4.5.4a, 4.5.4b*

Printable *Grammar 4.5.4*

 INSTRUCTIONAL VOCABULARY

- **adjectives** words used to describe a person, place, or thing
- **compare** to examine the differences and/or similarities between people, places, or things
- **comparison** the act of looking at things to see how they are similar

Review Making Comparisons

- Show **Display and Engage: Grammar 4.5.4a**. Remind students that **adjectives** can be used to **compare** two or more things in a sentence using *-er* and *-est* endings.

- With long adjectives, use *more* to compare two. Use *most* to compare three or more.

- Remind students that some adjectives change forms when used to compare things: *good, better, best, worse, worst.*

- Have students share sentences that include each of the following: *good, better, best, worse, worst.*

- Have students complete the activity on **Display and Engage: Grammar 4.5.4b**.

- Have students complete **Printable: Grammar 4.5.4** for practice with **comparisons**.

- Have students edit a writing draft using comparisons.

DISPLAY AND ENGAGE: Grammar 4.5.4a and 4.5.4b

Online

Review Making Comparisons

There are different ways to compare persons, places, and things.

Comparing Two	Comparing Three or More
Add *-er* to the end of most adjectives	Add *-est* to the end of most adjectives
Use the word *more* before a long adjective	Use the word *most* before a long adjective
Change *good* to *better*	Change *good* to *best*
Change *bad* to *worse*	Change *bad* to *worst*

 ENGLISH LEARNER SUPPORT: Scaffolded Practice

ALL LEVELS Arrange students in mixed-proficiency groups and assign each to make a comparison of two or three of their favorite foods. Have them use *-er/-est* or *more/most* to make comparisons, depending on how many items they are comparing. Have students continue by using *good/better/best* and *bad/worse/worst*. Ask volunteers to read aloud their sentences

LEARNING OBJECTIVES

- **Language** Write comparisons correctly.
- **Language** Use comparisons correctly in speaking and writing.

MATERIALS	Online

Display and Engage *Grammar 4.5.5*

Printable *Grammar 4.5.5*

 INSTRUCTIONAL VOCABULARY

- **adjectives** words used to describe a person, place, or thing
- **compare** to examine the differences and/or similarities between people, places, or things
- **comparison** the act of looking at things to see how they are similar

Connect and Teach

- Show **Display and Engage: Grammar 4.5.5**. Remind students that sentence fluency makes their writing clearer and easier to read. Display the sentences below and ask which is better.
  Repetitive Sentences: *This is the scariest bug. It is also the most intelligent.*
  Combined Sentences: *This is the scariest and most intelligent bug.*

- Ask students to combine these sentences to make the writing clearer: *This is the sunniest day we have had all week. It is also the most scorching day we have had all week. This is the sunniest and most scorching day we have had all week.*

Engage and Apply

- Have students combine the following sentences into one.
  Spiders are the slimiest bugs in the garden. They are also the most important. Spiders are the slimiest and most important bugs in the garden.

- Have students complete **Printable: Grammar 4.5.5** for practice with comparisons.

- Have students edit a writing draft using comparisons.

 ENGLISH LEARNER SUPPORT: Scaffolded Practice

ALL LEVELS Provide practice combining sentences that are repetitive. *She is the fastest runner in school. She is also the highest jumper in school.* Have students underline the words that describe the subject in each sentence. *the fastest runner, the highest jumper* Have students cross out the repetitive words in the second sentence. *She is, in school.* Suggest that *also* can be replaced with *and* when combining sentences. *She is the fastest runner and the highest jumper in school.*

LEARNING OBJECTIVES

- **Language** Introduce prepositions.
- **Language** Use prepositions correctly in speaking and writing.

MATERIALS	Online

Display and Engage *Grammar 4.6.1a, 4.6.1b*

Printable *Grammar 4.6.1*

INSTRUCTIONAL VOCABULARY

- **preposition** word that shows a connection between other words in a sentence

Connect and Teach

- Show **Display and Engage: Grammar 4.6.1a**. Explain that a **preposition** is a word that shows a connection between other words in a sentence. Some prepositions describe time and others describe place.

- Model identifying the preposition in the example sentence: *My favorite book is about an unusual animal.*

  THINK ALOUD *To identify the preposition, I ask:* What word shows a connection between other words in the sentence? *The word* about *connects other words in the sentence. Therefore,* about *is the preposition in this sentence. It gives specific information about the book.*

- Have students identify the preposition in each of the following sentences: *The movie is about good friends. about The keyboards are located between the books and posters. between The salad dressing would not be tasty if we made it without the yogurt. without*

Engage and Apply

- Complete items 1–5 on **Display and Engage: Grammar 4.6.1b** with students.

- Write the following sentences on the board. Have students identify the preposition in each sentence. *The horse leaped over the fence. over It ran down the trail. down*

- Have students complete **Printable: Grammar 4.6.1** for practice using prepositions.

- Have students edit a writing draft for practice using prepositions.

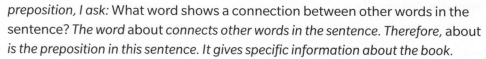
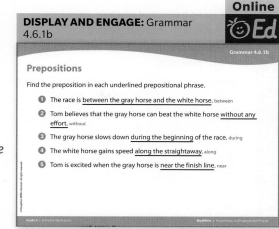
 ENGLISH LEARNER SUPPORT: Scaffolded Practice

SUBSTANTIAL

Complete the following sentence frames with various prepositions to show how they change the meaning of the phrase. *The baby crawls _____ his mother. to My cat loves to sit _____ the window sill. on*

MODERATE

Have students use the following sentence frames to describe a room. Responses may vary. *My bed is _____. in the corner I study _____. at my desk*

LIGHT

Have student pairs take turns orally describing a room using prepositional phrases.

LEARNING OBJECTIVES

- **Language** Introduce prepositional phrases.
- **Language** Use prepositional phrases correctly in speaking and writing.

MATERIALS	Online Ed

Display and Engage *Grammar 4.6.2a, 4.6.2b*

Printable *Grammar 4.6.2*

 INSTRUCTIONAL
VOCABULARY

- **preposition** word that shows a connection between other words in a sentence
- **prepositional phrase** group of words that begins with a preposition and ends with a noun or pronoun

Connect and Teach

- Show **Display and Engage: Grammar 4.6.2a**. Explain that a **prepositional phrase** begins with a **preposition** and ends with a noun or a pronoun. Point out that these words and all the words in between them make up the prepositional phrase.

- Model identifying the prepositional phrase in this sentence: *The hungry basketball team ate three dozen eggs for their breakfast.*

  THINK ALOUD *To identify a prepositional phrase, I ask:* What phrase begins with a preposition and ends with a noun or a pronoun? *I know that* for *is a preposition and the noun that ends the phrase is* breakfast. *So, the prepositional phrase is* for their breakfast.

- Have students identify the preposition and the prepositional phrase in the following sentence: *Please shelve the dictionary between the thesaurus and the new rhyming dictionary.* between *the thesaurus and the new rhyming dictionary*

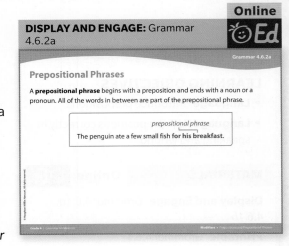

Engage and Apply

- Complete items 1–4 on **Display and Engage: Grammar 4.6.2b** with students.

- Write the following sentences on the board. Have students complete each sentence with a prepositional phrase.
  The prairie dog poked its head _____. out of the burrow
  The hungry bird chirped _____. for its mother

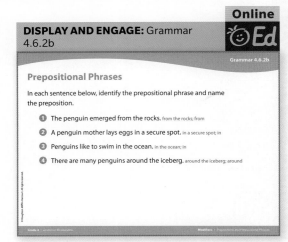

- Have students complete **Printable: Grammar 4.6.2** for practice using prepositional phrases.

- Have students edit a writing draft for practice using prepositional phrases.

 ENGLISH LEARNER SUPPORT: Scaffolded Practice

ALL LEVELS Review the idea that a preposition is one word that shows a connection between other words in a sentence. Reinforce identifying prepositions and prepositional phrases by displaying the following sentences. Work with students to identify the preposition and locate the prepositional phrase in each.

- *Sam ran away from the house. (tells where)* away, preposition; away from the house, prepositional phrase
- *His mother was not happy after she found out. (tells when)* after, preposition; after she found out, prepositional phrase
- *She spoke to him in a serious voice. (tells how)* in, preposition; in a serious voice, prepositional phrase

LEARNING OBJECTIVES

- **Language** Use prepositional phrases to provide details.
- **Language** Use prepositional phrases to provide details correctly in speaking and writing.

MATERIALS Online Ed

Display and Engage *Grammar 4.6.3a, 4.6.3b*

Printable *Grammar 4.6.3*

 INSTRUCTIONAL VOCABULARY

- **preposition** word that shows a connection between other words in a sentence
- **prepositional phrase** group of words that begins with a preposition and ends with a noun or pronoun

Connect and Teach

- Show **Display and Engage: Grammar 4.6.3a**. Remind students that a **prepositional phrase** gives more detail in a sentence. Tell students that a prepositional phrase can provide details such as *where*, *when*, and *how*.

- Model identifying the prepositional phrase in the the following sentence: *The child built a snowman with her own two hands.*

  THINK ALOUD *To think about a sentence with a prepositional phrase, I ask:* What is the prepositional phrase in the sentence? What details does it give about the sentence? *I know that* with *is a preposition, and the noun that ends the phrase is* hands. *So, the prepositional phrase is* with her own two hands. *The prepositional phrase tells how the child built a snowman.*

- Repeat the modeling with the other example sentences, and ask students to provide oral sentences that contain prepositional phrases.

Engage and Apply

- Complete items 1–6 on **Display and Engage: Grammar 4.6.3b** with students.

- Have students correctly use prepositional phrases to give details about classroom objects related to where, when, and how they are used.

- Have students complete **Printable: Grammar 4.6.3** for practice using prepositional phrases to provide details.

- Have students edit a writing draft for practice using prepositional phrases to provide details.

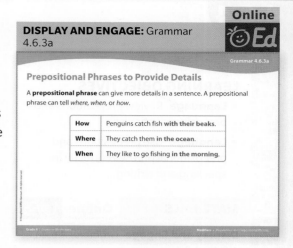

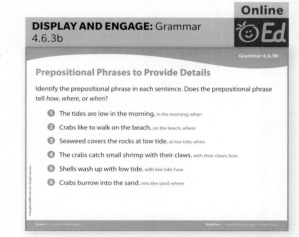

 ENGLISH LEARNER SUPPORT: Scaffolded Practice

ALL LEVELS Provide mixed-proficiency groups of students with an object to describe. Have them use prepositional phrases to describe the location and other details about the object. Then have groups present their sentences to each other. Have other groups identify the prepositional phrases in each sentence.

MODIFIERS • PREPOSITIONS AND PREPOSITIONAL PHRASES

LEARNING OBJECTIVES

- **Language** Review prepositions and prepositional phrases.
- **Language** Use prepositions and prepositional phrases correctly in speaking and writing.

MATERIALS   Online

Display and Engage *Grammar 4.6.4a, 4.6.4b, 4.6.4c*

Printable *Grammar 4.6.4*

 INSTRUCTIONAL VOCABULARY

- **preposition** word that shows a connection between other words in a sentence
- **prepositional phrase** group of words that begins with a preposition and ends with a noun or pronoun

Review Prepositions and Prepositional Phrases

- Show **Display and Engage: Grammar 4.6.4a** and then **Display and Engage: Grammar 4.6.4b**. Read aloud the sentences as students identify the **prepositions** and **prepositional phrases**.

- Remind students that a preposition is a word that shows a connection between other words in a sentence. A prepositional phrase begins with a preposition and ends with a noun. Write the following sentences on the board. Have students identify the preposition and prepositional phrase in each.

  » *Mike has a job working on a construction site. on a construction site*

  » *In the summer, he is especially busy. in the summer*

  » *He likes working with the backhoe. with the backhoe*

  » *If it's very hot, he brings extra water with him. with him*

  » *The water gives him relief from the heat. from the heat*

  » *Mike sometimes goes swimming after work. after work*

- Have students complete the activity on **Display and Engage: Grammar 4.6.4c**.

- Have students complete **Printable: Grammar 4.6.4** for practice using prepositions and prepositional phrases.

- Have students edit a writing draft for practice using prepositions and prepositional phrases.

Grammar 4.6.4a

Review Prepositions and Prepositional Phrases

A **preposition** is a word that shows a connection between other words in a sentence.

preposition
We finally found the key **under** the door.

 ENGLISH LEARNER SUPPORT: Scaffolded Practice

ALL LEVELS Reinforce the concept of prepositions and prepositional phrases by using visual aids for students in mixed-proficiency groups. Place a book in several positions on or around a table while having students describe where it is. For example: *under the table, on the table, beside the table.*

MODIFIERS • PREPOSITIONS AND PREPOSITIONAL PHRASES

Connect and Teach

- Show **Display and Engage: Grammar 4.6.5**. Explain to students that they can add interesting and helpful information to their writing by using **prepositional phrases**.

- Point out that an important part of revising is looking for sentences that can be made more descriptive by adding prepositional phrases.

- Invite a volunteer to read aloud the example sentences. Ask students to explain why the second sentence in each sentence pair is more effective. *The second sentence gives greater detail and makes the sentence more interesting.*

- Explain that like prepositional phrases, transitions can connect ideas. Examples include: *however, in conclusion, such as.* Write the following sentences and discuss how the transitions make the ideas flow and connect.
  The doctor was running late. However, Maya did not have school today. She had things to do while she waited, such as reading a book. In conclusion, Maya didn't mind waiting for her appointment.

Engage and Apply

- Write these sentence frames on the board. Have students orally give a prepositional phrase to complete each sentence.
  The pitcher thought _____. about throwing the ball
  The batter ran _____. around the bases
  The outfielder threw the ball _____. in to home plate

- Have students complete **Printable: Grammar 4.6.5** for practice using prepositions and prepositional phrases.

- Have students return to a piece of their writing. Have them review it to look for examples of prepositions and prepositional phrases and identify places where the phrases may have been used incorrectly or where they could provide more detail about the topic. Have them correct the writing in pencil and read the edited sentences aloud to a partner.

 ENGLISH LEARNER SUPPORT: Scaffolded Practice

ALL LEVELS Display the following sentences. Guide students to work in mixed-proficiency groups to identify the prepositional phrases.
The coach sat on the sidelines. on the sidelines
He yelled instructions at the players. at the players

DISPLAY AND ENGAGE: Grammar 4.6.5   Online Ed

Grammar 4.6.5

Connect to Writing: Using Prepositional Phrases

In your writing, you can use prepositional phrases to add helpful and interesting information to your sentences. Adding details to your sentences helps the reader visualize what you are describing.

Less Descriptive Sentence	More Descriptive Sentence
The white rabbit sniffed at my hand.	The white rabbit with floppy ears sniffed at my hand.
I followed my friend.	I followed my friend along the winding road.

LEARNING OBJECTIVES

- **Language** Identify negatives.
- **Language** Use negatives correctly in speaking and writing.

MATERIALS
Online

Display and Engage *Grammar 5.1.1a, 5.1.1b*

Printable *Grammar 5.1.1*

 INSTRUCTIONAL VOCABULARY

- **negative** a word that makes a sentence mean "no"
- **contraction** a word that combines two other words

Connect and Teach

- Show **Display and Engage: Grammar 5.1.1a**. Explain that a word that makes a sentence mean *no* is called a **negative**. A contraction made with a verb and the word *not* is a negative **contraction**. An apostrophe takes the place of the letter *o* in each contraction with *not*.

- Model identifying a contraction with *not* in this sentence: *There aren't many polar bears at the zoo in Miami.*

  THINK ALOUD *To identify a contraction with* not, *I ask: What word is a contraction made with a verb and the negative word* not? *The contraction* aren't *is a combined form of the verb* are *and* not.

Engage and Apply

- Complete the items on **Display and Engage: Grammar 5.1.1b** with students.

- Write the following sentences on the board. Have students write the contraction for the underlined words. *I <u>cannot</u> play in the game tonight. can't You <u>should not</u> eat two pieces of cake. shouldn't*

- Have students complete **Printable: Grammar 5.1.1** for practice using contractions with *not*.

- Have students edit a writing draft using contractions with *not*.

DISPLAY AND ENGAGE: Grammar 5.1.1a

Online

Contractions with *Not*

A contraction made with a verb and the negative word *not* is a negative that means "no." An apostrophe takes the place of the letter *o* in each **contraction with not**.

| contraction with not |
| There **weren't** many cars in the parking lot. |

Contractions are often used in conversation and casual or informal writing. For formal presentations or writing, use contractions carefully.

There is a difference in formal and informal tone in each example.

| We **don't** want big shopping malls, so we **won't** let them build here. |
| We **do not** appreciate large shopping centers, so we **will not** approve their permit. |

DISPLAY AND ENGAGE: Grammar 5.1.1b

Online

Contractions with *Not*

Identify the contraction for the underlined word or words.

1. California <u>was not</u> a state until 1850. wasn't
2. Texas <u>did not</u> become a state until 1845. didn't
3. Gold <u>had not</u> been found in California until 1848. hadn't
4. California <u>is not</u> a land-locked state. isn't
5. Many pioneer towns <u>would not</u> have flourished without gold. wouldn't
6. Many men got sick and <u>could not</u> mine for gold. couldn't
7. There <u>are not</u> a lot of active gold mines left in California. aren't
8. The history of the California gold rush <u>should not</u> be forgotten. shouldn't

EL **ENGLISH LEARNER SUPPORT: Facilitate Linguistic Connections**

In Spanish, Tagalog, and Cantonese, helping verbs may not be used in negative statements. Students may omit them in English, as in *I no want to do that.* Provide extra practice with helping verbs. For example, *I don't want to do that.*

Scaffolded Practice

ALL LEVELS Write several contractions with *not* and underline the apostrophe in each one. Discuss what words make up the contraction and work together as a class to identify the letters the apostrophes replace.

LEARNING OBJECTIVES

- **Language** Identify negatives.
- **Language** Use negatives correctly in speaking and writing.

MATERIALS   Online

Display and Engage *Grammar 5.1.2a, 5.1.2b*

Printable *Grammar 5.1.2*

 INSTRUCTIONAL VOCABULARY

- **negative** a word that makes a sentence mean "no"

Connect and Teach

- Show **Display and Engage: Grammar 5.1.2a**. Review that a word that makes a sentence mean *no* is called a **negative**. Explain that words, such as *nobody, not, nowhere,* and *never,* are negatives.

- Model how a positive sentence can be changed to have a negative meaning: *I will go to practice on Wednesday. I will not go to practice on Wednesday.*

  THINK ALOUD *To make a positive sentence have a negative meaning, I ask:* What word will change the sentence to have a negative meaning? Does the sentence still make sense? *The word* not *changes the meaning to negative, and the sentence still makes sense.*

Engage and Apply

- Complete the items on **Display and Engage: Grammar 5.1.2b** with students.

- Write the following sentences on the board. Have students say each sentence so it has a negative meaning. *All of us went to the movies.* **None** *Everyone liked the movie.* **No one** *We will go to the movies again.* **won't**

- Have students complete **Printable: Grammar 5.1.2** for practice with negatives.

- Have students edit a writing draft using negatives correctly.

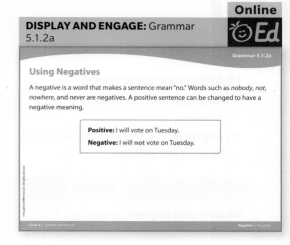

Online
DISPLAY AND ENGAGE: Grammar 5.1.2a

Using Negatives

A negative is a word that makes a sentence mean "no." Words such as *nobody, not, nowhere,* and *never* are negatives. A positive sentence can be changed to have a negative meaning.

> **Positive:** I will vote on Tuesday.
> **Negative:** I will not vote on Tuesday.

Online
DISPLAY AND ENGAGE: Grammar 5.1.2b

Using Negatives

Reword each sentence so that it has a negative meaning.

1. Everyone was at the beach today.
   No one was at the beach today.
2. All beach chairs will be put away.
   No beach chairs will be put away.
3. The ocean is warm enough to swim.
   The ocean is not warm enough to swim.
4. The lifeguards were on the beach watching the swimmers.
   The lifeguards were not on the beach watching the swimmers.
5. I always bring a friend to the beach with me.
   I never bring a friend to the beach with me.

EL **ENGLISH LEARNER SUPPORT: Scaffolded Practice**

ALL LEVELS Provide additional practice recognizing negative statements by displaying the following sentences. Guide students of mixed proficiencies to identify the negative sentences.

- *Many kids go to my elementary school.*
- *Jack has never been to my school.* negative
- *No classes are taking place today.* negative

LEARNING OBJECTIVES

- **Language** Identify double negatives.
- **Language** Use negatives correctly in speaking and writing.

MATERIALS   Online

Display and Engage *Grammar 5.1.3a, 5.1.3b*

Printable *Grammar 5.1.3*

 INSTRUCTIONAL VOCABULARY

- **negative** a word that makes a sentence mean "no"
- **double negative** using two negatives in a single sentence
- **contraction** a word that combines two other words

Connect and Teach

- Show **Display and Engage: Grammar 5.1.3a**. Explain that using two **negatives** together in a sentence is called a **double negative**. Never use two negatives together in a sentence. Review words that are negative, such as *nothing* and *never*.

- Model identifying the double negative in this example sentence:
  They didn't have nothing delicious to eat for dessert.

  THINK ALOUD *To identify the double negative, I ask:* What two negatives are used together in the sentence? *The negatives* didn't *and* nothing *are used together. To correct the sentence, I must remove one of the negatives:* They didn't have anything delicious to eat for dessert. *Or I could say:* They had nothing delicious to eat for dessert.

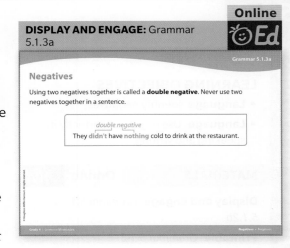

Engage and Apply

- Complete the items on **Display and Engage: Grammar 5.1.3b** with students.

- Write the following sentence on the board and have students identify the double negative and the **contraction** with *not: Jack wasn't never able to go to practice. never; wasn't*

- Have students complete **Printable: Grammar 5.1.3** for practice identifying and avoiding double negatives.

- Have students edit a writing draft for practice identifying and avoiding double negatives.

EL **ENGLISH LEARNER SUPPORT: Scaffolded Practice**

ALL LEVELS Write negative words and contractions. Help students understand that negative words and negative contractions should not be used together. Explain that sentences with double negatives can be fixed either by removing the negative contraction or removing the negative word. Guide students to correct the following sentences:

I don't never want to try surfing. I never want to try surfing. I don't want to try surfing.
There wasn't nothing good to eat. There wasn't anything good to eat. There was nothing good to eat.

Divide students into mixed-proficiency groups and have them write two sentences with double negatives. Have groups exchange papers and revise the sentences.

LEARNING OBJECTIVES

- **Language** Identify negatives.
- **Language** Use negatives correctly in speaking and writing.

MATERIALS   Online

Display and Engage *Grammar 5.1.4a, 5.1.4b, 5.1.4c*

Printable *Grammar 5.1.4*

 INSTRUCTIONAL VOCABULARY

- **negative** a word that makes a sentence mean "no"
- **double negative** using two negatives in a single sentence
- **contraction** a word that combines two other words

Connect and Teach

- Show **Display and Engage: Grammar 5.1.4a** and **Grammar 5.1.4b**. Review with students that a **negative** is a word that makes a sentence mean "no." Words such as *nobody, not, nowhere,* and *never* are negatives.

- Review that using two negatives together is called a **double negative**. Never use two negatives together in a sentence.

- Complete the items on **Display and Engage: Grammar 5.1.4c** with students.

- Write the following sentences on the board and have students rewrite the sentences in the negative.
  The sun is shining today. The sun is not shining today.
  The sun has been shining all week. The sun hasn't been shining all week.
  I wish it would rain. I wish it wouldn't rain.

- Have students complete **Printable: Grammar 5.1.4** to review using negatives.

- Have students edit a writing draft to review using negatives correctly.

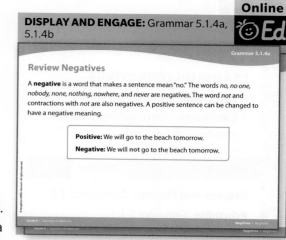

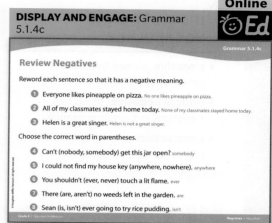

EL **ENGLISH LEARNER SUPPORT: Scaffolded Practice**

ALL LEVELS Some nonnative speakers of English may need additional practice recognizing contractions. Provide practice in forming contractions with these word pairs: *we will, we'll; I am, I'm; he is, he's.* Explain that contractions do not change the meaning of the text but they do create a less formal, more conversational tone.

LEARNING OBJECTIVES

- **Language** Identify negatives.
- **Language** Use negatives correctly in speaking and writing.

MATERIALS   Online Ed

Display and Engage *Grammar 5.1.5*

Printable *Grammar 5.1.5*

 INSTRUCTIONAL VOCABULARY

- **negative** a word that makes a sentence mean "no"
- **double negative** using two negatives in a single sentence
- **contraction** a word that combines two other words

Connect and Teach

- Show **Display and Engage: Grammar 5.1.5**. Review with students that following the rules for **contractions** makes their writing clear and easy to understand. Discuss the two examples below.

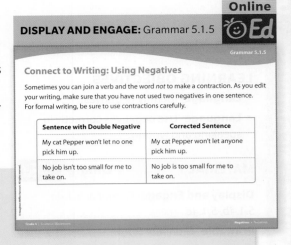

DISPLAY AND ENGAGE: Grammar 5.1.5

Online Ed

Grammar 5.1.5

Connect to Writing: Using Negatives

Sometimes you can join a verb and the word *not* to make a contraction. As you edit your writing, make sure that you have not used two negatives in one sentence. For formal writing, be sure to use contractions carefully.

Sentence with Double Negative	Corrected Sentence
My cat Pepper won't let no one pick him up.	My cat Pepper won't let anyone pick him up.
No job isn't too small for me to take on.	No job is too small for me to take on.

> incorrect
> I didn't like none of the pizzas at the restaurant.
>
> correct
> I didn't like any of the pizzas at the restaurant

THINK ALOUD *To identify the double negative, I ask:* What two **negatives** are used together in the sentence? *The negatives* didn't *and* none *are used together. To correct the sentence, I must remove one of the negatives:* I didn't like any of the pizzas at the restaurant. *Remove* none *and replace with* any.

- Point out that the second sentence is correct because the contraction is written correctly and because the **double negative** has been eliminated.

Engage and Apply

- Display sentences such as the following. Guide students to revise each sentence to eliminate the double negative.

  John wouldn't let nobody keep him from playing soccer. wouldn't let anyone
  He didn't wait for none of the others to get to the field. didn't wait for any

EL **ENGLISH LEARNER SUPPORT: Scaffolded Practice**

ALL LEVELS Students may use more than one negative in a sentence. They may say *nobody said nothing* instead of *nobody said anything*. Guide students to complete these sentence frames with standard English negatives.

He _____ (won't ever/won't never) eat pizza. won't ever
We don't have _____ (none/any). any

LEARNING OBJECTIVES

- **Language** Identify quotation marks with direct speech.
- **Language** Use quotation marks correctly in writing.

MATERIALS

Online

Display and Engage *Grammar 6.1.1a, 6.1.1b*

Printable *Grammar 6.1.1*

INSTRUCTIONAL VOCABULARY

- **dialogue** what people say to each other in a story or play
- **direct quotation** the exact words someone says
- **quotation** the exact words taken from a text
- **quotation marks** punctuation used to show the exact words someone says or the exact words taken from a text

Connect and Teach

- Show **Display and Engage: Grammar 6.1.1a**. Explain that a **quotation** is the exact words that someone says. **Quotation marks** are used before and after a **direct quotation** to set it apart from the other words in the sentence. In a story or play, the words characters say to one another are called **dialogue**.

- Explain that words, such as *Sam said*, come before or after a direct quotation to tell who is speaking.

- Model using quotation marks and other punctuation with direct speech in the example: *Caige said, "Let's go to the game tonight."*

  THINK ALOUD *To figure out how to use quotation marks, I ask:* What words tell that someone is speaking? What are the exact words that person says? *The words* Caige said *tells me that Caige is speaking. His exact words are* Let's go to the game tonight. *I know this because there are quotation marks before Caige's words and after the punctuation.*

Engage and Apply

- Complete the items on **Display and Engage: Grammar 6.1.1b** with students.

- Write the following sentences on the board. Have students add the proper punctuation.

  The kids said, Thank you for taking us ice skating! The kids said, "Thank you for taking us ice skating!"

  If Jack's mom hadn't taken them, they might not have gone ice skating at all, said Sarah. "If Jack's mom hadn't taken them, they might not have gone ice skating at all," said Sarah.

- Have students complete **Printable: Grammar 6.1.1** for practice using quotation marks with direct speech.

- Have students edit a writing draft using quotation marks with direct speech correctly.

ENGLISH LEARNER SUPPORT: Scaffolded Learning

ALL LEVELS Review the terms *dialogue, quotation,* and *quotation marks*. Explain that dialogue is set off with special marks. Display the following sentences. Guide students to identify the direct speech and add the missing punctuation.

Mr. Brooks said, "Books are kept in the library." "Books can also be kept at home," said Steve.

LESSON 6.1.2 SPLIT QUOTATIONS

LEARNING OBJECTIVES

- **Language** Identify and use split quotations.
- **Language** Use split quotations correctly in writing.

MATERIALS   Online

Display and Engage *Grammar 6.1.2a, 6.1.2b*

Printable *Grammar 6.1.2*

INSTRUCTIONAL VOCABULARY

- **dialogue** what people say to each other in a story or play
- **direct speech** the exact words someone says
- **quotation** the exact words taken from a text
- **quotation marks** punctuation used to show the exact words someone says or the exact words taken from a text
- **split quotation** direct speech that is interrupted in the middle by words that tell who is speaking

Connect and Teach

- Show **Display and Engage: Grammar 6.1.2a**. Explain that sometimes **direct speech** is interrupted by words that tell who is speaking. This is called a **split quotation**.

- Explain that a comma is still used to separate the first part of the **quotation** from the rest of the sentence. Review that the first word of each quote is capitalized, and the punctuation at the end of each part of the quotation is inside the quotation marks.

- Model using **quotation marks** and other punctuation with the example of a split quotation: *"We love to watch movies," Paul said, "so we download a movie every weekend."*

  THINK ALOUD *To punctuate a split quote correctly, I ask:* Is the quotation broken into parts? Where does the punctuation belong? *The words* said Paul *interrupt the exact words he is saying. So, I put quotation marks around* We love to watch movies *and* so we download a movie every weekend. *I put a comma after* movies *and a period at the end of the sentence.*

Engage and Apply

- Complete the items on **Display and Engage: Grammar 6.1.2b** with students.

- Have students complete **Printable: Grammar 6.1.2** for practice using split quotations.

- Have students edit a writing draft using split quotations correctly.

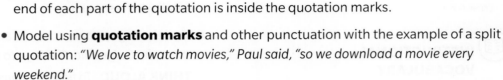

DISPLAY AND ENGAGE: Grammar
6.1.2a   Online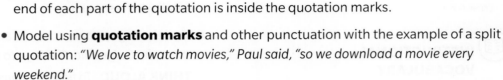

Split Quotations

A **split quotation** is one in which the exact words a person says are broken into two parts. Quotation marks are used to show each part. A comma separates the first quotation from the words that tell who is speaking. Use a period after the speaker.

The punctuation mark at the end of each quotation is inside the quotation mark.

The first word of each quotation is capitalized.

split quotation
"We love to read books," said Paul. **"So we go to the library once a week."**

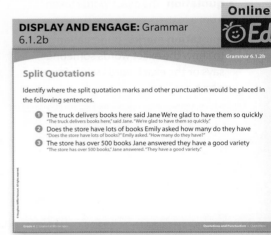

DISPLAY AND ENGAGE: Grammar
6.1.2b   Online

Split Quotations

Identify where the split quotation marks and other punctuation would be placed in the following sentences.

1. The truck delivers books here said Jane We're glad to have them so quickly
   "The truck delivers books here," said Jane. "We're glad to have them so quickly."
2. Does the store have lots of books Emily asked how many do they have
   "Does the store have lots of books?" Emily asked. "How many do they have?"
3. The store has over 500 books Jane answered they have a good variety
   "The store has over 500 books," Jane answered. "They have a good variety."

ENGLISH LEARNER SUPPORT: Scaffolded Practice

ALL LEVELS Provide sentence strips for students to manipulate to help them understand the concept of split quotations. Have them practice moving the speaker of the quotation from the beginning to middle to end of the sentence.

LEARNING OBJECTIVES

- **Language** Identify quotations from a text.
- **Language** Use quotations from a text correctly in writing.

MATERIALS   Online

Display and Engage *Grammar 6.1.3a, 6.1.3b*

Printable *Grammar 6.1.3*

INSTRUCTIONAL VOCABULARY

- **dialogue** what people say to each other in a story or play
- **quotation** the exact words taken from a text
- **quotation marks** punctuation used to show the exact words someone says or the exact words taken from a text

Connect and Teach

- Show **Display and Engage: Grammar 6.1.3a**. Explain that sometimes writers include an author's exact words in their own writing. **Quotation marks** are used to show that these words, or **quotations**, come from a book or other text. Explain that quotations from text are punctuated the same way as direct speech.

- Point out that writers should include the author and the source of the quotation taken from text.

- Model correctly using quotation marks and other punctuation for the example: *In Francisco Jiménez's book* Breaking Through, *he said "I lived in constant fear for ten long years, from the time I was four until I was fourteen years old."*

  THINK ALOUD *To punctuate the quotation correctly, I ask:* What are the author's exact words? Where does the punctuation belong? *I put quotation marks around the author's words:* I lived in constant fear for ten long years, from the time I was four until I was fourteen years old. *I use a comma to separate these words from the rest of the sentence.*

Engage and Apply

- Complete items 1–3 on **Display and Engage: Grammar 6.1.3b** with students.

- Have students complete **Printable: Grammar 6.1.3** for practice using quotations from text.

- Have students edit a writing draft for correct usage of quotations from text.

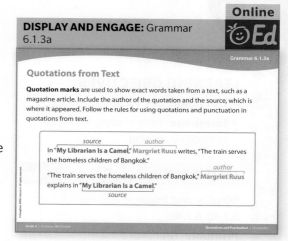

DISPLAY AND ENGAGE: Grammar
6.1.3a

Online Ed

Grammar 6.1.3a

Quotations from Text

Quotation marks are used to show exact words taken from a text, such as a magazine article. Include the author of the quotation and the source, which is where it appeared. Follow the rules for using quotations and punctuation in quotations from text.

In "**My Librarian Is a Camel**," **Margriet Ruus** writes, "The train serves the homeless children of Bangkok."

"The train serves the homeless children of Bangkok," **Margriet Ruus** explains in "**My Librarian Is a Camel**."

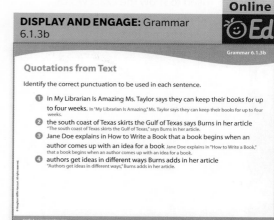

DISPLAY AND ENGAGE: Grammar
6.1.3b

Online Ed

Grammar 6.1.3b

Quotations from Text

Identify the correct punctuation to be used in each sentence.

1. In My Librarian Is Amazing Ms. Taylor says they can keep their books for up to four weeks. In "My Librarian Is Amazing," Ms. Taylor says they can keep their books for up to four weeks.
2. the south coast of Texas skirts the Gulf of Texas says Burns in her article "The south coast of Texas skirts the Gulf of Texas," says Burns in her article.
3. Jane Doe explains in How to Write a Book that a book begins when an author comes up with an idea for a book Jane Doe explains in "How to Write a Book," that a book begins when an author comes up with an idea for a book.
4. authors get ideas in different ways Burns adds in her article "Authors get ideas in different ways," Burns adds in her article.

ENGLISH LEARNER SUPPORT: Scaffolded Practice

SUBSTANTIAL

Help students understand that dialogue is what characters say in the story. Display simple dialogue and add quotation marks and commas:
"My math class is a lot of fun," said Marc.

Read the dialogue aloud, changing your tone for the dialogue and the speaker tag.

MODERATE

Help students understand how to write quotations by writing the following quotation, putting lines where the punctuation should be. Write: *Jiménez said_____But what I feared most happened that same year._____* Work with students to punctuate the sentence. (*Jiménez said, "But what I feared most happened that year."*) Use another example from a classroom text. Continue to use lines to mark where punctuation should go.

LIGHT

Have students find a sentence from a classroom text and work with a partner to copy it using proper punctuation. Remind students to include the author and source of the quotation taken from the text.

LEARNING OBJECTIVES

- **Language** Review quotations.
- **Language** Review using quotations correctly in writing.

MATERIALS   Online

Display and Engage *Grammar 6.1.4a, 6.1.4b, 6.1.4c*

Printable *Grammar 6.1.4*

 INSTRUCTIONAL VOCABULARY

- **dialogue** what people say to each other in a story or play
- **quotation** the exact words taken from a text
- **quotation marks** punctuation used to show the exact words someone says or the exact words taken from a text

Review Quotations

- Show **Display and Engage: Grammar 6.1.4a** and **Grammar 6.1.4b**. Remind students that **quotation marks** are used in writing to show the exact words someone says or the exact words from a text. Review the use of a comma to separate the **quotation** from who is speaking. Point out and analyze the punctuation in the following sentences:
  James said, "I love basketball." "I don't have practice today," shouted Lucy.

- Complete items 1–5 on **Display and Engage: Grammar 6.1.4c** with students.

- Write the following sentences on the board. Have students fill in the appropriate punctuation. *Your bike is fixed now said Roberto. Gregory asked What was wrong with it? Roberto replied The chain fell off.*
  "Your bike is fixed now," said Roberto. Gregory asked, "What was wrong with it?" Roberto replied, "The chain fell off."

- Have students complete **Printable: Grammar 6.1.4** for practice using quotations from text.

- Have students edit a writing draft using quotations from text.

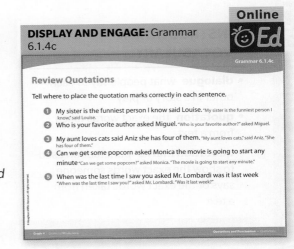

 ENGLISH LEARNER SUPPORT: Scaffolded Practice

SUBSTANTIAL

Ask: *Where do you get books?* Model writing students' responses as a quotation. (*Pablo says, "I get books from the library."*) Have students circle the quotation marks and underline the speaker.

MODERATE

Have students ask each other questions about books. Guide them to write their answers as quotations. Ask students to circle the quotation marks and underline the speaker.

LIGHT

Have students work in groups to gather quotations from different people about books they like. Tell students to record the quotations, remembering to punctuate them correctly.

LEARNING OBJECTIVES

- **Language** Identify and use quotations and split quotations.
- **Language** Use quotations and split quotations correctly in writing.

MATERIALS   Online

Display and Engage *Grammar 6.1.5*
Printable *Grammar 6.1.5*

 INSTRUCTIONAL VOCABULARY

- **dialogue** what people say to each other in a story or play
- **direct speech** the exact words someone says
- **quotation** the exact words taken from a text
- **quotation marks** punctuation used to show the exact words someone says or the exact words taken from a text
- **split quotation** direct speech that is interrupted in the middle by words that tell who is speaking

Connect and Teach

- Show **Display and Engage: Grammar 6.1.5**. Explain that good writers correctly punctuate **direct speech**, **dialogue**, and **quotations** from text to make their writing clear and understandable to readers.

- Point out that an important part of revising is checking for the correct punctuation with direct speech, dialogue, and quotations from text.

DISPLAY AND ENGAGE: Grammar 6.1.5   Online

Grammar 6.1.5

Connect to Writing: Using Quotations

Using quotation marks can be tricky. If you use them incorrectly, you can confuse readers. When you proofread your writing, be sure that you include only the speaker's exact words inside the quotations. Also make sure that you have placed the comma in the correct place to make it clear who is speaking.

Incorrect Quotation	Correct Quotation
"Do you think you could help me with these groceries?" Mrs. Sanchez asked. Of course replied her son.	"Do you think you could help me with these groceries?" Mrs. Sanchez asked. "Of course," replied her son.

Engage and Apply

- Display the following quotations. Guide students to use quotation marks and other punctuation correctly.

  Jessica asked, Have you read this book by Mark Twain? "Have...Twain?" Yes replied Tom. I liked it a lot. "Yes,"; "I...lot."

  Me too agreed Jessica. Twain said many important things. "Me too,"; "Twain...things." I thought so, too Tom nodded "I...too,"; nodded.

  Matt Hower, the author of <u>Books Can Teach</u>*, has said books help educate people. said,; "Books...people."*

- Have students complete **Printable: Grammar 6.1.5** for practice using quotations.

- Have students edit a writing draft to use quotations correctly.

EL **ENGLISH LEARNER SUPPORT: Scaffolded Practice**

ALL LEVELS Different languages sometimes indicate direct quotations with different marks from those used in English. For example, quotations in Spanish are often set off with marks that look like double "greater than" or "lesser than" signs (« and ») or with a dash (—) at the beginning of a quotation, with no mark at the end. Display how direct quotations are displayed in different languages and discuss how the marks function the same—to set off exactly what a speaker says.

LEARNING OBJECTIVES

- **Language** Identify and use end of sentence punctuation.
- **Language** Use end of sentence punctuation correctly in writing.

MATERIALS Online

Display and Engage *Grammar 6.2.1a, 6.2.1b*

Printable *Grammar 6.2.1*

 INSTRUCTIONAL VOCABULARY

- **punctuation** marks or signs in writing that help make meaning clear and separate parts of sentences

Connect and Teach

- Show **Display and Engage: Grammar 6.2.1a**. Explain that **punctuation** consists of marks or signs in writing that help make meaning clear and separate parts of sentences. Punctuation is especially important at the end of a sentence, because it shows where a sentence ends and tells the type of sentence.

- Review with students the different types of punctuation each type of sentence requires.

- Model using end-of-sentence punctuation in the example sentence: *Do you know the way to the train station?*

  THINK ALOUD *I ask:* "What kind of punctuation does the sentence need?" *When I read this sentence, I see it begins with* Do you know. *That tells me this sentence is a question and it should end with a question mark.*

Engage and Apply

- Complete items 1–4 on **Display and Engage: Grammar 6.2.1b** with students.

- Display a variety of sentences on the board. Have students identify the proper end-of-sentence punctuation for each one and why this is the proper punctuation. *Do you like apples? I would like apples for a snack. I love apples!*

- Have students complete **Printable: Grammar 6.2.1** for practice using end-of-sentence punctuation.

- Have students edit a writing draft for correct usage of end-of-sentence punctuation.

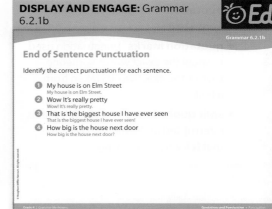

ENGLISH LEARNER SUPPORT: Scaffolded Practice

ALL LEVELS Create an end-of-sentence punctuation chart with explanations of each mark and example sentences.

period: used at the end of a statement or command
Lin went to the movies.

exclamation point: used at the end of a sentence to show strong feeling
That movie was great!

question mark: Used at the end of a question
Did you like that movie?

Then write several sentence parts and end punctuation marks on strips of paper. Have students of mixed proficiencies work in groups to put the sentences together using the proper punctuation mark. Invite students to share their sentences and explain why they used certain end marks.

QUOTATIONS AND PUNCTUATION • PUNCTUATION

LEARNING OBJECTIVES

- **Language** Identify and use capital letters and punctuation in quotations.
- **Language** Use capital letters and punctuation in quotations in writing.

MATERIALS   Online

Display and Engage *Grammar 6.2.2a, 6.2.2b*

Printable *Grammar 6.2.2*

INSTRUCTIONAL VOCABULARY

- **punctuation** marks or signs in writing that help make meaning clear and separate parts of sentences
- **quotation marks** punctuation used to show the exact words someone says or the exact words taken from a text
- **capitalization** using a capital letter to show a name or beginning of a sentence or quotation

Connect and Teach

- Show **Display and Engage: Grammar 6.2.2a**. Discuss that the first word of a **quotation** is capitalized, **quotation marks** are placed before the quotation begins and after the quotation ends, and the **punctuation** is usually placed on the inside of the last quotation mark.

- Point out that a comma separates the words that tell who is speaking from the speaker's exact words in a quotation. Also explain that if the words that tell who is speaking come after a quote that ends in a question mark or exclamation point, no comma is used.

- Model using **capitalization** and punctuation in quotations in the example sentence: *Lulu asked, "What time is the game?"*

  THINK ALOUD *To use capital letters and punctuation in quotations correctly, I ask:* "What kind of sentence is this quotation?" *It is a question.* "Does the quotation come first or last in the sentence?" *It comes last.*

Engage and Apply

- Complete items 1–3 on **Display and Engage: Grammar 6.2.2b** with students.

- Have students ask themselves where the quotation comes in the sentence and who is saying the words to determine how to correctly capitalize and punctuate quotations.

- Have students complete **Printable: Grammar 6.2.2** for practice using capital letters and punctuation in quotations.

- Have students edit a writing draft to correctly use capital letters and punctuation in quotations.

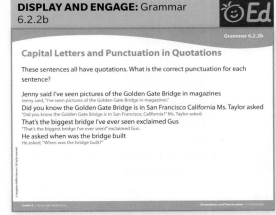

DISPLAY AND ENGAGE: Grammar
6.2.2a
Online

Grammar 6.2.2a

Capital Letters and Punctuation in Quotations

Quotation marks are used to indicate when a person is speaking. Always capitalize the first word of a quotation. Use a comma to separate a quotation from the person who is speaking.

comma   capital letter   end mark
Ms. Taylor asked, "Have you seen the Golden Gate Bridge?"

DISPLAY AND ENGAGE: Grammar
6.2.2b
Online

Grammar 6.2.2b

Capital Letters and Punctuation in Quotations

These sentences all have quotations. What is the correct punctuation for each sentence?

Jenny said I've seen pictures of the Golden Gate Bridge in magazines
Jenny said, "I've seen pictures of the Golden Gate Bridge in magazines."
Did you know the Golden Gate Bridge is in San Francisco California Ms. Taylor asked
"Did you know the Golden Gate Bridge is in San Francisco, California?" Ms. Taylor asked.
That's the biggest bridge I've ever seen exclaimed Gus
"That's the biggest bridge I've ever seen!" exclaimed Gus.
He asked when was the bridge built
He asked, "When was the bridge built?"

ENGLISH LEARNER SUPPORT: Scaffolded Practice

ALL LEVELS Review that dialogue and quotations are the exact words that people or characters say. Display the sentences below and guide students to recognize the dialogue in each.

The teacher said, "Dinosaur bones can be millions of years old."

"Dinosaurs lived on earth a long time ago," said Ana.

"Where did dinosaurs live?" I asked.

LEARNING OBJECTIVES

- **Language** Identify and use punctuation for effect.
- **Language** Use punctuation for effect correctly in writing.

MATERIALS Online Ed

Display and Engage *Grammar 6.2.3a, 6.2.3b*

Printable *Grammar 6.2.3*

 INSTRUCTIONAL VOCABULARY

- **punctuation** marks or signs in writing that help make meaning clear and separate parts of sentences
- **exclamation point (!)** end-of-sentence punctuation that shows feeling
- **ellipsis (. . .)** shows ideas have been omitted or an interruption in thought
- **dash (—)** shows an abrupt break in thought or emphasizes a certain idea
- **colon (:)** introduces a list or new but related ideas

Connect and Teach

- Show **Display and Engage: Grammar 6.2.3a**. Explain that **punctuation** can help express ideas and can have different effects on readers. An **exclamation point** can show excitement. An **ellipsis** can create tension. A **dash** can be used for emphasis. A **colon** introduces new but related information in a sentence.

- Model using punctuation for effect using the example sentence: *Our vacation to the theme park was amazing! We went on many rides—the Twister was my favorite.*

  THINK ALOUD *I ask:* What's the best punctuation for the first sentence? *The exclamation point indicates strong feeling. I know the person was excited to visit the theme park. The second sentence has a dash. The dash emphasizes the second part of the sentence.*

DISPLAY AND ENGAGE: Grammar 6.2.3a, 6.2.3b

Online Ed

Grammar 6.2.3a

Punctuation for Effect

Punctuation can affect the reader.

An **exclamation point** (!) shows excitement or emotion.

A **dash** (—) can be used for emphasis.

> excitement or emotion
> John is putting up his tent faster than everyone else!
> emphasis
> Camping is fun—but beware of bears!

Engage and Apply

- Complete items 1–3 on **Display and Engage: Grammar 6.2.3b** with students.

- Write these sentences on the board. Have students punctuate them properly. *Please bring the things we need hats, gloves, and hand warmers. Please bring the things we need—hats, gloves, and hand warmers. I'll bet it's going to be very cold I'll bet it's going to be very cold. But we will be fine we have warm clothing. But we will be fine—we have warm clothing.*

DISPLAY AND ENGAGE: Grammar 6.2.3c

Online Ed

Grammar 6.2.3c

Punctuation for Effect

Identify the punctuation for each sentence that will have the most effect on the reader.

A camper walked through the campground. Suddenly, he saw a bear
A camper walked through the campground. Suddenly, he saw a bear...

There are many different types of bears grizzly, polar, and black
There are many different types of bears: grizzly, polar, and black.

Look out. There's a bear over there.
Look out! There's a bear over there!

The bear he was right there walked away
The bear—he was right there—walked away!

- Have students complete **Printable: Grammar 6.2.3** for practice using punctuation for effect.

- Have students edit a writing draft using punctuation for effect.

EL **ENGLISH LEARNER SUPPORT: Scaffolded Practice**

ALL LEVELS To help students understand the different punctuation marks, make a chart of punctuation that can be used for effect. Have students copy the chart.

Create sentence strips and punctuation marks on paper and have students work with a partner to create sentences using punctuation for effect. Ask volunteers to share their sentences.

LEARNING OBJECTIVES

- **Language** Review punctuation.
- **Language** Review using punctuation correctly in writing.

MATERIALS

Online

Display and Engage *Grammar 6.2.4a, 6.2.4b*

Printable *Grammar 6.2.4*

 INSTRUCTIONAL VOCABULARY

- **punctuation** marks or signs in writing that help make meaning clear and separate parts of sentences
- **quotation marks** punctuation used to show the exact words someone says or the exact words taken from a text
- **exclamation point (!)** end-of-sentence punctuation that shows feeling
- **ellipsis (. . .)** shows ideas have been omitted or an interruption in thought
- **dash (—)** shows an abrupt break in thought or emphasizes a certain idea
- **colon (:)** introduces a list or new but related ideas

Review Punctuation

- Show **Display and Engage: Grammar 6.2.4a** and **Grammar 6.2.4b**. Review with the students that **punctuation** is especially important at the end of a sentence because it shows where a sentence ends and tells what kind of sentence it is.

- Remind students that the first word of a **quotation** is capitalized, quotation marks are placed before the quotation begins and after the quotation ends, and the punctuation is usually placed on the inside of the last **quotation mark**.

- Remind students that punctuation can help express ideas and can have different effects on readers. An **exclamation point** can show excitement. An **ellipsis** can create tension. A **dash** can be used for emphasis. A **colon** introduces new but related information in a sentence.

- Complete items 1–6 on **Display and Engage: Grammar 6.2.4c** with students.

- Have students complete **Printable: Grammar 6.2.4** for practice using punctuation.

- Have students edit a writing draft using proper punctuation.

DISPLAY AND ENGAGE: Grammar 6.2.4a and 6.2.4b

Online

Grammar 6.2.4a

Review Punctuation

Punctuation helps make writing clear. Different types of sentences require different punctuation. Punctuation can also be used for effect.

> We are having pancakes for breakfast.
> Would you like pancakes for breakfast?
> Yes! Pancakes are my favorite!

Quotation marks are used to indicate when a person is speaking. Capitalize the first word and use a comma to separate a quotation from the person who is speaking.

> Mina asked, "Where is my backpack?"

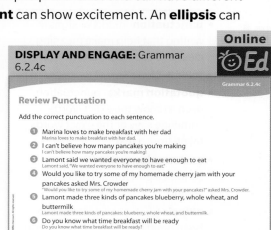

DISPLAY AND ENGAGE: Grammar 6.2.4c

Online

Review Punctuation

Add the correct punctuation to each sentence.

1. Marina loves to make breakfast with her dad
   Marina loves to make breakfast with her dad.
2. I can't believe how many pancakes you're making
   I can't believe how many pancakes you're making!
3. Lamont said we wanted everyone to have enough to eat
   Lamont said, "We wanted everyone to have enough to eat."
4. Would you like to try some of my homemade cherry jam with your pancakes asked Mrs. Crowder
   "Would you like to try some of my homemade cherry jam with your pancakes?" asked Mrs. Crowder.
5. Lamont made three kinds of pancakes blueberry, whole wheat, and buttermilk
   Lamont made three kinds of pancakes: blueberry, whole wheat, and buttermilk.
6. Do you know what time breakfast will be ready
   Do you know what time breakfast will be ready?

 ENGLISH LEARNER SUPPORT: Scaffolded Practice

ALL LEVELS Review with students that end punctuation marks are important because they tell what kind of sentence it is, how to read the sentence, and where a thought ends. Reinforce examples of each end-of-sentence punctuation mark:

Grace bought a new book.
What book did she buy?
That's my favorite book!

Have students work in mixed-proficiency groups to write sentences using each end-of-punctuation mark. Remind them to use the chart they created earlier. Have groups exchange sentences and identify the end mark and why it was used.

QUOTATIONS AND PUNCTUATION • PUNCTUATION

LEARNING OBJECTIVES

- **Language** Identify and use punctuation correctly.
- **Language** Use punctuation correctly in writing.

MATERIALS   Online Ed

Display and Engage *Grammar 6.2.5*

Printable *Grammar 6.2.5*

INSTRUCTIONAL VOCABULARY

- **punctuation** marks or signs in writing that help make meaning clear and separate parts of sentences
- **quotation marks** punctuation used to show the exact words someone says or the exact words taken from a text
- **exclamation point (!)** end-of-sentence punctuation that shows feeling
- **ellipsis (. . .)** shows ideas have been omitted or an interruption in thought
- **dash (—)** shows an abrupt break in thought or emphasizes a certain idea
- **colon (:)** introduces a list or new but related ideas

Connect and Teach

- Show **Display and Engage: Grammar 6.2.5**. Explain that good writers use **punctuation** to make their ideas clear and to create certain effects on readers.

- Point out that an important part of revising is checking to make sure that all punctuation is correct. Revising also includes varying punctuation to have different effects on readers.

- Tell students that another important aspect of revising is using quotations correctly, including the punctuation, quotation marks, and capitalization.

Engage and Apply

- Have students work with a partner to write a paragraph that uses effective and correct punctuation. Then have students rewrite the paragraph without punctuation marks, exchange papers with another group, and then fill in the punctuation marks.

- Have students complete **Printable: Grammar 6.2.5** for practice using correct punctuation.

- Have students edit a writing draft using correct punctuation.

 ENGLISH LEARNER SUPPORT: Facilitate Linguistic Connections

In Spanish and other languages, dialogue is often set off by colons and dashes. Explain that in written English, commas and quotation marks are always needed to show that someone is speaking. Provide examples, such as these: *Mama said, "A sequoia is a beautiful tree."* (In Spanish: *Mamá dijó:—La secuoya es un árbol muy bello.*)

Scaffolded Practice

SUBSTANTIAL

Write: *the ocean is home to many creatures, she explained* Have students add quotation marks, capitalization, and end punctuation. *"The ocean is home to many creatures," she explained.*

MODERATE

Display for students several written sentences that have incorrect punctuation. Have partners work together to correct the errors.

Let me know when you're done with the oven said James

"Let me know when you're done with the oven," said James.

do you want some hummus

Do you want some hummus?

Sarah said let's meet after school

Sarah said, "Let's meet after school."

LIGHT

Have students write sentences with a variety of punctuation mark errors. Have them exchange with a partner and correct the punctuation in their partner's sentences.

LEARNING OBJECTIVES

- **Language** Use commas and quotation marks to mark direct speech and quotations from a text.
- **Language** Use commas correctly in speaking and writing.

MATERIALS   Online 🔴Ed

Display and Engage *Grammar 6.3.1a, 6.3.1b*

Printable *Grammar 6.3.1*

INSTRUCTIONAL VOCABULARY

- **comma** punctuation mark that separates elements or ideas

Connect and Teach

- Show **Display and Engage: Grammar 6.3.1a**. Explain that **commas** are used to introduce direct speech—the exact words someone says.

- Review that quotation marks are used before and after the words someone says to set them apart from the other words in the sentence.

- Explain that when a speaker is addressing someone, a comma is used to set off the person's name.

- Model using commas in the sentence, *Juan asked, "Julia, can you help me with my homework?"*

  THINK ALOUD *To figure out the use of commas and quotation marks, I ask: "Does the sentence include an introductory word or the name of a person being addressed? Does the quotation include words that tell who is speaking?" Julia is the person being addressed. So, I put a comma after her name. Juan is speaking, so I put a comma after* asked *and before the quotation mark.*

- Repeat the modeling with the sentence, *"Yes, Juan, I can help you," replied Julia.*

Engage and Apply

- Complete items on **Display and Engage: Grammar 6.3.1b** with students.

- Have students complete **Printable: Grammar 6.3.1** for practice using commas with direct speech and names.

- Have students edit a writing draft to correctly use commas with direct speech and names.

DISPLAY AND ENGAGE: Grammar 6.3.1a

Grammar 6.3.1a

Commas with Direct Speech and Names

Use a comma or commas to set off the name of a person being addressed directly.
Use a comma after introductory words such as *yes, no,* and *well* to show a pause.
Use a comma to set off the words in a quotation that tell who is speaking.

> name of person being addressed
> The desert, Bryan, is home to many different animals.
> introductory word
> Yes, there are snakes and scorpions in the desert.
> who is speaking
> "Snakes are cool," Bryan said.

DISPLAY AND ENGAGE: Grammar 6.3.1b
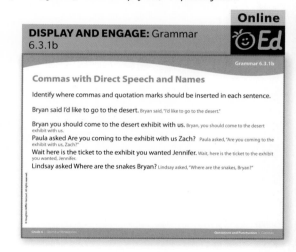

Grammar 6.3.1b

Commas with Direct Speech and Names

Identify where commas and quotation marks should be inserted in each sentence.

Bryan said I'd like to go to the desert. Bryan said, "I'd like to go to the desert."

Bryan you should come to the desert exhibit with us. Bryan, you should come to the desert exhibit with us.

Paula asked Are you coming to the exhibit with us Zach? Paula asked, "Are you coming to the exhibit with us, Zach?"

Wait here is the ticket to the exhibit you wanted Jennifer. Wait, here is the ticket to the exhibit you wanted, Jennifer.

Lindsay asked Where are the snakes Bryan? Lindsay asked, "Where are the snakes, Bryan?"

 ENGLISH LEARNER SUPPORT: Scaffolded Practice

ALL LEVELS Review the use of commas to set off direct speech. Display the following sentences. Work with students to identify which one shows direct speech.

Dr. Bob said that the chemistry experiment was successful.

Janis said, "Look at the way everyone is reading quietly together." speech

He said his dog's name is Fido.

LEARNING OBJECTIVES

- **Language** Use commas in compound sentences.
- **Language** Use commas in compound sentences correctly in speaking and writing.

MATERIALS   Online

Display and Engage *Grammar 6.3.2a, 6.3.2b*

Printable *Grammar 6.3.2*

 INSTRUCTIONAL VOCABULARY

- **comma** punctuation mark that separates elements or ideas

Connect and Teach

- Show **Display and Engage: Grammar 6.3.2a**. Review that a compound sentence is made up of two simple sentences joined by a coordinating conjunction. A coordinating conjunction is a word, such as *and, but, or,* and *so.* Point out that in a compound sentence, a **comma** is used before the coordinating conjunction.

- Model using commas in compound sentences in the example sentence.
  I love lions, but giraffes are my favorite animal.

  Think Aloud *To identify where to use a comma, I ask:* Which word is the coordinating conjunction? Where does the comma go in the sentence? *I see the coordinating conjunction* but. *I put a comma before it, after the word* lions.

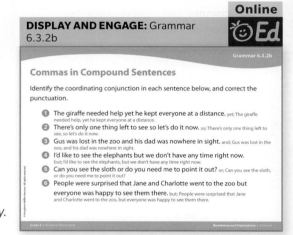

DISPLAY AND ENGAGE: Grammar 6.3.2a

Online **Ed**

Grammar 6.3.2a

Commas in Compound Sentences

In a compound sentence, a comma is used before a coordinating conjunction such as *and, but, so, yet,* and *or.*

> *coordinating conjunction*
> I love lions, but giraffes are my favorite animal.
> *comma*

Engage and Apply

- Complete items 1–6 on **Display and Engage: Grammar 6.3.2b** with students.

- Write the following sentence on the board. Have students identify the conjunction and say where to place a comma.
  James was told that there could be an avalanche so he didn't go skiing that day.
  so; comma after avalanche.

DISPLAY AND ENGAGE: Grammar 6.3.2b

Online **Ed**

Grammar 6.3.2b

Commas in Compound Sentences

Identify the coordinating conjunction in each sentence below, and correct the punctuation.

1. The giraffe needed help yet he kept everyone at a distance. yet; The giraffe needed help, yet he kept everyone at a distance.
2. There's only one thing left to see so let's do it now. so; There's only one thing left to see, so let's do it now.
3. Gus was lost in the zoo and his dad was nowhere in sight. and; Gus was lost in the zoo, and his dad was nowhere in sight.
4. I'd like to see the elephants but we don't have any time right now. but; I'd like to see the elephants, but we don't have any time right now.
5. Can you see the sloth or do you need me to point it out? or; Can you see the sloth, or do you need me to point it out?
6. People were surprised that Jane and Charlotte went to the zoo but everyone was happy to see them there. but; People were surprised that Jane and Charlotte went to the zoo, but everyone was happy to see them there.

- Have students complete **Printable: Grammar 6.3.2** for practice using commas in compound sentences.

- Have students edit a writing draft to correctly use commas in compound sentences.

 ENGLISH LEARNER SUPPORT: Scaffolded Practice

ALL LEVELS Remind students that commas serve many purposes. Provide additional support, identifying how commas are used with examples such as these:

compound sentence: *I went to the zoo, but I didn't see a hippo.*

yes/no response: *Yes, I'd like to learn more about tortoises.*

lists: *We helped brush, feed, and walk the animals.*

LEARNING OBJECTIVES

- **Language** Identify and use commas in serial, dates, city/state.
- **Language** Use commas correctly in speaking and writing.

MATERIALS

Online

Display and Engage *Grammar 6.3.3a, 6.3.3b*

Printable *Grammar 6.3.3*

INSTRUCTIONAL VOCABULARY

- **comma** punctuation mark that separates elements or ideas

Connect and Teach

- Show **Display and Engage: Grammar 6.3.3a**. Explain that **commas** are used to separate items in a series. Also, explain that a comma is used in dates to separate the day and year and in place names to separate the city and state.

- Model the correct use of commas in these example sentences: *When I go to Chicago, Illinois, I want to see Michigan Avenue, Navy Pier, and Grant Park.*

  THINK ALOUD *I ask:* How are commas used to separate items in the series? *I use a comma to separate each item in the series. I also use a comma before* and. *"How are commas used in place names?" I use a comma between the city and state and after the name of the state.*

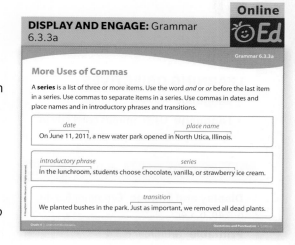

DISPLAY AND ENGAGE: Grammar
6.3.3a

Online Ed

Grammar 6.3.3a

More Uses of Commas

A **series** is a list of three or more items. Use the word *and* or *or* before the last item in a series. Use commas to separate items in a series. Use commas in dates and place names and in introductory phrases and transitions.

date	place name
On June 11, 2011, a new water park opened in North Utica, Illinois.

introductory phrase	series
In the lunchroom, students choose chocolate, vanilla, or strawberry ice cream.

transition
We planted bushes in the park. Just as important, we removed all dead plants.

Engage and Apply

- Complete items 1–5 on **Display and Engage: Grammar 6.3.3b** with students.

- Write this sentence on the board. Have students supply the commas where needed.

  I found great shrimp lobster and crab in Portland Maine.

  I found great shrimp, lobster, and crab in Portland, Maine.

- Have students complete **Printable: Grammar 6.3.3** for practice using commas in items in a series, dates, and cities and states.

- Have students edit a writing draft to correctly use commas in items, dates, and cities and states.

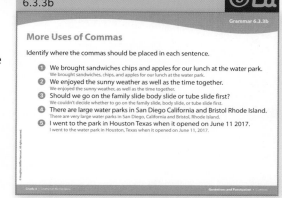

DISPLAY AND ENGAGE: Grammar
6.3.3b

Online Ed

Grammar 6.3.3b

More Uses of Commas

Identify where the commas should be placed in each sentence.

1. We brought sandwiches chips and apples for our lunch at the water park.
   We brought sandwiches, chips, and apples for our lunch at the water park.
2. We enjoyed the sunny weather as well as the time together.
   We enjoyed the sunny weather, as well as the time together.
3. Should we go on the family slide body slide or tube slide first?
   We couldn't decide whether to go on the family slide, body slide, or tube slide first.
4. There are large water parks in San Diego California and Bristol Rhode Island.
   There are very large water parks in San Diego, California and Bristol, Rhode Island.
5. I went to the park in Houston Texas when it opened on June 11 2017.
   I went to the water park in Houston, Texas when it opened on June 11, 2017.

ENGLISH LEARNER SUPPORT: Scaffolded Practice

SUBSTANTIAL

Write: *I am going to San Diego California. I am going to swim surf and hike.* Have students add commas where they are needed.

MODERATE

Have students write *I will graduate on June 2 2021.* and *I will go to college in Bloomington Indiana.* Then have them add commas where they are needed and read the sentences aloud.

LIGHT

Have partners write two sets of sentences with places, dates, or items in a series. Then have partners read each set to the class, having students tell where commas belong.

LESSON 6.3.4 — REVIEW COMMAS

LEARNING OBJECTIVES
- **Language** Review commas.
- **Language** Use commas correctly in speaking and writing.

MATERIALS — Online Ed

Display and Engage *Grammar 6.3.4a, 6.3.4b, 6.3.4c*

Printable *Grammar 6.3.4*

INSTRUCTIONAL VOCABULARY
- **comma** punctuation mark that separates elements or ideas

Connect and Teach

- Show **Display and Engage: Grammar 6.3.4a** and **Grammar 6.3.4b**. Remind students that a series is a list of three or more items. Use **commas** to separate the items in a series. Put a comma after each item except the last one.

- Use a comma to separate dates and place names.

- Model using commas in the example sentence, date, and place: *There are elephants, giraffes, and zebras in the zoo. January 31, 1776 Niagara, New York*

  THINK ALOUD *I ask: "How are commas used to separate items in the series?" I use a comma to separate each item in the series. I also use a comma before* and. *"How are commas used in dates and place names?" I use a comma between the day and year and between the city and state.*

- Review that commas are used to introduce direct speech. Quotation marks are used before and after the words someone says to set them apart from the other words in the sentence. When a speaker is addressing someone, a comma is used to set off the person's name. Commas are also used after introductory words like *yes* and *no*.

Engage and Apply

- Complete items 1–6 on **Display and Engage: Grammar 6.3.4c** with students.

- Have students write a short story about an adventure they had one day with their friends. Tell them to include sentences with a series of three or more words. Have partners share their stories.

- Have students complete **Printable: Grammar 6.3.4** for practice using commas.

- Have students edit a writing draft using commas.

DISPLAY AND ENGAGE: Grammar 6.3.4a, 6.3.4b — Online Ed

Review Commas — Grammar 6.3.4a

Use a **comma** or commas to set off names in direct address, introductory words, transitions, and quotations.

In a compound sentence, a comma is used before a coordinating conjunction such as *and, but, so, yet,* and *or.*

> Salma, I really wish you would join us for dinner.
> Yes, there is a vegetarian option.
> "We should play a game after dinner," said Lexa.
> I can go to dinner, but I can't stay for a game.
> Luca enjoyed dinner. In addition, he loved the game.

DISPLAY AND ENGAGE: Grammar 6.3.4c — Online Ed

Review Commas — Grammar 6.3.4c

Identify where commas should be inserted in each sentence.

1. Yes we will play a game after dinner. Yes, we will play a game after dinner.
2. You seem surprised yet you knew about this dinner since yesterday. You seem surprised, yet you knew about this dinner since yesterday.
3. We're making a new recipe so we need to go to the grocery store. We're making a new recipe, so we need to go to the grocery store.
4. We can have rice pudding ice cream or carrot cake for dessert. We can have rice pudding, ice cream, or carrot cake for dessert.
5. Similarly we can have tea or punch to drink. Similarly, we can have tea or punch to drink.
6. Have you been to the new restaurant in Jackson New Jersey? Have you been to the new restaurant in Jackson, New Jersey?

ENGLISH LEARNER SUPPORT: Scaffolded Practice

SUBSTANTIAL
Write: *Yes I like to read.* and *Luisa do you know how to swim?* Have students add commas where they are needed.

MODERATE
Have students write *Jenny do you want to hear a joke?* and *Yes please tell me a joke.* Then have them add commas and quotation marks where they are needed.

LIGHT
Have partners write two sets of questions and answers with names and introductory phrases. Then have partners exchange papers and add commas where they belong.

LEARNING OBJECTIVES

- **Language** Identify and use commas.
- **Language** Use commas correctly in speaking and writing.

MATERIALS   Online

Display and Engage Grammar 6.3.5

Printable Grammar 6.3.5

 INSTRUCTIONAL VOCABULARY

- **comma** punctuation mark that separates elements or ideas

Connect and Teach

- Show **Display and Engage: Grammar 6.3.5**. Explain that good writers use **commas** correctly to make their writing clear and understandable for readers.

- Point out that an important part of revising is making sure that commas are used where they are needed. Commas should be used correctly so that the reader understands the ideas in each sentence.

Engage and Apply

- Display the following sentences. Guide students to choose the correct use of commas.

  Samantha smiled and asked "Ella what are you doing here?" asked, Ella,

  I love comedy horror and musical movies. comedy, horror,

  We could play checkers or we could go shopping. checkers,

- Have students complete **Printable: Grammar 6.3.5** for practice using commas.

- Have students edit a writing draft to correctly use commas.

 ENGLISH LEARNER SUPPORT: Scaffolded Practice

ALL LEVELS Work with students to make a chart for the different uses for commas: in a series, in dates, between cities and states, in compound sentences, with quotations, and after names and introductory words. Then have students work in small groups to write three sentences using commas. Each sentence should use a comma in a different way. Have volunteers share their sentences with the class. Ask students to explain why they used each comma.

LEARNING OBJECTIVES

- **Language** Use capitalization.
- **Language** Use capitalization and titles correctly in writing.

MATERIALS   Online

Display and Engage *Grammar 6.4.1a, 6.4.1b*

Printable *Grammar 6.4.1*

INSTRUCTIONAL VOCABULARY

- **mechanics** the correct use of capitalization and punctuation
- **capitalization** using capital letters for proper nouns, such as titles, names, and places

Connect and Teach

- Show **Display and Engage: Grammar 6.4.1a**. Explain to students that they should pay attention to proper **mechanics** as they read and write. Point out that mechanics include **capitalization**, punctuation, and conjunction usage.

- Explain that the first word, the last word, and each important word in a title should be capitalized. Remind students that titles of books, magazines, and newspapers are underlined. Point out that titles of short stories, poems, songs, and articles are surrounded by quotation marks.

- Model correctly forming a title with the example book title, *I Am the Ice Worm*.
  THINK ALOUD *To decide how a title should be capitalized and if I should underline the title or use quotation marks, I ask, "Which words in this title should be capitalized? Does this title name a long work or a short work?" The title is* <u>I Am the Ice Worm</u>, *and all the important words should be capitalized. Because this is a book, the title should be underlined.*

- Use the above process to complete an example of a short story, such as "The Gift of the Magi."

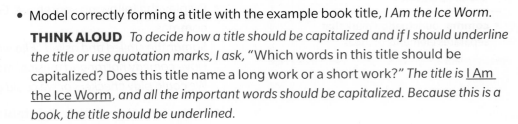

DISPLAY AND ENGAGE: Grammar 6.4.1a

Capitalization and Writing Titles

Capitalize the first, the last, and each important word in every title. **Underline** titles of long works such as books, magazines, newspapers, movies, and works of art. Put **quotation marks** around the titles of shorter works such as short stories, poems, songs, and articles.

Examples:
Title of book: <u>My Trip to Mars</u>
Title of song: "Johnny the Spaceman"

Engage and Apply

- Complete items 1–5 on **Display and Engage: Grammar 6.4.1b** with students.

- Have students complete **Printable: Grammar 6.4.1** to practice capitalization and writing titles.

- Have students edit a writing draft to practice using correct capitalization and writing titles.

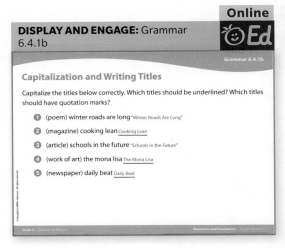

DISPLAY AND ENGAGE: Grammar 6.4.1b

Capitalization and Writing Titles

Capitalize the titles below correctly. Which titles should be underlined? Which titles should have quotation marks?

1. (poem) winter roads are long "Winter Roads Are Long"
2. (magazine) cooking lean Cooking Lean
3. (article) schools in the future "Schools in the Future"
4. (work of art) the mona lisa The Mona Lisa
5. (newspaper) daily beat Daily Beat

 ENGLISH LEARNER SUPPORT: Scaffolded Practice

SUBSTANTIAL

Write on the board: The Chicago tribune and The wall Street journal. Ask students if the titles are capitalized correctly. Work with students to correct the errors. The Chicago Tribune, The Wall Street Journal Then tell students that because these are the titles of newspapers, they should be underlined.

MODERATE

Provide a list of songs, books, and newspapers. Use all lowercase letters. Have students rewrite the titles with correct capitalization and punctuation. To help with punctuation, identify each type. the star spangled banner (song), huckleberry finn (book), the new york post (newspaper) "The Star Spangled Banner," <u>Huckleberry Finn</u>, <u>The New York Post</u>

LIGHT

Have students write two sentences using titles of favorite books, songs, or magazines. Guide them to use proper capitalization and punctuation.

LEARNING OBJECTIVES

- **Language** Use end punctuation.
- **Language** Use end punctuation correctly in speaking and writing.

MATERIALS   Online

Display and Engage *Grammar 6.4.2a, 6.4.2b*

Printable *Grammar 6.4.2*

 INSTRUCTIONAL VOCABULARY

- **punctuation** marks that help readers better understand text

Connect and Teach

- Show **Display and Engage: Grammar 6.4.2a**. Explain that some **punctuation** marks end a sentence. A period (.) ends a statement. A question mark (?) ends a question. An exclamation point (!) ends an exclamation.

- Use the following sentences to model how to determine the correct end punctuation: *Kate loves science. Do you enjoy doing experiments? I love doing science experiments!*

  THINK ALOUD *To decide which of the three kinds of end punctuation marks I should use, I ask:* What kind of sentence is it? Does the sentence tell something, ask a question, or show excitement? *The first sentence is a statement, so I use a period. The second sentence asks a question, so I use a question mark. The third sentence expresses excitement about science experiments, so I use an exclamation point.*

Engage and Apply

- Complete items 1–8 on **Display and Engage: Grammar 6.4.2b** with students.

- Have students write complete sentences and explain the correct type of end punctuation.

- Have students complete **Printable: Grammar 6.4.2** to use end punctuation.

- Have students edit a writing draft to use correct end punctuation.

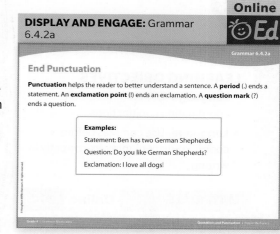

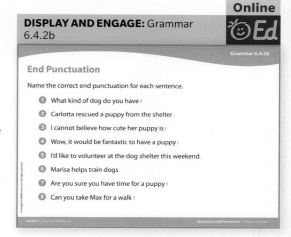

 ENGLISH LEARNER SUPPORT: Scaffolded Practice

SUBSTANTIAL/MODERATE

Write several sentences on the board with missing end punctuation:
Jon is reading
What is he reading
Do you like to read
I love to read
Ask yes/no questions to help students determine what punctuation mark to use. For example: *Is the first sentence telling something?* (yes) *Do periods end sentences that tell something?* (yes) Then write the punctuation mark.

LIGHT

Pair students and have them write simple sentences: one question, one statement, and one exclamation. Have them omit the end punctuation and then exchange sentences with another pair. Have students add the missing punctuation to the sentences. Review examples and ask why certain punctuation marks were used.

LEARNING OBJECTIVES

- **Language** Use commas before coordinating conjunctions.
- **Language** Use commas before coordinating conjunctions correctly in writing.

MATERIALS   Online Ed

Display and Engage *Grammar 6.4.3a, 6.4.3b*

Printable *Grammar 6.4.3*

 INSTRUCTIONAL VOCABULARY

- **coordinating conjunction** a word, such as *and, but, for, or,* and *so* that joins other words or groups of words

Connect and Teach

- Show **Display and Engage: Grammar 6.4.3a**. Explain that a compound sentence has two independent clauses joined by a comma and a **coordinating conjunction**.

- Coordinating conjunctions include *and, but, or,* and *so*. A comma is used before a coordinating conjunction.

- Use the example sentences to model how to combine two independent clauses: *Jane likes going to the park, but Cy doesn't.*

    THINK ALOUD *First, I ask:* How many independent clauses are in the sentence? What word should connect the clauses? *There are two separate clauses with related ideas, so I can combine them into a single compound sentence. Because Jane likes going to the park and Cy doesn't, I use the conjunction* but *to show the contrast. I also add a comma between the clauses:* Jane likes going to the park, but Cy doesn't.

Engage and Apply

- Complete items 1–4 on **Display and Engage: Grammar 6.4.3b** with students.

- Have students combine the following clauses: *Next year, we will want to go on a vacation. We will go to the beach. Next year, we will want to go on a vacation, so we will go to the beach.*

- Have students complete **Printable: Grammar 6.4.3** to practice using commas before coordinating conjunctions.

- Have students edit a writing draft to practice using commas before coordinating conjunctions correctly.

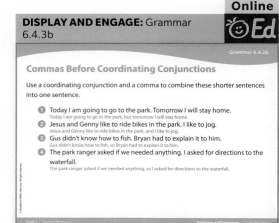

DISPLAY AND ENGAGE: Grammar 6.4.3a   Online Ed

Commas Before Coordinating Conjunctions

A **coordinating conjunction** is a word used to connect clauses in a sentence. Coordinating conjunctions include *and, but, or,* and *so*.

A comma is used before the coordinating conjunction.

> **Simple Sentences:**
> Jane likes going to the park. Cy doesn't.
>
> **Compound Sentence:**
> Jane likes going to the park, but Cy doesn't.

DISPLAY AND ENGAGE: Grammar 6.4.3b   Online Ed

Commas Before Coordinating Conjunctions

Use a coordinating conjunction and a comma to combine these shorter sentences into one sentence.

① Today I am going to go to the park. Tomorrow I will stay home.
   Today I am going to go to the park, but tomorrow I will stay home.
② Jesus and Genny like to ride bikes in the park. I like to jog.
   Jesus and Genny like to ride bikes in the park, and I like to jog.
③ Gus didn't know how to fish. Bryan had to explain it to him.
   Gus didn't know how to fish, so Bryan had to explain it to him.
④ The park ranger asked if we needed anything. I asked for directions to the waterfall.
   The park ranger asked if we needed anything, so I asked for directions to the waterfall.

 ENGLISH LEARNER SUPPORT: Scaffolded Practice

ALL LEVELS Write the coordinating conjunctions and explain the purpose of each. For example *but* combines opposite ideas; *and* combines similar ideas. Reinforce combining sentences using sentence strips. Guide students to use the strips to create sentences using a conjunction. Remind them to use a comma before the conjunction. For example, *We read the book, and we liked it.*

QUOTATIONS AND PUNCTUATION • PROPER MECHANICS

LEARNING OBJECTIVES

- **Language** Review proper mechanics.
- **Language** Use proper mechanics in writing.

MATERIALS Online

Display and Engage *Grammar 6.4.4a, 6.4.4b, 6.4.4c*

Printable *Grammar 6.4.4*

INSTRUCTIONAL VOCABULARY

- **coordinating conjunction** a word, such as *and, but, for, or,* and *so* that joins other words or groups of words
- **capitalization** using capital letters for proper nouns, such as titles, names, and places

Review Proper Mechanics

- Show **Display and Engage: Grammar 6.4.4a** and **Grammar 6.4.4b**. Remind students that the first word, the last word, and each important word in a title should be **capitalized**. Titles of books, magazines, and newspapers are underlined. Titles of short stories, poems, songs, and articles are surrounded by quotation marks.

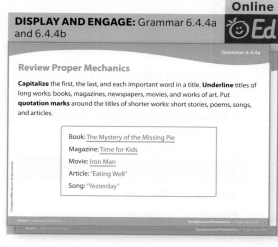

- Review that some punctuation marks end a sentence. A period (.) ends a statement. A question mark (?) ends a question. An exclamation point (!) ends an exclamation.

- **Coordinating conjunctions** include *and, but, or,* and *so.* A comma is used before a coordinating conjunction to join two independent clauses.

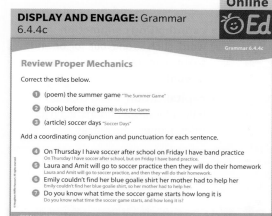

- Complete items 1–7 on **Display and Engage: Grammar 6.4.4c** with students.

- Have students complete **Printable: Grammar 6.4.4** to practice proper mechanics.

- Have students edit a writing draft to use practice proper mechanics correctly.

 ENGLISH LEARNER SUPPORT: Scaffolded Practice

ALL LEVELS Reinforce end punctuation, commas, and conjunctions using sentence strips. Include strips for end punctuation, commas, and conjunctions. Before students begin, add end punctuation, review each type of punctuation mark, and give examples. Then guide students to create sentences with the proper end punctuation. For example, *The girls are great at hockey, so they won the school championship. What sport do you play?*

LESSON 6.4.5

QUOTATIONS AND PUNCTUATION • PROPER MECHANICS

LEARNING OBJECTIVES

- **Language** Use proper mechanics.
- **Language** Use proper mechanics correctly in writing.

MATERIALS   Online

Display and Engage *Grammar 6.4.5*
Printable *Grammar 6.4.5*

 INSTRUCTIONAL VOCABULARY

- **mechanics** the correct use of capitalization and punctuation
- **coordinating conjunction** a word, such as *and, but, for, or,* and *so* that joins other words or groups of words
- **capitalization** using capital letters for proper nouns, such as titles, names, and places

Connect and Teach

- Remind students that using the proper **mechanics** and conventions when writing helps to understand the content and keeps them focused and interested.

Engage and Apply

- Complete the items on **Display and Engage: Grammar 6.4.5** with students.

- Review that errors in **capitalization** and punctuation may confuse readers. Display a paragraph, such as the following, and have students correct the capitalization and punctuation. *My brother gave me the article industry in the past It's a new article by his favorite author? do you want to read it when Im done!* My brother gave me "Industry in the Past." It's a new article by his favorite author. Do you want to read it when I'm done?

- Guide students to write a few complete sentences, using correct punctuation and capitalization. Tell them to be sure each sentence has a subject and a predicate. Students should include compound sentences with the correct punctuation and use of **coordinating conjunctions**.

- Tell them that as they edit their writing, they should make sure they have used correct punctuation, capitalization, quotation marks, and conjunctions and that each sentence is complete and correct.

- Have students complete **Printable: Grammar 6.4.5** to practice using proper mechanics.

- Have students edit a writing draft to correctly use proper mechanics.

 ENGLISH LEARNER SUPPORT: Scaffolded Practice

SUBSTANTIAL/MODERATE

Write sentences to review the different end punctuations marks, capitalizing titles, and joining independent clauses with coordinating conjunctions. Then have students work in small groups to write their own sentences. Review their work and revise punctuation and capitalization as needed.

LIGHT

Pair students and have them write three sentences with proper mechanics. One sentence should include a title of a work. One sentence should be a compound sentence with correct punctuation and coordinating conjunction. Invite volunteers to read their sentences aloud. Have the class state what punctuation mark was used.

LESSON 7.1.1

TO, TOO, AND TWO

LEARNING OBJECTIVES

- **Language** Distinguish and use *to, too,* and *two*

- **Language** Use *to, too,* and *two* in writing.

MATERIALS Online

Display and Engage *Grammar 7.1.1a, 7.1.1b*

Printable *Grammar 7.1.1*

 INSTRUCTIONAL VOCABULARY

- **homophones** words that sound the same but have different spellings and meanings

---

Connect and Teach

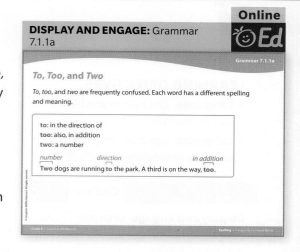

DISPLAY AND ENGAGE: Grammar 7.1.1a

To, Too, and Two

To, too, and *two* are frequently confused. Each word has a different spelling and meaning.

> to: in the direction of
> too: also, in addition
> two: a number

number   *direction*   *in addition*

Two dogs are running to the park. A third is on the way, **too.**

- Show **Display and Engage: Grammar 7.1.1a**. Explain that *to, too,* and *two* are frequently confused. They sound the same, but they are spelled differently and have different meanings. Such words are called **homophones**.

- Explain that *to* spelled *t-o* indicates "in the direction of." *Too* spelled *t-o-o* means "also" or "in addition." *Two* spelled *t-w-o* is a number.

- Model using *to, too,* and *two* correctly in the example sentence: *Two dogs are running to the park. A third is on the way, too.*

  THINK ALOUD *To determine whether to use to, too, or two, I ask: Which word makes sense in the sentence? When I want to say how many dogs there were, I use t-w-o, the number. I see that the sentence says that they are running somewhere—to the park. Since t-o means "in the direction," I know to use t-o. A third dog is also running to the park, so I know I should use t-o-o, which means "also."*

- Use the above process to complete the other examples.

Engage and Apply

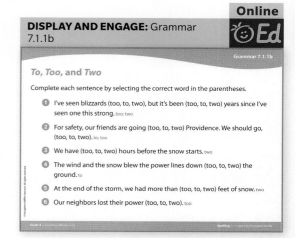

DISPLAY AND ENGAGE: Grammar 7.1.1b

To, Too, and Two

Complete each sentence by selecting the correct word in the parentheses.

1. I've seen blizzards (too, to, two), but it's been (too, to, two) years since I've seen one this strong. too; two

2. For safety, our friends are going (too, to, two) Providence. We should go, (too, to, two). to; too

3. We have (too, to, two) hours before the snow starts. two

4. The wind and the snow blew the power lines down (too, to, two) the ground. to

5. At the end of the storm, we had more than (too, to, two) feet of snow. two

6. Our neighbors lost their power (too, to, two). too

- Complete items 1–6 on **Display and Engage: Grammar 7.1.1b** with students.

- Ask students to give sentences using *to, too,* and *two* and to spell each frequently confused word.

- Have students complete **Printable: Grammar 7.1.1** to practice using *to, too,* and *two.*

- Have students edit a writing draft to practice using *to, too,* and *two* correctly.

 ENGLISH LEARNER SUPPORT: Scaffolded Practice

SUBSTANTIAL
Write *to, two,* and *too.* Then write these sentences: *I'm giving this to Katya. Here are two pencils. I have a pencil, too.* Say each sentence and have students repeat them. Underline the words *to, two,* and *too.*

MODERATE
Write *to, two,* and *too.* Have students take turns using each word in a sentence. Record students' sentences and talk about the different spellings and meanings.

LIGHT
Have students write sentences of their own using frequently confused words *to/two/too.* Have partners trade sentences and check spelling and usage of each word.

LEARNING OBJECTIVES

- **Language** Distinguish and use *there*, *they're* and *their*.
- **Language** Use *there*, *they're* and *their* correctly in speaking and in writing.

MATERIALS   Online

Display and Engage *Grammar 7.1.2a, 7.1.2b*

Printable *Grammar 7.1.2*

 INSTRUCTIONAL VOCABULARY

- **homophones** words that sound the same but have different spellings and meanings

Connect and Teach

- Show **Display and Engage: Grammar 7.1.2a**. Explain that *there*, *they're*, and *their* are often confused. They sound the same, but they are spelled differently and have different meanings. Such words are called **homophones**.

- Explain that *there* spelled *t-h-e-r-e* means "in that place." *They're* spelled *t-h-e-y apostrophe r-e* is a contraction of they are, and *their* spelled *t-h-e-i-r* means "belonging to them." *Their* shows ownership.

- Model correct use of *there*, *they're*, and *their* in the example sentences: *Their books are over there. They're going to need those books.*

  THINK ALOUD *To determine whether to use there, they're, or their, I ask:* Which word makes sense in the sentence? *I know that* their *shows ownership. Since the book belongs to them, I use* their. *The word* there *tells me a place. The books are by the table. I know that* they're *is a contraction of* they are, *so I use* they're *to say "they are going to need those books."*

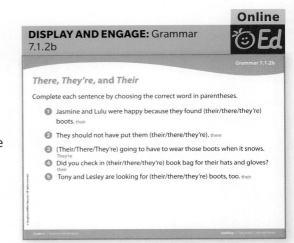

Online
DISPLAY AND ENGAGE: Grammar 7.1.2a

There, They're, and Their

There, their, and *they're* are frequently confused. Each word has a different spelling and meaning.

> **there:** in that place
> **they're:** a contraction of *they are*
> **their:** belonging to them
> *belonging to them   in that place*
> **Their** boots are over **there**.
> *They are*
> **They're** going to need those boots this winter.

Engage and Apply

- Complete items 1–5 on **Display and Engage: Grammar 7.1.2b** with students.

- Ask students to give sentences using *there*, *they're*, and *their* and to spell the frequently confused words.

- Have students complete **Printable: Grammar 7.1.2** to practice using *there*, *they're* and *their*.

- Have students edit a writing draft to practice using *there*, *they're*, and *their* correctly.

Online
DISPLAY AND ENGAGE: Grammar 7.1.2b

There, They're, and Their

Complete each sentence by choosing the correct word in parentheses.

1. Jasmine and Lulu were happy because they found (their/there/they're) boots. their
2. They should not have put them (their/there/they're). there
3. (Their/There/They're) going to have to wear those boots when it snows. They're
4. Did you check in (their/there/they're) book bag for their hats and gloves? their
5. Tony and Lesley are looking for (their/there/they're) boots, too. their

 ENGLISH LEARNER SUPPORT: Facilitate Linguistic Connections

Although homophones occur infrequently in Spanish, you may wish to give Spanish speakers these words as examples of words that are spelled differently but pronounced the same: *casar/cazar; hola/ola*. The first pair, *casar* and *cazar* are pronounced the same in some regions of the Spanish-speaking world but differently in others.

Scaffolded Practice

SUBSTANTIAL

Display a set of homophones and read each word aloud, guiding students to hear that all words sound the same. Then point out how the spelling is different, and explain that these words all have different meanings.

MODERATE

Display a set of homophones and work together to write sentences using each one. Discuss the different meanings and spellings.

LIGHT

Have pairs identify a set of homophones and write sentences using each one.

LESSON 7.1.3

ITS AND *IT'S*

LEARNING OBJECTIVES

- **Language** Distinguish and use *its* and *it's*.

- **Language** Use *its* and *it's* correctly in speaking and writing.

MATERIALS
Online **Ed**

Display and Engage *Grammar 7.1.3a, 7.1.3b*

Printable *Grammar 7.1.3*

 INSTRUCTIONAL VOCABULARY

- **homophones** words that sound the same but have different spellings and meanings

---

Connect and Teach

- Show **Display and Engage: Grammar 7.1.3a**. Explain that *its* and *it's* are frequently confused. They sound the same, but they are spelled differently and have different meanings. Such words are called **homophones**.

- Discuss that each word has a different meaning and spelling. *Its* spelled *i-t-s* means "belonging to it." Explain that we usually show possession by adding *-'s* to a word. However, to show possession with it, we simply add *-s*. Then explain that *it's* spelled with an apostrophe after the *t* is a contraction for *it is* or *it has*.

- Model correctly using *its* and *it's* in the example sentences: *It's possible to find almost anything on the Internet. If you want to know about France, you can find information about its culture.*

  THINK ALOUD *To determine whether to use its or it's with the apostrophe, I ask: Which word makes sense in the sentence? In the first sentence, I use It's to mean "it is." In the second sentence, I use its because that form tells me that the culture belongs to France.*

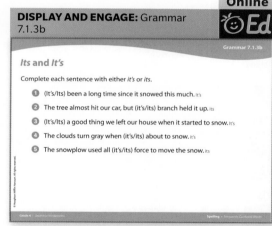

DISPLAY AND ENGAGE: Grammar 7.1.3a — Online Ed

Its and It's

Its and *it's* are frequently confused. Each word has a different spelling and meaning.

its: "belonging to it"
it's: a contraction of *it is*

It is — belonging to it
It's going to be a snowy winter. Our town will be testing **its** snow removal system.

Engage and Apply

- Complete items 1–5 on **Display and Engage: Grammar 7.1.3b** with students.

- Ask students to give sentences using *its* and *it's*. Write these sentences on the board. Before writing *its* or *it's,* ask students to supply the correct word and to spell it.

- Have students complete **Printable: Grammar 7.1.3** to practice using *its* and *it's*.

- Have students edit a writing draft to practice using *its* and *it's* correctly.

DISPLAY AND ENGAGE: Grammar 7.1.3b — Online Ed

Its and It's

Complete each sentence with either *it's* or *its*.

1. (It's/Its) been a long time since it snowed this much. It's
2. The tree almost hit our car, but (it's/its) branch held it up. its
3. (It's/Its) a good thing we left our house when it started to snow. It's
4. The clouds turn gray when (it's/its) about to snow. It's
5. The snowplow used all (it's/its) force to move the snow. its

---

 ENGLISH LEARNER SUPPORT: Facilitate Linguistic Connections

Contractions may be unfamiliar to nonnative speakers of English. Review that a contraction is a shorter way of saying two words. Reinforce the spellings of *they're* and *it's* by reviewing *they are* and *it is*.

Scaffolded Practice

SUBSTANTIAL
Help students understand the difference between *its* and *it's*. Point out items that student possess and use *it's* in a sentence: *It's your book.* Point out something in the classroom and use *its: The plant is in its pot.*

MODERATE
Write *it is* and *its*. Discuss which matches up to *it's* and why. Then have students practice using *it's* to show possession and *its* to show belonging. Provide sentence frames *It's your _____. This is its _____.*

LIGHT
Have pairs write two sentences using *its* and *it's.* Have volunteers share their sentences.

LEARNING OBJECTIVES

- **Language** Review frequently confused words.
- **Language** Use frequently confused words correctly in speaking and writing.

MATERIALS — Online

Display and Engage *Grammar 7.1.4a, 7.1.4b, 7.1.4c*

Printable *Grammar 7.1.4*

 **INSTRUCTIONAL VOCABULARY**

- **homophones** words that sound the same but have different spellings and meanings

Review Frequently Confused Words

- Show **Display and Engage: Grammar 7.1.4a** and **Grammar 7.1.4b**. Remind students that frequently confused words are **homophones**, or words that sound the same but have different spellings and meanings.

- Write the following words on the board:

  too   there   its
  two   their   it's
  to

  Display the following sentences. Guide students to choose the correct word. Then have students explain what that word means.

  We are going (two, to) the museum. to; *in the direction of*
  (Its, It's) one of our favorite places. it's; *contraction for it is*
  Our friends are meeting us (their, there). there; *at that location*
  We have to take (to, two) vans. two; *the number two*
  Our friends brought (their, there) cousin, Eddie. their; *belonging to*
  We can't wait to see the museum and all (it's, its) exhibits. its; *shows possession*

- Complete items 1–7 on **Display and Engage: Grammar 7.1.4c** with students.

- Have students complete **Printable: Grammar 7.1.4** to review frequently confused words.

- Have students edit a writing draft to correct frequently confused words.

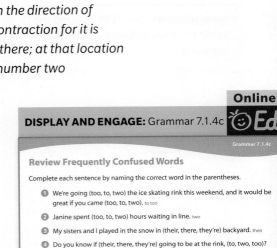

 ENGLISH LEARNER SUPPORT: Scaffolded Practice

ALL LEVELS Display sentence frames, such as the following, to reinforce the correct use of the frequently confused words. Have students complete the sentences with the correct words and say the complete sentence. Provide students with additional sentence frames as needed.

I have _____ pencils. two
I will take this pencil _____ my desk. to
_____ my favorite one. It's
My friends Juan and Clara said it's _____ favorite kind of pencil, too. their
_____ using those pencils for _____ math test. They're, their

LEARNING OBJECTIVES

- **Language** Identify the correct homophone.
- **Language** Use the correct homophone in writing.

MATERIALS   Online

Display and Engage *Grammar 7.1.5*
Printable *Grammar 7.1.5*

 **INSTRUCTIONAL VOCABULARY**

- **homophones** words that sound the same but have different spellings and meanings

Connect and Teach

- Show **Display and Engage: Grammar 7.1.5**. Explain that good writers always use the correct words to make their writing clear and understandable to readers.

- Point out that an important part of revising is checking for **homophones**, or words that sound like other words but have different spellings and meanings, and correcting those words as needed.

Online

DISPLAY AND ENGAGE: Grammar 7.1.5

Grammar 7.1.5

Connect to Writing: Using the Correct Word

Using an incorrect word can confuse your readers. When you proofread your writing, look for words that sound like other words but have different meanings and spellings. Make sure you're using the correct word. If you're not sure, look up the word in a dictionary.

Incorrect	Correct
Their will be to many people too count at they're ice skating party.	There will be too many people to count at their ice skating party.

Grade 6 | Grammar Worksheets   Spelling • Frequently Confused Words

Engage and Apply

- Display the following sentences. Guide students to correct the frequently confused words.

  The snowstorm there predicting sounds like its going to be dangerous. they're; it's
  Many places will have more than too feet of snow. two
  The county is going too need all of it's resources and aid from other counties, to. its; to
  The people in the village did there best to help out. their
  We did not send anyone too our sister county in the north. to

- Have students complete **Printable: Grammar 7.1.5** to practice using the correct homophone.

- Have students edit a writing draft to practice using the correct homophone.

___

EL **ENGLISH LEARNER SUPPORT: Scaffolded Practice**

ALL LEVELS Write the frequently confused words. Ask *yes/no* or simple questions to elicit what each word means. Then divide students into mixed-proficiency groups and have them write a sentence using each set of frequently confused words. After the sentence, have them write what the word means. Invite volunteers to read their sentences to the class. Have the class say which word was used.

LEARNING OBJECTIVES

- **Language** Identify abbreviations for people and places.
- **Language** Use abbreviations for people and places correctly in writing.

MATERIALS Online

Display and Engage *Grammar 7.2.1a, 7.2.1b*

Printable *Grammar 7.2.1*

 **INSTRUCTIONAL VOCABULARY**

- **abbreviation** a shortened form of a word

Connect and Teach

- Show **Display and Engage: Grammar 7.2.1a**. Explain that an **abbreviation** is a shortened form of a word. Point out that many abbreviations begin with a capital letter and end with a period.

- Model identifying the abbreviations in the example: *Dr. Kathy Sutherland, 28 Logjam Rd., Bristol, IA 54820*

  THINK ALOUD *To identify the abbreviation I ask:* What parts of the address are shortened forms of words? Dr., Rd. *and* IA *are all abbreviations in this address. The abbreviation* Dr. *is short for* Doctor, Rd. *is short for* Road, *and* IA *is short for* Iowa.

Engage and Apply

- Complete items 1–8 on **Display and Engage: Grammar 7.2.1b** with students.

- Write the following groups of words on the board. Ask students to identify where abbreviations can be used.
  27 Southwood Lane Lane–Ln.
  Mister Thomas Payne, Junior Mister–Mr.; Junior–Jr.

- Have students complete **Printable: Grammar 7.2.1** to practice using abbreviations for people and places.

- Have students edit a writing draft to practice using correct abbreviations for people and places.

DISPLAY AND ENGAGE: Grammar 7.2.1a

Online

Abbreviations for People and Places

An **abbreviation** is a shortened form of a word. Most abbreviations begin with a **capital letter** and end with a **period**. Both letters in the abbreviation of state names are capital letters, and no period is used.

> **person**
> Mr. Christopher Alcazar
> **place**
> 12 Ranger Rd.
> **place**
> Hollis, NH 03049

DISPLAY AND ENGAGE: Grammar 7.2.1b

Online

Abbreviations for People and Places

Name the abbreviation for the blue word.

1. Post Office Box 1526 PO
2. Mister William Kravitz Mr.
3. Federman Supply Company Co.
4. 1322 Racine Boulevard Blvd.
5. Portland, Oregon OR
6. Doctor Jeffrey Santos Dr.
7. Pedro Durante, Junior Jr.
8. 43 Chestnut Street St.

EL **ENGLISH LEARNER SUPPORT: Scaffolded Practice**

ALL LEVELS Display the following list of abbreviated names. Guide students to identify and say the abbreviated words. Model spoken words as necessary. Reinforce that the words are pronounced the same whether written fully or abbreviated.

Mr. Jones Mister

Mrs. Camillia Nord Missus

Dr. Quiceno Doctor

LEARNING OBJECTIVES

- **Language** Identify abbreviations for mailing addresses.
- **Language** Use abbreviations for mailing addresses correctly in writing.

MATERIALS Online

Display and Engage *Grammar 7.2.2a, 7.2.2b*

Printable *Grammar 7.2.2*

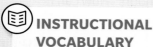 **INSTRUCTIONAL VOCABULARY**

- **abbreviation** a shortened form of a word

Connect and Teach

- Show **Display and Engage: Grammar 7.2.2a**. Point out that **abbreviations** are shortened forms of whole words. Explain how they are used in addresses to write street names and state names. Tell students that floor, suite, and apartment can be abbreviated.

- Model abbreviating the following

687 Main Street	*687 Main St.*
Apartment 16B	*Apt. 16B*
Vine, Vermont 05469	*Vine, VT 05469*

  THINK ALOUD *To identify the abbreviation, I ask:* "What parts of an address can I make shorter?" Street, Apartment, Vermont "How can I shorten the whole word?" St., Apt., VT

- Point out that both letters in the abbreviation of state names are capital letters and periods are not used.

Engage and Apply

- Complete items 1–9 on **Display and Engage: Grammar 7.2.2b** with students. Remind students to use correct capitalization and punctuation.

- Have students complete **Printable: Grammar 7.2.2** to practice using abbreviations for mailing addresses.

- Have students edit a writing draft to practice using correct abbreviations for mailing addresses.

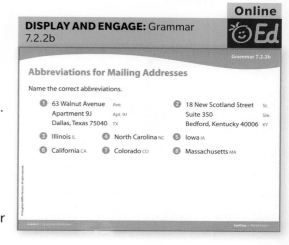

 ENGLISH LEARNER SUPPORT: Scaffolded Practice

SUBSTANTIAL

Use picture cards to support understanding of states and street. Write on the board: *Ocean Boulevard* and *California.* Then write the abbreviation for each and point out the shared letters, explaining that each refers to the same word.
Ocean Blvd; CA

MODERATE

Draw an envelope on the board with the following address: *Doctor Sal Burke The Burke Company73 West Jansen Avenue Westmoreland, California 90372* Guide students to form each abbreviation. Have them read the address aloud.
Dr. Sal Burke
The Burke Co.
73 W. Jansen Ave.
Westmoreland, CA 90372

LIGHT

Have students use abbreviations to write addresses. Have students exchange papers and check that the abbreviations are correct.

SPELLING • ABBREVIATIONS

LEARNING OBJECTIVES

- **Language** Identify abbreviations for time and measurement.
- **Language** Use abbreviations for time and measurement correctly in writing.

MATERIALS   Online

Display and Engage *Grammar 7.2.3a, 7.2.3b*

Printable *Grammar 7.2.3*

 **INSTRUCTIONAL VOCABULARY**

- **abbreviation** a shortened form of a word

Connect and Teach

- Show **Display and Engage: Grammar 7.2.3a**. Explain that **abbreviations** for days and months begin with a capital letter and end with a period. Point out that many abbreviations for measurements begin with a lowercase letter.

- Model abbreviating the following example:
  Friday, February 23, 1775
  12 inches of snow in 6 hours

  THINK ALOUD *To identify the abbreviation, I ask:* "What parts can I make shorter?" time: Friday, February; measurements: inches, hours "How can I shorten the whole word?" Fri., Feb., in., hr.

Engage and Apply

- Complete items 1–8 on **Display and Engage: Grammar 7.2.3b** with students.

- Have students write the days of the week and months of the year in a column. Then have them write the abbreviation for each day and month in a second column.

- Have students complete **Printable: Grammar 7.2.3** to practice using abbreviations for time and measurement.

- Have students edit a writing draft to practice using abbreviations for time and measurement correctly.

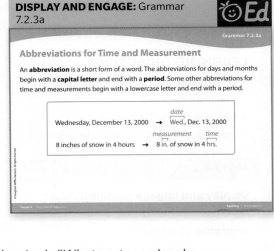

DISPLAY AND ENGAGE: Grammar 7.2.3a   Online

DISPLAY AND ENGAGE: Grammar 7.2.3b   Online

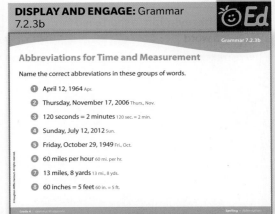

 ENGLISH LEARNER SUPPORT: Facilitate Linguistic Connections

In Spanish, days of the week and months, as well as their abbreviations, are not capitalized. Reinforce that capital letters are used for all English day and month names, whether full or abbreviated.

Scaffolded Practice

SUBSTANTIAL

Use a clock and a calendar to reinforce abbreviations for time. Explain that *Monday, October 13* is a date. Write *Mon., Oct. 13* and explain that it is still said as *Monday, October thirteen*. Repeat for hours/hr. and minutes/min.

MODERATE

Make a list of all the time and measurement words students know. Write the abbreviation next to each word and work together to identify how the word is shortened.

LIGHT

Have pairs look around the room and see what sentences they can write using time and measurement abbreviations.

LEARNING OBJECTIVES

- **Language** Review abbreviations
- **Language** Use abbreviations correctly in writing.

MATERIALS   Online

Display and Engage *Grammar 7.2.4a, 7.2.4b, 7.2.4c*

Printable *Grammar 7.2.4*

 INSTRUCTIONAL VOCABULARY

- **abbreviation** a shortened form of a word

Review Abbreviations

- Show **Display and Engage: Grammar 7.2.4a** and **7.2.4b**. Remind students that an **abbreviation** is a shorter way to write a word. There are many common abbreviations for titles, street and state names, measurements, months, and days.

- Review the types of words that can be abbreviated: days, months, time, dates, places, and titles. Ask students to share examples of each type of abbreviation. Write the full word and its abbreviation on the board, pointing out which abbreviations are capitalized and which ones remain lowercase.

Engage and Apply

- Complete items 1–6 on **Display and Engage: Grammar 7.2.4c** with students.

- Have pairs work together to make a list of all the abbreviations they know. Ask them to put a star next to the abbreviations that are capitalized because they are proper nouns.

- Have students complete **Printable: Grammar 7.2.4** to review abbreviations.

- Have students edit a writing draft to review abbreviations.

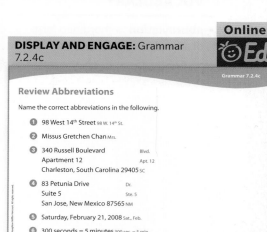

DISPLAY AND ENGAGE: Grammar
7.2.4a, 7.2.4b

Online Ed

Grammar 7.2.4a

Review Abbreviations

An **abbreviation** is a shortened form of a word. Most abbreviations begin with a **capital letter** and end with a **period**. Both letters in the abbreviation of state names are capital letters, and no period is used.

Abbreviations are used in an address to write street and state names. *Floor, suite,* and *apartment* are also parts of an address that use abbreviations.

> Dr. Angela Drucker
> 67 Maple St.
> Apt. 2
> Chicago, IL 60131

DISPLAY AND ENGAGE: Grammar
7.2.4c

Online Ed

Grammar 7.2.4c

Review Abbreviations

Name the correct abbreviations in the following.

1. 98 West 14th Street 98 W. 14th St.
2. Missus Gretchen Chan Mrs.
3. 340 Russell Boulevard   Blvd.
   Apartment 12   Apt. 12
   Charleston, South Carolina 29405 SC
4. 83 Petunia Drive   Dr.
   Suite 5   Ste. 5
   San Jose, New Mexico 87565 NM
5. Saturday, February 21, 2008 Sat., Feb.
6. 300 seconds = 5 minutes 300 sec. = 5 min.

 ENGLISH LEARNER SUPPORT: Scaffolded Practice

ALL LEVELS Remind students that proper nouns, such as names or titles, are always capitalized. Guide them to connect capitalizing abbreviations for the same nouns. Show them that time or measurement abbreviations are not capitalized because they are not proper nouns.

SPELLING · ABBREVIATIONS

LEARNING OBJECTIVES

- **Language** Identify abbreviations.
- **Language** Use abbreviations correctly in writing.

MATERIALS   Online

Display and Engage *Grammar 7.2.5*

Printable *Grammar 7.2.5*

 INSTRUCTIONAL VOCABULARY

- **abbreviation** a shortened form of a word

Connect and Teach

- Show **Display and Engage: Grammar 7.2.5**. Explain that good writers use **abbreviations** when writing titles, addresses, days, months, and measurements in special kinds of writing.

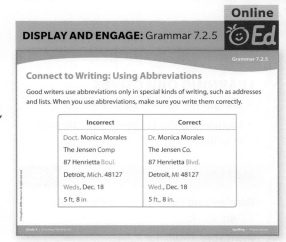

Engage and Apply

- Review the examples on **Display and Engage: Grammar 7.2.5** with students.

- Display the following name and address. Guide students to identify which words should be abbreviated and how to abbreviate them.

  Captain Francis Skully Captain–Capt.

  1563 Robins Way Way–Wy.

  Portland, Oregon 00143 Oregon–OR

- Write the following words on the board. Have students write the abbreviations for each word.

  Road Rd.   July Jul.

  miles mi.   Thursday Thurs.

  inches in.   Court Ct.

- Have students complete **Printable: Grammar 7.2.5** to practice using abbreviations.

- Have students edit a writing draft to practice using abbreviations correctly.

EL **ENGLISH LEARNER SUPPORT: Facilitate Linguistic Connections**

Some students may need help with pronunciations when reading aloud or speaking in a more formal register. Students may have trouble voicing /r/ at the end of words such as *Mister* or *Doctor*. They may omit the /r/ sound and voice the words as *Mistuh* and *Doctuh*. Write this sentence on the board: *Mr. Jones lives on River St.* Read the sentence aloud, emphasizing the /r/ sound in *Mister* and *River*. Have students echo your reading several times.

Scaffolded Practice

ALL LEVELS Work together to write a short letter to the principal. Guide students to help you write the abbreviations in the letter. For example:

River St. School
406 Smith Blvd.
Grove, IL

Fri., Nov. 12

Dear Mrs. Cruz,
Our class would like to thank you for watching our presentations. We had so much fun learning about Mr. and President Lincoln. We liked that the president was 6 ft. tall!

LEARNING OBJECTIVES

- **Language** Identify homophones.
- **Language** Use homophones correctly in writing.

MATERIALS
Online

Display and Engage *Grammar 7.3.1a, 7.3.1b*

Printable *Grammar 7.3.1*

 **INSTRUCTIONAL VOCABULARY**

- **homophones** words that sound alike but are spelled differently

Connect and Teach

- Show **Display and Engage: Grammar 7.3.1a**. Sometimes two words that sound alike are spelled differently and have different meanings. These words are called **homophones**.

- Some examples of commonly used high-frequency homophones are: *hear/here, buy/by, weather/whether, bear/bare, break/brake, complement/compliment, aloud/allowed, capital/capitol,* and *principle/principal.*

- Model determining which homophone to choose using this example: *The fifth grade class visited the capitol building. The school principal chaperoned the trip.*

  THINK ALOUD *When I am writing a sentence and come across a word that sounds like another word, I ask:* What word makes the most sense here? How can I use the context to figure out what word I need? *These sentences contain homophones:* capitol *and* principal. *To figure out which word I need and how to spell it, I think about how the word is being used. In the first sentence,* capitol *is referring to a building, so I know the word is* capitol *because the homophone* capital *refers to a letter. In the second sentence, I know the word* principal *is referring to a person. The homophone* principle *refers to a belief, so I know the first spelling is correct.*

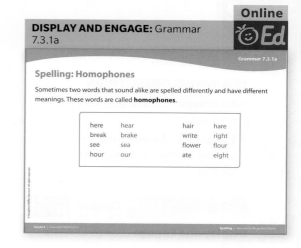

Engage and Apply

- Complete items 1–7 on **Display and Engage: Grammar 7.3.1b** with students.

- Have students complete **Printable: Grammar 7.3.1** to practice spelling homophones.

- Have students edit a writing draft to practice spelling homophones correctly.

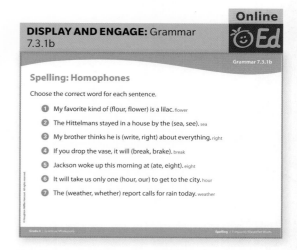

 ENGLISH LEARNER SUPPORT: Scaffolded Practice

ALL LEVELS Review the difference between the commonly used homophones *hear/here* and *by/buy*. First, review the definition of each word. Then have the students use the correct form to complete the sentence frames.

Isabelle wants to _____ a new sweater. buy
The ball is _____ the tree. by
Sheila didn't _____ the bell ring. hear
The book is over _____. here

LEARNING OBJECTIVES

- **Language** Identify noun and verb endings.
- **Language** Use noun and verb endings correctly in speaking and writing.

MATERIALS   Online

Display and Engage *Grammar 7.3.2a, 7.3.2b*

Printable *Grammar 7.3.2*

INSTRUCTIONAL VOCABULARY

- **word endings** *-s, -es, -ed, -ing* added to words to change the verb tense or to change a singular noun to a plural noun

Connect and Teach

- Show **Display and Engage: Grammar 7.3.2a**. Explain that words follow certain spelling patterns and rules. There are several common rules to follow when adding **word endings**.

- Explain the CVC rule and adding endings. In CVC words, such as *nap*, double the ending consonant before adding *-ed* or *-ing*: *napped, napping*.

- Explain the CVCe rule. If a word ends in *e*, drop the *e* before adding the ending: *raked, raking*.

- Explain the *y* to *i* rule. When a noun ends in *y*, change the *y* to an *I* before adding *-s* or *-es*: *lady—ladies; copy—copies*.

Engage and Apply

- Complete items 1–6 on **Display and Engage: Grammar 7.3.2b** with students.

- Have students complete **Printable: Grammar 7.3.2** to practice spelling words with ending.

- Have students edit a writing draft to practice correctly spelling words with endings.

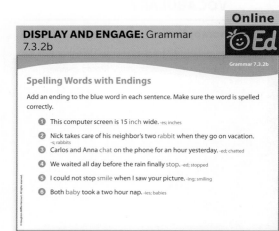

DISPLAY AND ENGAGE: Grammar 7.3.2a   Online Ed

Grammar 7.3.2a

Spelling Words with Endings

There are rules on how to add endings to words. For short vowel words that have the consonant-vowel-consonant pattern, CVC, double the last consonant. For long vowel words that end in *e*, drop the *e* before adding the ending. For nouns that end in *y*, change the *y* to an *i* before adding most endings.

Double Consonant	Drop the *e*	Change *y* to *i*
-ed and *-ing*	*-ed* and *-ing*	*-es* and *-ed*
napped	hoped	copies
getting	making	dried
robbed	using	ladies

DISPLAY AND ENGAGE: Grammar 7.3.2b   Online Ed

Grammar 7.3.2b

Spelling Words with Endings

Add an ending to the blue word in each sentence. Make sure the word is spelled correctly.

1. This computer screen is 15 inch wide. -es; inches
2. Nick takes care of his neighbor's two rabbit when they go on vacation. -s; rabbits
3. Carlos and Anna chat on the phone for an hour yesterday. -ed; chatted
4. We waited all day before the rain finally stop. -ed; stopped
5. I could not stop smile when I saw your picture. -ing; smiling
6. Both baby took a two hour nap. -ies; babies

ENGLISH LEARNER SUPPORT: Scaffolded Support

ALL LEVELS Some of the rules for spelling plural nouns are the same in Spanish as they are in English. Discuss some of these rules and compare them to English spelling rules. For example, if a noun ends in a vowel, add an *-s*. However, some rules are different. For example, in Spanish, the plural of the word *color* is *colores*. Explain that in English, most words that end with a consonant just add *-s*. The exceptions are *f, s, x, sh,* and *ch*. Ask students to share other spelling rules in their home language and compare them to English spelling rules. Reinforce the English spelling rules by having students write the singular and plural form of English words.

LEARNING OBJECTIVES

- **Language** Identify suffixes.
- **Language** Use suffixes correctly in speaking and writing.

MATERIALS   Online Ed

Display and Engage *Grammar 7.3.3a, 7.3.3b*

Printable *Grammar 7.3.3*

 INSTRUCTIONAL VOCABULARY

- **root** the main part of a word
- **suffix** word part that is added to the end of a root word to change the meaning of the word

Connect and Teach

- Show **Display and Engage: Grammar 7.3.3a**. Explain that a **suffix** is a word part that is added to the end of a **root** word to change its meaning. Commonly used suffixes include: *-ful, -ly, -less, -ness, -ment, -ion/-tion/-ation, -able/-ible,* and *-ence.*

- Explain that some words change spelling when a suffix is added. For example, when a word ends in a *y,* the *y* changes to an *i* before adding the suffix: *beauty— beautiful; pretty—prettier; pretty—prettily; plenty—plentiful; pity— pitiful.* Write the words on the board.

- If a word ends with an *e,* the *e* is dropped when adding a suffix that begins with a vowel. Write the following words on the board so students understand the rule: *sense—sensible; tense—tension; invite—invitation; communicate—communication.*

- Remind students that when a suffix is added to the word, the meaning of the word changes.

Engage and Apply

- Complete items 1–6 on **Display and Engage: Grammar 7.3.3b** with students.

- Have students complete **Printable: Grammar 7.3.3** to practice spelling words with suffixes.

- Have students edit a writing draft to practice spelling words with suffixes correctly.

DISPLAY AND ENGAGE: Grammar 7.3.3a

Online 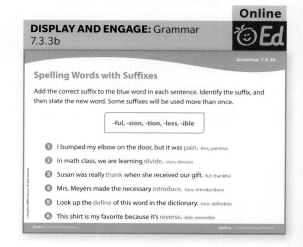 Ed

 ENGLISH LEARNER SUPPORT: Scaffolded Practice

ALL LEVELS Have students talk about things they do that require care. Ask them to write two sentences using the word care with the endings *-ful* and *-less.* Talk about how adding the endings changes the meaning of the word *care.*
My work was slow and careful.
My work was careless.

SPELLING • FREQUENTLY MISSPELLED WORDS

LEARNING OBJECTIVES

- **Language** Review correct spelling with high-frequency homophones, endings, and suffixes.
- **Language** Use correct spelling in writing.

MATERIALS   Online

Display and Engage *Grammar 7.3.4a, 7.3.4b, 7.3.4c*

Printable *Grammar 7.3.4*

INSTRUCTIONAL VOCABULARY

- **homophones** words that sound alike but are spelled differently
- **word endings** *-s, -es, -ed, -ing* added to words to change the verb tense or to change a singular noun to plural
- **suffix** word part that is added to the end of a root word to change the meaning of the word

Review Spelling

- Show **Display and Engage: Grammar 7.3.4a** and **7.3.4b**. Remind students that **homophones** are words that sound alike but are spelled differently. Review some high-frequency homophones, such as *buy/by, hear/here, bare/bear,* and *principle/principal*.

- Review the spelling rules and patterns for adding **word endings** *-s, -es, -ing,* and *-ed*. In CVC words, such as *nap,* double the ending consonant before adding *-ed* or *-ing*. If a word ends in *e,* drop the *e* before adding the ending. When a noun ends in *y,* change the *y* to an *I* before adding *-s* or *-es*.

- Remind students of the spelling rules that some words follow when adding **suffixes**.

- Complete items 1–6 on **Display and Engage: Grammar 7.3c** with students.

- Have students complete **Printable: Grammar 7.3.4** to practice spelling with high-frequency homophones, endings, and suffixes.

- Have students edit a writing draft to practice correctly spelling high-frequency homophones, endings, and suffixes.

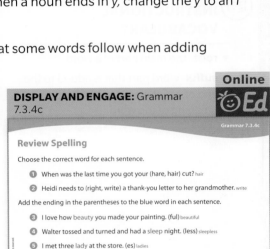

DISPLAY AND ENGAGE: Grammar 7.3.4a, 7.3.4b   Online

Grammar 7.3.4a

Review Spelling

Homophones are two words that sound alike but are spelled differently and have different meanings.

| principle/principal | whether/weather |

When adding endings to words, the spelling changes. Letters are added, dropped, or changed.

> napped, napping
> bake, baking
> baby, babies

DISPLAY AND ENGAGE: Grammar 7.3.4c   Online

Grammar 7.3.4c

Review Spelling

Choose the correct word for each sentence.

1. When was the last time you got your (hare, hair) cut? hair
2. Heidi needs to (right, write) a thank-you letter to her grandmother. write

Add the ending in the parentheses to the blue word in each sentence.

3. I love how beauty you made your painting. (ful) beautiful
4. Walter tossed and turned and had a sleep night. (less) sleepless
5. I met three lady at the store. (es) ladies
6. After four hours, the snow finally stop. (ed) stopped

 ENGLISH LEARNER SUPPORT: Scaffolded Practice

ALL LEVELS Review the spelling rules and patterns. Provide students with a list of high-frequency words that follow simple spelling patterns. For example, *baby, lady, nap, tap, rake,* and *bake*. Have students work with partners to add the endings *-s, -es, -ed,* or *-ing*. Review their responses. Ask students to explain what spelling rule or pattern they followed.

LEARNING OBJECTIVES

- **Language** Identify correct spelling with homophones, endings, and suffixes.
- **Language** Use correct spelling in writing.

MATERIALS   Online

Display and Engage *Grammar 7.3.5*

Printable *Grammar 7.3.5*

 **INSTRUCTIONAL VOCABULARY**

- **homophones** words that sound alike but are spelled differently
- **word endings** *-s, -es, -ed, -ing* added to words to change the verb tense or to change a singular noun to plural
- **suffix** word part that is added to the end of a root word to change the meaning of the word

Connect and Teach

- Show **Display and Engage: Grammar 7.3.5**. Remind students that using spelling words correctly will make their writing easier to read and understand.

  Write the following sentences and ask the students to correct the errors.

  Did you here that noise? Change here to hear

  The whether forecast said there would be rain tomorrow. Change whether to weather

  She was successful because she was care. Change care to careful

  Carla painted a beautyful portrait. Change beautyful to beautiful

  Sarah cookked yesterday. Change cookked to cooked

  Jackson bakeed a cake for Lisa's birthday. Change bakeed to baked

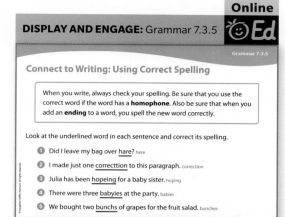

Engage and Apply

- Complete items 1–5 on **Display and Engage: Grammar 7.3.5** with students.
- Have students complete **Printable: Grammar 7.3.5** to use correct spelling.
- Have students edit a writing draft to use correct spelling.

 ENGLISH LEARNER SUPPORT: Scaffolded Practice

ALL LEVELS Write the following sentences. Have students choose the correctly spelled word. Challenge them to explain why the word is correctly spelled.

Marta will (buy/by) a new book. buy

Is that a (bear/bare) over there? bear

The (puppys/puppies) are so cute. puppies

I (rubed/rubbed) my sore arm. rubbed

Resources

Online

FIND MORE ONLINE!

Scope and Sequence

Reproducible Rubrics

Standards Correlations

Language Differences
- Alphabet
- Phonological Features
- Grammatical Features

Professional Learning

Look up these professional resources to learn more about the research foundations for *Into Reading: Writing Workshop*.

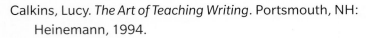

Calkins, Lucy. *The Art of Teaching Writing*. Portsmouth, NH: Heinemann, 1994.

Calkins, Lucy, Amanda Hartman, and Zoe Ryder White. *One to One: The Art of Conferring with Young Writers*. Portsmouth, NH: Heinemann, 2005.

Calkins, Lucy. *A Guide to the Writing Workshop: Primary Grades*. Portsmouth, NH: Heinemann, 2017.

Carroll, Joyce Armstrong. *The Best of Dr. JAC*. Spring, TX: Absey & Company, Inc., 1998.

Carroll, Joyce Armstrong. *Dr. JAC's Guide to Writing with Depth*. Spring, TX: Absey & Company, Inc., 2002.

Carroll, Joyce Armstrong. "Finding the Genesis for a Thesis." *School Library Monthly* 29, no. 6 (March 2013):17–19.

Carroll, Joyce Armstrong. "Teaching the Thesis." *School Library Monthly* 29, no. 2 (November 2012):18–20.

Carroll, Joyce Armstrong, and Jill Aufill. *Authentic Strategies for High-Stakes Tests: A Practical Guide for English Language/Arts*. Spring, TX: Absey & Company, Inc., 2007.

Carroll, Joyce Armstrong, Kelley Barger, Karla James, and Kristy Hill. *Guided by Meaning in Primary Literacy: Libraries, Reading, Writing, and Learning*. Santa Barbara, CA: Libraries Unlimited, 2016.

Carroll, Joyce Armstrong, and Edward E. Wilson. *Acts of Teaching: How to Teach Writing: A Text, A Reader, A Narrative*. 2nd Ed. Portsmouth, NH: Heinemann, 2008.

Carroll, Joyce Armstrong, and Edward E. Wilson. *Brushing Up on Grammar: An Acts of Teaching Approach*. Santa Barbara, CA: Libraries Unlimited, 2010.

Cruz, M. Colleen. *The Unstoppable Writing Teacher: Real Strategies for the Real Classroom*. Portsmouth, NH: Heinemann, 2015.

Dawson, Peg, and Richard Guare. *Smart but Scattered: The Revolutionary "Executive Skills" Approach to Helping Kids Reach Their Potential*. New York, NY: Guilford Press, 2009.

Durlak, Joseph A., Celene E. Domitrovich, Roger P. Weissberg, and Thomas P. Gullotta, eds. *Handbook of Social and Emotional Learning: Research and Practice*. New York, NY: Guilford Press, 2016.

Durlak, Joseph A., Roger P. Weissberg, Allison B. Dymnicki, Rebecca D. Taylor, and Kriston B. Schellinger. "The Impact of Enhancing Students' Social and Emotional Learning: A Meta-Analysis of School-Based Universal Interventions." *Child Development* 82, no. 1 (January/February 2011): 405–432.

Dweck, Carol S. *Mindset: The New Psychology of Success*. New York, NY: Ballantine Books, 2007.

Fisher, Douglas, and Nancy Frey. *Better Learning Through Structured Teaching: A Framework for the Gradual Release of Responsibility*. 1st ed. Association for Supervision & Curriculum Development, 2008.

Gartland, Lauren B., and Laura B. Smolkin. "The Histories and Mysteries of Grammar Instruction: Supporting Elementary Teachers in the Time of the Common Core." *The Reading Teacher* 69, no. 4 (January/February 2016): 391–399.

Gerde, Hope. K., Gary. E. Bingham, and Barbara A. Wasik. "Writing in Early Childhood Classrooms: Guidance for Best Practices." *Early Childhood Education Journal* 40, no. 6 (2012): 351–59.

Graham, Steve. "Want to Improve Children's Writing? Don't Neglect Their Handwriting." *American Educator* (Winter 2009–2010): 20–27, 40.

Graham, Steve, Alisha Bollinger, Carol Booth Olson, Catherine D'Aoust, Charles MacArthur, Deborah McCutchen, and Natalie Olinghouse. *Teaching Elementary School Students to Be Effective Writers*. Washington, DC: Institute of Education Sciences, 2012.

Graham, Steve, and Karen R. Harris. "A Path to Better Writing: Evidence-Based Practices in the Classroom." *The Reading Teacher* 69, no. 4 (January/February 2016): 359–365.

Graham, Steve, and Karen Harris. *Writing Better: Effective Strategies for Teaching Students with Learning Disabilities*. 1st ed. Baltimore, MD: Brookes Publishing, 2005.

Graham, Steve, Karen Harris, and Michael Hebert. *Informing Writing: The Benefits of Formative Assessment*. Washington, DC: Carnegie Corporation of New York, Alliance for Excellent Education, 2011.

Graham, Steve, and Dolores Perin. *Writing Next: Effective Strategies to Improve Writing of Adolescents in Middle and High Schools—A Report to Carnegie Corporation of New York*. Washington, DC: Alliance for Excellent Education, 2011.

Harris, Karen, Steve Graham, Linda Mason, and Barbara Friedlander. *Powerful Writing Strategies for All Students*. 1st ed. Baltimore, MD: Brookes Publishing, 2007.

Horn, Martha, and Mary Ellen Giacobbe. *Talking, Drawing, Writing: Lessons for Our Youngest Writers*. Portland, ME: Stenhouse Publishers, 2006.

Kirby, Amanda, and Lynne Peters. *100 Ideas for Supporting Pupils with Dyspraxia and DCD*. London: Bloomsbury Academic, 2007.

Lonigan, Christopher. J., and Timothy Shanahan. "Executive Summary." *Developing Early Literacy: Report of the National Early Literacy Panel*. Washington, DC: National Institute for Literacy, 2009.

McGrath, Constance. *The Inclusion-Classroom Problem Solver: Structures and Supports to Serve All Learners*. Portsmouth, NH: Heinemann, 2007.

Mo, Ya, Rachel A. Kopke, Lisa K. Hawkins, Gary A. Troia, and Natalie G. Olinghouse. "The Neglected 'R' in a Time of Common Core." *The Reading Teacher* 67, no. 6 (March 2014): 445–453.

Richards, Regina G. *When Writing's a Problem: Understanding Dysgraphia & Helpful Hints for Reluctant Writers*. Riverside, CA: RET Center Press, 2015.

Richards, Todd L., Virginia W. Berninger, Pat Stock, Leah Altemeier, Pamela Trivedi, and Kenneth R. Maravilla. "Differences Between Good and Poor Child Writers on fMRI Contrasts for Writing Newly Taught and Highly Practiced Letter Forms." *Reading and Writing* 24, no. 5 (May 2011): 493–516.

Rogers, Katie, and Julia Simms A. *Teaching Argumentation: Activities and Games for the Classroom*. Bloomington, IN: Marzano Research, 2015.

Serravallo, Jennifer. *The Writing Strategies Book: Your Everything Guide to Developing Skilled Writers*. Portsmouth, NH: Heinemann, 2017.

Sloan, Megan. *Into Writing: The Primary Teacher's Guide to Writing Workshop*. Portsmouth, NH: Heinemann, 2009.

Teaching Elementary School Students to Be Effective Writers Practice Guide Summary. Washington, DC: Institute of Education Sciences, September 23, 2014.

Troia, Gary A., ed. *Instruction and Assessment for Struggling Writers: Evidence-Based Practices*. Challenges in Language and Literacy. New York, NY: Guilford Press, 2010.

Troia, Gary A. "Research in Writing Instruction: What We Know and What We Need to Know." In *Shaping Literacy Achievement: Research We Have, Research We Need*, edited by Michael Pressley, Allison K. Billman, Kristen H. Perry, Kelly E. Reffitt, and Julia Moorhead Reynolds, 129–156. New York City: Guilford Press, 2007.

Troia, Gary A., and Steve Graham. "Effective Writing Instruction Across the Grades: What Every Educational Consultant Should Know." *Journal of Educational and Psychological Consultation* 14 (2003): 75–89.

Troia, Gary A., and Steve Graham, eds. *Students Who Are Exceptional and Writing Disabilities: Prevention, Practice, Intervention, and Assessment*. *Exceptionality: a Special Education Journal*. London: Routledge, 2017.

Troia, Gary A., Rebecca K. Shankland, and Anne Heintz, eds. *Putting Writing Research into Practice: Applications for Teacher Professional Development*. New York, NY: Guilford Press, 2010.

Van Sluys, Katie. *Becoming Writers in the Elementary Classroom: Visions and Decisions*. Principles in Practice. Urbana, IL: National Council of Teachers of English, 2011.

Washington, Julie. "Language Development in Young Children." Early Learning Webinars. Houghton Mifflin Harcourt, October 20, 2016. http://www.hmhco. com/classroom/ evaluate-and-sample/webinars/professional-webinars/ early-learning?elqTrackId=36 6ad0c9423e486691852cd55a 08e45b&elqaid=3697 &elqat=2.

Winn, Maisha T., and Latrise Johnson. *Writing Instruction in the Culturally Relevant Classroom*. Principles in Practice. Urbana, IL: National Council of Teachers of English, 2011.

Credits

Photo Credits

Handwriting

Individual students have various levels of handwriting skills, but they all have the desire to communicate effectively. To write correctly, they must be familiar with concepts of

- size (tall, short).
- open and closed letters.
- capital and lowercase letters.
- manuscript vs. cursive letters.
- letter and word spacing.
- punctuation.

Explain Stroke and Letter Formation

Tell students that most manuscript letters are formed with a continuous stroke, so students will not often pick up their pencils when writing a single letter. Explain that when they begin to use cursive handwriting, students will have to lift their pencils from the paper less frequently and will be able to write more fluently. Provide students with a copy of the manuscript and cursive handwriting models on pages R7–R9 for future reference.

Teach Writing Position

Establishing the correct posture, pen or pencil grip, and paper position for writing will help prevent handwriting problems.

Posture Tell students to sit with both feet on the floor and with hips to the back of the chair. They can lean forward slightly but should not slouch. Ask them to make sure their writing surface is smooth and flat. It should be at a height that allows their upper arms to be perpendicular to the surface and their elbows to be under their shoulders.

Writing Instrument Have students use an adult-sized number-two lead pencil for their writing assignments. Explain that as they become proficient in the use of cursive handwriting, they can use pens to write final drafts.

Paper Position and Pencil Grip Explain to students that as they write in cursive, the position of the paper plays an important role. The paper should be slanted along the line of the student's writing arm, and the student should use his or her nonwriting hand to hold the paper in place. Tell them to hold their pencils or pens about one inch from the tip.

Then ask students to assume their writing position. Check each student's position, providing adjustments as necessary.

Develop Handwriting

The best instruction builds on what students already know and can do. Given the wide range in students' handwriting abilities, a variety of approaches may be needed. Use the following activities as you choose to provide regular handwriting practice to students of all proficiency levels.

Write in Cursive
Project or display
Anchor Chart: Cursive Handwriting. Point out the characteristics of cursive writing and the differences from the manuscript alphabet, as needed. Then duplicate for each student the model of the cursive alphabet on page R7. Have students trace each lowercase and uppercase letter. Then have students write each letter in both lowercase and uppercase on a separate sheet of lined paper.

ANCHOR CHART: Cursive Handwriting — Online Ed

Cursive Handwriting

In **cursive handwriting,** the letters in each word are connected.

This is cursive handwriting.

Practice connecting the letters. Be sure the connecting lines are not too short or too long.

Look at my cursive writing!

a b c d e f g

Think about the **size** and **shape** of each letter. Practice forming each letter neatly and correctly.

Handwriting *(continued)*

Slant Letters Correctly Tell students that most cursive letters slant very slightly to the right. Have them practice writing the lowercase alphabet. Tell them to check that they have slanted their letters correctly by drawing a faint vertical line through the middle of each letter. If they have correctly slanted each letter, the lines will all be parallel to each other.

Letter Spacing Explain to students that when writing in cursive, they should leave an equal amount of space between each letter in a word. Tell students that if they leave too little or too much space between letters, their writing will be difficult to read. Write the following words on the board and have students write them on a sheet of lined paper: *batch, reject, vanish, sloppy, rhythm.*

Word Spacing Tell students that it is important to leave the correct amount of space between each word in a sentence. Tell students to leave a space about the width of a pencil between words. Demonstrate how to do this. Then have students practice letter and word spacing by writing phrases that describe the weather, such as *hot and dry.*

Join Uppercase and Lowercase Letters Tell students that when writing most proper nouns in cursive, they must join an uppercase and a lowercase letter. Have students practice joining uppercase and lowercase letters by writing the following state names: Alabama, California, Florida, New York. Then explain that some uppercase letters, such as D, P, T, V, and W, do not join with a lowercase letter. Have students practice writing the following proper nouns, making sure not to join the first and second letter: Dallas, Phoenix, Texas, Virginia, Washington.

Answer Questions Have students practice writing sentences by answering "how" questions about things they see and do on a daily basis. For example, you might ask, *How do you get to school?* Tell students to write their answers in complete sentences and use their best cursive writing.

Write Sentences Have students write five original sentences about their daily routines. Remind them to slant their letters correctly and to leave the correct amount of space between the letters in each word and between each word in a sentence. Have them trade papers with a classmate and give feedback on the legibility of their partner's cursive writing.

Write a Paragraph Have students write an original paragraph about a favorite book, sport, or other activity. Remind them to use the correct posture for writing, paying special attention to leaving appropriate spacing between letters in a word and between words in a sentence.

Assess Handwriting

To assess students' handwriting skills, review samples of their written work. Note whether they use correct letter formation and appropriate size and spacing. Note whether students follow the conventions of print, such as correct capitalization and punctuation. When writing messages, notes, and letters, or when publishing their writing, students should write legibly in cursive, leaving appropriate spacing between letters and words to make the work readable for their audience.

HANDWRITING Cursive Alphabet

A B C D E F G H

I J K L M N O P

Q R S T U V W

X Y Z

a b c d e f g h

i j k l m n o p

q r s t u v w

x y z

HANDWRITING Manuscript Alphabet

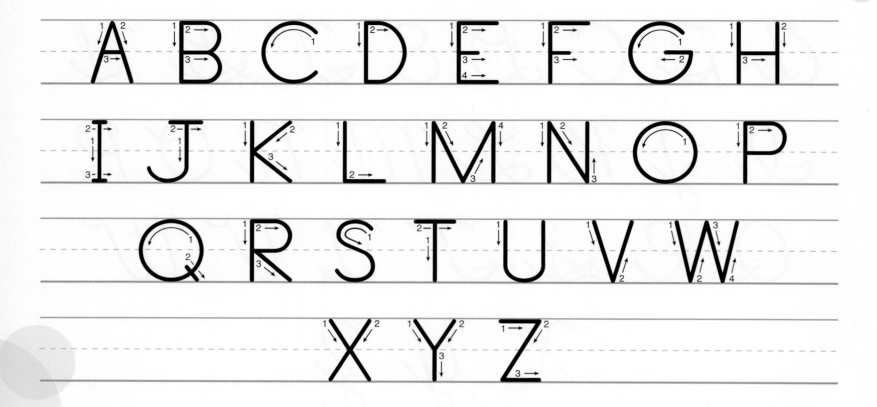

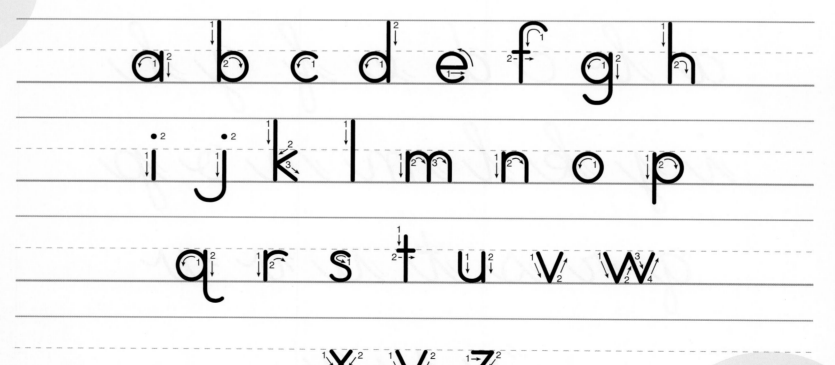

CONTINUOUS STROKE Manuscript Alphabet

A B C D E F G H
I J K L M N O P
Q R S T U V W
X Y Z

a b c d e f g h
i j k l m n o p
q r s t u v w
x y z

Instructional Vocabulary Glossary

A

abbreviation a shortened form of a word

action verb a verb that tells what its subject does

adjective a word that gives information about a noun

adverb a word that describes a verb or an adjective

allusion a reference to another person, place, thing, event, or literary work

antecedent the noun that a pronoun replaces

antonym a word that is opposite in meaning to another word

apostrophe punctuation used to show possession

argument a type of writing that makes a statement and supports it in order to convince readers, or a reason or set of reasons that supports an idea

B

be a verb that tells what something is or is like

bibliography a list of sources referred to in a text, usually included at the end of that text

C

call to action words that urge a reader to do, think, or believe something

capital letter a letter that comes at the beginning of a proper noun and is uppercase

caption words or sentences about an illustration or a photograph

central idea the main idea of a text or what the text is mostly about

character a person or animal in a story

chronological order the order in which events happen or steps in a process should be done

claim the main argument

clause group of words that has a subject and a predicate

coherence the logical or sensible connection of sentences that show how ideas are related

colon a punctuation mark that introduces a list or new but related ideas

comma a punctuation mark that shows a pause in a sentence

command/imperative sentence a type of sentence that gives a command

comma splice a comma incorrectly connecting two thoughts without a conjunction

common noun a word that names a person, place, or thing

comparative adjective a type of adjective that compares two persons, places, or things

comparative adverb a type of adverb that compares the action of two things

compare to examine the differences and similarities between people, places, or things

comparison the act of looking at things to see how they are similar

complete predicate all the words that tell what the subject is or does

complete sentence has a subject and predicate and expresses one complete thought

complete subject all the words that tell who or what is doing the action

complex sentence a sentence made up of an independent clause and a dependent clause joined with a subordinating conjunction

compound predicate a predicate with two or more actions joined by a conjunction

compound sentence a sentence that has two simple sentences joined by a comma and a conjunction, such as *and, or, but*, or *so*

compound subject two or more subjects joined by a conjunction

conclusion the ending of a piece of writing

conflict something in a story that creates a challenge for the characters; also called *problem* or *struggle*

contraction a short way of writing two words, using an apostrophe to replace one or more letters

coordinating conjunction a word that connects other words or groups of words in a sentence

counterclaim an argument against a writer's claim

couplet a two-line poem that rhymes

current recent

D

dash a punctuation mark that indicates a pause or an abrupt break in thought; it is used to set a group of words off from the rest of a sentence

demonstrative pronoun a pronoun, such as *this*, that talks about something nearby or far away

dependent clause a clause with both a subject and a sentence that is not a complete sentence on its own and is connected to an independent clause in a sentence using a subordinating conjunction

description informational text that gives details about a topic that help readers picture it

detail a fact or idea that supports or tells more about a central or main idea

dialogue the words that characters in a story or drama say aloud to each other

dialogue tag the words near dialogue that tell who is speaking

direct address when a person or thing is directly named in a sentence

direct dialogue the exact words that a character says

double negative using two negatives in a single sentence

E

editorial an article that expresses an opinion

ellipsis a punctuation mark made up of three periods; it is used to show a pause or an omission of words from a quotation that is not needed for meaning.

evaluate to decide what is most important to know

events what happens in a story

exclamation/exclamatory sentence a type of sentence that shows strong feelings

exclamation point end-of-sentence punctuation that shows feeling

experts people who know a lot about a topic

F

facts information that can be proven to be true

figurative language words or expressions used in a way that means something different from their dictionary definitions

formal language a style for speaking or writing, following the rules of English

freewriting a strategy for getting ideas onto paper without worrying about structure or grammar

future progressive verb tense tells about an action that will happen over a period of time in the future

future tense shows action that will happen

G

genre a type or category of writing, such as fiction, informational text, or opinion writing

glossary an alphabetical list of words and their meanings in the back of a book

graphic feature a visual that gives information or supports text

H

haiku a three-line poem with 17 syllables—5 in the first line, 7 in the second line, and 5 in the third line

helping verb a verb that comes before a main verb and tells more about the action

homophone a word that sounds the same, but has a different meaning and/or spelling, as another word

hook a literary device, usually at the beginning of a story, which keeps readers engaged

I

independent clause a clause that is a complete sentence on its own

index the section of a book that lists the major topics and their pages numbers

Instructional Vocabulary Glossary

indirect dialogue a rewording or summary of what a character says

inference a smart guess that readers make, based on clues in text and what they already know

informal language a style for speaking or writing that you use with people you know, such as friends and family

informational text writing that presents factual information to expand a reader's knowledge

internal documentation a note in text showing the source that a quote or specific piece of information comes from

introduction the beginning of a piece of writing

irregular verb a verb that does not end in -ed in the past tense

L

limerick a humorous poem of three long and two short lines with the rhyme scheme AABBA

M

main idea the central idea of a text, or what the text is mostly about

mechanics the correct use of capitalization and punctuation

meter the pattern of stressed and unstressed syllables in a poem

modal auxiliary a helping verb that shows how things could be or should be

N

narrative a type of writing that tells a series of events

narrator the person who tells a story

negative a word that makes a sentence mean "no"

notes written information about a topic

noun a word that names a person, place, or thing

O

object pronoun a type of pronoun that tells who or what receives the action of the verb

ode a poem that celebrates or praises a person, place, thing, or idea

opinion an idea or belief that cannot be proven

P

paraphrase to put someone else's ideas in your own words

participial phrase describes a noun

participle a verb form that can be used as an adjective

past participle a verb form that can be used to form past tenses

past progressive verb tense tells about an action that happened over a period of time in the past, but is no longer going on

past tense shows action that has already happened

personal narrative story of an important event or time in the author's life

persuade to try to convince someone of an idea or to try to get the person to do something

plagiarism copying someone else's work without giving credit

plural possessive a plural noun that shows ownership

poetry a form of literature that uses rhythmic elements and often rhyme to express feelings and ideas

possessive noun a noun that shows ownership

possessive pronoun a pronoun that shows ownership, such as *mine, yours, his,* and *theirs*

predicate the part of a sentence that tells what action is being done

preposition word that shows a connection between other words in a sentence

prepositional phrase group of words that begins with a preposition and ends with a noun or pronoun

present participle expresses present tense by adding -ing

present progressive verb tense tells about an action happening over a period of time in the present

present tense a verb that tells what is happening now or that happens over and over

primary source an original document, interview, or information from someone who has witnessed an event

progressive verb tense tells about an action that happens over a period of time

pronoun a word, such as *he*, *she*, or *they*, that takes the place of one or more nouns

proper noun a word that names a particular person, place, or thing and is capitalized

punctuation marks or signs in writing that help make meaning clear and separate parts of sentences

Q

quatrain a four-line poem with a specific rhyme scheme

question/interrogative sentence a type of sentence that asks a question

quire four sheets of paper that are folded to form eight leaves

quotation the exact words a person says or from a text

quotation marks punctuation used to show the exact words someone says or the exact words taken from a text

R

realistic fiction story that includes people and places that could exist in the real world

reason a statement or fact that explains an idea

rebuttal reasons why a counterclaim is wrong

reflexive pronoun a type of pronoun that tells when the subject of a sentence does something to itself

relative adverb a type of adverb used to introduce a dependent clause that gives information about time, place, or reason

relative pronoun a type of pronoun used to introduce a dependent clause that gives more information about a noun

relevant relates to the topic

reliable from a qualified source that can be trusted

research to study and find out about a subject

research plan a plan for how you will learn about topic in depth

research report informational text written after conducting detailed research and analysis

resolution how the conflict in a story is solved

rhetorical question a question that a writer or speaker uses for effect

rhyme scheme the pattern of end rhymes in a poem

riddle a poem that cleverly describes a person, place, thing, or idea without naming it. The reader is supposed to guess what the riddle is describing.

root the main part of a word

run-on sentence a sentence that has two complete thoughts, or sentences, that run into each other

S

secondary source books, articles, or reports based on research someone else did

sensory language words that describe sights, sounds, smells, touches, and tastes to help the reader create a mental picture

sentence fragment a group of words that does not tell a complete thought

setting where and when a story takes place

shades of meaning small differences between words that mean almost the same thing

simple predicate the main word that tells what the subject does or is

simple subject is the main word that is the focus of the sentence

split quotation direct speech that is interrupted in the middle by words that tell who is speaking

stanza a group of lines that forms part of a poem

statement/declarative sentence a type of sentence that tells something

statistic numerical evidence

subject the part of a sentence that tells who or what is doing the action

subject pronoun a type of pronoun that tells who or what does the action of the sentence

Instructional Vocabulary Glossary

subordinating conjunction   a word or phrase that links a dependent clause to an independent clause

suffix word   part that is added to the end of a root word to change the meaning of the word

summary   a restatement of the most important information, or main ideas, in a text in your own words

superlative adjective   a type of adjective that expresses the extreme degree of comparison

superlative adverb   a type of adverb that compares the action of more than two things; a word that expresses the extreme degree of comparison

support   information that helps explain an idea

supporting evidence   details in a text that helps to explain the central idea

survey   the answers to questions, usually reported as statistics

symbolism   the use of an image to represent a larger idea

synonym   word that means the same or almost the same as another word

T

tanka   a haiku with two additional 7-syllable lines at the end

tercet   a couplet with one added line that rhymes

testimony   a personal statement of support

text organization   the way a text is arranged to help readers understand the information

text structure   the way information in a text is organized to help readers understand it

transition words   words or phrases that link ideas

V

verb   word that shows action

W

word endings   letters, such as *-s*, *-es*, *-ed*, or *-ing*, added to words to change the verb tense or to change a singular noun to plural

RUBRIC • Narrative Writing Rubric

	SCORE			
	4	**3**	**2**	**1**
ORGANIZATION/ PROGRESSION	• The writing is clearly appropriate for the particular topic, purpose, and audience. • The writing skillfully uses literary devices within a purposeful structure. • The writing is well controlled and progresses through plot elements.	• The writing is mostly appropriate for the particular topic, purpose, and audience. • The writing uses literary devices within an adequate structure. • The writing is controlled and progresses through plot elements.	• The writing may not always be appropriate for the particular topic, purpose, and audience. • The writing may use literary devices within some structure. • The writing may not always be controlled. Progression through plot elements may be weak.	• The writing is not appropriate for the particular topic, purpose, and audience. • The writing uses no literary devices and may not be organized. • The writing is not controlled. Lack of progression through plot elements makes the narrative hard to follow.
DEVELOPMENT OF PLOT	• The writing develops an engaging plot with relevant details. • The writing demonstrates a thorough understanding of the task, using genre characteristics and craft such as setting and characters.	• The writing develops a plot with relevant details. • The writing demonstrates an adequate understanding of the task, using genre characteristics and craft such as setting and characters.	• The writing minimally develops a plot. Details may be inappropriate or too brief. • The writing demonstrates a limited understanding of the task.	• The writing does not develop a plot. Details are inappropriate or too brief. • The writing demonstrates a lack of understanding of the task.
USE OF LANGUAGE/CONVENTIONS	• Purposeful and controlled sentence structure and variety contribute to the effectiveness of the narrative. • Word choice is precise, is appropriate to the task, and contributes to the clarity of the essay. • The writer demonstrates a consistent command of Standard English conventions, including grammar, usage, capitalization, punctuation, and spelling. Minor errors do not detract from the effectiveness of the writing.	• Adequately controlled sentence structure and variety mostly contribute to the effectiveness of the narrative. • Word choice is mostly precise, is appropriate to the task, and usually contributes to the clarity of the essay. • The writer demonstrates an adequate command of Standard English conventions, including grammar, usage, capitalization, punctuation, and spelling. Some errors do not detract from the effectiveness of the writing.	• Awkward or only somewhat controlled sentence structure and variety may weaken the effectiveness of the narrative. • Word choice may be general and not precise, showing only basic awareness of the task. Word choice may not contribute to the clarity of the essay. • The writer demonstrates a partial command of Standard English conventions, including grammar, usage, capitalization, punctuation, and spelling. Some distracting errors may interfere with the effectiveness of the writing.	• Awkward or uncontrolled sentence structure and variety limit the effectiveness of the narrative. • Word choice may be vague, showing little or no awareness of the task. Word choice does not contribute to the clarity of the essay. • The writer demonstrates little or no command of Standard English conventions, including grammar, usage, capitalization, punctuation, and spelling. Distracting errors interfere with the effectiveness of the writing.

RUBRIC • Informational Writing Rubric

	SCORE			
	4	**3**	**2**	**1**
ORGANIZATION/PROGRESSION	• The writing is clearly appropriate for the particular topic, purpose, and audience. • The writing is skillfully organized with a purposeful structure around a clear central idea. • The writing logically progresses with a clear introduction, meaningful transitions, and a strong conclusion.	• The writing is mostly appropriate for the particular topic, purpose, and audience. • The writing is organized with an adequate structure around a clear central idea. • The writing progresses with an introduction, meaningful transitions, and a conclusion.	• The writing may not always be appropriate for the particular topic, purpose, and audience. • The writing is organized with some structure. The central idea may be weak or unclear. • The writing may not always progress logically. It may not include an introduction or a conclusion. Transitions may be too weak to show relationships between ideas.	• The writing is not appropriate for the particular topic, purpose, and audience. • The writing may not be organized. The central idea is missing or unclear. • The writing may not always progress. It may not include an introduction or a conclusion. Lack of transitions make the writing hard to follow.
DEVELOPMENT OF IDEAS	• The writing develops a central and engaging idea with relevant details. • The writing demonstrates a thorough understanding of the task, using genre characteristics and craft.	• The writing mostly develops a central idea with relevant details. • The writing demonstrates an adequate understanding of the task, using genre characteristics and craft.	• The writing minimally develops a central idea. Details may be inappropriate or too brief. • The writing demonstrates a limited understanding of the task.	• The writing does not develop a central idea. Details are inappropriate or too brief. • The writing demonstrates a lack of understanding of the task.
USE OF LANGUAGE/CONVENTIONS	• Purposeful and controlled sentence structure and variety contribute to the effectiveness of the essay. • Word choice is precise, is appropriate to the task, and contributes to the clarity of the essay. • The writer demonstrates a consistent command of Standard English conventions, including grammar, usage, capitalization, punctuation, and spelling. Minor errors do not detract from the effectiveness of the writing.	• Adequately controlled sentence structure and variety mostly contribute to the effectiveness of the essay. • Word choice is mostly precise, is appropriate to the task, and usually contributes to the clarity of the essay. • The writer demonstrates an adequate command of Standard English conventions, including grammar, usage, capitalization, punctuation, and spelling. Some errors do not detract from the effectiveness of the writing.	• Awkward or only somewhat controlled sentence structure and variety may weaken the effectiveness of the essay. • Word choice may be general and not precise, showing only basic awareness of the task. Word choice may not contribute to the clarity of the essay. • The writer demonstrates a partial command of Standard English conventions, including grammar, usage, capitalization, punctuation, and spelling. Some distracting errors may interfere with the effectiveness of the writing.	• Awkward or uncontrolled sentence structure and variety limit the effectiveness of the essay. • Word choice may be vague, showing little or no awareness of the task. Word choice does not contribute to the clarity of the essay. • The writer demonstrates little or no command of Standard English conventions, including grammar, usage, capitalization, punctuation, and spelling. Distracting errors interfere with the effectiveness of the writing.

RUBRIC • Poetry Writing Rubric

	SCORE			
	4	**3**	**2**	**1**
ORGANIZATION/ PROGRESSION	• The writing is clearly appropriate for the particular topic, purpose, and audience. • The writing skillfully uses literary devices within a purposeful structure appropriate to the poetic form. • The writing is well controlled, with meaningful transitions that enrich the progression of the poem.	• The writing is mostly appropriate for the particular topic, purpose, and audience. • The writing uses literary devices within an adequate structure mostly appropriate to the poetic form. • The writing is controlled, with meaningful transitions that support the progression of the poem.	• The writing may not always be appropriate for the particular topic, purpose, and audience. • The writing may use literary devices within some structure, although it may not be appropriate to the poetic form. • The writing may not always be controlled. Transitions may be too weak to support the progression of the poem.	• The writing is not appropriate for the particular topic, purpose, and audience. • The writing uses no literary devices and its structure may not be appropriate to the poetic form. • The writing is not controlled. Lack of transitions makes the poem hard to follow.
DEVELOPMENT OF IDEAS	• The writing develops an engaging idea with relevant details. • The writing demonstrates a thorough understanding of the task, using genre characteristics and craft.	• The writing develops an idea with relevant details. • The writing demonstrates an adequate understanding of the task, using genre characteristics and craft.	• The writing minimally develops an idea. Details may be inappropriate or too brief. • The writing demonstrates a limited understanding of the task.	• The writing does not develop an idea. Details are inappropriate or too brief. • The writing demonstrates a lack of understanding of the task.
USE OF LANGUAGE/CONVENTIONS	• When appropriate to the form, purposeful and controlled sentence structure and variety contribute to the effectiveness of the poem. • Word choice is precise, is appropriate to the task, and contributes to the clarity of the poem. • When appropriate to the form, the writer demonstrates a consistent command of Standard English conventions, including grammar, usage, capitalization, punctuation, and spelling. Minor errors do not detract from the effectiveness of the writing.	• When appropriate to the form, adequately controlled sentence structure and variety mostly contribute to the effectiveness of the poem. • Word choice is mostly precise, is appropriate to the task, and usually contributes to the clarity of the poem. • When appropriate to the form, the writer demonstrates an adequate command of Standard English conventions, including grammar, usage, capitalization, punctuation, and spelling. Some errors do not detract from the effectiveness of the writing.	• When appropriate to the form, awkward or only somewhat controlled sentence structure and variety may weaken the effectiveness of the poem. • Word choice may be general and not precise, showing only basic awareness of the task. Word choice may not contribute to the clarity of the poem. • When appropriate to the form, the writer demonstrates a partial command of Standard English conventions, including grammar, usage, capitalization, punctuation, and spelling. Some distracting errors may interfere with the effectiveness of the writing.	• When appropriate to the form, awkward or uncontrolled sentence structure and variety limit the effectiveness of the poem. • Word choice may be vague, showing little or no awareness of the task. Word choice does not contribute to the clarity of the poem. • When appropriate to the form, the writer demonstrates little or no command of Standard English conventions, including grammar, usage, capitalization, punctuation, and spelling. Distracting errors interfere with the effectiveness of the writing.

RUBRIC • Correspondence Writing Rubric

	SCORE			
	4	**3**	**2**	**1**
ORGANIZATION/PROGRESSION	• The writing is clearly appropriate for the particular topic, purpose, and recipient. • The writing is skillfully organized with a purposeful structure around a clear central idea. • The writing logically progresses with a clear introduction, meaningful transitions, and a strong conclusion.	• The writing is mostly appropriate for the particular topic, purpose, and recipient. • The writing is organized with an adequate structure around a clear central idea. • The writing progresses with an introduction, meaningful transitions, and a conclusion.	• The writing may not always be appropriate for the particular topic, purpose, and recipient. • The writing is organized with some structure. The central idea may be weak or unclear. • The writing may not always progress logically. It may not include an introduction or a conclusion. Transitions may be too weak to show relationships between ideas.	• The writing is not appropriate for the particular topic, purpose, and recipient. • The writing may not be organized. The central idea is missing or unclear. • The writing may not always progress. It may not include an introduction or a conclusion. Lack of transitions makes the writing hard to follow.
DEVELOPMENT OF IDEAS	• The writing develops a central and engaging idea with relevant details. • The writing demonstrates a thorough understanding of the task, includes a clear request for information, and includes an appropriate greeting and closing.	• The writing mostly develops a central idea with relevant details. • The writing demonstrates an adequate understanding of the task, includes a mostly clear request for information, and includes a greeting and closing.	• The writing minimally develops a central idea. Details may be inappropriate or too brief. • The writing demonstrates a limited understanding of the task. It may include a request for information but may not include a greeting and closing.	• The writing does not develop a central idea. Details are inappropriate or too brief. • The writing demonstrates a lack of understanding of the task. It may not include a request for information or a greeting and closing.
USE OF LANGUAGE/CONVENTIONS	• Purposeful and controlled sentence structure and variety contribute to the effectiveness of the correspondence. • Word choice is precise, is appropriate to the task, and contributes to the clarity of the correspondence. • The writer demonstrates a consistent command of Standard English conventions, including grammar, usage, capitalization, punctuation, and spelling. Minor errors do not detract from the effectiveness of the writing.	• Adequately controlled sentence structure and variety mostly contribute to the effectiveness of the correspondence. • Word choice is mostly precise, is appropriate to the task, and usually contributes to the clarity of the correspondence. • The writer demonstrates an adequate command of Standard English conventions, including grammar, usage, capitalization, punctuation, and spelling. Some errors do not detract from the effectiveness of the writing.	• Awkward or only somewhat controlled sentence structure and variety may weaken the effectiveness of the correspondence. • Word choice may be general and not precise, showing only basic awareness of the task. Word choice may not contribute to the clarity of the correspondence. • The writer demonstrates a partial command of Standard English conventions, including grammar, usage, capitalization, punctuation, and spelling. Some distracting errors.	• Awkward or uncontrolled sentence structure and variety limit the effectiveness of the correspondence. • Word choice may be vague, showing little or no awareness of the task. Word choice does not contribute to the clarity of the correspondence. • The writer demonstrates little or no command of Standard English conventions, including grammar, usage, capitalization, punctuation, and spelling. Distracting errors interfere with the effectiveness of the writing.

RUBRIC • Argument Writing Rubric

	SCORE			
	4	**3**	**2**	**1**
ORGANIZATION/PROGRESSION	• The writing is clearly appropriate for the particular topic, purpose, and intended audience or reader. • The writing is skillfully organized with a purposeful structure around a clear central claim. • The writing logically progresses with a clear introduction, meaningful transitions, and a strong conclusion.	• The writing is mostly appropriate for the particular topic, purpose, and intended audience or reader. • The writing is organized with an adequate structure around a clear central claim. • The writing progresses with an introduction, meaningful transitions, and a conclusion.	• The writing may not always be appropriate for the particular topic, purpose, and intended audience or reader. • The writing is organized with some structure. The central claim may be weak or unclear. • The writing may not always progress logically. It may not include an introduction or a conclusion. Transitions may be too weak to show relationships between ideas.	• The writing is not appropriate for the particular topic, purpose, and intended audience or reader. • The writing may not be organized. The central claim is missing or unclear. • The writing may not always progress. It may not include an introduction or a conclusion. Lack of transitions makes the writing hard to follow.
DEVELOPMENT OF CLAIMS	• The writing defends a central claim with relevant facts, reasons, and/or other support. • The writing demonstrates a thorough understanding of the task, using genre characteristics and craft.	• The writing mostly defends a central claim with relevant facts, reasons, and/or other support. • The writing demonstrates an adequate understanding of the task, using genre characteristics and craft.	• The writing minimally defends a central claim. Support may be inappropriate or too brief. • The writing demonstrates a limited understanding of the task.	• The writing does not defend a central claim. Support is inappropriate or too brief. • The writing demonstrates a lack of understanding of the task.
USE OF LANGUAGE/CONVENTIONS	• Purposeful and controlled sentence structure and variety contribute to the effectiveness of the essay. • Word choice is precise, is appropriate to the task, and contributes to the clarity of the essay. • The writer demonstrates a consistent command of Standard English conventions, including grammar, usage, capitalization, punctuation, and spelling. Minor errors do not detract from the effectiveness of the writing.	• Adequately controlled sentence structure and variety mostly contribute to the effectiveness of the essay. • Word choice is mostly precise, is appropriate to the task, and usually contributes to the clarity of the essay. • The writer demonstrates an adequate command of Standard English conventions, including grammar, usage, capitalization, punctuation, and spelling. Some errors do not detract from the effectiveness of the essay.	• Awkward or only somewhat controlled sentence structure and variety may weaken the effectiveness of the essay. • Word choice may be general and not precise, showing only basic awareness of the task. Word choice may not contribute to the clarity of the essay. • The writer demonstrates a partial command of Standard English conventions, including grammar, usage, capitalization, punctuation, and spelling. Some distracting errors.	• Awkward or uncontrolled sentence structure and variety limit the effectiveness of the essay. • Word choice may be vague, showing little or no awareness of the task. Word choice does not contribute to the clarity of the essay. • The writer demonstrates little or no command of Standard English conventions, including grammar, usage, capitalization, punctuation, and spelling. Distracting errors interfere with the effectiveness of the writing.

Index

Resources

Index

Index

I

ideas

  connect, W82, W132

  generate, W6

  organize, W7, W78

  revise for, W174

  strengthen, W100

idea-support map, W42, W44, W96, W132, W135

illustration, for descriptions, W33

illustrator

  Brace, Eric, W125

  Comport, Sally Wern, W53

  Ford, Gilbert, W71

  Magoon, Scott, W107

  Silva, Simón, W1

  Young, Ed, W179

imaginative literature, types of, W113

imaginative story, W107–W124

imperative sentence, W222–W224

independent clauses, W136, W306

index, W163

indirect dialogue, W11

inference, W92

informal language, W94, W207

information, gather, W24

informational text, W145, W199

  description, W17–W34

  expository essay, W71–W88, W161–W178

  research report, W143–W160

Instructional Vocabulary, W3, W7, W9, W11, W13, W15 *and throughout lessons*

internal documentation, W169

interrogative sentence, W221, W223, W224

introduction, defined, W7

introductions, W27, W205

irregular verbs, W286–W290

  connect to writing, W290

  helping verbs, W288

  review, W289

  verb *be*, W287

L

languages, capitalizing, W238

Learning Mindset

  Belonging, W71, W73, W77, W78, W83

  Curiosity, W179, W181, W189, W192, W196

  defined, W8, W20

  Grit, W143, W145, W149, W150, W154, W157

  Growth, W1, W3, W5, W8, W10

  Noticing, W17, W19, W23, W25, W28, W31

  Perseverance, W197, W199, W204, W212

  Persistence, W209

  Planning Ahead, W125, W127, W131, W134, W137

  Problem Solving, W161, W163, W170, W172, W178

  Resilience, W53, W55, W59, W62, W69

  Seeking Challenges, W35, W37, W41, W44, W46

  Self-Reflection, W107, W109, W114, W116, W121

  Wonder, W89, W91, W98, W100, W106

letter, W89–W106

limericks, W184

linking verbs, W268

listening skills. *See* participate, as a listener

M

main idea, W24

main verbs, W267

mechanics

  editing for, W31, W49, W67, W85, W175, W211

  proofreading for, W139

mechanics, proper, W346–W350

  capitalization and writing titles, W346

  commas before coordinating conjunctions, W348

  connect to writing, W350

  end punctuation, W347

  review, W349

meter, W184, W188

Index

Index

Index